The Whole Library Handbook

Current Data, Professional Advice, and Curiosa about Libraries and Library Services

ala
editions

AN IMPRINT OF THE AMERICAN LIBRARY ASSOCIATION
CHICAGO • 2013

Cover design by Casey Bayer.
Composition by Priority Publishing. Selected artwork from ClipArt.com.

The paper used in this publication meets the minimum requirements of American National Standard for Information Sciences—Permanence of Paper for Printed Library Materials, ANSI Z39.48-1992.

ISBNs: 978-0-8389-1090-0 (print); 978-0-8389-9648-5 (PDF).

Library of Congress Cataloging-in-Publication Data

The whole library handbook 5 : current data, professional advice, and curiosa / edited by George M. Eberhart.
pages   cm
Includes bibliographical references and index.
ISBN 978-0-8389-1090-0
1. Library science—United States—Handbooks, manuals, etc.
2. Libraries—United States—Handbooks, manuals, etc. I. Eberhart, George M. II. Title: Whole library handbook five.
Z665.2.U6W493 2013
020.0973—dc23   2012041726

Printed in the United States of America.

17   16   15   14   13   5   4   3   2   1

CONTENTS

PREFACE

The Whole Library Handbook 5
by George M. Eberhart

SINCE THE LAST EDITION of *The Whole Library Handbook* was published in 2006, Facebook and Twitter have transformed the way we communicate, ebooks have begun to come of age, and smartphones and tablets are becoming our display of choice. It seems wildly inappropriate, in all this explosion of information, to call something "the whole" anything. Yet the high quality of many texts in library and information science is still recognizable, even though making selections for a collection like this is devilishly difficult.

Once again, I have tried to present the most informative, practical, and entertaining tips, lists, statistics, and guidelines. About 98% of *WLH5* is completely new or substantially revised from previous editions. However, I would keep those earlier books on the shelf for a few years more. *WLH4* has essays on music and map collections, milestones in African-American library service, and a fairly comprehensive list of allegedly haunted libraries. *WLH3* (2000) has advice on how to identify a first edition, tips on preparing a bibliography, and a history of the card catalog. *WLH2* (1995) offers suggestions on how to photograph your library, a salute to Ranganathan, and an overview of 20th-century bookbindings. Even the first handbook (1991) contains still-insightful essays on Soviet librarianship, methods for moving books, and how barcodes work.

There should be something in here for anyone who wants to find out how libraries work and what issues librarians are facing. As in the earlier editions, please keep in mind that many of the selections are only extracts from larger books or longer articles. The originals are always worth seeking out.

Finally, I would like to thank the many authors in this edition, among them Larry Nix, Will Manley, Kathy Rosa and Judy Hoffman, Jean Weihs, and James LaRue. Also, my deepest appreciation goes to my wife, Jennifer Henderson, who is always turning up new films with libraries and librarians in them, as well as to all of the library students, librarians, support staff, and library advocates who have found something useful in these handbooks over the years.

LIBRARIES

CHAPTER ONE

Thou dear and well-loved haunt of happy hours,
How often in some distant gallery,
Gained by a little painful spiral stair,
Far from the halls and corridors where throng
The crowd of casual readers, have I passed
Long, peaceful hours seated on the floor
Of some retired nook, all lined with books,
Where reverie and quiet reign supreme!

—Amy Lowell, "The Boston Athenaeum" (1912)

BASIC INFORMATION

What is a library?
by George M. Eberhart

A LIBRARY IS a collection of resources in a variety of formats that is (1) organized by information professionals or other experts who (2) provide convenient physical, digital, bibliographic, or intellectual access and (3) offer targeted services and programs (4) with the mission of educating, informing, or entertaining a variety of audiences (5) and the goal of stimulating individual learning and advancing society as a whole.

SOURCE: George M. Eberhart, *The Librarian's Book of Lists* (Chicago: American Library Association, 2010), 1.

Libraries: Conditions and trends
by Kathy Rosa and Judy Hoffman

WHILE LIBRARIES CONTINUE to circulate books, connect people to the information they need, and offer a variety of public programs, they have also evolved into providers of digital access and centers of community engagement. Public, school, and academic libraries all have an increased demand for internet and digital resources. The US population has increased, and so has the number of people who find their way to library resources and the expertise of librarians.

Several agencies assist in collecting data about the expenditures, staff, services, and facilities of libraries in the United States. The US National Center for Education Statistics, a branch of the US Department of Education, conducts surveys on academic and school libraries; its academic library survey takes place every two years, and the school library survey—a component of the Schools and Staffing Survey—is conducted every three years. The Institute of Museum and Library Services surveys public libraries on an annual basis. The American Library Association's *Public Library Funding and Technology Access Study* (PLFTAS) is a multiyear project that looks at public access to computers and the internet in U.S. public libraries. The ALA American Association of School Librarians (AASL) collects data on school libraries annually in its *School Libraries Count!* longitudinal survey. Information about library networks and consortia comes from data collected by the ALA Association of Specialized and Cooperative Library Agencies.

The American Library Association also conducts household surveys to understand how people perceive the value of public, school, and academic libraries. In surveys taken in 2009–2011, ALA found that:

- In 2011, almost two-thirds of Americans (65%) reported using their public library either in person, by telephone, or online during the past year.

Libraries in the United States

College and university libraries		3,689
Public libraries		8,951*
Central buildings*	8,770	
Branch buildings	7,647	
Total buildings	16,417	
School libraries		99,180
Public schools	81,920	
Private schools	17,100	
BIA (Bureau of Indian Affairs)	160	
Special libraries		8,014
Armed forces libraries		275
Government libraries		1,060
Total		**121,169**

* The number of central buildings is different from the number of public libraries because some public library systems have no central building and some have more than one.

SOURCES: *Academic Libraries: 2010 First Look* (Washington, D.C.: National Center for Education Statistics, 2011); *Public Libraries in the United States: Fiscal Year 2010* (Washington, D.C.: Institute of Museum and Library Services, 2013); *Characteristics of Public and Bureau of Indian Education Elementary and Secondary School Library Media Centers in the United States: Results from the 2007–08 Schools and Staffing Survey* (Washington, D.C.: National Center for Education Statistics, 2009); *2008 Digest of Education Statistics*, Private school libraries, 1999–2000, Table 421 (Washington, D.C.: National Center for Education Statistics, 2009); *American Library Directory, 2012–2013* (Medford, N.J.: Information Today, 2013).

- The 33% who did not visit a library were most likely to be men over 55, men aged 18–34, or those with some high school or less education.
- Three in 10 Americans (about 45.4 million adults) who visited a library in 2009 reported increasing library use in the previous six months; 35% reported increasing online library use in the same period.
- Almost six in 10 Americans (58%) reported owning a library card in 2011. This is a slight decline from 2010, when 62% reported owning a library card.
- When comparing the public library to other tax-supported services, 31% ranked the library at the top of the list in 2011, and 57% ranked it in the middle.
- More than 223 million Americans agreed that because it provides free access to materials and resources, the public library plays an important role in giving everyone a chance to succeed. This is up from 216.6 million reported in 2006.

Libraries in Canada

Academic libraries	346
Public libraries	2,046
Special libraries	854
Government libraries	275
Total	**3,521**

SOURCE: *American Library Directory, 2012–2013* (Medford, N.J.: Information Today, 2013).

- When asked what their children did in the library, 86% reported they checked out books, 73% read for fun, 46% checked out movies, 43% did research for school or to get homework help, and 41% went to attend study hour or other programming.

When asked about school libraries:

- 97% of Americans agreed that school library programs are an essential part of the education experience because they provide resources to students and teachers.
- 96% agreed that school libraries are important because they give every child the opportunity to read and learn.
- 92% agreed that school library programs are a good value for their tax dollars.

When asked about academic libraries:

- 95% of Americans agreed that college and research libraries are an essential part of the learning community.
- 97% agreed that college and research libraries connect users with a world of knowledge.

Public libraries

The number of public libraries increased by nearly 2% between 2000 and 2009; however, the national population increased by nearly 12%, resulting in a decrease in the number of public libraries per capita.

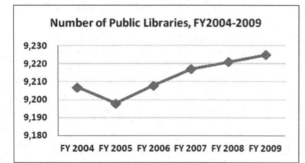

Number of Public Libraries, FY2004-2009

9,230
9,220
9,210
9,200
9,190
9,180

FY 2004 FY 2005 FY 2006 FY 2007 FY 2008 FY 2009

The number of users served by public libraries is determined by each state library. Depending upon the year, about 1%–3% of the total US population live outside a public library service area. However, an individual may pay to use a public library even though the community does not provide tax support for its own library or for one in another community. These individuals are often referred to as nonresident borrowers. Although they may not be reported in the legal service area of a public library, their use is reported in other data—visits, circulation, or program attendance. Therefore, it is difficult to get a final count of individuals without tax-supported access to a public library.

Expenditures. Public library budgets consist of tax-supported revenues (local, state, and federal) as well as fees, fines, donations, local fundraising, grants, and other sources. Total public library operating expenditures change little year to year and typically align with inflation rates (3%–6% annually). Larger urban libraries and suburban library systems account for the majority of these increases, while libraries in smaller communities account for far less public library spending overall; their budgets show little change year to year. In fact, per capita operating expenditures, in constant 2008 dollars, increased less than $5 between 2000 and 2009. In 2009, the range of per capita expenditures varied from a high of $77.34 (District of Columbia) to a low of $16.46 (Mississippi).

Staff salaries and benefits account for the largest portion of public library expenses, followed by programming, utilities, technology and infrastructure, and collections. During the recession years of 2008–2009, more than 40% of public libraries reported operating budget increases of up to 4%, but these increases barely kept pace with inflation. In addition, 22.9%–25.9% reported no change in their operating budgets. Put plainly, 69.2% of public libraries in 2008 and 67.7% in 2009 saw little or no meaningful increases. In 2009, only 38% of libraries reported increases at or above inflation. The picture is further complicated by the fact that salaries, health benefits, and utility costs increased faster than inflation.

A November 2011 survey of Chief Officers of State Library Agencies (COSLA) found 23 states (46% of responses) reporting decreases in local funding to public libraries, with more than one-third 5% or higher and 14% of states reporting greater than 10%.

Staffing. The chart on the right presents public library workforce figures. For the most part, library staffing remained stable during the period 2000–2009. But decreased funding reported in 2010 and 2011 has affected staffing levels at many libraries at a time when usage is skyrocketing. The number one challenge affecting libraries' ability to help job seekers in an economic downturn is a lack of adequate staff. Almost 50% of libraries surveyed in 2011 agreed that the library does not have enough staff to help patrons. About 41% thought that their staff did not have the necessary skills to meet patron demand.

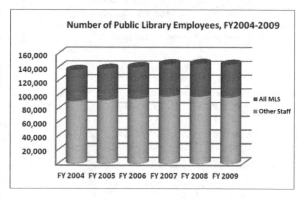

Number of Public Library Employees, FY2004-2009

Services. Total circulation of public library materials has grown each year. In 2009, total circulation was more than 2.41 billion items, up 5.2% from 2008. Circulation increased by 26.1% during the 10-year period from 2000 to 2009. Circulation of children's materials accounted for 32.9%–35% of total public library circulation in 2004–2009.

In the 2011 COSLA survey, 12 states reported they were aware of public library closures in the previous 12 months. Most of these states reported closures of five or fewer libraries, although New Jersey reported closures in the 10–15 range, and Michigan reported more than 20 closures.

Although reference transactions declined slightly between 2002 and 2009, there was considerable growth in the use of public internet computers by library visitors. In the 2011–2012 PLFTAS survey, about 65% agreed their library had too few public computers to meet the demand and 42% reported their connection speeds are insufficient. Two-thirds of libraries reported being the only free access to computers and the internet in their communities.

Libraries report providing services to job seekers as the most vital public internet service they offer, with 92.2% of all libraries reporting they provide access to jobs databases and other job opportunity resources.

Continuing a trend reported beginning in 2006, public libraries increasingly assist patrons applying for or accessing e-government services. About 97% of libraries reported offering this service, compared with 54% in 2008. More than two-thirds of public libraries assist patrons completing government forms. One in three public libraries is collaborating with other agencies to provide e-government services, up from 13.4% in 2008.

US libraries are increasingly turning to social media and mobile applications to increase their community interactions. For the first time, the 2011–2012 PLFTAS survey asked libraries to report on their use of specific social media tools. Nearly 71% of libraries report using social networking tools (such as Facebook), and 45.6% report using communications tools (Twitter). Over 14% of public libraries have websites optimized for mobile devices, nearly 12% use scanned codes (QR codes), and over 7% have smartphone apps.

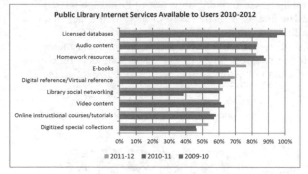

Despite what the media may present about everything being on the internet and the need for public libraries diminishing, data reported by libraries regarding visits paints a very different picture. The bar chart on the left shows total visits between 2002 and 2008. Library visits increased about 3.2% in 2003 from 2002, and about 5% in 2008 from 2007. Public library visits per capita were about 5.1 in 2008, up from about 4.5 in 2002. Reference transactions also rose in 2008, by 2.9% from 2007.

Newly reported for the first time in 2012, 39.1% of libraries provide e-readers for checkout, and 76.3% reported offering ebooks, an increase of 9% from 2011.

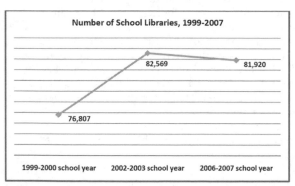

School libraries

The number of school libraries has risen by about 6% from the 1999–2000 and 2006–2007 school years. This increase is a result of population growth and the need for more elementary and secondary public schools, as well as consolidation of smaller schools into larger school districts and the need for additional school libraries to serve students and teachers. The graph above shows the number of public school librar-

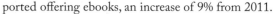

ies between school years 1999–2000 and 2006–2007. Private school libraries are not included in the data presented from the NCES school library surveys. Private schools are separately surveyed and no longer are asked about the presence of a library.

Expenditures. The percentage change in estimated school library operating expenditures from 1999–2000 to 2002–2003 was 154.2%, and it increased again between the 2002–2003 and 2006–2007 school years by 114.2%. This can be explained partly by the increase in the number of schools during this period due to population growth and school consolidation.

The AASL annual surveys of school library media programs indicate that almost all schools experienced a decrease in funding in 2007–2009 for information resources (print and nonprint materials, licensed databases, and other electronic access to information) except for a very small percentage of schools. The median per student expenditure in 2008 was just over $12. This is about two-thirds the cost of a fiction title or about one-third the cost of a single nonfiction title.

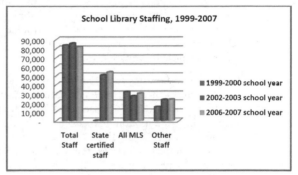

Staffing. The graph on the right shows the total number of school library staff, those with state certification, and those in the MLS and other categories. Beginning in 2002–2003, state-certified school library staff were identified as a separate employee classification, including staff members also counted in the total as well as those in the MLS and other staff categories.

Services. Circulation of materials in school libraries increased about 9.5% from the 1999–2000 to the 2006–2007 school years. Half of schools responding to a 2008 survey reported that at least 20 classes or other groups and 150 individuals visited their media centers during a typical week.

Academic libraries

The National Center for Education Statistics conducts a survey of academic libraries every two years. During 2010, 3,689 degree-granting colleges and university libraries responded to the survey, approximately 4% fewer respondents than in the 2008 survey. The decrease in respondents was primarily in the categories of specialized and associate's degree–granting institutions.

Expenditures. Overall operating expenditures rose by less than 1% from 2008 to 2010. The expenditures for all materials rose by less than 1%; however, the expenditures for electronic book and serial back files rose by 12.3%, from $133.6 million in 2008 to $152 million in 2010.

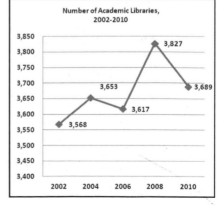

Staffing. Staffing in academic libraries remained stable between 2004 and 2010. The graph below presents total staff and category of employee—librarians, other staff, and student assistants. Although overall staffing declined by approximately 1.5%, those reductions are attributed to other staff (−3.6%) and students (−4.7%). The number of full-time-equivalent librarians increased 5.4% during this period.

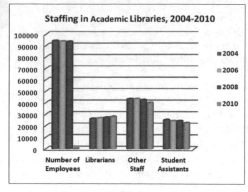

Staffing in Academic Libraries, 2004-2010

Services. Visits to academic libraries increased slightly (.08%) in 2010 from 2008. Group instruction also increased slightly during this same period. Librarians and other library staff provided about 35 million information-service transactions to library visitors. Information services include providing assistance that involves the knowledge, use, recommendation, interpretation, or instruction in the use of one or more information sources.

- Academic libraries reported more than 11 million books, journal articles, and other materials circulating through interlibrary loan transactions in 2010, an increase of 118,477 from 2008. Libraries reported receiving 10.2 million items from other institutions, a decrease of about 500,000 from 2008. This is due in part to fewer documents received from commercial services (services that charge for interlibrary loan).
- During a typical week in 2010, academic libraries had more than 22 million visits and provided more than 520,122 informational services to groups attended by more than 9.7 million students and faculty. Visits to academic libraries increased about 93.7 million from 2008, as did services to groups by about 22,000.
- The number of academic libraries providing reference service by email or online increased to about 76% in 2010, up from 72% in 2008. The number reporting digitization projects increased to 40.8% from 35.7%.

The number of serial subscriptions, electronic reference sources, and aggregation services declined, while the number of ebooks increased. Academic libraries added more than 32 million ebooks during 2010, compared to about 20 million in 2008, an increase of 38%.

Networks and consortia

Library networks and consortia are legally established organizations that serve libraries, not the public, and provide a range of services to their member libraries. For the most part, they are regional (multicounty) and serve multiple library types. Of the 204 eligible networks responding to a 2005–2006 baseline survey, 125 (61%) were regional, another 52 (26%) were local, and 24 (12%) were statewide organizations.

Public libraries are served by 167 networks and consortia (82%), academic libraries by 121 (59%), and school libraries by 99 (49%). Special libraries are served by only 93 (46%)—the most frequent special library members being medical, nonprofit, and institutional.

The most common services and activities include communication with member libraries, resource sharing, professional development, consulting and technical assistance, and cooperative purchasing or group discounts. Other frequent activities include automation and other technology services, library advocacy, public relations, marketing, information and referral services, and document delivery services. Less frequent activities include standards and guidelines development or support, services to special populations, library and information science professional collections, rotating or other shared collections, and digitization or other preservation efforts.

Revenue sources include state government (28%), membership fees (9%), local and federal governments (including e-rate funds) combined (<10%), and other (53%). Networks spend less than libraries on staff as a proportion of overall operating expenditures. Total expenditures reported in 2005–2006 were $365 million. Products and services for member libraries accounted for 44% of total operating expenditures and staff about 30%.

SOURCE: Specially prepared by the ALA Office for Research and Statistics.

Library workers: Facts and figures

compiled by the AFL-CIO Department for Professional Employees

IN 2011, there were 198,000 librarians, 37,000 library technicians, and 140,000 other education, training, and library workers. Between 2010 and 2020, the number of librarians is expected to increase by 7%, while library technicians increase by 9%. Total employment in the US is expected to increase by 14%.

Employment

Most *librarians* work in school and academic libraries, but nearly one-third work in public libraries. The remainder work in special libraries, including those in businesses, law firms, nonprofits, and scientific organizations.

In 2011, 26% of librarians worked part-time. Public and college librarians often work weekends and evenings, as well as some holidays. School librarians usually have the same workday and vacation schedules as classroom teachers. Special librarians usually work normal business hours, but in fast-paced industries such as advertising or legal services often work longer hours when needed. This also applies to *library technicians.*

More than half of all *library assistants* are employed by local government in public libraries; most of the remaining employees work in school libraries. About 63% of all library assistants work part-time.

Diversity

Librarians, technicians, and assistants are predominantly white. According to a 2007 American Library Association (ALA) report, there is a persistent lag in racial diversity and persons with disabilities.

In 2011, 15% of all librarians were minorities: 10.1% were black or African American, 3.9% were Hispanic or Latino, and 2.6% were Asian.

Minorities accounted for approximately 20% of all other education, training, and library workers in 2011: 7.7% were black or African American, 3.4% were Asian, and 9.2% were Hispanic or Latino.

Among members of the Association of Research Libraries (ARL), 16.2% of the professional staff is composed of minorities. Asian/Pacific Islanders account for 6.8% of the professional staff, blacks or African Americans for 4.4%, Latinos or Hispanics for 2.6%, and American Indian/Alaskan natives for 0.3%.

The percentage of minorities varies significantly between geographical regions. Minorities make up 18.2% of professional employees in ARL libraries in the South Atlantic Region, while comprising 3.4% of professionals in East South Central ARL libraries.

In 2005, just 21% of librarians were under age 39, while 41% were between ages 50 and 59.

Women's work

Library workers have been, and will continue to be, mostly female. Most MLS degrees conferred in the 2009–2010 school year went to women. Women comprise 81% of ALA-accredited MLS enrollment. Black women comprise 4.1% of MLS graduates, Hispanic women comprise 4.9%, and Asian women comprise 3.7%.

In 2011, women accounted for 86.2% of all librarians and 71.2% of all other education, training, and library workers.

A 2010 ARL survey found 62% of research librarians are female. Among research library directors, women are in the majority (58%).

While men accounted for only 38% of university library professionals in 2011, they accounted for approximately 42% of university library directors.

The wage gap

Pay inequity remains a persistent and pervasive problem in our society. In 2010, median weekly earnings for women were 81% those of men. For most women of color, the earnings gap is even larger: African American women earned just 72 cents for every dollar earned by men in 2010. Hispanic and Latina women earned just 62 cents for every dollar men earned. Only Asian American women's earnings were closer to parity with men's: in 2010, they earned 94% that of all men. However, they earned 83% as much as Asian American men.

In 2011, female librarians had median weekly earnings of $813, compared to $1,052 for men, a disparity of 29.4%. The overall salary for women research librarians was 96% that of men in 2011–2012, compared to 94.4% in 2003–2004.

In a 2011–2012 survey of academic librarians, even when years of experience in a particular job category were equal, men still outpaced women in salary by 3.8%: $73,348 for women and $76,225 for men. On average, women have more years of experience than men, but still men's salaries are higher in nearly all experience cohorts.

Regional and institutional variance

Nationally, the mean annual wage for librarians was $57,020 in 2011. However, wages varied from state to state. The states with the highest salaries were the District of Columbia, Maryland, California, Connecticut, and New Jersey, where the average annual wage among the five states was $67,736. The five lowest-paying states were South Dakota, Idaho, Vermont, Mississippi, and Oklahoma, where the average annual wage was $41,308. The West and North Atlantic states, which have high union membership rates, consistently have the highest median salaries for library workers.

The salary of a director depends on the type of library. In 2007, directors of very small university libraries (with fewer than 50 staff) had average salaries of $183,989. In contrast, directors of very large university libraries (more than 110 staff members) made $258,544. Librarians employed by local governments earned an average salary of $51,140 in 2011. Elementary and secondary school librarians earned an average salary of $59,190 in 2011.

In 2010, directors of public libraries were paid an average salary of $100,106, while librarians made $52,851. Directors of academic libraries earned $97,767, while librarians earned $55,732.

Benefits

Nearly 12% of public libraries do not offer a pension and 17.4% do not offer retirement savings. Among academic libraries, 23.3% do not offer a pension and 20% do not offer retirement savings.

Almost 40% of public libraries do not offer vision insurance and 16% do not offer dental insurance. Among academic libraries, 42.9% do not offer vision insurance and 17.9% do not offer dental insurance.

Some 34% of public libraries do not offer disability insurance and almost 17% do not offer prescription coverage; in academic libraries, 19.7% do not offer disability insurance and 23.1% do not offer prescription coverage.

Unionization

In 2011, workers in education, training, and library occupations had the highest unionization rates for any occupation group.

In 2011, 23.7% of librarians, 18.4% of library technicians, and 17.2% of library assistants were union members. Twenty-two percent of other education, training, and library workers were union members.

Union librarians earned an average of 64% more than nonunion librarians in 2011. Union library technicians earned an average of 32.3% more than non-union librarian technicians in 2010 (the last year available). Union library assistants earned nearly 148% more than nonunion library assistants in 2011.

Union workers in other education, training, and library fields earned an average of 24.2% more than their nonunion counterparts. In March 2011, 93% of union workers had access to medical care benefits, compared with only 69% of nonunion workers; 84% of unionized workers had paid sick leave, compared with 64% of nonunion workers.

Libraries in the recession

In a December 2008 op-ed piece in the *Huffington Post*, ALA President Jim Rettig noted, "As the nation continues to experience a sharp and jarring economic downturn, local libraries are providing valuable free tools and resources to help Americans of all ages through this time of uncertainty. . . . [N]ow more than ever, libraries are proving that they are valued and trusted community partners."

Nationwide more people applied for library cards in 2008 than at any time since records have been kept. Families visiting libraries are often looking for less expensive ways to find entertainment and access to the internet, while many adults are looking for new jobs.

Libraries continue to receive strong support from their communities. Between December 1, 2009, and November 30, 2010, ballot measures asking voters to support increases in operating revenue passed 87% of the time. Ballot measures seeking funds to build libraries passed 55% of the time.

At a time when libraries and librarians are facing increasing demands, many states and municipalities are threatening to cut their budgets and close branches as a result of budget shortfalls. Libraries and librarians are faced with meeting the challenges of increased usage without increased budgetary support. As a result of the recession, libraries and librarians have had to confront challenges like homelessness, increased crime, and violent incidents in their work environment.

SOURCE: "Library Workers: Facts and Figures," 2012, dpeaflcio.org/programs-publications/issue-fact-sheets/library-workers-facts-figures/. Reprinted with permission.

ACADEMIC LIBRARIES

The largest university research libraries, 2010–2011

THE FOLLOWING FIGURES are based on an investment index developed by the Association of Research Libraries (ARL) to measure the relative size of its university library members.

Starting with 2005–2006 data, ARL has used a Library Investment Index as an alternative to the historical index known as the ARL Membership Criteria Index (using the data elements for numbers of volumes held, number of volumes added, number of current serials received, total operating expenditures, and number of professional and support staff). The Library Investment Index is highly correlated with the older Membership Criteria Index and less affected by the rapidly changing context of library collections. The methodology behind this new index is described by Bruce Thompson in his October 2006 paper, "Some Alternative Quantitative Library Activity Descriptions/Statistics that Supplement the ARL Logarithmic Index," www.arl.org/bm~doc/bruce_3mk.pdf. The index does not attempt to measure a library's services, quality of collections, or success in meeting the needs of users.

The four data elements in the new index's formula are: total expenditures, salaries and wages of professional staff, total library materials expenditures, and total number of professional and support staff.

ARL does not claim that this ranking incorporates all the factors necessary to give a complete picture of research library quality. However, it is a measuring device that has proven reliable over the years for specific internal and comparative purposes.

Total expenditures includes money spent on materials purchases, binding, salaries, and general operations, but does not include capital expenditures for buildings, expenditures for plant maintenance, and fringe benefits. Figures for Canadian libraries are expressed in U.S. dollars.

Professional salaries excludes salaries and wages for support staff.

Materials is the portion of total expenditures on materials purchases alone.

Total staff includes professionals and support staff, but not student assistants.

	Rank	Total expenditures	Prof. salaries	Materials budget	Total staff
Harvard University	1	111,574,120	41,095,798	32,341,358	938
Yale University	2	75,334,128	20,277,163	31,340,632	546
University of Toronto	3	68,231,488	14,811,055	26,969,613	501
Columbia University	4	61,537,559	20,346,338	26,445,238	514
University of Michigan	5	63,957,474	16,017,883	23,002,928	569
New York University	6	52,604,525	11,142,488	20,461,642	367
University of California, Berkeley	7	50,050,063	17,488,347	17,846,646	414
Princeton University	8	49,653,805	11,070,207	23,156,840	344
Pennsylvania State University	9	50,451,411	11,637,032	17,953,463	529
University of Texas at Austin	10	45,469,795	9,345,115	17,392,118	415
University of Alberta	11	45,090,932	7,605,073	19,446,396	297
Univ. of California, Los Angeles	12	46,006,514	11,496,193	12,393,660	414
Cornell University	13	44,199,742	12,788,362	14,917,133	376
University of North Carolina at Chapel Hill	14	41,802,228	10,926,630	16,970,946	361
Duke University	15	40,696,213	12,204,695	17,528,304	298
University of Pennsylvania	16	42,126,455	8,902,620	15,547,546	297
University of Illinois at Urbana-Champaign	17	40,577,401	11,716,762	15,281,388	392
Texas A&M University	18	40,192,993	9,176,007	18,443,037	278
University of Minnesota, Twin Cities	19	40,734,130	8,271,828	17,008,958	309
University of Washington	20	40,322,337	11,960,645	14,842,396	356
University of Southern California	21	39,516,945	9,515,234	19,125,627	278
Univ. of Wisconsin–Madison	22	39,840,839	14,554,551	11,522,129	372
Ohio State University	23	40,373,445	10,286,053	11,954,846	313
University of British Columbia	24	38,921,146	9,978,233	16,142,816	307
University of Chicago	25	35,293,147	5,346,281	18,143,564	243
Emory University	26	33,592,247	7,569,205	16,496,488	212
Indiana University	27	33,898,136	8,719,246	13,490,434	341
Johns Hopkins University	28	31,816,227	6,813,353	14,568,011	242
University of Pittsburgh	29	31,327,783	6,835,120	15,605,569	273
Rutgers University	30	31,937,803	7,672,965	10,510,456	325
Université de Montréal	31	31,150,210	7,732,904	11,811,475	347
University of Arizona	32	30,719,703	5,433,223	14,386,012	209
University of Virginia	33	31,487,948	7,178,055	10,352,942	305
Northwestern University	34	29,933,068	8,392,073	13,631,528	259
Brigham Young University	35	29,878,235	7,996,456	13,388,500	178
University of Iowa	36	29,668,041	6,447,265	15,060,052	207
McGill University	37	28,991,577	5,545,724	13,823,892	214
North Carolina State University	38	29,394,144	7,992,821	9,782,748	229
Georgetown University	39	27,762,272	6,827,796	12,109,640	211
Michigan State University	40	27,591,184	5,383,778	13,407,332	196

	Rank	Total expenditures	Prof. salaries	Materials budget	Total staff
University of Connecticut	41	27,242,619	9,614,941	10,315,248	143
University of Miami	42	27,120,660	5,497,021	13,598,382	201
Univ. of California, San Diego	43	27,749,870	7,268,865	9,548,345	297
University of Florida	44	27,242,279	5,888,886	12,004,335	305
University of Calgary	45	27,112,060	6,005,590	12,120,784	217
George Washington University	46	27,157,092	6,210,004	11,509,525	185
Washington Univ. in St. Louis	47	26,757,893	6,470,977	12,274,398	200
Texas Tech University	48	25,632,190	5,477,734	11,938,700	244
University of Notre Dame	49	25,412,893	5,381,203	11,837,829	226
University of Maryland	50	24,953,475	8,002,200	10,677,197	197
York University	51	25,699,722	6,042,577	9,781,731	161
Vanderbilt University	52	24,872,400	6,101,150	11,312,373	193
Massachusetts Institute of Technology	53	24,550,670	8,611,527	9,000,247	174
Purdue University	54	24,201,236	5,648,218	11,244,162	172
Arizona State University	55	24,573,912	3,921,818	10,805,462	227
University of Oklahoma	56	22,723,720	3,298,230	13,952,020	151
Temple University	57	22,752,180	5,286,728	11,937,615	162
University of Ottawa	58	22,811,421	3,676,674	11,420,342	163
University of Tennessee	59	22,234,695	4,956,126	11,912,941	203
University of Kansas	60	22,590,331	6,129,953	9,536,565	215
University of Georgia	61	22,568,889	4,157,414	10,489,974	235
Université de Laval	62	22,262,905	4,136,246	11,252,948	213
University of Manitoba	63	22,586,370	5,631,730	8,405,158	195
University of Utah	64	23,326,789	4,515,559	6,728,095	235
University of Colorado	65	22,096,966	3,279,210	11,420,186	165
Boston University	66	21,793,684	5,594,286	9,645,325	197
University of Kentucky	67	21,178,982	5,188,542	10,936,239	189
University of Western Ontario	68	21,079,314	4,674,613	11,318,696	177
University of Cincinnati	69	21,096,528	5,646,217	10,259,873	135
Brown University	70	20,982,750	5,004,998	9,701,826	162
Wayne State University	71	20,806,976	5,613,204	8,601,311	192
Boston College	72	20,338,858	5,758,591	9,529,516	140
University at Buffalo	73	20,062,539	7,345,399	8,214,014	160
University of Houston	74	20,294,011	3,358,567	10,548,198	137
University of California, Irvine	75	20,159,689	4,447,825	9,714,066	170
University of Alabama	76	19,902,602	4,244,327	9,798,773	156
Dartmouth College	77	19,740,990	4,401,255	9,421,474	167
University of Louisville	78	19,553,275	3,076,088	9,467,444	141
University of South Carolina	79	19,500,404	3,832,782	8,882,438	170
University of Rochester	80	18,941,344	5,531,117	8,514,371	156
University of Delaware	81	18,961,932	4,511,411	9,169,159	149
University of Saskatchewan	82	18,891,576	4,441,754	9,427,558	135
University of New Mexico	83	19,388,843	5,028,247	7,160,258	178
Syracuse University	84	18,372,392	4,786,369	8,401,813	165
University of Missouri	85	18,080,926	3,826,845	9,751,527	157
Queen's University	86	18,232,789	3,753,248	9,169,623	138
McMaster University	87	17,698,226	4,258,043	8,551,365	130
University of California, Davis	88	17,923,706	4,234,501	7,462,149	171
University of Hawaii at Manoa	89	17,455,232	5,536,404	7,258,502	171
Oklahoma State University	90	17,635,952	5,119,922	7,074,884	137

	Rank	Total expenditures	Prof. salaries	Materials budget	Total staff
University of Illinois at Chicago	91	17,648,664	3,463,592	8,210,441	159
Iowa State University	92	17,132,300	3,140,064	9,078,625	138
Florida State University	93	16,849,352	3,644,439	8,749,087	171
Tulane University	94	16,416,459	3,182,768	9,380,699	132
Rice University	95	15,767,079	3,423,981	10,015,546	105
University of Oregon	96	16,022,100	4,204,820	6,143,178	157
University of Nebraska–Lincoln	97	15,565,260	3,619,010	6,797,403	151
Virginia Polytechnic Institute and State University	98	15,164,519	2,438,267	8,428,572	120
University of Waterloo	99	15,476,852	2,843,525	7,052,563	124
Southern Illinois University	100	15,045,791	2,963,976	7,090,979	141
University of Massachusetts	101	14,817,481	3,639,890	6,066,496	133
Case Western Reserve Univ.	102	14,271,584	3,846,213	7,076,887	105
Colorado State University	103	14,264,719	3,125,882	7,021,010	94
University of California, Santa Barbara	104	14,851,101	2,926,340	4,807,044	164
Stony Brook University	105	13,640,247	4,901,784	6,634,380	111
University of Guelph	106	14,130,368	3,410,082	6,212,065	116
Washington State University	107	13,943,581	3,052,415	5,935,225	123
Univ. of California, Riverside	108	12,319,332	3,560,226	4,983,504	103
Georgia Institute of Technology	109	12,171,689	2,965,805	5,751,353	115
Auburn University	110	12,137,778	3,029,393	5,621,146	87
Ohio University	111	12,208,591	2,613,794	5,283,994	108
University at Albany, SUNY	112	11,597,750	3,885,388	5,193,274	121
Louisiana State University	113	11,650,393	2,952,232	5,682,352	120
Kent State University	114	11,335,095	3,001,890	4,403,740	131
Howard University	115	8,320,804	1,949,674	3,155,926	82

SOURCE: Martha Kyrillidou, *ARL Library Investment Index: Description and Worksheets* (Washington, D.C.: Association of Research Libraries, 2011), www.arl.org/stats/index/index.shtml. Reprinted with permission.

Standards for libraries in higher education

THE 2011 *Standards for Libraries in Higher Education* are designed to guide academic libraries in advancing their role as partners in educating students, achieving their institutions' missions, and positioning them as leaders in assessment and continuous improvement on their campuses. Libraries must demonstrate their value and document their contributions to overall institutional effectiveness and be prepared to address changes in higher education. These *Standards* were developed through study and consideration of new and emerging issues and trends in libraries, higher education, and accrediting practices. They differ from previous

Cornell University's Olin Library. Photo by George M. Eberhart.

versions by articulating expectations for library contributions to institutional effectiveness.—*GME.*

Principles and performance indicators

Institutional effectiveness. Libraries define, develop, and measure outcomes that contribute to institutional effectiveness and apply findings for purposes of continuous improvement.

The library defines and measures outcomes in the context of institutional mission.

The library develops outcomes that are aligned with institutional, departmental, and student affairs outcomes.

The library develops outcomes that are aligned with accreditation guidelines for the institution.

The library develops and maintains a body of evidence that demonstrates its impact in convincing ways.

The library articulates how it contributes to student learning, collects evidence, documents successes, shares results, and makes improvements.

The library contributes to student recruitment, retention, time to degree, and academic success.

The library communicates with the campus community to highlight its value in the educational mission and in institutional effectiveness.

Professional values. Libraries advance professional values of intellectual freedom, intellectual property rights and values, user privacy and confidentiality, collaboration, and user-centered service.

The library resists all efforts to censor library resources.

The library protects each library user's right to privacy and confidentiality.

The library respects intellectual property rights and advocates for balance between the interests of information users and rights holders through policy and educational programming.

The library supports academic integrity and deters plagiarism through policy and education.

The library commits to a user-centered approach and demonstrates the centrality of users in all aspects of service design and delivery in the physical and virtual environments.

The library engages in collaborations both on campus and across institutional boundaries.

Flickr photo by Taber Andrew Bain, used CC A 3.0.

Educational role. Libraries partner in the educational mission of the institution to develop and support information-literate learners who can discover, access, and use information effectively for academic success, research, and lifelong learning.

Library personnel collaborate with faculty and others regarding ways to incorporate library collections and services into effective education experiences for students.

Library personnel collaborate with faculty to embed information-literacy learning outcomes into curricula, courses, and assignments.

Library personnel model best pedagogical practices for classroom teaching, online tutorial design, and other educational practices.

1

Library personnel provide regular instruction in a variety of contexts and employ multiple learning platforms and pedagogies.

Library personnel collaborate with campus partners to provide opportunities for faculty professional development.

The library has the IT infrastructure to keep current with advances in teaching and learning technologies.

Discovery. Libraries enable users to discover information in all formats through effective use of technology and organization of knowledge.

The library organizes information for effective discovery and access.

The library integrates library resource access into institutional web and other information portals.

The library develops resource guides to provide guidance and multiple points of entry to information.

The library creates and maintains interfaces and system architectures that include all resources and facilitates access from preferred user starting points.

The library has technological infrastructure that supports changing modes of information and resource discovery.

The library provides one-on-one assistance through multiple platforms to help users find information.

Collections. Libraries provide access to collections sufficient in quality, depth, diversity, format, and currency to support the research and teaching missions of the institution.

The library provides access to collections aligned with areas of research, curricular foci, or institutional strengths.

The library provides collections that incorporate resources in a variety of formats, accessible virtually and physically.

The library builds and ensures access to unique materials, including digital collections.

The library has the infrastructure to collect, organize, provide access to, disseminate, and preserve collections needed by users.

The library educates users on issues related to economic and sustainable models of scholarly communication.

The library ensures long-term access to the scholarly and cultural record.

Space. Libraries are the intellectual commons where users interact with ideas in both physical and virtual environments to expand learning and facilitate the creation of new knowledge.

The library creates intuitive navigation that supports self-sufficient use of virtual and physical spaces.

The library provides safe and secure physical and virtual environments conducive to study and research.

The library has the IT infrastructure to provide reliable and robust virtual and physical environments needed for study and research.

The library uses physical and virtual spaces as intellectual commons, providing access to programs, exhibits, lectures, and more.

The library designs pedagogical spaces to facilitate collaboration and learning, and the creation of new knowledge.

The library's physical space features connec-

The Anderson Memorial Library (dedicated in 1901) was the first Carnegie library west of the Mississippi and the first for an academic institution, the College of Emporia, Kansas.

tivity and up-to-date, adequate, well-maintained equipment and furnishings.

The library provides clean, inviting, and adequate space, conducive to study and research, with suitable environmental conditions and convenient hours for its services, personnel, resources, and collections.

The library's physical and virtual spaces are informed by consultation with users.

Management and administration. Libraries engage in continuous planning and assessment to inform resource allocation and to meet their mission effectively and efficiently.

The library's mission statement and goals align with and advance those developed by the institution.

Library personnel participate in campus decision making needed for effective library management.

The library allocates human and financial resources effectively and efficiently to advance the library's mission.

The library's budget is sufficient to provide resources to meet the reasonable expectations of library users when balanced against other institutional needs.

The library partners with multiple institutions (for example, via collections consortia) for greater cost-effectiveness and to expand access to collections.

The library plans based on data and outcomes assessment using a variety of methods both formal and informal.

The library communicates assessment results to library stakeholders.

Library personnel model a culture of continuous improvement.

The library has the IT infrastructure needed to collect, analyze, and use data and other assessments for continuous improvement.

Personnel. Libraries provide sufficient number and quality of personnel to ensure excellence and to function successfully in an environment of continuous change.

Library personnel are sufficient in quantity to meet the diverse teaching and research needs of faculty and students.

Library personnel have education and experience sufficient to their positions and the needs of the organization.

Library personnel demonstrate commitment to ongoing professional development, maintaining and enhancing knowledge and skills for themselves and their coworkers.

Library personnel contribute to the knowledge base of the profession.

Library personnel are professionally competent, diverse, and empowered.

Personnel responsible for enhancing and maintaining the library's IT infrastructure keep current with library technology applications and participate in ongoing training.

External relations. Libraries engage the campus and broader community through multiple strategies in order to advocate, educate, and promote their value.

The library contributes to external relations through communications, publications, events, and donor cultivation and stewardship.

The library communicates with the campus community regularly.

Library personnel convey a consistent message about the library and engage in their role as ambassadors in order to expand user awareness of resources, services, and expertise.

SOURCE: *ACRL Standards for Libraries in Higher Education,* October 2011, ala.org/acrl/standards/standardslibraries.

Linking the information commons to learning

by Joan K. Lippincott

MANY INSTITUTIONS ARE RENOVATING their libraries to become information commons or learning commons. Frequently, the information commons occupies one floor of a library facility, generally a main service floor, which often includes or replaces the library's reference area. Most information commons are currently in library spaces that have been renovated; a minority are in totally new buildings. A small number of information commons are in nonlibrary buildings.

Information commons have drawn students by offering environments that address their needs, bringing together technology, content, and services in a physical space that results in an environment different from that of a typical library. The technology in an information commons is intentionally more pervasive than in most traditional academic libraries.

Some information commons have vision or mission statements that directly address the relationship between the commons and the learning mission of the university. Making this linkage operational can be a challenge.

Enabling student work

Walking into a busy information commons on a weekday evening, an observer would likely see groups of students clustered around computers, some chatting, others talking on cellphones, some with headphones listening to audio while they work on computers, and some working on their own, perhaps on a laptop, with coffee and snacks, books and notebooks spread out on a table. It would be difficult to tell, without peering over their shoulders, exactly what types of activities the students were engaged in, particularly whether they're recreational or academic. Are they playing computer games? Buying things on the internet? Sending and receiving instant messages? Or are they involved in more scholarly pursuits, such as accessing journals licensed by the library, using art image collections, writing papers, editing videos for course projects, or accessing assignments through a course management system? The students probably are doing some of each.

Today's students mix academic and social activities. Some see their multitasking as a troublesome lack of ability to concentrate, but it is a logical strategy for students who grew up in a world with media in many formats at their fingertips 24 hours a day. Information commons, with their large numbers of computers, range of software, and spaces configured for groups, provide an ideal environment for students to collaborate with others and multitask. Developing spaces where students can collaborate outside class provides support for an increased emphasis on teamwork, both in and outside higher education.

One satisfied student at the University of Tennessee stated, "Every time I have been in the library after hours, the commons has been packed full of students. Some students were finishing assignments, some doing group projects, and some just relaxing with friends. The group study areas are of the perfect number and size, and the computers have all the programs I could need on them."

Students spend much of their time learning outside classrooms by reading, exploring, creating, and communicating. The information commons creates an environment that nurtures these activities by providing content in a variety of formats, technologies that might not be affordable to individual students, and spaces built to encourage collaboration and interaction. Outside the classroom, students extend their understanding of the basic course concepts and make the learning their own by investigating a topic and producing a product that integrates it with the content of the course. Doing this type of work engages students in their coursework and the discipline.

A key purpose of an information commons is to leverage the intersection of content, technology, and services in a physical facility to support student learning. For example, a student in a 20th-century film course might develop a paper, primarily text, that embeds film clips and related images from other sources (perhaps illustrating events or costumes from the era of the film) and draws on film criticism from books and journals; or a student in a marketing course might create a PowerPoint presentation using data from the US census, statistical software, images to illustrate points, and materials from business journals to develop the presentation. Then, the student can rehearse the presentation in a specially designed "practice presentation" room set up with a podium, computer projector and screen, and chairs for an audience of friends who can critique the presentation. For projects like these, students need access to hardware, software, print and digital content; assistance from individuals with a broad range of expertise; and a place in which all these things are available.

Advertising available services

For students first walking into an information commons, their initial impression is that a lot of technology is available, but it is not clear for what purpose. To advertise the range of activities possible in the commons, libraries can provide visual cues to inform students of the rich information resources, the range of software, and the services offered. Some information commons have used colorful banners to promote services. The computer default screens and mouse pads in the information commons can promote the content, software, and services students can access. Libraries can display digital resources on large screens to illustrate the rich content available for use in course projects. The information commons can exhibit student products developed as a result of work in the commons. Staff can collaborate with student focus groups to refine the language of signs that indicate services available. For example, merely adding the word "research" to a sign designating reference services seemed to greatly improve student understanding of what types of questions they might ask at that service point.

Students exploring college choices as well as students new to campus may initially explore the library through its website. In many cases, it is difficult, if not impossible, to find information about the library's information commons on the library's web pages. The information commons pages could foster the close connection of its resources to learning by emphasizing how the content, hardware, software, and space that it provides are useful for course projects.

Linking to courses

Librarians can seek out likely courses and work with the faculty to forge a closer relationship between the resources available in the information commons and course assignments. For example, in a course where students do oral history projects, the librarian could work with faculty to develop a guide to sources of context (newspapers, books, image collections, diaries) that would assist students in shaping their projects, and then offer a class or online tutorial to help them use equipment and software to record and edit oral histories that they capture themselves, providing the tools they need to develop a narrative presentation.

Information on the hardware, software, and services offered in the information commons that would be useful for course projects could be embedded into a course-management system as well.

Often learning can be strengthened by integrated services. Physical colocation can lead staff to reconfigure services. For example, at Dartmouth College the library reference staff, information technology service staff, and writing center are located on one floor of the library. They have developed a program in which they jointly provide intensive training to a group of students who serve as peer tutors for locating information (library) resources, using technology, and improving writing for course assignments. Normally, these three functions are separate, but students' needs often cross administrative boundaries. The students advertise their services by making brief presentations in writing-intensive classes and scheduling appointments in a library tutoring center.

Leveraging technology

Providing new types of technology can help the information commons enhance learning. An option called TeamSpot is available in libraries at the University of Washington, which calls its implementation Collaboration Studios. The setup allows a small group of students to connect their laptops to a large display screen that participants can individually control from their desktops (or using a digital pen or remote control), facilitating collaborative work.

Collaboration Studios at the University of Washington.

Classrooms

Many information commons incorporate classrooms equipped with a variety of technologies, including computers and projectors, smartboards, video editing equipment, and videoconferencing capabilities. Often one or two classrooms are set aside for the library's information literacy instruction program. Classrooms available for general use are either assigned by the registrar or scheduled by the library. On many campuses, concerns have arisen that some faculty request the technology-enabled classrooms because of their location or newness rather than a need to incorporate technology into the learning process. Given the limited number of these classrooms, it would be to the institution's advantage to verify that the classes using these spaces genuinely use the technology. The information commons staff can also make a special effort to develop tools and services for the courses held in their facility.

Conclusion

With careful planning, an information commons can be a collaborative learning space, not just a glorified computing lab; it can be a place to access, use, and create information, not just a reference area with rows of computers; and it can provide transparent user services, not fiefdoms of service points.

SOURCE: Joan K. Lippincott, "Linking the Information Commons to Learning," in Diana Oblinger, ed., *Learning Spaces* (Boulder, Colo.: Educause, 2006), www.educause.edu/research-and-publications/books/learning-spaces. Reprinted with permission.

PUBLIC LIBRARIES

14 ways public libraries are good for the country

IN 1995, *American Libraries* published an article on "12 Ways Libraries Are Good for the Country" to help library advocates explain to the public why libraries are essential community institutions. In 2013, when library budgets, staff, hours, and services are being threatened in many areas, it's more important than ever to issue these reminders. For this edition of *The Whole Library Handbook,* I have shortened the message and added two that were missing before.

1. **Public libraries encourage democracy.** Libraries provide access to information and multiple points of view so that citizens can make informed decisions on public policy.
2. **Public libraries break down boundaries.** Libraries offer services and programs for people at all literacy levels, readers with little or no English skills, homebound senior citizens, prisoners, homeless or impoverished individuals, and persons with physical or learning disabilities.
3. **Public libraries level the playing field.** Libraries make resources available to everyone in the community, regardless of income or social status.
4. **Public libraries value independent thought.** Libraries offer choices between mainstream and alternative viewpoints, between traditional and visionary concepts, and between monocultural and multicultural perspectives.
5. **Public libraries nourish creativity.** By providing an atmosphere that stimulates curiosity, libraries create opportunities for unstructured learning and serendipitous discovery.
6. **Public libraries offer sanctuary.** By providing an atmosphere conducive to reflection, libraries induce a feeling of serenity and transcendence that opens the mind to new ideas and interpretations.
7. **Public libraries animate young minds.** Children's and young adult librarians offer story hours, book talks, summer reading activities, career planning, art projects, gaming competitions, and other programs to spark youthful imaginations.
8. **Public libraries extend family activities.** Libraries offer an alternate venue for parents and their children to continue and enhance activities traditionally conducted at home, such as homework centers, parenting collections, after-school programs, outreach, one-on-one reading, and early-literacy programs.
9. **Public libraries build 21st-century skills.** Library services and programs foster critical-thinking skills, problem-solving aptitude, visual and scientific literacy, cross-disciplinary thinking, information and media literacy, productivity and leadership skills, civic literacy, global awareness, and health and environmental literacy.

10. **Public libraries serve as technology hubs.** Libraries offer a wide range of public-access computing and internet access services at no charge to users. In 2012, more than 62% of US libraries reported that they were the only provider of free computer and internet access in their communities.
11. **Public libraries offer a lifeline to the unemployed.** Library patrons search for jobs online, polish résumés with word processing software, fill out applications, research new professions, sign up for career workshops, and look for financial assistance.
12. **Public libraries return high dividends.** Public libraries return to their communities anywhere from $1.30 to $10.00 in services for every $1.00 invested in them. In 2009, public librarians delivered more than 300 million hours of service annually (144,261 US librarians x 40 hours a week x 52 weeks). How valuable is your local library? Use the handy Library Value Calculator created by the Massachusetts Library Association (www.ilovelibraries.org/getinformed/getinvolved/calculator).
13. **Public libraries build communities.** People gather at the library to find and share information, experience and experiment with the arts and media, and engage in community discussions and games.
14. **Public libraries preserve the past.** Libraries are repositories of community history, oral narratives, and audiovisual records of events and culture. When these local resources are digitized and placed online as digital libraries, communities and cultures 1,000 miles away can share in the experience.

SOURCE: George M. Eberhart, *The Librarian's Book of Lists* (Chicago: American Library Association, 2010), 82–83.

Public library records

Most bookmobiles—7: St. Louis County (Mo.) Library District.
Most branches—98: Toronto (Ont.) Public Library.
Most self-service kiosks—250: King County (Wash.) Library System.
Highest director's salary—$230,000: Los Angeles Public Library.*
Highest entry-level salary—$88,199: Ajax (Ont.) Public Library.
Most paid MLS librarians—463.5: Toronto (Ont.) Public Library.
Most reference transactions—8,767,705: County of Los Angeles Public Library.
Most interlibrary loans to others—957,465: Cleveland (Ohio) Public Library.
Most interlibrary loans from others—888,064: Madison (Wis.) Public Library.
Most holdings per capita—90.09: Bison (S. Dak.) Public Library.
Highest collection turnover—41.96: Carson City (Nev.) Public Library.
Highest circulation of electronic materials (including ebooks)—2,970,471: Allen County (Ind.) Public Library.
Highest attendance at programs—865,495: Toronto (Ont.) Public Library.
Highest registrations as % of population served—565%: Delta Community Library, Delta Junction, Alaska.

* The New York Public Library Branch Libraries did not report the director's salary, and the NYPL Research Libraries did not participate in this survey.

SOURCE: Public Library Data Service Statistical Report database, FY2011, www.plametrics.org.

The 20 largest public libraries

THE NUMBER OF VOLUMES a library owns is not a measure of the quality of library service. But as Herman Fussler noted in 1949, "Yet the reverence for size continues. The library that has the most books is likely to be regarded as, ipso facto, the best." Volume counts do have a certain fascination. The following are among the largest public libraries in North America, according to 2011 data in the annual *Public Library Data Service Statistical Report*, which surveyed 1,498 libraries.—*GME*.

Boston Public Library	16,140,023
Public Library of Cincinnati and Hamilton County	8,819,759
Toronto Public Library	8,694,461
Detroit Public Library	7,070,433
New York Public Library, the Branch Libraries	7,001,664
County of Los Angeles Public Library	6,795,552
Queens Borough Public Library	6,544,609
Los Angeles Public Library	6,459,552
Chicago Public Library	5,790,289
San Diego Public Library	5,535,415
Free Library of Philadelphia	5,043,943
Dallas Public Library	4,972,494
Hennepin County (Minn.) Library	4,961,514
Cleveland Public Library	4,273,202
Brooklyn Public Library	4,233,304
King County (Wash.) Library System	4,044,907
Hawaii State Public Library System	3,776,405
Miami-Dade (Fla.) Public Library System	3,674,651
Broward County (Fla.) Libraries	3,477,312
Mid-Continent Consolidated Library District, Independence, Mo.	3,419,516

SOURCE: Public Library Data Service Statistical Report database, FY2011, www.plametrics.org.

Public libraries as internet providers
by Charles R. McClure and Paul T. Jaeger

ON THE BASIS OF OUR RESEARCH over recent years—including national public library and internet surveys; focus groups with public librarians, users, and community members on uses and applications of technology in public libraries around the country; and development of statewide digital libraries and library services—we see several internet-enabled social roles and responses now being developed and provided by the public library community. Here is a summary of some of the most important.

Place for public access to the internet. All community residents have the opportunity to come to the library and access and use the array of services and resources available on the internet. For a majority of communities, the public library is the only place where free access to the internet is available. This service response requires staff who are trained in assisting users locate the services and resources available and requires that the library have a high-quality technology infrastructure such as adequate workstations, bandwidth, and up-to-date equipment and software.

E-government services provider. Community residents rely on the public library to access federal, state, and local information and to interact effectively with these government units to obtain specific services such as completing benefits forms and obtaining child support. Staff must be knowledgeable about the range of federal, state, and local e-government services available and being requested, they must be able to assist the user in completing these forms, and they must be able to help users obtain additional information from the agencies as needed.

Emergency and disaster relief provider. In times of local community emergencies—hurricanes, tornadoes, terrorist attacks— the public library is a source of current information and a means for residents to communicate with other local residents and people outside their community. Public library staff are trained to assist both residents and emergency/disaster relief staff in accessing, managing, and providing current information. Internet-enabled resources and computing technology provide the basis for the provision of these services.

Wi-Fi services in use at the San Diego County (Calif.) Public Library.

Internet and technology trainer. Community residents rely on the public library to learn how to access and use the internet, how to use various software applications to solve individual needs, how to use new information technologies, and how to use such internet services as email. These services include one-on-one assistance that teaches users how to complete job applications and government forms and to access and understand, for example, medical information. Library staff are both knowledgeable about these technologies and applications and high-quality trainers. The library has training facilities such that instruction can be easily and effectively provided.

Youth educational support provider. Increasingly, the public library provides a broad range of support to youth in need of assistance in accessing electronic information for formal education and homeschooling educational needs. Indeed, many public libraries have specific internet-enabled programs that are intended primarily to help youths (and parents) be successful in their educational efforts.

Computers in use at the Carrollton Library, West Georgia Regional System.

Staff must be knowledgeable about these sources, be able to assist youths in their use, and have the skills to work with youths and young adults to apply this information to specific assignments and other projects. The library must have physical facilities that support these applications and access to these applications.

Connector of friends, families, and others. An important service response of public libraries in the networked environment is serving as a means for individuals to stay in touch via email and other applications with friends, family, and other individuals. Tourists use the public library to contact children and friends;

in natural disasters, people use the public library to track their family members and friends; immigrants stay in touch with families back home (wherever that is); and a range of business and other communication is conducted electronically at the library. To meet this service response, the library must have an adequate number of public-access workstations to meet user demand throughout the day and staff who can assist those who need basic training to access various communication services.

Anyplace, anywhere, anytime individualized information provider. Local residents and others can now access services such as Ask-a-Librarian electronically through email, chat, handheld devices, and in some instances video streaming and blogs. Significantly, users can access such service anyplace, anytime, and from virtually anywhere. Librarians must be trained to use interactive internet-enabled communication software, develop etiquette skills, and use a range of electronic resource-sharing approaches to make this information available.

Digital library manager. For many users of public libraries, the primary access and use of the library is through the library's digital website. Indeed, many library services and resources are easier to access and use electronically than in person. The construction of a public library's virtual digital library via the web is significantly different than the provision of services and resources in a physical facility. To be successful in this service response, the library staff must have knowledge of the design and management of digital libraries, determine how best to provide electronic resources to its virtual users, and have a modern and high-quality technology information infrastructure platform for the digital library.

Virtual, seamless, and endless electronic resources provider. Residents may not know where a resource is located, who owns it, or how it can be quickly obtained. They only know that they need the item *now*. Public libraries respond by having statewide and nationally developed electronic resource-sharing networks that are virtual, seamless, extensive, and almost instantaneous in the provision of these resources—often in full text. The public library must participate in such networks, understand how to make these resources available "just-in-time," and have the technology infrastructure and bandwidth for such resources to be delivered directly to the user.

Digital workplace/space. The public library provides digital tools, resources, and services that residents can use whenever they wish (from the library or remotely). These tools may include blogs, wikis, digital cameras, RSS feeds, threaded discussion lists, and more. Access to this workplace and workspace allows residents to use and experiment with current technologies to which they might not otherwise have access. Being a digital workplace/space requires the library to have state-of-the-art information technology and support as well as extremely knowledgeable staff who can work with residents on these various applications.

Digital ombudsperson. Public librarians may go well beyond making internet resources and services available to their users and training them on the use of these resources and services. In this service response, the librarian provides advice and specific techniques for applying and integrating various digital and internet-enabled services and resources to meet specific needs of the user. Once again, providing a digital ombudsperson service response requires the library to have state-of-the-art information technology and support as well as extremely knowledgeable staff who can work with residents on creative and innovative solutions in various digital applications.

SOURCE: Charles R. McClure and Paul T. Jaeger, *Public Libraries and Internet Service Roles: Measuring and Maximizing Internet Services* (Chicago: American Library Association, 2009), 49–51.

SCHOOL LIBRARIES

School library checklist for principals

by Doug Johnson

RAPID CHANGES IN TECHNOLOGY, learning research, and the library profession in the past 20 years have created a wide disparity in the effectiveness of school library media programs. Is your school's library media program keeping current? The checklist below can be used to quickly evaluate your building's program.

Professional staff and duties
- Does your library media center have the services of a fully licensed school library media specialist (SLMS)?
- Is that person fully engaged in professional duties? Is there a written job description for all library media personnel: clerical, technical, and professional?
- Does the SLMS understand the changing roles of the SLMS as described in *Empowering Learners: Guidelines for School Library Media Programs* (Chicago: ALA American Association of School Libraries, 2009)?
- Does the SLMS offer staff development opportunities in information literacy, information technologies, and integration of these skills into the content area?
- Is the SLMS an active member of a professional organization?
- Is the SLMS considered a full member of the teaching faculty?

Professional support
- Is sufficient clerical help available to the SLMS so that she/he can perform professional duties rather than clerical tasks?
- Is sufficient technical help available to the SLMS so that she/he can perform professional duties rather than technical tasks?
- Is there a district media supervisor, leadership team, or department chair who is responsible for planning and leadership?
- Do the building principal, site leadership committee, and staff development team encourage the library media personnel to attend workshops, professional meetings, and conferences that will update their skills and knowledge?
- Does the SLMS participate in a Professional Learning Community and Personal Learning Networks?

Collection size and development
- Does the library media center's book and audiovisual collection meet the needs of the curriculum? Has a baseline print collection size been

Word cloud created in Wordle based on the words in this and the following article.

established? Is the collection well weeded?

- Is a variety of media available that will address different learning styles?
- Have electronic and online resources been added to the collection when appropriate? Are there sufficient hardware and internet bandwidth for groups of students to take advantage of these resources?
- Has a recent assessment been done that balances print collection size and electronic resources? Have some print materials been supplanted by online subscriptions? Has space formerly used to house print materials been effectively repurposed?
- Are new materials chosen from professional selection sources and tied to the curriculum through collection mapping?

Facilities

- Is the library media center located so it is readily accessible from all classrooms? Does it have an outside entrance so it can be used for community functions evenings and weekends? Can computer labs be reached directly from a hallway instead of through the library media center?
- Does the library media center have an atmosphere conducive to learning with serviceable furnishings, instructional displays, and informational posters? Is the library media center carpeted with static-free carpet to reduce noise and protect electronic devices? Is the library media center climate-controlled so that materials and equipment will not be damaged by high heat and humidity, and so that it can be used for activities during the summer?
- Does the library contain general instructional areas, a story area (in elementary schools), and spaces for individuals to work?
- Does the library media center contain a computer lab or wireless laptops/netbooks for students and teachers working with a class or independently in the library and for the SLMS to use to teach? Does the library contain and support multimedia workstations and digital video production facilities?
- Is the library media center fully networked with voice, video, and data lines in adequate quantities? Does the library media center serve as the hub of these information networks with routers, file servers, video head ends, and technical staff housed there?
- Does the library maintain a useful, up-to-date online presence with resources for students, staff, and families?

Curriculum and integration

- Is the SLMS an active member of grade-level and/or team-planning groups?
- Is the SLMS an active member of content curriculum writing committees?
- Is the SLMS a part of grade-level or content-area professional learning communities?
- Are library media center resources examined as a part of the content areas' curriculum review cycle?
- Are library media and information technology skills taught as part of content areas rather than in isolation? Are the information literacy skills of evaluating, processing, and communicating information being taught as well as accessing skills?
- Is the safe and appropriate use of online resources a part of the information and technology literacy curriculum?

Resource-based teaching

- Does the SLMS (with assistance from building and district leadership) promote teaching activities that go beyond the textbook?
- Do teachers and administrators view the SLMS as an instructional design and authentic assessment resource? Does the library program support inquiry-based and student-centered learning activities throughout all curricular areas? Does the SLMS collaborate with students and teachers to create a wide range of opportunities that enable the development and practice of critical-thinking skills and responsible digital citizenship?
- Does flexible scheduling in the building permit the SLMS to be a part of teaching teams with classroom teachers, rather than only covering teacher preparation time?
- Is a clear set of information literacy and technology benchmarks written for all grade levels available? Are these benchmarks assessed in a joint effort of the SLMS and classroom teacher? Are the results of these assessments shared with the student and parents?

Information technology

- Does the library media center give its users access to recent information technologies such as:
  a. computerized library catalog and circulation system for the building collection?
  b. access to a computerized union catalog of district holdings as well as access to the catalogs of public, academic, and special libraries from which interlibrary loans can be made?
  c. full online access to the internet?
  d. a wide variety of online reference tools like full-text periodical indexes, encyclopedias, atlases, concordances, dictionaries, thesauri, readers' advisors, and almanacs?
  e. a wide variety of computerized productivity programs appropriate to student ability level such as word processors, multimedia and presentation programs, spreadsheets, databases, desktop publishing programs, graphic creation programs, and still and motion digital image-editing software?
  f. access to collaborative learning/networking tools such as wikis, blogs,

and other online sharing programs and cloud computing resources
such as online productivity tools and file storage?

g. production hardware, such as multimedia computers, still and video
digital cameras, scanners, and LCD projection devices?

h. educational television programming and services?

i. access to desktop conferencing equipment and software?

j. educational computer programs including practices, simulations, and
tutorials that support the curriculum?

- Are the skills needed to use these resources being taught to and with
teachers by the SLMS?

Telecommunications
- Is the school linked by a telecommunications network for distance
learning opportunities for students? Are there interactive classrooms in
the building?
- Does the library media program coordinate programming that can be
aired on the local public access channel?
- Does the library program coordinate in-house video broadcast programming?

Reference, networking, and interlibrary loan
- Does your SLMS have the expertise needed to provide effective and
timely reference services to students and staff?
- Is your school a member of a regional multitype system or library consortium?
- Does the SLMS use interlibrary loan to fill student and staff requests
that cannot be met by building collections?
- Does the SLMS participate in cooperative planning opportunities with
other schools, both locally and distant?

Planning/yearly goals
- Does the library media program have a district-wide set of long-range
goals?
- Does the SLMS set yearly goals based on the long-term goals that are
tied directly to building and curriculum goals in collaboration with
building leadership?
- Is a portion of the SLMS's evaluation based on the achievement of the
yearly goals?
- Is the library media program represented on the building technology
planning committee or the district technology planning committee?

Budgeting
- Is the library media program budget zero- or objective-based? Is the
budget tied to program goals?
- Does the SLMS write clear rationales for the materials, equipment, and
supplies requested?
- Does the budget reflect both a maintenance and growth component for
the program?
- Does the SLMS keep clear and accurate records of expenditures?
- Does the SLMS write grant applications when available?

Policies/communications
- Are board policies concerning selection and reconsideration policies

current and enforced? Is the staff aware of the doctrines of intellectual freedom and library user privacy? Do these policies extend to digital resources?

- Does the district have a safe and acceptable-use policy for internet and technology use?
- Does the SLMS serve as an interpreter of copyright laws? Does the SLMS help others determine the rights they wish to put on their own intellectual property?
- Does the SLMS have a formal means of communicating the goals and services of the program to the students, staff, administration, and community? Is the library's web presence professional, easy to navigate, current, and useful?

Evaluation

- Does the SLMS determine and report ways that show the goals and objectives of the program are being met and are helping meet the building and district goals? Does the SLMS create an annual library report for administrators, staff, and parents that includes qualitative and quantitative measurements?
- Do all new initiatives involving the library media and technology program have an evaluation component?
- Does the district regularly evaluate the library media program using external teams of evaluators as part of any accreditation process?
- Do the SLMS and school participate in formal studies conducted by academic researchers when requested?

SOURCE: Doug Johnson, "13 Point Library Media Program Checklist for School Principals, 2009," Blue Skunk Blog, October 23, 2009, doug-johnson.squarespace.com/blue-skunk-blog/2009/10/23/13-point-checklist-2009.html. Reprinted with permission.

Selected activities of school librarians

THREE ACTIVITIES of school librarians are key to their roles as teachers, administrators, and instructional collaborators.

Delivering instruction. Of these three activities, not surprisingly, delivering instruction is the one that demands the most time. In half of the schools that responded to the 2007 *School Libraries Count!* survey, librarians spent at least 12 hours per week—or almost two and a half hours per day—on this activity. This number has continued to increase; by 2012, the average number of hours spent on delivering instruction had increased to 14.4 hours per week. The top quarter of schools reported 20 or more hours per week of instructional delivery—half of the time of a single full-time equivalent. The top 5% of schools reported that delivering instruction took up 31–32 hours per week in 2011–2012—roughly three-quarters of a single FTE.

Overseeing the library media center budget. School library budget oversight required at least two hours per week for half of responding schools, at least four hours for the top quarter of schools, and 10 hours or more per week for the top 5% of respondents.

Planning with teachers. For collaborative planning of instructional units with classroom teachers, responding libraries reported surprisingly low numbers of hours per week. In 2012, half of the respondents spent one hour per week or less on this important activity. The top quarter of schools reported three or more hours per week of collaborative planning—on average, a little more than a half hour per day—and the top 5% reported seven or more hours for this activity—less than an hour and a half per day.

Doubtless, two reasons above all others explain these figures. Many librarians have little or no support staff to cover the library while they meet with teachers. Likewise, many librarians are in schools that do not embrace flexible scheduling of visits to the library—very often because fixed schedules are utilized to provide solitary planning periods to teachers, while librarians and other staff are required to supervise students during those periods.

School libraries reported being open roughly the same number of hours from 2007 to 2012, with the average ranging from 31.8 to 34; the availability of flexible hours also remains consistent. Additionally, the hours worked by school librarians has increased an average 2.0 hours in the same time period; however, in 2012 the number of hours decreased slightly across schools outside the Midwest. On average, survey participants reported a decline of 2.8 hours worked by overall library staff from 2007 to 2012.

Studies show that students are more likely to be successful if they have the benefit of school library programs led by a state-certified school librarian, and that higher test scores are linked to the presence of quality school library programs and the involvement of full-time school librarians in the learning process.

SOURCE: *School Libraries Count! A National Survey of School Library Media Programs* (Chicago: ALA American Association of School Librarians, 2007), 4; *School Libraries Count! A National Longitudinal Survey of School Library Programs* (Chicago: ALA American Association of School Librarians, 2012), 5–7; SupportSchool Libraries!, ilovelibraries.org.

SPECIAL LIBRARIES

Choosing law librarianship
by Mary Whisner

I WAS FORTUNATE to have some good advice when I was thinking about my move to law librarianship. By now, well into my career, I have many observations of my own to share with readers who are now thinking about that move.

Even people who have spent considerable time in law libraries often do not have a good idea of what law librarians do. For instance, law students and lawyers see reference librarians at the reference desk, but have no idea of what they do away from the desk—let alone what catalog librarians, acquisitions librarians, and others do. A library paraprofessional might have a good idea of what the librarians she works with most closely do, but not know about other librarians in the institution or in other types of libraries.

Law librarianship is characterized by variety. There are different types of law libraries (serving law firms, government agencies, law schools, courts, corporate law departments). There are different sizes of law libraries—from a one-person library serving a law firm with 30 attorneys to the Law Library of Congress. And there are different law librarian positions (from catalog librarian to library director, from computer services librarian to rare books librarian).

Service. Librarianship is fundamentally a service profession. The staff members of a law library serve the larger organization—law school, court, agency, or law firm. If you like customer service and you enjoy coming up with ways to serve your organization better, you could have a long, happy life in the profession. On the other hand, if you do not like the idea of setting your project aside because Professor Procrastinator or Larry the Last Minute Litigator has a deadline, then you might find some parts of law librarianship vexing.

Juggling. Most law librarians I know juggle many different duties and projects. In a given week, a reference librarian might work at the reference desk, do research for a partner or professor, serve on a committee, edit a newsletter, conduct a training session, and clear a printer jam. Meanwhile, a technical services librarian might catalog some books, supervise the paraprofessional who is checking in serials, negotiate a contract with a bibliographic utility, serve on a university committee, and write a policy manual.

Organizing. An essential feature of library work is that it involves organizing. Librarians organize materials (cataloging and classifying). They organize information (creating bibliographies, setting up brief banks, structuring an intranet site). They organize people and projects. Librarians also tend to think institutionally about policies and procedures—for example, setting up a system for assigning study carrels that will be fair to all the law students in a school or setting up a check-out system for a firm library that is likely to be used by all the attorneys in a firm.

Role in decision-making. Most librarians are involved in setting library policy and making decisions about personnel and resources. Some people think it is rewarding to be involved in the decision-making. Others think it is awful to have to figure out how to balance a budget or decide when to discipline an employee who is not performing well. The good news is having a say, but it's not good news for you if you don't want to do the work of sitting in meetings, writing and reviewing proposals, and hammering out compromises.

Communicating. Like most professional work, law librarianship requires good communication—in many settings, using many media. Are you interested in leading a class or training session? Could you explain the pros and cons of subscribing to a new database to colleagues in a selection committee meeting? Would you like to write research guides or create websites? If you had to summarize research results in a memo to a law professor or a judge, would you convey professionalism and intelligence?

Professional involvement. Librarians often belong to regional and national associations where they can be involved by serving on committees, holding office, speaking, and so on. Some professional involvement includes public service projects (for example, educating the public about law and legal research, even if you aren't in a library that's open to the public). At many institutions, librarians get support for this involvement (having leave time and a travel budget to attend a conference). Librarians also often write for publication. In some academic settings, librarians must publish in order to receive tenure or promotion.

Self-education. Law librarianship and legal research are always changing, so it is important for professionals to devote substantial efforts to continuing self-education. This includes reading professional publications, monitoring discussion lists, and attending training sessions.

Job market. Law librarianship has a national job market. As a librarian you could apply for—and might even be recruited for—jobs in other parts of the country. The good news is that you can go many places in the field. The bad news is that—depending on your city—you might need to move in order to get the sort of position you want. For example, if you want to work in an academic law library and the one law school in your city does not have any openings now, you will need to apply elsewhere. Law librarianship also has local job markets. For instance, many (perhaps most) law firm jobs are advertised and filled locally.

Status and stereotypes. Law librarians are generally valued contributors within the organizations they serve. However, just as they do not get the biggest salaries, they do not have other markings of status: the corner office, the best parking space, and so on. Those will go to the partners, deans, and judges.

Some organizations have some ignorant, rude individuals in positions of authority who do not treat librarians (or any support staff) with the respect they deserve. They are an occupational hazard.

Changing professions can mean swapping stereotypes. Some lawyers who become librarians miss the positive stereotypes of lawyers (smart, powerful, important) and regret the negative stereotypes of librarians (dull, mousy, prim). On the other hand, it can be refreshing to lose the negative stereotypes of lawyers (greedy, argumentative, unscrupulous, arrogant) in favor of the positive stereotypes of librarians (smart, knowledgeable, helpful, committed, energetic).

Through our own conduct, we all help to shape the stereotype. The people who come to our libraries and see us in action know that librarians are accomplished, highly trained professionals.

Find out more. One way to get a sense of what law librarians do is to talk to us. We are a chatty lot and many of us are happy to talk to people who are considering the profession. Talk to the librarians at the law library you use or contact your local chapter of the American Association of Law Libraries.

SOURCE: Mary Whisner, "Update to Choosing Law Librarianship: Thoughts for People Contemplating a Career Move," LRRX.com, April 4, 2008, www.llrx.com/features/lawlibrarianship.htm. Reprinted with permission.

Medical libraries: A clinician's guide

by Jamie Graham

HEALTH SCIENCE LIBRARIES perform critical functions in universities for both medical students and faculty. Here is a summary of the services offered by librarians at the New York University Health Sciences Libraries.—*GME.*

You may have seen us at clinical rounds, faculty council, or institutional review board sessions. You may have wondered why a medical librarian would be present outside the library. Our exact function is often a mystery to clinicians, so we are taking this opportunity to tell you everything we have to offer.

Professional librarians at the NYU Health Sciences Libraries have a masters in library science and often hold additional degrees in specific subject matters. Many attain further credentialing by the Academy of Health Professionals and a few possess doctorates as well. In addition, the Medical Library Association offers continuing education seminars that keep medical librarians attuned to developments in the various health professions. In this way, we stay current on topics such as accreditation, changes in evidence-based practice, and consumer health information.

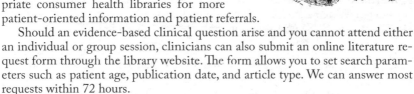

In our role as librarians, we can certainly help any clinician acquire specific research materials and documents. However, our job is not limited to providing assistance solely within the library. Another major function is to participate in clinical rounds by answering questions that arise regarding the current practice of evidence-based medicine in patient care. We can address issues during the meetings or afterwards through individual sessions or small group workshops. We can also direct clinicians to the appropriate consumer health libraries for more patient-oriented information and patient referrals.

Should an evidence-based clinical question arise and you cannot attend either an individual or group session, clinicians can also submit an online literature request form through the library website. The form allows you to set search parameters such as patient age, publication date, and article type. We can answer most requests within 72 hours.

Furthermore, framing your query in a PICO format can help clarify your request, streamline the search process, and ensure a quicker response. PICO represents a widely used method of asking clinical questions by directly specifying the patient Population, Intervention, Control, and Outcome of interest.

Our librarians also provide scheduled training classes throughout the year on topics such as evidence-based medicine practice, research management, clinical resources, and grant funding. Additionally, we can teach individual sessions and offer small group presentations by request. Popular topics include using resources such as RefWorks, creating table-of-contents alerts in Ovid, finding bibliometrics, and preparing manuscripts according to current National Institutes of Health mandates. Sessions are held either in the library or at outside offices.

One recent initiative involves assisting the NYU School of Medicine faculty in finding multimedia resources to incorporate into their lectures and Learning Activity Management System or LAMS. In this way, our goal is to enhance the online Advanced Learning Exchange (ALEX) system and we hope to expand the role of our librarians with ALEX in the near future.

Our medical librarians wear a variety of different hats in the health care arena and our services can be tailored to fit individual needs. Finally, if clinicians ever find themselves in need of immediate information support, they can always use our Ask-a-Librarian service.

SOURCE: Jamie Graham, "What Exactly Do You Do? A Clinician's Guide to the Medical Librarian," *Clinical Correlations,* September 25, 2009, www.clinicalcorrelations.org/?p=1869. Reprinted with permission.

NATIONAL LIBRARIES

Library of Congress 2012 fact sheet

TODAY'S LIBRARY OF CONGRESS is an unparalleled world resource. The collection of more than 151 million items includes more than 34.5 million cataloged books and other print materials in 470 languages; more than 66.6 million manuscripts; the largest rare book collection in North America; and the world's largest collection of legal materials, films, maps, sheet music, and sound recordings. In fiscal year 2012, the Library of Congress:

Welcomed nearly 1.7 million on-site visitors.

Responded to more than 700,000 congressional reference requests and delivered to Congress more than 1 million research products and approximately 30,000 volumes from the library's collections.

Provided reference services to 540,489 individuals (in person, by telephone, and through written and electronic correspondence).

Held a total of 155,357,302 items in the collections, including:

23,276,091	cataloged books in the Library of Congress classification system.
12,638,773	books in large type and raised characters, incunabula (books printed before 1501), monographs and serials, bound newspapers, pamphlets, technical reports, and other printed material.
119,442,438	items in the nonclassified (special) collections. These included:
3,420,599	audio materials, such as discs, tapes, talking books, and other recorded formats.
68,118,899	manuscripts.
5,478,123	maps.
16,746,497	microforms.
6,589,199	pieces of sheet music.
15,704,268	visual materials, including 1,354,126 moving images, 13,640,325 photographs, 104,270 posters, and 605,547 prints and drawings.

Circulated more than 25 million copies of Braille and recorded books and magazines to more than 800,000 blind and physically handicapped reader accounts.

Circulated more than 1 million items for use within the library.

Preserved 6 million items from the library's collections.

Registered 511,539 claims to copyright.

Recorded more than 87 million visits and 545 million page views on the library's website. At year's end, the library's online primary source files totaled 37.6 million.

Employed a permanent staff of 3,312 employees.

Operated with a total fiscal 2012 appropriation of $629.2 million, including authority to spend $41.9 million in receipts.

SOURCE: Library of Congress, www.loc.gov/about/generalinfo.html.

The Vatican Library

by Cardinal Jean-Louis Tauran

THE VATICAN APOSTOLIC LIBRARY has a long history. It was founded on April 30, 1451, by Pope Nicholas V, who had the idea of opening a public library in the Vatican that would no longer be for the exclusive use of the pontiff.

The popes were, for the most part, great humanists. The library of the popes who resided in Avignon, France, had become one of the greatest in Europe, with 1,677 Latin codices. However, historical upheavals and the changes in papal residences left Nicholas with a library of only 350 manuscripts. He therefore decided to add his personal collection to these and create a library that aimed to be "of common use to men of knowledge." Nicholas had facilities prepared inside the Palace of the Vatican and began to collect books for a "universal" library, in accordance with the humanistic criteria of the time—not only theology or law, but also literature (with Latin and Greek codices), medicine, astronomy, and mathematics.

Nicholas's efforts were successful, since when he died in 1455 the Vatican Library contained more than 1,200 manuscripts. This was how our library, at that time the largest in Europe, came into being.

Today, the Vatican Apostolic Library houses one of the most important collections of manuscripts and books in the world as a result of continuous growth over the centuries. The history of its development coincides with the history of literature, culture, and art in the West and elsewhere. [The library closed for refurbishing in 2007–2010 and in 2012 began a five-year project to digitize many of its manuscript holdings.—*GME.*]

The manuscripts kept in the library cover literature and history, art and law, astronomy and mathematics, natural sciences and medicine, liturgy, patristics, and theology. The total number of manuscripts is around 150,000 (including volumes in the archives). The majority date from the Middle Ages and Renaissance, with a few important documents from antiquity and many others from the modern era. There are about 60,000 of the so-called "Latins," or those written in the Latin alphabet in many languages (Latin, Italian, French, English, Spanish, German, Provençal, etc.); about 5,000 in the Greek alphabet; about 800 in Hebrew; more than 9,000 in other Middle Eastern languages, including Arabic, Coptic, Syriac, Armenian, and Ethiopian; and about 2,000 in Chinese, Korean, and Japanese.

This enormous collection is accompanied by a considerable patrimony of early printed material: about 8,300 incunabula, books from the 16th and 17th centuries, prints, drawings, objects, coins and medals (about 400,000 items, one of the largest numismatic cabinets in the world), as well as modern printed books (about 1.6 million).

To cite a few examples, we hold some of the most ancient copies of Homer, Euclid, Cicero, Virgil, and Dante. Among the numerous codices of the Bible, the most famous are the Codex Vaticanus (Vat. gr. 1209) of the 4th century and the Papyrus Bodmer VIII from the 3rd century, which contains the oldest copy of St. Peter's letters.

Pope Sixtus IV Appoints Bartolomeo Platina Prefect of the Vatican Library, fresco by Melozzo da Forlì, 1477.

Hebraica in the Vatican. The Vatican Library has remained true to the universal nature desired by its founder, and it is indeed in this spirit of universality that it has also contributed to Jewish and Islamic studies.

The collection of Jewish manuscripts and books at the Vatican Library has been promoted and increased with the help of Jewish scholars. The first nucleus of Jewish manuscripts in the Vatican Secret Archives dates back to a few years after the Sack of Rome in 1527, a traumatic event that eradicated the memory of any previous interest shown by the popes in Jewish sacred books. The first collection was developed by the Jewish convert Ottavio Franceschi (1543–1601), a future bishop of Forli and scriptor hebraicus of the Vatican Library from 1558; and after 1633 by his successor Federico Carlo Borromeo, who cataloged the Jewish manuscripts present at that time.

With the acquisition in 1657 of the collection of the dukes of Urbino, the library obtained a large part of the precious collection of Jewish manuscripts that originally belonged to the merchant Menahem ben Aharon Volterra, which had been acquired by Federico da Montefeltro for his personal library after he ransacked Volterra in 1472.

During the first half of the 20th century, the Vatican Library not only promoted the specialized studies of Jewish scholars, but also provided them with shelter and protection. They included Umberto Cassuto, a rabbi and professor at

Anna Maria
Agnoletti

the University of Rome, as well as a bibliographer for the library from 1933 until 1938 when he left to become a professor at the University of Jerusalem; Giorgio Levi Della Vida, an illustrious linguist who was fired from his post at the University of Rome in 1932 for refusing to take a loyalty oath to Mussolini and who worked in the Vatican Library until 1939; and the Allied partisan and archivist Anna Maria Enriques Agnoletti, who cared for the Archive of St. Peter until 1943 and was executed by Italian fascists in June 1944.

Of the numerous Hebrew manuscripts (about 800) in the Vatican Library, I recall the codices Rossiani 554 and 556, containing respectively the Old Testament and the Psalms, both produced in Rome in the 13th century, which are some of the earliest known illuminated Jewish texts; Rossiani 498 and 555, which constitute a part of the Mishneh Torah by Maimonides and the Arba'ah Turim by Jacob ben Asher, complete with splendid miniatures. The library also has the oldest known manuscript of rabbinic literature, the Vaticanus Ebraicus 66 (a 9th-century commentary on Leviticus), and Neofiti 1 (1504), an important Palestinian targum.

Islamic materials. The inventory compiled by the first Vatican librarian, Bartolomeo Platina, recorded 20 paper manuscripts in Arabic. The Vatican's early interest in Arabic books focused on discovering early Christian documents in Arabic as well as the recovery of classical knowledge by way of the East.

Here are two examples of these two aspects: the Codex Vaticanus Arabus 13, one of the oldest Arabo-Christian New Testament manuscripts extant, which dates back to the 9th century; and the Vaticanus Arabus 310 (10th century), a parchment copy of a treatise by the famous Arabic-speaking Jewish physician Isaac Israeli ben Solomon.

Interest in Arabic doctrine dates back to the time of Sixtus IV, as the Contrastum Muhameti cum Philaton, which formerly belonged to the first collection, attests. The syncretic Vaticanus Ebraicus 357 is also worthy of note, consisting of a Judeo-Arabic treatise on pharmacopeia and a Judeo-Arabic Qur'an with an interlinear handwritten Latin translation, the work of Raimondo Moncada

(Flavius Mithridates), Pico della Mirandola's teacher. Also preserved among the Arabic texts is the only known example of a Spanish Muslim illustrated manuscript (Vaticanus Arabus 638).

With the founding of the Maronite College in 1584 and the resulting influx of Arabic speakers to Rome, there was a significant growth in the number of scholars with some knowledge of Arabic, who not only had access but also contributed to the collections of Arabic works in the Vatican Library. Such a climate culminated with the Maronite Giuseppe Simone Assemani, appointed custodian of the library in 1739. However, not until the beginning of the 20th century was there a rebirth of an authentic tradition of meticulous Islamic studies, with the fundamental contribution of Italy's major Semitic linguist, Giorgio Levi Della Vida, who placed his immense knowledge at the service of the library. By cataloguing its Islamic manuscripts, he laid the foundation for any further study of the Middle Eastern treasures preserved in the Vatican collections.

SOURCE: Cardinal Jean-Louis Tauran, "The Contribution of the Vatican Library to Christian, Jewish, and Islamic Studies: A Mission of Peace," *Amici,* no. 40 (Fall 2006), reprinted in *Catholic Library World* 77, no, 3 (March 2007): 210–213. Reprinted with permission. Tauran was director of the Vatican Library and Vatican Secret Archives from 2003 to 2007.

The Royal Library of Belgium
by Stuart A. P. Murray

BELGIUM'S NATIONAL LIBRARY has roots in the 15th century, when the earliest known libraries belonged to monasteries and to the Dukes of Burgundy. The 900 manuscript titles of the Burgundian library were part of the Belgian royal library when it was established in 1837.

Belgium's diverse and rich cultural heritage includes more than 2,500 public libraries, although the country's population is less than 11 million. Its book heritage is also considerable, with Antwerp one of Europe's major printing centers since 1876.

The Royal Library is bilingual (Flemish and French) in keeping with Belgium's national composition. Its respective names are Koninklijke Bibliotheek and Bibliothèque Royale. It is a scientific institution belonging to the national government and acquires information in every scientific discipline. Since 1966 it has been a legal deposit library responsible for cataloging and collecting every Belgian publication.

The library collects and conserves items from Belgium's national heritage, including books and periodicals, maps and engravings, coins, medals, and printed music. Among the collections are many items from Belgium's musical heritage, including the Fétis archives, made up of the work and books of 19th-century Belgian musicologist, composer, and critic François-Joseph Fétis.

Frontispiece to the *Chroniques de Hainaut,* painted by Rogier van der Weyden and held by the Royal Library of Belgium.

There are 4 million bound volumes, including a rare-book collection numbering 45,000 works. The library has more than 700,000 engravings and drawings, and 150,000 maps and plans. There are more than 250,000 objects, from coins to scales and monetary weights. The coin collection reputedly holds one of the most valuable coins in the entire field of numismatics: a 5th-century B.C. Sicilian tetradrachm.

The Royal Library is host to the Center for American Studies, which offers a master of arts degree program. The center was established by several Belgian universities as a new institute of higher learning, and has its own Library of American Studies (30,000 titles), Library of American Civilization (20,000 computerized volumes on pre–World War I United States), and the American Research Library (3,000 recent online periodicals).

SOURCE: Stuart A. P. Murray, *The Library: An Illustrated History* (New York: Skyhorse, 2009), 249–250.

STATE LIBRARIES

What state library agencies do

A STATE LIBRARY AGENCY is the official agency of a state that is charged by state law with the extension and development of public library services throughout the state and that has adequate authority under state law to administer state plans in accordance with the provisions of the Library Services and Technology Act (LSTA) (P.L. 111–340, passed in December 2010).

Beyond these two roles, state library agencies vary greatly. They are located in various departments of state government and report to different authorities. They are involved in various ways in the development and operation of electronic information networks. They provide different types of services to different types of libraries. They provide important reference and information services to state governments and administer the state libraries and special operations such as state archives, libraries for the blind and physically handicapped, and the state centers for the book.

The state library agency may function as the state's public library at large, pro-

California State Library and Courts building, Sacramento.

viding library services to the general public. Some state libraries perform allied operations—that is, services not ordinarily considered a state library agency function. These allied operations may include maintaining state archives, managing state records, conducting legislative research for the state, or operating a museum or art gallery.

The state library agencies of the District of Columbia, Hawaii, and Maryland are different from other state libraries in a variety of ways. They are administrative offices without a separate state library collection. In the District of Columbia, which is treated as a state for reporting purposes, the Martin Luther King Memorial Library (the central library of the District of Columbia Public Library) functions as a resource center for the district government. In Hawaii, the state library is located in the Hawaii State Public Library System. State law designates Enoch Pratt Free Library's central library as the Maryland State Library Resource Center.

State library services

State library agencies provide many services to libraries, including financial assistance, support for collections maintenance, and facilitating access to technology. In 2010, state library agencies provided $712.1 million in financial assistance to public libraries. This was the lowest amount of assistance provided over the study period, resulting in a 10-year decrease of 28.5%. The highest amount of financial assistance, $996.5 million (2010 constant dollars), was provided in 2001.

State library agencies play an important role in promoting reading and literacy within their respective states. In 2010, more than two-thirds of state library agencies funded literacy programs in public libraries. This has declined by 23.4% over the past 10 years, from a high of 47 states in 2001. Since 2006, 50 state library agencies have funded summer reading programs in public libraries.

State library agencies also fund library programs and services that promote lifelong learning in general. These include homework help programs, after-school programs, English for speakers of other languages (ESOL) classes, information- and computer-literacy training, and online education. Spending on lifelong learning grew from $30.9 million in 2005 to a high of $42.6 million in 2008. LSTA expenditures on programs and services for lifelong learning were $37.9 million in 2010.

State library agencies provide digitization services to aid with the preservation and conservation of materials. In 2010, 32 state library agencies funded or facilitated digitization or digital programs or services to public libraries and library cooperatives. These efforts include any program or activity that provides for the digitization of documents, publications, or sets of records or artifacts to be made available for public use. Since 2005, the number of states that provided digitization support for public libraries has remained stable. Sixteen state library agencies provided preservation and conservation services to libraries.

State library agencies facilitate access to technology and information resources for libraries. One way they accomplish this is by supporting library access to the internet through direct funding, equipment, and internet databases and directories. Twenty-four states provided public libraries with direct funding for internet access in 2010, continuing a downward trend from a high of 37 states in 2001.

More states (29) provided equipment necessary for internet access, including hardware, software, and peripherals. Although there was a slight increase in state library agency equipment support in 2006 and 2007, this service has also been decreasing since 2001. In addition to directly funding internet access and providing equipment to allow access, state library agencies also make more content available online for library patrons. In 2010, all state library agencies provided access to directories, databases, or online catalogs via the internet and managed a website, file server, bulletin board, or electronic mailing list, services that they have been providing since 2002. In 2010, $94.8 million (58.7%) of LSTA funds were spent on library technology, connectivity, and services. Although this is a decrease of 5.6% from 2005 levels, LSTA expenditures on technology have increased by 9.8% from a low of $86.3 million in 2008.

State library agencies often serve as coordinator of library services in their states. In this role, many of them purchase database licenses for public libraries, public school media centers, and library cooperatives. Because the state library agency can leverage the bargaining power of the state and the collective buying power of the entities that it represents, it can negotiate lower prices for access to databases than would otherwise occur if individual libraries and administrative entities had to negotiate agreements themselves, thus leading to an overall savings. In 2010, 48 state library agencies purchased statewide database licenses for public libraries, 42 purchased licenses for school library media centers (elementary and secondary public schools), and 34 purchased licenses for library cooperatives.

Across the United States, expenditures on statewide database licenses have increased by 7% over the past 10 years. During this time, expenditures have fluctuated between $56.9 million in 2003 and $67.8 million in 2005. In 2010, state library agencies spent $65.2 million on statewide database licensing. In 2010, federal and state contributions to funds for statewide database licensing were comparable, at $31.8 million (48.8%) and $29.6 million (45.4%), respectively. This represents a dramatic change over the 10-year study period. In 2001, state contributions comprised the lion's share of funds for statewide database licensing at $37.9 million (76.2%). In contrast, the federal contribution in 2001 was $11.8 million (23.8%). Federal sources have accounted for the largest absolute increase in funding over the study period ($17.3 million), representing a 119.8% increase. Taken as a whole, this demonstrates that federal and other sources of revenue have grown in importance over the past decade.

State library agencies fund continuing education events for library staff in public libraries, academic libraries, public school media centers, special libraries, and library cooperatives. Almost all states provided continuing education events for library professionals. In 2010, there were 9,974 continuing education events offered nationwide, a 133.1% increase since 2001. Attendance at continuing education events in 2010 was 142,811, a 30.9% increase from 2001.

State library agency revenue totaled $1.08 billion in 2010, having fallen by $344.2 million since 2001, a 10-year decline of 24.1%. Revenue increased in 2007, but overall has continued on a downward trajectory in recent years. Similarly, expenditures fell by 23.5%, from $1.4 billion in 2001 to $1.07 billion in 2010.

SOURCE: *State Library Agency Survey: Fiscal Year 2010* (Washington, D.C.: Institute of Museum and Library Services, January 2012), www.imls.gov/assets/1/AssetManager/stla2010.pdf.

MOBILE LIBRARIES

The first bookmobile

THE FIRST BOOKMOBILE in the United States was introduced in Washington County, Maryland, in 1905. Mary L. Titcomb, the first librarian of Washington County Free Library, considered seriously the need for the library to become a county library. Her task was to get books in homes throughout the county, not just in Hagerstown, the county seat. The first step was to send boxes of books on the Library Wagon to the general store or the post office in small towns and villages throughout the county. By 1904, boxes with 30 volumes each were sent to 66 deposit stations, to extend the reach of the library and manage the practical distribution of the books.

Mary L. Titcomb

But Miss Titcomb was not satisfied. As she wrote in *The Story of the Washington County Free Library:*

Would not a Library Wagon, the outward and visible signs of the service for which the Library stood, do much more in cementing friendship? Would the upkeep of the wagon after the first cost be much more than the present method? Is not Washington County with its good roads especially well adapted for testing an experiment of this kind, for the geography of the County is such that it could be comfortably covered by well planned routes? These and other aspects of the plan were laid before the Board of Trustees—who approved of the idea, and forthwith the librarian began interviewing wagon makers and trying to elucidate her ideas with pen and pencil. The first wagon, when finished with shelves on the outside and a place for storage of cases in the center, resembled somewhat a cross between a grocer's delivery wagon and the tin peddler's cart of bygone New England days. Filled with an attractive collection of books and drawn by two horses, with Mr. Thomas the janitor both holding the reins and dispensing the books, it started on its travels in April 1905.

Joshua Thomas, the janitor at the Washington County Free Library, became the driver of the book wagon between 1905 and 1910.

No better method has ever been devised for reaching the dweller in the country. The book goes to the man, not waiting for the man to come to the book. Psychologically too the wagon is the thing. As well try to resist the pack of a peddler from the Orient as the shelf full of books when the doors of the wagon are opened by Miss Chrissinger at one's gateway.

The wagon, driven by Joshua Thomas, covered many miles over the county roads delivering books to remote houses. There was some initial resistance:

> When directions were given as to painting, we had the fear of looking too much like the laundry wagon before our eyes, and the man was strictly enjoined, not to put any gilt or scroll work on it but to make even the lettering, "Washington County Free Library," plain and dignified, directions carried out only too well, for in the early days of our wagoning, as our man approached one farm house, he heard a voice charged with nervous trepidation, call out, "Yer needn't stop here. We ain't got no use for the dead wagon here." Suffice it to say, that we promptly painted the wheels red, and picked off the panels of the doors with the same cheerful color.

In August 1910, the original book wagon was destroyed. While crossing the Norfolk and Western Railroad track at St. James, a freight train ran into it, leaving literally nothing but fragments. In 1912 a motorized book wagon was introduced, the first of a long fleet of vehicles taking books to the men, women, and children of Washington County, Maryland, not just those in the rural areas, but those in senior citizen homes, Head Start Programs, schools, and many other county residences.

As Miss Titcomb noted: "Any account of this first Book Wagon, the first in the United States, would be incomplete without the statement that this method of rural library extension has been adopted in many states in the Union, and that new book wagons are being put in operation each year." Indeed bookmobiles are now found as part of many library systems around the world, utilizing vans and buses, but also boats, camels, and even donkeys. From the first "perambulating library" in Warrington, England, in 1858 to the first 20th-century book wagon in the United States in 1905, and to the more modern book and media delivery systems of today, libraries are still taking their wares to an appreciative public.

SOURCE: Western Maryland Regional Library, Hagerstown, Maryland, www.whilbr.org/bookmobile/index.aspx. Reprinted with permission.

A tribute to mobile libraries

by Larry T. Nix

PRECEDING BOOKMOBILES as a primary method of library outreach to rural areas were small, rotating collections of books called traveling libraries.

These small libraries, usually from 30 to 100 books, were located in a post office, a store, or someone's home with a volunteer acting as the caretaker of the collection. Under the leadership of Melvil Dewey, the state of New York initiated a state-funded traveling library system in 1892. In New York the collections stayed in one location for six months before they were rotated. Michigan initiated a similar system in 1895. Iowa and Wisconsin followed in 1896. Many other states also adopted this model of public library extension, including California, Idaho, Illinois, Nebraska, Ohio, Oregon, Pennsylvania, and Virginia. Other interesting traveling library efforts were the Seaboard Airline Railway Free Traveling Library System and the United States Lighthouse Service Traveling Library.

A Stout traveling library in Wisconsin, 1890s, named after State Sen. James Huff Stout.

There were also some commercial traveling libraries such as those provided by the H. Parmelee Library Company, founded in Iowa in 1882. It developed a rotating "package" collection that it called the University of the Traveling Library. The company relocated to Chicago in 1898 where it continued to market its rotating package library as a way of providing "a thoroughly equipped and permanent library in every town and hamlet in America."

Like many historical library artifacts, the book cases and boxes that transported and housed traveling libraries have largely disappeared. Those that remain can be found at the following locations:

- Ashland (Wis.) Historical Society Museum
- Russell J. Rassbach Heritage Museum, Menomonie, Wisconsin
- McMillan Memorial Library, Wisconsin Rapids, Wisconsin
- Potawatomi Lighthouse, Rock Island State Park, Wisconsin
- Mystic Seaport Museum Library, Connecticut
- Idaho State Library, Boise
- Idaho State Historical Society, Boise
- Boonsboro (Md.) Free Library
- Special Collections, Columbia University, New York City

- Heceta Head Lighthouse, near Yachats, Oregon
- Library of Virginia, Richmond
- Smithsonian Institution, Washington, D.C.

There are few visions of library service more inspiring than that of a bookmobile and its staff providing books to young children. The concept and reality of bookmobile service started in Hagerstown, Maryland, in April 1905 when Mary L. Titcomb, the librarian of the Washington County Free Library, sent out the first book wagon in the United States. Washington County Free Library was also one of the first libraries in the United States to use a motorized vehicle as a bookmobile.

In 1952, the Maryland State Department of Education issued a booklet in the shape of a bookmobile (right) to promote its mobile library services.

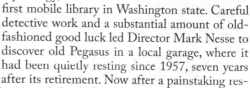

The prohibitive expense of operating branches in remote communities prompted the Everett (Wash.) Public Library to invest in a Model T Ford truck modified to serve as a book wagon, which began service in May 1924.

Named "Pegasus" (left) after the flying horse of mythology, it was the first mobile library in Washington state. Careful detective work and a substantial amount of old-fashioned good luck led Director Mark Nesse to discover old Pegasus in a local garage, where it had been quietly resting since 1957, seven years after its retirement. Now after a painstaking restoration, Pegasus accompanies the library's Book Cart Drill Team in city parades. It is probably the oldest existing bookmobile in the world.

The Smith branch of the New Orleans Public Library was made unusable as a result of Hurricane Katrina in 2005. The librarians, Friends of Libraries, and other citizens of Medina, Ohio, came to the rescue by refitting their recently retired bookmobile and donating it to New Orleans in 2006 to serve the area formerly served by the Smith branch. This prompted Theresa Laffey, outreach services manager for the Medina County District Library, to observe: "Some bookmobiles never die; they just change locations."

SOURCE: Larry T. Nix, "A Tribute to the Bookmobile," Library History Buff Blog, www.libraryhistorybuff.com/bookmobile.htm, and "Traveling Libraries," www.libraryhistorybuff.com/traveling-us.htm. Reprinted with permission.

Recipes from pack horse librarian scrapbooks

by Jason Vance

OLD RECIPES OFFER CLUES about a region's culture and people. For example, recipes from Kentucky's Depression-era Appalachian region include small game, like opossum and groundhog, pointing to mountaineers' use of hunting for obtaining food, controlling garden pests, and sport. Recipes for vegetables offer glimpses of gardens filled with shuck beans, pumpkins, and corn. Pickled walnuts and canned elderberries were picked in the fall and preserved for eating in the winter months. Today, these glimpses of the Appalachian dinner table, garden, and pantry are made possible by Kentucky's pack horse librarians.

Kentucky's pack horse libraries were federally funded Works Progress Administration programs that paid carriers to deliver books and other reading material to isolated Appalachian homes, schools, and community centers during the Great Depression from 1936 to 1940. The librarians, mostly women, traveled routes that were impassable by cars and modern bookmobiles to deliver library material by horse and mule.

Pack horse librarians, mostly women, traveled the remote sections of Kentucky by horse and mule, meeting up at headquarters to replenish the stock. WPA photo, 1938.

By 1940, 182 pack horse librarians operated out of 33 counties in eastern Kentucky. While the WPA provided money for carriers' salaries, supplies, and training, it did not fund the purchase of books and other reading material. The pack horse libraries were heavily dependent on donated books, magazines, and newspapers. Some of these items were so ragged and worn that they were cannibalized to create scrapbooks. According to some reports, the librarians would meet weekly at their local centers and create these scrapbooks as supplements to their circulating collections.

By April 1940, 2,582 of these self-published works were loaned and read by families in eastern Kentucky, but today only a few remain. The Franklin D. Roosevelt Presidential Library in Hyde Park, New York, has a small collection of pack horse library scrapbooks, each of which is thematically arranged. The themes include Bible lessons, nature pictures, quilts and crafts, and recipes.

The subject of recipes and cooking is treated two different ways in the FDR Library's collection of pack horse library scrapbooks. One scrapbook, compiled by pack horse librarians in Harlan County, Kentucky, contains recipes from popular women's magazines like *Good Housekeeping* and *Ladies' Home Journal*. The content of this scrapbook is wholly unoriginal, though the selection and arrangement of the recipes tell an interesting story about the availability of resources for the pack horse library collections. In another scrapbook, the librarian presents a list of 18 typewritten recipes collected from community patrons along the pack horse library routes. This collection seeks to preserve local culture and memory through its recipes.

Recipes from Harlan County

The collection of recipes offered by the Harlan County pack horse library scrapbook is wide in scope, sparsely illustrated, and is compiled entirely of clippings from magazines, labels, and other printed ephemera. An introductory note that accompanies this scrapbook (presumably written for its presentation to the FDR Library) reads: "Cook books are popular. Anything to do with canning or preserving is welcomed. Recipes in Women's Magazines were so much hungered for by the women in the communities that there was a temptation to cut out recipes from the magazines." The creation of these recipe scrapbooks was seen as a way to curb the readers' temptation to deface the libraries' magazines and books.

The recipes were crudely pasted into a spiral-bound composition book that contains 38 lined pages. Many of the recipes in this collection are labeled, "A *Good*

1

Housekeeping Tested Recipe." Others bear the marks of brand names like All-Bran, Eagle Brand, and Wonder. The recipes are sparsely illustrated with pictures that don't always match the content of the page. For example, on one page, a color illustration from an advertisement for Heinz tomato juice is used to illustrate a page containing five recipes in which tomato juice is not an ingredient. Other illustrations contain handwritten annotations for the pictures. One cake is accompanied by a note that reads, "A beautiful cake. . . ."

The selection and arrangement of the recipes in this scrapbook seem somewhat haphazard and dictated by the source materials at hand, not a systematic and careful organization of collected clippings. One page contains recipes for Halloween, like "Skull bone cake," "Owl boats," and "Frosted Halloween Doughnuts." Other pages seem to have no connecting theme or common ingredient and list recipes like "Bean goulash," "Graham cracker raisin cakes," and "Pumpkin waffles," all on the same page.

Despite its loose arrangement, the Harlan County pack horse library recipe scrapbook shows signs of use. Some pages are covered with food spatter or are marked with cup rings. Though these collections of clipped recipes were popular along the pack horse library routes, they did not reflect local tradition or culture. The popularity of recipes for "Oyster pie," "Grape leaf bundles," and "Tropical strawberry shortcake" says less about the mountaineers' gardens and available resources than it does their curiosity and appetite for new experimental dishes.

Recipes from local readers

In addition to cannibalizing magazines, books, and other ephemera for printed recipes, librarians also collected recipes from patrons along their delivery routes. These contributed recipes are more regional in nature and reflect the availability of local game and vegetables. Southern staples like spoon bread and cracklin bread are listed along with less common recipes for pickled green walnuts and canned elderberries.

The FDR Library's scrapbooks contain 18 such recipes, transcribed onto four typewritten pages contained in the introduction to the scrapbook collection. These include local vernacular language and southern expressions like "shuck beans" and "pot likker." One recipe for "Bean soup dumpling" claims to have been made in "slave time."

Many of the cooking instructions require a certain level of cooking proficiency, and aren't as "numerically rigid" and prescribed as recipes in modern cookbooks. Some recipes, like the one for ash cakes, call for the use of an open fireplace to cook in hot coals.

Other recipes, like "A Love Charm or Broiled Steak" tell an actual story. In this recipe, the writer tells of a young woman who thought she was losing her husband's affection. According to the recipe, she went to the "seventh daughter of a seventh daughter for a love powder." Instead of a potion, the "mystery woman" gave her the recipe for broiled steak. At the end of the recipe, the author adds a parenthetical note saying, "The charm was a perfect success."

Even when the narrative isn't so obvious, each of the pack horse library scrapbook recipes tells a story. The pack horse scrapbooks offer a unique window into another era and illustrate the librarians' dual roles of shaping and preserving local culture and memory.

SOURCE: Jason Vance, "A Taste of History: Recipes from Pack Horse Librarian Scrapbooks," *Kentucky Libraries* 73, no. 4 (Fall 2009): 4–7. Reprinted with permission.

Seven arguments for building new libraries

by James LaRue

RECENTLY, ONE OF OUR EMPLOYEES moved to the Midwest to become the director of a library whose main building was destroyed by a thousand-year flood. On the one hand, many members of the community are working to restore that library.

On the other hand, this former employee tells me he's hearing more and more often the refrain that building libraries just isn't necessary. Not in the 21st century. Not in the age of the internet.

I disagree. After I thought about it for a bit, I could come up with at least seven arguments for why we still need to build libraries. But I don't see why we have to stop at seven. Feel free to add to the list.

Argument 1. The library is an anchor store and traffic generator. Libraries pull a cross-section of the public, all ages, all day long, through our doors. We are the business that never goes out of business. (Of course, the closing of four out of seven libraries in Aurora, Colorado, at the end of 2009 indicates that this rule, too, has its exceptions.) Yet it remains true that even in a down economy, library use goes *up*. You want your business to be by a library. If you're planning a development, you want the liveliness of a public building in the heart of it.

Argument 2. Library construction is a powerful economic stimulus, especially in a recession. People often overlook that a public construction project employs architects, general contractors, local tradespeople, local suppliers, and so on, which in turn generates sales for local restaurants, gas stations, etc.

Argument 3. Library buildings are a bridge over the digital divide. Libraries are about access, and our record of allowing digitally disadvantaged people—poor, young, elderly—to use public technology to bootstrap themselves out of technological ghettos is real.

Argument 4. The internet encourages, not replaces, library use. Every time we add more internet terminals, the use of everything else goes up—more books checked out, more browsing, more magazines read, more reference questions, more program attendance. There's a lot of data about this, going all the way back to 1999, and still holding true (see Colorado State Library, Library Research Service, *Fast Facts*, no. 163, Dec. 21, 1999, www.lrs.org/documents/fastfacts/163cirvinet.pdf).

Argument 5. Library buildings foster community, both through providing meeting spaces and hosting programs that foster lifelong learning. Genetically, socially, we are wired for interaction. Libraries serve the role of both common and neutral ground.

Argument 6. Library buildings manifest and reinforce a statement of community values. The library is a tangible sign of a community's commitment to individual inquiry, a safety net for the young and old, a secular sanctuary for people who need public space either for public contact or for private pondering. I remember pondering this comment from a member of the Greatest Generation: "In my day, we lived in modest homes, but built significant public monuments. These days, we live in palaces, and build government buildings out of split-face concrete."

Argument 7. Library buildings are an investment in our children's brains. The children's storytime—featuring real live people from your own community—is our nation's single most potent strategy for sowing literacy in the land. The library is a space where even preschool children meet live performers, then are loaded up with materials to further deepen the experience. The presence of location offering trained staff to promote literacy and learning through readers' advisory work, reference work, teaching, adds a resource to a community that not only employs local people today, but helps raise people who are employable tomorrow.

But that's just off the top of my head. I'd be interested from hearing more from our community. What's the value of a library building?

SOURCE: James LaRue, "7 Arguments for Building New Libraries," LaRue's Views, Douglas County (Colo.) Libraries, December 17, 2009, douglascountylibraries.org/AboutUs/Publications/ LaRuesViews/121709. Reprinted with permission.

Project professionals

by Lynn M. Piotrowicz and Scott Osgood

ONCE YOU HAVE LOOKED at your building plans critically, the next step is to find professionals you can trust to help you achieve your project goals. This is a guide to the key players and their responsibilities.

Needs-assessment phase

Taxpayers pay for any building improvements.

Library governing board facilitates the building improvement process. *Reports to* taxpayers and local government officials. *Oversight:* Creating a building advisory committee.

Building advisory committee consists of the library director, representatives from library staff, library governing board, Friends group, community members, and local government officials. Assesses the needs of the community, translates those needs into an RFP, hires an architectural firm, finds the money for the project, and provides publicity and support for the project. *Reports to* taxpayers, library governing board, and local government officials.

Architectural firm responds to the RFP and meets with the building advisory committee to listen to the goals, dreams, aspirations, and limitations of the library. *Reports to* building advisory committee.

Building advisory committee reviews the cost proposal submitted by the chosen architectural firm. *Reports to* taxpayers, library governing board, and local government officials. *Oversight:* Engages in the quality-based selection process, whereby the architectural plan is compared to the committee's expectations with a special focus on the cost.

Design phase

Architectural firm completes all phases of the design process from concept to final construction documents. *Reports to* building advisory committee, which reviews all phases of the process and provides timely feedback, concerns, and approvals so the architect can proceed to the next stage of the process.

Architectural firm's stable of experts

Licensed engineer creates a site plan of the design to guarantee that your ground can accommodate the building process. *Reports to* architectural firm, local building and zoning officials, and your neighbors. *Oversight:* That your building project does not impact existing structures.

Hazardous remediation surveyor conducts destructive testing to determine if any known hazardous materials will be impacted by your building improvement process. *Reports to* building advisory committee and the architectural firm. *Oversight:* The consideration and removal of any toxic materials.

Structural engineer determines how your building will be supported. *Reports to* architectural firm. *Oversight:* Designing the bones of the building.

Mechanical engineer determines how and where your plumbing, heating, cooling, and air-quality equipment will be located. *Reports to* the commissioning agent, who is hired to verify that the initial mechanical design and the final installation meet the design intent. *Oversight:* Making sure that the air is fresh, the building is heated and cooled, the water is delivered, and the sewage is removed.

Electrical engineer interprets the National Electric Code and places panels, transformers, and circuits in correct locations and quantities. *Reports to* architectural firm. *Oversight:* Lights and outlets work and don't present a fire hazard.

Fire protection engineer determines where boxes, annunciator panels, and sprinkler systems are to be located. *Reports to* local fire chief. *Oversight:* If there is a fire in the building, notification and management of catastrophe.

Lighting designer takes into consideration the uses of the area and proposes the type of lighting systems that can be used for maximum efficiency. *Reports to* architectural firm. *Oversight:* Appropriate lights for each type of use or task.

Acoustic designer deals with noise suppression requirements. *Reports to* architectural firm. *Oversight:* Making sure that sound stays where it is supposed to be.

Data designer looks at the data needs of the facility and adds appropriate wiring to accommodate all computers and other electronic equipment. *Reports to* building advisory committee and architectural firm. *Oversight:* Computer lines and system equipment are adequate for the needs of the building occupants.

Security consultant plans for safety and emergency needs. *Reports to* building advisory committee and architectural firm. *Oversight:* Keeping everyone safe.

Interior designer presents a "color board" for approval of interior finishes such as flooring, wall treatments, furnishings. *Reports to* architectural firm, building advisory committee, and library governing board. *Oversight:* How the building looks and functions within the structure.

Postdesign phase

Clerk of works serves as the advocate, advisor, and watchdog for the owner. *Reports to* building advisory committee. *Oversight:* The entire building process.

Job captain oversees the subconsultants once the design is settled. *Reports to* architectural firm. *Oversight:* The successful implementation of the design plan through the employment of skilled personnel.

Consultants and subcontractors

Competent person provides a safe work setting while digging the foundation. *Reports to* job captain (OSHA-mandated). *Oversight:* That the site is safe.

Dig safe compliance officer locates and marks all existing underground services. *Reports to* job captain. *Oversight:* Maintenance of all existing services that run the property.

Mason builds the foundation. *Reports to* structural engineer, job captain, and clerk of works. *Oversight:* Whatever method of foundation is decided upon, this person is responsible for doing the work.

Steel detailer draws up plans for needed steel based on the structural engineer's design. *Reports to* structural engineer, job captain, and clerk of works. *Oversight:* Defines what steel shapes to buy, what lengths to cut and weld, and where to put the holes for bolting.

Roofers build the roof members to support the needs of the roof and equipment to be placed on the roof. *Reports to* structural and mechanical engineers, job captain, and clerk of works. *Oversight:* Guarantees that the hardest working component of the building is structurally sound and keeps the elements out of the building.

Independent inspector for roofing observes the work being done on your roof and is able to identify problems and quickly make decisions to resolve any issues. *Reports to* job captain and clerk of works. *Oversight:* That your roofing job is done to specifications and all issues are resolved.

Window professionals provide a connection between the inside of your building and the outside world. *Reports to* job captain and clerk of works. *Oversight:* Aesthetically pleasing and energy-efficient openings to the neighborhood.

Drywallers add the interior wall in preparation for finish work. *Reports to* job captain and clerk of works. *Oversight:* Walls.

Tapers cover the seams of the drywall with successive coats of mud. *Reports to* job captain and clerk of works. *Oversight:* Walls that are solid.

Sanders smooth out the roughness of the mud and prepare the surface for the finish work (paint, wallpaper, or cabinetry). *Reports to* job captain and clerk of works. *Oversight:* Walls that are smooth.

Painters apply a primer and coats of paint to achieve the desired finish. *Reports to* job captain and clerk of works. *Oversight:* Walls that are covered with paint.

Wallpaperers apply the sizing and product of choice. *Reports to* job captain and clerk of works. *Oversight:* Walls that are covered.

Millwork carpenter takes the design and translates it into pieces of wood to be assembled on-site. *Reports to* job captain and clerk of works. *Oversight:* Interior wood components.

Flooring expert installs the flooring finishes. *Reports to* job captain and clerk of works. *Oversight:* Cement, wood, terrazzo, or carpet.

Ceiling expert installs the ceiling finishes. *Reports to* job captain and clerk of works. *Oversight:* Painted or tiled, a quality job that is safe.

SOURCE: Lynn M. Piotrowicz and Scott Osgood, *Building Science 101: A Primer for Librarians* (Chicago: American Library Association, 2010), 78–83.

Great libraries of the world

by George M. Eberhart

I HAVE CHOSEN 250 LIBRARIES that are notable for their exquisite architecture, historic collections, and innovative services. Unfortunately, I only have room to showcase seven of them here. The entire list has been appearing in *American Libraries Direct* and imaged on pinterest.com/amlibraries, and it is also available on www.alaeditions.org/webextras. If you find yourself on vacation nearby, stop by any one of these splendid libraries for a visit.

Beinecke Rare Book and Manuscript Library, Yale University, New Haven, Connecticut. The library, designed by architect Gordon Bunshaft, is the largest building in the world reserved exclusively for the preservation of rare books and manuscripts. Six stories of book stacks are surrounded by a windowless, rectangular building with walls made of a translucent Danby white marble, which provides protection from direct light. Three floors of stacks extend below ground level. Since its opening in 1963, the Beinecke has become a repository for books printed anywhere before 1601, books printed in Latin America before 1751, books printed in North America before 1821, newspapers and broadsides printed in the United States before 1851, European tracts and pamphlets printed before 1801, East European and Asian books through the 18th century, and other special collections. *Website:* www.library.yale.edu/beinecke/.

Thomas Fisher Rare Book Library, University of Toronto, Canada. The library houses the university's Department of Rare Books and Special Collections and its official archives. Built in 1973, the facility was named after an early settler of Upper Canada whose great-grandsons Sidney and Charles Fisher donated their own collections of Shakespeare, various 20th-century authors, and the etchings of 17th-century Bohemian artist Wenceslaus Hollar. Other rare items held are the *Nuremberg Chronicle* (1493), Shakespeare's First Folio (1623), Isaac Newton's *Principia* (1687), and Charles Darwin's proof copy (with annotations) of *On the Origin of Species* (1859). *Website:* www.library.utoronto.ca/fisher/.

Strahov Monastery Library, Prague, Czech Republic. This library dates back to the establishment of the Premonstratensian abbey in 1143, although most of

its collections were plundered by the Swedish army in 1648 at the end of the Thirty Years' War. After the Peace of Westphalia, the monastery's books were housed in the Theological Hall built in 1671–1679, a splendid Baroque room with a beautifully ornate ceiling painted by Siard Nosecký; the room is now lined with astronomical globes and displays a facsimile of the 9th-century Strahov New Testament with its bejeweled 17th-century binding. The expanding collections required the construction of additional space, completed in 1783–1797 and known as the Philosophical Hall, where Franz Anton Maulbertsch painted a ceiling fresco in six months in 1794 with the help of just one assistant. The richly gilded and carved walnut bookcases are the work of carpenter Jan Lahofer. The highest rows of books are only accessible from a gallery; hidden spiral staircases, masked with false book spines, lead up to the corners of the gallery. An adjacent Cabinet of Curiosities features the preserved remains of an extinct dodo bird, sea fauna, insects, minerals, handcuffs, and Hussite peasant weapons. In 1953, the library was nationalized as a Museum of National Literature, and the monastic archives, music collection, picture gallery, and exhibits were dispersed to other state institutions. Soon after 1989, following the collapse of state communism, the library was returned to the monks. *Website:* www.strahovskyklaster.cz/webmagazine/page.asp?idk=294.

Amsterdam Central Public Library, Netherlands. Designed by architect Jo Coenen, the 28,000-square-meter building opened in 2007 as the largest public library in Europe. It features more than 700 public computers, business meeting rooms, a theatre, restaurant, radio station, and pianos. *Website:* www.oba.nl.

British Library, London, United Kingdom. The library's new facility in St. Pancras has 11 reading rooms, each specializing in different subject areas or types of material, where readers can access most of the library's 150 million items. Collections of British and overseas newspapers are available in another reading room in North London, and a research collection of 7 million items can be found in a third facility in Boston Spa in West Yorkshire. The Online Gallery provides access to 30,000 images from sacred or significant books, such as the Lindisfarne Gospels, together with certain exhibition items in a proprietary page-turning format. Among the library's treasures are the world's earliest dated printed book, the *Diamond Sutra,* from 868 A.D.; two Gutenberg Bibles; two copies of the 1215 Magna Carta; and the sole surviving manuscript copy of the Anglo-Saxon poem *Beowulf. Website:* www.bl.uk.

Saint Catherine's Monastery Library, Sinai Desert, Egypt. This library of the oldest working Christian monastery contains the second largest collection of early codices and manuscripts in the world (some 3,300), outnumbered only by the Vatican Library. Its strength lies in Greek, Arabic, Armenian, Hebrew, Georgian, Syriac, and Udi texts. There are many early and important editions of the bible, patristic and classical texts, and Orthodox service books. The Syriac Sinaiticus palimpsest is one of only two manuscripts that preserve the text of the Old Syriac translation of the Gospels. The Codex Sinaiticus, a 4th-century manuscript that contains the oldest

Photo: Berthold Werner, used CC A-SA 3.0

complete New Testament, was housed here until 1859 when the German scholar Constantin von Tischendorf removed it to Russia for study; it was sold in 1933 to the British Museum, where the greater portion of it now resides. *Website:* www.sinaimonastery.com.

State Library of New South Wales, Sydney, Australia. The library traces its origins to the opening of the Australian Subscription Library in 1826. The collection moved to its current location when the Mitchell Building opened in 1910 to house the unsurpassed collections of Australiana bequeathed by Sydney bibliophile David Scott Mitchell. The central section of the building includes a portico with Ionic columns, the main reading room, and an ornate vestibule with a reproduction of the 1644 Abel Tasman Map in marble mosaic and a contemporary glass sculpture created by Jon Hawley that is based on the earliest depiction of the stars of the Southern Cross in 1516. A Shakespeare Room features richly embellished Tudor motifs and a plaster ceiling modeled on Cardinal Wolsey's Closet at Hampton Court Palace. The Dixson Wing was added on the south side in 1929 to provide space for the extensive collection of colonial books, manuscripts, and paintings presented by William Dixson. *Website:* www.sl.nsw.gov.au.

12 trends in academic library design
by Thomas Sens

MANY ACADEMIC PLANNERS assumed that the coming of the internet would lead to the decline of the library as we know it. To the contrary, many academic libraries have experienced significantly *increased* patron use in recent years.

College students have heightened expectations and demands for academic libraries based on new approaches to learning. While the internet can provide 24/7 access to information, it can also isolate learners. In contrast, the new academic library model provides a forum for students to collaborate, enjoy fellowship, engage in healthy debate, create and challenge ideas, and experience learning and discovery in a multitude of meaningful ways. The following 12 trends define how the library has evolved to maintain its essential position within the academic landscape.

1. Envision the library as place. Today's libraries serve four key functions, in addition to their traditional role of housing printed materials.

First, they are a *locus for collaboration.* Spaces where students can openly discuss and debate without having to keep their voices down are the new norm.

Second, there is also a need for *individual, contemplative space*—not the long library tables of the past, but a variety of spaces to suit the individual needs and learning styles of today's students. A blend of formal and informal spaces can create environments where all students can have their needs met.

The third function of libraries is to provide *a home for services,* such as writing, communication, tutoring centers, and advanced lab spaces.

2. Invite students and other stakeholders to the table. Students should be invited to participate early in the planning process. Their input can help the library planning committee understand students' needs for today and tomorrow, while opening the way for potentially innovative ideas to surface. Town hall-style meetings, student focus groups, and student representation on advisory councils are three proven ways to bring them into the planning process.

Be sure to bring these other user groups into the discussion:

- *Library staff* are familiar not only with the library's everyday workings but also with new trends and technologies that the library might benefit from. A student worker who staffs the front desk might have valuable insights into how the whole staff could be more efficient in their work.
- *Faculty involvement* is necessary, to help the planning group understand how professors utilize space for classes.
- *Student activities groups* can benefit from the library as an excellent place for their headquarters or meeting areas.
- *IT personnel* are crucial to involve from the start to afford the planning committee the opportunity to learn about exciting new information technologies that might benefit the project.

3. Make collaboration a must. Working and learning in isolation is no longer an option. Collaboration has changed nearly every facet of pedagogy and every aspect of university design. In the past, teaching was focused on the transfer of knowledge from professor to student, but today's students learn by accessing knowledge and exploring new ideas among their peers. Clearly the paradigm has shifted: the "sage on the stage" has become the "guide on the side."

This collaborative approach to learning and teaching parallels the rapid expansion of information. Designing for collaboration allows more productive academic work to take place.

4. See that technology drives the bus. Every space in a university library should be informed by technology. From providing more power outlets for laptop users to installing complex 3D simulators, library spaces must be planned with appropriate technological amenities in mind. These may include:

- wireless internet and printing access
- readily accessible public computers with basic software and internet connections
- distance learning classrooms that provide videoconferencing capabilities and electronic flip charts to share information both graphically and electronically
- practice presentation rooms equipped with projection systems and conference tables
- advanced computing centers with the latest video, graphics, and science software
- lockers with built-in outlets for charging personal devices such as cellphones and laptops
- 3D visualization spaces such as Fakespace or CAVE (Cave Automatic Virtual Environment), which provide realistically simulated situations that allow students to interact in virtual environments

D. H. Hill Library at North Carolina State University created spaces with extensive power outlets to support students with laptops.

5. Plan for change. Libraries being built today must also look to the future. The best way to do that is to maximize flexibility in spaces and infrastructure. Building core infrastructure, such as vertical circulation, natural lighting, and HVAC, to support future renovation ensures a smoother transition.

Short-term flexibility is also important. Movable furniture and temporary wall partitions serve not only the long-term function of space but also short-term needs for flexible work environments. When students are allowed to reconfigure their work environment, they will find ways to create the most conducive environment for collaboration and optimal learning.

6. Use the library to attract and retain top students. Prospective students are often customers, placing high demands on the universities they are considering attending. The library can be a strong selling point for the top high school seniors that many colleges and universities are competing for.

The library can also reinforce the university's brand. There are opportunities throughout a library to convey the university's goals and mission through graphics and environmental branding. The library should become a physical manifestation of the university's philosophies.

7. Optimize spaces between spaces. Some of the most successful and well-used spaces in a library can grow from so-called "spaces between spaces." For example, a corridor can become a gallery for student or faculty art exhibits. Widening a corridor outside study rooms and providing seating can create a student gathering space. Unused wall space near an entrance can become a bulletin board for student messages. Converting unused areas into spaces that encourage interaction can bring the environment to life.

8. Consolidate emerging specialty spaces. Academic libraries are becoming hubs for specialty spaces. Services that used to be scattered across the campus can become readily available to students when relocated to the library. Some examples of specialty spaces are tutoring centers, writing centers, group study rooms, presentation rooms, distance learning rooms with access to videoconferencing software, and art galleries.

9. Take advantage of the commons. The commons model has become a blend of computer technology services and classical library reference and research resources. Today's commons break many of the old rules of library behavior. In the commons area, nobody hushes students who want to talk, food and drink is allowed, collaborative behavior is encouraged,

Porter Henderson Library at Angelo State University created a number of niches throughout the building, each housing one to six students.

and cafés and vending machines are de rigueur. Many information commons operate 24/7.

10. Rethink library space. In the past, library space usually involved a formula to estimate necessary square footage as stacks grew. Today, such calculations are not as critical. Determining the best way to allocate and organize space is a puzzle that requires many considerations:

- Reserve the first floor for public functions such as the commons, group study areas, collaboration zones, and library help and circulation areas.
- Uses for academic programs often work better on upper floors of the building, away from public zones and prime areas.
- Use the basement for archives and stacks that may be able to utilize compact shelving systems better suited to slab-on-grade conditions due to their concentrated weights.
- Consider what kind of security is needed for 24/7 spaces versus areas that are only open during regular library hours. This may inform how to zone the library with respect to security.
- Keep floor plans open and spacious with a logical workflow.

A four-story living wall improves indoor air quality in Centennial College's Library in Toronto.

11. Design for environmental sustainability. Going green can have a positive impact on your budget. With proper environmental design, the overall life cycle cost of the building can be decreased through use of efficient systems. More to the point, green buildings—notably green libraries—can be a drawing card for students. Whenever possible, use green techniques to visually impact the library; display characteristics of sustainable architecture that make students aware of the efforts the university makes to support a sustainable environment.

Areas where sustainability can be immediately apparent include recycled, renewable, and sustainable materials; renewable energy (PVs, wind turbines); rainwater-harvesting cisterns and efficient plumbing fixtures; daylighting systems; and natural ventilation.

12. Get creative with funding. Virtually all institutions are struggling with funding, so planning for a new academic library requires stretching dollars effectively. Lay out exactly what the physical demands of the future library will be so that dollars are used toward creating a functional, forward-looking space.

On most campuses, libraries are interdepartmental and cannot obtain funding via study-related grants. Bringing new tenants into the library and creating specialty spaces for them can be an effective way to tap new funding sources. For example, including science centers or presentation spaces for the business school could bring in funding from these sometimes wealthier departments. For a library that BHDP Architecture designed, the café was funded by the university's housing, dining, and guest services department. Seeking donor-funded spaces like laboratories or writing/tutoring centers can also augment funding.

The message is clear: If you want your library project to become a reality, you've got to be creative in finding the funds to build it.

These trends were identified through numerous discussions with library deans, directors, staff, and patrons. Discuss them early on in the library planning process, while debating the future vision, mission, and purpose to ensure a library design that accommodates the learner of today and tomorrow.

SOURCE: Thomas Sens, "12 Major Trends in Library Design," *Building Design + Construction* 50, no. 12 (December 2009): 38–42. © 2009 SGC Horizon LLC. Reprinted with permission.

DIGITAL LIBRARIES

Putting digitized collections of unpublished materials online

THE PRIMARY RESPONSIBILITIES of cultural materials repositories— stewardship and support for research and learning—require us to provide access to materials entrusted to our care. This document establishes a reasonable community of practice that increases and significantly improves access to collections of unpublished materials by placing them online for the purpose of furthering research and learning. Although it promotes a well-intentioned, practical approach to identifying and resolving rights issues that is in line with professional and ethical standards, note that this document does not concern itself with what individuals who access particular items may do with them. While the document was developed with United States law in mind, it is hoped that the spirit of the document will resonate in non-U.S. contexts.

Unpublished U.S. Geological Survey field notes.

If your institution has legal counsel, involve them in adopting this approach; after the approach has been adopted, only seek their advice on specific questions.

Select collections wisely. Keep your mission in mind and start with a collection of high research value or high user interest. Assess the advantages and risks of relying on fair use (in the United States) to support public access.

Some types of materials may warrant extra caution when considering rights issues, such as:

- contemporary literary papers;
- collections with sensitive information, such as Social Security numbers

or medical data;
- materials that are likely to have been created with commercial intent (because they are more likely to have economic value);
- very recent materials that were not intended to be made public.

If research value is high and risk is high, consider compromises, such as making a sensitive series accessible on-site only, until a suitable time has passed.

Use archival approaches to make decisions. Check donor files and accession records for permissions, rights, or restrictions. Assess rights and privacy issues at the appropriate level, most often at the collection or series level.

Attempt to contact and get permission from the rights holder, if there's an identifiable rights holder at that level.

Include what you know about the rights status in the description of the collection, including if the collection is in the public domain, if the institution holds the rights, or if the rights holder has given the institution permission to place the digitized collection online.

Document your processes, findings, and decisions and share them with your professional community.

Provide take-down policy statements and disclaimers. Adopt a liberal take-down policy, such as: "These digitized collections are accessible for purposes of education and research. We've indicated what we know about copyright and rights of privacy, publicity, or trademark. Due to the nature of archival collections, we are not always able to identify this information. We are eager to hear from any rights owners, so that we may obtain accurate information. Upon request, we'll remove material from public view while we address a rights issue."

Use an appropriate disclaimer at the institutional level, such as "[Institution] makes digital versions of collections accessible in the following situations:

- They are in the public domain.
- The rights are owned by [institution].
- [Institution] has permission to make them accessible.
- We make them accessible for education and research purposes as a legal fair use.
- There are no known restrictions on use.

To learn what your responsibilities are if you'd like to use the materials, go to [link]."

Prospectively, work with donors. Identify possible intellectual property issues and get relevant contact information. Ask donors to state any privacy concerns and identify sensitive materials that may be in the collection.

Suggest that donors transfer copyright to the institution or license their works under a Creative Commons license.

Include statements in your collecting policies and in your deeds of gift or transfer documents that:

- ensure that no restrictions are placed on content that is already in the public domain,
- grant license to digitize the materials for unrestricted access even when donors retain the rights,
- and guard against limitations or restrictions on fair use rights.

SOURCE: OCLC Research, *Well-Intentioned Practice for Putting Digitized Collections of Unpublished Materials Online* (Dublin, Ohio: OCLC, 2010), www.oclc.org/research/activities/rights/practice.pdf. Reprinted with permission.

The digital Bibliotheca Alexandrina

by Noha Adly

1

FOUNDED IN THE BEGINNING of the third century B.C., the Ancient Library of Alexandria was a major center for scholars and scientists for centuries. It was the world's hub for human knowledge and the largest and most famous center of learning and excellence in the ancient world. When it was destroyed, a glorious era of human knowledge was demolished as well. In 2002, the new Library of Alexandria—the Bibliotheca Alexandrina (BA, www.bibalex.org)— was built in almost exactly the same spot, intended to recapture the spirit of the ancient library and to inherit its goals while keeping pace with the world's most advanced technological developments.

The International School of Information Science, a research institute affiliated with the BA, aims to further the BA's goal of promoting research and development related to digital libraries. ISIS has embarked on an array of ambitious projects, including hosting a mirror site for the Internet Archive, participating in the Million Book Project, organizing the digital archive of the Gamal Abdel Nasser collection, digitizing 113 years of *al-Hilal* magazine, presenting the first-ever complete digital version of *Description de l'Égypte* (1809–1829), conducting advanced research for the Arabic component of the UN-sponsored Universal Networking Language translation program, and offering the most advanced 3D virtual imaging techniques in an immersive environment for science and technology applications.

The BA has built its own digital laboratory, equipped with state-of-the-art technologies. A staff of 120 technicians works seven days a week, two shifts per day, digitizing various media including slides in multiple formats, negatives, books, manuscripts, pictures, and maps. The laboratory is equipped with the necessary tools for indexing, archiving, and managing digital media, thus allowing for centralized digital control of the entire workflow.

The Digital Assets Repository was developed to create and maintain digital library collections and preserve them for future generations. Public access is provided through web-based search and browsing facilities. DAR is also concerned with automating the digitization workflow and integrating it with the repository. The management tools developed within DAR help the BA preserve, manage, and share its digital assets. In April 2009, BA announced the launch of the largest Arabic Digital Library worldwide

The Digital Assets Repository, showing one of its holdings.

as part of the DAR. To date, the digitized collection of Arabic books totals 130,000 searchable books and is increasing daily—a significant contribution to the limited Arabic content on the internet.

Another project is the Memory of Modern Egypt digital repository, which contains more than 60,000 objects of various digitized material pertaining to the last 200 years of Egypt's

Memory of Modern Egypt webpage.

history. What distinguishes this digital repository is the interrelation of the different forms of material (documents, pictures, videos, audio, maps, articles, stamps, coins) with specific themes. The repository is designed in a user-friendly interface with appropriate browsing tools and search facilities.

The library's ICT infrastructure includes four mutually reinforcing components to provide a wide array of services to researchers:

1. It provides **high-bandwidth connectivity** to its users. Although 155 Mbps bandwidth is small relative to Western standards, it is extremely high in this area of the world. The BA is exercising major efforts to establish massive links with Internet2 and GÉANT2, which will allow researchers from Egypt, Europe, Japan, or the United States to work online simultaneously using live databases in Europe and elsewhere.

2. It maintains a **fully operational data analysis facility**, termed VIS-TA (Virtual Immersive Science and Technology Applications), a 3D virtual-reality simulation tool aimed at providing researchers in the region with state-of-the-art, immersive VR. It is a powerful tool, one that allows researchers to test out ideas in virtual reality, trying many combinations and permutations before actually touching the complex, fragile, or expensive physical experiment.

3. It makes available **mass storage devices** for storing enormous amounts of data, reaching 3.7 petabytes. The archival facility holds the web collections of the Internet Archive from 1996 through 2008. The archival material is digitized within the BA but is open to hold massive datasets necessary for research.

4. It has established a **supercomputer facility** to allow for massive data analysis and problem-solving. The High Performance Computing cluster offers a new scope for scientific research at higher education levels. The supercomputer accommodates a computational ability at a rate equivalent to trillions of operations per second, an incredible speed that can make a difference in domains and applications such as bioinformatics, data mining, computer vision, image processing, physics simulation, weather forecasting, finite elements, oil and underground exploration, astrophysics, and cloud computing.

A scanner in the BA's digital laboratory.

The BA is committed to pursuing its mission as a center of excellence for the production and dissemination of knowledge and as a leading institution in the digital age. With the simple credo of "Access to all information, for all people, at all times," the library deploys new technologies to honor the past, celebrate the present, and embrace the future.

SOURCE: Noha Adly, "Bibliotheca Alexandrina: A Digital Revival," *Educause Review* 44, no. 6 (November/December 2009): 8–9. Reprinted with permission.

PEOPLE

CHAPTER TWO

Some speculate that [catalogers] are aliens from a faraway galaxy who have come to Earth to tidy things up a bit.

—Will Manley, *American Libraries*, July/August 1994

RECRUITMENT

The interview

by Joan Giesecke and Beth McNeil

THE CLIMATE CREATED in the interview is important. Create a welcoming atmosphere, away from noise and interruptions. Introduce yourself to the candidate. Determine the candidate's preferred name and use it during the interview. Set a tone for a friendly exchange of comments and allow communication to develop freely in order to build mutual confidence.

Describe the job and the library. Keep in mind that an interview is a two-way process. The candidate needs to know about the position, your department, salary information, training opportunities, and other information that will help him or her make a decision about accepting the position if it is offered. You want to learn as much as possible about the candidate's qualifications for the position.

Asking applicants for examples from their past work history or educational experiences will reveal areas of knowledge, skills, and abilities required for them to be successful on the job. By the close of the interview, you want to have an accurate and balanced picture of the applicant's qualifications and job motivation. Behavioral, situational, and competency-based interview questions will provide the best information for determining if the applicant can do the job. If you have a formal set of core competencies for your library or unit, it will be important to ask interview questions that will be helpful in determining whether your applicant meets or could meet a level of competency in areas important to your unit. Regardless of whether you have formal competencies, you will most likely have a set of knowledge, skills, behaviors, and attributes (the components of formal core competencies lists) that are important for the particular position and important to your organization. To elicit information about candidates' knowledge, skills, behaviors, and attributes, you might ask the following questions.

If analytical skills or problem solving is a competency, examples of questions to consider asking include the following:

- Walk me through a situation in which you had to get information by asking many questions of several people. How did you know what to ask?
- Describe a time you had to ask questions and listen carefully to clarify the exact nature of an internal/external customer's problem.

If creativity is a competency, you might ask questions like this:

- Tell me about a way in which you worked with other staff to develop creative ideas to solve problems.
- Describe how you've gone about learning a new technical task.
- In your current position, what have you done differently than your predecessors?
- Tell me about a creative idea you had to improve a library service.
- Tell me about a unique approach you took to solve a problem.

If working in groups (teamwork) is important for the position, consider asking:

- Can you give me an example of a group decision you were involved in recently? What did you do to help the group reach the decision?
- Describe a time you worked with a group or team to determine project responsibilities. What was your role?

If you value flexibility and adaptability in employees in your unit, consider asking:

- Tell me about an important project/task/assignment you were working on in which the specifications changed. (What did you do? How did it affect you?)
- Tell me about a time you had to meet a scheduled deadline while your work was being continually interrupted. What caused you to have the most difficulty and why?
- Going from position to position must have been difficult. Tell me about a challenge that occurred when making that transition. (How did you handle it?)
- Describe a time you had to significantly modify work procedures to align with new strategic directives.

To determine leadership ability or potential, consider asking:

- Tell rne about a time you inspired someone to work hard to do a good job.
- Describe a face-to-face meeting in which you had to lead or influence a very sensitive individual.
- Tell me about a time you were able to convince someone from outside (your department) to cooperate with you on an important project.
- What strategies have you used to communicate a major change to employees? Which strategies have worked and which have not?
- Describe a situation in which you had to translate a broad or general plan into specific goals.

For positions where customer service is important, consider asking:

- In your current job, how do you know if your internal/external customers are satisfied? (Give a specific example.)
- Tell me about a time when you were able to respond to an internal/external customer's request in a shorter period of time than expected. Contrast that situation with a time you failed to meet an internal/external customer's expectations. (What was the difference?)
- As a [position], how did you ensure that you were providing good service?
- Sometimes it's necessary to work with a customer who has unusual requests. Please describe a time when you had to handle an unusual request that seemed unreasonable. What did you do?
- Some days can be very busy with requests from customers and coworkers. Please describe a time recently when you didn't have enough time to completely satisfy a particular customer. How did you handle the situation?

If planning skills are critical to the position, consider asking:

- Walk me through yesterday (or last week) and tell me how you planned the day's (or week's) activities.
- What procedure have you used to keep track of items that need attention? Tell me about a time you used that procedure.
- What objectives did you set for this year? (What steps have you taken to make sure that you're making progress on all of them?)
- Sometimes deadlines don't allow the luxury of carefully considering all options before making a decision. Please give an example of a time this happened to you. What was the result of your decision?
- Tell me about a time you were faced with conflicting priorities. In scheduling your time, how did you determine what was a priority?

To determine the applicant's level of technical knowledge or expertise, consider asking:

- Describe a project, situation, or assignment that challenged your skills as a [position]. What did you do to effectively manage the situation?
- Sometimes complex projects require additional expertise. Describe a situation in which you had to request help.
- Have you ever had to orient a new employee on a technical task or area? How did you do it?
- Describe a time you solved a technical problem.
- What equipment have you been trained to operate? How proficient are you?
- What word-processing packages can you use? How proficient are you?
- Give me an example of a project that demonstrates your technical expertise in [web page development].
- Describe how you've gone about learning a new technical task.
- How much experience have you had operating a [mouse, keyboard, word processor, etc.]?
- Describe the most challenging work you've done.

To determine the level of a candidate's interpersonal skills, consider asking:

- Working with people from diverse backgrounds or cultures can present specific challenges. Can you tell me about a time you faced a challenge adapting to a person from a different background or culture? (What happened? What did you do? What was the result?)
- Our relationships with coworkers are not always perfect. Tell me about the most challenging relationship you had with a coworker. Why was it challenging? What did you do to try to make it work?

In addition to the kinds of questions just outlined, you may find that a candidate who is enthusiastic and willing to learn is a better fit for this new venture than someone with a lot of technical skills but poor interpersonal skills. In other words, hire talent and remember you can teach skills. Recruiting an enthusiastic learner can be more successful in the long run than someone who does not fit well in the organization and is not enthusiastic about the challenge of starting a new project.

During the interview, your job is to listen, ask follow-up questions when necessary, and evaluate the candidate's answers to try to predict future performance. Practice good communication skills, such as active listening, reflecting, and reframing, and you will learn much about the candidate.

If you find the candidate is giving short answers and you are not learning enough about the person, ask follow-up questions. Continue to probe the answers until you feel comfortable that you have learned all you need to from the candidate. Candidates can be quite nervous, particularly if they are new to the job market. You can help the person by asking questions that help her explain her skills and interests. Do not settle for a "yes" or "no" answer if you want more information. Ask again if needed. This is your chance to learn about the candidate. Don't be shy. Ask and ask and ask and listen and listen and listen.

When you have finished asking your list of questions, ask the candidate if she has any additional information related to the position that she would like you to know. This gives the applicant the chance to mention or reiterate any strengths she brings to the position. Then ask the candidate if she has any questions for you.

If an applicant voluntarily offers information that you would never ask for legal reasons, human resources specialists recommend that you not write down the information she volunteers. Instead, guide the interview back to issues specifically related to the job.

At the end of the interview, thank the applicant for her interest in the position, outline what will happen next, and give the applicant a sense of when you will make your decision.

SOURCE: Joan Giesecke and Beth McNeil, *Fundamentals of Library Supervision,* 2d ed. (Chicago: American Library Association, 2010), 84–88.

Tips for applicants in a tight market
by Meredith Farkas

FOR SO MANY LIS STUDENTS, the job search is going to be a struggle. In a tight market, having a good cover letter and résumé can mean the difference between getting a phone interview and ending up in the round file. I made many rookie mistakes when I was looking for my first professional position—mistakes that I've seen made time and time again when looking through other people's cover letters and résumés. I'm writing out these tips in the hopes that others can avoid those mistakes when they're applying for jobs.

Do's

- Tailor your cover letter to the job you're applying for. Most importantly, address the specific requirements in the job ad. You may be particularly proud of how you designed your library's intranet, but if the job you're applying for has nothing to do with any of the skills you exhibited during that project, it's not worth detailing in the cover letter. In the search committee I was on, we would go through each cover letter and résumé with a list of required and preferred qualifications and would see which ones the applicant addressed. If they didn't show evidence of one of the required qualifications, they'd be out of the running. Period.

- Tailor your résumé to some extent to the job you're applying for. Highlight things that you've done or skills that you have that are on the list of requireds and preferreds for that job.
- Tell me why you want to work here and why you want this job. When I see a cover letter from someone who clearly wants the job they're applying for (as opposed to wanting any job), I am much more likely to want to interview them. When we were hiring for a distance learning librarian, I gave the most weight to people whose letters made it seem like they really wanted to be a distance learning librarian.
- Learn about the organization. This is important early on, but it's especially important when you get to the interview. If they are too lazy to research the library and the search committee members, they will apply themselves similarly to their day-to-day work.
- Include experience outside of libraries that might be relevant (school, other jobs). I always made an effort to describe how the skills I'd developed as a psychotherapist were relevant to reference and instruction work. If you're applying for a library job where you're working with the public, retail experience is a great asset.
- Include any extracurricular professional activities you've engaged in, such as speaking gigs, committee memberships, or articles written. Personally, I am jazzed when I see a new grad or soon-to-be-grad who has published, presented, or otherwise contributed to the profession beyond library schoolwork. It tells me that they have a passion for going above and beyond and that they'll probably do that in this job as well.

- Express enthusiasm and confidence. Write your cover letter as if you know you're the right person for the job (though don't be full of yourself either).
- Read the application requirements carefully. We once required that applicants send us a link to at least one example of a website they created. Many people didn't send us anything, which meant we wouldn't consider them.
- Unless the reason is particularly sensitive, do explain gaps in your résumé or frequent job hopping. Whatever the search committee will imagine is probably worse than your actual reason.
- If you currently work in a different type of library (or have only taken coursework towards working in a different area), address why you are now applying for this job. We got a lot of applications for a distance learning librarian position from folks who were catalogers or archivists. Had they said, "I'm really interested in getting more experience in online instruction," we would have given them greater consideration. Otherwise, it just looks like they don't really want to work in that area.
- If there's a reason why you want the job beyond the position itself (like you want to relocate to the area, or you have ties to the area) do state that. It can let people know that you're seriously interested in relocating. Just make sure it doesn't sound like it's your *only* reason for applying.

Don'ts

- Apply for a job you know you wouldn't want (because of location, duties, or hours). You're not only wasting your time, but you're wasting the time of the people who are interviewing you. And definitely make sure you are really interested in a job before you go for an in-person interview (especially if it requires travel funding). There's nothing wrong with realizing after interviewing that a place isn't a good fit, but if you're interviewing for a job you'd never want, you're wasting people's time.
- Send a generic cover letter. Passing off a generic cover letter makes you look like you don't want the job that much. And usually it's obvious that a cover letter is the same one you've used to apply for 10 other jobs.
- List everything you've done in your cover letter. Specifically address what the search committee cares about—the required and preferred qualifications.
- If you're applying for a job that requires technical skills, be honest about your level of skill. A small stretching of the truth is okay, but if it's a big stretch, it's likely that you'll be found out.
- Talk about your personal hobbies. I can't tell you how many résumés I've seen that talk about people's interests in gardening and genealogy or their involvement in the Boy Scouts. Nice, but unless these somehow relate to the job requirements, they don't belong in a professional résumé.
- Have a generic objective on your résumé. I personally never put an objective on my résumé, but if you're going to, make it meaningful or leave it off. I love ones that say things like "to obtain a position where I can apply my knowledge, experience, and education in the field of librarianship." How is this useful?
- Write well, but don't use lots of big words to impress. Many applicants actually use those words incorrectly. I have seen this happen way too many times and it makes candidates look dumber than if they'd just used terms they were familiar with.
- Apply for a job that requires an MLIS if you don't have one or aren't close to getting one. A few months away is usually acceptable, but if you're just starting an MLIS program, don't bother.
- Maybe it's just me, but I hate when people write things like, "My background and accomplishments seem to be a good match for your needs."
- Unless the job requires specific subject expertise, I don't want to see a list of the databases you've used. If you have general reference experience in an academic library, I'll assume that you are competent at searching most databases and can learn the ones you're not familiar with.
- List your GPA unless something in the job description asks you to address academic achievement.
- Make your cover letter more than one-and-one-third pages and less than a half page. Personally, I prefer a cover letter that is exactly one page long.
- Just tell us generic things like you're "detail oriented" or "innovative"— illustrate it in some way with things you've done.

SOURCE: Meredith Farkas, "Tips for Library Job Applicants in a Tight Market," *Information Wants to be Free*, May 18, 2010, meredith.wolfwater.com/wordpress/. Reprinted with permission.

Phone interviews

by Rachel E. Cannady and Daniel Newton

THE NEXT STEP after completing a successful application is the phone interview. Phone interviews, initially, might seem like a handicap because you are unable to read the interviewing panel's nonverbal cues. This lack of physical interaction can work to your benefit, however, as it allows you to have a list of accomplishments, experiences, and other notes that you want to mention sitting right in front of you. Use this advantage to stay confident and relaxed. Additionally, complete some research on the library and university. By knowing their mission and vision statements, you are demonstrating that you are interested, prepared, and serious about the position.

You can also prepare by practicing interview questions. If you do a simple internet search for "commonly asked librarian interview questions," you can find a few comprehensive lists. Regardless of whether you use one of these lists or another, be sure to practice answering questions about yourself prior to the interview. The more you practice, the more comfortable you will become talking about yourself and your accomplishments. The most commonly asked question is something akin to "Why are you the best candidate for this job?" Be ready with a few reasons for why you are the best applicant.

 Phone interviews require a quiet setting where you can concentrate, hear, and be heard. If you have animals, be sure to put them in another room so that they will not distract you. If you have roommates, children, or spouses, put out a sign so that they will not interrupt you. If you are working, double-check that your supervisor approves of your time spent, and then find a quiet place where you will not be interrupted.

Now that you have found a quiet spot for the phone interview, try to find a place of mental calm before the phone rings. The search committee members will call within a minute or two of the designated call time, so be prepared. Regardless of your preparation, it is hard to judge the search committee's reaction to your answers. Take advantage of your personality and sense of humor, when appropriate, to set you apart from the other candidates. Always make sure you know who is interviewing you so that you can write an email thanking them for their time after the phone interview. If you do not know the names of those on the search committee prior to the interview, print out the library's staff directory and highlight the search committee members' names as they introduce themselves.

In our experience, phone interviews range from 13 to 90 minutes, and, in both instances, face-to-face interviews were offered. The length of time for the interview is not a determining factor for how successful it is. On average, most phone interviews last around 30 minutes. In most cases, if the university or college was interested, they usually followed up within two weeks of the phone interview.

Job searching is difficult, but it is not impossible. Your future position might not be what you initially expected, so strike a balance between being open-minded and narrow in focus when searching. By looking at yourself and your talents from many angles, you will be able to find something that fits you.

SOURCE: Rachel E. Cannady and Daniel Newton, "Making the Best of the Worst of Times: Global Turmoil and Landing Your First Library Job," *College & Research Libraries News* 71, no. 4 (April 2010): 205–207, 212.

Still waiting

by Edwin B. Maxwell

YOU BATTLED A TOUGH MLIS program. "Here comes the easy part," you thought to yourself: landing your dream library job. Then as the pages of your calendar peeled away without as much as a return phone call, you began to question the whole thing. As a fairly recent MLS graduate and an experienced member of a highly successful library job development program, I was asked to sit on an ALA Annual Conference panel, "The Job Hunt: What to Do While You Wait." I faced a dilemma. What am I going tell a room full of frustrated recent grads who can't even get an interview? I asked the advice of colleagues and classmates, and from their wisdom I distilled three proven tactics for job-hunting success.

Don't wait. New graduates sometimes forget that receiving their degree is not the end of their education. Librarianship is a profession, not a job, and any professional should constantly refine old skills and acquire new ones. Never allow your expertise to depreciate while waiting for your dream job to materialize. Even working librarians are constantly engaging in professional development programs and workshops. Use this time to sharpen your tools and gain an edge on the competition. Observe those who hold jobs you envy, analyze what skills put them there, and educate yourself accordingly. Library professional organizations offer countless webinars, classes, and workshops that teach applicants how to become more employable. If there is one thing I learned from working with library human resource departments it is that they absolutely love a proactive candidate.

Volunteer. How do you gain experience to get the job when no one will hire you? The answer is one that job-ready new graduates dread. But volunteering allows you to showcase your passion, enthusiasm, and knowledge to your potential employer. Organizations are increasingly asked to do more with less; as a result, many employers ask volunteers to relieve the workload of their overburdened employees. Once the financial situation turns around (and it will), the first people organizations consider hiring are their own volunteers.

Join a professional organization. The library world seems immense to new graduates. But that professional world is made up of many niche communities. Find your niche, align yourself with the committee that shares your passion, and dedicate yourself to service. You will quickly find yourself on the short list of go-to people. Believe me: Word spreads fast. If your passion doesn't seem to have an organization or subgroup supporting it, create it. There are numerous accounts of information professionals identifying a need within their community (many times stemming from a library school or extracurricular project), developing a solution, and then turning it into a promising career.

Job searching can be extremely difficult. Experts estimate that an average job search in a good economy can last three to six months. In an economic downturn, search time can double. The *New York Times* reported that the average unemployed person in America has been looking for work for more than nine months. Try not to take the state of your employment personally; remember that this crisis affects all occupations at all hiring levels, and that the economy will eventually improve. In the meantime, continue to develop your professional tool kit so that when the opportunity approaches, you will be in motion, ready to catch it.

SOURCE: Edwin B. Maxwell, "Still Waiting," *Library Worklife,* November 2011.

LIBRARIANS

Librarian salaries, 2005–2012
by Kathy Rosa

EACH YEAR the American Library Association, in partnership with the ALA–Allied Professional Association, conducts a sample survey of public and academic libraries to benchmark salaries. The study samples six types of positions in public and academic libraries. The positions are:

- Director, dean, or chief officer
- Deputy, associate, or assistant directors
- Department heads, branch managers, senior managers
- Managers or supervisors of support staff
- Librarians who do not supervise
- Beginning librarians

The average (mean) salary for librarians increased modestly each year during 2005–2012, with a slight decline reflected in the 2009 data reported. The net average increase for the eight-year period was approximately 13.6%, or $7,293.

The 2012 median librarian salary estimated by the ALA-APA study was $56,760, in line with the median estimate ($55,300) published by the U.S. Bureau of Labor Statistics in its May 2011 Occupational Employment Statistics (Librarians), online at www.bls.gov/oes/current/oes254021.htm (see Table 1 and 2).

Table 1. Salaries, percentage change in mean/median, 2005–2012

	2005	2006	2007	2008	2009	2010	2012*
Number of salaries reported	24,814	10,631	7,564	16,258	17,018	11,554	11,315
Mean	$53,779	$56,259	$57,809	$58,960	$58,860	$60,734	$61,072
Mean change	3.0%	4.6%	2.8%	2.0%	–0.2%	3.2%	0.6%
Median	$50,274	$50,976	$53,000	$53,521	$54,500	$55,883	$56,760
Median change	3.0%	1.4%	4.0%	1.0%	1.8%	2.5%	1.6%

*No survey was conducted in 2011.

SOURCE: ALA–Allied Professional Association annual salary surveys.

Table 2. Percentile wage estimates for this occupation, 2011

Percentile	10%	25%	50% (median)	75%	90%
Hourly wage	$16.08	$21.00	$26.59	$33.30	$40.80
Annual wage	$33,440	$43,690	$55,300	$69,260	$84,850

SOURCE: Bureau of Labor Statistics, Occupational Employment Statistics, May 2011.

Deputy directors saw the largest percentage increase in salaries from 2004 to 2012 (Table 3), followed by nonsupervisory librarians and directors. Detail on number of positions and libraries reporting for each type of library (public and academic) for 2012 appear in Table 4.

Table 3. Rank order of position types by mean salary, 2004 and 2012

	Mean regional Salary 2004	Mean regional Salary 2012	Percentage change
Director/dean/chief officer	$80,823	$98,213	21.5%
Deputy/associate/assistant director	66,497	85,609	28.7%
Department head/branch manager/ coordinator/senior manager	56,690	66,606	17.5%
Manager/supervisor of support staff	46,648	56,033	20.2%
Librarians who do not supervise	45,554	55,474	21.8%
Beginning librarian	38,918	45,660	17.3%

SOURCE: ALA–Allied Professional Association annual salary surveys.

Table 4. Rank order of position types by mean of salaries paid, public and academic libraries, 2012

Public	Regional Salary mean	Number of employees
Director/dean/chief officer	$96,187	332
Deputy/associate/assistant director	80,044	371
Department head/branch manager/ coordinator/senior manager	63,531	2,521
Manager/supervisor of support staff	53,877	1,115
Librarians who do not supervise	50,276	3,305
Beginning librarian	46,168	603

Academic	Regional Salary mean	Number of employees
Director/dean/chief officer	$100,852	255
Deputy/associate/assistant director	90,934	355
Department head/branch manager/ coordinator/senior manager	66,895	237
Librarians who do not supervise	58,209	1,739
Manager/supervisor of support staff	56,734	363
Beginning librarian	45,560	119

SOURCE: ALA–Allied Professional Association annual salary surveys.

Association of Research Libraries

The Association of Research Libraries' 2011–2012 salary survey reported from 115 institutions and 9,910 staff positions an average (mean) salary of $74,437 and median salary of $68,407. Similar to the ALA survey, the average salary increased $2,200 from the previous year and median salaries rose by more than $2,140.

Overall, men earned slightly more than women with the average salary for men being $76,225 compared with $73,348 for women. Male assistant directors reported average salaries 9% higher than that of their female counterparts. The average salaries for selected positions reported by ARL member libraries are listed in Table 5.

Table 5. Average ARL salaries, rank order, 2012

Position	Salary (mean)
Director	$208,787
Associate director	122,296
Assistant director	109,135
Department head, computer systems	94,660
Head, branch	87,069
Department head, rare books and manuscripts	85,743

SOURCE: Association of Research Libraries, Annual Salary Survey, 2011–2012.

Special librarians

Average salaries of information professionals in the United States and Canada rose in 2009, the third consecutive year they increased, according to the salary survey sponsored by the Special Libraries Association (Table 6). The average salary of an information professional in the United States was $73,880 in 2009, compared with $71,812 reported in 2008. (2012 data from the SLA survey was not available at press time.)

Table 6. Salary distribution by primary job responsibility, special librarians, 2009

	United States	Canada*
10th Percentile	$43,000	$50,200
First Quartile, 25%	$52,450	$60,000
Median, 50%	$68,000	$70,000
Third Quartile, 75%	$89,000	$83,500
90th Percentile	$112,000	$100,000
Number	2,478	341
Mean	$73,880	$72,705
Mean % change	3.1%	2.8%

* Canadian salaries are reported in Canadian dollars. The exchange rate on April 1, 2009, was Can$1.26 = $1.00 U.S.

SOURCE: SLA Annual Salary Survey, 2009.

BLS industry profile

Additional advice on librarian salaries is available from the Bureau of Labor Statistics, which provides profiles for librarians working in various industries. In 2011, BLS listed the following as "top" industries and "top paying" industries.

Table 7. Top levels of employment within the occupation of librarian

Industry	Employment	Hourly mean wage	Annual mean wage
Elementary and secondary schools	60,650	$28.46	$59,190
Local government	42,910	$24.59	$51,140
Colleges, universities, professional schools	19,610	$29.61	$61,590
Other information services	6,030	$24.15	$50,230
Junior colleges	4,620	$29.74	$61,870

Table 8. Top paying industries within the occupation of librarian

Industry	Employment	Hourly mean wage	Annual mean wage
Federal executive branch	1,640	$38.54	$80,170
Legal services	1,730	$33.06	$68,750
Management, scientific, and technical consulting services	280	$32.91	$68,440
Offices of physicians	50	$32.61	$67,830
Computer systems design	130	$32.55	$67,710

SOURCE: Bureau of Labor Statistics, Occupational Employment Statistics, May 2011.

Librarians in the United States, 1880–2009

by Sydney Beveridge, Susan Weber, and Andrew A. Beveridge

THE U.S. CENSUS first collected data on librarians in 1880, four years after the founding of the American Library Association. They only counted 636 librarians nationwide. Indeed, one respondent reported on his census form that he was the "Librarian of Congress." The U.S. Census, which became organized as a permanent bureau in 1902, can be used to track the growth of the library profession. The number of librarians grew over the next 110 years, peaking at 307,273 in 1990. Then the profession began to shrink, and as of 2009 it had dropped by nearly a third to 212,742. The data enable us to measure the growth, the gender split in this profession known to be mostly female, and to explore other divides in income and education, as they changed over time.

We examined a number of socioeconomic trends over the duration, and focused on 1950 (the first year that detailed wage data were recorded), 1990 (the peak of the profession), and 2009 (the most currently available data). We looked at data within the profession and made comparisons across the work world.

Our analysis is based upon the original census materials organized by the Minnesota Population Center. They are available online as the Integrated Public Use Micro-data Samples at www.ipums. org. In 1880, the samples include all of the census responses in the entire country. For most decades the data only include a sample, generally one or five percent. These results are subject to sampling error, as well as issues related to census response in general.

For the first 110 years of data, the number of librarians increased, especially after World War II. In 1990, the trend reversed. Over the past 20 years, the number of librarians has dropped by 31%, though the decline has slowed.

ALA members relax at the Delaware Water Gap after the 1897 Annual Conference in Philadelphia. Left to right: James G. Barnwell (Library Company of Philadelphia); John Thomson and Edith Brinkman (Free Library of Philadelphia); Mary Wright Plummer (Pratt Institute); and Rose G. Stewart (Free Library of Philadelphia).

Considering the nation today, the states with the largest librarian populations are Pennsylvania, Illinois, New York, Texas, and California. Meanwhile, the states with the highest concentrations of librarians (or librarians per capita) are Vermont, District of Columbia, Rhode Island, Alabama, and New Hampshire.

Median earnings

The Census Bureau has kept records of librarian wages since 1940. Median librarian wages (whether full-time or part-time) increased until 1980, though they were a lower percentage of the median wages of all workers. Indeed, between 1970 and 1980 librarian wages declined nearly $4,000—more than twice the drop of median wages across all professions. (This wage drop was in the context of the oil embargo in the mid-1970s, and the economic fallout that it caused.) In 1990, librarian median wages declined further and were the same as those for all workers, but by 2009 they had gained in relative terms, and reached their peak of $40,000. (All these figures are adjusted for inflation.) By 2009, the typical librarian earned more than one-third more than a typical U.S. worker. According to the census results, librarians have enjoyed consistently high employment rates. For instance in 2009, the unemployment rate among librarians was just 2%—one-fifth the national rate.

A feminine profession

Today, 83% of librarians are women, but in the 1880s men had the edge, making up 52% of the 636 librarians enumerated. By 1930, male librarians were truly rare, making up just 8% of the librarian population.

Gender and education wage differences						
	Librarians			Everyone		
Median wages	Total	Men	Women	Total	Men	Women
1950	$21,174	$27,481	$21,174	$18,471	$22,975	$11,253
1990	$27,680	$34,600	$25,950	$29,237	$37,749	$21,509
2009	$39,979	$39,280	$39,979	$29,984	$34,982	$24,987
Median wages (1950)						
Age 25+	$22,976	$27,481	$22,976	$20,273	$24,778	$12,164
No BA	$18,921	$27,481	$18,471	$20,273	$23,877	$11,263
BA	$27,931	$32,887	$27,481	$29,283	$35,590	$22,075
Median wages (1990)						
Age 25+	$31,140	$43,250	$29,410	$34,600	$43,250	$25,085
No BA	$21,798	$28,545	$21,279	$29,410	$38,060	$21,665
BA	$41,496	$47,087	$39,790	$51,900	$63,422	$39,790
Median wages (2009)						
Age 25+	$41,279	$43,977	$40,179	$34,282	$39,979	$28,785
No BA	$19,990	$34,982	$19,990	$27,985	$32,983	$22,988
BA	$44,977	$44,977	$44,877	$51,973	$64,966	$44,976

Librarians working full-time earned more than the national median income in 1950 and 2009, but incomes dipped below the national median in 1990. Female librarians consistently outearned women elsewhere in the labor market. However, when tracking education and wages, librarians with bachelor's or graduate degrees consistently earn less than their counterparts elsewhere in the labor market.

Looking at gender, male librarians outearned female librarians in 1950 and

1990, but by 2009, median wages for the two sexes were within $100 of each other. The gender wage gap has essentially closed for librarians with college degrees, but among library workers without college degrees, the gap remains and is 50% larger than for those working in other professions.

Race. The librarian field has been and continues to be a predominately white profession. In 1920, the first nonwhite librarians were recorded in the census sample. Asian and Native American librarians were not identified until 1960. In 1950, there were 990 African-American librarians, representing 2% of the total librarian population. In 1990, that number rose to 27,958, or 9% of the total librarian population, much closer to the African-American population nationwide (11%). As of 2009, there were 15,128 African-American librarians, representing 7% of the population. (In 2009, 89% of librarians were white, while the entire U.S. population was 82% white.)

Marriage. In 1880, one in three librarians were married. The wedding-bell rate declined to less than 10% in 1920 before turning around and rising for the next several decades. Today, the marriage rate among librarians is the highest it has ever been with 62% of librarians married in 2009.

Education. In 1940, when education data for librarians debuted, 45% of librarians had completed at least four years of college. That proportion has risen over the decades to 86% in 2009, more than three times the national rate of 28%.

Age. Librarians skew older with 64% of them 45 years or older, and 40% of them more than 55 years old. The librarian population has aged over the past couple of decades. In 1950 and 1990, only 42% of librarians were 45 years or older, but by 2000, 64% were at least 45 years old.

School librarians in Topeka, Kansas, 1939. Works Progress Administration photo.

Public and private. In 1950, 37% of librarians worked in the private or nonprofit sector while 62% worked in a public setting (the remaining 1% were self-employed). In 1990, 48% of librarians worked in the private or nonprofit sector, with men and women represented in almost equal numbers. In 2009, the number of librarians in the private or nonprofit sector decreased to 32%. Thus a large fraction of the decline in the number of librarians has come from their decline in the nonpublic sectors.

Conclusion

Starting from a very small beginning, librarians grew into a large profession in the mid-20th century. As with other professions related to the media—books, newspapers, magazines, recorded music, and movies—the internet seems to be having an effect on the field, as it has faced a significant decline since 1990. That decline seems to have slowed substantially since 2000, as librarians find new roles in the internet age and the extensive increase in information that it has brought about.

SOURCE: Sydney Beveridge, Susan Weber, and Andrew A. Beveridge. "Librarians in the U.S. from 1880–2009," OUPBlog, June 20, 2011, blog.oup.com/2011/06/librarian-census/. Reprinted with permission.

Ten Commandments of the new professional

by Natalie Baur

LIBRARY SCHOOL DIPLOMA hot off the press, check. Applications and cover letters sent out to dream jobs, check. Weeks (and weeks) of waiting, phone interviews, and on-site interviews, check. An accepted job offer and start date, check! For many new librarians, the long, angst-filled path from graduation to job offer is a journey that consumes every last ounce of attention, making it all too easy to forget that a career is indeed waiting for them after getting that job offer. After breathing a sigh of relief that the bills will get paid on time, reality sets in: This is your very first professional position. Soon after, that little voice inside your head rings the alarm bells: I have no idea what I'm doing.

Don't listen to that little devil on your shoulder. Instead, look the other way and channel your will power and self-confidence that got you through graduate school while serving multiple internships and gaining work experience. Use the time you have in the Purgatory of the Freshly Hired, the stage between the job offer and your first day, to study the catechism of the new professional. Are you ready? Yes.

The following Ten Commandments will give you sound guidance for starting your long and rewarding career on the professional staff rosters.

1. **Jack of all trades, master of none.** You do not want to be Jack. Instead of overwhelming yourself by getting involved in everything, everywhere, just step back for those first critical few months and figure out which areas of librarianship most excite you, and where you want to concentrate your efforts. Select and join a core of professional organizations (too many memberships get expensive, anyway). Find that one committee or round table that really gets you fired up to donate your volunteer hours. Little steps will still get you to where you're headed.

2. **Study your organization's hierarchy.** You can easily ask for the organizational chart before your first day on the job. Know who is who and, more importantly, who answers to whom. After all, you will want to get things done in your new role, and you need to know who to ask and in what order.

3. **Get to know the workplace culture.** Is it laid back or formal? What is the dress code? Are schedules flexible or do you need to punch in and out at exact times? What is the working relationship between professional and paraprofessional staff members? Before you start, it might be a good idea to get in touch with some of the folks on your search committee or your HR contact to discuss the ins and outs of fitting in.

4. **Take the initiative.** Contact your new boss before you start. Ask her about what kinds of things you will be working on right out of the gate. You don't have to ask a million questions. Just let her know that you are thinking about your new roles and responsibilities.

5. **Expectations.** What does the library expect of its newest professionals? Are you expected to publish, present, and/or attend and participate in professional conferences and meetings? If you didn't get this infor-

mation in the interview process, make sure you have all of the details. You will need to be on top of this from day one, as many libraries require these types of activities before you are considered for retention, promotion or, in some cases, tenure.

6. **Find a mentor.** This person can be someone at your new library or a former professor or supervisor. In any case, this person will be your ally in helping you wade through the ins and outs of professional librarianship. Soon enough you won't be the newbie anymore, and then it will be your turn to guide the next generation to the path of success.

7. **Find your stride.** The first few weeks or months will be an adjustment and very busy, but consider what kind of work-life balance is best for your lifestyle and family situation. You'll save yourself from burning out before your vacation time accrues. And take those vacation days. That's what they're for.

8. **Introduce yourself.** Don't wait for everyone to introduce themselves to you. Your coworkers and librarians in other departments are busy, too. Do your best to introduce yourself to folks you don't know, don't remember, or didn't get the chance to meet during your interview.

9. **Explore.** Find out about all of the fringe benefits your organization offers. Many organizations offer employees such perks as exercise facilities and discounted entertainment, museum tickets, and travel. If HR doesn't clue you into this, make sure to ask. It will help you achieve that perfect work-life balance. Double bonus.

10. **Be yourself.** It's a cliché, but this is the best thing you can do, and you can do it from day one. Follow your true interests and passions and you will find that most likely your library will have an outlet for you to pursue them to the fullest. It's up to you to show your fellow librarians just what makes you tick.

Starting your first professional position is daunting, but everyone started out somewhere. Clear your mind of those jitters and doubts. Having a positive attitude from day one will make the transition much easier for you and your new coworkers. Good luck!

SOURCE: Natalie Baur, "The Ten Commandments of the New Professional," *Library Worklife,* July 2012.

A plague on both your Hepburns

by Leigh Anne Vrabel

THE DAY I RECEIVED MY MLIS, one of my professors shook my hand, gave me a very nice coffee mug as a token of the school's appreciation, and proudly proclaimed, "Congratulations, Leigh Anne! You're a change agent!"

I was somewhat nonplussed by this. Remember, it was 2004, and the phrase hadn't yet become a buzzword—at least, I don't think it had. Despite the fact that I opted for electives in both management and library marketing, I'd never heard it. I figured it was a compliment, though, because the professor looked so happy. So I smiled and said "thank you," and that was the end of that . . . for the moment.

The memory hasn't faded, though. Off and on over the course of my career I've asked myself what that phrase means, or could mean, and how it compares to leadership. I've been watching leaders and managers for a while now, operating under the premise that I want to be a leader. But what if I'm just a really good change agent instead?

Not that the two are mutually exclusive. Which brings us to Audrey and Katharine Hepburn.

A theory, with disclaimers

Broad, sweeping generalizations are fairly odious; moreover, I am the least qualified person on the planet to speak to possible archetypes of *male* librarianship. Although I've admired the gentlefolk from both afar and anear for many a day, I would not presume to try to describe what it's like to be a "guybrarian." So one of you will simply have to pick up the "Gary Cooper / Cary Grant / Harry Caray" metaphor and run with it. Or craft something utterly delightful of your own. Or be a good sport and try to find your inner Kate 'n' Audrey as you read along.

Even within the limitations of the archetype structure, it seems to me that you can tell a lot about librarians by determining whether they are more like Audrey Hepburn or Katharine Hepburn. To illustrate, I will examine both archetypes, listing strengths and weaknesses, and determine whether their qualities tend toward leadership or change agentship.

Please note that by no stretch of the imagination am I speaking of the historical personages Audrey and Katharine, the ones who had private lives and histories that obviously went much deeper than a superficial library blog-gloss can go. I refer, however, to the iconic Kate and Audrey we've built up in our minds, the ones we think of when we hear the name "Hepburn." That is the whole point, after all, of an archetype: It's a broad portrait of a certain ethos, not a granular portrait of a complex human being.

One final warning: You may already think you know where you are on this particular spectrum. Try to suspend your judgment until you get to the end of the essay. You may be surprised by what you find in yourself.

Audrey Hepburn: The ladylike leader

Three words: little black dress. Three more: *Breakfast at Tiffany's*. One more for good measure: Givenchy. The Audrey type is redolent with class and sophistication, gentleness and grace, poise and good manners, humor and kindness. An

open face with a lovely smile. Everybody loves Audrey, because you simply can't hate her—she's too darned *nice*. Even if you did hate her, she'd probably continue to be sweet and kind to you anyway.

The Audrey librarian is service-oriented to the point of self-sacrifice. Even if she's drowning in her own work, she'll gladly help you with yours, and never complain about it. The surliest of problem patrons melts in her presence because nothing ever seems to faze her, and she knows how to turn bad transactions into good ones with skillful listening and speaking. She has an uncanny knack of knowing when to enforce a policy and when to bend it, and because she is always kind and gracious to everybody, she can never be accused of playing favorites.

Audreys serve on every committee that invites them and volunteer for every extra opportunity they can. They're also prone to bringing in donuts, cookies, or other baked goods to the office, most likely baked from scratch. If she does bring store-bought, she springs for the *cute* cupcakes from the gourmet cupcake emporium in the hip neighborhood. And again, all of this would be utterly unbearable if they weren't *really good cupcakes*.

She's good at readers' advisory, reference, cataloging, Web 2.0, Web 3.0, storytimes, and organizing teen art clubs and Super Mario Kart tournaments. If the circulation desk is short-staffed, she volunteers to pitch in. If the library is closed due to weather, she starts calling down the phone tree. She gives 110% all day, every day, and never complains, even though she hasn't had a raise in five years.

Lest you think Audreys are too perfect to exist, let me assure you they have a dark side. Audreys have a bad habit of squelching their true feelings and accepting poor working conditions, because they don't feel they have a right to complain. If they are not given enough praise and recognition by their supervisors, they will start to feel bitter. Audreys are also prone to overwork and martyrdom, and if they keep their frustrations bottled up too long, little things can set them off. Audreys also have a hard time asserting themselves, and tend to avoid conflict like the plague. Audreys may also grow to resent always being asked to take the leadership role, but are often unwilling or unable to delegate responsibilities to colleagues. Audreys are prone to burnout, and tend to suffer when their high ideals don't match up to the sometimes dull realities of library service, especially in its administrative aspects.

Katharine Hepburn: The challenging change agent

Two words: *Desk Set*. One more: trousers. Kates are loud, vivacious, and opinionated. They actively question policies, eye "the way we've always done it" with suspicion, and subscribe to the theory that it's easier to ask for forgiveness rather than permission. Kates avidly read professional journals and library blogs looking for cool new things to try in their libraries, and when they're at the reference desk, the problem patrons tend to give them a wide berth, because they know no shenanigans will be tolerated.

Katharines love to learn new things. If they're reference librarians, they're curious about cataloging; if they're children's librarians,  they want to know more about adult services. They loathe getting bogged down in the minutiae of administration, but at the same time they want to be a part of the bigger picture of library service. Kates are generalists rather than specialists, and don't like to be pigeonholed as any one kind of librarian.

Much to the dismay of people around them, especially the Audreys in their organization, Kates like blunt, direct communication. If you want a Kate to do something, you can't hint around or be subtle. However, once you tell her exactly what you want and when you want it, she will bend over backwards to deliver it. Kates don't tolerate abusive behavior from peers or patrons, and they ask pointed questions about new policies or initiatives. If the emperor has no clothes, they not only say so, they take a photograph and put it up on their library blogs, and if you want constructive criticism about anything, you should ask a Kate first.

Like their Audrey counterparts, Kates too have a dark side that must be acknowledged. While they sincerely love and respect their colleagues, Kates don't always play well with others, and may have difficulty finding a job situation where they fit in with the group. Kates don't "do" the social graces very well, perceiving them as fake and phony, and may therefore come across as tactless, thoughtless, or just plain rude. Kates want to move forward as quickly as possible, both with their ideas and within the organizational structure, so they may become impatient, frustrated, and angry with those in her organization who resist change. They don't always know how to communicate their visions in such a way that the rest of the group can relate to, and they may sometimes be overly critical of colleagues whose work styles and habits are very different from theirs.

Hepburns as leaders and change agents

I'd like to stress that while the archetypes are very different, there's no *wrong* way to Hepburn. After a lot of thought, I've come to the conclusion that both Kates and Audreys could make very effective leaders, and that the variances are primarily of style rather than skill set: Audreys, who tend to catch more flies with honey, are excellent choices to lead departments whose employees already have strong working relationships; although their fear of conflict makes them less effective in situations where there are interpersonal conflicts, an Audrey who is willing to work with her shadow qualities can learn to become a compassionate, yet firm, leader who can graciously lay down the law, an iron fist in a velvet glove.

Kates, I must confess, lend themselves far better to being change agents. Change is scary and unsettling for most people, but Katharines thrive on it, and are extremely skillful at creating things that don't yet exist. It's not that Kates can't be good leaders—the problem is, their visions are usually so outrageous that people might be afraid to follow. And unless a Kate is willing to work with *her* shadow qualities, and smooth down her rough edges a little, she may have a hard time convincing people that the horizons she's pursuing are worthwhile ones.

In an ideal situation, you'd have coleadership situations where an Audrey was paired with a Kate—say, an Audrey manager with a Kate senior staffer, or a Kate dean of students with an Audrey head librarian. Since the real is always far less than the ideal, however, a good place to start is with yourself: Are you more like Katharine or Audrey? In which ways? What do you need to work on a little? Is there a Kate or an Audrey in your organization who could help you with that?

Now look at the organization as a whole. What's the Kate-to-Audrey ratio? Who holds the major position of power—a Kate or an Audrey? How do you feel about that? What archetypal qualities of either figure would best move your organization forward? How can you cultivate those?

Because this is a philosophical ramble, and not a scholarly study, I'm sure there are gaping holes in what I'm trying to do here. But I think it's off to a good start.

SOURCE: Leigh Anne Vrabel, "A Plague on Both Your Hepburns: Leaders, Change Agents, and Library Archetypes," Library Alchemy, February 19, 2010, libraryalchemy.wordpress.com. Reprinted with permission.

MANAGERS

Who's the boss?

by Jamie E. Helgren and Linda Hofschire

THE SURVIVAL OF MANY PUBLIC LIBRARIES has been threatened as their funding has dried up in recent years. City and county officials are casting about for a lifesaver, and some have snagged a promising catch in the form of private companies that take over the management of public libraries. A September 26, 2010, *New York Times* article describing this occurrence in Santa Clarita, California—the first city with a relatively healthy library system to privatize its management—triggered a heated debate in the library community.

The Library Research Service (LRS), a unit of the Colorado State Library, picked up on this debate and developed a 60-Second Survey to gauge the library community's thoughts on the topic of privatizing public library management. Narrow by intent, these online surveys capture the perceptions of respondents on a single timely topic. They are

The newly independent Santa Clarita (Calif.) Public Library opened its Old Town Newhall branch in 2012.

publicized through local, regional, and national library discussion lists, blogs, and other channels.

For the privatization survey, a series of questions asked respondents to identify whether they thought public or private management would achieve better outcomes in regard to various services. LRS posted the survey online for a four-week period in November and December 2010. A total of 2,509 respondents completed the survey, representing every state and several foreign countries. More than half (58%) worked in public libraries, 17% in academic, and 10% in school libraries. About half of the respondents were in supervisory positions: 25% were directors and 26% were managers or supervisors.

Accompanying the responses were 1,500 comments—some quite lengthy—that offered more nuanced insight into respondents' varied thoughts on privatized management. Not only does this level of feedback support the obvious conclusion that privatization of public libraries is a controversial subject, but it also reveals the many different angles from which people connected to libraries view it.

The main goal of this study was to assess the perspectives of practicing librarians on privatization. However, we also interviewed Mark Smith, a vice president of library operations at Library Systems and Services, Inc. (LSSI), the primary private company in the United States offering library management services, to provide insight into the private sector's perspective.

The debate

Privatizing public library management has been on ALA's radar for more than a decade. It created an Outsourcing Task Force in 1997 to advise the Association on outsourcing and privatization and adopted a policy statement in 2001 opposing "the shifting of policy making and management oversight of library services from the public to the private for-profit sector."

Given this precedent, it is not surprising that library professionals are skeptical about relinquishing management to a third party. When asked to choose between two options—whether public library management should remain in the public sector to avoid a focus on profit or whether management should be privatized if it means providing better services at lower costs—a full 87% of survey respondents agreed with the former. Outsourcing cataloging or processing to third parties has by now become common practice for many American libraries, but the prospect of turning over responsibilities as community- or library-specific as management and collection development to the private sector raises significant questions about who retains authority over what, and whether the library's mission and users will remain top priorities.

Survey responses revealed that many library professionals fear that privatizing management would adversely affect public library services. "The mission of the library would be absolutely compromised through privatization, including patron privacy and access to a nonbiased canon of information," one respondent remarked.

When choosing whether they thought public- or private-sector management was more likely to achieve a list of outcomes for public libraries, at least three in four respondents identified public-sector management as the best way to improve

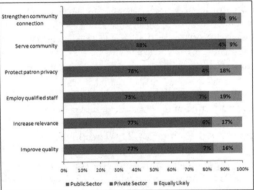

Chart 1. What type of management is more likely to achieve the following outcomes in public libraries?

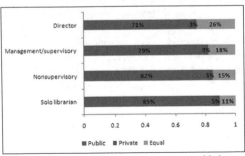

Chart 2. What type of management is more likely to protect patron privacy in public libraries?

the quality of library services, increase the relevance of libraries' collections, employ qualified staff to meet community needs, and protect patron privacy. Public-sector management drew even more support—from nearly nine out of 10 respondents (88%)—when respondents considered the library's ability to serve all the members of its community and the strength of the library's connection to its community (Chart 1).

The types of positions respondents held made a difference in how they answered these questions. Directors were often the most likely to indicate that both types of management—public and private sector—were equally likely to achieve the above outcomes. This pattern was most pronounced when it came to the protection of patron privacy (Chart 2).

Librarians are right to count matters such as collection relevance and patron privacy among their major concerns, as they are central to any public library's mission. According to Mark Smith, a private company must consider these matters as primary interests as well.

In an email interview, he explained that the policies of each LSSI-operated library, including patron privacy and collection development, are set by the library's governing body, not LSSI. LSSI and the libraries it operates are bound by state statutes to protect the confidentiality of patron records. The company does offer support in policy-making when requested, and Smith said LSSI recommends that the libraries formally adopt the ALA Library Bill of Rights.

"We encourage our library staff members performing selection to buy materials broadly to serve the diverse reading, listening, and viewing interests of each of our library communities," Smith commented. "We regularly provide justifications for purchases to our city and county partners when materials in the collection are challenged."

A survey respondent who worked for a privatized library system noted that the process and outcome for assessing challenged materials in his or her library "were exactly what they would have been" before the management switch.

One apprehension that repeatedly arose in survey comments was whether a large national company could remain in touch with the needs of local communities or if it would produce "cookie cutter" libraries. This is a concern about which Smith said he was aware. "LSSI-operated libraries must be highly responsive to community needs because if they were not, our contracts would end," Smith maintained. "We are held accountable to a higher standard than most public library managers, not only because we are governed by annual agreements, but because there is an unusually high level of scrutiny within the library profession of everything we do."

Although respondents expressed major concerns about the impact of privatization on the issues discussed above, they were more likely to recognize its potential benefits on outcomes such as reducing costs and increasing efficiency. More than two-thirds of respondents thought that private management was just as likely as, if not more likely than, public management to achieve these outcomes.

The best of both worlds

Is it possible there is a middle ground in this debate? Survey results indicated that while most respondents opposed outright privatization, they were open to incorporating business practices into library management. While a little more than half indicated that public libraries should be run like a public service, a sizeable percentage (42%) thought that they should be run like both a public service and a business (Chart 3). Notably, just 2% of respondents thought public libraries should be run like a business. Taken together, these findings show that the library community—as represented by those who responded

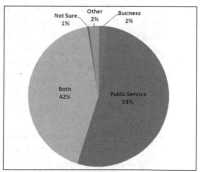

Chart 3. Should a public library be run like a public service or a business?

to the survey—at most wants to tweak the public service model, not abandon it.

Interestingly, about half (52%) of the respondents in supervisory positions (director or manager), who presumably would be most aware of the complexities involved in running a successful library, indicated that libraries should be run like both a public service and a business. In comparison, only about one-third (35%) of respondents in nonsupervisory positions agreed with this statement. Similar response patterns for those in supervisory roles were found for all of the survey questions, suggesting that serious consideration should be (and already is) given to how the business model can be best applied to public-sector management.

While nearly three-fourths (73%) of survey comments contained pro–public management sentiments, close to one-fourth (23%) were either pro-private or discussed alternatives to the black-and-white, public-versus-private debate. For example, several respondents suggested incorporation as a private, nonprofit entity (such as the New York Public Library) or implementation of business practices into libraries' current management structures.

"Ultimately, I think libraries should be publicly managed, but they really need to learn some lessons about efficient and cost-effective management from the business sector," one respondent commented. "We gripe about budget problems, but rarely are willing to make the tough decisions that would be better for libraries in the long run. We need to find a way to be sustainable, not just solving the money crisis for another few months."

What happens to the staff?

For better or worse, privatization may offer cost savings by centralizing services and streamlining processes for libraries that are struggling financially. Many of the survey respondents expressed concerns that additional cost reduction results from cutting services and shrinking salaries; more than 8 in 10 respondents (82%) thought that job security and benefits would be negatively impacted by privatization, and two-thirds were concerned about job prospects for MLIS librarians.

"I work for a privatized library," one survey respondent wrote. "They save money by paying us less. When qualified staff leave, they replace them with unqualified staff for much less pay. The only reason customers don't notice a decrease in quality soon after privatization is because the staff cares and tries really hard to provide good service. In a few more years, the rot will show."

While it is unknown if this respondent works for an LSSI-run library, Smith likewise addressed issues of service, qualified staff, and compensation. "We minimize staff time and material resources in processes that do not contribute to providing direct library service," Smith explained. "This does not mean we eliminate services that are deemed too costly, as is often suggested. The primary factor driving management decisions should be service—how to provide the best possible library service for the least cost. That is the definition of efficiency."

Part of running an efficient library is hiring the right people for the right jobs. Smith acknowledged that some library work requires an MLIS librarian and noted that LSSI must offer competitive salaries for librarians with the degree in order to attract qualified candidates to those positions.

Many librarians are prepared to meet the challenges of implementing business practices in a public institution, but doubt has contributed to an air of mistrust pervading nearly all angles of the discussion surrounding privatizing public library management. In spite of these professional concerns, some survey respondents tried to turn the conversation back to the focal point of all library work: the users.

"It really doesn't matter what I think—it's what the communities providing funding think that counts," one respondent proclaimed. "What has a community defined as 'better?' It's up to us to make the case, and if public agencies can't make the case that they can do a 'better' job for their communities, then privatization will be a trend that will continue growing."

SOURCE: Jamie E. Helgren and Linda Hofschire, "Who's the Boss?" *American Libraries*, July 12, 2011, americanlibrariesmagazine.org/features/07122011/who-s-boss.

What I've learned from 30 years of managing libraries

by J. Robert Verbesey

2

RECENTLY, IN PREPARATION for a lecture, I was pondering what I have learned from more than 30 years of managing public and academic libraries, from studying and teaching management at three graduate library school programs and one undergraduate business program for 20 years, and from watching colleagues do both well and poorly managing libraries.

I have learned—sometimes through bitter experience—the following.

Employees are not interchangeable cogs in a wheel. They are flesh and blood; they are individuals. The manager's responsibility is to put people where their talents can shine and their weaknesses are minimized (as much as possible). Understand, too, that people and jobs change. That means the manager has to continuously assess and adapt to changing situations.

We learn best from our mistakes, **so let people make mistakes** and do not punish them— unless they keep repeating the same mistake. Employees need to be given freedom. As they thrive and produce and prove themselves, they should be given more of it. Making mistakes is part of this process. To quote Thomas Edison: "Results? Why man, I have gotten a lot of results. I know several thousand things that won't work."

Basketball coaches are fond of saying that you cannot teach "height." In the same way, you cannot teach "brains." **So hire the smartest people you can,** give them the resources they need, listen to and learn from them, and then get out of their way—unless again, you are much smarter than they are collectively. And believe me, if you think you are, you probably are not.

Parcel out the praise, and take the blame. The manager's task is to praise and protect his or her employees. It is not to look for someone to blame. Recognizing and rewarding employees for good performance on a regular basis is important. Take the time and make the effort to do it. Do everything you can to take a few minutes to recognize employee achievements. If you do, both performance and morale are likely to improve.

Employees need clear and unambiguous goals and objectives. That means the organization needs clear, unambiguous goals and objectives. When appropriate, there should be clearly defined deadlines that are both challenging and realistic. Clear goals and objectives enable employees to make decisions without constantly needing to go to a manager.

After someone tells you something important, rephrase what they have said. This will let them and you know for sure that you've accurately heard what has been said.

When it comes to communication, too many agencies operate on a need-to-know basis. I suggest operating on a *need-to-not-know* basis. Unless there is a compelling reason not to divulge information, just share it. The need-to-know is often misused to stifle scrutiny or to increase personal power. Trust your employees and they will be more likely to trust you.

Continuous two-way feedback is essential. This is especially so with new employees. The purpose is not to micromanage but to nurture. Annual performance reviews serve no purpose but to kill trees and raise anxiety levels. Employees should know every week exactly what they are doing well and need to do better. That means the manager and the employee should be in almost daily contact. And, if it is truly two-way communication, it means managers have to listen. In the 1980s this was referred to as "management by walking around."

High-maintenance people are seldom worth it. The corollary to this is that there are happy people and unhappy people. Again, if you have a choice, hire happy people. In general a manager cannot undo what parents, genes, and early childhood experiences have done to an employee. So do not try, unless you have a lot of free time, expertise in psychology, and the employee in question has extraordinary talent in some areas that are important to your organization.

If you find someone who is both task-oriented and process-oriented, pay them whatever it takes to keep them. Such gems are hard to find and harder to replace. Some employees are so concerned about the process—the "people" side of the equation—that the completion time and quality of the work suffer. Others engage full-bore on the task at hand and ignore the needs of the people with whom they work. Those who are good at completing the task while simultaneously working with colleagues in a collegial manner are worth their weight in gold; so value them accordingly.

Leave a job before, not after, "they" want you to. There are few things sadder than watching someone who has overstayed their usefulness, clawing to hang onto a position they no longer do well—but cannot afford or simply do not want to leave.

Managing people is an art. You cannot learn it well by only reading books or memorizing rules. You can only learn it well by carefully observing, by doing, making errors, learning from those errors, mending your ways, picking the brains of successful experienced managers, and thereby incrementally improving.

Never give yourself special perks that will stick in the craw of your employees or the public you serve. The parking space closest to the door should go to the employee who arrives first. Playing golf during the middle of the day and calling it work probably will not sit well with some of your employees.

Call your organization when you are out of the office. In many instances, you will be unpleasantly shocked. The telephone is so important to businesses, yet many callers are likely to get caught in an endless loop of "press two, then press five" and then find out no one answers. Whenever possible have a person answer the phone rather than a recording.

The prize should go not to the person who complains about workmates or the rules or the equipment, but to the person who ignores all that and does his/her

best. **Value highly those employees who do a good job because they have pride in themselves and have a desire to do a thing well for its own sake.** Anyone who says they would do a better job if they were paid more is someone you do not want in your organization.

Very few people truly like change, but shy away from those who cannot deal with it. Twenty-five hundred years ago Heraclitus (left) said, "Nothing endures but change." He is as right today as he was then. But change today is at warp speed.

Finally, laugh—at yourself and with others.

SOURCE: J. Robert Verbesey, "What I've Learned from 30 Years of Managing Libraries," *Catholic Library World* 79, no. 3 (March 2009): 192–94. Reprinted with permission.

Some fundamentals of library supervision

by Joan Giesecke and Beth McNeil

MANAGEMENT USED TO BE SIMPLE. The manager or supervisor told employees what to do and employees did what they were told. That world does not exist today. Today's managers, supervisors, team leaders, project managers, and unit heads face a more complex environment. But if you enjoy bringing people together and helping them do their best, you are ready to be a manager. Enjoy the complexities and challenges that make up this exciting world.

Written communication

As a supervisor, you will find that you need good written communication skills. You will be responsible for preparing reports, writing evaluations of your staff, developing policy statements, and communicating with your supervisors. In addition, in today's world of email communication, you will also be writing information to your staff that traditionally may have been communicated orally.

Good writing takes practice. Think about the message you want to convey and how you want that message to be delivered. Are you preparing a formal report to be shared with those above you in the organization? Are you sending a procedural change notification to your department? Are you communicating with groups outside of your organization?

Each audience is different and has different needs. You want to be sure that your writing style is appropriate for the audience. For example, an academic-style report may be appropriate for a professional journal article but may not be effective for conveying information to your unit. A library-use policy may need two versions, one for print on paper and another for the library's website; the content will be the same, but the arrangement on the paper and screen may need to vary in order to effectively communicate with the two different audiences. An informal, chatty memo to your group may be fine to alert them to a minor change in policy. This same style, though, is not appropriate for your annual report. Be sure, then, that your style of writing fits with your audience and with the purpose of your communication.

Next, in preparing to write, you should review or outline the purpose of your communication. What do you want to accomplish with your writing? Do you want to entice the public to a program or convey a policy change? Both actions are important but have very different purposes.

Third, consider the message you want to relay. What are the facts you want to get across to others? What are the key points you want to be sure your audience recognizes in your writing?

Once you have identified your audience, sufficiently outlined your purpose, and decided your main message, you are ready to begin drafting your piece. Your draft may go through many versions before it is ready. Writing requires effort and editing. It is rare that a person can sit down and compose a memo or a report without needing to make changes and edit the document. Think about the order in which you convey the information. Your primary and important points should appear first. The readers should not have to guess at what you want them to remember. Put the most important message first. Then add in your next most important items, and so on until you have included all the points you wish to make. Finally, write a concluding paragraph or section to summarize your key points and close your piece.

Now comes the hard part. You need to review your work and edit the piece to make it as clear as possible. Some word-processing software packages have tools that can help with this, but human review is still necessary. Eliminate any extraneous and unnecessary words. Do not use five words if three will do. Use active sentence structures to maintain clarity.

Check for grammar. Do all your nouns and verbs agree with each other? Have you started a paragraph each time you have a new thought or idea to express? Do you have long sentences that cannot be easily understood? Look at how you can shorten and revise your work to increase clarity and understanding while still conveying all the points that you wish to make.

One helpful hint is to read your writing out loud. How does it sound? Do the words flow easily? Are the ideas clear? Reading your work out loud can help you catch grammatical errors, as well as discover when you have used more words than you need.

Good written communication is a core skill for supervisors. Taking your time and reviewing your work before you distribute it will help you become an effective writer.

Email

Some dangers in the world of communication involve the misuse of and mistakes made through email communication. It is too easy sometimes to think you can just sit down and compose an email and fire it off without review. Poorly written email messages can be as dangerous for a supervisor as a poorly written report. With email, as with all communication, be sure you practice good etiquette. Be careful with your use of abbreviations. For example, not everyone knows instant messaging abbreviations that dominate some emails. Be sure you explain the abbreviations you do include.

Be thoughtful about when you use email. It makes very little sense to send someone an email message when you are sitting next to the person and can simply

 turn and talk to him. Email should not be used as a way to avoid oral communication. You will also want to be careful about whom you send emails to and how you reply to messages sent to you. Do not copy everyone imaginable on an email message unless the information is truly needed by everyone in the organization or group. Do not reply to all on a discussion list message if you are sending a private reply to the sender. Not everyone on the list wants to know about your lunch plans. Keep your business emails business-oriented and do not confuse business and social communication.

One other trap to avoid with email is the tendency to send out an email reply when you are upset or angry. That is not the time to be sending messages, even to close friends, as the message could be forwarded to others. Email is not a secure communication channel. Rather, treat it as you would a postcard and assume everyone around will be able to see the message.

Dangers of email "reply all." The library board decides to postpone the annual fundraiser this year due to staff shortages. Tony's unit typically organizes and staffs the fundraiser, so he lets his unit know and he sends an email to all library staff indicating that the fundraiser will be postponed this year. A supervisor of another unit, who enjoys the fundraiser himself and often receives input from patrons and staff about it, reacts angrily and responds to Tony's message questioning Tony's authority, accidentally copying to all staff. Tony feels undermined by his colleague; Tony's colleague is embarrassed by his email gaffe and ultimately apologizes to Tony; staff members who had initially accepted that the postponement was necessary and unavoidable now experience lowered morale and wonder about the library supervisors' working relationship.

Email can be very effective when used correctly. Email is an efficient communication medium and can help you inform everyone in a group at the same time about a change. It can also help you document that you have relayed needed information to your group. It can help you send updates and non–time-sensitive information to a large number of people.

As a supervisor, think about what you want to communicate with your writing and then pick the best way to get your ideas across to your audience. Whether you are composing an email message, jotting down a list of bullet points you want to mention at a staff meeting, or writing a formal report, remember to think about your audience, review your purpose, and then outline your message. Finally, edit, edit, edit! A well-written and edited email will help you send the kind of message you want to send to your group. A poorly written or repetitive report can just as easily hurt you. Communicating well is an art. Take time as a supervisor to practice the art of good writing each time you write.

Supervisor's role in teams

By now you may be wondering what your role as a manager is in the team environment. Are you a team leader, a team member, or just one of the crowd? What role do you play in this type of organizational structure? As team leader you are responsible for the following tasks.

Understand and be committed to the team concept. First, as a manager, you need to understand the team concept. If you play favorites or reward and promote individual achievement over group goals, you will undermine team efforts. If you are not committed to a team structure, you will not be effective as a team leader.

Select team members. As team leader, you are responsible for choosing the members of your team. Look for complementary skills so you can build a group of people with the variety and depth of skills you need for success.

Develop people skills. As a manager, you need to recognize and acknowledge team members' skill-building efforts. Even something as simple as saying "Good job" or "That's a good effort" will support people-building skills. Recognizing that different people want different types of recognition is important, too. Some people like public recognition; others prefer a personal letter. As a team leader, you need to understand your team members as individuals at the same time you promote group coordination and collaboration. Being responsive to and supportive of team members will help maximize individual performance and contribute to team success.

Facilitate information flow. Another major role for you as leader is to facilitate, support, and promote the flow of information. You bring in information from the rest of the organization. You facilitate the sharing of information about your unit with the organization. And you support the coordination of effort within the group through the sharing of information. As team leader, you are responsible for encouraging quieter team members to participate and to express their opinions while working with more forceful members to learn to listen to their colleagues.

Coordinate with your peers. As team leader, you are charged with working effectively with other team leaders to advance the goals of the organization. In interlibrary loan, for example, you may be working with an acquisition unit to be sure that heavily requested items are considered for purchase. You may coordinate searching activities with a reference unit. You may work with a cataloging unit to be sure the catalog records contain enough detail for your unit to use to verify ownership of a particular item. In each of these venues, you want to represent the goals and needs of your team while sharing the concerns of other units with your group.

Pay attention to first meetings. As team leader, you will set the tone for how the group initially interacts. If you show that you are flexible, committed to team goals, and responsive to the group, you will set a positive tone that will carry the group through its first few meetings. By sending a clear signal that you support the team as a team, you will encourage the development of good team guidelines and processes.

Set clear rules for behavior. Help the group establish clear ground rules as they begin to form as a group. Agreements on attendance, discussion options, confidentiality, meeting process, and other issues should be established early on in the process so the team can function effectively as a group while they build their skills to become a true team. Disagreements or resentments over simple items such as the time allowed for personal phone calls or the length of breaks can destroy team trust and make the group dysfunctional. A positive working environment that promotes true harmony within the team, without covering up tensions or disagreements, will lead to a productive team.

Spend lots of time together. As a leader, you need to spend time with your team. Absentee management will not work in a team environment. Delegating work to the group and then disappearing from the unit will not work. Team efforts require the group to work together. As team leader, you need to be a part of the group at the same time that you provide leadership and help set direction.

Provide positive feedback and constructive advice. As team leader, you are also responsible for providing feedback to the group. The team needs to know how they are performing as a group, how they are meeting goals, and how they are interacting. Effective leaders provide appropriate coaching, feedback, and advice even as they function as part of the team.

Keep goals relevant. As team leader, you can help guide the group to ensure that agreed-upon goals and purpose mesh well with the overall goals of the organization. When teams are working on multiple goals, confusion can arise when goals appear to be in conflict. As team leader, you will need to watch for such situations and help coordinate or sort through team activities so that the team stays focused on the overall organizational objectives. Gina, as head of a reference unit, knows that her organization values customer service. She also knows that there are a variety of ways to measure customer service. She works with her team, then, to develop goals for limiting the number of patron complaints or increasing the number of patrons served. Matching unit goals to organizational goals is crucial if the team is to remain relevant to the organization.

Create opportunities for others. Team leaders cannot take all the desirable assignments, praise, or glory and expect to have a successful team. Rather, true team leaders share opportunities, plum assignments, and rewards with the team. Watching staff develop into successful team members is a reward to a true team leader.

Do real work. Team leaders are important members of the team. While the role of team leader means that you have responsibilities outside of the team, you also have real work responsibilities inside the team. A team leader in interlibrary loan will help with lending requests or borrowing requests when needed and not just sit around while team members struggle to complete a day's set of requests.

Performance evaluations

Most organizations will have a system for annual performance evaluations. The process may include a standardized form and a numerical rating system. Or the system may use open-ended letters, leaving the process up to the supervisor. No matter what system you use, a good supervisor will write a clear analysis of the staff member's performance. Vague statements that read like a horoscope will not be helpful to the staff member, nor will it provide the employee with any advice on what is working well. You should present a balanced view of the staff member's performance, noting strengths and accomplishments. Emphasizing strengths will help a staff member focus on successes and will help provide

a more motivating environment. A performance evaluation is also a means to document any concerns about a person's performance. Again, balance is a key. Do not overemphasize recent experiences or ignore past events. The evaluation should reflect the entire year.

To complete a successful performance evaluation, follow these steps:

1. Review the staff member's position description, standards, and expectations. Be sure you know what the employee is supposed to be doing.
2. Review your notes on the person's performance for the year. Identify major successes and areas of outstanding performance. Note, too, any areas that need improvement.
3. Complete the evaluation form or write the evaluation letter. Be sure to focus on the current year's performance. Note improvements from the last evaluation. Do not raise past issues that have been resolved more than a year ago. Tie performance to expectations so that the staff member knows how the work he has done is reflected in the evaluation.
4. The evaluation should contain no surprises. If you have not addressed a problem this year, you should not blame the staff member for not improving. You may list this as an area for growth, but it should not adversely affect a staff member's overall rating.
5. Once the form is complete, give it to the staff member to review prior to any discussion about performance. Some organizations will specify how many workdays the staff member has to review a written evaluation prior to an oral conference. Carefully follow your organization's procedures.
6. Plan the oral conference. Do not read the written form to the employee. Rather, decide on strengths to highlight, accomplishments to review, and concerns to discuss.
7. At the oral conference, outline strengths. Note areas of improvement. Answer any questions the staff member may have. Listen carefully to his concerns. Be sure to address any uncertainty, disagreements, or confusion.

8. Review any concerns you have about the person's performance. Discuss plans to address these concerns.
9. Discuss goals and objectives for the coming year. Include plans to address concerns but also include ways to build on the staff member's strengths to improve performance and reach excellence.
10. Close the conference by signing forms as needed. Review any follow-up that is planned.
11. Because performance evaluations are confidential personnel papers, be sure to file the forms as outlined in your organization's procedures immediately after the oral conference. Do not carelessly leave evaluation forms lying around your office. You must keep them safe.

Once the conference is completed and the forms are safely processed, do not ignore performance issues for a year. Do follow-up as needed. Meet regularly with your staff, discuss their accomplishments, and review areas for growth.

SOURCE: Joan Giesecke and Beth McNeil, *Fundamentals of Library Supervision,* 2d ed. (Chicago: American Library Association, 2010), ix, x, 26–29, 57–59, 123–24.

CONSULTANTS

The role of a consultant
by Ulla de Stricker

FOR THOSE WORKING in full-time jobs, the lifestyle of a consultant may appear to be one of ease and leisure. They may envy the flexibility in scheduling work—for example, the luxury of being able to decide which projects to accept—and the benefits of working from home, to name but a few of the major perceived advantages. Although those advantages most certainly are appealing, there are realities to deal with as well: the tendency for work to be uneven, the challenge of managing expectations within preset budget envelopes, the considerable time and effort going into networking—again, to name just a few.

Why are consultants needed?

As individuals, we take for granted the need to seek out and pay for the services of an expert who can help us deal with a specific situation we wouldn't dream of tackling—or couldn't tackle—ourselves. We gladly pay for the services of mechanics. Library managers follow the same paradigm when they call on a consultant to help plan the interior of a new library, fashion a communications strategy, or select and implement a content management system for the intranet.

Of course, the practice of purchasing professional assistance when needed goes far beyond such relatively few-and-far-between occasions as outfitting a new library. Most libraries and similar knowledge-based entities (competitive intelligence units, marketing departments, risk analysis teams) lack the personnel to carry out all the projects that must be undertaken. When a library system must be upgraded, when it's time to market an expanded range of services to existing and new clients, when a body of material needs to be digitized, or when libraries in a region need to develop new ways to collaborate—consultants are called in to plan, guide, and assist in processes that do not fall within the day-to-day operations.

Generally, it is understood that the value of a consultant's expertise more than justifies the cost. Here's why:

Engaging consultants makes business sense. Library directors are keenly aware of the benefits resulting from just-in-time procurement of expertise. More important, the variety of business, technical, and strategic challenges facing most libraries and library-like entities is so great that no other option exists but to lean on targeted expertise when special circumstances arise. For example, the development from scratch of a program to support a distance-learning initiative could require experience falling outside that of current staff in an academic library.

Consultants bring a fresh perspective. A compelling benefit to engaging the services of consultants is the fact that they are unencumbered by the past. They have no traditions lurking in the backs of their minds as they go about their projects; in fact, it can be a risk for a consultant to become too closely entwined in the client's operations. Conversely, consultants bring along experience from their previous projects in other settings. No amount of benchmarking can match breadth of expertise.

Consultants represent a time-limited commitment for the client. When the consultant's report is in hand, the client is free to consider whether to proceed with the consultant's recommendations. Although all consultants hope their clients implement the recommended approach—immediately—reality says otherwise. Sometimes clients aren't ready for the changes recommended, budget limitations get in the way, or sudden new developments put plans on hold.

Consultants are a solution to a communications challenge. Inasmuch as the "hard truth" can be easier to accept if it comes from an outsider, consultants are sometimes asked to take care of a function that could be difficult for a manager to perform. As a result, consultants may find themselves bearing an uncomfortable message, thus needing considerable finesse in the area of communications.

Consulting roles

Consulting activities are extremely varied, yet they share characteristics. In your consulting career, you may get to function in every role from summer relief to miracle worker, and you will intuitively recognize that different work tasks and tangible outputs are appropriate according to the nature of a given project. Assignments can be quite straightforward, as in "Select and install a new library management system"—or more nuanced, as in "Please help us determine how we can best meet the needs of the students in the distance learning program."

For successful outcomes, the roles consultants play must be clearly understood, both by the consultant and by the client. There is trouble ahead if it turns out the client and the consultant have different views of what the consultant should contribute to a given project.

The following examples illustrate the range of roles consultants may find themselves performing. Naturally, individual consultants may gravitate to certain types of roles and focus their offerings accordingly.

An extra pair of hands. A hiring freeze may prevent adding new staff, but a contractor can be engaged to:
- Fill in for someone on leave.

- Supervise the completion of a cataloging backlog.
- Manage the merger of two libraries or collections.

The consultant works within preexisting guidelines and may have limited opportunity to be creative.

Special-purpose assistance. No one on staff is available to carry out a special project:

- Teach staff how to use a new system or tool.
- Prepare a special exhibit.
- Conduct market research: What do current and potential clients need?

The consultant may work under the direction of a manager on staff and may not have much scope for bringing about significant change.

Unique expertise. The client needs advice on how to deal with a particular challenge:

- How can we improve work flow in technical services?
- What are the best options when it comes to staffing up and selecting software for a new intranet?
- How can we make the new library wing blend in with the original building and yet stand out as a strong architectural statement?
- What technology infrastructure will be adequate for current and future needs?

In this role, the consultant is sought out specifically to bring to bear expertise that is not already on hand. Typically the consultant conducts a study of "how things are now" and prepares a set of recommendations for concrete actions, designs, purchases, and so forth.

Been there, done that. The client wants to minimize risk by engaging someone who is very familiar with activities similar to the project at hand:

- How can we figure out what services to prioritize and what services to terminate?
- How can we improve the visibility of the resource center among the market analysts?

In many situations, the client is particularly keen on knowing that the consultant has carried out similar projects and therefore can apply proven techniques. If receptivity to new approaches is limited, it is the consultant's challenge to convince the client to try something novel.

Visionary strategist. "Help us chart the way":

- We know we need some kind of knowledge repository for the call center agents, but we have no idea where to begin.
- We need to strengthen our role in, and contribution to, the community we serve; what are the components in meeting such a challenge?

This role requires a mix of broad expertise across the gamut of the project's components as well as considerable skills in managing complex projects.

Agent of change. Organizational and psychological challenges stand in the way of moving forward:

- Design and lead a series of exercises to help staff arrive at conclusions and insights that will facilitate their acceptance of change.
- Facilitate exploratory sessions to identify friction points and opportunities.

In some library and library-like settings, strong traditions exist for how things are done, and it can be difficult for the current director to get staff members excited about new priorities, services, or processes. In such a case, the consultant's role is to facilitate changes in employee attitudes.

Rescuer. Specific events require specialized expertise:
- A fire has caused sprinkler damage to irreplaceable materials. Now what?
- Several of the senior staff have taken early retirement, and a sudden illness has left a gap in staffing. How can we get through the next few months, and how do we deal with the planning for human resources?

Though it would be nice if skills such as salvaging wet books were not needed, the fact is that accidents do happen, and consultants who know what to do are needed—now. The best laid plans of library directors can't prevent a staffing crisis; it is fortunate that some consultants specialize in dealing with such situations.

SOURCE: Ulla de Stricker, *Is Consulting for You? A Primer for Information Professionals* (Chicago: American Library Association, 2008), 3–8.

TRUSTEES

A trustee's guide to relationships
by Mary Y. Moore

YOUR RELATIONSHIPS WITH other board members, the library director, the staff, and the community you represent are vital to your success as a trustee, yet this aspect of the job is often overlooked. The typical term for a library board member is three to five years. Reappointment usually occurs if you are willing to serve and have represented your community well. Considering the time you will be spending with all these different people, you will want to make sure that your communication lines are open and your trust levels are high—just as they should be in a good marriage.

Relationships with other board members

People decide to serve on a library's board of trustees for a variety of reasons. The most laudable reason has to do with the desire to serve their community in an area to which they can bring some knowledge or talent. Unfortunately, people with personal agendas are often elected or appointed to library boards, and they can cause serious problems. Consider why the following people might be problematic:

- The person who is on the board because he or she wants to cut taxes and does not care where or how.
- The person who is on the board because he or she thinks it will look good on a political résumé.
- The person who thinks board service might be a nice social thing to do—a kind of "good works" that one can talk about at a cocktail party.
- The board member who is a political activist and has one issue or concern for which he or she campaigns to the exclusion of other issues.

- The board member who believes that he or she alone knows what is moral and what is immoral when it comes to the material in the library.

You can imagine that meeting month after month with these folks might be difficult. So what can you do?

First of all, examine your reasons for being on the library board. Perhaps you had no reason other than that you were flattered to be asked. Or perhaps you started out with one thing in mind but have changed your perspective now that you know what is expected of you. A successful library board member will be open-minded, objective, and reasonable. There will be times when you have to put your own prejudices aside to do what is best for the library and the community.

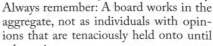
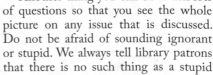
Des Plaines Public Library Board of Trustees Meeting October 18, 2011

Always remember: A board works in the aggregate, not as individuals with opinions that are tenaciously held onto until others give up.

Another thing you can do is ask lots of questions so that you see the whole picture on any issue that is discussed. Do not be afraid of sounding ignorant or stupid. We always tell library patrons that there is no such thing as a stupid question; true ignorance occurs when someone doesn't ask, but assumes instead that others will know. You may even be doing a favor for someone who is less assertive than you. You may also prevent someone from pushing something through without telling the whole story.

Finally, if someone on your board is behaving unethically, the best thing you can do is call the person on it. It need not be done offensively. Use an "I" message such as, "I feel that when you constantly miss meetings or arrive late, perhaps you are not as committed to this responsibility as I am. Can you clarify this for me? Do we need to change the date of the meetings?" This message is very clear, but it will not offend the person because it also expresses concern for his or her welfare.

If you use these techniques, you will improve communication at your meetings and demonstrate your value as a board member.

Relationships with the library director

In terms of a relationship between you as a board member and the library director, there are two basic points to keep in mind.

1. It is your job to work with other board members on the governance of the library. It is the library director's job to manage the library.
2. A governing board is responsible for hiring, evaluating, and, if necessary, firing the library director. In other words, the library director is your employee. The rest of the staff are hired, evaluated, and, if necessary, fired by the director or his or her designee. With an advisory board, it is someone else's responsibility to employ the library director, although board members should be able to advise the employer on various aspects of the director's employment.

All that formality aside, the best relationship between board members and a library director is as a team working together for the good of the library and the community it serves. With any luck, you will honestly like and respect the library director for the talents and management expertise he or she brings to the job.

You might even become close friends, although that could lead to difficulties. Remember that one of your responsibilities is to evaluate the library director's performance, and you must do so with objectivity and compassion. You can't let personal feelings get in the way.

Good communication is the most powerful tool you have in establishing a solid working relationship with your director. If you have questions or concerns, talking candidly with the library director is the best course of action. Most of us try to avoid conflict. We tend to talk to a third party if there is something about a person that bothers us. Somehow it seems safer—less fraught with potential conflict. However, an honest sharing of concerns or questions with your director can usually clear things up in a hurry. If what concerns you would be inappropriate to discuss with the director, the next best person to talk to is the chair of the board.

Relationships with the community

You are representing either a whole community or a part of one. It should be made clear at the outset that you are representing a neighborhood, an age group, an ethnicity, a business community, or perhaps a particular town or county. To that end, you need to know what your constituents want from the library or the library system. You are not expected to send out surveys or hold focus groups; that's the job of the library staff. But there are other ways to keep your finger on the pulse of your community. You can gauge the degree to which your community is being served by attending community meetings, asking questions at gatherings, and listening to what people are saying about the library.

Alice Ihrig, a library trustee from the Midwest and past president of the American Library Trustees Association (now United for Libraries), used to tell wonderful stories about her methods of getting feedback on her library. One of her tactics was to "accidentally" nudge the cart of the shopper ahead of her in the supermarket checkout line. When noticed, she would smile brightly, apologize, and immediately introduce herself as one of the local library's trustees. She would then ask if the shopper was a library customer and what he or she thought of the library. That approach may seem a bit daunting, particularly if you are an introvert, but it certainly worked for her.

Relationships with library staff

A trustee's relationship with the staff of a library is probably one of the trickiest. If you are already friends with staff members, the best rule of thumb is to be discreet. Sometimes confidential matters are discussed in library board meetings, whether you are on a governing board or an advisory board. And sometimes you have to make hard budget or policy decisions that could have unfortunate effects upon your friends.

It is tempting for staff members who know a board member personally to complain about work matters or supervisors. The most common complaint is usually about the library director. Unfortunately, libraries are often managed in a hierarchical style, with several layers of personnel at different pay scales and levels of responsibility. This can cause poor morale. It is often hard for line staff to understand why librarians are paid more than they are, and at times they are resentful. When one is unhappy with one's work, the easiest person to blame is the boss.

Some of the complaints about the library director or a supervisor might be justified, but board members should not discuss these issues with staff. The wisest course of action is to review the management style and capability of the director during regular evaluation sessions. Many people in library administration received only cursory management training in library school. They need additional training and professional development on the job.

Relationships with staff can be cordial and courteous. You should care about their welfare because they are the backbone of the library service. They also represent the library's greatest resource, since staff salaries use 60% or more of an annual budget. However, you should not court close friendships with staff people while you are on the board. Discretion, tact, and diplomacy will serve you well in these relationships.

Relationships with political entities

The most important relationships you can have, as far as the library is concerned, are those with local, state, and federal political representatives. Government bodies at all three levels have a powerful impact on public libraries. If your library board serves a county or city, regardless of size, the county commissioners or city council members make decisions that are critical to the library's welfare. Not only do they determine the size of the county's or city's contribution to the annual library budget but they can also be instrumental in zoning decisions, bond issues, security, and other matters.

It's a good idea to attend county commission or city council meetings on a regular basis, not only to keep tabs on local matters but also to see where the community is heading in terms of its leadership. It is important to know the goals of the body that is funding the library. If its goals are not compatible with those of the library, the funding organization may not look kindly on the library. Asking questions and making appropriate comments within the context of the meetings, or talking to county and city officials following the meetings, will get you known as someone who cares about the county or city and its library.

How well do you know your state government representatives? Do you know who they are, and do you feel at ease picking up the phone or emailing them when you are concerned about an issue? If not, you need to find out how to contact them. The state government makes many decisions that affect libraries. Some states provide funding for public libraries, and state legislatures make the laws that govern the way your library operates. So you can see that the state government relationship is a pivotal one.

Finally, the federal government has been generous to libraries over the last 50 years. Not only does it supply state library agencies with federal funds, but it also gets involved in First Amendment issues, copyright issues, telecommunications costs, and other key concerns. It's great if you are on speaking terms with your members of Congress because emails, letters, and phone calls do have an impact.

Attending local political gatherings and meeting your representatives face to face can help your cause. Then they can put a face with a name when you contact them on behalf of libraries. Your relationships are critical to your success as a library trustee. Make sure that they are all they can be.

SOURCE: Mary Y. Moore, *The Successful Library Trustee Handbook*, 2d ed. (Chicago: American Library Association, 2010), 9–14.

How to organize a library Friends group

EVERY LIBRARY NEEDS FRIENDS. Whether you are a community member or librarian, by starting a Friends group you'll be giving an important gift to the community.

1. If you are a librarian, reach out to some of your most faithful and energetic volunteers or a few of your most devout patrons to start a small steering committee. If you are a library lover who wants to start a group, contact your librarian and share your plans. It is critical to the success of the group that the librarian and the Friends' steering committee work closely together.

2. The steering committee should reflect the community. Again, it should include the librarian and a small core of active volunteers or patrons. It is important to have access to an attorney, public relations and advertising talent, and high-profile leaders.

3. Determine the group's purpose and mission so that you can plan an organizational structure to accomplish them. This structure will include the types of standing committees you'll need to carry out your work.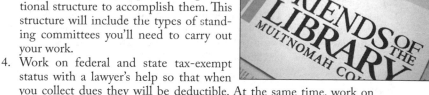

4. Work on federal and state tax-exempt status with a lawyer's help so that when you collect dues they will be deductible. At the same time, work on developing the group's constitution and by-laws. Visit the United for Libraries website for materials that will provide you with sample by-laws and assistance for writing your constitution.

5. Determine what your dues structure will be. Consider a structure that will optimize both the number of members who will join and your ability to raise funds through dues. Starting with a low student or retired rate and increasing the dues incrementally for "higher" categories of giving should accomplish both objectives.

6. Once you have developed an organizational structure and have 501(c)(3) tax-exempt status, you will want to embark on a membership drive. This will probably include a direct mailing and a membership brochure to hand out at the library, doctor's offices, grocery stores, and other places where members might be recruited.

7. Design a professional-looking brochure for the membership drive. The brochure doesn't have to be expensive but it does have to look professional. Be sure that you include a space for new members to become active participants and volunteers in the organization. Follow up right away to involve those who want to volunteer.

8. Hold your first "all member" meeting following the membership drive. This meeting should include a program component to attract a high

attendance. At this program/meeting, elect officers and committee chairs to set and accomplish the group's goals.

9. Develop a long-range plan for your Friends group that includes participation from library staff so that your group's goals can stay in alignment with the library's vision and goals.

10. Join United for Libraries to get access to our special toolkit for members only, "Starting a New Friends Group, or Revitalizing the Group You Have," as well as "Incorporating and Tax Exempting Procedures for Friends," and host of other materials and advice to help you do what you do even better.

SOURCE: ALA United for Libraries, "How to Organize a Friends Group," Fact Sheet no. 1, ala.org/united/sites/ala.org.united/files/content/friends/factsheets/unitedff1.pdf.

Friends' Literary Landmarks

THE LITERARY LANDMARKS ASSOCIATION was founded in 1986 by former Friends of Libraries U.S.A. president Frederick G. Ruffner to encourage the dedication of historic literary sites. The first dedication was at Slip F18 in Bahia Mar, Florida, the anchorage of the *Busted Flush,* the houseboat home of novelist John D. MacDonald's protagonist Travis McGee. Since that time, more than 100 Literary Landmarks have been dedicated across the country.

Dedications have included homes of famous writers, libraries and museum collections, and literary scenes. Local Friends groups or state Friends may apply to dedicate a Literary Landmark. When an appropriate landmark is identified, the sponsoring group can plan a dedication ceremony and apply to ALA's United for Libraries division for official recognition. These are the landmarks that have been dedicated since 2006 through mid-2012.

2006

Des Moines (Iowa) Public Library. Forrest Spaulding, director of the Des Moines Public Library from 1917 to 1919 and again from 1927 to 1952, wrote the Library Bill of Rights that was adopted by the Des Moines Public Library board on November 21, 1938, and adopted by the American Library Association on June 18, 1948. *Website:* dmpl.org/about_us/index.html.

Handy Writers' Colony, Marshall, Illinois. *From Here to Eternity* author James Jones cofounded the Handy Writers' Colony (1949–1964) at the west edge of Marshall with his mentor Lowney Turner Handy and her husband, Harry. Jones wrote *Some Came Running* here before moving to New York and writing other books. Several other colony writers completed and published novels during those years. The house Jones built at the edge of the colony grounds in 1953 still stands. *Website:* www.uis.edu/archives/handy.html.

Curwood Castle, Owosso, Michigan. This castle, now a museum, contained the writing studio of James Oliver Curwood in one of its turrets. Curwood was the author of many books, stories, magazine articles, and films, and was a zealous conservationist. *Website:* www.michigan.org/property/detail.aspx?p=G5298.

Curwood Castle, by Joanna Poe, used CC A 3.0.

2

Tennessee Williams House, New Orleans. Tennessee Williams owned this 19th-century townhouse from 1962 until his death in 1983. Here he worked on his autobiography, *Memoirs,* in which he wrote, "I hope to die in my sleep . . . in this beautiful big brass bed in my New Orleans apartment, the bed that is associated with so much love." He always considered New Orleans his spiritual home. *Website:* www.flickr.com/photos/wallyg/2484859160/.

Charles C. Wise Jr. Library, West Virginia University, Morgantown. The writings and personal papers of Louise McNeill, poet laureate of West Virginia from 1977 to 1993, are housed in the West Virginia and Regional History Collection. McNeill is beloved for her depiction of West Virginia's life and lore in *Paradox Hill,* the historical *Gauley Mountain* and *Elderberry Flood,* and the autobiographical *Milkweed Ladies. Website:* www.libraries.wvu.edu/wvcollection/.

Sequoyah's Cabin, Sallisaw, Oklahoma. This historic log cabin was the home of Sequoyah, the Cherokee genius who developed the syllabary that brought literacy to his people. The cabin was built by Sequoyah's own hands. *Website:* www. okhistory.org/outreach/homes/sequoyahcabin.html.

B. S. Ricks Memorial Library, Yazoo City, Mississippi. This library was dedicated a Literary Landmark in recognition of Willie Morris (1934–1999), journalist, editor, author, and Mississippian. *Website:* www.yazoo.lib.ms.us/B_S_Ricks_Memorial_Library/Home.html.

Collier Library, Special Collections, University of North Alabama, Florence, Alabama. T. S. Stribling (1881–1965), was a graduate of State Normal College at Florence (1903) and Pulitzer Prize winner (1933) for *The Store.* Stribling's writings, research materials, and memorabilia are located in the archives and special collections department. *Website:* www.una.edu/library/collections/t.s.-stribling. html.

2007

Kate Chopin House, St. Louis. Novelist and short story writer Kate Chopin (1850–1904) lived in this house at 4232 McPherson Avenue in the autumn of 1903. It was in this house that she wrote her last poem, "To the Friend of My Youth: To Kitty," and her last story, "The Impossible Miss Meadows." It was also in this house that she died of a cerebral hemorrhage on August 22, 1904. The house is the only existing St. Louis building associated with her life and work. *Website:* www.katechopin.org/biography.shtml.

Frederick Douglass National Historic Site (right), Washington, D.C. This site preserves the last residence of Frederick Douglass (1818–1895), one of the most prominent African-American leaders of the 19th century. A fiery orator, dedicated editor, bestselling author, and presidential advisor, Douglass crusaded for human rights as an abolitionist, a strong advocate for women's suffrage, and a 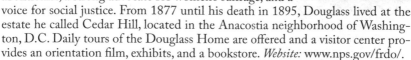 voice for social justice. From 1877 until his death in 1895, Douglass lived at the estate he called Cedar Hill, located in the Anacostia neighborhood of Washington, D.C. Daily tours of the Douglass Home are offered and a visitor center provides an orientation film, exhibits, and a bookstore. *Website:* www.nps.gov/frdo/.

Will Rogers Memorial Museum, Claremore, Oklahoma. Will Rogers wrote to entertain, to enlighten, and to educate. His words were stilled far too soon. The site on which the museum now resides was purchased by Will and Betty Rogers to build their Oklahoma home. It is on a bluff overlooking the city. The museum was built as a gift of the people of Oklahoma in memory of their native son. *Website:* www.willrogers.com/memorial/memorial/about.html.

2008

Idlewild (Mich.) Public Library. Idlewild is the Black Eden of 20th-century African-American history. It was the vacation destination for such writers as Charles Chesnutt, Zora Neale Hurston, Langston Hughes, and W. E. B. Du Bois. At Idlewild, writers and entertainers created a separate place for African-American culture and thought to blossom in one of the few locations where African-Americans were welcome to vacation and relax. *Website:* www.michigan.gov/documents/hal/lm_Idlewild_Brochure_245831_7.pdf.

American Philosophical Society Library, Philadelphia. Home of the Col. Richard Gimbel Collection of Thomas Paine papers. An important 18th-century radical republican theorist and political writer, Paine was a leading figure in the American Revolution. Despite his humble beginnings and lack of formal education, his reasoned and persuasive writings not only influenced nascent American republican ideology, but profoundly affected the perception of government in England and France as well. His three most influential works are *Common Sense* (1776), *The Rights of Man* (1791–1792), and *The Age of Reason* (1794, 1795, 1807). *Website:* www.amphilsoc.org/library/manuscri.

Mother Colony House, Anaheim, California. The Mother Colony House is the oldest frame building in Anaheim. It was here in 1876 that Helena Modjeska resided with Henryk Sienkiewicz (left), one of the most popular Polish authors, who was awarded the Nobel Prize in Literature in 1905 for his "outstanding merits as an epic writer." He is best known as the author of *Quo Vadis.* While in Anaheim he wrote *Listy z podróży* (*Letters from a Journey*) and was inspired to write two short stories, both set in Anaheim. *Website:* library.anaheim.net/Library/Default3.aspx?Folder=Title&Folder2=Mother Colony House &articleID=131.

2009

Lorenzo de Zavala State Archives and Library Building, Austin, Texas. Noted Texas authors, including James Michener, Walter Prescott Webb, and cartoonist Jack "Jaxon" Jackson used the state archives for research and inspiration. Laura Bush, then Texas First Lady, spoke at the building's dedication as a Literary Landmark. *Website:* www.tsl.state.tx.us.

Osage Tribal Museum, Pawhuska, Oklahoma. John Joseph Mathews worked to preserve the culture and history of the Osage Nation through his writing. He authored four nonfiction books and one fiction book in his lifetime, including *Wah'kon-tah: The Osage and the White Man's Road* (1932), which was the first university press book selected by the Book-of-the-Month Club, and sold 50,000 copies. *Website:* www.osagetribe.com/museum/.

Jones Library, Amherst, Massachusetts. The Jones Library originally dedicated its Frost Room in 1959, with poet Robert Frost and Charles Green, founding director of the Jones Library, in attendance. Green started what is now one of the richest Frost collections in the world. Fifty years later, the library was dedicated a Literary Landmark in honor of Frost. *Website:* www.joneslibrary.org/specialcollections/.

Eudora Welty Library, Jackson, Mississippi. The Eudora Welty Library, the main library of the Jackson-Hinds Library System, was recognized as part of the Eudora Welty Centennial Celebration. Eudora Welty had a major role in Mississippi's library heritage, supported public libraries, and was a lifelong resident of Jackson. *Website:* www.jhlibrary.com/mainlib/ew_main.htm.

Wethersfield, Connecticut, was the setting for Elizabeth George Speare's Newbery Award–winning book *The Witch of Blackbird Pond.* The novel tells the story of Kit Tyler, who is forced to leave her Caribbean home for the Connecticut colony in 1687 and is accused of being a witch. Speare lived in Wethersfield when she wrote the novel in 1958. *Website:* www.wethersfieldlibrary.org.

2010

Marguerite deAngeli Branch of the Lapeer District Library, Lapeer, Michigan. Marguerite deAngeli, an author and illustrator of children's books, was a Lapeer native. In 1950, she was awarded the Newbery Medal for *The Door in the Wall.* The Lapeer City Library, which has an extensive collection of her materials, was renamed in her honor on August 22, 1981. *Website:* www2.library.lapeer.org/locations-hours/marguerite-deangeli-branch.html.

Boyhood Home of Stanley Kunitz, Worcester, Massachusetts. Pulitzer Prize–winning poet and U.S. Poet Laureate Stanley Kunitz (1905–2006) lived at this house at 4 Woodford Street from 1919 to 1925. Gregory and Carol Stockmal, who purchased the house in 1979, maintained a 20-year relationship with Kunitz, who dedicated his poem "My Mother's Pears" to the Stockmals. *Website:* wcpa.homestead.com/footsteps2009.html.

Betsy's House and **Tacy's House**, Mankato, Minnesota. The childhood home of Maud Hart Lovelace was dedicated a Literary Landmark along with the childhood home of her best friend, Frances "Bick" Kenney. Lovelace's series of Betsy-Tacy books was based on her and Bick's adventures growing up in Mankato. *Website:* www.betsy-tacysociety.org/houses.

Mark Twain Boyhood Home and Museum, Hannibal, Missouri. The site includes six properties on the National Register of Historic Places, including Mark Twain's boyhood home (built in the 1840s and opened to the public in 1912) and two interactive museums. Twain lived in Hannibal from age 4 to 17. The experiences that Samuel Clemens took from Hannibal became part of American culture through his writings as Mark Twain. *Website:* www.marktwainmuseum.org.

Ernest Hemingway Home and Museum, Key West, Florida. Hemingway lived and wrote here from 1931 to 1939. The Literary Landmark dedication was on the occasion of Key West's "One Island, One Book" event, when the citizens of Key West celebrated Hemingway's novel *To Have and Have Not. Website:* www.hemingwayhome.com.

2011

Beauregard-Keyes House, New Orleans. Author Frances Parkinson Keyes made the house at 1113 Chartres Street her winter residence from 1945 until her death in 1970 at the age of 85. Of her 51 books, *The Chess Players* and *Madame Castel's Lodger* are set at the house and tell of its construction and early habitation. It was at the house that she wrote *Dinner at Antoine's*, her best-known work. *Website:* www.bkhouse.org.

Tahlequah (Okla.) Public Library. Woodrow Wilson Rawls (1913–1984) was the author of two children's books, *Where the Red Fern Grows* and *Summer of the Monkeys*. Rawls's early childhood was spent on his mother's Cherokee allotment 13 miles northeast of Tahlequah, along the Illinois River in Cherokee County. Rawls visited the Carnegie Library in Tahlequah when he was young. *Website:* www.tahlequah.lib.ok.us.

Mansfield (Tex.) Public Library. John Howard Griffin lived on a farm in Mansfield during the time he conducted the social experiment chronicled in his book *Black Like Me*. He darkened his skin in the fall of 1959 and lived as a black man for seven weeks while traveling through Louisiana, Mississippi, Georgia, and Alabama. *Black Like Me* has been translated into 14 languages and has sold more than 10 million copies. *Website:* www.mansfield-tx.gov/departments/library/.

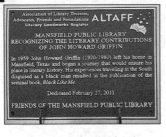

2012

Hackley Public Library, Muskegon, Michigan. Children's book author and storyteller Verna Aardema (1911–2000) used the Hackley Public Library to research folk tales from various cultures, which she rewrote as children's stories. She credited Hackley librarians for their invaluable help with her research. An elementary school teacher for more than 25 years, she was known as Muskegon's "Story Lady." Aardema is the author of *Why Mosquitoes Buzz in People's Ears*, which won the Caldecott Medal in 1976. *Website:* www. hackleylibrary.org.

SOURCE: ALA United for Libraries. The full list is online at ala.org/united/products_services/ literarylandmarks.

16 ways to make more money at your book sale

by the Friends of Indiana Libraries

1. Collect lots of donations. Keep reminding the community that you will accept donations of books, magazines, records, tapes, videos, puzzles, games, whatever.
2. Make it easy for people to donate. Have a collection spot in the library; perhaps at other locations. Offer to pick up donations for people who can't transport their books.
3. Sort. Once the sale is bigger than eight tables, it really will help to sort into categories. For a small sale, categories can be as simple as "Fiction," "Nonfiction," "Children's."
4. Make it look good. Discard musty, ragged, totally unusable items. Box or arrange with like sizes together, titles facing the same way.
5. Make the space appealing. Keep the room clean and tidy, warm in winter, cool in summer. Attractive, readable signs. Enough light. Three-foot (minimum!) aisles.
6. Market the sale; get lots of buyers to come. Newspaper stories, radio PSAs, posters, bookmarks. Highlight any interesting or unusual items.

7. If at all possible, keep it open for more than one day.
8. Raise prices. A sample from around the country indicates that the usual low basic prices are: hardcover books $1, paperbacks 50 cents, magazines 10 cents or 25 cents, records $1. [*Note:* These prices are from 1999.]
9. Price the good stuff higher than the base price. Some examples of "good stuff": coffee-table books, books in excellent condition, cookbooks, art books, collectibles.
10. Try a silent auction of the real treasures.
11. Treat the Friends to a members-only presale. (Accept new memberships at the door, too.)
12. Make the sale a good place to be, a real party, a community event. Balloons, popcorn, clowns, storytellers, live music, smiling cashiers, a cheerful atmosphere.
13. Keep reminding everyone—workers and buyers—that it benefits the library.
14. Celebrate your success. Publicize the results. Thank everybody.
15. Sell, sell, sell. Try half-price for the last day, or a bag sale, or both. Get rid of all the leftovers and start fresh for the next sale.
16. Make it a regularly scheduled event, so donors and buyers look forward to it.

SOURCE: Sandy Dolnick, *The Essential Friends of Libraries: Fast Facts, Forms, and Tips* (Chicago: American Library Association, 2005), CD supplement, Folder 5.

SUPPORT STAFF

Training shelvers
by Patricia Tunstall

YOU NEED TO BE SURE that a new page can shelve accurately, but you don't want to make her uncomfortable by constantly looking over her shoulder as she puts her first cart of books away. It's also true that you have better things to do with your valuable time. The answer to this conundrum is to use training slips. These are brightly colored pieces of paper the size of a bookmark with your library logo and "Training Slip" printed on them. They should also display a message for patrons, letting them know that it is okay to check out a book that has a training slip in it.

Start the process by asking your new employee to put a cart of books in order in the sorting area. Have her tuck a training slip inside each book at the same time, leaving a third of the slip sticking out at the top. It's important to be positive and encouraging from the beginning, so when you introduce the concept of the training slips, avoid putting a negative slant on it. Telling someone who has been in the building for only an hour that using these slips is going to help you find all her mistakes strikes entirely the wrong note. It's far better to say that the training slips will show you at once how well she is doing and will give you both a chance to talk about anything that needs clarification. Once your trainee has the cart ready, check that everything is in order and have her correct any errors before you head out to the stacks. Give some thought to the way you draw attention to these errors. Remember that your aim should be to boost confidence, so I recommend that you *never* use any variations of the following:

"I can see three mistakes on this cart already."

"You're not being very careful, are you?"

"You did much better than this on your test."

Remarks like these make people feel as if you regard them as idiots—certainly no way to begin a working relationship. It's much better to let your trainee know that she is experiencing a learning curve that is absolutely normal. So you could instead say:

This boy has no understanding of library protocols

From "Librarian" video by Haunted Love.

"Some of these long Dewey numbers can be very confusing."

"This one catches everyone out at first."

"It looks as if you have nearly everything in the right place."

When you get to the stacks, be specific about how you want the job done. This is the time when you can lay the foundations of efficient working habits. It's a good idea to shelve the first few books yourself. As you do so, you can talk about and illustrate the following guidelines:

- Park your cart across the end of the book stack, leaving the aisle clear for patrons.
- Check the books on either side of each one that you shelve in case there is an error in the sequence.
- Reshelve any books that you find out of order.
- Be especially careful at the ends and beginnings of shelves so that the correct sequence of materials is not interrupted or confused.
- Concentrate on accuracy.
- Straighten up the books on the shelf as you go, and pull the books forward to the shelf edge.
- Push bookends into place.
- Shift books to the next, or the previous, shelf if they are overcrowded.
- Pick up and reshelve any books that have been left lying on the floor or piled up at the ends of the shelves.
- Bring any damaged or wrongly labeled items you find back to the sorting area.

Ask your new page to leave the books she shelves sticking out a couple of inches so that you can spot them easily later.

It is a good idea to let your trainee know that patrons are allowed to touch, and even walk away with, the materials that she has just put away. I neglected to do this once and came back to find my new shelver and a member of the public in the middle of a rather tense standoff. Also stress that if a patron asks her a question, she should reply that she is a brand-new employee and direct the patron to staff at the nearest public desk. Finally, tell her that since she did so well on her tests, you are sure she will do a splendid job. And then go away and leave her to her work.

After half an hour or so, check on her progress. It's not unusual to find that she has made half-a-dozen errors. People often don't realize at first just how careful they have to be with Dewey numbers, especially the long ones, or they don't know that a group of fiction books written by the same author should be further alphabetized by title. When you find an error, draw the trainee's attention to the book in question and ask her if she notices anything about it. Often trainees see at once where they went wrong and can then have the satisfaction of putting things right themselves. If they don't understand why a book is in the wrong place, point out where the error lies and then ask them to try again. Be patient and stay calm. If the neophyte shelver is really struggling with an item, just show her where it goes. Be sure to draw attention to the fact that she has managed to shelve most of the cart accurately. In my experience, new employees get past these small hiccups very quickly, and they are not worth dwelling on. You can expect the next cart to still have one or two errors, but the third cart will usually have none. Some people take a little longer to get to the point where they are error-free, so from time to time you may need to use the training slips for up to the first half-dozen carts. And then the training slips can be put away.

Occasionally you may come across an employee who, in spite of all your guidance, does not reach the standard of accuracy you are looking for. I once hired someone who made six to eight errors on each of his first three carts. This was a new experience for me, but I was prepared to go on working with him. The next time he came to work, I used the training slips again, and the error rate remained steady for the next three carts. I took the person to one side and asked him how he thought he was doing. He was under the impression that he was doing splendidly. At this point, I could not see a way forward and had to explain that I could not spare the time to check every book he shelved and would have to let him go. If you find yourself in a similar position, be polite and as kind as you can, but be firm. You can't afford to keep a chronic error-maker on your team. And, yes, this shelver had passed the tests at the interview stage.

I never told my new pages that I expected them to have a cart of books shelved within a certain amount of time. I was always far more concerned with accuracy. If you give your employees the time and space to establish good shelving skills, they usually pick up speed naturally.

Each time that you introduce a trainee to a new duty, make sure that you explain and demonstrate exactly what is required. If you get into a habit of doing this, it should help your new staff acquire competence at an encouraging pace. Of course there will be times when you think you have shown someone all she needs to know about a task, only to come back later and find her going about it entirely the wrong way. When that happens, try to avoid any displays of annoyance. If you embarrass or humiliate a trainee, she is much less likely to be receptive to any further instructions that you give her. It's best to accept right away that her lack of understanding could be your fault. A useful phrase in circumstances like this is, "It looks as if I didn't explain this very clearly. What I would like you to do is. . . ." I always found that this approach worked very well and that my staff respected me for being prepared to admit that I could be at fault.

It's important to remember that the areas where materials are checked in and sorted can look completely chaotic to a newcomer. Do not expect new pages to immediately know the difference between carts that contain checked-in items, which can be taken away

and shelved, and carts that contain unchecked items. If you do not have a system in place where each cart is clearly marked with brightly colored labels, I strongly suggest that you set one up.

You need your employees to turn up on time, get busy, and stay busy in order to cope with the constant flow of returned materials. It's best to be clear about your expectations from the beginning. If breaks are meant to be 15 minutes long, you need to make that plain on the first day and follow up with instant reminders if you notice anyone taking longer. And of course you will get far more cooperation in this matter if you are back from your own breaks on time. It also does no harm to point out from the first day that breaks should be taken in the middle of a shift and may not be saved until the end in order to leave work early.

Shelvers are always going to spend a high proportion of their time working alone in the stacks, and it is worth making it clear from the start that the library expects them to avoid the following distractions:

- Friends and family members who are visiting the library should certainly be greeted, but long conversations must be politely discouraged or postponed until break time or the end of a shift.
- Shelvers should be encouraged to acknowledge patrons in a friendly manner and give them appropriate assistance but should avoid being drawn into long social chats.
- In the course of their work, shelvers inevitably come across all manner of interesting and absorbing books. They must understand that they cannot take time out to browse or read them. They can check them out and take them home instead.
- If another shelver is working a couple of stacks over, shelvers may find it tempting to stop what they are doing and socialize. This not only wastes time but gives the appearance of wasting time to any nearby patrons.

When you are making points like these, it's helpful to avoid phrases that begin with "Don't." People are generally more receptive to instructions that are given in a positive way. Even if you are giving what amounts to a command, you can bookend it with remarks that will make it sound more like a suggestion—for example:

- "You'll probably come across a lot of books that interest you when you shelve, and there just isn't time to stop and read them, but please feel free to check out whatever you'd like to enjoy later."
- "We all enjoy seeing our friends when they come here, but of course we have to remind them they'll have to wait until we have finished working if they want to talk to us for any length of time."

Occasionally I have had new shelvers ask me if they could listen to music while they work. My answer was always no, for the following reasons.

- If your ears are blocked by headphones, you may not hear a patron who is trying to ask for assistance.
- Patrons may not feel they can approach you at all if they see the headphones.
- If you are in a quiet area by yourself, you should be aware of who else is around for safety reasons.
- You should be giving your work your full attention.

I did not allow the use of cellphones during work periods. People were free to make all the calls they liked during their breaks, as long as they did not disturb other staff members.

Any time that you are about to tell people what to do, try to imagine how you would like to be given the same instructions yourself. If you treat your employees with courtesy and are patient and good-humored, they will be more inclined to give you their full attention and their best efforts.

All shelvers spend a lot of time pushing heavy carts around a building that is populated by other staff members and by patrons. Always assume that the following advice to trainees is necessary:

- Never run with a cart under any circumstances.
- Always check the area around you carefully before moving off. Small children can be hard to see if they are directly in front of your cart.
- Never let children ride on your cart.
- Never attempt to ride on a cart yourself.
- Move slowly across the ends of the aisles. Patrons can emerge from them very suddenly.
- Never try to squeeze you and your cart onto an elevator if it is already full of patrons.
- Let patrons with wheelchairs or strollers go ahead of you and, if necessary, instead of you.
- Steer your cart around the building as carefully as you can. Make an effort to avoid collisions with walls, library furniture, elevator doors, and so forth.

Some of these instructions are obviously aimed at younger and more high-spirited trainees who might be tempted to take part in a cart race or to sit on an empty cart while riding in an elevator. It can be surprising, though, how careless even some mature adults can be about scraping inanimate objects or crashing into them, so I recommend that you give all new employees some book cart "driver's ed."

SOURCE: Patricia Tunstall, *Hiring, Training, and Supervising Library Shelvers* (Chicago: American Library Association, 2010), 16–21.

Rights and duties of library volunteers

by Preston Driggers and Eileen Dumas

WHAT KEEPS VOLUNTEERS coming back? What makes the volunteer experience a positive one for the library as well as the individual? The answers are partly found in the planning process. It is important to take into account the rights, responsibilities, and duties of the volunteer as a contributing member of the paid and unpaid staff team and the reciprocal expectations on behalf of the library. These go hand in hand.

Basic volunteer rights

The importance of understanding the rights, responsibilities, and duties of a volunteer cannot be overestimated. All community volunteers have a right to expect that their library duties represent work that

- is meaningful (not "make-do work") to the functioning of library operations
- is based on skills, interests, and backgrounds whenever possible
- provides training time adequate for success
- contributes to the library's overall management plan
- can be completed within the agreed volunteer time commitment
- has clearly defined job descriptions, whether short-term, project-specific, or ongoing
- has supervising staff willing to provide clear instructions and performance feedback
- is done in a physically safe work environment free of harassment and hostility
- is recognized as a contribution of the volunteer's personal time and talent to the success of the job or project.

Adding to positive volunteer motivation is an understanding of how assigned tasks fit into the larger context of library operations. Copying, collating, and stapling a six-page information booklet 50 times can seem to be nothing but dull repetition unless the volunteer understands how these booklets are important for an upcoming program and reflect the quality of the library in the community. Explanations do not have to be overly extensive to show how one task affects others, but volunteers want to know how their tasks relate to the larger library mission.

In addition to the above rights, volunteers have the right to a designated workspace. It may be a shared desk or a table in the reference area or just part of a backroom work table. Nothing alienates someone faster than starting a job only to find out on day one that there is no place to work. A volunteer scrambling to find an appropriate work area is not only uncomfortable but also counterproductive.

Finally, volunteers have the right to some limited control and input over their assigned tasks. This input contributes to volunteer buy-in of the project and fos-

ters an atmosphere of participation within the library organization. Drawing upon the above example, there may be half-a-dozen ways to print, collate, and staple booklets together. Let the individual evolve a personalized way to accomplish the end result. Using close supervision to tell the volunteer just what to do every step of the way is one way to drive off many good volunteers. There are library tasks that must be done in sequence and in precise ways, yet even paid staff evolve their own approaches. This happens with volunteers as well, who may find more efficient approaches than the one used by others.

Personal respect. Every community volunteer has the right to be respected as a unique individual who is contributing time and energy to the library. Respect can be shown in many ways, but the easiest is when paid staff acknowledge volunteers by name and treat them as coworkers. Using a name tag with the first name is one way of demonstrating respect for the individual volunteer.

Orientation to the library. Every library volunteer has the right to a general library orientation, a brief explanation of library volunteer policies and procedures

2

and where to find them, and introductions to relevant staff. In large libraries, orientation training may be done on a particular weekly schedule for an hour. In small community libraries, orientation is often accomplished through a walk-around, a single page of user-friendly volunteer guidelines with discussion, and informal introductions to the library staff and other volunteers. The goal of new-volunteer orientation is to help the volunteer transition from being an outsider to an insider. Feeling part of the team is one important element in creating a successful experience.

Training. Every library volunteer has the right to receive adequate training based on the assigned tasks and personal skills and backgrounds. This includes training in safety procedures appropriate to the tasks. Additionally, volunteers have a right to expect ongoing training and educational opportunities when ap-propriate. These opportunities can be used to strengthen a ré-sumé, boost personal knowledge, or serve as encouragement to take on more difficult library assignments. If the cost of training volunteers would be prohibitive, sometimes a staff member with specialized knowledge can be assigned to provide the training. This is often the case for computer-literate volunteers who help customers with computer issues but receive specialized library training from reference or information technology staff.

Grievance procedures and conflict resolution. Every volunteer has a right to be treated fairly and to be able to air grievances during times of conflict. Conflicts can occur with other volunteers or with staff members. It is important to have a grievance procedure in place for volunteers. A volunteer who feels mistreated by the library staff will likely share the negative experiences with others in the com-munity and possibly with those in influential community positions. Depending on circumstances, this angered volunteer can create a negative image in the com-munity for you, the library, and the library director.

Most volunteer conflicts arise from minor misunderstandings that fester into strong feelings. If a particular conflict is faced early and quickly, it can often be resolved or at least mitigated. Your challenge as volunteer services manager is that you might not know about the conflict until it takes on its own life. In your posi-tion, you can set up a grievance and conflict-resolution procedure that follows a traditional chain of command (staff supervisor to library director). You can use an open-door procedure in which you listen to the volunteer and the charges of unfairness. Then you can work toward a solution, subject to the library director's approval. If you follow such a resolution procedure, a volunteer who ultimately leaves is more likely to do so with a feeling that the conflict was heard fairly rather than with intense anger.

Recognition. Volunteers have a right to expect some type of recognition for the work they perform. Recognition can take the form of a simple verbal thank-you from the supervisor, a written thank-you note from the volunteer services manager, or a formal luncheon or evening reception. Even a quick thank-you by email is appreciated. The most important and enduring recognition is respect and consideration for a job well done.

Responsibilities and duties

Once accepted, library volunteers need to honor their responsibilities and duties in order to continue to serve as volunteers. Lists of responsibilities should be part of a volunteer policy manual and provided to volunteers as well as posted on bulletin boards and the library intranet. For many small libraries operating on informal relationships, the list of responsibilities shown below may seem excessive. In some large jurisdictions, however, specific responsibilities are required to be legally stated on the volunteer application form.

Not all of the following responsibilities and duties apply to all volunteer programs or to every type of volunteer. For example, volunteers providing homebound services, those working with children or vulnerable adults, and those in contact with customers outside library premises may be subject to criminal background checks, whereas those working in the public area within the library may not require such checks. As the volunteer services manager, you need to develop your own list of responsibilities, including those based on jurisdictional legal requirements or accepted conventions within your library.

Work commitment responsibilities
- Perform assigned tasks following the job description in a proficient manner.
- Perform duties to the best of one's abilities and be receptive to training.
- Regard volunteering as a serious commitment.
- Show up on time and follow the mutually agreed-upon work schedule.
- Notify supervisor as soon as possible if unable to work as scheduled.

- Carry out assignments in good spirits and accept supervision.
- Maintain an attitude of open-mindedness.
- Follow through on any library work commitments made to others.
- Seek the assistance of the supervisor or another staff person whenever a customer question occurs or a task project is completed.
- Respect the duties of the library staff and contribute to maintaining smooth working relationships.
- Follow the established library rules and policies regarding personal conduct.
- Dress appropriately for the assigned tasks, including any special programs, events, and public meetings.
- Stay informed about information posted on volunteer bulletin boards.
- Read email and pertinent announcements.
- Stay informed about any ongoing changes that may impact the assigned work.
- Commit to the mission, values, goals, and policies of the library.
- Provide the supervisor with adequate notice before leaving and the reason, if possible.

Customer service responsibilities
- Maintain confidentiality of all information and records pertaining to library customers.
- Show respect to library customers by being friendly, courteous, and cooperative, and guide them to staff members when necessary.
- Remember that all volunteers work in a public setting as representatives of the library.

Employment responsibilities
- Agree to criminal background checks on local and national databases.
- Agree to have references checked as listed on the application form.

- Agree to be fingerprinted and tested for substance abuse.
- Grant full permission to be identified by first name in photographs and other recordings for any publicity or promotional purposes including newspapers, television, and radio announcements or on the library website.
- Agree to carry car insurance when using one's own car while performing assigned tasks.
- Acknowledge that there is no salary or other compensation for performing volunteer work.
- Recognize that volunteering does not provide special advantage for any future full-time library position.
- Agree to the library's right to end the volunteer relationship for poor performance.

SOURCE: Preston Driggers and Eileen Dumas, *Managing Library Volunteers*, 2d ed. (Chicago: American Library Association, 2011), 25–30.

Mentoring volunteers
by Marta K. Lee

VOLUNTEERS NEED DIRECTION as they complete assigned jobs in the workplace. Mentoring the volunteer is an opportunity to provide interesting jobs, or at least make the work appear to be appealing. This is important in that all tasks need to be completed and are vital for the library's operation. How does mentoring come into play in volunteer work? Nearly every work opportunity with volunteers offers a chance to be a mentor. Yet often volunteers have bestowed on me as much mentoring as I have given them; it is a two-way street. Two-way mentoring benefits both individuals involved. Remember that mentoring does not always mean the same thing in every situation. Mentoring volunteers is different than mentoring or supervising an internship for a library school student. Many volunteers have no official training in the library field, which can mean that they do not understand the big picture of library work. Volunteers often do not desire to handle certain jobs they feel are beneath them. However, any type of mentoring can benefit both the teacher and the student.

Mentoring public library volunteers

Some public libraries use volunteers to assist with special projects, and mentoring is needed to teach the volunteers the necessary tasks. For example, a public library in Denver came up with a unique program involving disabled middle-school students. The librarian "posed the idea of having the teens do some simple volunteer tasks on their weekly visits, to channel their energy into a more focused direction." Jobs that the students assisted with included alphanumeric sorting, tidying up the board books, collating handouts, and shelving materials. All the jobs made the student volunteers feel important, and they did jobs that the staff did not have to complete. Another public library system has volunteers take reading materials to homebound seniors. This program is rapidly expanding, as both the volunteers and the seniors like the one-on-one interactions.

A public library in Indiana utilizes teens as volunteers; this fosters good relations with the public. The Friends of the Library have collected donations to inaugurate a college scholarship program that would reward the students for their hard work. In 2001, four students who worked in the library were granted $500 scholarships for college. Some public libraries have special projects that are operated solely by volunteers. These projects include assisting the children's librarian with the story time for preschoolers; the volunteers are called the Story Time Ladies. This program is so popular that the library had to increase the number of story times per week.

York County (Va.) Public Library utilizes volunteers to assist with many jobs. Some 95% of the volunteers working in this public library system are willing to do various jobs that need to be completed. Even so, as Library Director Kevin Smith notes, "Volunteers are very enthusiastic about working for the library until the first day of work, when they [become] dismayed that [the library staff] do more than sit around and read books all day." This can be a typical reaction of many individuals who have never thought about the day-to-day operations of a library prior to volunteering. These same volunteers are surprised to find that shelving books can be tedious. In addition, some volunteers are amazed to realize that while shelving books, they can encounter some rather unpleasant patrons. Mentoring such individuals requires sharing with them some of the realities of library work and assuring them that many good times come along with the not-so-good times.

Once York County Public Library had a volunteer who liked to clean and polish the books. Often the volunteer would be so involved with cleaning the books that patrons would be "delayed from leaving until all of the books were nice and shiny." While shelving, the volunteer would clean books, so not many books could be reshelved. But library volunteers have implemented many successful programs and services. For example, the summer reading program could not be completed without the teen volunteers. One individual who is trained in repairing books enables the library to save money on binding and repairing of materials.

While working at a public library system near Richmond, Virginia, Smith mentored a high-school–student library volunteer. The student went from volunteer to page to several different paid library positions and has now gone to library school to become a library professional. According to Smith, the experience of providing guidance to someone along his or her career path was very rewarding.

Mentoring school and special library volunteers

The media specialist delivers more than access to library materials; he or she is also teacher, an instructional partner, and an information specialist. The media specialist handles technology along with assisting every student who attends the school. Larger school systems have media specialists for each school but often have to rely on volunteers to help in the library. Schools that cannot afford a media specialist often depend on parents to volunteer in the library.

Special libraries rely on volunteers just as museums rely on docents. Docents give tours that might not occur if the museum had to rely on paid staff. Some docents or volunteers give their time because they enjoy the topic or history of the institution.

At the Mariners' Museum in Newport News, Virginia, many of the volunteers and docents help in researching topics for museum displays. The volunteers utilize the museum's extensive library in their research. The library depends on volunteers to assist the archivist in processing and cataloging materials, researching projects, and answering patron requests. Mentoring in special libraries provides an opportunity to instruct others in administering quality service to the patron while presenting appropriate materials and teaching about a specialized area. Specialized areas might be about maritime history, law, or corporate issues.

Mentoring academic library volunteers

2

Academic libraries also depend on volunteers to complete jobs. Regent University Library in Virginia Beach has depended on volunteers for a number of years. In the fall of 2007, one potential LIS school student approached the library dean about the possibility of shadowing a librarian in order to explore the field as a possible career choice. The student met with me, the mentor, to discuss her interests. She was interested in reference as a career choice; this helped me set up projects for her. Times for her to come to the library were established along with scheduled time for her to meet with staff members. An overview of the library's operation gave her a better understanding of the library as a workplace.

After she spent time in each section of the library and with each librarian, she and I sat down to discuss librarianship as a profession. I even had her talk to the paraprofessionals in circulation, acquisitions, periodicals, and interlibrary loan, as these jobs are usually supervised by a librarian. Librarians need to know how these jobs are completed in order to be a better librarian. Because the student had no library experience, I asked her if she had time to volunteer in any library. She did have time, and she volunteered in the library two half days per week. Any type of experience is better than having no library experience on a résumé when applying for a professional position, and this volunteer work would look impressive on her résumé. Because she was new to library work but wanted to be a librarian, I thought that it would be good for her to gain experience from the bottom up, so she began in circulation, shelving, checking materials in and out, and assisting with other jobs.

After several weeks, we expanded her experience by adding labeling materials in technical services. The volunteer student was shown how to do the job so that she could work independently when she arrived. An important part of mentoring any individual is imparting the confidence to do a job, and do it well. Thus, in both departments, she was trained by supervisors who fully understood the work and could help her understand it—and enjoy it—as well. Both circulation and technical services appreciated the extra help as the student assistant budget had been cut in half.

Mentoring long-term volunteers

Working with a long-term volunteer or a volunteer program offers different challenges. For one thing, each day the volunteer comes to work, time needs to be taken by the supervisor to find out how things are going both with the job and at home (with volunteers, especially, home situations can affect work schedules and performance). As with all mentoring, be prepared for minor interruptions to answer questions or to address problems. Remember, the volunteer is giving up his or her time to aid the library; be sensitive to the volunteer's time, and find ways to show your appreciation.

Working with volunteers means planning ahead so that jobs are ready when the volunteer arrives at work. Plus, a certain amount of supervision by a staff member is necessary to ensure that the job is completed in a satisfactory way and in a specified amount of time. Decisions need to be made by a paid staff member, who will be responsible for the outcome. If supervising a volunteer takes a large amount of time, then it would probably be best to handle the job yourself instead.

Some believe that it is important to maintain a quality program if the library goes ahead with volunteers. Quality programs involve having jobs for the volunteer to handle that are important to the library and not just busywork. However, the library can assign a full- or part-time staff member to manage the volunteer program.

Does the cost outweigh the benefits of volunteers? Certainly, there is a downside to working with volunteers. Some volunteers may not take the position seriously, which can mean dealing with their not showing up when they said that they would. This can be difficult when they are assigned to a service point, like the circulation desk. In addition, staff can be affected by the volunteer's idiosyncrasies (we had one volunteer who liked to clean the books with Goo Gone). Even so, the benefits of working with volunteers outnumber the problems, so do not hesitate to work with a volunteer or start a volunteer program.

My experience with volunteers in an academic setting has meant spending a small amount of time thinking about the jobs that the volunteer can do for the library but receiving a great return. There are more jobs than I can ever conceive of completing, and with a bit of mentoring, volunteers can help. Having such help allows me to concentrate on the bigger picture and services.

SOURCE: Marta K. Lee, *Mentoring in the Library: Building for the Future* (Chicago: American Library Association, 2011), 71–77.

Retired librarians as volunteers

by Renee B. Bush

WHY VOLUNTEER? You are finally going to have more free time, time for which you may have been longing for years, or perhaps secretly dreading. Most retirees will still need to tend to family demands and their home as well as other continuing personal commitments. However, many do find (sometimes to their great surprise) that the transition from decades of heavily scheduled days with many commitments to days with little structure and few constraints can be difficult. For those people, and even for others who move into retirement with ease, there are some good reasons to give serious thought to volunteering. If any of the following pique your curiosity, consider giving this option a closer look:

- exploring new territory, developing new skills, and discovering talents you never knew you had, all while performing a service;
- developing a sense of satisfaction in helping to address the needs of others and the social or environmental problems that have meaning for you;
- forming new connections in your community;
- moderating a sense of loss associated with lack of contact with colleagues and the social opportunities afforded by the workplace;
- finding you can be appreciated and respected by others working in new contexts, thus enhancing your sense of purpose;
- investigating possibilities and building a résumé for a new career.

Volunteerism has been on the rise in the United States and is a research topic of considerable interest to psychologists and sociologists. It is clear that doing things for others can help people feel a greater sense of purpose; retirees may find that a well-chosen volunteer position restores much of what was beneficial to them in their work life. Even the process of exploring possibilities can be surprisingly stimulating, and the notions you had about what volunteer work looks like could significantly change. It is quite possible there are opportunities out there—or ones you could create—that you never imagined.

Begin by taking stock. What activities, familiar as well as unexplored, and volunteer environments seem attractive to you?

- Have you wished for an opportunity to spend more time outdoors, or would something in a quiet office space sound just right?
- Would you prefer interacting with many different people or being more on your own?
- Have you been hoping for more contact with children, animals, or homeless persons?
- Do you long to travel?
- Would you like to experience more theater and musical performances or have more contact with artists and artisans?

What skills and talents do you have or would you like to develop?

- Would you happily transfer to another situation in which you find and organize information, design websites, teach, or write?
- Is there anything you've been wishing you could do better or try for the first time that has nothing at all to do with the work world you are leaving? For example, do you want to learn how to rehabilitate injured wildlife, become more self-sufficient with home repairs, or brush up your foreign-language skills?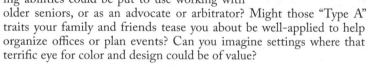
- Do you feel that your patient nature and listening abilities could be put to use working with older seniors, or as an advocate or arbitrator? Might those "Type A" traits your family and friends tease you about be well-applied to help organize offices or plan events? Can you imagine settings where that terrific eye for color and design could be of value?

What is it you know you do not want to do? What activities would physical constraints prevent you from doing?

- Are you certain you no longer want the responsibility of managing people or large budgets? Burned out dealing with the public? Glad you'll never have to make another presentation?
- Is manual labor such as painting, gardening, moving, or unpacking boxes out of the question?

To what extent is location a limiting factor?

- Do you need to stay local? Would you want and be able to travel to volunteer?
- Will a need to rely on public transportation be a factor?
- Would the cost of fuel and parking be a constraint?

How are you able and how do you wish to allocate your free time?

- What are the existing demands on your time and energy?

- Do you believe you can easily and happily make a regular commitment of a few hours or a few days per week? A couple of days per month?
- Do you have health problems or other limiting factors that would make a regular commitment difficult but still wish to contribute when you are able? Could you commit to working on a particular day or a specific number of days agreed upon in advance? How about agreeing to be on a call list and then participating when you can?
- Would you prefer to take on tasks you could do at home?

What might you do and where? You have taken stock and now you want get a sense of where you could find a role that would meet your criteria. If you have a clear idea about the sort of (or which specific) organization and type of work you are intent upon, you may be able to zero in on something great with little effort. But most people do not know what the possibilities are and would like to explore their options. There are three primary areas you will want to keep in focus as you begin your search—although you may well find these changing as you learn more about what is being done and what might be done in service to others:

1. The population or cause served (the elderly, orphaned animals, historic architecture preservation, literacy).
2. The setting in which you see yourself (nursing homes, animal shelters, private foundations, educational centers).
3. The actual work you would like to do (telephoning, animal care, grant writing, tutoring).

Most issues of any newspaper, national or local, large or small, have articles that at least mention not-for-profit organizations and often report on specific projects for volunteers. Magazines of all sorts cover organizations of interest and volunteer efforts from many different angles.

Monitor local media, such as network and cable TV websites and community weeklies, for the area in which you would wish to volunteer. Even if you are not interested in business per se, you will find that many organizations and community projects are mentioned in publications aimed at the business community.

Start networking. Contact people you know who do volunteer work and find out how they found their positions and ask for suggestions or contacts they can provide. Find out why they chose what they are doing and what they find satisfying about it. If you have been participating in online social networks (Facebook, LinkedIn), this is a great way to make use of them.

Check with any organization with which you are or have been affiliated or that has always sounded interesting. National not-for-profits, local community organizations, and religious groups are all logical places to make inquiries about the work they do and whether there might be a place for you. Your alumni association or the human resources department of your former employer may also provide opportunities for volunteers.

Watch for calls for volunteers for specific local events. Fundraisers such as races or walks or wrapping holiday gifts in stores are the most common, but there are many other projects that require only a short-term commitment. These can be a great way to test out your notions about what you would enjoy and what you should avoid. It can also afford a closer look at that particular organization.

You should also be aware that there may be instances in which volunteering for the organization that interests you is not possible. Some of the places you think are suitable may have collective bargaining agreements with unions. This can include not-for-profit organizations such as state universities, federal parks, or nature preserves. In these cases, there may be very strict regulations about what volunteers may or may not do. Often, Friends groups exist within organizations to help raise money and coordinate volunteers in support of some facets of their mission.

Traveling to volunteer. If making your contribution away from home, perhaps very far from home, sounds appealing, you will be delighted to find that opportunities abound:

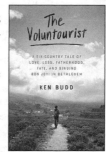

- If you are already interested in some national or international organizations, check out their websites first.
- Many opportunities will require expenditures on your part; depending on the organization and the location, it may be a considerable amount.
- Be sure you determine in advance whether difficult or dangerous conditions and sensitive cultural situations might be encountered.
- Pertinent search terms to use include volunteer travel, volunteer vacations, volunteer abroad, voluntourism, long-distance volunteering, working vacations, eco-voluntourism, agritourism, and edu-voluntourism.

Working from home. Opportunities for virtual volunteering (performing volunteer service using the internet) are increasing, and not all require advanced technical skills. Should your software expertise extend beyond the usual Microsoft Office suite, however, you may find some exciting opportunities in service organizations to apply those skills. If you value Wikipedia, consider supporting it by applying your librarian's expertise there.

If spending more time at a computer is not what you are looking for, but you are unable to commit to projects away from home, take heart. Organizations still need people to perform tasks that need not be done somewhere else, such as telephoning shut-ins, knitting for preemie hospital units, mailing letters to armed forces personnel abroad, or being a pen pal to a person learning English in another country.

Creating your own service projects. Perhaps you would like to create your own projects rather than become part of an existing organization. There are countless exciting possibilities, but it is important to know where the service you wish to provide will fit into the larger scheme of things and how best to maximize the benefits you generate without having a negative impact on the efforts of others. The best place to begin is the Corporation for National and Community Service's Resource Center (www.nationalserviceresources.org/via), which provides a wealth of information on volunteer self-organizing to get you moving in the right direction.

Time banking. Strictly speaking, this is not volunteer work in that the rewards gained by your efforts are somewhat more tangible. You spend an hour doing something for someone in your community, and you earn a Time Dollar that you use to pay someone to do something for you. It is, actually, an alternative economic system that ultimately builds stronger communities. Time Banks, aka Service Exchanges or Time Trades, provide incentives for work that is often done by volunteers.

Not retired yet? All the better. Take stock before you retire so that you have a better idea of what you believe would best suit you. Many people find the transition from full-time employment to retirement much easier to navigate if there are some regular activities that lend structure to their days and prevent them from feeling the loss of contact with colleagues or others. If you know ahead of time that volunteer work would be a good fit, you can take advantage of opportunities to prepare for a volunteer position you could really love. Here are a few ways to do just that:

- Enroll in continuing education courses available to you at your place of employment or in your community (some are helpful at work as well as useful after you leave), such as time management, supervisory skills, or software applications.
- Employers often partner with local charities and provide time off for employees' participation, so keep an eye on what they have lined up and talk with coworkers who have some experience with the program.
- If your employer has not formed such relationships in the community, consider being the one to introduce the idea or even volunteer to organize a suitable partnership or sponsorship.
- Consider volunteering for single events or projects that do not require a long-term commitment. Such experiences can help you sort out your preferences and identify constraints.

One last word: burnout. Volunteer burnout is not uncommon. It is better for everyone involved if you make your commitment knowing this is a possibility and make a conscious effort to avoid it, rather than leaving later, exhausted and unhappy. Decide how much time you can devote to the position and communicate that clearly. If you are unsure, it's better to underestimate and perhaps add  more time later than to have to scale back or quit. If you have a tendency to take on more than you can comfortably handle or find it difficult to refuse requests for your time, you will need to be vigilant about how your position is affecting you and your family, and communicate any problems as soon as they become evident. Personality traits may not be the only factors in burnout situations, however. Poor management, unrealistic expectations, or lack of support on the part of the organization can contribute as well. You could possibly address these situations to everyone's satisfaction, but you must do so as soon as you realize there is a problem.

If you have decided to organize your own service project, you may also be in danger of ending up overwhelmed and unsatisfied with your efforts. If you have never done a project similar to what you intend to take on, try to find others who have; you may discover that some aspects require more time and effort than you had thought. Pace yourself, delegate when you can, and be flexible about parameters or deadlines you have set that can be changed without creating problems for you or for others.

Start with something you feel sure you can do. Enjoy the sense of accomplishment and happiness that comes from making a contribution, and look forward to more interesting opportunities to generate those feelings again.

SOURCE: Renee B. Bush, "Volunteering in Retirement," in Carol Smallwood, ed., *Pre-and Post-Retirement Tips for Librarians* (Chicago: American Library Association, 2012), 143–153.

THE PROFESSION

CHAPTER THREE

They don't teach witchcraft in library school. Vermin—check. Mold and mildew—check. Difficult patrons—check. But there was no course in witchcraft, no syllabus for sorcery. If only I'd been properly prepared for my first real job.

—Mindy Klasky, *Girl's Guide to Witchcraft*
(Don Mills, Ont.: Red Dress Ink, 2006)

EVENTS

Calendar to 2019

2013

January

22–25	Assoc. for Library & Info. Sci. Education	Seattle, Wash.
25–29	American Library Assoc. (Midwinter)	Seattle, Wash.
30–Feb. 2	Ontario Library Assoc.	Toronto, Ont.

February

| 6 | Digital Learning Day | |
| 27–Mar. 2 | Music Library Assoc. | San Jose, Calif. |

March

| 10–16 | Teen Tech Week | |

April

10–13	Assoc. of College & Research Libraries	Indianapolis, Ind.
12	National Drop Everything and Read Day	
14–20	National Library Week	
21–27	Preservation Week	
24–26	Washington Library Assoc.	Vancouver, Wash.
24–27	Texas Library Assoc.	Fort Worth, Tex.
25–28	Alberta Library Conference	Jasper, Alta.
25–29	Art Libraries Society/N.A.	Pasadena, Calif.
30	Children's Day/Book Day	

May

3–8	Medical Library Assoc.	Boston, Mass.
7–8	National Library Legislative Day	
29–June 1	Canadian Library Assoc.	Winnipeg, Man.

June

9–11	Special Libraries Assoc.	San Diego, Calif.
19–22	American Theological Library Assoc.	Charlotte, N.C.
27–July 2	American Library Assoc. (Annual)	Chicago, Ill.

July

| 13–16 | American Assoc. of Law Libraries | Seattle, Wash. |

August

| 11–17 | Society of American Archivists | New Orleans, La. |
| 17–23 | IFLA World Library Congress | Singapore |

September

25–27	South Dakota Library Assoc.	Sioux Falls, S. Dak.
25–28	New York Library Assoc.	Niagara Falls, N.Y.
29–Oct. 5	Banned Books Week	

October

13–19	Teen Read Week	
20–22	New England Library Assoc.	Portland, Maine
20–23	Pennsylvania Library Assoc.	Seven Springs, Pa.
22–25	Wisconsin Library Assoc.	Green Bay, Wis.

November

6–9	Charleston Conference	Charleston, S.C.
14–17	American Assoc. of School Librarians	Hartford, Conn.

2014

January

21–24	Assoc. for Library & Info. Sci. Education	Philadelphia, Pa.
24–28	American Library Assoc. (Midwinter)	Philadelphia, Pa.

February

26–Mar. 2	Music Library Assoc.	Atlanta, Ga.

March

11–15	Public Library Assoc.	Indianapolis, Ind.

April

8–11	Texas Library Assoc.	San Antonio, Tex.
13–19	National Library Week	
30	Children's Day/Book Day	

May

16–21	Medical Library Assoc.	Chicago, Ill.
28–31	Canadian Library Assoc.	Victoria, B.C.

June

8–10	Special Libraries Assoc.	Vancouver, B.C.
18–21	American Theological Library Assoc.	New Orleans, La.
26–July 1	American Library Assoc. (Annual)	Las Vegas, Nev.

July

12–15	American Assoc. of Law Libraries	San Antonio, Tex.

August

10–16	Society of American Archivists	Washington, D.C.

September

27–Oct. 4	Banned Books Week	
28–Oct. 1	Pennsylvania Library Assoc.	Lancaster, Pa.

3

October

1–3	South Dakota Library Assoc.	Pierre, S. Dak.
12–18	Teen Read Week	
19–21	New England Library Association	Boxborough, Mass.

November

4–7	Wisconsin Library Assoc.	Wisconsin Dells
5–8	Charleston Conference	Charleston, S.C.

2015

January

27–30	Assoc. for Library & Info. Sci. Education	Chicago, Ill.
29–Feb. 3	American Library Assoc. (Midwinter)	Chicago, Ill.

April

14–17	Texas Library Assoc.	Austin, Tex.
25–28	Assoc. of College & Research Libraries	Portland, Oreg.

May

15–20	Medical Library Assoc.	Austin, Tex.

June

3–6	Canadian Library Assoc.	Ottawa, Ont.
14–16	Special Libraries Assoc.	Boston, Mass.
17–20	American Theological Library Assoc.	Denver, Colo.
25–30	American Library Assoc. (Annual)	San Francisco

July

18–21	American Assoc. of Law Libraries	Philadelphia, Pa.

September

27–Oct. 3	Banned Books Week	

November

4–7	Charleston Conference	Charleston, S.C.

2016

January

22–26	American Library Assoc. (Midwinter)	Boston, Mass.

April

5–9	Public Library Assoc.	Denver, Colo.
19–22	Texas Library Assoc.	Houston, Tex.

June

1–4	Canadian Library Assoc.	Halifax, N.S.
23–28	American Library Assoc. (Annual)	Orlando, Fla.

July

| 16–19 | American Assoc. of Law Libraries | Chicago, Ill. |

September

| 25–Oct. 1 | Banned Books Week | |

November

| 2–5 | Charleston Conference | Charleston, S.C. |

2017

January

| 20–24 | American Library Assoc. (Midwinter) | Atlanta, Ga. |

March

| 29–Apr. 1 | Assoc. of College & Research Libraries | Nashville, Tenn. |

April

| 25–28 | Texas Library Assoc. | San Antonio, Tex. |

June

| 22–27 | American Library Assoc. (Annual) | Chicago, Ill. |

July

| 15–18 | American Assoc. of Law Libraries | Austin, Tex. |

November

| 8–11 | Charleston Conference | Charleston, S.C. |

2018

February

| 9–13 | American Library Assoc. (Midwinter) | Denver, Colo. |

March

| 20–24 | Public Library Assoc. | Philadelphia, Pa. |

April

| 10–13 | Texas Library Assoc. | Dallas, Tex. |

June

| 21–26 | American Library Assoc. (Annual) | New Orleans, La. |

2019

January

| 25–29 | American Library Assoc. (Midwinter) | Seattle, Wash. |

June

| 20–25 | American Library Assoc. (Annual) | Washington, D.C. |

3

Past ALA Annual Conferences

A LIST OF ALL ALA Annual Conference dates and locations, with attendance figures, contrasted with total ALA membership (from 1900 on).

Date	Place	Attendance	Membership
1876, Oct. 4–6	Philadelphia	103	[N/A
1877, Sept. 4–6	New York	66	for
1877, Oct. 2–5	London, England	21*	1876–
1878	[No meeting]		1899]
1879, June 30–July 2	Boston	162	
1880	[No meeting]		
1881, Feb. 9–12	Washington, D.C.	70	
1882, May 24–27	Cincinnati	47	
1883, Aug. 14–17	Buffalo, N.Y.	72	
1884	[No meeting]		
1885, Sept, 8–11	Lake George, N.Y.	87	
1886, July 7–10	Milwaukee, Wis.	133	
1887, Aug. 30–Sept. 2	Thousand Islands, N.Y.	186	
1888, Sept. 25–28	Catskill Mountains, N.Y.	32	
1889, May 8–11	St. Louis, Mo.	106	
1890, Sept. 9–13	Fabyans (White Mts.), N.H.	242	
1891, Oct. 12–16	San Francisco	83	
1892, May 16–21	Lakewood, N.Y., Baltimore, Washington	260	
1893, July 13–22	Chicago	311	
1894, Sept. 17–22	Lake Placid, N.Y.	205	
1895, Aug. 13–21	Denver & Colorado Springs	147	
1896, Sept. 1–8	Cleveland	363	
1897, June 21–25	Philadelphia	315	
1897, July 13–16	London, England	94*	
1898, July 5–9	Lakewood, N.Y.	494	
1899, May 9–13	Atlanta	215	
1900, June 6–12	Montreal, Québec	452	874
1901, July 3–10	Waukesha, Wis.	460	980
1902, June 14–20	Boston & Magnolia, Mass.	1,018	1,152
1903, June 22–27	Niagara Falls, N.Y.	684	1,200
1904, Oct. 17–22	St. Louis, Mo.	577	1,228
1905, July 4–8	Portland, Me.	359	1,253
1906, June 29–July 6	Narragansett Pier, R.I.	891	1,844
1907, May 23–29	Asheville, N.C.	478	1,808
1908, June 22–27	Lake Minnetonka, Minn.	658	1,907
1909, June 28–July 3	Bretton Woods, N.H.	620	1,835
1910, June 30–July 6	Mackinac Island, Mich.	533	2,005
1910, Aug. 28–31	Brussels, Belgium	46*	
1911, May 18–24	Pasadena, Calif.	582	2,046
1912, June 26–July 2	Ottawa, Ontario	704	2,365
1913, June 23–28	Kaaterskill, N.Y.	892	2,563
1914, May 25–29	Washington, D.C.	1,366	2,905
1915, June 3–9	Berkeley, Calif.	779	3,024

* U.S. attendance

Date	Place	Attendance	Membership
1916, June 26–July 1	Asbury Park, N.J.	1,386	3,188
1917, June 21–27	Louisville, Ky.	824	3,346
1918, July 1–6	Saratoga Springs, N.Y.	620	3,380
1919, June 23–27	Asbury Park, N.J.	1,168	4,178
1920, June 2–7	Colorado Springs	553	4,464
1921, June 20–25	Swampscott, Mass.	1,899	5,307
1922, June 26–July 1	Detroit	1,839	5,684
1923, April 23–28	Hot Springs, Ark.	693	5,669
1924, June 30–July 5	Saratoga Springs, N.Y.	1,188	6,055
1925, July 6–11	Seattle, Wash.	1,066	6,745
1926, Oct. 4–9	Atlantic City, N.J.	2,224	8,848
1927, June 20–27	Toronto, Ontario	1,964	10,056
1927, Sept. 26–Oct. 1	Edinburgh, Scotland	82 *	
1928, May 28–June 2	West Baden, Ind.	1,204	10,526
1929, May 13–18	Washington, D.C.	2,743	11,833
1929, June 15–30	Rome and Venice, Italy	70 *	
1930, June 23–28	Los Angeles	2,023	12,713
1931, June 22–27	New Haven, Conn.	3,241	14,815
1932, April 25–30	New Orleans	1,306	13,021
1933, Oct. 16–21	Chicago	2,986	11,880
1934, June 25–30	Montreal, Québec	1,904	11,731
1935, May 20–30	Madrid, Seville, & Barcelona, Spain	42 *	
1935, June 24–29	Denver	1,503	12,241
1936, May 11–16	Richmond, Va.	2,834	13,057
1937, June 21–26	New York	5,312	14,204
1938, June 13–18	Kansas City, Mo.	1,900	14,626
1939, June 18–24	San Francisco	2,869	15,568
1940, May 26–June 1	Cincinnati	3,056	15,808
1941, June 19–25	Boston	4,266	16,015
1942, June 22–27	Milwaukee, Wis.	2,342	15,328
1943	[No meeting]		14,546
1944	[No meeting]		14,799
1945	[No meeting]		15,118
1946, June 16–22	Buffalo, N.Y.	2,327	15,800
1947, June 29–July 5	San Francisco	2,534	17,107
1948, June 13–19	Atlantic City, N.J.	3,752	18,283
1949:	Regional conferences	[N/A]	19,324
Aug. 22–25	(Far West) Vancouver, B.C.		
Sept. 2–5	(Trans-Miss.) Fort Collins, Colo.		
Oct. 3–6	(Middle Atlantic) Atlantic City, N.J.		
Oct. 12–15	(New England) Swampscott, Mass.		
Oct. 26–29	(Southeastern) Miami Beach, Fla.		
Nov. 9–12	(Midwest) Grand Rapids, Mich.		
Nov. 20–23	(Southwestern) Fort Worth, Tex.		
1950, July 16–22	Cleveland	3,436	19,689
1951, July 8–14	Chicago	3,612	19,701
1952, June 29–July 5	New York	5,212	18,925

* US attendance

Date	Place	Attendance	Membership
1953, June 21–27	Los Angeles	3,258	19,551
1954, June 20–26	Minneapolis	3,230	20,177
1955, July 3–9	Philadelphia	4,412	20,293
1956, June 17–23	Miami Beach, Fla.	2,866	20,285
1957, June 23–30	Kansas City, Mo.	2,953	20,326
1958, July 13–19	San Francisco	4,400	21,716
1959, June 21–27	Washington, D.C.	5,346	23,230
1960, June 19–24	Montreal, Québec	4,648	24,690
1961, July 9–15	Cleveland	4,757	25,860
1962, June 17–23	Miami Beach, Fla.	3,527	24,879
1963, July 14–20	Chicago	5,753	25,502
1964, June 28–July 4	St. Louis	4,623	26,015
1965, July 3–10	Detroit	5,818	27,526
1966, July 10–16	New York	9,342	31,885
1967, June 25–July I	San Francisco	8,116	35,289
1968, June 23–29	Kansas City, Mo.	6,849	35,666
1969, June 22–28	Atlantic City, N.J.	10,399	36,865
1970, June 28–July 4	Detroit	8,965	30,394
1971, June 20–26	Dallas	8,087	29,740
1972, June 24–30	Chicago	9,700	29,610
1973, June 24–30	Las Vegas	8,539	30,172
1974, July 5–13	New York	14,382	34,010
1975, June 29–July 5	San Francisco	11,606	33,208
1976, July 18–24	Chicago (Centennial)	12,015	33,560
1977, June 17–23	Detroit	9,667	33,767
1978, June 25–30	Chicago	11,768	35,096
1979, June 24–30	Dallas	10,650	35,524
1980, June 29–July 4	New York	14,566	35,257
1981, June 26–July 2	San Francisco	12,555	37,954
1982, July 10–15	Philadelphia	12,819	38,050
1983, June 25–30	Los Angeles	11,005	38,862
1984, June 23–28	Dallas	11,443	39,290
1985, July 6–11	Chicago	14,160	40,761
1986, June 26–July 3	New York	16,530	42,361
1987, June 27–July 2	San Francisco	17,844	45,145
1988, July 9–14	New Orleans	16,530	47,249
1989, June 24–29	Dallas	17,592	49,483
1990, June 23–28	Chicago	19,982	50,509
1991, June 29–July 4	Atlanta	17,764	52,893
1992, June 25–July 2	San Francisco	19,261	54,735
1993, June 24–July 1	New Orleans	17,165	55,836
1994, June 23–30	Miami Beach	12,627	55,356
1995, June 24–28	Chicago	19,146	56,444
1996, July 4–10	New York	18,027	56,688
1997, June 26–July 3	San Francisco	19,339	55,643
1998, June 25–July 1	Washington	24,844	55,573
1999, June 24–30	New Orleans	22,598	58,777
2000, July 6–12	Chicago	24,913	61,103
2001, June 14–20	San Francisco	26,820	63,424
2002, June 13–19	Atlanta	21,130	64,211

Date	Place	Attendance	Membership
2003, June 19–25	Toronto	17,570	63,793
2004, June 24–30	Orlando	19,546	64,222
2005, June 23–29	Chicago	27,962	66,127
2006, June 22–28	New Orleans	16,964	64,689
2007, June 21–27	Washington	28,499	64,729
2008, June 26–July 2	Anaheim, Calif.	22,047	64,884
2009, July 9–15	Chicago	22,762	61,379
2010, June 24–29	Washington	26,201	61,198
2011, June 23–28	New Orleans	20,125	60,040
2012, June 21–26	Anaheim, Calif.	20,134	59,471

3

Attending non-library conferences
by Joseph Nicholson

PROFESSIONAL LIBRARY ASSOCIATIONS provide many excellent opportunities for career development, including networking, programs, and committee work. However, focusing one's efforts solely on library associations limits the possibilities for staff development, especially if your library position involves subject mastery outside library science. Associations outside of libraries, but focused on subjects of interest to staff and the institution, offer significant opportunities to build subject expertise, career opportunities, and leadership skills.

Attending a conference outside libraries can be intimidating. Unlike our library association meetings, where most attendees understand the professional language and structures, attending a conference outside libraries requires adjusting to new issues, terms, jargon, and even social groupings. As with any conference, taking the time to prepare ahead of the event can help to maximize the benefit for both the institution and the new employee.

Navigating a new conference

Having successfully written my application and been awarded one of the stipends, I prepared to attend my first American Public Health Association annual meeting. Attending the conference on this stipend had several benefits. One of the requirements of the stipend was that you shadow someone who had attended the meeting in the past, attending a scientific session with them and learning on a personal basis how they handle the meeting and how attendance benefits them.

A second requirement of the stipend was to attend a meeting with all the other stipend recipients and other librarians who also attend the conference. Having a meeting with other librarians in the field who are in attendance may not be easy to arrange, but it is incredibly beneficial. These more ex-perienced librarians who have previously attended and participated in the meetings can really help you navigate. In addition, the networking benefits of meeting with a group of professionals with similar interests are numerous. Ultimately, making connections with like-minded individuals in the group can create a comfort zone in what could otherwise be a foreign environment.

Deciding what sessions to go to is one of the most

daunting tasks of going to a new conference, especially one as large as the APHA annual meeting. Part of the aim of having a person to shadow is to have someone help you narrow down what sessions may be of interest to you. Also, part of being able to meet with the other librarians in attendance is to get suggestions regarding what sessions to attend. However, the needs and interests of your user group and your library might not be the same as those of the librarians and professionals with whom you speak.

Participating in the conference. Once you have figured out your way around the conference, your focus should be on finding ways to participate and interact with the other attendees. First, you should attend the business meetings and socials of the sections or groups that are of interest to you. If you are outgoing and introduce yourself to people, saying that you are a new member and a librarian, you will surely get some interest. Public health professionals, for example, are always excited to have information professionals interested in helping them. At every meeting I attended, participants seemed to know that a librarian was in the room and could potentially help them with their information needs.

Second, you should volunteer to work at a booth in the exhibit hall, so you can connect with others at your workplace (if your institution has a booth) or meet other conference members of sections you're interested in and learn more about what they do. Spending an hour or two working a booth will enable you to meet a large cross-section of the conference population.

Benefits of participation

Attendance at a non-library conference offers many potential benefits to your library. Not only do you benefit directly—the library staff, the library patrons, and the library's reputation also will profit from your participation.

How the new employee benefits. The direct benefits to the new employee are probably the easiest ones to notice. Knowledge, prestige, and experience are three things a new employee can gain from participating in a non-library conference. They are certainly interconnected and all serve well in career development, both immediately and in the long run.

Networking with colleagues in and out of the library world increases exposure to new thoughts, ideas, and resources. This exposure increases knowledge of the topic, which is beneficial in the short term for making collection-development decisions, giving presentations, or even answering reference questions. This new knowledge will continue to serve the individual down the road, especially if he or she continues to participate and keep abreast of new developments in the field.

The more sessions you attend, the more people with whom you network, the more papers you present, the more experience you will have under your belt. Experience pays off more in the long term than in the immediate benefits of new knowledge. Naturally, having a lot of good experience is also a great résumé-builder.

The continuous buildup of experience eventually leads to prestige. *Prestige* may seem too strong of a word for having merely participated in a conference, but I believe it is an appropriate word, especially after continuing to participate actively. Prestige, in this sense, is the kind of obvious importance associated with successful people. Stepping up to the plate year after year, being able to contribute to the conference and the field on national and international levels, and being able to bring back lessons and apply them to the library and job are the kinds of experiences that lead to prestige. Following continued participation, people begin to recognize names and faces and seek out these familiar faces for special projects. The individual can become an in-demand librarian among the audience with whom he or she mingled at conference. It can, and does, take much experience to build up this prestige, but it is certainly worthwhile for long-term career development.

How your library benefits. Following the conference the benefits are immediate and continuous. Everyone involved in your library gains from participation as the attendees disseminate their knowledge, experience, and prestige gained from the conference. The clear recipients of these benefits are the library patrons. Active participation in their subject or field allows for better service to them. The library will be more adept at answering complicated reference questions, and it can build a better collection through knowing different resources. Having a better, stronger, and more focused collection is another great service you can provide. It will take some more work on your part, but spreading your information to the library staff is an excellent way to develop staff knowledge and increase their awareness of hot topics that may be of importance to patrons.

SOURCE: Joseph Nicholson, "Non-Library Conferences for Development," in Georgie L. Donovan and Miguel A. Figueroa, eds., *Staff Development Strategies That Work! Stories and Strategies from New Librarians* (New York: Neal-Schuman Publishers, 2009), 201–204. Reprinted with permission.

Meet me in St. Louis

by George M. Eberhart

IMAGINE AN ALA ANNUAL CONFERENCE where for six days you meet in one large room from 9:30 a.m. to only half past noon, after which you are free to go wandering around an exhibit and amusement area 13 times the size of Disney's Magic Kingdom in Florida.

Imagine a conference where, after listening to a "characteristic address" by Melvil Dewey—"full of the enthusiasm of invention and the ardor of prophecy, which never fails to kindle a responsive spark in his audience"—you venture out to ride on the biggest Ferris Wheel in the world, eat a new-fangled treat called an ice cream cone, watch Alexander Graham Bell participate in a kite-flying contest, listen to rousing performances by John Philip Sousa's band, or thrill to reenactments of Spanish-American War naval battles and the Boer War Battle of Colenso.

October 17–22, 1904, was American Library Association Week at the St. Louis World's Fair, formally known as the Louisiana Purchase Exposition in commemoration of Thomas Jefferson's acquisition of most of the Midwest 100 years earlier. Like many other organizations, ALA saw the fair as a wonderful opportunity to hold its annual meeting in a historic venue that offered unlimited educational benefits.

And, why not? ALA itself was founded and first met at the 1876 Centennial Exposition in Philadelphia, then went on to meet in Chicago in 1893 for the World's Columbian Exposition—although the conference arrangements there were a bit chaotic and attendees apparently goofed off more than usual because they couldn't get to the sessions. But St. Louis fair promoters were out to

one-up Chicago in any way they could, and they made it easy for ALA to round up its members for the program. *Library Journal* (the official organ before the *ALA Bulletin* launched in 1907) reported in its November issue, "The great body of the audience came to listen and learn, and nothing could divert even the younger folk from that stern duty and pleasant privilege."

The majority of the ALA attendees stayed at the Inside Inn, the only hotel that was actually inside the fairgrounds. Visitors could stay for as little as $1.50 per day on the European plan, or $3.00 per day on the American plan, which included three meals. Both plans covered admission to the fair, which ordinarily would cost 50 cents daily (the equivalent of $10 today). After a sweltering St. Louis summer, the weather had just started to turn in October, and some librarians complained about the hotel's chilly beds and lack of elevators in a building that covered 10 acres and offered 2,257 rooms. (Little did they know that the Inside Inn, run by the soon-to-be-famous hotel magnate E. M. Statler, had lined each room with asbestos as a fire-protection measure.)

In the morning, conference-goers hopped on the Intramural Railway for 20 minutes to get to their meeting room in the Hall of Congresses, a large building with 40 auditoriums. The room was described as "pleasant and satisfactory, well ventilated, and with good acoustics" and ALA claimed that fair officials said no other convention "had been attended so largely and continuously" as the ALA sessions. The only mix-up occurred when deaf and blind writer and activist Helen Keller was assigned the ALA room by mistake for her speech, and attendees had to push through an overflow crowd to meet in a smaller room down the corridor.

Amazingly, you can still visit the very spot where ALA met and Helen Keller spoke. Washington University was about to move from downtown St. Louis to a site at the edge of the city when fair organizers asked about renting the newly constructed buildings in 1903 and 1904 as headquarters for the exposition. The university agreed and postponed its move until after the fair. One of the new

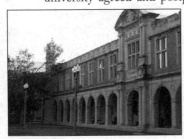

buildings was the Hall of Congresses, which became the university's Ridgley Hall in January 1905 and housed (appropriately) the main library until the 1960s. Ridgley Hall still stands (left) and is the home of the departments of Germanic and Romance languages and literatures. The ALA meeting room was transformed first into Ridgley Library's reading room, then into a lounge area, and now it endures as the renovated Holmes Lounge, a popular place to dine on campus.

Ridgley Hall, photo by Baili Min.

An article titled "Seven Days at the St. Louis Fair: The Lighter Side of the Conference" appeared in *Library Journal* as part of the conference proceedings. Written by "One at Headquarters"—an ironic designation, since ALA at the time was without a central office, with correspondence handled by ALA Secretary James Ingersoll Wyer in Nebraska, the ALA Publishing Board in Boston, and the *LJ* editors in New York—the piece was probably penned by none other than *LJ* Editor and Founder Richard Rogers Bowker.

Bowker waxed eloquent about the fairgrounds, which he visited on Sunday when the fair was closed: "Seen thus, in stillness and comparative solitude, the

Fair was a picture long to be remembered—the Sunken Gardens, bordered by the columned arcades of the great buildings on either side; the magnificent semicircle of the Colonnade of States outlining the noble terraces flanking Festival Hall; the vistas of cascades, lagoons, and beautiful structures, all grouped in harmony—at no other time were the magnitude and beauty of its conception so evident and overpowering."

He also reveals that the magnificent Tyrolean Alps Restaurant (left) became the after-hours "recognized headquarters of the Association," set in an authentic Alpine village (complete with specially constructed fake mountains) where diners could drink beer or lemonade and listen to the melodies of "Kounzak's magnificent orchestra." In fact, Bowker admits to having so much fun there that he forgot he had been entrusted with tickets to an October 19 "moonlight launch trip on the lagoons during a special illumination of buildings and grounds" that made the fair "gleam with a many-colored radiance that made the sky look like black velvet and the moon seem insignificant." He sheepishly turned up late for the event.

Another special perk arranged by the local committee was an evening at Hagenbeck's Animal Circus and Zoological Paradise, which featured continuous animal extravaganzas in a 3,000-seat arena and such special shows as elephants plummeting down a gigantic water slide. "Somebody from Headquarters" (Bowker) arrived to distribute the tickets this time to librarians but was mistaken for a showman and not the "ALA man." He wrote, "This is said to have hurt him cruelly, for he had hoped that he looked the bibliothecal part assigned to him on life's stage."

Among the 577 attendees were 30 delegates from 17 foreign countries. One of the visitors was the droll L. Stanley Jast, librarian of Croydon (England) Public Library, whose memorable jest at the opening session bears repeating. After a welcoming oration by Fair President and former Missouri Governor David R. Francis, Jast responded on behalf of the overseas librarians, saying, "I am inclined to think, sir, that perhaps the two most valuable and satisfactory characteristic products of American civilization are the librarian, on the one hand, and the cocktail on the other. I will not attempt, sir, the delicate question of deciding which is best, but I am given to understand that some of us have sampled both and found them equally satisfactory and equally stimulating."

The roster of US librarians in attendance included a total of 26 former, current, or future ALA presidents who would span nearly a half century of Association history.

I would be remiss if I didn't mention ALA's own exhibit at the St. Louis World's Fair, which actually won an award. The ALA Model Li-

(Left to right) ALA President-Elect Ernest Cushing Richardson, former ALA President Reuben Gold Thwaites, and ALA President Herbert Putnam. Richardson wears one of the white buttons that identifies him as an ALA conference attendee.

brary, installed in the Missouri Building, was run as a branch of the St. Louis Public Library and consisted of a collection of 5,000 volumes selected by ALA as essential, some 1,500 works by Missouri authors, and several thousand books, newspapers, and magazines from St. Louis Public Library. The books could circulate to exposition employees. Melvil Dewey's Library Bureau supplied bookshelves, counters, desks, and tables, and the Library of Congress furnished cards for the catalog. The fair awarded ALA a "grand prize" for the Model Library and gave a gold medal to St Louis Public Library Director Frederick Crunden for his services at the exhibit.

Unfortunately, the Missouri Building was destroyed by a fire that broke out around 6 p.m. on November 19, less than two weeks before the fair closed. *LJ* reported in its January 1905 issue: "The bulk of the furniture and the books were at once removed from the building, and the only damage was to several hundred books which remained in the building and were ruined by water. . . . Mr. Crunden and other members of the Public Library staff reached the grounds shortly after the fire and assisted the salvage corps in protecting the books by tarpaulins."

The Library of Congress also had an exhibit at the United States Government Building, featuring a sectional model of the library, a set of catalog cards showing the evolution from handwritten to printed cards, pages from President James Monroe's journals, and a collection of Civil War music.

After St. Louis, ALA managed to hold its Annual Conference concurrently with a world's fair in five more cities. But the St. Louis World's Fair represented the first blossoming of 20th-century technology that emerged from the Victorian Era. The average American in 1904 rarely traveled 20 miles from home. Few living outside the major cities had any knowledge of the wider world or developing technologies. For many, it was their first chance to see airships, wireless telegraphy, baby incubators, massive displays of electrical lighting, or foreigners of any type. It was a perfect venue for an ALA conference.

SOURCE: George M. Eberhart, "Meet Me in St. Louis," *American Libraries* CentenniAL Blog, June 19, 2007.

10 steps to promote learning in your conference presentation

by Peter Bromberg

A SMALL MEME developed on Twitter recently, prompted by the following tweet by David Wedamen, "Just had a GREAT idea from @brandeislibn. Conferences should be built around TEACHING not PRESENTING. Wouldn't that be something?"

Alice Yucht built on the idea with her tweet, "How about Conferences should be about LEARNING, not Show-n-Tell?", which got me thinking about how we approach conferences and conference presentations in the library profession. If the goal of the conference is that attendees will learn, what do conference presentations have to look like to achieve that goal?

I believe the goal of presenting should be to create a change in the listener; a change of behavior, thinking, and/or feeling. Any good teacher or trainer will tell you that to be effective in creating that change, you must begin with the learning objective in mind, and work backwards from there to design the lesson or the talk.

The cart before the horse?

Many library conferences seem to be designed around topics that presenters wish to present on, more than they are designed around or focused on the learning that participants need. In too many conference presentations, speakers design their talks as core dumps of data, or long, dry recountings of "how we did it good," without giving enough attention to the key question, "As a result of hearing me speak, people will do/think/feel_____" (fill in the blank).

The answer to that question is the main organizing principle, the guiding star, of any well-constructed talk. Leaving out all of the other variables (emotion, humor, pacing, eye contact, vocal variety, body language, visuals, questions, room environment, acoustics), it is very difficult to have an effective presentation if what constitutes success is a mere afterthought.

3

Promote learning with your talk

1. **Ask, "What do I want them to do, think, and/or feel as a result of hearing this program?"** Ask and answer this question before you write one word or create one slide. The answer to this question is your *objective*. Let the objective guide you continually as you construct your presentation, throwing aside anything that does not help achieve the goal of the talk.

2. **Share your objectives with the audience** at some point during your presentation—preferably during the first few minutes. If the audience knows what you intend to achieve with the talk, it will give them context that will help them make meaning and ground the learning. It will also help them evaluate whether you have effectively achieved your goal. Or not.

3. **Have a strong opening.** The first two minutes of your talk gives you a great opportunity to grab and hold the audience's attention, but it's likely that you already *have* their attention during the first two minutes. It's the next 58 that present the challenge! So what do I mean by a strong opening? I mean an opening that engages the audience, creates some positive expectation for the rest of the talk, or provides a framework for the learning that is about to take place. Olivia Mitchell suggests three possible openings—Organized Opening, Story Opening, Dramatic Opening.

4. **Use examples to illustrate your points**. For example: Don't just say, "Merchandising your collection is good." Say, "When we created a 'recently returned' display at the front door and displayed them all covers out, 98% of them recirculated within the same day and our circulation stats increased 20%." Examples support the learning by attesting to the truth of your message, and also help ground the learning by clarifying and fleshing out your meaning.

5. **Use simple, clear, engaging visuals to reinforce your points** (or don't use them at all). Good visuals can help you focus the audience's attention, help them make meaning, and promote future recall, by connecting intellectual ideas with visual representations. As for bullet points: I'm not one of those people who believes bullet points should *never* be

used, but if you use them, do it sparingly, with a large readable font, and a supporting image (if room permits).

6. **Tell stories**. Our brains are actually wired to enjoy stories. And because stories have the power to simultaneously engage the listener both cognitively and emotionally, they are highly effective in getting your point across.

7. **Appeal to emotions as well as reason**. Unless you are presenting on the planet Vulcan, your audience probably consists of human beings, and research shows that it is our emotions that lead us to *act*. If your goal is get listeners to *do something*, you need to rouse some feeling within them by appealing to their empathy, their self-interest, or some combination of both. As Chip and Dan Heath suggest in *Made to Stick*, you want to appeal "not only to the people they are right now but also to the people they would like to be."

8. **Practice, practice, practice.** There is no substitute for practicing your talk, preferably in front of others, to work out the kinks, identify and clarify muddied points, and become comfortable with the material. When you know your talk cold you will relax, let you personality show, and more easily connect with the audience.

9. **Have a strong closing and telegraph when it's coming**. You don't have to bring tears to the audience's eyes, or bring them to their feet. But you do need to let them know that you're wrapping it up, and use the closing as an opportunity to reinforce your goal. You can do this by simply restating your main points and asserting why/how the listener will benefit by doing what you want them to do. Or you can end with a provocative question (engaging them cognitively), or with a story (engaging them emotionally). However you choose to close your presentation, use vocal variety and word choice to telegraph that you are concluding, so the audience realizes that it is time to clap wildly.

10. **What are your ideas?** I'm leaving #10 blank for your own observations. What do you do to effectively promote learning in your talks? What have speakers done that have helped you as a learner/listener?

SOURCE: Peter Bromberg, "10 Steps to Promote Learning in Your Conference Presentation," ALA Learning, February 2, 2010, alalearning.org/2010/02/02/10steps/.

Mastering moderation
by Steven J. Bell

YOU JUST FOUND OUT you're going to moderate a conference program or webcast. Congratulations. Now what? What exactly are you going to do? If what you do is emulate what you've seen most moderators do at library conferences, both physical and virtual, chances are you'll politely ask attendees to take their seats before you start reading off the presenters' names and their canned biographical statements. Then you'll sit down and disappear for the rest of the program. If that doesn't sound very exciting or productive, it's the unfortunate outcome of programs planned with little thought to what a moderator can and should bring to a library program of an type.

Instead, let me describe a role that moderators can play that will add value to any program. Taking the role of moderator seriously means being proactive about working with the speakers to design a well-thought-out program with a singular goal: delivering an outstanding program experience to the audience.

Getting things off to a good start. Instead of thinking of the moderator as a librarian randomly assigned to a panel or program, consider it an important design decision to integrate the moderator into the program as an equal, if not more important, participant.

Several years ago I organized a debate between two teams arguing for and against "good enough" research. It was a huge success primarily because we chose a moderator who was the focal point of the program, commenting wisely after each team made its points, becoming one of the audience in order to compel attendees to line up to make their voices heard, and ultimately whipping up the crowd into a frenzy before they voted on the debate winner. Every moderator can decide whether he or she will simply be an awkward appendage to the main event or become an integral part of the proceedings. I argue that the latter option is attendee-centered program design.

Setting the stage. When asked to serve as a moderator in any capacity, and before making a commitment, the first task is to ask questions and determine what the program organizer expects. If the only expectation is to read names and biographies off a sheet, you need to decide if that's all you wish to do. Be courageous and suggest that the moderator should take a more active role in the program. Assuming that the planners and participants agree, you should immediately agree to take responsibility for managing the program. Here are some of the primary responsibilities the moderator should agree to accept:

- Develop a timeline for preparation leading up to the program.
- Create a script or timeline that gives structure to the presentation.
- Bring presenters together for program planning.
- Identify strategies to engage the audience.
- Keep the speakers on time and the attendees involved.
- Orchestrate the program with flexibility.
- Wrap up the proceedings with authority.

Designing the program. When attendees experience a great program, it's usually the result of intentional design. Most panelists will embrace a moderator who takes the reins and leads the presentation planning effort. A savvy moderator has a knack for planning the program, but avoids one so tightly scheduled that it offers no room for spontaneity or deviation from the plan. The moderator should set the tone early by establishing a timetable for preparing for the big day, and then taking responsibility for organizing the meetings, preparing agendas, and then leading the meetings. The panelists or presenters are the content experts; they bring the material and generate the discussion. It's the moderator who makes sure all presenters get their moment to shine, but more importantly creates the setting for those attending to play a major role in any program.

As the conference approaches, the moderator should plan a series of virtual meetings at which the participants will design the program. Think of it as a script that identifies the order of speakers, time allotted for each presentation, how the moderator will participate, and audience involvement. The more activity there is, the more detail should be included in the script. I moderated a program that combined multiple video segments, speaker commentary, and a question-and-answer segment with the audience. With that much activity and quick shifts between each, a script covering what happens when, and who does what for how long, greatly increases the odds of success—and we had over 25 attendees come to the microphones to comment or ask questions in just one hour. The key to success is advance preparation; but the moderator must be the production expert who brings it all together.

Looking for Phil Donahue. Pretty much anyone can read canned speaker introductions, but it takes a librarian with presence to moderate. Skilled moderators know how to create a dynamic between the presenters and the audience. The moderator and presenters, in their planning stages, should determine what level of audience participation they desire. That should be the starting point for all that follows.

The moderator should be physically located in the audience area, equipped with wireless microphone, to prompt questions and comments. Good moderators, much like talk-show hosts, know how to get the audience involved and keep the proceedings on topic, as well as how to deal with disruptions and potential problems, such as an attendee who monopolizes time during a discussion segment.

Poor timing is the downfall of most conference programs. To avoid getting derailed, the moderator needs to ensure that all panelists get their fair share of presentation time. A well-designed timetable should eliminate overcrowding the program with activity. I recall being asked to moderate a program where another member of the program planning committee structured the event. I was told to take 20 minutes to summarize and respond to the other speakers. Not only were there too many speakers on the program, but one went 10 minutes beyond his allotted time. I ended up giving a rushed four-minute response. Lesson learned.

With proper preparation each presenter should know exactly how much time he or she has. In advance, the moderator should set a clear expectation for all to adhere to that agreement, and indicate how each presenter will be signaled when the time is nearly gone. Moderators who sit idly while a single presenter hogs other speakers' time do a disservice to the entire panel and the audience. To further ensure a well-run program the moderator should arrive early to make sure everything is ready to go, that the technology is in place and tested, and that each speaker is ready.

Bringing it all home. Nothing's worse than a conference session that ends on a flat or dull note, so think in advance about ways to bring the session to a finish that strives for a bit more than that tired, old "Anyone have a question" standby. What if no one does have a question? Is that it? There are other possibilities. If nothing else, the moderator should prepare questions in advance to ask the speakers. Often just one is enough to stimulate the audience to follow with their own questions.

Take your wireless microphone and wade into the audience. Ask attendees what they might do with these new ideas when they get back to their libraries. If you have a friend or two planning to attend, ask them if they'd be willing to be your first audience participant. It's all part of the preparation.

Don't let your session fail. While preparing this article I read a blog post by veteran speaker Scott Berkun titled "Why Panel Sessions Suck (and How to Fix Them)." Here are some final tips based on Berkun's points that offer all would-be moderators advice on how to make sure their session is the great experience everyone involved wants it to be.

- Be an active moderator. Have good questions at the ready in case the audience is slow to speak up. Keep the presenters on time. Challenge the panelists to follow up on a statement or comment. If something isn't go-ing right—with the presenters, technology, or whatever—take personal responsibility for doing something about it. Don't just sit there.

- Planning makes the difference. Use your gut instincts to change what seems to be going wrong as you and the speakers plan the program. Instead of those stale, canned introductions, find something unique and pithy to say about each one. Decide on a Twitter hashtag and promote it before and during the session.

- Controversy is not a dirty word. It's all right for the speakers to debate a topic and have opposing viewpoints. Consider asking the speakers to pick one side of an issue or debate and defend their decision. Keep it under control with respect to time and negativity; keep it respectful

- Offer the presenters advance feedback on their visuals. Avoid a program that's a series of mind-numbing slides. Urge the speakers to use video or more of a debate-style presentation. Mentor less experienced speak-ers who show the need for support. Make sure introverted panelists are equally involved; be equally aware of panelists with huge egos who may bully moderators or other panelists. Work with the speakers to create a conversation with the audience. Encourage the speakers to tell their stories rather than offer facts.

- Be a leader. Bring energy and passion to the pro-gram; it's infectious. Start it off with enthusiastic remarks that set the tone. Know when to shut up; give others the lead when appropriate. Be the person on the team who brings out the best in your teammates. It helps to have the natural abil-ity to think fast on your feet and ad lib for ef-fect, but consider having a humorous or engaging  short anecdote at hand to share if needed. And you're not a late-night TV show host, so no canned monologues or jokes.

The web offers yet more advice on how to be a great moderator, much of it found in the presentation blogs. Explore this territory for what it's worth if you seek ideas beyond what's offered here (search "great moderator" or "master mod-erator"). But expect some surprising or conflicting ideas.

In the end each moderator should decide what works best for each individual program, the speakers, and the audience. But there is little in the way of advice to offer in acquiring those intangible skills—timing, confidence, poise, emotion, passion, dynamism, and tact—that great moderators possess. They are learned through time and experience. Try watching videos of great moderators and pre-senters, then take every opportunity to practice. Remember, it's not about perfec-tion; it's about presence.

A moderator can make or break the program. The complacent ones play no part in planning or running of the program, and that leaves wide open the pos-sibility of a session that is completely dysfunctional and disastrous. Ultimately the best moderators, like the best presenters, are passionate in how they care about the attendees. There is much more to the role of the moderator beyond just naming the presenters' names, but it all starts with focusing on the audience and doing whatever it takes to make sure they have a great program experience.

SOURCE: Steven J. Bell, "Mastering Moderation," *American Libraries* 41, no. 6/7 (June/July 2010): 48–50.

GRANTS & AWARDS

Scholarships, grants, and awards

MANY OPPORTUNITIES EXIST in the field of library and information science for its practitioners to obtain assistance for their research and to gain recognition for their achievements. The following list provides information on grants, scholarships, and awards given by ALA and other national associations in the United States and Canada.

The arrangement is topical under three major headings: **scholarships** (monetary aid in support of a degree); **grants** (remuneration for things you are going to do); and **awards** (recognition for things you have already done). Considered topically, this list can be viewed as a measure of what we value most in our profession.

Scholarships are on pp. 140–143. Under grants, the subheads are:
>   **for programs** (pp. 143–146); and
>   **for publications, research, and travel** (pp. 146–153).

Under awards, the subheads for achievements are:
>   **for individual or group achievement** (pp. 153–160);
>   **to libraries for excellence** (pp. 160–161);
>   **for service to children and young adults** (pp. 161–162);
>   **for service to the underserved** (pp. 162–163);
>   **for advocacy and marketing** (pp. 163–164);
>   **for intellectual freedom** (pp. 164–165);
>   **for literacy and social responsibility** (p. 165);
>   **for special collections and archives** (pp. 165–166);
>   **for technology** (pp. 166–168).

Awards for books or other publications are in the following categories:
>   **for articles, papers, and research** (pp. 168–171);
>   **for children's and young adult literature** (pp. 171–173);
>   **for non-print media** (p. 174); and
>   **for reference and adult books** (pp. 174–176).

Scholarships

AALL Educational Scholarships. Scholarships in support of library and law school degrees, non-law degrees, and CE courses for both law school graduates and non–law school graduates. American Association of Law Libraries, www.aallnet.org.

AALL George A. Strait Minority Scholarship. Awarded to members of a minority group with law library experience who are enrolled in library or law school. American Association of Law Libraries, www.aallnet.org.

AALL Marcia J. Koslov Scholarship. Provides funding for AALL members who serve as librarians in state, court, or county libraries to attend continuing education seminars or programs. American Association of Law Libraries, www.aallnet.org.

AECT Legacy Scholarship. An award of $1,000 presented to a school librarian in pursuit of a master's degree or professional certificate. Association for Educational Communications and Technology, aect.site-ym.com.

AECT McJulien Minority Graduate Scholarship Award. Presented to a minority graduate student in educational communications and technology. Association for Educational Communications and Technology, aect.site-ym.com.

AECT Master's Scholarship Award. An award of $1,000 presented to a student currently accepted or enrolled in master's program in the field of educational communications and technology. Association for Educational Communications and Technology, aect.site-ym.com.

AECT ect Mentor Endowment Scholarship. A $3,000 scholarship intended for use by a doctoral student in educational communications and technology to pursue studies in this field. Association for Educational Communications and Technology, aect.site-ym.com.

AILA Virginia Mathews Memorial Scholarship. A $2,000 scholarship to an American Indian or Alaskan Native student who is enrolled in, or has been accepted in, an ALA-accredited master's degree program. American Indian Library Association, www.ailanet.org.

AJL Student Scholarship. A $1,000 scholarship to a library school student who intends to pursue a career in Judaica librarianship. Association of Jewish Libraries, www.jewishlibraries.org.

ALA David H. Clift Scholarship. A $3,000 scholarship to an individual pursuing a master's degree in library science from an ALA-accredited program. ALA Scholarships, ala.org.

ALA Marshall Cavendish Scholarship. A $3,000 scholarship to an individual pursuing a master's degree in library science from an ALA-accredited program. ALA Scholarships, ala.org.

ALA Mary V. Gaver Scholarship. A $3,000 scholarship to an individual specializing in youth services who is pursuing a master's degree in library science. ALA Scholarships, ala.org.

ALA Miriam L. Hornback Scholarship. A $3,000 award given to an ALA or library support staff person to support studies toward a master's degree in library and information studies. ALA Scholarships, ala.org.

ALA Peter Lyman Memorial/SAGE Scholarship in New Media. A $2,500 award given to an individual specializing in new media who is pursuing a master's degree in library and information studies. ALA Scholarships, ala.org.

ALA Tom and Roberta Drewes Scholarship. Scholarship of $3,000 to a library support staff person currently working in a library, pursuing a master's degree in library science. ALA Scholarships, ala.org.

ALA Tony B. Leisner Scholarship. A $3,000 award to a library support staff person currently working in a library, pursuing a master's degree in library science. ALA Scholarships, ala.org.

ALA/ALSC Bound to Stay Bound Books Scholarships. Four $7,000 awards to assist individuals who wish to work in the field of library service to children. ALA Association for Library Service to Children, ala.org/alsc/.

ALA/ALSC Frederic G. Melcher Scholarships. Two annual $6,000 scholarships established to encourage and assist people who wish to enter the field of library service to children. ALA Association for Library Service to Children, ala.org/alsc/.

ALA/ERT Christopher J. Hoy Scholarship. A $5,000 award to an individual pursuing a master's degree in library science. ALA Scholarships, ala.org/ert/.

ALA/FAFLRT Cicely Phippen Marks Scholarship. An annual scholarship of $1,500 for a library school student specializing in federal librarianship. ALA Federal and Armed Forces Libraries Round Table, ala.org/faflrt/.

ALA/GODORT W. David Rozkuszka Scholarship. A $3,000 award for financial assistance to an individual currently working with government documents in a library and working on a master's degree in library science. ALA Government Documents Round Table, ala.org/godort/.

ALA/LITA Christian Larew Memorial Scholarship. A $3,000 scholarship for qualified persons who plan to follow a career in library and information technology, and who demonstrate a strong commitment to the use of automated systems. ALA Library and Information Technology Association, ala.org/lita/.

ALA/LITA LSSI Minority Scholarship in Library and Information Technology. A $2,500 scholarship for qualified persons who plan to follow a career in library automation and who are members of a principal minority group. ALA Library and Information Technology Association, ala.org/lita/.

ALA/LITA OCLC Minority Scholarship in Library and Information Technology. A $3,000 scholarship for qualified persons who plan to follow a career in library automation and who are members of a principal minority group. ALA Library and Information Technology Association, ala.org/lita/.

ALA/OFD Spectrum Scholarships. Provides 50 annual scholarships of $5,000 each to minority students representing African-American, Asian–Pacific Islander, Latino/Hispanic, and Native American populations to encourage admission and graduation from an ALA-accredited master's degree program in library and information studies. ALA Office for Diversity, ala.org/spectrum/.

APALA Scholarship. Provides financial assistance to a student of Asian or Pacific background who is enrolled, or has been accepted in, an ALA-accredited master's or doctoral degree program. Asian Pacific American Library Association, www.apalaweb.org.

ARL Initiative to Recruit a Diverse Workforce. A stipend of up to $10,000 to attract students from underrepresented groups to careers in academic and research libraries. Association of Research Libraries, www.arl.org.

ARLIS/NA Internship Award. A grant of $2,500 to support a library student during a period of internship in an art library or visual resources collection. Art Libraries Society of North America, www.arlisna.org.

ARLIS/NA Robertson Rare Book School Scholarship. An annual award of tuition waiver for one course at the Rare Book School at the University of Virginia. Art Libraries Society of North America, www.arlisna.org.

ASDAL D. Glenn Hilts Scholarship. A $1,500 award to a member of the Seventh-day Adventists Church to attend an ALA-accredited program. Association of Seventh-day Adventist Librarians, www.asdal.org.

ASIS&T Thomson Reuters Doctoral Dissertation Proposal Scholarship. An award of $1,500 and up to $500 in travel support to foster research in information science by assisting doctoral students in the field with their dissertation research. American Society for Information Science and Technology, www.asis.org.

ATLA Leadership Development Program Scholarships. Assists ATLA members in attending leadership development programs to a maximum of $1,500. American Theological Library Association, www.atla.com.

ATLA Scholarships to Promote Diversity in Theological Librarianship. Three $1,200 scholarships to assist underrepresented minorities to explore careers in theological librarianship. American Theological Library Association, www.atla.com.

BCALA E. J. Josey Scholarship Awards. Two unrestricted grants of $2,000 awarded annually to African-American students enrolled in or accepted by ALA-accredited programs. Black Caucus of the American Library Association, www.bcala.org.

Beta Phi Mu Blanche E. Woolls Scholarship. Award of $2,250 to a student beginning library and information studies at an ALA-accredited school with the intention of pursuing a career in school library media service. Beta Phi Mu, www.beta-phi-mu.org.

Beta Phi Mu Eugene Garfield Doctoral Dissertation Fellowship. Six awards to library and information science students working on doctoral dissertations. Beta Phi Mu, www.beta-phi-mu.org.

Beta Phi Mu Frank B. Sessa Scholarship. Award of $1,500 for continuing education of a Beta Phi Mu member. Beta Phi Mu, www.beta-phi-mu.org.

Beta Phi Mu Harold Lancour Scholarship. Award of $1,750 for graduate study in a foreign country related to the applicant's work or schooling. Beta Phi Mu, www.beta-phi-mu.org.

Beta Phi Mu Sarah Rebecca Reed Scholarship. Award of $2,250 for study at an ALA-accredited library school. Beta Phi Mu, www.beta-phi-mu.org.

CALA Huang Tso-ping and Wu Yao-yu Scholarship. A $200 award for a student of Chinese heritage in an ALA-accredited program in library and information science. Chinese American Librarians Association, cala-web.org.

CALA Scholarship of Library and Information Science. A $1,000 award for a student of Chinese heritage in an ALA-accredited program in library and information science. Chinese American Librarians Association, cala-web.org.

CALA Sheila Suen Lai Scholarship. A $500 award for a student of Chinese heritage in an ALA-accredited program in library and information science. Chinese American Librarians Association, cala-web.org.

CALL Diana M. Priestly Memorial Scholarship. An award of $2,500 (Can.) to a Canadian citizen to support professional development in law librarianship. Canadian Association of Law Libraries, www.callacbd.ca.

CALL Education Reserve Fund Grant. An award to CALL members to further their education in pursuits that do not fit the guidelines of already established scholarships. Canadian Association of Law Libraries, www.callacbd.ca.

CLA Dafoe Scholarship. An award of $5,000 (Can.) for a Canadian citizen or landed immigrant to attend an accredited library school. Canadian Library Association, www.cla.ca.

CLA H. W. Wilson Scholarship. An award of $2,000 (Can.) for a Canadian citizen or immigrant to pursue studies at an accredited library school. Canadian Library Association, www.cla.ca.

CLA Rev. Andrew L. Bouwhuis Memorial Scholarship. A $1,500 scholarship for graduate study towards a master's degree in library science. Catholic Library Association, www.cathla.org.

CLIR A. R. Zipf Fellowship. A cash award to a student in the early stages of graduate school who shows exceptional promise for leadership and technical achievement in information management. Council on Library and Information Resources, www.clir.org.

CNI Paul Evan Peters Fellowship. An award of $5,000 for two consecutive years to assist a student pursuing graduate studies in information sciences or librarianship who demonstrates commitment to the use of digital information and advanced technology to enhance scholarship, intellectual productivity, and public life; support of civic responsibilities and democratic values; and humor and imagination. Awarded every two years. Coalition for Networked Information, www.cni.org.

MLA Continuing Education Awards. Grants of $100–$500 to develop MLA members' knowledge of the theoretical, administrative, or technical aspects of librarianship. Medical Library Association, www.mlanet.org.

MLA Scholarship. A scholarship of up to $5,000 for a student who is entering an ALA-accredited library school. Medical Library Association, www.mlanet.org.

MLA Scholarship for Minority Students. A scholarship of up to $5,000 for a minority student who is entering an ALA-accredited library school. Medical Library Association, www.mlanet.org.

MLA Thomson Reuters Doctoral Fellowship. A fellowship given every two years in the amount of $2,000 to encourage superior students to conduct doctoral work in an area of health sciences librarianship. Medical Library Association, www.mlanet.org.

NASIG Fritz Schwartz Serials Education Scholarship. A $3,000 scholarship to a library science graduate student who demonstrates excellence in scholarship and the potential for accomplishment in a serials career. North American Serials Interest Group, www.nasig.org.

Reforma Rose Treviño Memorial Scholarship. Provides funding for a Hispanic or Latino/a student to attend an ALA-accredited library school. Reforma, www.reforma.org.

Reforma Scholarships. Grants of up to $1,500 to Hispanic or Latino/a students attending an ALA-accredited library school. Reforma, www.reforma.org.

SAA F. Gerald Ham Scholarship. Two scholarships of $7,500 to support the graduate archival education of a second-year student who is studying at a United States university that meets the criteria for graduate education set forth by SAA. Society of American Archivists, www.archivists.org.

SAA Josephine Forman Scholarship. A scholarship of $10,000 to provide financial support to a minority student pursuing graduate education in archival science. Society of American Archivists, www.archivists.org.

SAA Mosaic Scholarship. Two scholarships of $5,000 are awarded annually to applicants who are pursuing graduate education in archival science. Society of American Archivists, www.archivists.org.

SALALM Scholarship. A scholarship of $1,000 for a master's candidate in archival studies or library school who has a strong interest in Latin America or the Caribbean. Seminar on the Acquisition of Latin American Library Materials, salalm.org.

TLA Brooks McNamara Performing Arts Librarian Scholarship. $500 in support of a student enrolled in a MLS or archival training program specializing in performing arts librarianship. Theatre Library Association, www.tla-online.org.

Grants

For programs

AALL Distinguished Lectureship Award. Supports an association member to present a lecture on the history, practice, or philosophy of law librarianship at the annual convention. American Association of Law Libraries, www.aallnet.org.

AALL Minority Leadership Development Award. Given to an AALL member to nurture leaders for the future and to introduce minority law librarians to leadership opportunities within the association American Association of Law Libraries, www.aallnet.org.

AIIP Roger Summit Award Lecture. Sponsors an industry leader or innovative thinker to speak at the annual AIIP Conference. Association of Independent Information Professionals, www.aiip.org.

ALA Emerging Leaders Program. Designed to enable up to 75 new librarians to get on the fast track to ALA and professional leadership. Participants are given the opportunity to work on a variety of projects, network with peers, and get an inside look into ALA structure and activities. ALA Office for Human Resource Development and Recruitment, ala.org/hrdr/.

ALA H. W. Wilson Library Staff Development Grant. $3,500 and a 24k-gold–framed citation to a library organization for a program to further its staff development goals. ALA Awards, ala.org.

ALA/AASL ABC-CLIO Leadership Grant. Up to $1,750 to be given to school library associations that are affiliates of AASL for planning and implementing leadership programs at the state, regional, or local level. ALA American Association of School Librarians, ala.org/aasl/.

ALA/AASL Beyond Words: Dollar General School Library Relief Fund. Provides up to $15,000 to replace or supplement books, media, and library equipment in public schools whose library programs have been affected by a natural disaster. ALA American Association of School Librarians, ala.org/aasl/.

ALA/AASL Innovative Reading Grant. An award of $2,500 to support the planning and implementation of a unique and innovative program for children that motivates and encourages reading, especially with struggling readers. ALA American Association of School Librarians, ala.org/aasl/.

ALA/ACRL e-Learning Scholarships. Twenty grants covering the cost of the ACRL e-Learning webcast registration fee. ALA Association of College and Research Libraries, ala.org/acrl/.

ALA/ALCTS Online Course Grants. One free seat per ALCTS online continuing educational course session provided to librarians and information professionals from developing countries. ALA Association for Library Collections and Technical Services, ala.org/alcts/.

ALA/ALSC Bookapalooza Program. Offers select libraries a collection of children's materials that will help transform their collection and provide the opportunity for these materials to be used in their community in creative and innovative ways. ALA Association for Library Service to Children, ala.org/alsc/.

ALA/ALSC BWI Summer Reading Program Grant. A grant of $3,000 to an ALSC member to implement an outstanding public library summer reading program for children. ALA Association for Library Service to Children, ala.org/alsc/.

ALA/ALSC Candlewick Light the Way Grant. A $3,000 grant awarded to a library proposing a program or service in support of special population children and their caregivers. ALA Association for Library Service to Children, ala.org/alsc/.

ALA/ALSC Maureen Hayes Author/Illustrator Visit Award. A $4,000 honorarium to pay for a visit from a nationally known author or illustrator who will speak to children who have not had the opportunity to hear an author or illustrator. ALA Association for Library Service to Children, ala. org/alsc/.

ALA/ALSC May Hill Arbuthnot Honor Lecture Award. An invitation to an individual of distinction to prepare and present a paper that will be a significant contribution to the field of children's literature and subsequently published in *Children and Libraries.* ALA Association for Library Service to Children, ala.org/alsc/.

ALA/EMIERT Coretta Scott King Book Donation Grant. Approximately 300 books by African-American authors and illustrators given to help build collections and bring books into the lives of children in latchkey, preschool programs, faith-based reading projects, homeless shelters, charter schools, and underfunded libraries. ALA Ethnic and Multicultural Information Exchange Round Table, ala.org/emiert/.

ALA/ORS Loleta D. Fyan Grant. One or more grants of up to $5,000 to a library, library school, association, or unit or chapter of ALA for the development and improvement of public libraries and the services they provide. ALA Office of Research and Statistics, ala.org/ors/.

ALA/PIO Arthur Curley Memorial Lecture. Funding intended to bring a distinguished author or performer to lecture or perform at the ALA Midwinter Meeting. ALA Public Information Office, ala.org/pio/.

ALA/PIO Scholastic Library Publishing National Library Week Grant. A $3,000 grant awarded to a library or library association for the best proposal for a public awareness campaign that supports the theme of National Library Week. ALA Public Information Office, ala.org/pio/.

ALA/PLA Baker & Taylor Entertainment Audio Music/Video Product Award. Designed to promote the development of a circulating audio music/video product collection in public libraries and increase the exposure of the format within the community, the grant consists of $2,500 worth of audio music or video products. ALA Public Library Association, ala.org/pla/.

ALA/PLA Romance Writers of America Library Grant. A grant of $4,500 for a public library to build or expand a romance fiction collection or host romance fiction programming. ALA Public Library Association, ala.org/pla/.

ALA/YALSA BWI Collection Development Grant. Up to two $1,000 grants for collection development materials to YALSA members who represent a public library and work directly with young adults. ALA Young Adult Library Services Association, ala.org/yalsa/.

ALA/YALSA Dollar General Summer Reading Grants. Twenty $1,000 grants to encourage outstanding summer reading programs and recognize YALSA members for outstanding program development. ALA Young Adult Library Services Association, ala.org/yalsa/.

ALA/YALSA Dollar General Teen Summer Interns Grants. Forty $1,000 grants to support teen interns for summer reading programs. ALA Young Adult Library Services Association, ala.org/yalsa/.

ALA/YALSA Frances Henne *Voice of Youth Advocates* Research Grant. An annual grant of $1,000 to provide seed money to an individual, institution, or group for small-scale projects to encourage research on library service to young adults. ALA Young Adult Library Services Association, ala.org/yalsa/.

ALA/YALSA Great Books Giveaway Competition. Each year the YALSA office receives approximately 1,200 newly published children's, young adult, and adult books; videos; CDs; and audiocassettes. YALSA and the cooperating publishers are offering one year's worth of review materials as a contribution to a library in need. ALA Young Adult Library Services Association, ala.org/yalsa/.

AMHL Small Grants Program. Grants of $500–$1,500 that enhance opportunities for members of AMHL to engage in research, scholarship, and creative endeavors. Association of Mental Health Librarians, www.mhlib.org.

Amigos Fellowship and Opportunity Award Program. Grants of up to $10,000 to library and information professionals in Amigos member libraries to fund individuals' development projects or encourage Amigos member libraries to innovate, cooperate, lead, and educate within their libraries, their communities, and the library profession. Amigos Library Services, www.amigos.org.

ATLA Consultation Grants. Assists theological libraries with consultant fees to assess operations and planning. American Theological Library Association, www.atla.com.

ATLA Grants for Continuing Education Programs. Assists institutional members or regional groups in funding continuing education programs. American Theological Library Association, www.atla.com.

ATLA International Collaboration Grant. Enables collaboration between ATLA institutions and groups abroad. American Theological Library Association, www.atla.com.

CLA John T. Corrigan, CFX Memorial Continuing Education Grant. Assists CLA chapters in their mission of providing quality continuing education opportunities. Catholic Library Association, www.cathla.org.

CLIR Cataloging Hidden Special Collections and Archives. Awarded to support innovative, efficient description of large volumes of material of high value to scholars. Council on Library and Information Resources, www.clir.org.

CLIR Digital Library Federation Data Curation Postdoctoral Fellowships. Provide recent PhDs with professional development, education, and training opportunities in data curation for the sciences and social sciences. Council on Library and Information Resources, www.clir.org.

CLIR Peterson Fellowship. This award recognizes an early-career IT professional or librarian who has led a collaborative effort to resolve a significant challenge or critical problem in IT/digital libraries. It covers travel, lodging, and registration costs associated with the fellow's participation in the National Institute for Technology in Liberal Education's annual spring symposium and CLIR's Digital Library Federation Forum, both national venues, www.clir.org.

CLIR Postdoctoral Fellowship in Academic Libraries. Awarded to recent PhDs who believe there are opportunities to develop meaningful linkages among disciplinary scholarship, libraries, archives, and evolving digital tools. Council on Library and Information Resources, www.clir.org.

IAMSLIC Grants. Support projects related to the recording, retrieval, and dissemination of information in aquatic and marine science through small grants to IAMSLIC regional groups and members. International Association of Aquatic and Marine Science Libraries and Information Centers, www.iamslic.org.

IASL Books for Children Project. An award of $1,000 to provide books for children in developing countries. International Association of School Librarianship, www.iasl-online.org.

IMLS Connecting to Collections Statewide Implementation Grants. A limited number of grants are awarded to implement plans or models created with the Statewide Planning grants to provide safe conditions for collections, develop an emergency plan, assign responsibility for collection care, and increase public and private support for collections care. Institute of Museum and Library Services, www.imls.gov.

IMLS Laura Bush 21st Century Librarian Program. Matching grants to libraries or institutions of higher education in amounts from $50,000 to $500,000 for library programs that support efforts to recruit and educate the next generation of librarians and the faculty who will prepare them for careers in library science. Institute of Museum and Library Services, www.imls.gov.

IMLS National Leadership Grants. Grants to libraries in amounts from $50,000 to $1 million for library programs that preserve culture, heritage, and knowledge; contribute to building technology infrastructures and information technology services; and provide 21st-century knowledge and skills to current and future generations in support of a world-class workforce. Programs must be in one of the following areas: advancing digital resources, research, demonstration, or library-museum collaboration. Institute of Museum and Library Services, www.imls.gov.

IMLS Native American Library Services Basic Grants. Annual grants to Indian tribes and Native Alaskan villages to support existing library operations and to maintain core library services. Institute of Museum and Library Services, www.imls.gov.

IMLS Native American Library Services Enhancement Grants. Annual grants to Indian tribes and Native Alaskan villages to enhance existing library services or implement new library services. Institute of Museum and Library Services, www.imls.gov.

IMLS Native Hawaiian Library Services Grants. Annual grants to nonprofit organizations primarily serving Native Hawaiians to expand and improve library services. Institute of Museum and Library Services, www.imls.gov.

IMLS Sparks! Ignition Grants for Libraries and Museums. Grants of up to $25,000 for programs that address problems, challenges, or needs of broad relevance to museums, libraries, or archives; test innovative responses to these problems; and make the findings of these tests widely and openly accessible. Institute of Museum and Library Services, www.imls.gov.

LBFAL Grants to School Libraries. Grants of up to $6,000 to expand, update, and diversify school library collections. Laura Bush Foundation for America's Libraries, www.laurabushfoundation.com.

MLA Janet Doe Lectureship. Awarded for a unique perspective on the history or philosophy of medical librarianship. The selected lecture is presented at the MLA annual meeting and published in the *Journal of the Medical Library Association*. Medical Library Association, www.mlanet.org.

MLA John P. McGovern Award Lectureship. For a significant national or international figure to speak on a topic of importance to health science librarianship at the MLA annual meeting. Medical Library Association, www.mlanet.org.

MLA Joseph Leiter NLM Lectureship. For a lecture on biomedical communications. Medical Library Association, www.mlanet.org.

MLA Rising Stars. A one-year leadership development program designed for MLA members who are interested in attaining leadership roles in MLA but who have not yet become active at a national level. Medical Library Association, www.mlanet.org.

NCFL Better World Books Libraries and Families Award. $10,000 grants awarded annually in three categories (Friends group, public or academic library, or urban library) to support existing library programming for families and expand the literacy-building practices of families in the library setting. National Center for Family Literacy, www.famlit.org.

NSN Brimstone Award for Applied Storytelling. A grant for a model storytelling project that is service-oriented, based in a community or organization, and replicable. National Storytelling Network, storynet.org.

NSN Member Grants. Funding of up to $1,000 for projects, community-based programs, or scholarly research in storytelling. National Storytelling Network, storynet.org.

ULC Joey Rodger Leadership Award. A grant awarded annually to provide financial assistance to a library leader for participation in a leadership development opportunity. Urban Libraries Council, urbanlibraries.org.

For publications, research, and travel

AALL Annual Meeting/Workshop Grants. To cover registration costs at association annual meetings or workshops. American Association of Law Libraries, www.aallnet.org.

AALL Research Grant. Sponsors research that is critical to the profession. American Association of Law Libraries, www.aallnet.org.

AALL Special Interest Section Sponsored Grants. These provide financial assistance for specialists to travel or conduct research. American Association of Law Libraries, www.aallnet.org.

AALL Wolters Kluwer Law and Business Grant. Sponsors research that will have a practical impact on the law library profession and inspire products and changes in the marketplace. American Association of Law Libraries, www.aallnet.org.

AALL/LISP Kathy Garner Grant. Covers registration and travel costs for attending an AALL annual meeting. American Association of Law Libraries, Legal Information Services to the Public Special Interest Group, www.aallnet.org.

AECT Dean and Sybil McClusky Research Award. A cash award of $500 for the most outstanding doctoral research proposal in educational technology. Association for Educational Communications and Technology, aect.site-ym.com.

AIIP Myra T. Grenier Award. A $600 stipend awarded to a new or aspiring independent information professional to attend the AIIP Annual Conference. Association of Independent Information Professionals, www.aiip.org.

AIIP Roger Summit Conference Sponsorship. Provides $1,000 and free registration for an individual who has been an AIIP member for at least two years and in business for at least three, and who has not attended an AIIP conference before. Association of Independent Information Professionals, www.aiip.org.

AIIP Sue Rugge Memorial Award. A complimentary conference registration and $500 cash stipend awarded to a full member of AIIP who has significantly helped another member through formal or informal mentoring. Association of Independent Information Professionals, www.aiip.org.

AILA DEMCO Travel Grant. Travel grants of $500 to allow attendance at the ALA Annual Conference. American Indian Library Association, www.ailanet.org.

ALA Carnegie-Whitney Grants. Annual grants of up to $5,000 to individuals, libraries, official ALA units, and other groups affiliated with ALA for the preparation and publication of popular or scholarly reading lists, indexes, and other guides to library resources that will be useful to users of all types of libraries. ALA Publishing, ala.org.

ALA EBSCO Annual Conference Sponsorships. Awards of up to $1,000 allowing librarians to attend ALA Annual Conference. An essay of no more than 250 words on a specified topic is required. ALA Awards, ala.org.

ALA EBSCO Midwinter Meeting Sponsorships. Awards of up to $1,500 allowing librarians to attend ALA Midwinter Meeting. An essay of no more than 250 words on a specified topic is required. ALA Awards, ala.org.

ALA/AASL Frances Henne Award. A grant of $1,250 to a school library media specialist with less than five years in the profession to attend an AASL national conference or ALA Annual Conference for the first time. ALA American Association of School Librarians, ala.org/aasl/.

ALA/AASL Research Grant. Two grants totaling $5,000 to conduct innovative research aimed at measuring and evaluating the impact of school library media programs on learning and education. ALA American Association of School Librarians, ala.org/aasl/.

ALA/ACRL De Gruyter European Librarianship Study Grant. An annual grant of $3,000 for an academic or research librarian to support research on the acquisition, organization, or use of European library resources. The grant covers air travel, transportation, room, and board for up to 30 consecutive days. ALA Association of College and Research Libraries, ala.org/acrl/.

ALA/ALCTS First Step Award. A $1,500 grant to provide librarians new to the serials field to attend an ALA Annual Conference for the first time. ALA Association for Library Collections and Technical Services, ala.org/alcts/.

ALA/ALCTS Jan Merrill-Oldham Professional Development Grant. A $1,250 cash grant to a librarian or paraprofessional working in preservation for airfare, lodging, and registration fees related to attendance at the ALA Annual Conference. ALA Association for Library Collections and Technical Services, ala.org/alcts/.

ALA/ALSC Louise Seaman Bechtel Fellowship. Grant of $4,000 for ALSC members with eight or more years professional service to children, to read and study at the Baldwin Library of Historical Children's Literature at the University of Florida. ALA Association for Library Service to Children, ala.org/alsc/.

ALA/ALSC Penguin Young Readers Group Award. Four $600 awards to children's librarians with less than 10 years of experience in school or public libraries to attend ALA Annual Conference. ALA Association for Library Service to Children, ala.org/alsc/.

ALA/FAFLRT Adelaide Del Frate Conference Sponsorship. Award of $1,000 for attendance at ALA Annual Conference, to encourage library school students to become familiar with federal librarianship and seek work in federal libraries. ALA Federal and Armed Forces Libraries Round Table, ala.org/faflrt/.

ALA/GODORT NewsBank/Readex Catharine J. Reynolds Awards. Grants of up to a total of

$2,000 to documents librarians for travel or study in the field of documents librarianship. ALA Government Documents Round Table, ala.org/godort/.

ALA/IRO Bogle Pratt International Travel Fund. A $1,000 award to assist ALA members to attend their first international library conference. ALA International Relations Office, ala.org/iro/.

ALA/IRO Guadalajara International Book Fair Free Pass. Provides free Book Fair registration and lodging for up to 100 librarians who work in the area of Spanish-language acquisitions and/or are working to build their Spanish-language collections to better serve their communities and users. ALA International Relations Office, ala.org/iro/.

ALA/IRO Hong Kong Book Fair Free Pass. Provides free Book Fair registration and lodging for selected librarians from the U.S. and Canada who collect Chinese-language materials. ALA International Relations Office, ala.org/iro/.

ALA/LRRT Jesse H. Shera Award for the Support of Dissertation Research. A prize of $500 for library dissertation research employing exemplary design and methodology approved by the doctoral candidate's dissertation committee that is about to be employed or is in the initial stage of use. ALA Office for Research and Statistics, ala.org/lrrt/.

ALA/NMRT 3M Professional Development Grant. A cash award to attend ALA Annual Conference for NMRT members to encourage professional development and participation in ALA and NMRT activities. ALA New Members Round Table, ala.org/nmrt/.

ALA/NMRT Annual Conference Professional Development Attendance Award. Offers professional development and networking opportunities to three NMRT members by providing tickets to attend the Newbery/Caldecott/Wilder Banquet at the ALA Annual Conference. ALA New Members Round Table, ala.org/nmrt/.

ALA/NMRT Shirley Olofson Memorial Award. A $1,000 award to an NMRT member to help defray costs of attending ALA Annual Conference. ALA New Members Round Table, ala.org/nmrt/.

ALA/OFD Diversity Research Grants. Three annual awards of $2,000 for original research in three selected topics on diversity issues within the library profession and $500 travel grants to attend and present research results at ALA Annual Conference. ALA Office for Diversity, ala.org/diversity/.

ALA/OGR White House Conference on Library and Information Services Taskforce Award. A $300 stipend granted to a non-librarian advocate participating in Library Advocacy Day activities for the first time. ALA Office of Government Relations, ala.org/ogr/.

ALA/OITP Robert L. Oakley Memorial Scholarship. A $1,000 grant supporting research and advanced study for librarians in their early or mid-careers who are interested or active in intellectual property, public policy, and copyright. ALA Office for Information Technology Policy, ala.org/oitp/.

ALA/ORS Carroll Preston Baber Research Grant. Up to $3,000 for innovative research that could lead to an improvement in library services to any specified group(s) of people. ALA Office for Research and Statistics, ala.org/ors/.

ALA/PLA DEMCO New Leaders Travel Grant. Awards of up to $1,500 each, designed to enhance professional development and improve the expertise of public librarians new to the field by making possible their attendance at major professional development activities. ALA Public Library Association, ala.org/pla/.

ALA/RMRT Norman Horrocks–Scarecrow Press Annual Conference Award. A grant of $1,000 to help retired members defray the costs of attending an ALA conference. ALA Retired Members Round Table, ala.org/rmrt/.

ALA/RUSA Atlas Systems Mentoring Award. A grant of $1,250 to aid a library practitioner who is new to the field of interlibrary loan, document delivery, or electronic reserves with travel expenses to attend the ALA Annual Conference; a mentor is assigned to the recipients to help them navigate through the conference experience. ALA Reference and User Services Association, ala.org/rusa/.

ALA/RUSA Emerald Research Grant Award. A grant of $5,000 awarded to individuals seeking support to conduct research in business librarianship. ALA Reference and User Services Association, ala.org/rusa/.

ALA/RUSA Gale Cengage Learning Student Travel Award. An annual travel award of $1,000 that enables a student enrolled in an ALA-accredited master's degree program to attend ALA conference, including a one-year membership in the Business Reference and Services Section. ALA Reference and User Services Association, ala.org/rusa/.

ALA/RUSA Morningstar Public Librarian Support Award. A travel award of $1,000 to a public librarian who has performed outstanding business reference service and who requires financial assistance to attend the ALA Annual Conference. ALA Reference and User Services Association, ala.org/rusa/.

ALA/United for Libraries Gale Outstanding Trustee Conference Grant. Two awards of $850 each, to members currently serving on a local public library board, for first attendance at an ALA Annual Conference. ALA United for Libraries: Association of Library Trustees, Advocates, Friends, and Foundations, ala.org/united/.

ALA/YALSA Baker & Taylor Conference Grants. Two annual grants of $1,000 each awarded to young adult librarians in public and school libraries to attend an ALA Annual Conference for the first time. ALA Young Adult Library Services Association, ala.org/yalsa/.

ALA/YALSA Board Fellow Program. A $500 stipend to support a nonvoting member of the YALSA board to help defray travel, registration, and hotel costs for one year. ALA Young Adult Library Services Association, ala.org/yalsa/.

ALA/YALSA Midwinter Paper Presentation. YALSA's past presidents sponsor a paper presentation at Midwinter Meeting each year on trends impacting young adult services. The selected presenter will receive up to $1,500 to defray registration and travel costs. ALA Young Adult Library Services Association, ala.org/yalsa/.

ALA/YALSA Supporting Diversity Conference Stipend. Allows two YALSA members with diverse backgrounds to attend the ALA Annual Conference. ALA Young Adult Library Services Association, ala.org/yalsa/.

ALA/YALSA Young Adult Literature Symposium Stipend. Biennial stipends of up to $1,000 are awarded—one to a library worker and one to a student—to enable two qualified recipients to attend YALSA's Young Adult Literature Symposium. ALA Young Adult Library Services Association, ala.org/yalsa/.

ALISE Doctoral Students to ALISE Grant. Up to two awards in the amount of $500 to defray travel expenses and ALISE Conference registration. Association for Library and Information Science Education, www.alise.org.

ALISE OCLC Library and Information Science Research Grant. Awards to faculty of library and information science schools for independent research that helps librarians integrate new technologies into areas of traditional competence. Association for Library and Information Science Education, www.alise.org.

ALISE Research Grant Competition. One or more grants totaling $5,000 to support research broadly related to education for library and information science. Association for Library and Information Science Education, www.alise.org.

ALISE University of Washington Information School Youth Services Graduate Student Travel Award. A grant of $750 to support travel to the ALISE Annual Conference for an LIS student with a concentration in youth services. Association for Library and Information Science Education, www.alise.org.

APALA Sheila Suen Lai Research Grant. A grant to encourage APALA members to engage in research in Asian/Pacific librarianship. Asian Pacific American Librarians Association, www.apalaweb.org.

APALA Travel Grant. A grant of $500 to support travel to the ALA Annual Conference. Asian Pacific American Librarians Association, www.apalaweb.org.

ARLIS/NA Andrew Cahan Photography Award. An award of $1,000 for ARLIS/NA members in the field of photography to attend the ARLIS/NA conference. Art Libraries Society of North America, www.arlisna.org.

ARLIS/NA AskART Conference Attendance Award. An award of $1,000 to ARLIS/NA members active in the field of American art to attend the ARLIS/NA conference. Art Libraries Society of North America, www.arlisna.org.

ARLIS/NA Conference Attendance Award. An award of $1,000 for committee members, chapter officers, and moderators to attend the ARLIS/NA conference. Art Libraries Society of North America, www.arlisna.org.

ARLIS/NA Howard and Beverly Joy Karno Award. An award of $1,000 for art librarians in Latin America to attend the ARLIS/NA conference. Art Libraries Society of North America, www.arlisna.org.

ARLIS/NA H. W. Wilson Foundation Research Award. Awards of up to $3,000 in support of research activities by ARLIS/NA individual members in the fields of librarianship, visual resources curatorship, and the arts. Art Libraries Society of North America, www.arlisna.org.

ARLIS/NA Judith A. Hoffberg Student Award for Conference Attendance. An award of $1,000 for library students considering a career in art librarianship to attend the ARLIS/NA conference. Art Libraries Society of North America, www.arlisna.org.

ARLIS/NA Merrill Wadsworth Smith Travel Award in Architecture Librarianship. An award of $1,000 to ARLIS/NA members who are architecture librarians to attend the ARLIS/NA conference. Art Libraries Society of North America, www.arlisna.org.

ARLIS/NA Puvill Libros Award. An award of $1,000 for art librarians in Europe to attend the ARLIS/NA conference. Art Libraries Society of North America, www.arlisna.org.

ARLIS/NA Samuel H. Kress Foundation Award for European Travel. An award to ARLIS/NA members to support participation and professional development at European conferences. Art Libraries Society of North America, www.arlisna.org.

ARLIS/NA Student Conference Attendance Award. An award of $1,000 to help finance attendance at the ARLIS/NA conference for a library school student who is an ARLIS/NA member and considering a career in art librarianship. Art Libraries Society of North America, www.arlisna.org.

ARLIS/NA Student Diversity Award for Conference Attendance. An award of $1,000 for library students in traditionally underrepresented groups who are considering a career in art librarianship to attend the ARLIS/NA conference. Art Libraries Society of North America, www.arlisna.org.

ARSL Bernard Vavrek Scholarship. A $500 stipend to a current library student to attend the ARSL annual conference. Association for Rural and Small Libraries, www.arsl.info.

ARSL Founders Scholarship. A $500 stipend to a library staff member working in a small or rural library to attend the ARSL annual conference. Association for Rural and Small Libraries, www.arsl.info.

ARSL Ken Davenport Scholarship. A $500 stipend to a library staff member working in a small or rural library to attend the ARSL annual conference. Association for Rural and Small Libraries, www.arsl.info.

ASIS&T History Fund Research Grant. A maximum of $1,000 for the best research in support of a proposal within the history of information science and technology. American Society for Information Science and Technology, www.asis.org.

ASIS&T New Leaders Award. Travel expense reimbursement of up to $700 the first year and $300 the second year to recruit, engage, and retain new ASIS&T members in their first three years of membership. American Society for Information Science and Technology, www.asis.org.

ASIS&T ProQuest Doctoral Dissertation Award. An award of $1,000 and up to $500 in travel support to recognize outstanding recent doctoral candidates, provide a forum for presenting their research, and assist them with some travel support. American Society for Information Science and Technology, www.asis.org.

ATLA Publication Grants. Grants of up to $4,000 to one or more recipients to aid in the development of a scholarly work that advances some aspect of theological librarianship or provides bibliographic access to a significant body of literature within theological or religious studies. American Theological Library Association, www.atla.com.

BSA Fellowships. Stipends of $1,500–$6,000 in support of travel, living, and research expenses to support bibliographical inquiry as well as research in the history of the book trades and in publishing history. Bibliographical Society of America, www.bibsocamer.org.

CALA C. C. Seetoo Conference Travel Scholarship. A $500 award for students of Chinese heritage in a graduate program in library and information science to attend ALA Annual Conference. Chinese American Librarians Association, cala-web.org.

CALA Conference Travel Grants. Up to four awards of $500 each for CALA members to travel to library and information science conferences. Chinese American Librarians Association, cala-web.org.

CALA Sally C. Tseng Professional Development Grant. Annual grants of up to $1,000 to CALA members in support of library research. Chinese American Librarians Association, cala-web.org.

CALL Eunice Beeson Memorial Bursary. Assists CALL members who wish to attend the annual meeting but are unable to do so for financial reasons. Canadian Association of Law Libraries, www.callacbd.ca.

CALL James D. Lang Memorial Scholarship. Supports attendance of a CALL member at a continuing education program. Canadian Association of Law Libraries, www.callacbd.ca.

CALL Janine Miller Fellowship. Provides funding of up to $2,500 (Can.) for a CALL member to attend the Law Via the Internet Conference, held annually. Canadian Association of Law Libraries, www.callacbd.ca.

CALL Northern Exposure to Leadership Grant. Assists with registration and travel costs to the

Northern Exposure to Leadership Institute. Canadian Association of Law Libraries, www.callacbd.ca.

CALL Research Grant. Up to $3,000 (Can.) to conduct research that promotes an understanding of legal information sources or law librarianship. Canadian Association of Law Libraries, www.callacbd.ca.

CHLA Professional Development Grant. A grant of $250 (Can.) to enhance access to professional development opportunities for individual CHLA members. Canadian Health Libraries Association, www.chla-absc.ca.

CHLA Rural and Remote Opportunities Grant. A cash grant of $300 (Can.) to support continuing education activities for members in rural or remote communities. Canadian Health Libraries Association, www.chla-absc.ca.

CILIP/IFLA Aspire Award. Provides travel funds for new professionals to attend CILIP and IFLA conferences. International Federation of Library Associations and Institutions, www.ifla.org.

CLA Chancellor Group Conference Grant. A $500 (Can.) travel grant to support attendance of newly qualified teacher-librarians at the CLA conference. Canadian Library Association, www.cla.ca.

CLA Library Research and Development Grants. One or more grants totaling $1,000 (Can.) awarded annually to personal members of the Canadian Library Association in support of theoretical and applied research in library and information science. Canadian Library Association, www.cla.ca.

CLA/CLSS Sister Sally Daly Memorial Grant. A $1,500 grant for a new member of the Children's Library Services Section to attend the CLA convention. Catholic Library Association, www.cathla.org.

CLIR Mellon Fellowships for Dissertation Research in Original Sources. Fifteen fellowships of $2,000 per month for 9–12 months to support dissertation research in the humanities in original sources. Council on Library and Information Resources, www.clir.org.

CLIR Rovelstad Scholarship in International Librarianship. Provides all expenses for a student of library and information science to attend the annual IFLA World Library and Information Congress. Council on Library and Information Resources, www.clir.org.

CSLA Pat Tabler Memorial Scholarship Award. Recognizes and pays conference expenses for a beginning librarian who has shown initiative and creativity in starting or renewing a congregational library. Church and Synagogue Library Association, cslainfo.org.

Educause Jane N. Ryland Fellowship Program. Grants established to expand opportunities for information technology professionals to attend Educause events. Educause, www.educause.edu.

Fulbright Specialist Program. Short-term grants of two to six weeks to U.S. scholars and professionals to consult, teach, or work in overseas academic institutions. Council for International Exchange of Scholars, www.cies.org/specialists/.

IASL Jean Lowrie Leadership Development Grant. $1,000 and conference fees for school librarians in developing nations to attend an IASL conference. International Association of School Librarianship, www.iasl-online.org.

IASL Ken Haycock Leadership Development Grant. $1,000 and conference fees for school librarians in any country to attend an IASL conference. International Association of School Librarianship, www.iasl-online.org.

IASL Takeshi Murofushi Research Award. A $500 grant to fund research in school librarianship. International Association of School Librarianship, www.iasl-online.org.

IFLA/OCLC Jay Jordan Early Career Development Fellowship. Up to six individuals, including a theological librarian, are selected for participation in this intensive five-week fellowship program. Four weeks are based at OCLC headquarters in Dublin, Ohio; one week is based at OCLC in Leiden, Netherlands. The program gives fellows opportunities to meet with leading information practitioners, visit libraries, and explore topics including information technologies, library operations and management, and global cooperative librarianship. International Federation of Library Associations and Institutions, www.ifla.org.

MELA George Atiyeh Prize. An annual cash award to attend the annual meetings of MELA and the Middle East Studies Association of North America. Middle East Librarians Association, www.mela.us.

MLA Cunningham Memorial International Fellowship. A fellowship for health sciences librarians from countries outside the United States and Canada to provide for observation and supervised work in one or more medical libraries in North America. The award is $6,000, with up to $2,000 additional for travel within these two countries. Medical Library Association, www.mlanet.org.

MLA David A. Kronick Traveling Fellowship. A $2,000 fellowship to cover the expenses involved in traveling to three or more medical libraries in the United States or Canada, for the purpose of studying a specific aspect of health information management. Medical Library Association, www.mlanet.org.

MLA Donald A. B. Lindberg Research Fellowship. An annual grant of $10,000 to fund research linking the information services provided by librarians to improved health care and advances in biomedical research. Medical Library Association, www.mlanet.org.

MLA EBSCO Annual Meeting Grant. Awards of up to $1,000 for travel and conference-related expenses to four health science librarians to attend the MLA meeting. Medical Library Association, www.mlanet.org.

MLA Research, Development, and Demonstration Project Grants. These provide support for projects that will help to promote excellence in the field of health sciences librarianship and information sciences. Grants range from $100 to $1,000. Medical Library Association, www.mlanet.org.

MLA/HLS Professional Development Grants. Given twice a year, this award provides librarians working in hospital and similar clinical settings with the support needed for educational or research activities. Medical Library Association, Hospital Libraries Section, www.mlanet.org.

MLA/MIS Career Development Grant. This award provides $1,500 to support a career development activity that will contribute to advancement in the field of medical informatics. Medical Library Association, Medical Informatics Section, www.mlanet.org.

MLA Carol June Bradley Award. A $1,000 grant to support research into the history of music libraries and music librarianship. Music Library Association, www.musiclibraryassoc.org.

MLA Dena Epstein Award. A $2,100 grant to support archival and library research in American music. Music Library Association, www.musiclibraryassoc.org.

MLA Kevin Freeman Travel Grant. Conference registration fee and a cash award of up to $750 to support travel and hotel expenses to attend the MLA annual meeting. Music Library Association, www.musiclibraryassoc.org.

MLA Lenore F. Coral IAML Travel Grant. Supports travel to the International Association of Music Libraries annual meeting. Music Library Association, www.musiclibraryassoc.org.

MLA Walter Gerboth Award. An award of up to $1,000 to MLA-member music librarians in the first five years of their professional careers, to assist research in progress. Music Library Association, www.musiclibraryassoc.org.

Mortensen Center Summer Associates Program. Offers library and information science professionals from outside the United States an opportunity to explore and engage with current issues and trends in the field. Mortensen Center, University of Illinois at Urbana-Champaign, www.library.illinois.edu/mortensen/associates/.

NASIG Horizon Award. Provides funding to attend NASIG annual conference for a practicing serials librarian. North American Serials Interest Group, www.nasig.org.

NASIG John Merriman Joint UK Serials Group Award. A $6,000 award supporting two people, one from each association, and consisting of travel to the sister conference, and accommodations for the duration of the conference. North American Serials Interest Group, www.nasig.org.

NASIG John Riddick Student Grants. Encourage participation at NASIG conferences by funding students enrolled in an ALA-accredited school who are interested in pursuing some aspect of serials work upon completion of their professional degrees. North American Serials Interest Group, www.nasig.org.

NASIG Marcia Tuttle International Grant. A $3,000 grant for a NASIG member working in serials to foster international communication and education. North American Serials Interest Group, www.nasig.org.

NASIG Rose Robischon Scholarship. Offers funding for a NASIG member to attend the NASIG annual conferemce. North American Serials Interest Group, www.nasig.org.

NASIG Serials Specialist Award. Provides funding for a serials paraprofessional to attend the NASIG annual conferemce. North American Serials Interest Group, www.nasig.org.

OHA Emerging Crises Research Fund. A grant of up to $3,000 to undertake oral history research in situations of crisis research in the United States and internationally. Oral History Association, www.oralhistory.org.

SAA Donald Peterson Student Travel Awards. Awards up to $1,000 to an archives student or recent graduate in support of registration, travel, and housing at the SAA Annual Conference. Society of American Archivists, www.archivists.org.

SAA Harold T. Pinkett Minority Student Award. Supports full registration and related expenses of hotel and travel to attend the SAA annual meeting. Awarded to a minority student who manifests an interest in becoming a professional archivist. Society of American Archivists, www.archivists. org.

SAA Oliver Wendell Holmes Award. Assists overseas archivists already in the United States or Canada for training, to travel to or attend the SAA annual meeting. Society of American Archivists, www.archivists.org.

SALALM Enlace Travel Awards. Assists Latin American or Caribbean librarians with travel to the SALALM conference. Seminar on the Acquisition of Latin American Library Materials, salalm. org.

SALALM Presidential Travel Fellowships. Provides up to $1,000 for Latin American studies librarians for travel to the SALALM conference. Seminar on the Acquisition of Latin American Library Materials, salalm.org.

Awards

For individual or group achievement

AALL Chapter Professional Development Awards. Recognizes significant achievements in designing outstanding professional development programs for its members and other librarians and to reward chapters for performing well. American Association of Law Libraries, www.aallnet.org.

AALL Emerging Leader Award. Recognizes newer members who have already made significant contributions to the association or to the profession. American Association of Law Libraries, www.aallnet.org.

AALL Hall of Fame Award. Recognizes members whose contributions to the profession and service to the association have been significant, substantial, and long-standing. American Association of Law Libraries, www.aallnet.org.

AALL Marian Gould Gallagher Distinguished Service Award. Recognizes sustained service to law librarianship, exemplary service to AALL, or contributions to the professional literature. American Association of Law Libraries, www.aallnet.org.

AALL Presidential Certificate of Appreciation/Merit. Awarded annually at the discretion of the AALL President in recognition of exceptional achievements and contributions to the profession. American Association of Law Libraries, www.aallnet.org.

AALL Volunteer Service Award. Honors members who have made a significant contribution to the work of AALL. American Association of Law Libraries, www.aallnet.org.

AALL/ALL Frederick Charles Hicks Award. Recognizes an individual or group who has made outstanding contributions to academic law librarianship. American Association of Law Libraries, Academic Law Libraries Special Interest Section, www.aallnet.org.

AALL/ALL Outstanding Service Award. Honors an ALL member who has made outstanding contributions to the section in section activity and professional service. American Association of Law Libraries, Academic Law Libraries Special Interest Section, www.aallnet.org.

AALL/FCIL Daniel L. Wade Outstanding Service Award. Honors an FCIL member who has made outstanding contributions in section activity and professional service. American Association of Law Libraries, Foreign, Comparative, and International Law Special Interest Section, www.aallnet.org.

AALL/FCIL Spirit of the FCIL-SIS Award. Honors a section member. American Association of Law Libraries, Foreign, Comparative, and International Law Special Interest Section, www.aallnet. org.

AALL/PLL Emerging Leader Award. Recognizes newer members who have made significant contributions to the profession. American Association of Law Libraries, Private Law Libraries Special Interest Section, www.aallnet.org.

AALL/PLL Service Award. Honors a member who has made a significant contribution to the work of the section. American Association of Law Libraries, Private Law Libraries Special Interest Section, www.aallnet.org.

AALL/SCCLL Bethany J. Ochal Award. Given to a member who has made a significant contribution to law librarianship and who is nearing the end of his or her library career or who has recently retired. American Association of Law Libraries, State, Court, and County Law Libraries Special Interest Section, www.aallnet.org.

AALL/TS Renee D. Chapman Memorial Award. Recognizes extended and sustained distinguished service to technical services law librarianship. American Association of Law Libraries, Technical

Services Special Interest Section, www.aallnet.org.

AASLH Award of Merit. Presented to an organization or individual to recognize excellence for projects (including civic engagement, special projects, educational programs, exhibits, publications, restoration projects), individual achievement, and organizational general excellence. American Association for State and Local History, www.aaslh.org.

ACL Emily Russel Award. A monetary gift and plaque given to honor foreign service, special achievement, publication, innovative initiatives, or organizational activities. Association of Christian Librarians, www.acl.org.

ACL Lifetime Achievement Award. Recognition of an ACL member for significant contributions to the association or the field. Association of Christian Librarians, www.acl.org.

ACMLA Honours Award. Recognizes distinguished service to the field of map librarianship, curatorship, or archives. Association of Canadian Map Libraries and Archives, www.acmla.org.

AECT Distinguished Service Award. Granted to a person who has shown outstanding leadership in advancing the theory and/or practice of educational communications and technology for over 10 years. Association for Educational Communications and Technology, aect.site-ym.com.

AECT Robert deKieffer International Fellowship Award. A cash award of $200 presented to an individual in recognition of professional leadership in the field of educational communications and technology in a foreign country. Association for Educational Communications and Technology, aect.site-ym.com.

AECT Special Service Award. Presented to an individual who has shown notable service to AECT over the past 10 years. Association for Educational Communications and Technology, aect.site-ym.com.

AECT/DDL/Information Age Publishers Distance Education Best Practices Award. Presented for a best practice in any aspect of distance education. Association for Educational Communications and Technology, aect.site-ym.com.

AIIP Marilyn Levine President's Award. Given in recognition of any person or institution that has demonstrated extraordinary support to the objectives of the association. Association of Independent Information Professionals, www.aiip.org.

AIIP Pam Wegmann International Award. Recognizes the contributions made by an AIIP member who lives outside of North America. Association of Independent Information Professionals, www.aiip.org.

AJL Fanny Goldstein Merit Award. Recognizes loyal and ongoing contributions to AJL and the profession of Jewish librarianship. Association of Jewish Libraries, www.jewishlibraries.org.

AJL Life Membership Award. Recognizes outstanding leadership and professional contributions to AJL and the profession of Jewish librarianship. Association of Jewish Libraries, www.jewishlibraries.org.

ALA Beta Phi Mu Award. A $1,000 award presented to a library school faculty member or an individual for distinguished service to education for librarianship. ALA Awards, ala.org.

ALA Elizabeth Futas Catalyst for Change Award. A $1,000 biennial award to honor a librarian who invests time and talent to make positive changes in the profession of librarianship. ALA Awards, ala.org.

ALA Honorary Membership. Conferred on a living citizen of any country whose contribution to librarianship or a closely related field is so outstanding that it is of lasting importance to the advancement of the whole field of library service. ALA Awards, ala.org.

ALA Joseph W. Lippincott Award. A $1,000 award to a librarian for an outstanding contribution to the profession. ALA Awards, ala.org.

ALA Melvil Dewey Medal. A citation presented to an individual or a group for recent creative achievement of a high order, particularly in those fields in which Melvil Dewey was interested, notably library management, library training, cataloging and classification, and the tools and techniques of librarianship. ALA Awards, ala.org.

ALA/ACRL Academic or Research Librarian of the Year Award. A $5,000 award for a significant national or international contribution to academic or research librarianship and library development. ALA Association of College and Research Libraries, ala.org/acrl/.

ALA/ACRL Award for Career Achievement in Women's Studies Librarianship. An award for outstanding contributions in women's studies through accomplishments and service to the profession. ALA Association of College and Research Libraries, ala.org/acrl/.

ALA/ACRL Award for Significant Achievement in Women's Studies Librarianship. An award for outstanding contributions in women's studies through accomplishments and service to the profession. ALA Association of College and Research Libraries, ala.org/acrl/.

ALA/ACRL Distinguished Education and Behavioral Sciences Librarian Award. This $2,000 award honors a distinguished academic librarian who has made an outstanding contribution as an education and/or behavioral sciences librarian. ALA Association of College and Research Libraries, ala.org/acrl/.

ALA/ACRL EBSCO Community College Learning Resources Leadership Award. An award of $500 to individuals or groups from two-year institutions to recognize significant leadership. ALA Association of College and Research Libraries, ala.org/acrl/.

ALA/ACRL Innovation in Science and Technology Librarianship. A $3,000 award that recognizes creative, innovative approaches to solving problems or improving products and services in science and technology librarianship. ALA Association of College and Research Libraries, ala.org/acrl/.

ALA/ACRL Marta Lange/CQ Press Award. This $1,000 award recognizes an academic or law librarian for contributions to bibliography and information service in law or political science. ALA Association of College and Research Libraries, ala.org/acrl/.

ALA/ACRL Miriam Dudley Instruction Librarian Award. A cash award of $1,000 to an individual who has made an especially significant contribution to the advancement of instruction in a college or research library environment. ALA Association of College and Research Libraries, ala.org/acrl/.

ALA/ACRL ProQuest Innovation in College Librarianship Award. A $3,000 award to recognize an innovative project in a college library primarily serving undergraduates. ALA Association of College and Research Libraries, ala.org/acrl/.

ALA/ACRL Routledge Distance Learning Librarianship Conference Sponsorship Award. An award of $1,200 to a librarian working in the field of distance learning librarianship to defray the costs of attending an ALA conference. ALA Association of College and Research Libraries, ala.org/acrl/.

ALA/ACRL Special Presidential Recognition Award. Highlights excellence among ACRL members who have provided outstanding service to the association and the profession. ALA Association of College and Research Libraries, ala.org/acrl/.

ALA/ACRL/LLAMA/LITA/ALCTS Hugh C. Atkinson Memorial Award. An annual cash award to recognize outstanding accomplishments by an academic librarian who has worked in the areas of library automation or management and made contributions (including risk-taking) toward the improvement of library services or library development and research. Jointly administered by ALA's ACRL, LLAMA, LITA, and ALCTS divisions. ALA Association of College and Research Libraries, ala.org/acrl/.

ALA/ALCTS Esther J. Piercy Award. An annual $1,500 award to recognize contributions by a librarian in technical services with not more than 10 years professional experience. ALA Association for Library Collections and Technical Services, ala.org/alcts/.

ALA/ALCTS George Cunha and Susan Swartzburg Award. An annual award of $1,250 that acknowledges and supports cooperative preservation projects or rewards individuals or groups that foster collaboration for preservation goals. ALA Association for Library Collections and Technical Services, ala.org/alcts/.

ALA/ALCTS Harrassowitz Award for Leadership in Library Acquisitions. This award of $1,500 is given to recognize the contributions by and outstanding leadership of an individual in the field of acquisitions librarianship. ALA Association for Library Collections and Technical Services, ala.org/alcts/.

ALA/ALCTS Margaret Mann Citation. An annual citation for outstanding professional achievement in cataloging or classification through publication, participation, or contributions over the previous five years. OCLC will donate a $2,000 scholarship to the U.S. or Canadian library school of the winner's choice. ALA Association for Library Collections and Technical Services, ala.org/alcts/.

ALA/ALCTS Paul Banks and Carolyn Harris Preservation Award. A $1,500 award to recognize the contribution of a professional preservation specialist who has been active in the field of preservation or conservation for library or archival materials. ALA Association for Library Collections and Technical Services, ala.org/alcts/.

ALA/ALCTS Presidential Citation. Honors ALCTS members who make significant contributions to the division and to the profession but whose accomplishments do not fall within the criteria for other awards. ALA Association for Library Collections and Technical Services, ala.org/alcts/.

ALA/ALCTS Ross Atkinson Lifetime Achievement Award. An annual award of $3,000 to recognize the contribution of a library leader through demonstrated exceptional service to ALCTS and its areas of interest (acquisitions, cataloging and classification, collection management and development, preservation and reformatting, and serials). ALA Association for Library Collections and Technical Services, ala.org/alcts/.

ALA/ALCTS Ulrich's Serials Librarianship Award. An annual $1,500 award for distinguished contributions to serials librarianship, including leadership in serials-related activities through participation in professional associations or library education programs, contributions to serials literature, research in the area of serials, or development of tools to enhance serials access or management. ALA Association for Library Collections and Technical Services, ala.org/alcts/.

ALA/ASCLA Cathleen Bourdon Service Award. A citation presented to recognize an ASCLA member for outstanding service and leadership to the division. ALA Association of Specialized and Cooperative Library Agencies, ala.org/ascla/.

ALA/ASCLA Leadership and Professional Achievement Award. A citation for leadership and achievement in consulting, multitype library cooperation, or state library development. ALA Association of Specialized and Cooperative Library Agencies, ala.org/ascla/.

ALA/EMIERT Distinguished Librarian Award. Honors significant accomplishments in library services that are national or international in scope and that include improving, spreading, and promoting multicultural librarianship. ALA Ethnic and Multicultural Information Exchange Round Table, ala.org/emiert/.

ALA/FAFLRT Achievement Award. Recognizes achievement in the promotion of library and information service in the federal community. ALA Federal and Armed Forces Library Round Table, ala.org/faflrt/.

ALA/FAFLRT Distinguished Service Award. Recognizes a FAFLRT member for outstanding and sustained contributions. ALA Federal and Armed Forces Library Round Table, ala.org/faflrt/.

ALA/IRO John Ames Humphry/OCLC/Forest Press Award. This $1,000 award is given to a librarian or other person who has made significant contributions to international librarianship. ALA International Relations Office, ala.org/iro/.

ALA/MAGIRT Honors Award. Cash award and a citation to recognize lifetime achievement and outstanding contributions to map librarianship. ALA Map and Geospatial Information Round Table, ala.org/magirt/.

ALA/NMRT Student Chapter of the Year Award. Given to an ALA student chapter in recognition of its outstanding contributions. ALA New Members Round Table, ala.org/nmrt/.

ALA/OFD Achievement in Library Diversity Research. Complimentary ALA Annual Conference registration awarded to an ALA member who has made a significant contribution to diversity research in the profession. ALA Office for Diversity, ala.org/diversity/.

ALA/PIO Carnegie Corporation of New York/*New York Times* I Love My Librarian Award. This annual award encourages library users to recognize the accomplishments of academic, public, or school librarians for their efforts to improve the lives of people in their communities. Up to 10 winners are selected to receive a $5,000 cash award, a plaque, and $500 travel stipend to attend an awards reception in New York City. ALA Public Information Office, ala.org/pio/.

ALA/PLA Allie Beth Martin Award. An award of $3,000 to a librarian who, in a public library setting, has demonstrated extraordinary range and depth of knowledge about books or other library materials and has distinguished ability to share that knowledge. ALA Public Library Association, ala.org/pla/.

ALA/PLA Charlie Robinson Award. A $1,000 award to a library director who, over a period of at least seven years, has been a risk-taker, innovator, or change agent in a public library. ALA Public Library Association, ala.org/pla/.

ALA/RUSA Gale Cengage Learning Award for Excellence in Business Librarianship. A $3,000 award given to recognize an individual who has made a significant contribution to business librarianship. ALA Reference and User Services Association, ala.org/rusa/.

ALA/RUSA Genealogical Publishing Company Award. A citation and $1,500 cash award to a librarian, library, or publisher to encourage professional achievement in historical reference and research librarianship. ALA Reference and User Services Association, ala.org/rusa/.

ALA/RUSA Isadore Gilbert Mudge Award. An annual award of $5,000 and a citation to an individual who has made a distinguished contribution to reference librarianship. ALA Reference and User Services Association, ala.org/rusa/.

ALA/RUSA Margaret E. Monroe Library Adult Services Award. A citation to honor a librarian who has made significant contributions to library adult services. ALA Reference and User Services Association, ala.org/rusa/.

ALA/RUSA MARS Achievement Recognition Certificate ("My Favorite Martian"). Given to an individual in recognition of service to the Machine-Assisted Reference Section. ALA Reference and User Services Association, ala.org/rusa/.

ALA/RUSA RSS Service Achievement Award. Given to a Reference Services Section member for a significant contribution to the work of the section. ALA Reference and User Services Association, ala.org/rusa/.

ALA/RUSA Virginia Boucher/OCLC Distinguished Interlibrary Loan Librarian Award. An award of $2,000 to an individual for outstanding professional achievement, leadership, and contributions to interlibrary loan and document delivery. ALA Reference and User Services Association, ala.org/rusa/.

ALA/United for Libraries Major Benefactors Honor Award. Recognition to individuals, families, or corporate bodies who have made major gifts to public libraries. ALA United for Libraries: Association of Library Trustees, Advocates, Friends, and Foundations, ala.org/united/.

ALA/United for Libraries National Friends of Libraries Week Award. Recognizes Friends groups for activities and programming presented during National Friends of Libraries Week. ALA United for Libraries: Association of Library Trustees, Advocates, Friends, and Foundations, ala.org/united/.

ALISE Award for Professional Contribution to Library and Information Science Education. For contributions that promote and enhance the status of library/information science education. Association for Library and Information Science Education, www.alise.org.

ALISE Award for Teaching Excellence in the Field of Library and Information Science Education. For regular and sustained excellence in teaching library and information science. Association for Library and Information Science Education, www.alise.org.

ALISE Norman Horrocks Leadership Award. An award of $500 that recognizes a new ALISE member who has demonstrated outstanding leadership qualities in professional ALISE activities. Association for Library and Information Science Education, www.alise.org.

ALISE Service Award. Given to an ALISE member for regular and sustained service through the holding of various offices and positions or fulfilling specific responsibilities for the organization. Association for Library and Information Science Education, www.alise.org.

ARLIS/NA Distinguished Service Award. Honors an individual in the field of art librarianship or visual resources curatorship who has made an outstanding contribution to art information. Art Libraries Society of North America, www.arlisna.org.

ARSC Award for Distinguished Service to Historical Recordings. This award honors a person who has made outstanding contributions to the field of recorded sound, outside of published works or discographic research. Association for Recorded Sound Collections, www.arsc-audio.org.

ASI Hines Award. Honors those members who have provided exceptional service to ASI. American Society of Indexers, www.asindexing.org.

ASI Order of the Kohlrabi. A pin given to ASI members for service and support to the organization. American Society of Indexers, www.asindexing.org.

ASIS&T Award of Merit. A Revere bowl and certificate to recognize an individual for noteworthy contributions to the field of information science. American Society for Information Science and Technology, www.asis.org.

ASIS&T James M. Cretsos Leadership Award. To recognize a new ASIS&T member who has demonstrated outstanding leadership qualities in association activities. American Society for Information Science and Technology, www.asis.org.

ASIS&T Thomson Reuters Outstanding Information Science Teacher Award. An award of $1,000 and up to $500 in travel support to recognize the unique teaching contribution of an individual as a teacher of information science. American Society for Information Science and Technology, www.asis.org.

ASIS&T Watson Davis Award. To recognize an ASIS&T member who has shown continuous dedicated service to the membership through active participation in and support of the association's programs. American Society for Information Science and Technology, www.asis.org.

BCALA Appreciation Awards. Given to BCALA members. Black Caucus of the American Library Association, www.bcala.org.

BCALA Distinguished Service Awards. Two awards given to BCALA members for outstanding service to the association and to the profession. Black Caucus of the American Library Association, www.bcala.org.

BCALA Professional Achievement Award. Given to a BCALA member. Black Caucus of the American Library Association, www.bcala.org.

BCALA Trailblazer's Award. Presented once every five years in recognition of an individual whose pioneering contributions have been outstanding and unique, and whose efforts have "blazed a trail" in the profession. Black Caucus of the American Library Association, www.bcala.org.

CALA Distinguished Service Award. To a CALA member for outstanding service to the profession. Chinese American Librarians Association, cala-web.org.

CALA President's Recognition Award. To a CALA member for service to the association. Chinese American Librarians Association, cala-web.org.

CALL Denis Marshall Memorial Award for Excellence in Law Librarianship. An award of $3,000 (Can.) to attend the CALL annual conference for a member who has provided outstanding service to the association or law librarianship. Canadian Association of Law Libraries, www.callacbd.ca.

CALL Honoured Members. Honors individuals who have made an outstanding contribution to the advancement of law librarianship. Canadian Association of Law Libraries, www.callacbd.ca.

CBHL Charles Robert Long Award. Given to a CBHL member for distinguished service and achievement. Council on Botanical and Horticultural Libraries, www.cbhl.net.

CHLA Canadian Hospital Librarian of the Year. Honors a hospital librarian who has made a significant contribution to health care or health librarianship in Canada. Canadian Health Libraries Association, www.chla-absc.ca.

CHLA Emerging Leader Award. Recognizes the contribution of a librarian in the early years of a career in health librarianship in Canada. Canadian Health Libraries Association, www.chla-absc.ca.

CHLA Flower Award for Innovation. An annual award to recognize Canadian librarians or teams who have created or demonstrated improvements in health sciences library services for their users or the profession through innovative thinking and approaches. Canadian Health Libraries Association, www.chla-absc.ca.

CHLA Margaret Ridley Charlton Award for Outstanding Achievement. Honors an individual who has made a significant contribution to the field of health sciences librarianship in Canada. Canadian Health Libraries Association, www.chla-absc.ca.

CLA Alan MacDonald Mentorship Award. An award in recognition of a commitment to mentoring activities either in the workplace or in an association. Canadian Library Association, www.cla.ca.

CLA Emerging Leader Award. Recognizes a CLA member with less than five years' experience in the library field who demonstrates leadership or active participation in association work. Canadian Library Association, www.cla.ca.

CLA Outstanding Service to Librarianship Award. An award for distinguished service in the field of Canadian librarianship. Canadian Library Association, www.cla.ca.

CLA Mary A. Grant Volunteer Service Award. Recognizes outstanding volunteer service to the association. Catholic Library Association, www.cathla.org.

CLA/PCLSS Aggiornamento Award. For an outstanding contribution to the renewal of parish and community life. Catholic Library Association, Parish and Community Library Services Section, www.cathla.org.

CSLA Award for Outstanding Congregational Librarian. Recognizes a church or synagogue librarian who exhibits distinguished service to his/her congregation and/or community through devotion to the ministry of congregational librarianship. Church and Synagogue Library Association, cslainfo.org.

CSLA Award for Outstanding Contribution to Congregational Libraries. Given to a person or institution that has provided inspiration, guidance, leadership, or resources to enrich the field of church or synagogue libraries. Church and Synagogue Library Association, cslainfo.org.

Educause Leadership Award. Recognizes exemplary leadership that has a significant and positive impact on advancing the theory and practice of information technology in higher education. Educause, www.educause.edu.

Educause Rising Star Award. Recognizes an information technology professional who, while early in his or her career, demonstrates exceptional leadership and accomplishment in the area of information technology in higher education. Educause, www.educause.edu.

FLICC Federal Librarian of the Year. This award recognizes and commends outstanding, innovative, and sustained professional achievements by a federal librarian. Federal Library and Information Center Committee, www.loc.gov/flicc/.

FLICC Federal Library Technician of the Year. This award recognizes and commends outstanding, innovative, and sustained achievements by a federal library technician. Federal Library and Information Center Committee, www.loc.gov/flicc/.

GIS Mary B. Ansari Distinguished Service Award. Recognizes significant contributions to the geoscience information profession. Geoscience Information Society, www.geoinfo.org.

IFLA Communicator of the Year Award. Honors the activities of any communicator of any IFLA member group. International Federation of Library Associations and Institutions, www.ifla.org.

IFLA Honorary Fellow. Conferred on an individual who has delivered long and distinguished service to IFLA. International Federation of Library Associations and Institutions, www.ifla.org.

IFLA Medal. Conferred on an individual in the country hosting the annual World Library and Information Congress who has made a distinguished contribution either to IFLA or to international librarianship. International Federation of Library Associations and Institutions, www.ifla.org.

MELA David H. Partington Award. Grants public recognition to MELA members who have displayed a high standard of excellence and accomplishments in and contributions to the field of Middle East librarianship, librarianship in general, and the world of scholarship. Middle East Librarians Association, www.mela.us.

MELA M. Lesley Wilkins Education Award. A $1,000 cash prize awarded in alternate years to an individual who made significant contributions to education and mentorship in Middle East librarianship. Middle East Librarians Association, www.mela.us.

MLA Carla J. Funk Governmental Relations Award. A $500 award that recognizes a medical librarian who has demonstrated outstanding leadership in the area of governmental relations at the federal, state, or local level and who has furthered the goal of providing quality information for improved health. Medical Library Association, www.mlanet.org.

MLA Distinguished Public Service Award. Presented to honor persons, most often legislators, whose exemplary actions have served to advance the health, welfare, and intellectual freedom of the public. Medical Library Association, www.mlanet.org.

MLA Estelle Brodman Award for the Academic Medical Librarian of the Year. A cash award that recognizes an academic medical librarian at mid-career level who demonstrates significant achievement, the potential for leadership, and continuing excellence. Medical Library Association, www.mlanet.org.

MLA Fellows and Honorary Members. Recognizes MLA members and nonmembers who have made outstanding contributions to the advancement of medical librarianship by conferring a special membership status. Medical Library Association, www.mlanet.org.

MLA Lois Ann Colaianni Award for Excellence and Achievement in Hospital Librarianship. Given to an MLA member who has made significant contributions to the profession through overall distinction or leadership in hospital library administration or service, production of a definitive publication related to hospital librarianship, teaching, research, advocacy, or the development of innovative technology to hospital librarianship. Medical Library Association, www.mlanet.org.

MLA Louise Darling Medal. Presented annually to recognize distinguished achievement in collection development in the health sciences. Medical Library Association, www.mlanet.org.

MLA Lucretia W. McClure Excellence in Education Award. Honors outstanding practicing librarians or library educators in the field of health sciences librarianship and informatics who demonstrate skills in teaching, curriculum development, mentoring, research, or leadership in education at local, regional, or national levels. Medical Library Association, www.mlanet.org.

MLA Marcia C. Noyes Award. Recognizes a career that has resulted in lasting, outstanding contributions to health sciences librarianship. Medical Library Association, www.mlanet.org.

MLA President's Award. Given to an MLA member for a notable or important contribution to medical librarianship in the past year. Medical Library Association, www.mlanet.org.

MLA T. Mark Hodges International Service Award. Honors outstanding individual achievement in promoting, enabling, or delivering improvements in the quality of health information internationally through the development of health information professionals, the improvement of libraries, or an increased use of health information services. Medical Library Association, www.mlanet.org.

MLA Virginia L. and William K. Beatty Volunteer Service Award. Recognizes a medical librarian for service to the association and health sciences librarianship. Medical Library Association, www.mlanet.org.

MLA A. Ralph Papakhian Special Achievement Award. An award recognizing extraordinary service to the profession of music librarianship over a relatively short period of time. Music Library Association, www.musiclibraryassoc.org.

MLA Citation. Awarded in recognition of distinguished service to music librarianship over a career. Music Library Association, www.musiclibraryassoc.org.

NGS Filby Award for Genealogical Librarianship. A $1,000 award to a public, special, or academic librarian whose primary focus is genealogy and who has significantly advanced genealogy and local history. National Genealogical Society, www.ngsgenealogy.org.

NSN Distinguished National Service Award. Presented to individuals, members, or groups who contribute their time and energy on the national level to advance the work of the National Storytelling Network, storynet.org.

NSN Lifetime Achievement Award. Presented annually to individuals who have dedicated their lives to the art form of storytelling and who have demonstrated meritorious service to the National Storytelling Network, as well as to the community of storytellers at large. National Storytelling Network, storynet.org.

OHA Martha Ross Teaching Award. A biennial award that recognizes a distinguished primary or secondary school teacher or professional involved in educational outreach at the precollegiate level who has incorporated the practice of oral history in the classroom. Oral History Association, www.oralhistory.org.

OHA Postsecondary Teaching Award. A biennial award that recognizes a distinguished postsecondary educator involved in undergraduate, graduate, continuing, or professional education who has incorporated the practice of oral history in the classroom. Oral History Association, www.oralhistory.org.

OHA Stetson Kennedy Vox Populi Award. A biennial award that honors outstanding achievement in the collecting and use of oral histories of individuals and organizations whose work has contributed to change for a better world. Oral History Association, www.oralhistory.org.

SLA Dialog Member Achievement Award. Presented to an SLA member for raising visibility, public awareness, and appreciation of the profession or the association. Special Libraries Association, www.sla.org.

SLA Diversity Leadership Development Program Award. Presented to an individual SLA member who represents a group traditionally underrepresented in the association. Special Libraries Association, www.sla.org.

SLA Dow Jones Leadership Award. A $2,000 cash award presented annually to an SLA member who exemplifies leadership as a special librarian through examples of personal and professional competencies. Special Libraries Association, www.sla.org.

SLA Fellow. Bestowed on an individual SLA member to recognize leadership as an information professional. Special Libraries Association, www.sla.org.

SLA Hall of Fame Award. Granted to an SLA member at or near the end of an active professional career to recognize service and contributions to the association. Special Libraries Association, www.sla.org.

SLA John Cotton Dana Award. Granted to an information professional to recognize a lifetime of achievement and exceptional service to special librarianship. Special Libraries Association, www.sla.org.

SLA Rising Star Award. Presented annually to recognize a new member who shows exceptional promise of leadership and contribution to the association and profession. Special Libraries Association, www.sla.org.

SLA Rose L. Vormelker Award. Presented to an SLA member in recognition of exceptional services in the area of mentoring students or practicing professionals in the field. Special Libraries Association, www.sla.org.

TLA Distinguished Service in Performing Arts Librarianship Award. Given to individuals whose vision, energy, and knowledge have extended the boundaries of performing arts librarianship. Theatre Library Association, www.tla-online.org.

TLA Honorary Membership. Conferred upon individuals who have demonstrated outstanding dedication to TLA. Theatre Library Association, www.tla-online.org.

To libraries for excellence

AASLH Albert B. Corey Award. Recognizes primarily volunteer-operated historical organizations that best display the qualities of vigor, scholarship, and imagination in their work. American Association for State and Local History, www.aaslh.org.

AASLH Award of Merit. Presented to an organization or individual to recognize excellence for projects (including civic engagement, special projects, educational programs, exhibits, publications, restoration projects), individual achievement, and organizational general excellence. American Association for State and Local History, www.aaslh.org.

ALA Marshall Cavendish Excellence in Library Programming Award. An annual $2,000 cash award recognizing either a school or public library with programs that have community impact and respond to community needs. ALA Awards, ala.org.

ALA/ACRL EBSCO Community College Library Program Achievement Award. An award of $500 to a two-year institution to recognize significant achievement in programs. ALA Association of College and Research Libraries, ala.org/acrl/.

ALA/ACRL Excellence in Academic Libraries Awards. Three awards of $3,000 granted annually to recognize outstanding community college, college, and university libraries. ALA Association of College and Research Libraries, ala.org/acrl/.

ALA/ALCTS Outstanding Collaboration Citation. Recognizes and encourages collaborative problem-solving efforts in the areas of acquisition, access, management, preservation, or archiving of library materials. ALA Association for Library Collections and Technical Services, ala.org/alcts/.

ALA/IRRT Presidential Citation for Innovative International Library Projects. Recognizes innovative contributions to international librarianship. ALA International Relations Round Table, ala.org/irrt/.

ALA/LLAMA AIA Library Building Awards. A biennial award presented by the American Institute of Architects and LLAMA to encourage excellence in the architectural design and planning of libraries. Citations are presented to the winning architectural firms and to libraries. ALA Library Leadership and Management Association, ala.org/llama/.

ALA/LLAMA IIDA Interior Design Awards. A biennial award presented by the International Interior Design Association and LLAMA for excellence in library interior design. ALA Library Leadership and Management Association, ala.org/llama/.

ALA/PLA EBSCO Excellence in Small and/or Rural Public Library Service Award. This $1,000 award honors a public library serving a population of 10,000 or less that demonstrates excellence of service to its community as exemplified by an overall service program or a special program of significant accomplishment. ALA Public Library Association, ala.org/pla/.

ALA/PLA Highsmith Library Innovation Award. This $2,000 award recognizes a public library's innovative and creative service program to the community. ALA Public Library Association, ala.org/pla/.

ALA/RUSA Gale Cengage Learning Award for Excellence in Reference and Adult Library Services. A citation and $3,000 cash award to a library for developing an imaginative resource to meet patrons' reference needs. Resources may include a bibliography, guide to literature of a specific subject, directory, database, or other reference service. ALA Reference and User Services Association, ala.org/rusa/.

CSLA Award for Outstanding Congregational Library. Honors a church or synagogue library that has responded in creative and innovative ways to the library's mission of reaching and serving members of the congregation and/or wider community. Church and Synagogue Library Association, cslainfo.org.

FLICC Federal Library or Information Center of the Year. Two awards recognizing and commending outstanding, innovative, and sustained achievements by a federal library or information center, one for agencies with 11 or more employees, and another for those with 10 or fewer. Federal Library and Information Center Committee, www.loc.gov/flicc/.

IMLS National Medal for Museum and Library Service. Given annually to recognize a museum's or a library's commitment to public service through exemplary and innovative programs and community partnerships. Institute of Museum and Library Services, www.imls.gov.

OHA Elizabeth B. Mason Project Award. Two biennial awards that recognize outstanding oral history projects. Oral History Association, www.oralhistory.org.

For service to children and young adults

ALA Scholastic Library Publishing Award. An annual award of $1,000 and a citation presented to a librarian for contributions to the stimulation and guidance of reading by children and young people. ALA Awards, ala.org.

ALA Sullivan Award for Public Library Administrators Supporting Services to Children. An annual award of a gift and citation to an individual who has shown exceptional understanding and support of public library service to children while having general management, supervisory, or administrative responsibility that has included public library service to children in its scope. ALA Awards, ala.org.

ALA/AASL Collaborative School Library Award. A $2,500 award to a school librarian and teacher who have worked together to execute a project, event, or program using school library resources. ALA American Association of School Librarians, ala.org/aasl/.

ALA/AASL Distinguished School Administrator Award. An award of $2,000 to a school administrator who has made worthy contributions to the operations of an exemplary school library and to advancing the role of the school library in the educational program. ALA American Association of School Librarians, ala.org/aasl/.

ALA/AASL Distinguished Service Award. A $3,000 award for an outstanding national contribution to school librarianship and school library development. ALA American Association of School Librarians, ala.org/aasl/.

ALA/AASL National School Library Program of the Year Award. Three awards of $10,000 each to school districts (large and small) and a single school for excellence and innovation in outstanding library programs. ALA American Association of School Librarians, ala.org/aasl/.

ALA/AASL President's Crystal Apple Award. Given at the discretion of the AASL president to an individual or group who has had significant impact on school libraries and students. ALA American Association of School Librarians, ala.org/aasl/.

ALA/ALSC Distinguished Service Award. A $1,000 award to honor an ALSC member who has made significant contributions to library service to children and/or ALSC. ALA Association for Library Service to Children, ala.org/alsc/.

ALA/PPO Sara Jaffarian School Library Program Award for Exemplary Humanities Programming. An annual award of $4,000 to an elementary or middle school for outstanding humanities programming. ALA Public Programs Office, ala.org/ppo/.

ALA/YALSA Greenwood Publishing Group Service to Young Adults Achievement Award. A $2,000 biennial award that ecognizes a YALSA member who has demonstrated unique and sustained devotion to young adult services through substantial work in several initiatives. ALA Young Adult Library Services Association, ala.org/yalsa/.

ALA/YALSA MAE Award for Best Literature Program for Teens. Honors a YALSA member for developing an outstanding reading or literature program for young adults. Winners receive $500 and an additional $500 for their libraries. ALA Young Adult Library Services Association, ala.org/yalsa/.

ALA/YALSA Presidential Citation. Honors those who have provided outstanding service to the division or the profession of young adult librarianship. ALA Young Adult Library Services Association, ala.org/yalsa/.

CLA Angela Thacker Memorial Award. Honors Canadian teacher-librarians who have made contributions to the profession through publications, productions, or professional development activities that deal with topics relevant to teacher-librarianship or information literacy. Canadian Library Association, www.cla.ca.

CLA/CLSS Philip F. Neau Memorial Award. Recognizes outstanding contributions to the section. Catholic Library Association, Children's Library Services Section, www.cathla.org.

CLA/HSYALSS St. Katharine Drexel Award. For an outstanding contribution to the growth of high school librarianship. Catholic Library Association, High School and Young Adult Library Services Section, www.cathla.org.

IASL LinksPlus Library Commendation Award. This $1,000 award recognizes outstanding and innovative school library projects, plans, publications, or programs that could serve as models for replication by individuals and associations. International Association of School Librarianship, www.iasl-online.org.

IASL School Librarianship Award. Recognizes IASL members for their contribution to the national development of school libraries and services within their own country or internationally. International Association of School Librarianship, www.iasl-online.org.

IASL Softlink International Excellence Award. $1,000 to recognize significant contributions to school librarianship by school library specialists, educators, or researchers. International Association of School Librarianship, www.iasl-online.org.

National Arts and Humanities Youth Program Awards. Awards of $10,000 each that recognize and support outstanding community arts and humanities programs celebrating the creativity of America's young people by providing them with learning opportunities and chances to contribute to their communities. President's Committee on the Arts and the Humanities, www.nahyp.org.

For service to the underserved

AALL/SCCLL O. James Werner Award. To honor a member who has made a significant contribution to serving directly or for arranging services to be provided to persons with disabilities. American Association of Law Libraries, State, Court, and County Law Libraries Special Interest Section, www.aallnet.org.

AILA Honoring Our Elders Award. An award to a current or former AILA member for distinguished service to Indian communities and extraordinary service to the association. American Indian Library Association, www.ailanet.org.

ALA/ASCLA Exceptional Service Award. A citation presented to recognize exceptional service to patients, to the homebound, to people who live in group residences, and to inmates, as well as to recognize professional leadership, effective interpretation of programs, pioneering activity, and significant research of experimental projects. ALA Association of Specialized and Cooperative Library Agencies, ala.org/ascla/.

ALA/ASCLA Francis Joseph Campbell Award. A citation and a medal presented to a person who has made an outstanding contribution to the advancement of library service for the blind and physically handicapped. ALA Association of Specialized and Cooperative Library Agencies, ala.org/ascla/.

ALA/ASCLA KLAS National Organization on Disability Award. A $1,000 award and certificate to a library for an innovative and well-organized project that has developed or expanded services for people with disabilities or to a library that has made its total services more accessible through changing physical or attitudinal barriers. ALA Association of Specialized and Cooperative Library Agencies, ala.org/ascla/.

ALA/OLOS Diversity and Outreach Fair. Gift certificates totaling $350 to fair participants for their institutions' programs, activities, and services supporting accessibility and underrepresented groups or communities. ALA Office for Literacy and Outreach Services, ala.org/olos/.

ALA/OLOS Jean E. Coleman Library Outreach Lecture. An invitation to an individual of distinction to prepare and present a paper on a library-access topic to ensure that all citizens, particularly Native Americans and adult learners, have access to quality library services. ALA Office for Literacy and Outreach Services, ala.org/olos/.

ALA/RUSA John Sessions Memorial Award. A plaque given to a library or library system to honor significant work with the labor community and to recognize the history and contributions of the labor movement toward the development of this country. ALA Reference and User Services Association, ala.org/rusa/.

ALA/RUSA Outstanding Service to Minority Business Communities Award. An annual award of $2,000 to a librarian or library for creating an innovative service for a minority business community or for recognition by that community as an outstanding service provider. ALA Reference and User Services Association, ala.org/rusa/.

ALA/RUSA Zora Neale Hurston Award. An annual award given to an individual RUSA member who has demonstrated leadership in promoting African-American literature. ALA Reference and User Services Association, ala.org/rusa/.

BCALA DEMCO Award for Excellence in Librarianship. An annual award of $500 to a librarian who has made significant contributions to promoting the status of African Americans in the library profession. Black Caucus of the American Library Association, www.bcala.org.

CLA W. Kaye Lamb Award for Service to Seniors. Biennial award recognizing a library that has developed an ongoing service, program, or procedure of benefit to seniors or a design and organization of buildings or facilities that improve access and encourage use by seniors. Canadian Library Association, www.cla.ca.

FNLM Michael E. DeBakey Library Services Outreach Award. Recognizes outstanding contributions to rural and underserved communities by a practicing health sciences librarian. Friends of the National Library of Medicine, www.fnlm.org.

Reforma Arnulfo D. Trejo Librarian of the Year Award. Granted to an individual who has promoted and advocated services to the Spanish-speaking and Latino/a communities. Reforma, www.reforma.org.

Reforma Estela and Raúl Mora Award. A $1,000 stipend presented annually to the most exemplary program celebrating Día de Los Niños/Día de Los Libros. Reforma, www.reforma.org.

For advocacy and marketing

AALL Excellence in Marketing Award. Honors outstanding achievement in public relations activities by an individual or group. American Association of Law Libraries, www.aallnet.org/about/award_eim.asp.

AALL Robert L. Oakley Advocacy Award. Recognizes an AALL member or group who has been an outstanding advocate. American Association of Law Libraries, www.aallnet.org/about/award_oakley.asp.

AALL/SCCLL Law Library Advocate Award. Presented to a law library supporter for contributions to a state, court, or county law library's service or visibility. American Association of Law Libraries, State, Court, and County Law Libraries Special Interest Section, www.aallnet.org.

ALA Gale Cengage Learning Financial Development Award. A citation and $2,500 to a library organization for an innovative, creative, well-organized project that successfully developed income from alternative sources. ALA Awards, ala.org.

ALA Honorary Membership. Conferred on a living citizen of any country whose contribution to librarianship or a closely related field is so outstanding that it is of lasting importance to the advancement of the whole field of library service. ALA Awards, ala.org.

ALA Ken Haycock Award for Promoting Librarianship. A citation and a $1,000 award to honor an individual for contributing significantly to the public recognition and appreciation of librarianship through professional performance, teaching, and/or writing. ALA Awards, ala.org.

ALA Paul Howard Award for Courage. $1,000 awarded every two years to a librarian, library board, library group, or an individual who has exhibited unusual courage for the benefit of library programs or services. ALA Awards, ala.org.

ALA/LLAMA Best of Show Competition. Recognizes the best individual pieces of public relations materials produced by libraries in the previous year. Many different categories and winners. ALA Library Leadership and Management Association, ala.org/llama/.

ALA/LLAMA John Cotton Dana Public Relations Award. An annual citation honoring outstanding strategic communication for libraries. ALA Library Leadership and Management Association, ala.org/llama/.

ALA/United for Libraries ALA President's Award for Advocacy. An annual award of $1,000 to a statewide advocacy campaign for the development of a program or programs for Friends and trustees at the state library association conference. ALA United for Libraries: Association of Library Trustees, Advocates, Friends, and Foundations, ala.org/united/.

ALA/United for Libraries Baker & Taylor Awards for Friends Groups. Financial awards recognizing Friends groups for outstanding efforts to support their libraries. ALA United for Libraries: Association of Library Trustees, Advocates, Friends, and Foundations, ala.org/united/.

ALA/United for Libraries Best Friends Awards. Recognizes a Friends group for its print and electronic materials that promote its special programs and projects. ALA United for Libraries: Association of Library Trustees, Advocates, Friends, and Foundations, ala.org/united/.

ALA/United for Libraries Public Service Award. Honors a legislator who has been especially supportive of libraries. ALA United for Libraries: Association of Library Trustees, Advocates, Friends, and Foundations, ala.org/united/.

ALA/United for Libraries Trustee Citations. Recognizes two outstanding public library trustees for distinguished service to library development on the local, state, regional, or national level. ALA United for Libraries: Association of Library Trustees, Advocates, Friends, and Foundations, ala.org/united/.

BCALA Library Advocacy Award. Given to BCALA members. Black Caucus of the American Library Association, www.bcala.org.

CLA Ken Haycock Award for Promoting Librarianship. A $1,000 (Can.) award to honor individuals who contribute significantly to the public recognition and appreciation of librarianship. Canadian Library Association, www.cla.ca.

IFLA International Marketing Award. Honors a library that has implemented a creative, results-oriented marketing project or campaign. International Federation of Library Associations and Institutions, www.ifla.org.

SAA J. Franklin Jameson Archival Advocacy Award. Honors an individual, institution, or organization not directly involved in archival work that promotes greater public awareness, appreciation, or support of archival activities or programs. Society of American Archivists, www.archivists.org.

ULC Urban Player Award. An honorarium presented to an individual who has positioned the public library as a vital resource in the broad agenda of a city or county and has enriched the community by creating a stronger presence for the public library. Urban Libraries Council, urbanlibraries.org.

For intellectual freedom

AALL Public Access to Government Information Award. Honors the achievements of those who have championed public access. American Association of Law Libraries, www.aallnet.org.

ALA Paul Howard Award for Courage. $1,000 awarded every two years to a librarian, library board, library group, or an individual who has exhibited unusual courage for the benefit of library programs or services. ALA Awards, ala.org.

ALA/AASL Intellectual Freedom Award. A $2,000 award to a school librarian who has upheld the principles of intellectual freedom. An award of $1,000 goes to a media center of the recipient's choice. ALA American Association of School Librarians, ala.org/aasl/.

ALA/IFRT Eli M. Oboler Memorial Award. $500 awarded biennially to an author of a published work in English, or in English translation, dealing with issues, events, questions, or controversies in the area of intellectual freedom. ALA Intellectual Freedom Round Table, ala.org/ifrt/.

ALA/IFRT John Phillip Immroth Memorial Award for Intellectual Freedom. $500 and a citation honoring intellectual freedom fighters who have demonstrated remarkable personal courage in resisting censorship. ALA Intellectual Freedom Round Table, ala.org/ifrt/.

ALA/OGR Eileen Cooke State and Local James Madison Award. Recognizes state or local individuals, groups, or other entities that have championed access to government information and the public's right to know. Presented yearly on Freedom of Information Day. ALA Office of Government Relations, ala.org/ogr/.

ALA/OGR James Madison Award. Honors those who have championed, protected, and promoted public access to government information and the public's right to know. Presented yearly on Freedom of Information Day. ALA Office of Government Relations, ala.org/ogr/.

ALA/OITP L. Ray Patterson Copyright Award. Honors those who have made significant and consistent contributions to the pursuit of balanced copyright principles while working in the area of information policy, law, libraries, or library education. ALA Office for Information Technology Policy, ala.org/oitp/.

ALA/PLA Gordon M. Conable Award. An award of $1,500 to an individual who has demonstrated a commitment to intellectual freedom and the Library Bill of Rights. ALA Public Library Association, ala.org/pla/.

CLA Award for the Advancement of Intellectual Freedom in Canada. Recognizes outstanding contributions to intellectual freedom in Canada by individuals or groups. Canadian Library Association, www.cla.ca.

EFF Pioneer Awards. Recognizes leaders on the electronic frontier who are extending freedom and innovation in the realm of information technology. Electronic Frontier Foundation, www.eff.org.

FTRF Roll of Honor Award. Recognizes those individuals who have contributed substantially to the foundation through adherence to its principles and/or substantial monetary support. Freedom to Read Foundation, ala.org/ftrf/.

For literacy and social responsibility

ALA Equality Award. $1,000 and a citation to an individual or group for an outstanding contribution that promotes equality in the library profession in such areas as pay equity, affirmative action, legislative work, and nonsexist education. ALA Awards, ala.org.

ALA/ACRL Innovation Award. This annual $3,000 award recognizes a project that demonstrates creative, innovative, or unique approaches to information literacy instruction or programming. ALA Association of College and Research Libraries, ala.org/acrl/.

IFLA Guust van Wesemael Literacy Prize. This biennial award sponsors a public or school library in a developing country to purchase books for activities in the field of literacy. International Federation of Library Associations and Institutions, www.ifla.org.

NCL Literacy Leadership Awards. Recognizes individuals and organizations that have made extraordinary contributions to improving literacy in the United States. National Coalition for Literacy, www.national-coalition-literacy.org.

For special collections and archives

ACA Fellows. Recognizes ACA members for distinguished service to the archival profession. Association of Canadian Archivists, archivists.ca.

ACA Membership Recognition Award. Given annually to an ACA member for professional achievements or significant contributions. Association of Canadian Archivists, archivists.ca.

ALA/ACRL Katharine Kyes Leab and Daniel J. Leab *American Book Prices Current* **Exhibition Catalogue Awards.** Three awards for outstanding catalogues published by American or Canadian institutions in conjunction with library exhibitions as well as digital exhibition catalogues of outstanding merit. ALA Association of College and Research Libraries, ala.org/acrl/.

ALA/GODORT Bernadine Abbott Hoduski Founders Award. Recognizes documents librarians who may not be known at the national level but who have made significant contributions to the field of state, international, local, or federal documents. ALA Government Documents Round Table, ala.org/godort/.

ALA/GODORT James Bennett Childs Award. An annual award presented to an individual who has made a lifetime and significant contribution to the field of government documents librarianship.

ALA Government Documents Round Table, ala.org/godort/.

ALA/GODORT LexisNexis "Documents to the People" Award. $3,000 to an individual, library, organization, or noncommercial group that most effectively encourages the use of government documents in library services. ALA Government Documents Round Table, ala.org/godort/.

SAA Archival Innovator Award. Recognizes an individual, group, repository, or organization for the greatest overall impact on the archives profession. Society of American Archivists, www.archivists.org.

SAA C. F. W. Coker Award. Certificate and cash award for finding aids, finding aid systems, projects that involve innovative development in archival description, or descriptive tools that enable archivists to produce more effective finding aids. Society of American Archivists, www.archivists.org.

SAA Council Exemplary Service Award. Recognizes a special contribution to the archives profession. Society of American Archivists, www.archivists.org.

SAA Distinguished Service Award. Recognizes a North American archival institution, organization, education program, or nonprofit or governmental organization that has given outstanding service to its public and has made an exemplary contribution to the archival profession. Society of American Archivists, www.archivists.org.

SAA Diversity Award. Recognizes an individual, group, or institution for outstanding contributions in advancing diversity within the archives profession. Society of American Archivists, www.archivists.org.

SAA Emerging Leader Award. Encourages early-career archivists who have completed archival work of broad merit, demonstrated significant promise of leadership, or performed commendable service to the archives profession. Society of American Archivists, www.archivists.org.

SAA Fellow. Awarded for outstanding contribution to the archival profession. Society of American Archivists, www.archivists.org.

SAA Fellows' Ernst Posner Award. Certificate and cash award that recognizes the author(s) of an outstanding article dealing with some facet of archival administration, history, theory, and/or methodology that was published during the preceding year in the *American Archivist*. Society of American Archivists, www.archivists.org.

SAA Philip M. Hamer–Elizabeth Hamer Kegan Award. Certificate and cash award that recognizes an archivist, editor, group of individuals, or institution that has increased public awareness of a specific body of documents through compilation, transcription, exhibition, or public presentation. Society of American Archivists, www.archivists.org.

SAA Preservation Publication Award. Recognizes the author(s) or editor(s) of an outstanding published work related to archives preservation published in North America during the preceding year. Society of American Archivists, www.archivists.org.

SAA Sister M. Claude Lane Memorial Award. Certificate and cash prize that recognizes individuals who have made a significant contribution to the field of religious archives. Society of American Archivists, www.archivists.org.

SAA Spotlight Award. This award recognizes the contributions of individuals who work for the good of the profession and of archival collections, and whose work would not typically receive public recognition. Society of American Archivists, www.archivists.org.

SAA Theodore Calvin Pease Award. Certificate and cash prize of $100 that recognizes superior writing achievements by students of archival administration. Society of American Archivists, www.archivists.org.

SAA Waldo Gifford Leland Award. Certificate and cash prize that encourages and rewards writing of superior excellence and usefulness in the field of archival history, theory, or practice. Monographs, finding aids, and documentary publications published in North America during the preceding year are eligible. Society of American Archivists, www.archivists.org.

For technology

AALL Innovations in Technology Award. Recognizes an association member, group, or library for innovative use of technology in the development of an application or resource for law librarians or legal professionals. American Association of Law Librarians, www.aallnet.org.

AALL New Product Award. Honors new commercial information products that enhance or improve access to legal information, the legal research process, or procedures for technical processing of library materials. American Association of Law Libraries, www.aallnet.org.

AALL/CS Kenneth J. Hirsh Distinguished Service Award. Honors a section member who has made outstanding contributions to CS, to AALL, and who is well regarded for his or her service to the profession. American Association of Law Libraries, Computing Services Special Interest Section, cssis.org.

AECT Annual Achievement Award. Honors the individual who during the past year has made the most significant contribution to the advancement of educational communications and technology. Association for Educational Communications and Technology, aect.site-ym.com.

AECT Outstanding Practice Award. For an outstanding design of instructional materials or systems. Association for Educational Communications and Technology, aect.site-ym.com.

AECT Richard B. Lewis Memorial Award. Presented to a school district for outstanding utilization of technology. Association for Educational Communications and Technology, aect.site-ym.com.

AECT/DDL/Information Age Publishers Crystal Award. Recognizes innovative multimedia-based distance learning courses and projects. Association for Educational Communications and Technology, aect.site-ym.com.

AIIP Technology Award. Recognizes the year's most valuable emerging tool for information professionals. Association of Independent Information Professionals, www.aiip.org.

ALA Information Today Library of the Future Award. An award of $1,500 to honor a library, library consortium, group of librarians, or support organization for innovative planning for, applications of, or development of patron training programs about information technology in a library setting. ALA Awards, ala.org.

ALA/AASL Information Technology Pathfinder Award. Awards of $1,000 to elementary and secondary school librarians for demonstrating vision and leadership through the use of information technology to build lifelong learners. An additional $500 goes to each library. ALA American Association of School Librarians, ala.org/aasl/.

ALA/ALCTS Coutts Award for Innovation in Electronic Resources Management. An annual award of $2,000 to recognize the contribution of an individual who has demonstrated innovation and excellence in the practice of electronic collection management and development. ALA Association for Library Collections and Technical Services, ala.org/alcts/.

ALA/LITA Frederick G. Kilgour Award for Research in Library and Information Technology. $2,000 for research relevant to the development of information technologies, especially work which shows promise of having a positive and substantive impact on any aspect of the publication, storage, retrieval, and dissemination of information, or the processes by which information and data is manipulated and managed. ALA Library and Information Technology Association, ala.org/lita/.

ALA/LITA *Library Hi Tech* Award. An award of $1,000 to recognize outstanding communication in continuing education within the field of library and information technology. ALA Library and Information Technology Association, ala.org/lita/.

ALA/PLA Polaris Innovation in Technology John Iliff Award. A $1,000 honorarium that recognizes the contributions of a library worker, librarian, or library that has used technology and innovative thinking as a tool to improve services to public library users. ALA Public Library Association, ala.org/pla/.

ALISE Pratt-Severn Faculty Innovation Award. A cash award of $1,000 to LIS faculty for incorporating evolving information technologies in the curriculum. Association for Library and Information Science Education, www.alise.org.

Bill and Melinda Gates Foundation Access to Learning Award. An annual award of up to $1 million to a public library or similar organization outside the United States to connect people to information through free access to computers and the internet. Bill and Melinda Gates Foundation, www.gatesfoundation.org.

CLA OCLC Award for Innovative Technology. Given annually to honor a member or members of the Canadian Library Association for innovative use and application of technology in a Canadian library setting. Canadian Library Association, www.cla.ca.

CNI/Educause/ARL Paul Evan Peters Award. Biennial award that recognizes notable, lasting achievements related to high-performance networks and the creation and use of information resources and services that advance scholarship and intellectual productivity. Coalition for Networked Information, www.cni.org.

IASL School Library Technology Innovation Award. An award of $1,000 (Austral.) recognizes school library programs or projects that effectively utilize current and emerging technologies for school libraries and information service delivery. International Association of School Librarianship, www.iasl-online.org.

MLA Thomson Reuters/Frank Bradway Rogers Information Advancement Award. Presented annually in recognition of outstanding contributions for the application of technology to the delivery of health science information, to the science of information, or to the facilitation of the delivery of health science information. Medical Library Association, www.mlanet.org.

For articles, papers, and research

AALL Joseph L. Andrews Bibliographical Award. For significant contribution to legal bibliographical literature. American Association of Law Libraries, www.aallnet.org.

AALL *Law Library Journal* Article of the Year. A cash award of $500 for outstanding achievement in research and writing published in *Law Library Journal.* American Association of Law Libraries, www.aallnet.org.

AALL Law Library Publications Award. Honors achievement in creating in-house library materials that are outstanding in quality and significance. American Association of Law Libraries, www.aallnet.org.

AALL LexisNexis Call for Papers Awards. A cash award to promote scholarship and provide an outlet for creativity. American Association of Law Libraries, www.aallnet.org.

AALL *Spectrum* Article of the Year Award. A cash award of $500 to honor outstanding achievement in writing an article that contributes to topics relating to law librarianship, practical applications for library work, legal materials, legal information, or professional and staff training and development in *AALL Spectrum.* American Association of Law Libraries, www.aallnet.org.

AALL/ALL Outstanding Article Award. For contributions to the enhancement of academic law librarianship through publishing. American Association of Law Libraries, Academic Law Libraries Special Interest Section, www.aallnet.org.

AALL/LHRB Morris L. Cohen Student Essay Competition. A $500 prize to a student in an LIS or law program for an essay on legal history, rare law books, or legal archives. American Association of Law Libraries, Legal History and Rare Books Special Interest Section, www.aallnet.org.

AALL/SCCLL Connie E. Bolden Publications Award. Given every third year for a scholarly publication that addresses the concerns of state, court, or county law librarians. American Association of Law Libraries, State, Court, and County Law Libraries Special Interest Section, www.aallnet.org.

ACA Gordon Dodds Prize. Recognizes superior research and writing on an archival topic by a student enrolled in a master's-level archival studies program at a Canadian university. Association of Canadian Archivists, archivists.ca.

ACA Hugh A. Taylor Prize. Awarded to honor the author of an *Archivaria* article published during the previous year that presents new ideas or refreshing syntheses in the most imaginative way. Association of Canadian Archivists, archivists.ca.

ACA W. Kaye Lamb Prize. Awarded to honor the author of the best *Archivaria* article published during the previous year. Association of Canadian Archivists, archivists.ca.

ACMLA Paper Award. An award of $200 for a feature article appearing in the *ACMLA Bulletin.* Association of Canadian Map Libraries and Archives, www.acmla.org.

ACMLA Student Paper Award. A prize of $250 and free ACMLA membership for an unpublished essay by a Canadian library student. Association of Canadian Map Libraries and Archives, www.acmla.org.

AECT *ETR&D* Young Scholar Award. A cash award of $500 for the best paper discussing a theoretical construct that could guide research and/or development in educational technology. The winning paper will be published in *Educational Technology Research and Development.* Association for Educational Communications and Technology, aect.site-ym.com.

AECT James W. Brown Publication Award. A cash award of $500 to the author(s) of an outstanding publication in the field of educational technology. Association for Educational Communications and Technology, aect.site-ym.com.

AECT Outstanding Journal Article Award. For an outstanding article in the field of instructional design. Association for Educational Communications and Technology, aect.site-ym.com.

AECT Qualitative Inquiry Award. A cash award of $2,000 for a research study using qualitative theories and methods. Association for Educational Communications and Technology, aect.site-ym.com.

AECT Robert M. Gagne Award for Graduate Student Research in Instructional Design. An award of $250 for a significant contribution to instructional design practices. Association for Educational Communications and Technology, aect.site-ym.com.

AECT Young Researcher Award. A cash award of $500 for the best paper reporting on a quantitative or qualitative study addressing a question related to educational technology. Association for Educational Communications and Technology, aect.site-ym.com.

AECT/Information Age Publishers Journal Article Award. For an outstanding article published within the last three years that describes best practices or research in distance education. Association for Educational Communications and Technology, aect.site-ym.com.

AIIP *Connections* Writer's Award. A $350 award for travel to the AIIP Annual Conference is given to the writer of the best article published in *AIIP Connections* each year. Association of Independent Information Professionals, www.aiip.org.

ALA ABC-CLIO/Greenwood Award for Best Book in Library Literature. A $5,000 award for a book dealing with topics and issues pertinent to library professionals. ALA Awards, ala.org.

ALA/ACRL Ilene F. Rockman Instruction Publication of the Year Award. This award recognizes an outstanding publication related to instruction in a library environment published in the preceding two years. ALA Association of College and Research Libraries, ala.org/acrl/.

ALA/ACRL Oberly Award for Bibliography in the Agricultural or Natural Sciences. A biennial cash award for the best English-language bibliography in the field of agriculture or a related science. ALA Association of College and Research Libraries, ala.org/acrl/.

ALA/ALCTS Edward Swanson Memorial Best of *LRTS* Award. Annual citation given to the author(s) of the best paper published in *Library Resources and Technical Services*. ALA Association for Library Collections and Technical Services, ala.org/alcts/.

ALA/ALCTS Outstanding Publication Award. A $250 award for the year's outstanding monograph, article, or original paper in the field of library technical services. ALA Association for Library Collections and Technical Services, ala.org/alcts/.

ALA/EMIERT David Cohen Multicultural Award. Honors articles on significant new research in multiculturalism in libraries. ALA Ethnic and Multicultural Information Exchange Round Table, ala.org/emiert/.

ALA/GODORT Margaret T. Lane/Virginia F. Saunders Memorial Research Award. Given annually to the author(s) of an outstanding research article in which government information, either published or archival in nature, forms a substantial part of the documented research. ALA Government Documents Round Table, ala.org/godort/.

ALA/GODORT Notable Government Documents. An annotated list that recognizes excellence in government publications, identifies documents of distinction, and commends individual works of a superlative nature. ALA Government Documents Round Table, ala.org/godort/.

ALA/IRO Emily Dean Heilman Award. Given to a fourth-year library science student in Turkey for a thesis that contributes to the progress and development of Turkish libraries. ALA International Relations Office, ala.org/iro/.

ALA/LHRT Donald G. Davis Article Award. A biennial award for the best article written in English in the field of United States and Canadian library history including the history of libraries, librarianship, and book culture. ALA Library History Round Table, ala.org/lhrt/.

ALA/LHRT Justin Winsor Prize for Library History. A biennial award of $500 to an author of an outstanding essay embodying original historical research on a significant subject of library history. The essay will be published in *Libraries and Culture*. ALA Library History Round Table, ala.org/lhrt/.

ALA/LHRT Phyllis Dain Library History Dissertation Award. A biennial award of $500 to outstanding dissertations treating the history of books, libraries, librarianship, or information science. ALA Library History Round Table, ala.org/lhrt/.

ALA/LITA Ex Libris Student Writing Award. $1,000 given for the best unpublished manuscript on a topic in the area of libraries and information technology written by a student or students enrolled in an ALA-accredited library and information studies graduate program. ALA Library and Information Technology Association, ala.org/lita/.

ALA/LRRT Beta Phi Mu Research Paper Award. A prize of $500 to recognize excellent research into problems related to the profession of librarianship. ALA Office for Research and Statistics, ala.org/lrrt/.

ALA/LRRT Jesse H. Shera Award for Distinguished Published Research. A prize of $500 for an outstanding and original research article related to libraries published in the previous year. ALA Office for Research and Statistics, ala.org/lrrt/.

ALA/PLA *Public Libraries* Feature Article Contest. A first prize of $500 and a second prize of $300 to the authors of the best features published in *Public Libraries* in the previous year. ALA Public Library Association, ala.org/pla/.

ALA/RUSA Louis Shores Award. A citation to an individual reviewer, group, editor, review medium, or organization to recognize excellence in book reviewing and other media for libraries. ALA Reference and User Services Association, ala.org/rusa/.

ALA/RUSA Reference Service Press Award. $2,500 award presented to recognize the most outstanding article published in *RUSQ* during the preceding two-volume year. ALA Reference and User Services Association, ala.org/rusa/.

ALISE Bohdan S. Wynar Research Paper Competition. A $2,500 honorarium for a completed research paper concerning any aspect of librarianship or information science. Association for Library and Information Science Education, www.alise.org.

ALISE Eugene Garfield Doctoral Dissertation Competition. A $500 award for a completed dissertation dealing with substantive issues related to library and information science. Association for Library and Information Science Education, www.alise.org.

ALISE ProQuest Methodology Paper Competition. A $500 honorarium for papers describing and discussing a research method or a technique associated with a particular research method. Association for Library and Information Science Education, www.alise.org.

APHA Annual Awards. Honors an individual or institution for a distinguished contribution to the study, recording, preservation, or dissemination of printing history, in any specific area or in general terms. American Printing History Association, www.printinghistory.org.

ARLIS/NA Gerd Muehsam Memorial Award. $500 cash and $300 in travel expenses to the ARLIS/NA conference to a graduate library student for a paper or project on a topic relevant to art librarianship. Art Libraries Society of North America, www.arlisna.org.

ARLIS/NA Melva J. Dwyer Award. Citation given to the creators of exceptional reference or research tools relating to Canadian art and architecture. Art Libraries Society of North America, www.arlisna.org.

ASI H. W. Wilson Award. A citation and $1,000 for the indexer, and a citation for the publisher to honor excellence in indexing of an English-language monograph or other nonserial publication published during the previous calendar year. American Society of Indexers, www.asindexing.org.

ASI Website Indexing Award. Presented for a publicly accessible index to a website. American Society of Indexers, www.asindexing.org.

ASIS&T History Fund Research Paper. A maximum of $500 for the best paper submitted in the history of information science and technology. American Society for Information Science and Technology, www.asis.org.

ASIS&T John Wiley & Sons Best *JASIST* Paper Award. A $1,500 cash award to recognize the best refereed paper published in the volume year of the *Journal of the American Society for Information Science and Technology* preceding the ASIS&T annual meeting. American Society for Information Science and Technology, www.asis.org.

ASIS&T Pratt Severn Best Student Research Paper. Up to $500 for travel expenses and full registration for the ASIS annual meeting for research and writing in the field of information science. American Society for Information Science and Technology, www.asis.org.

ASIS&T Research in Information Science Award. To recognize an individual or individuals for an outstanding research contribution in the field of information science. American Society for Information Science and Technology, www.asis.org.

BSA St. Louis Mercantile Library Prize in American Bibliography. A prize of $2,000 awarded every three years for scholarship in the bibliography of American history and literature. Bibliographical Society of America, www.bibsocamer.org.

BSA William L. Mitchell Prize for Research on Early British Serials. An award of $1,000 for bibliographical scholarship on 18th-century periodicals published in English or in any language but within the British Isles and its colonies and former colonies. Bibliographical Society of America, www.bibsocamer.org.

CALA Jing Liao Award for the Best Research in All Media. A $500 award to a CALA member for excellence in research in print or electronic format. Chinese American Librarians Association, cala-web.org.

CALL *Canadian Law Library Review* Feature Article Award. An award of $250 (Can.) given annually to the author of a feature-length article published in *Canadian Law Library Review*. Canadian Association of Law Libraries, www.callacbd.ca.

CALL Hugh Lawford Award for Excellence in Legal Publishing. An annual award to recognize excellence in Canadian legal publishing. Canadian Association of Law Libraries, www.callacbd.ca.

CBHL Annual Literature Award. Given to both the author and publisher of a work that makes a significant contribution to the literature of botany or horticulture. Council on Botanical and Horticultural Libraries, www.cbhl.net.

CHLA Login Canada Student Paper Prize. Awarded annually to a library student who submits the best unpublished paper on health sciences librarianship. Canadian Health Libraries Association, www.chla-absc.ca.

CLA Robert H. Blackburn Distinguished Paper Award. For notable research by a CLA member published in a peer-reviewed journal. Canadian Library Association, www.cla.ca.

CLA Student Article Contest. An honorarium of $200 (Can.) and publication in *Feliciter* for articles by students or recent graduates of Canadian library schools. Canadian Library Association, www.cla.ca.

CLA Chapter Newsletter Award. Recognizes excellence in CLA chapter and section newsletters. Catholic Library Association, www.cathla.org.

CLA John Brubaker Memorial Award. For the best article in *Catholic Library World* in the previous year. Catholic Library Association, www.cathla.org.

CLA/ALALES Jerome Award. Presented annually for excellence in Catholic scholarship. Catholic Library Association, Academic Libraries, Archives, and Library Education Section, www.cathla.org.

GIS Best Paper Award. For the best paper published in the field of geosciences information during the previous year. Geoscience Information Society, www.geoinfo.org.

MLA Ida and George Eliot Prize. Award presented annually for a work published in the preceding calendar year that has been judged most effective in furthering medical librarianship. Medical Library Association, www.mlanet.org.

MLA Murray Gottlieb Prize. Awarded annually for the best unpublished essay on the history of medicine and allied sciences written by a health sciences librarian. Medical Library Association, www.mlanet.org.

MLA Rittenhouse Award. Given for the best unpublished paper (bibliographical, issue- or topic-based, or report of research results) or web-based project on health sciences librarianship or medical informatics written by a student in an ALA-accredited school of library science or a trainee in an internship. Medical Library Association, www.mlanet.org.

MLA Eva Judd O'Meara Award. An annual award for the best review published in *Notes.* Music Library Association, www.musiclibraryassoc.org.

MLA Richard S. Hill Award. An annual award for the best article on music librarianship or article of a music-bibliographic nature. Music Library Association, www.musiclibraryassoc.org.

MLA Vincent H. Duckles Award. Annual award for the best book-length bibliography or other research tool in music. Music Library Association, www.musiclibraryassoc.org.

NSN Talking Leaves Literary Award. Presented to individuals who have made outstanding contributions to the literary body of storytelling as authors, editors, or collectors. National Storytelling Network, storynet.org.

OHA Article Award. Biennial award that recognizes a published article or essay that uses oral history to make a significant contribution to contemporary scholarship. Oral History Association, www.oralhistory.org.

SALALM José Toribio Medina Award. An honorarium of $250 for outstanding bibliographies, reference works, and sources that facilitate access to research or contribute to the understanding, use, or development of Latin American collections. Seminar on the Acquisition of Latin American Library Materials, salalm.org.

For children's and young adult literature

AILA American Indian Youth Literature Award. Honors the very best writing and illustrations by and about American Indians. American Indian Library Association, www.ailanet.org.

AJL Sydney Taylor Book Awards. Presented annually to outstanding books for children and teens that authentically portray the Jewish experience. Association of Jewish Libraries, www.jewishlibraries.org.

AJL Sydney Taylor Manuscript Award. A cash award of $1,000 for the best fiction manuscript appropriate for readers ages 8–11, written by an unpublished author. Association of Jewish Libraries, www.jewishlibraries.org.

ALA *Booklist* Editors' Choice: Adult Books for Young Adults. The *Booklist* youth books editors choose the year's best personal reading for teenagers among adult books published the previous year. ALA *Booklist,* www.booklistonline.com.

ALA *Booklist* Editors' Choice: Books for Youth. The *Booklist* youth books editors select best-of-the-year fiction, nonfiction, and picture books for young, middle, and older readers. ALA *Booklist,* www.booklistonline.com.

ALA Schneider Family Book Awards. Three annual awards of $5,000 each to honor an author or illustrator for a book that embodies an artistic expression of the disability experience for child and adolescent audiences. ALA Awards, ala.org.

ALA/ALSC John Newbery Medal. A medal presented annually to the author of the most distinguished contribution to American literature for children published in the United States in the preceding year. ALA Association for Library Service to Children, ala.org/alsc/.

ALA/ALSC Laura Ingalls Wilder Medal. A medal presented every two years to an author or illustrator whose books, published in the United States, have over a period of years made a substantial and lasting contribution to children's literature. ALA Association for Library Service to Children, ala.org/alsc/.

ALA/ALSC Mildred L. Batchelder Award. A citation presented to an American publisher for a children's book considered to be the most outstanding of those books originally published in a foreign language in a foreign country and subsequently translated into English and published in the United States. ALA Association for Library Service to Children, ala.org/alsc/.

ALA/ALSC Notable Children's Books. An annual annotated list of the best children's books for younger, middle, older, and all ages. ALA Association for Library Service to Children, ala.org/alsc/.

ALA/ALSC Pura Belpré Medal. Annual award to a Latino/Latina author and illustrator whose works best portray, affirm, and celebrate the Latino cultural experience in an outstanding work of literature for children and youth. ALA Association for Library Service to Children, ala.org/alsc/.

ALA/ALSC Randolph Caldecott Medal. A medal presented annually to the illustrator of the most distinguished American picture book for children published in the United States in the previous year. ALA Association for Library Service to Children, ala.org/alsc/.

ALA/ALSC Robert F. Sibert Informational Book Medal. Awarded annually to the author of the most distinguished informational book published in English during the preceding year. ALA Association for Library Service to Children, ala.org/alsc/.

ALA/ALSC Theodor Seuss Geisel Award. Awarded to the author(s) and illustrator(s) of the most distinguished contribution to the body of American children's literature known as beginning reader books published in the United States during the preceding year. ALA Association for Library Service to Children, ala.org/alsc/.

ALA/EMIERT Coretta Scott King Book Awards. Awards given to an African-American author and to an African-American illustrator for outstanding books for young adults and children that reflect the African-American experience. The awards consist of a plaque and $1,000 to the author and $1,000 to the illustrator. ALA Ethnic and Multicultural Information Exchange Round Table, ala.org/emiert/.

ALA/EMIERT Coretta Scott King–John Steptoe Award for New Talent. Citation for an outstanding book designed to bring visibility to a black writer or artist at the beginning of his/her career as a published book creator. ALA Ethnic and Multicultural Information Exchange Round Table, ala.org/emiert/.

ALA/EMIERT Coretta Scott King–Virginia Hamilton Award for Lifetime Achievement. A biennial cash award of $1,500 that recognizes an African-American author or illustrator for a body of published books for children or young adults who has made a significant and lasting literary contribution. ALA Ethnic and Multicultural Information Exchange Round Table, ala.org/emiert/.

ALA/GLBTRT Stonewall Book Award–Children's and Young Adult Literature Award. Cash awards to authors of children's and young adult literature relating to the gay/lesbian/bisexual/transgender experience published in the United States. ALA Gay, Lesbian, Bisexual, Transgender Round Table, ala.org/glbtrt/.

ALA/GLBTRT/SRRT Rainbow Project Book List. An annotated list of recommended books dealing with gay, lesbian, bisexual, trangender, and questioning issues and situations for children up to age 18. ALA Gay, Lesbian, Bisexual. Transgender Round Table, ala.org/glbtrt/.

ALA/SRRT Amelia Bloomer Book List. An annual annotated book list (or bibliography) of well-written and well-illustrated books with significant feminist content, intended for young readers (ages birth through 18). ALA Social Responsibilities Round Table, ala.org/srrt/.

ALA/YALSA Alex Awards. Citations to 10 authors of English-language adult books that have special appeal to young adults, ages 12–18. ALA Young Adult Library Services Association, ala.org/yalsa/.

ALA/YALSA Award for Excellence in Nonfiction for Young Adults. An award for the best nonfiction book for young adults (ages 12–18) published the previous year. ALA Young Adult Library Services Association, ala.org/yalsa/.

ALA/YALSA Best Fiction for Young Adults. The best fiction titles written for teens in the past 16 months. ALA Young Adult Library Services Association, ala.org/yalsa/.

ALA/YALSA Best of the Best of the University Presses. Best books from university presses that reflect a viewpoint and topical coverage not typically reflected in standard selection tools. ALA Young Adult Library Services Association, ala.org/yalsa/.

ALA/YALSA Great Graphic Novels for Teens. An annotated list of graphic novels published in the past 16 months that are recommended reading for teens aged 12–18. ALA Young Adult Library Services Association, ala.org/yalsa/.

ALA/YALSA Margaret A. Edwards Award. A $2,000 award given to an author whose books have helped adolescents become aware of themselves and address questions about their role and importance in relationships, society, and in the world. ALA Young Adult Library Services Association, ala.org/yalsa/.

ALA/YALSA Michael L. Printz Award. Honors the the the best book written for young adults in the previous year that exemplifies literary excellence. ALA Young Adult Library Services Association, ala.org/yalsa/.

ALA/YALSA Outstanding Books for the College Bound. A list of reading recommendations to students of all ages who plan to continue their education beyond high school. ALA Young Adult Library Services Association, ala.org/yalsa/.

ALA/YALSA Popular Paperbacks for Young Adults. Annual lists of popular paperback books, representing a broad variety of accessible themes and genres, that are intended to encourage young adults to read for pleasure. ALA Young Adult Library Services Association, ala.org/yalsa/.

ALA/YALSA Quick Picks for Reluctant Young Adult Readers. An annual list of books for recreational reading for young adults (ages 12–18) who do not like to read. ALA Young Adult Library Services Association, ala.org/yalsa/.

ALA/YALSA Readers' Choice List. The most popular teen titles in a given year, organized by broad genres. ALA Young Adult Library Services Association, ala.org/yalsa/.

ALA/YALSA Teens' Top Ten. An annual "teen choice" list, where teens nominate and choose their favorite books of the previous year. ALA Young Adult Library Services Association, ala.org/yalsa/.

ALA/YALSA William C. Morris Debut YA Award. Honors a debut book published by a first-time author writing for teens. ALA Young Adult Library Services Association, ala.org/yalsa/.

ALA/YALSA Writing Award. Honors the best writing in YALSA's blogs and journals. ALA Young Adult Library Services Association, ala.org/yalsa/.

ALISE *LMC* Paper Award. A $1,000 award for an outstanding paper reporting innovative research in library services to young people. A version of the paper will be published in *Library Media Connection*. Association for Library and Information Science Education, www.alise.org.

APALA Literature Awards. Given to the writers or illustrators of adult or children's books about Asian/Pacific Americans. Asian Pacific American Library Association, www.apalaweb.org.

BSA Justin G. Schiller Prize for Bibliographical Work on Pre–20th-Century Children's Books. An award of $2,000 for scholarship in the bibliography of historical children's books. Bibliographical Society of America, www.bibsocamer.org.

CLA Amelia Frances Howard-Gibbon Illustrator's Award. For an illustrator of an outstanding children's book published in Canada the previous year. Canadian Library Association, www.cla.ca.

CLA Book of the Year for Children Award. For an outstanding children's book published in Canada the previous year by a Canadian author. Canadian Library Association, www.cla.ca.

CLA Young Adult Book Award. Recognizes an author of an outstanding English-language Canadian book appealing to young adults. Canadian Library Association, www.cla.ca.

CLA/CLSS Regina Medal. A silver medal awarded to an author or illustrator for a lifetime contribution to children's books. Catholic Library Association, Children's Library Services Section, www.cathla.org.

CSLA Helen Keating Ott Award for Outstanding Contribution to Children's Literature. A person or organization selected and honored for significant contribution in promoting high moral and ethical values through children's literature. Church and Synagogue Library Association, cslainfo.org.

CSLA Rodda Book Award. Recognizes a book that exhibits excellence in writing and has contributed significantly to congregational libraries through promotion of spiritual growth. The award is given to books for adults, young adults, and children on a three-year-rotational basis. Church and Synagogue Library Association, cslainfo.org.

For nonprint media

ALA *Booklist* Editors' Choice: Media. The *Booklist* editors select best-of-the-year documentary and feature films and audiobooks. ALA *Booklist,* www.booklistonline.com.

ALA/ALSC Andrew Carnegie Medal. A medal presented annually to an American producer for outstanding video production for children issued in the United States in the previous calendar year. ALA Association for Library Service to Children, ala.org/alsc/.

ALA/ALSC Great Web Sites for Kids. A compilation of websites recommended for young people. ALA Association for Library Service to Children, ala.org/alsc/.

ALA/ALSC Notable Children's Recordings. An annual annotated list of the best children's recordings. ALA Association for Library Service to Children, ala.org/alsc/.

ALA/ALSC Notable Children's Videos. An annual annotated list of the best children's videos. ALA Association for Library Service to Children, ala.org/alsc/.

ALA/ALSC/*Booklist*/YALSA Odyssey Award for Excellence in Audiobook Production. Given to the producer of the best audiobook made for children or young adults available in English in the United States. ALA Association for Library Service to Children, ala.org/alsc/.

ALA/RUSA ABC-CLIO Online History Award. A biennial citation and $3,000 cash award to recognize the production of a freely available online historical collection, an online tool tailored for the purpose of finding historical materials, or an online teaching aid stimulating creative historical scholarship. ALA Reference and User Services Association, ala.org/rusa/.

ALA/RUSA Listen List. A list of outstanding audiobook titles that merit special attention by general adult listeners and the librarians who work with them. ALA Reference and User Services Association, ala.org/rusa/.

ALA/VRT Notable Videos for Adults. A list of 15 outstanding programs released on video within the previous two years and suitable for all libraries serving adults. ALA Video Round Table, ala. org/vrt/.

ALA/YALSA Amazing Audiobooks for Young Adults. An annual annotated list of notable audio recordings significant to young adults released in the previous two years. ALA Young Adult Library Services Association, ala.org/yalsa/.

ALA/YALSA Fabulous Films for Young Adults. An annotated list of films based on a theme that will appeal to young adults in a variety of settings. ALA Young Adult Library Services Association, ala.org/yalsa/.

ARLIS/NA Worldwide Books Award for Electronic Resources. To recognize outstanding electronic publications by ARLIS/NA individual members in librarianship, visual resources curatorship, or the arts. Art Libraries Society of North America, www.arlisna.org.

GIS Best Website Award. Presented to a geosciences website that exemplifies outstanding standards of content, design, organization, and overall site effectiveness. Geoscience Information Society, www.geoinfo.org.

OHA Nonprint Format Award. Recognizes a film, video, performance piece, radio program or series, exhibition, or drama that makes significant and outstanding use of oral history to interpret an historical event, person, place, or way of life. Oral History Association, www.oralhistory.org.

For reference and adult books

AAC&U Frederic W. Ness Book Award. A $2,000 award recognizing a book that contributes to the understanding and improvement of liberal education. Association of American Colleges and Universities, www.aacu.org.

ACL Nonfiction Book Award. For excellence in writing and research that inspires serious discussion in the Christian community. Association of Christian Librarians, www.acl.org.

AECT Outstanding Book Award. For an outstanding book in the field of instructional design. Association for Educational Communications and Technology, aect.site-ym.com.

AECT/Information Age Publishers Distance Education Book Award. For an outstanding book published within the last three years that describes important aspects of distance education or theory. Association for Educational Communications and Technology, aect.site-ym.com.

AJL Judaica Reference and Bibliography Awards. For outstanding bibliographies and reference books in Judaica. Association of Jewish Libraries, www.jewishlibraries.org.

ALA *Booklist* Editors' Choice: Adult Books. The *Booklist* adult books editors select titles as representative of the year's outstanding books for public library collections. ALA *Booklist,* www. booklistonline.com.

ALA *Booklist* Editors' Choice: Reference Sources. The *Booklist* adult books editors select reference titles intended for a general readership at the high-school level and up. ALA *Booklist*, www. booklistonline.com.

ALA *Booklist*/RUSA Andrew Carnegie Medals for Excellence in Fiction and Nonfiction. An award established in 2012 to recognize the best fiction and nonfiction books for adult readers published in the U.S. the previous year. ALA Awards, ala.org/awardsgrants/carnegieadult.

ALA W. Y. Boyd Literary Award for Excellence in Military Fiction. $5,000 to an author for the best fiction set in a period when the United States is at war. ALA Awards, ala.org.

ALA/ACRL *Choice* Outstanding Academic Titles. The best scholarly titles reviewed by *Choice* magazine. ALA Association of College and Research Libraries, ala.org/acrl/.

ALA/GLBTRT Over the Rainbow Project Booklist. Recognizes current quality nonfiction and fiction books that authentically express gay, lesbian, bisexual, and transgender experiences. ALA Gay, Lesbian, Bisexual, and Transgender Round Table, ala.org/glbtrt/.

ALA/GLBTRT Stonewall Book Award–Barbara Gittings Literature Award. Cash awards to authors of fiction of exceptional merit relating to the gay/lesbian/bisexual/transgender experience published in the United States. ALA Gay, Lesbian, Bisexual, and Transgender Round Table, ala. org/glbtrt/.

ALA/GLBTRT Stonewall Book Award–Israel Fishman Nonfiction Award. Cash awards to authors of nonfiction of exceptional merit relating to the gay/lesbian/bisexual/transgender experience published in the United States. ALA Gay, Lesbian, Bisexual, and Transgender Round Table, ala.org/glbtrt/.

ALA/LHRT Eliza Atkins Gleason Book Award. An award presented every three years to recognize the best book written in English in the field of library history, including the history of libraries, librarianship, and book culture. ALA Library History Round Table, ala.org/lhrt/.

ALA/RUSA Dartmouth Medal. A medal presented to honor the creation of a reference work of outstanding quality and significance. ALA Reference and User Services Association, ala.org/rusa/.

ALA/RUSA Notable Books for Adults. An annual list of 25 very good, very readable, and at times very important fiction, nonfiction, and poetry books for the adult reader. ALA Reference and User Services Association, ala.org/rusa/.

ALA/RUSA Outstanding Reference Sources. An annual list of the best reference publications for small and medium-sized libraries. ALA Reference and User Services Association, ala.org/rusa/.

ALA/RUSA Reading List. Awards for outstanding genre fiction that merits special attention by general adult readers and the librarians who work with them. ALA Reference and User Services Association, ala.org/rusa/.

ALA/RUSA Sophie Brody Award. An award for the U.S. author of the most distinguished contribution to Jewish literature for adults. ALA Reference and User Services Association, ala.org/rusa/.

ALA/United for Libraries Literary Landmark. Officially recognizes any special location that is tied to a deceased literary figure or author or his or her work. ALA United for Libraries: Association of Library Trustees, Advocates, Friends, and Foundations, ala.org/united/.

APALA Literature Awards. Given to the writers or illustrators of adult or children's books about Asian/Pacific Americans. Asian Pacific American Library Association, www.apalaweb.org.

ARLIS/NA George Wittenborn Memorial Book Award. Annual award for outstanding art books published in North America. Art Libraries Society of North America, www.arlisna.org.

ARLIS/NA Worldwide Books Award for Publications. To recognize outstanding publications by ARLIS/NA members. Art Libraries Society of North America, www.arlisna.org.

ARSC Lifetime Achievement Award. Presented to an individual in recognition of a life's work in research and publication on recorded sound. Association for Recorded Sound Collections, www. arsc-audio.org.

ASIS&T Best Information Science Book. Recognizes the outstanding book in information science published during the preceding year. American Society for Information Science and Technology, www.asis.org.

BCALA Literary Awards. The three annual BCALA Literary Awards (fiction, nonfiction, and first novelist) of $500 each recognize outstanding works by African-American authors. Citations are also provided for Honor Books and for Outstanding Contribution to Publishing. Black Caucus of the American Library Association, www.bcala.org.

CSLA Rodda Book Award. Recognizes a book that exhibits excellence in writing and has contributed significantly to congregational libraries through promotion of spiritual growth. The award is given to books for adults, young adults, and children on a three-year-rotational basis. Church and Synagogue Library Association, cslainfo.org.

GIS Best Guidebook Award. For the best geological guidebook published in the previous year.

Geoscience Information Society, www.geoinfo.org.

GIS Mary B. Ansari Best Geoscience Reference Work Award. For the best reference book in the field of geosciences or astronomy in the previous year. Geoscience Information Society, www. geoinfo.org.

OHA Book Award. Recognizes a published book that uses oral history to make a significant contribution to contemporary scholarship. Oral History Association, www.oralhistory.org.

TLA George Freedley Memorial Award. Given annually for an English-language book of exceptional scholarship published in the United States that examines some aspect of live theatre or performance. Theatre Library Association, www.tla-online.org.

TLA Richard Wall Memorial Award. Given annually for an English-language book of exceptional scholarship published in the United States in the field of recorded performance. Theatre Library Association, www.tla-online.org.

LIBRARY EDUCATION

Accredited library programs

THE FOLLOWING GRADUATE LIBRARY and information studies programs are accredited (as of June 2012) by the American Library Association under its *Standards for Accreditation*. All programs offer a master's-level degree; those marked with an asterisk (*) offer a doctorate; those marked with a plus sign (+) offer post-master's certification; those marked with a computer symbol (🖥) offer a degree that can be acquired through 100% online instruction.

+**Catholic University of America,** School of Library and Information Science, 620 Michigan Avenue NE, Washington, DC 20064; (202) 319-5085. *Website:* slis.cua.edu. L. R. Poos, interim dean.

+🖥**Clarion University of Pennsylvania,** Department of Library Science, 222 Carlson Library Building, 840 Wood Street, Clarion, PA 16214-1232; (814) 393-2271. *Website:* www.clarion.edu/1095/. Janice M. Krueger, chair.

Dalhousie University, School of Information Management, Kenneth C. Rowe Management Building, 6100 University Avenue, Suite 4010, Halifax, NS, Canada B3H 4R2; (902) 494-3656. *Website:* sim.management.dal.ca. Louise Spiteri, director.

*+**Dominican University,** Graduate School of Library and Information Science, Crown Library 300, 7900 West Division Street, River Forest, IL 60305; (708) 524-6845. *Website:* www.dom.edu/gslis. Susan Roman, dean.

*+🖥**Drexel University,** College of Information Science and Technology, 3141 Chestnut Street, Philadelphia, PA 19104-2875; (215) 895-2474. *Website:* www.ischool.drexel.edu. David E. Fenske, dean.

*+**Emporia State University,** School of Library and Information Management, 1200 Commercial Street, Emporia, KS 66801; (620) 341-5203. *Website:* slim. emporia.edu. Gwen Alexander, dean.

*+🖥**Florida State University,** School of Library and Information Studies, 142 Collegiate Loop, P.O. Box 3062100, Tallahassee, FL 32306-2100; (850) 644-5775. *Website:* slis.fsu.edu. Corinne Jörgenson, director.

*+**Indiana University,** School of Library and Information Science, 1320 E. 10th

Street, LI 011, Bloomington, IN 47405-3907; (812) 855-2018. *Website:* www. slis.iu.edu. Debora Shaw, dean.

+**Kent State University,** School of Library and Information Science, P.O. Box 5190, 314 University Library, Kent, OH 44242-0001; (330) 672-2782. *Website:* www.kent.edu/slis/. Don A. Wicks, interim director.

*+**Long Island University,** Palmer School of Library and Information Science, C. W. Post Campus, 720 Northern Boulevard, Brookville, NY 11548-1300; (516) 299-2866. *Website:* www.liu.edu/palmer/. Jody K. Howard, director.

▣**Louisiana State University,** School of Library and Information Science, 267 Coates Hall, Baton Rouge, LA 70803; (225) 578-3158. *Website:* slis.lsu.edu. Beth M. Paskoff, dean.

*+**McGill University,** School of Information Studies, 3661 Peel Street, Montreal, QC, Canada H3A 1X1; (514) 398-4204. *Website:* www.mcgill.ca/sis/. France Bouthillier, director.

▣**North Carolina Central University,** School of Library and Information Sciences, P.O. Box 19586, 1801 Fayetteville St., Durham, NC 27707; (919) 530-6485. *Website:* www.nccuslis.org. Irene Owens, dean.

+**Pratt Institute,** School of Information and Library Science, 144 W. 14th Street, 6th Floor, New York, NY 10011; (212) 647-7682. *Website:* www.pratt.edu/academics/information_and_library_sciences/. Tula Giannini, dean.

+**Queens College, City University of New York,** Graduate School of Library and Information Studies, 65–30 Kissena Boulevard, Rosenthal Library, Room 254, Flushing, NY 11367-1597; (718) 997-3790. *Website:* www.qc.cuny.edu/Academics/Degrees/DSS/gslis/Pages/default.aspx?. James Marcum, director.

*+▣**Rutgers, the State University of New Jersey,** Department of Library and Information Science, 4 Huntington Street, New Brunswick, NJ 08901-1071; (732) 932-7500, ext. 8218. *Website:* comminfo.rutgers.edu. Maric L. Radford, chair.

St. Catherine University, Master of Library and Information Science, 2004 Randolph Avenue, #4125, St. Paul, MN 55105; (651) 690-6802. *Website:* www.stkate.edu/academic/mlis/. Deborah S. Grealy, program director.

+**St. John's University,** Division of Library and Information Science, 8000 Utopia Parkway, Jamaica, NY 11439; (718) 990-6200. *Website:* www.stjohns.edu/academics/graduate/liberalarts/departments/lis/. Jeffery E. Olson, director.

*▣**San Jose State University,** School of Library and Information Science, One Washington Square, San Jose, CA 95192-0029; (408) 924-2490. *Website:* slisweb.sjsu.edu. Sandra Hirsh, director.

*+**Simmons College,** Graduate School of Library and Information Science, 300 The Fenway, Boston, MA 02115-5898; (617) 521-2800. *Website:* www. simmons.edu/gslis/. Michèle V. Cloonan, dean.

▣**Southern Connecticut State University,** Information and Library Science Department, 501 Crescent Street, New Haven, CT 06515; (203) 392-5781. *Website:* www.southernct.edu/ils/. Chang Suk Kim, chairperson.

*+**Syracuse University,** School of Information Studies, 343 Hinds Hall, Syracuse, NY 13244-4100; (315) 443-2911. *Website:* ischool.syr.edu. Elizabeth D. Liddy, dean.

*▣**Texas Woman's University,** School of Library and Information Studies, 404 Stoddard Hall, P.O. Box 425438, Denton, TX 76204-5438; (940) 898-2602. *Website:* www.twu.edu/slis/. Ling Hwey Jeng, director.

***Université de Montréal,** École de bibliothéconomie et des sciences de l'information, 3150 rue Jean-Brillant, Montréal, QC, Canada, H3T 1N8.

Website: (514) 343-6044; www.ebsi.umontreal.ca. Clément Arsenault, director.

*▢**University of Alabama,** School of Library and Information Studies, Box 870252, 513 Gorgas Library, Tuscaloosa, AL 35487-0252; (205) 348-4610. *Website:* www.slis.ua.edu. Heidi Julien, director.

*+**University at Albany, State University of New York,** Information Studies Department, Draper 113, 135 Western Avenue, Albany, NY 12222; (518) 442-5110. *Website:* www.albany.edu/informationstudies/index.php. Philip B. Eppard, chair.

***University of Alberta,** School of Library and Information Studies, 3–20 Rutherford South, Edmonton, AB, Canada T6G 2J4; (780) 492-4578. *Website:* www.slis.ualberta.ca. Ernie Ingles, director.

*+**University of Arizona,** School of Information Resources and Library Science, 1515 East First Street, Tucson, AZ 85719; (520) 621-3565. *Website:* sirls.arizona.edu. Bryan Heidorn, director.

*+**University of British Columbia,** School of Library, Archival, and Information Studies, Irving K. Barber Learning Centre, 1961 East Mall, Suite 470, Vancouver, BC, Canada V6T 1Z1; (604) 822-2404. *Website:* www.slais.ubc.ca. Caroline Haythornthwaite, director.

+▢**University at Buffalo, State University of New York,** Department of Library and Information Studies, 534 Baldy Hall, Buffalo, NY 14260-1020; (716) 645-2412. *Website:* gse.buffalo.edu/lis/. Jianqiang Wang, interim chair.

*+**University of California, Los Angeles,** Department of Information Studies, Graduate School of Education and Information Studies Building, Box 951520, Los Angeles, CA 90095-1520; (310) 825-8799. *Website:* is.gseis.ucla.edu. Gregory H. Leazer, chair.

University of Denver, Library and Information Science Program, 1999 E. Evans Avenue, Denver, CO 80208-1700; (303) 871-2509. *Website:* www.du.edu/education/programs/lis/. Mary Stansbury, domain chair.

*+**University of Hawaii,** Library and Information Science Program, 2550 McCarthy Mall, Honolulu, HI 96822; (808) 956-7321. *Website:* www.hawaii.edu/lis/. Andrew B. Wertheimer, chair.

*+**University of Illinois at Urbana-Champaign,** Graduate School of Library and Information Science, 501 East Daniel Street, Champaign, IL 61820-6211; (217) 333-3280. *Website:* www.lis.illinois.edu. Allen Renear, interim dean.

University of Iowa, School of Library and Information Science, 3087 Main Library, Iowa City, IA 52242-1420; (319) 335-5707. *Website:* slis.grad.uiowa.edu. Daniel A. Berkowitz, interim director.

*▢**University of Kentucky,** School of Library and Information Science, 320 Little Fine Arts Library, Lexington, KY 40506-0224; (859) 257-8876. *Website:* cis.uky.edu/lis/. Jeffrey T. Huber, director.

*▢**University of Maryland,** College of Information Studies, 4105 Hornbake Building, College Park, MD 20742; (301) 405-2038. *Website:* ischool.umd.edu. Jennifer J. Preece, dean.

***University of Michigan,** School of Information, 4322 North Quad, 105 S. State Street, Ann Arbor, MI 48109-1285; (734) 647-3576. *Website:* www.si.umich.edu. Jeffrey K. MacKie-Mason, dean.

***University of Missouri,** School of Information Science and Learning Technologies, 303 Townsend Hall, Columbia, MO 65211; (573) 884-2670. *Website:* lis.missouri.edu. Daniel Clay, dean, College of Education.

*+**University of North Carolina at Chapel Hill,** School of Information and Library Science, CB #3360, 100 Manning Hall, Chapel Hill, NC 27599-3360;

(919) 962-8366. *Website:* sils.unc.edu. Gary Marchionini, dean.

University of North Carolina at Greensboro, Department of Library and Information Studies, 446 School of Education Building, P.O. Box 26170, Greensboro, NC 27402-6170; (336) 334-3477. *Website:* lis.uncg.edu. Clara M. Chu, chair.

*+**University of North Texas,** Department of Library and Information Sciences, 3940 N. Elm, E292, Denton, TX 76207; (940) 565-2445. *Website:* www.lis. unt.edu/main/. Suliman Hawamdeh, chair.

+**University of Oklahoma,** School of Library and Information Studies, 401 West Brooks, Room 120, Norman, OK 73019-6032; (405) 325-3921. *Website:* slis. ou.edu. Cecelia Brown, director.

*+**University of Pittsburgh,** School of Information Sciences, 135 N. Bellefield Avenue, Pittsburgh, PA 15260; (412) 624-5230. *Website:* www.ischool.pitt. edu. Ronald L. Larsen, dean.

⌨**University of Puerto Rico,** Escuela Graduada de Ciencias y Tecnologías de la Información, P.O. Box 21906, San Juan, PR 00931-1906; (787) 763-6199. *Website:* egcti.upr.edu. Luisa Vigo Cepeda, acting director.

+**University of Rhode Island,** Graduate School of Library and Information Studies, Rodman Hall, 94 W. Alumni Avenue, Kingston, RI 02881; (401) 874-2878. *Website:* www.uri.edu/artsci/lsc/. Renee Hobbs, interim director.

*+⌨**University of South Carolina,** School of Library and Information Science, 1501 Greene Street, Columbia, SC 29208; (803) 777-3858. *Website:* www. libsci.sc.edu. Samantha K. Hastings, director.

+**University of South Florida,** School of Information, 4202 East Fowler Avenue, CIS 1040, Tampa, FL 33620-8100; (813) 974-3520. *Website:* si.usf.edu. James E. Andrews, director.

⌨**University of Southern Mississippi,** School of Library and Information Science, 118 College Drive, #5146, Hattiesburg, MS 39406-0001; (601) 266-4228. *Website:* www.usm.edu/library-information-science. Melanie J. Norton, director.

*⌨**University of Tennessee,** School of Information Sciences, 451 Communication Building, 1345 Circle Park Drive, Knoxville, TN 37996-0341; (865) 974-2148. *Website:* www.sis.utk.edu. Edwin M. Cortez, director.

*+**University of Texas at Austin,** School of Information, 1616 Guadalupe Street, Suite 5.202, Austin, TX 78701-1213; (512) 471-3821. *Website:* www.ischool. utexas.edu. Andrew Dillon, dean.

*+**University of Toronto,** Faculty of Information, 140 St. George Street, Room 211, Toronto, ON, Canada M5S 3G6; (416) 978-3234. *Website:* www.ischool. utoronto.ca. Seamus Ross, dean.

*+⌨**University of Washington,** Information School, 370 Mary Gates Hall, Box 352840, Seattle, WA 98195-2840; (206) 685-9937. *Website:* ischool.uw.edu. Harry Bruce, dean.

***University of Western Ontario,** Faculty of Information and Media Studies, North Campus Building, Room 240, London, ON, Canada N6A 5B7; (519) 661-3542. *Website:* www.fims.uwo.ca. Thomas Carmichael, dean.

*+**University of Wisconsin-Madison,** School of Library and Information Studies, 4217 Helen C. White Hall, 600 North Park Street, Madison, WI 53706; (608) 263-2900. *Website:* www.slis.wisc.edu. Kristin Eschenfelder, director.

*+⌨**University of Wisconsin-Milwaukee,** School of Information Studies, Northwest Quad Building B, 2025 E. Newport, Milwaukee, WI 53211; (414) 229-4707. *Website:* www4.uwm.edu/sois/. Wooseob Jeong, interim dean.

Valdosta State University, Master of Library and Information Science Program, 1500 N. Patterson Street, Valdosta, GA 31698-0133; (229) 333-5966. *Website:* www.valdosta.edu/mlis/. Wallace Koehler, director.

+🖥**Wayne State University,** School of Library and Information Science, 106 Kresge Library, Detroit, MI 48202; (313) 577-1825. *Website:* slis.wayne.edu. Sandra G. Yee, director.

SOURCE: ALA Office for Accreditation, September 2012.

Library leadership opportunities

THESE STRUCTURED PROGRAMS offer leadership training and career skills for librarians who wish to build their management skills.

ALA Emerging Leaders Program. A leadership development program that enables newer library workers from across the country to participate in problem-solving work groups, network with peers, gain an inside look into the structure of the American Library Association, and have an opportunity to serve the profession in a leadership capacity. It puts participants on the fast track to ALA committee volunteerism as well as other professional library-related organizations. *Website:* ala.org/ala/educationcareers/leadership/emergingleaders/.

ALA Spectrum Doctoral Fellowship. Provides full tuition support and stipends to 10 full-time library and information science doctoral students for all four years of study. The Fellowship is open to applicants of American Indian/Alaska Native, Asian, Black/African American, Hispanic/Latino, or Native Hawaiian/Other Pacific Islander heritage. *Website:* ala.org/offices/diversity/spectrum/phd.

Archives Leadership Institute. Funded by the National Historical Publications and Records Commission, this University of Wisconsin-Madison program examines the leadership needs of the archives profession and prepares participants to influence policy and effect change for the benefit of the profession. *Website:* www.slis.wisc.edu/continueed-ArchLeader.htm.

ARL Leadership and Career Development Program. An 18-month program to prepare mid-career librarians from traditionally underrepresented racial and ethnic minority groups to take on increasingly demanding leadership roles in member libraries of the Association of Research Libraries. *Website:* www.arl.org/diversity/lcdp/index.shtml.

2011–2012 ARL Leadership and Career Development Program Fellows, January 2011. Photo by J. T. MacMillan.

ARL Research Library Leadership Fellows Program. Offers an opportunity for development of future senior-level leaders in large research libraries. The program exposes and engages library staff who have the desire and potential for leadership at member libraries of the Association of Research Libraries to themes and institutions that will enhance their preparedness. *Website:* www.arl.org/leadership/rllf/index.shtml.

Aurora Institute for Emerging Leaders. This program is for those who have been identified as potential leaders by their own organizations and have had two years experience in a supervisory or management role. With the increasing interrelationship of the library, information, and cultural industries, the program will appeal to a wide range of organizations, including libraries, galleries, museums, archives, and records management. *Website:* www.aurorafoundation.org.au/index. php?_a=viewDoc&docId=5.

Certified Public Library Administrator Courses. This series of continuing education programs is designed to meet both the requirements for CPLA certification and the needs of library managers wanting to enhance their skills outside of the CPLA framework. The workshops have been designed to be practical rather than theoretical and include interactive exercises and group work. *Website:* ala.org/pla/education/cpla.

Eureka! Leadership Program. Sponsored by the California State Library and Infopeople, this program offers librarians in California with 3–10 years of professional library experience an opportunity to take part in an intensive week-long training institute, as well as follow-up activities. *Website:* eurekaleadership.org.

Frye Leadership Institute. This Atlanta-based institute engages those who are already leaders in libraries, information services, and higher education and further develops their skills, particularly in the area of advocacy. *Website:* www. fryeinstitute.org.

Harvard Leadership Institute for Academic Librarians. Provides important leadership concepts and applies them to the practical challenges of leading and managing the contemporary academic library. The curriculum addresses three areas—planning, organizational strategy and change, and transformational learning—with an overarching goal of increasing leadership and management capacity. *Website:* www.gse.harvard.edu/ppe/programs/higher-education/portfolio/leadership-academic-librarians.html.

HBCU Library Alliance Leadership Program. Funded by a grant from the Andrew W. Mellon Foundation, the program provides theoretical and practical instruction and useful resources to encourage the development of leadership skills within the Historically Black College and University library community and on their own campuses. *Website:* www.hbculibraries.org/html/leadership.html.

ILEAD U: Illinois Libraries Explore, Apply, Discover. A three-year continuing education initiative offered by the State Library of Illinois to address the need to expand Illinois librarians' leadership abilities to use participatory technology and effectively engage their libraries' constituents. *Website:* www.webjunction. org/partners/illinois/il-programs/ileadu.html.

Maryland Library Leadership Institute. Created by the Maryland Library Association, the institute focuses on the development of individual leadership skills. *Website:* www.mdlib.org/leadership/.

Minnesota Institute for Early Career Librarians. Every two years, the University of Minnesota Libraries offer a week-long training institute for 25 early-career academic librarians who are from traditionally underrepresented groups and are in the first three years of their professional career. *Website:* www.lib.umn. edu/sed/institute/.

MLA Leadership Academy. The Michigan Library Association offers a series of training sessions on leadership essentials, team building, communications and listening, change management, conflict resolution, and consensus building. *Website:* www.mla.lib.mi.us/events/leadership/.

Mortensen Center Associates Program. This program, sponsored by the Mortensen Center at the University of Illinois at Urbana-Champaign, offers library and information science professionals from outside the United States an opportunity to explore and engage with current issues and trends in the field. *Website:* www.library.illinois.edu/mortenson/associates/.

MPLA Leadership Institute. The Mountain Plains Library Association brings identified leadership candidates into close relationship with the association's products of training and professional development. *Website:* www.mpla.us/leadership/.

NCLA Leadership Institute. The North Carolina Library Association's learning experience for individuals who lead or hope to lead the state's libraries. *Website:* www.nclaonline.org/professional-development/ncla-leadership-institute/.

New England Library Leadership Symposium. An intensive course offered by the New England Library Association to foster mentoring and development of leaders for state and regional library associations. *Website:* www.nelib.org/nells/.

Northern Exposure to Leadership Institute. The institute assists professional librarians aspiring to leadership roles to develop, strengthen, and evolve their leadership potential so that they may be better equipped to lead Canada's libraries or information service organizations or programs in the 21st century. *Website:* www.ls.ualberta.ca/neli/.

NYLA Leadership and Management Academy. An educational program for emerging leaders in the library profession sponsored by the New York Library Association. *Website:* www.nyla.org/max/4DCGI/cms/review.html?Action=CMS_Document&DocID=51.

PNLA Leadership Institute. Designed by the Pacific Northwest Library Association to provide opportunities for emerging library leaders in the Northwest to cultivate their leadership skills and potential. *Website:* www.pnla.org/institute/.

Senior Fellows at UCLA. A professional development program for senior level academic librarians that offers a unique combination of management perspectives, strategic thinking, and practical and theoretical approaches to the issues confronting academic institutions and their libraries. *Website:* is.gseis.ucla.edu/events/seniorfellows/index.htm.

Sunshine State Library Leadership Institute. This State Library and Archives of Florida institute assists in preparing library leaders to provide the highest quality library services to the citizens of the state. *Website:* dlis.dos.state.fl.us/bld/leadership/institute.cfm.

TALL Texans Leadership Institute. The institute provides advanced leadership and management education in service to all the libraries of Texas and the communities they serve. Participants are mid-career library and information science practitioners (degreed and non-degreed) who are employed in the field and have at least five years of experience in a professional-level position in library or information science. *Website:* www.txla.org/?q=node/400.

Tribal College Librarians Professional Development Institute. The institute is held annually at Montana State University in Bozeman and has promoted professional development activities for tribal college librarians since 1990. *Website:* www.lib.montana.edu/tcli/.

Women's Leadership Institute. A special program for women seeking to become leaders in higher education administration and student affairs, coproduced by 19 higher education associations. Presentations, structured wellness time, and small group discussions emphasize problem-solving strategies for college and university leaders. *Website:* ala.org/acrl/womensleadership.

Wyoming Library Leadership Institute. Offered by the Wyoming State Library, this institute provides opportunities for learning, mentoring, and developing leadership skills to promote the personal and professional growth of the Wyoming library community. *Website:* www-wsl.state.wy.us/training/wlli.html.

Top row: Annie Eliza Hutchins, Eliza S. Talcott. *Second row:* Kate Bonnell, Frank Chauncy Patten, Janey Elizabeth Stott, Melvil Dewey (faculty), Florence Woodworth, George H. Baker (faculty), Frances S. Knowlton, Walter Stanley Biscoe (faculty), Lilian Howe Chapman, Lillian Denio. *Third row:* Salome Cutler Fairchild (faculty), Harriet Sherman Griswold, Annie Brown Jackson, May Seymour, Richard F. Armstrong (honorary), Mrs. George Watson Cole (honorary), Mrs. Annie Dewey (honorary), Eulora Miller, Harriet Converse Fernald. *Fourth row:* George Catlin, Mary Wright Plummer, Martha Furber Nelson, Harriet P. Burgess. *Reclining:* George Watson Cole.

The first library school students, 1887–1888

by George M. Eberhart

MELVIL DEWEY founded the first professional school for librarians at Columbia College in New York City where he served as college librarian. The School of Library Economy opened its doors January 5, 1887, with 20 students enrolled—17 women and three men (two other women came aboard later to join the Class of 1888). The faculty consisted of Dewey, who taught library economy; George H. Baker (bibliography); Walter Stanley Biscoe (cataloging and classification); and several guest lecturers.

Dewey took a gigantic risk admitting women into the school. At the time, Columbia trustees allowed women to study independently at the library in order to pass an examination for a bachelor's degree, but they were prohibited from taking classes. Although he had the verbal permission of President Frederick A. P. Barnard, Dewey had nothing in writing allowing him to enroll women. The day before the school opened, Dewey was informed by the chairman of Columbia's committee on buildings that he could not use any campus classrooms for coeducational instruction. Within 24 hours, he had cleared a storeroom within the library to prepare it as an instructional area. But Dewey had made some enemies, and his unauthorized experiment ultimately led to his resignation a year later. Although some of its graduate schools began allowing women in the 1890s, the undergraduate Columbia College did not become fully coeducational until 1983.

Dewey wrote in the March 1887 issue of *Library Notes*: "Most of the students have been so persistent in their study and practice that they have seemed to live in the library. Lunch is brought up to those wishing it by the school page assigned to wait on the class, and for 14 hours daily there is opportunity for work."

He doted on this first class of library students and tried to repay their enthusiasm for the profession with some perks: "With all this work, time has been found for many enjoyable extras. Many courtesies have been extended, including complimentary tickets for the entire class for various entertainments and lectures. . . . Alternate Friday evenings have been spent socially at the home of the director of the school, where music, simple refreshments, and general good fellowship helped to develop the esprit de corps evident in the pioneer class."

The first students enrolled for only three months, but after only six weeks they petitioned for an extra month; most of the class eventually opted for a full two years of study. After or between courses, the school found apprentice positions for some of the students. In 1889, the school followed Dewey to the New York State Library, located in Room 31 of the Capitol Building in Albany, New York, when he was appointed director. It became the New York State Library School.

Many of Dewey's first students became prominent in the profession. Here is the roster for the Class of 1888 and what became of them.

Bonnell, Kate (d. 1890), from San Francisco. She left school in May 1887 to become a cataloger at the New York Free Circulating Library.

Burgess, Harriet P. (d. 1896), from New York City. She left school in May 1887.

Catlin, George, from Birmingham, England, where he was assistant city librarian. He left school in June 1887 and became a cataloger at the University Club in New York City in the winter of 1887.

Chapman, Lilian Howe (d. 1916), came from Cottage City (now Oak Bluffs), Massachusetts, where she was librarian for the Cottage City Library Association. She stayed at school through December 1887, then spent her later years as a technical services specialist in Vineyard Haven and Cottage City libraries in Massachusetts; Plainville, Woodstock, and Windsor public libraries in Connecticut; Brooklyn (N.Y.) Public Library; and the Morgan Memorial Library in Boston.

Cole, George Watson (1850–1939). After practicing law in Connecticut for nine years, Cole (left) turned to librarianship at Melvil Dewey's urging. In 1885–1886 he compiled the printed catalog of the Fitchburg (Mass.) Public Library. From Fitchburg he moved to Brooklyn in the autumn of 1886 to become librarian of the Pratt Institute, attending library school at the same time. After graduating in 1888, Cole went to work with William F. Poole at the Newberry Library in Chicago, which he left in January 1891 to become director of the Free Public Library of Jersey City. In December 1895, because of a bout with typhoid fever, Cole resigned and devoted the next five years to travel and bibliographic research. In December 1901 he began compiling a seven-volume catalog of the library of American and English literature and miscellany owned by wealthy collector Elihu Dwight Church, of Brooklyn, which established him as an outstanding American bibliographer. In New York City in October 1915, Cole became the personal librarian of railroad magnate and bibliophile Henry E. Huntington, who had amassed one of the country's largest collections of rare books and manuscripts, including the Church collection. Cole moved with Huntington's library when it was transferred in 1920 to its present location in San Marino, California, becoming librarian emeritus in 1924. Cole was president of the Bibliographical Society of America in 1917–1918. He collected picture postcards as a hobby and in 1935 published a brochure on their systematic arrangement.

Denio, Lillian (d. 1901), from Albion, New York. During her studies in library school, Denio worked at Wellesley College Library and as cataloger for the Union for Christian Work in Brooklyn. After graduating in January 1889, she became cataloger at Grand Rapids (Mich.) Public Library in 1889–1890 and director of the Bryson Library at Columbia University Teachers College in 1890–1896.

Fernald, Harriet (Hattie) Converse (1866?–1932), from Orono, Maine. During library school, Fernald worked in technical services at the Saugus (Mass.) Public Library; Bowdoin College in Brunswick, Maine; and the Union for Christian Work in Brooklyn. After graduating in January 1889, she worked as a cataloger in the Maine State College library (now the University of Maine, Orono), becoming its first professional library director from 1890 to 1897 and the only woman member of a college faculty in Maine. She established a course in library economy there in 1894. She married attorney John Alvin Pierce in 1897 and moved to Spokane, Washington, but her husband died in 1907 and she returned to Maine.

Godfrey, Lydia Boker, from Wellesley, Massachusetts. Godfrey worked as superintendent of the Wellesley College Library cataloging department from 1883 until her graduation in April 1888, then served as Wellesley reference librarian in 1888–1893 and director in 1893–1903. In 1896, she compiled a sampler of English plays with Katharine Lee Bates titled *English Drama* (Boston: Robinson).

Goodrich, Harriet (d. 1926), from Grand Rapids, Michigan. She left school in February 1887. In 1924–1926, she was in charge of the architectural reading room of the University of Michigan Library in Ann Arbor.

Griswold, Harriet Sherman (d. 1889), from Batavia, New York. Before attending library school, Griswold was director of the Batavia (N.Y.) Public Library in 1883–1886, and became librarian of the New York City YWCA in 1887–1888.

Hutchins, Annie Eliza (d. 1912), from Cambridge, Massachusetts. With working experience at Harvard University, Boston Public, and Cornell and Columbia College libraries, Hutchins became an instructor in dictionary cataloging after attending library school. She moved on to positions at the Newberry Library and Yale University in 1890–1910.

Jackson, Annie Brown, from North Adams, Massachusetts. Jackson was a stockholder in Melvil Dewey's commercial operation, the Library Bureau. She served on the North Adams Public Library book committee from 1885 to 1896 and as president of its board of trustees from 1896 to at least 1922.

Jones, Ada Alice (d. 1943), from Chester, Ohio. Jones (right) was a cataloger at Wellesley College library before going to library school. While studying for her degree, she served as assistant librarian for the New York City YWCA, then moved on to a cataloging position at Columbia College in 1887–1888 and followed Dewey to the New York State Library from 1889 to 1892, where she also taught cataloging through 1911. Jones was described as "meticulous in her teaching, inspiring ideals of accuracy and thoroughness." She took time out to be the director of the Woman's Library at the World's Columbian Exposition in Chicago in 1893, returning to Albany as head cataloger from 1892 to at least 1922.

Knowlton, Frances (Fannie) S., from Holland Patent, New York. She left school in April 1887.

Miller, Eulora (d. 1939). Miller (right) was the first woman to graduate from Purdue University in 1878, becoming Purdue's first professional library director in 1878 and assistant librarian at the Lafayette (Ind.) Public Library from 1882 to 1887. She returned to Lafayette as director after getting her degree in 1888, then took a position as director of the Pratt Institute Library in Brooklyn. She married Rufus Platt Jennings in 1890 and moved to Berkeley, California. As Eulora M. Jennings, she gained minor fame as a dramatist, having published four plays, including *Mrs. Oakley's Telephone* (1904), *Tom's Fiancée* (1906), *Dinner at the Club* (1906), and *Die Prinzessin von Barnhof* (1906).

Nelson, Martha Furber (b. 1853), from Trenton, New Jersey. The assistant librarian of the New York Free Circulating Library, Nelson left library school in June 1887 to become a classifier in the Pratt Institute Library in Brooklyn. She soon took a position as director of the Women's Christian Temperance Union library in Trenton from 1887 to 1895, then as instructor in bibliography at the New Jersey State Normal School in Trenton (now the College of New Jersey) from 1895 to 1920.

Patten, Frank Chauncy (1855–1934), from Ripon, Wisconsin. Patten made his first trip to Texas in 1879, traveling some 1,750 miles on foot to organize a school for about 25 African Americans at Live Oak Point (now Rockport), where he taught until January 1880. Before coming to library school, Patten was assistant librarian at Ripon College library. He worked as a cataloger in the New York Free Circulating Library and as evening reference clerk at Columbia College library while getting his degree. He stayed on at the New York State Library as catalog and shelf curator from 1889 to 1892, then took a job as director of the Helena (Mont.) Public Library in 1892–1899. In 1903 Patten was appointed to supervise the completion of the Rosenberg Library in Galveston, Texas, the first free public library in the state, which opened in June 1904. Under his supervision the Negro branch opened in 1905. Patten emphasized children's services, reference, public lectures, and Galveston and Texas history. In 1918 he published a biography of the library's benefactor, Henry Rosenberg (1824–1893).

 **Plummer, Mary Wright** (1856–1916) was the only graduate of the first library school class to become president of the American Library Association (1915–1916). After library school, Plummer (left) took charge of the cataloging department at St. Louis Public Library in 1888–1890. She then moved to the Pratt Institute Library in Brooklyn, where she became director in 1896 and created the second school for library studies. Plummer is credited as being the first librarian to create a separate room for the children's collection and the first to promote special training for children's librarians. She served as a contributing editor for *Public Libraries* from 1896 until her death. In 1900, Plummer was the official U.S. delegate to the International Library Congress during the Exposition Universelle in Paris in 1900 and was in charge of the ALA exhibit there. After leaving Pratt, she founded the New York Public Library School in 1911–1916. Plummer wrote poetry, children's books (including *Roy and Ray in Mexico,* 1907, and *Stories from the Chronicle of the Cid,* 1910), *Training for Librarianship* (1907) and *Hints to Small Libraries* (1911) for ALA, and a history of the New York State Library School in Albany. In 1916 she was too ill from cancer to deliver her ALA presidential address and died in September. Recognizing her national standing as well as her active role in the field, Princeton University Librarian Ernest Cushing Richardson declared that no other individual except for Herbert Putnam had

"contributed so much constructively to the elevation and dignity of the library profession in America" (*Library Journal,* December 1916, p. 879).

Seymour, May (d. 1921), from Binghamton, New York. During breaks in library school, Seymour worked as a cataloger at the Osterhout Free Library in Wilkes-Barre, Pennsylvania, and at Columbia College Library. After graduating in 1889, she was put in charge of classification at the New York State Library in Albany, and became an instructor in the school and education librarian in 1891. An accomplished editor, Seymour became a close confidante of Melvil Dewey and assisted him in the preparation of the 1904 *A.L.A. Catalog,* an annotated bibliography of some 8,000 essential books for public libraries. Dewey said of her accomplishment, "she has given not only every working hour that could be taken from other duties but has added evenings, holidays, and vacations. After plans were completed, the editor left their execution to her, and in 30 years' experience he has never been better satisfied with the performance of delegated duties." In August 1906, she moved permanently to Dewey's Lake Placid Club, where she worked tirelessly on the 4th–11th editions of the Dewey Decimal Classification in return for free lodging, as long as she spent half her time on club publications. Dewey called her a "specialist in omniscience." In *Irrepressible Reformer,* Wayne Wiegand wrote: "In 1920 May Seymour had a large cottage called White Birches built on club grounds, and made it large enough to accommodate her in one section, and Melvil and Annie Dewey in another. White Birches quickly became the Deweys' social center; they regularly entertained there and turned it into a family circle."

Stott, Janet Elizabeth, from New York City. Stott worked as assistant librarian at the New York Free Circulating Library from 1882 until 1889, when she married Richard Lavery.

Talcott, Eliza Sophia (1846–1933), from Elmwood, Connecticut. A Vassar College graduate, Talcott worked as a cataloger at the Connecticut Mutual Life Insurance Company in Hartford and the Union for Christian Work in Brooklyn after library school, then moved on to the Hartford Public Library, where she worked as assistant librarian from 1888 to 1895. She became a trustee of the West Hartford Public Library in 1900–1919, which was then housed at the First Church of Christ, Congregational.

Woodworth, Florence (d. 1950), from St. Louis. Woodworth worked with May Seymour as a cataloger at the Osterhout Free Library in Wilkes-Barre, Pennsylvania, and at Columbia College Library until April 1889, when she followed the library school to the New York State Library. In Albany, she worked both as an instructor in the school and as a cataloger and various other positions in the library until her retirement in 1925. As a teacher, Woodworth was described as "devoted, self-effacing, offering personal interest and help." In 1900, she prepared the ALA exhibit for the Exposition Universelle in Paris. Her relationship to Dewey was as a close friend; both she and May Seymour moved into Melvil and Annie Dewey's large house as boarders in the 1890s. Woodworth became a surrogate mother to Dewey's son Godfrey during Annie's absences, and she accompanied Annie to the Battle Creek (Mich.) Sanitarium when she became seriously ill in 1905.

SOURCE: "Register of the New York State Library School," *Bulletin of the New York State Library School,* no. 48 (July 15, 1922): 10–12; and scattered additional sources. For more insight into Melvil Dewey's library school, see Wayne Wiegand, *Irrepressible Reformer: A Biography of Melvil Dewey* (Chicago: American Library Association, 1996); Grosvenor Dawe, *Melvil Dewey: Seer, Inspirer, Doer* (Essex County, N.Y.: Lake Placid Club, 1932); and articles in the January 1996 issue of *American Libraries.*

WRITING

Editing your writing

by Beth Nieman

GETTING A FIRST DRAFT ON PAPER is quite an accomplishment, but a writer's job doesn't end there; you must edit your work to make it presentable for a publisher and suitable for readers to enjoy.

Make time for editing. Allow yourself plenty of time to write your article, and then let your rough draft sit unread for a day or so before you pick it up to edit

it. You'll see it as though you were reading it for the first time. Awkward sentences, spelling errors, and grammar problems will be more obvious to you.

Read your writing aloud with pen in hand. It is helpful to print your work out double-spaced, perhaps with larger-than-normal print, so that you have plenty of room on the page to mark corrections. Circle phrases or paragraphs that sound awkward as you read your work out loud. Head back to the word processor, make the changes you marked, and read the corrected passages aloud again to make sure they flow well and convey your ideas. You can repeat this step several times.

Look for common writing mistakes. The following five areas are troublesome to many writers:

1. **Clichéd phrases.** Clichés are overused phrases that add absolutely nothing to your writing. Instead of writing "It rained cats and dogs," come up with a fresh way to describe a sudden, intense downpour. Sometimes a cliché is what comes to mind as you're writing your early draft; that's OK, as long as you go back later and remove it during the editing process.

2. **Passive sentence structure.** A passive sentence here and there isn't going to ruin your writing, but a book or article full of passive sentences often makes for dull reading and adds unnecessary words. "The ball was thrown by Sally" is an example of a passive sentence. To rewrite that sentence, try "Sally threw the ball." This easy rewrite cut out two unnecessary words that added no meaning to the sentence. It also made Sally the subject of the sentence instead of the ball.

3. **Weak verbs.** Colorful verbs give energy and impact to your writing, while weak verbs make for anemic writing that interests no one. Compare "George drove quickly around the track" to "George sped around the track" and "George raced around the track." "George drove" conveys the basic meaning, but drove is a boring verb that needed the adverb quickly to help it along. A verb such as *sped, raced,* or even *zoomed* adds zest to the sentence and needs no modifier.

4. **Grammar, spelling, and usage errors.** When sending your proposals

or articles to editors, remember that your writing is the first impression of you that an editor will receive. It's important to proofread your writing carefully. Computer spell-checkers and grammar-checkers can help, but they're not infallible. Writers who want to see their work in print must have an excellent command of standard English and turn in their very best work to editors. If you need help improving your writing, consider taking a community college class to sharpen your skills. Also, there are many reference works available for you to study. Get one. Use it.

5. **Fuzzy thinking.** If you find it difficult to rewrite an awkward sentence or paragraph, it's possible you just don't know what you're talking about. Are you writing around your idea instead of getting right to the point? Ask yourself, "What is it I'm trying to say in this sentence?" If you can't answer that question, try cutting it altogether; your writing will probably be better for it.

3

Don't be afraid to rearrange the furniture as you're editing. You may have a lot of great ideas for an article or book chapter, but they don't necessarily emerge from your keyboard in the most effective order. You might find that you wrote the perfect opening sentence somewhere in the middle of your first draft. With the aid of your word processor, it's just a matter of seconds to rearrange your sentences or even entire paragraphs without retyping.

Make sure you have your facts straight before submitting your writing for publication. Check for accuracy on facts and dates, citations, and the spelling of proper nouns and personal names. Don't count on your editor to do this important step for you.

The best thing you can do to improve your writing is to cut unnecessary words for improved clarity. This step tightens your writing, making it crisp, clean, and readable. The American humorist Mark Twain once wrote to a friend, "I didn't have time to write a short letter, so I wrote a long one instead." It does take more effort to write a well-polished, short article because you must make each word, phrase, and sentence work hard—there simply isn't room for flab. You'll be amazed at how fresh and clear your lean final draft is.

After you have cleaned up your draft, have a colleague review your work if possible. Choose someone whose judgment you respect and who will be honest with you rather than someone who will just say nice things to make you feel good. Remember, you don't have to use every suggestion your colleague makes—just use what is useful to you. Be prepared to graciously accept whatever criticism is offered and don't take it personally. If you've chosen your reader well, he or she will tell you where your ideas are unclear, where there may be typographical errors, and perhaps even ask a couple of probing questions to draw you out and help you get more information into your article.

Finally, give special attention to the first and last paragraphs of your article. The first paragraph should introduce your topic with an interesting hook to make the reader want to find out more, while the final paragraph should sum up your points in a neat, memorable way.

Creating a solid rough draft is an important step to producing a great article, but good editing is equally important for a professional result. Make time for editing, and editors will make time for you.

SOURCE: Beth Nieman, "Editing Your Writing," in Carol Smallwood, ed., *Writing and Publishing: The Librarian's Handbook* (Chicago: American Library Association, 2010), 41–42.

10 reasons to publish an online column

by Ruth Pennington Paget

WHEN I WORKED FOR ACCOUNTING and consulting firms in Chicago and Paris, I learned how those firms used writing articles and books to establish their professional expertise in the business world. Businesses would come to these firms seeking proposals for audits and consulting in part because of the professional stature of the firms that staff publications created. Librarians can use this same technique of using the written word to create expertise as a means of currying public support for our organizations through online columns.

The following reasons for writing online columns figure among those that I have gleaned from my experience in writing the "Global Librarian" column during two years for the *Bayline* newsletter of the San Francisco Bay Area chapter of the Special Libraries Association.

Landing an online column is easier than landing a print one. If you have expertise in an area but have not published before, an online outlet may be ideal for you. It helps to query and then give editors two or three columns so that they can immediately place them in a publishing schedule. Standards are not lower on the web, but cost and space limitations are much lower than in print, which makes it easier to add columnists. The secret is to remember to write for the reader's benefit and not your self-glorification.

One trend that I have noticed recently in my local paper is that it runs online columns in what appears to be a trial to gauge readership. The newspaper can see how the public responds to online columnists before giving them a column in the print newspaper. The online column promotes interaction with the paper as well when readers comment on the articles online.

Creating a business card with brio. An online column establishes expertise and provides a ready source of downloadable public relations material. For example, if you do presentations at your local chamber of commerce, you could staple your business card to printouts of your column and distribute them. Not only would attendees have your information, but also it would be easier for them to make personal recommendations to others about your library's services if they have something to share with their colleagues.

Staying abreast of new trends. Writing a column will prompt you to stay current in your field of expertise. Your search for column ideas will cause this, and sometimes your readers or your editor will present you with ideas to write about.

Keeping your message in the public eye longer. Print newspaper articles appear online in full text for about one to two weeks. After that, they show up in search engines in a newspaper's archives with only one or two sentences describing the content; for full text, you generally have to pay for the article.

Online newsletter columns generally appear in search engines as full-text versions. Having expertise-laden articles available to the public free of charge could make the difference in obtaining an article in the newspaper or a television spot when the media is researching a topic, getting the public to vote on a library bond, or encouraging donors to fund programs at your library.

Using online columns as a networking tool. As a column writer, you have a perfect forum for interviewing movers and shakers in and out of the library world. If you cannot physically go to a different part of the country, try a telephone interview or even an email interview.

Writing outside the library field. Other librarians know how our field works and how vital it is. To expand that knowledge to other audiences, librarians must be present in other venues. The sampling of areas here shows how librarians can create a presence in fields outside of library science:

- helping a small business with marketing research in a chamber of commerce newsletter
- providing health and wellness information resources for a gymnasium's newsletter
- contributing to student success in a school online newsletter
- discussing sources for funding for a nonprofit's newsletter
- describing how to do genealogical research at the library in a genealogy newsletter
- providing reading readiness tips to a day-care association's newsletter
- sharing literacy skills information with an adult school newsletter

Honing your writing skills. Practice and a skillful editor's techniques will make the blank page or blank screen hold no qualms for you. If you need a creative budge, Twyla Tharp's *The Creative Habit* may be what you need.

Promoting your library's benefits to the public. Collect your online columns, print them out, and put them in a binder for the public and visitors to peruse at your library. This collection informs the public and would, in the ideal case, encourage them to make personal recommendations about how your library benefits the public to other patrons, the media, politicians, and foundations.

Promoting employee knowledge. Not only do online columnists learn from their writing, but the entire staff can benefit from reading these columns as well. Placing hyperlinks with article annotations on library intranets provides staff with access to the latest trends and norms in the profession.

Setting the agenda. The best benefit of writing an online column is that you can create topics of discussion among audiences that may have never been aware that a library does more than lend books. Instead of waiting for others to recognize and write about the contributions of libraries to the economy, education, and community, librarians can spread that message themselves with online columns in the right venues.

SOURCE: Ruth Pennington Paget, "Ten Reasons to Publish an Online Column," in Carol Smallwood, ed., *Writing and Publishing: The Librarian's Handbook* (Chicago: American Library Association, 2010), 141–143.

What makes a good reviewer?
by Brad Hooper

SUCCESSFUL REAL-ESTATE AGENTS swear by the adage that the three most important factors in guaranteeing a sale are location, location, location, and, as noted, this concept could be well adapted to book reviewing: The three most important factors in becoming a successful reviewer are experience, experience, experience.

First, experience reading books or listening to audiobooks; second, experience reading reviews; and finally, experience writing reviews. Generally, the individual who has an interest in writing reviews is usually referred to as a "book person." (That tagging can be taken either flatteringly or disparagingly, depending on how one senses the labeler's attitude toward someone who spends considerable time with his or her nose in a book.)

To become a good reviewer, the book person must learn to read books and listen to audiobooks critically and not simply for enjoyment. In fact, reading critically is often accomplished at the expense of a certain degree of the sheer enjoyment of reading or listening. This point cannot be expressed too emphatically: A person interested in reviewing needs to read, read, and read (or listen) critically before beginning to think about writing reviews.

At the same time, while you are involved in your program of critical reading, you should also be reading reviews. And read even more reviews. Try reading a new book (or listening to an audiobook) that you know is making a splash. Save all the reviews you see written about it, but do not read the reviews until you have finished reading (or listening to) the book. Then compare your reactions to the reactions of the reviewer.

Or vice versa: Read all the reviews you can about a new book, and keeping them close at hand, now read the book, all the while searching out all the points the reviewers have made. (This will result in a not particularly smooth read, but think of it as an anatomy course; you have the textbook in hand as you dissect the body, and it helps you to identify each organ and gland. And in our case, you use the reviews to dissect the book as you read it.)

Just as dissection of the human body is an absolutely necessary requisite in a medical education, dissection of books or audiobooks is absolutely necessary for an education in reviewing. As indicated previously, it will not be the same reading or listening experience as before. You cannot simply sit back and enjoy. You must constantly analyze, forever dissecting the book or audiobook and identifying its component parts.

Getting started

You do not want to disassemble a book? You want only to enjoy it—in its wholeness and completeness—or just learn from it, if it is an educational book? Then don't be a reviewer, as simple as that. It is your choice.

But for those who seriously want to review, there comes a point when you

Booklist Associate Editor Donna Seaman

have been reading critically for some time, and you have been reading all the reviews you can get your hands on (and using them to help analyze the works you have been reading or listening to); and now it is time to try your hand at writing reviews.

The short review. Start with a short review, about 175 words. You will be surprised at how necessary it is to practice concision when facing a 175-word limit. It certainly is not easy to express yourself about a book or audiobook in 175 words, because you have to remember that, even in a short review, you must answer both of the crucial questions that always must be answered in a review: What is the book (or audiobook) about? How good is it?

If you find you do not have 175 words to say about the item you are reviewing, then perhaps you should try another book or audiobook. If the second time you still can't come up with 175 words for a review, then it would be wise to reconsider whether reviewing is really an endeavor you should pursue.

The full-length review. After you have practiced the art of concision in several 175-word reviews, then allow yourself—or compel yourself, as the case may be— to go full length: 500 words, the average length of a feature review in a newspaper

---

The top 20 most annoying book reviewer clichés
by Michelle Kerns

In *1984,* George Orwell created newspeak, a language "whose vocabulary gets smaller every year." While newspeak exists only in fiction (or does it?) an even more pervasive, destructive language-killer has infiltrated the newspapers, news sites, and literary blogs of the world—reviewerspeak.

Let's take a look at the 20 most annoying clichés book reviewers use (and I am a chief offender here, though I am entering rehab even as we speak) as a substitute for original and substantive thought:

1. **Gripping.**
2. **Poignant.** If anything at all sad happens in the book, it will be described as poignant.
3. **Compelling.**
4. **Nuanced.** In reviewerspeak, this means, "The writing in the book is really great. I just can't come up with the specific words to explain why."
5. **Lyrical.** See definition of nuanced above.
6. **Tour de force.**
7. **Readable.**
8. **Haunting.**
9. **Deceptively simple.** As in "deceptively simple prose."
10. **Rollicking.** A favorite for reviewers when writing about comedy/adventure books.
11. **Fully realized.**
12. **At once.** As in "Michael Connelly's *The Brass Verdict* is at once a compelling mystery and a gripping thriller." See, I just used three of the most annoying clichés without any visible effort. Piece of cake.
13. **Timely.**
14. **"X meets X meets X."** As in "Stephen King meets Charles Dickens meets Agatha Christie in this haunting yet rollicking mystery."
15. **Page-turner.**
16. **Sweeping.** Almost exclusively reserved for books with more than 300 pages.
17. **That said.** As in "Stephenie Meyer couldn't identify quality writing with a compass and a trained guide; that said, *Twilight* is a harmless read."
18. **Riveting.**
19. **Unflinching.** Used to describe books that have any number of unpleasant occurrences—rape, war, infidelity, death of a child, etc.
20. **Powerful.**

The problem with these words is that, when reviewers use them to death (as they have), book reviews cease to have any purpose or meaning.

SOURCE: Michelle Kerns, "The Top 20 Most Annoying Book Reviewer Clichés and How to Use Them All in One Meaningless Review," Examiner.com, March 11, 2009, www.examiner.com/book-in-national/the-top-20-most-annoying-book-reviewer-cliches-and-how-to-use-them-all-one-meaningless-review. Reprinted with permission.

review section, whether in print or online. If you are writing a 500-word review of a novel, do not simply fill the review with plot description. Remember the other elements of a fiction review: character, theme, setting, and style. Recall, too, that you must answer the how-good-is-it question. Five hundred words simply recapitulating for the reader that "she did this, and then she did that" will not suffice. Readers will forget two minutes after they have read your review most of the facets of the plot that you have ever-so-carefully charted for them. It is best to remember that a long retelling of the plot—a lengthy mapping of what happens next—will make a review tiresome to read and consequently make the book or audiobook sound boring even if it most definitely is not.

No overwriting allowed

We have established that experience is crucial—no, vital—in a good reviewer. Experience reading books, experience reading reviews, and experience writing reviews.

But in addition to experience, good writing skills are absolutely necessary to be a successful reviewer. What is meant by good writing skills is not an ability to spell, or to make subject and verb agree, or to possess a good arsenal of adjectives and adverbs useful in analysis. What is meant by good writing skills is the ability to express oneself in well-wrought language that has, at once, color and flourish but without being overly wrought. Floweriness has no place, in other words.

It is not difficult for reviewers, even ones with experience under their belts, to fall into the unfortunate habit of competing with the book or audiobook they are reviewing. They draw attention to themselves by overwriting. It is all perfectly well and good—necessary, in fact—for a reviewer to be forthcoming in proffering answers to the questions of what the book is about and how good it is. A review is nothing if not a setting for the reviewer's answers to these questions. But sometimes reviewers unconsciously—perhaps even consciously—desire to impress the reader of the review with their own writerly talents, as if to insist that even though they are only writing a review, offering a critique of someone else's creativity, they have to prove, at the same time, their creativeness as well; and consequently, they draw attention to their writing style, as opposed to their critical skills, by overwriting. Consider the following hypothetical example:

> This breathtaking, groundbreaking, earth-shattering novel, brimming with wisdom that soars into the stratosphere and writerly talent that storms through the narrative like the fiercest typhoon, depicts a dysfunctional family whose individual and collective sufferings make the reader wince with pinpricking recognition and yelp with the poignant frustration of not being able to enter the novel's pages oneself and help direct these characters out of the miasma into which they've sunk like precious gems that have been dropped overboard and apparently lost forever.

Overwriting in a review usually takes the form of using so many big, long, uncommon words that the writing suggests the reviewer had a thesaurus handy, in which to find a more impressive but, in truth, a more obscure word for nearly every one the reviewer ordinarily would have used. Or overwriting can involve soaring metaphors whose meaning is muddied because the image the reviewer intended to create has no concrete value. Spun from thin air and purple language, the metaphor brings to the reader no graphic, resonant visualization—and that is the whole purpose of a metaphor. But if it is just fancy language with no real meaning, then it simply draws attention to itself as such: fancy but empty language. That certainly makes the reviewer look bad, especially because the reviewer's job at hand is judging someone else's writing ability.

No one can be a successful reviewer without good analytical skills in combination with good writing skills. Again, experience plays a determinant role here—in bringing good analysis to bear on reviewing books and being able to express your analytical ideas in the most effective language. Reviewers must grasp the criteria by which a book should be judged; furthermore, these skills in judgment must be practiced to be made not only sharp but also reasonable and definitely geared to the particular book or audiobook at hand, and not simply generalized commentary that could apply to most any book.

The analytical skills of the reviewer—the acumen of the reviewer in estimating the quality of a book—means very little if the reviewer's wise, judicious, and perceptive opinions are not borne on effective language. The reviewer's ability to express an idea, whether it is in answer to the question of how good the book is or even in answer to the question of what the book is about, will make the difference in the reader of the review not only understanding the reviewer's ideas but also enjoying the review.

In sum, good critical ideas must remain inseparable from good writing skills, and both must be practiced and practiced again.

A generous nature

In covering the subject of what makes a good reviewer, the word generous must surface in our discussion. A good reviewer is generous. By that I do not mean soft, easy, uncritical, and only too willing to applaud any book that comes down the publishing pike simply because it is a book. What I do mean is that the reviewer must be open-minded and munificent.

Book lovers by definition certainly hold books in high regard; they regard the very concept of a book as sacred. (That is the nature, of course, of being a devotee of something.) Most book lovers consider having written and published a book the most honorable, even thrilling, reward life can offer.

But a book lover needs to realize that the publication of someone's book does not automatically mean the book is good. All kinds of bad books get published, which really should come as no surprise to anyone. On the other hand, a book reviewer should never be resentful of someone getting a book published; and a good book reviewer cannot be someone who believes the whole book publishing industry is rotten, overly commercial, and has turned its back on cultural excellence—and thus every review written should take the industry to task.

Be critical, not crabby

Personal taste, as noted, naturally plays a part in the way a reviewer looks at a book or audiobook. That's an absolute given in reviewing. But the personal issues of the reviewer should not be a part of the review. A review is no place for a reviewer to grind axes about his or her personal opinions on the book industry, on the author's personality or reputation (other than critical reputation, which is fair game for discussion or even just mention in a review), or even on the subject matter at hand. Be accepting of what people want to write about and how they chose to write about it. The good reviewer will always remind himself of this.

When it comes to subject matter, reviewers simply cannot be mean in their outlook on what kind of books should and should not be published—not simply subject matter in nonfiction but also subject matter in fiction. If a reviewer realizes that a book's subject is not one that he or she feels comfortable reading about, then the book should be given up and allowed to be reviewed by someone for whom the subject matter presents no problem.

The following comment (purely made up, by me) illustrates what I am talking about:

> This book is about aristocratic life in France in the century prior to the Revolution. A book about this time and place should be an examination of the peasantry and lower classes in the cities rather than a visit to the frivolous upper class and the ridiculous life at the royal court.

It is simply unfair to criticize a book on the basis of it being about something you are not interested in—or feel distressful about because it hits too close to home. If the subject of abortion, for instance, makes you uncomfortable or angry, then never should you review a book on the subject; if novels that deal deeply and authoritatively with family dysfunction make you break out in a cold sweat of recognition and resentment, and you simply cannot bear the truth the novel presents, you shouldn't review the book, because you are not going to be fair in judging it.

If science does not interest you, do not review a book on science. If domestic fiction bores you, do not review domestic fiction. You cannot fault a book for what it is about. Never forget that. Conversely, a potential reviewer should not be a prima donna and turn down books that don't exactly fit into his or her tight parameters of a "reviewing field." Reviewers must read and learn and expand not only their reviewing but also their knowledge and worldview.

A good reviewer has to strike a balance between being too detached from what he or she is reviewing and getting too wrapped up in it. If a reviewer should never slam a book simply based on subject matter, then never should a reviewer praise a book solely on the same basis; for example, although historical novels may be your forte, not all historical novels are good simply because they are historical novels. By the same token, a book advocating a liberal or a conservative social and economic agenda is not necessarily good simply because you agree with the author's political stance.

Finally, a good reviewer is able to at once stand back and see the whole forest and stand up close to observe the individual trees. But note that never does a good reviewer lose sight of the first view—the whole forest, that is—while he or she is making observations about the individual trees. The good reviewer should not get so entangled in sharing the details of a book, even if the review is to be a long one (500 words, say), that he or she does not stand back and give impressions of the book as a whole.

SOURCE: Brad Hooper, *Writing Reviews for Readers' Advisory* (Chicago: American Library Association, 2010), 55–62.

MATERIALS
CHAPTER FOUR

And it is a well-known fact that books devour space. You can't reverse this law. However much space you give them, it's never enough. First they occupy the walls. They continue to spread wherever they can gain a foothold. Only ceilings are spared the invasion. New books keep arriving, and you can't bear to get rid of a single one. And so, slowly and imperceptibly, the volumes crowd out everything before them. Like glaciers.

> —Serbian writer Zoran Živković, from the story "Home Library," in his mosaic novel *The Library* (*Biblioteka*), 2002

BOOKS

The first big format change: From scroll to codex

by Leila Avrin

ACCORDING TO HERODOTUS (*Histories* V, 58), the Greeks used papyrus as their primary writing material once the Phoenician alphabet was introduced. He noted that the Ionians wrote on the hides of sheep and goats, as was common among barbarians in his own day. (A barbarian originally was one who did not speak Greek, but undoubtedly the name carried a pejorative connotation.) Papyrus could have been introduced first to the Greek islands, but not used regularly, as early as the 10th or 9th century B.C., when the Phoenicians first introduced the alphabet. We know from the Story of Wenamun that Egypt exported papyrus through Byblos in the early 11th century B.C. But because it was not until after 750 B.C. that Greek expansion, trade, and colonization flourished, the late 8th century B.C. would be a more realistic date for the first practical use of papyrus on a large scale in the Greek world. Papyrus was known to be one of the important

Scroll of the Book of Esther.

Mediterranean trade items in the 7th century, and it must have been quite common in Greece by the early 6th century. The Greeks who had established their own colonies in Egypt by the 7th century naturally wrote on papyrus.

The name of the Phoenician port town of Byblos (Gubla in Phoenician, later Gebal) is thought to be the origin of the Greek word for the papyrus reed, *biblion*, and for book, *biblos*. Our *Bible* and *bibliography* and the French *bibliothèque* are derived from these Greek words. Many other book-related materials take their names from this port of trade. Perhaps these modern terms are from the town's name, or perhaps the Egyptian *ppr* sounded like *bbl* to the Greek ear. Papyrus, both leaf and sheet, was also called *chartes* in Greek, which became the term *charta* in Latin.

Hellenistic and Roman papyrus was thicker and not as perfectly formed as it had been in earlier dynastic Egypt, and in general the Greek scroll was shorter and smaller than its Egyptian ancestor. The average-sized scroll was long enough for writing one play, or two or three short books of Homer's works. The division of the *Iliad* and *Odyssey* into "books" may have been determined originally by the scroll's standard length.

The papyrus manufacturer continued to paste sheets into ready-made rolls of 20 sheets in Roman times, no matter what the ultimate purpose of the papyrus would be, with joins overlapping about one-half inch (1–2 centimeters), running downhill, as did the scrolls of dynastic Egypt, so that the scribe's nib would not get caught. In Hellenistic times the Ptolemaic court controlled the manufacture and trade of papyrus. They marked the beginning of each scroll with their *proto-*

col, a practice that continued in the papyrus trade in the Byzantine Empire (but not in the Roman, as far as we know) into the Islamic period, when there were bilingual protocols in Greek and Arabic. The term *protocol* is still with us today in diplomatic and medical practice.

The introduction of the codex

The major change in the structure of the book, from scroll to codex, occurred at the end of the first Christian century. Whereas earlier cultures in Mesopotamia, Greece, and Etruria from time to time used luxury or ordinary wax tablets, Romans wrote on *pugillares* or codices regularly, for personal letters, dispatches, schoolwork, authors' first drafts, diplomas, notices, documents, and especially for legal matters (hence our legal "codes" and "codicils"). Polyptychs, fastened together like our three-ring notebooks, numbered up to 10 tablets.

For convenience, in the first centuries B.C. and A.D., *membranae* sometimes substituted for wood panels. There is no Greek precursor for the Latin *membranae; dipthera* simply meant "hides" until the meaning was extended to notebooks. Martial said *membrana* was used for classical literature as well, but we have no examples from such an early date. Quintilian (ca. 30–100 A.D.) mentioned that students used *membranae* for lecture notes. The first person to do this probably did not think himself an innovative book designer. We do not have examples from this date to tell us whether *membrana* was made in the manner of the parchment we know from the Middle Ages, or whether it was like the thin leather of the Dead Sea Scrolls. But scholars such as Colin Roberts and Theodore Cressy Skeat consider ca. 100 A.D. as the date for the first parchment codex.

The Roman Empire had a well-developed postal system. Although papyrus was shipped to all parts of the empire, it may not have been quite so accessible at the northern and western borders. The postal service undoubtedly discouraged cumbersome wooden tablets (what bureaucrat could limit himself to a one-*diptycha* report?), so one may surmise that *membranae,* thin animal skins, leather, or parchment began to replace wooden *tabellae* even in the first century B.C. Many scholars are now of this opinion.

The first reference to the codex as the form of a book was made by Martial. Parchment codices were particularly suited to the traveling missionaries of the early church, but pagan writers also commented on their portability, noting that fragile papyrus scrolls should be left in the library. The codex also could be concealed more easily than a scroll, when necessary. In addition, it was far easier to find a quotation by consulting an Old Testament codex than to search for the exact wording of a proof-text in a cumbersome scroll. Another advantage of the parchment book was that both sides of the sheet could be written on without difficulty and without prejudice against the author or publisher for being cheap.

The earliest Christian Bible codices that have been preserved come from Egypt, 16 of them on papyrus. Seven were of the New Testament, but there were also parts of the Pentateuch, Isaiah, and Psalms, the favorite scriptural books of early Christians. These were not written in the scribe's formal book hand known later from monastic scriptoria, but in a neat documentary script. Undoubtedly they were made for the use of the Egyptian Christian community by its own members. Papyrus codices

A folio from Papyrus 46, an early New Testament codex in Greek, circa A.D. 175-225.

were prepared with their quires gathered first for binding, then they were written upon, just as papyrus scrolls had been premanufactured. The exact number of lines per page was not always planned in advance for the whole codex, as they were to be in later codices. The missionary activity of St. Mark, who may have written his Gospel in codex form, and the influence of the Roman Church on Egypt have been suggested as the reasons for the early introduction of codices into the community there. From 2nd-century Egypt, all of the surviving Christian works are codices, while non-Christian codices represent only 2% of the manuscripts found. This statistic has led to the conclusion that pagan works continued, due to their conservatism, to be written on scrolls.

Papyrus was not as suitable a material as parchment for the bound codex, because folding and sewing weakened it just where it needed to be the strongest—at the spine. After many years, those papyrus codices fortunate enough to have withstood time and the elements had to be reinforced at the spine with parchment. As the quality of papyrus and its production and export from Egypt declined in the early centuries of Christianity, so did the scroll production. The nature of the materials, then—papyrus and parchment—had much to do with the form the book ultimately took. Folding papyrus made it brittle, so the scroll form was better suited to it. Sewing ruined it. Parchment could not be pasted easily and permanently, but sewing suited it, especially in the fold, and did not weaken the material if the book was bound properly. The parchment scroll was quite heavy, as we know from Hebrew Torah scrolls. A scroll written on both sides was neither practical nor aesthetically pleasing. Far more text could be written on a codex of approximately the same size as the bulkier scroll.

Even though Christian scribes did not consider the roll a proper form of book, they still clung to earlier traditions of layout. Although some of the first books

display one column per page, the finest early and nearly complete Bible codices extant today (from the 4th and 5th centuries) were planned with three or four columns per page. When one opens an early Christian or Byzantine luxury manuscript, such as the Codex Sinaiticus, one sees eight columns across two pages, which gives the impression of an open

The 4th century Codex Sinaiticus, held by the British Library.

scroll. Another Greek manuscript, the Codex Vaticanus, of the middle or late 4th century, was written in three columns per page. The earliest Hebrew Bible codices from the 10th–12th centuries show three columns per page. Later the number was reduced to two in both Hebrew and Latin European Bibles. Today the two-column tradition still exists in Bibles, dictionaries, and encyclopedias. The latter are sometimes paginated by column rather than by page for quick reference. Was the two-column layout retained because the narrow column is easier for the eye to scan? Today's book designer may rationalize it in this way, but an underlying reason is that tradition always dictated that a Bible and a dictionary should be in two columns.

The parchment codex is often considered a Christian innovation, associated with the city of Rome, where St. Mark wrote his Gospel. This location is emphasized by both Colin Roberts and Paul Needham. In the early years of Christianity, it was the professional scribes and publishers in Rome who had access to papyrus scrolls. Christians would not have been using their services or buying their pagan books because they were not interested in the subject matter. Some historians have asserted that Christians could not afford the expensive papyrus, but Roberts points out that we have no information on the relative cost of *membrana* and papyrus, Christianity was illegal and Christians were often persecuted, and missionaries kept a low profile. In recording their own literature they were left to their own devices, and therefore they could have been more practical and, in the end, more creative makers of books. Parchment notebooks used by Jews and new Christians therefore were the models for Gospel books and writings of the early Church fathers.

So while book evolution from roll to codex and from papyrus surface to parchment began in the first centuries B.C. and A.D., and the popularity of the parchment codex grew steadily in the 2nd and 3rd centuries A.D., the parchment codex

---

Colonial American books

Spanish America led the way in book publishing, as the New World's first printing press was set up in Mexico, where in 1539 the first North American title was printed. This was a book of religious instruction, written in both Spanish and native Nahuatl.

No British colonial titles were published until the mid-1600s. The first printing press in the English-speaking colonies arrived in Massachusetts in 1638, and was set up in the home of Henry Dunster, first president of Harvard College in Cambridge. In 1663 this shop produced the earliest Bible published in British North America. As with the first Spanish book, it was intended for native readers and was the first book printed wholly in a Native American language—Algonquian.

A large number of the bound books in the colonies were official ledgers and court dockets kept by government offices. The practice of manufacturing blank books for the use of clerks and secretaries became common in the 1700s. Their volumes of public records made up the first reference libraries, used by officials, legislators, and lawyers.

To the north, New France possessed no printing presses, its culture and economy tightly controlled by a dictatorial governor based in Quebec. Canada's small population of native peoples and French colonials was mainly employed in producing furs and lumber for the profit of the crown. There were only 2,200 Europeans in New France in 1663, when Quebec's Jesuit seminary, now Laval University, established the first Canadian library—one of the oldest in North America.

Although no books were printed in New France, some wealthy Canadians had impressive private libraries. According to Pehr Kalm, the 18th-century Swedish traveler and botanist, Canadians seemed more interested in science and literature than were colonials in British America.

The first Canadian printing press arrived in 1752, brought to Nova Scotia by British settlers. The first Canadian newspaper appeared in Quebec in 1764, soon after the fall of New France to the British after the French and Indian War. By then, printers in British America had, for decades, been producing books, stationery, business handbills, and legal documents, as well as local newspapers. These periodicals were filled with classified advertising and announcements of the arrival and departure of merchant ships with lists of cargoes and goods for sale. As colonial unrest brought about a "continental" spirit of resistance to British colonial policies, newspapers began to report the latest political developments in the colonies and Britain.

More than ever before, the printed word was a force for change in British America, where by 1770 a well-read middle class had come to power.

SOURCE: Stuart A. P. Murray, *The Library: An Illustrated History* (Chicago: American Library Association, 2009), 140–141.

4

as the form of luxury manuscript was not firmly established until the 4th century.

Papyrus did not disappear altogether from the European continent. A few literary works were written on it in the 6th century, and it was still used for official documents by the Merovingian kings of France in the 6th century, for deeds in France in the 7th century, and for commercial documents in Ravenna between the 5th and 10th centuries. It apparently was in daily use in the papal chancery until the middle of the 11th century. The last papal bull written on papyrus was dated 1057, but there are even later references to the use of papyrus in the pope's chancery. All the while in the Near East, papyrus remained the standard writing material, especially in Egypt, where it was the surface for official documents, business accounts, and correspondence well into the Islamic period, until paper began to replace it in the late 8th century.

Sinai Codex 339, parchment, 11th–12th century.

While we must thank the Romans for our codex form of book, it was the Christian church that provided the magic combination of parchment and codex to make the medieval book in Europe and Byzantium the vehicle of knowledge and the object of beauty it was to become.

SOURCE: Leila Avrin, *Scribes, Script, and Books: The Book Arts from Antiquity to the Renaissance* (Chicago: American Library Association, 1991), 144–146, 173–175.

A primer on graphic novels

by Francisca Goldsmith

IF YOU AS THE READERS' ADVISOR, or members of your readers' advisory staff, lack a background in personal reading experience that includes a range of graphic novels, here is a crash course in what to read to get yourself up to the starting line. The titles listed here are presented in the order recommended for you to read, and the annotations include key concepts and questions to hold in mind as you approach each one.

How does reading a graphic novel work? Start with a title that requires you to attend to narrative flow, using both images and words to follow the story. I'd recommend Carol Lay's *The Big Skinny* (Villard, 2008), a nonfiction graphic novel about one woman's success in losing and keeping off weight, or James Sturm's

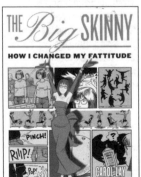

The Golem's Mighty Swing (now collected in *James Sturm's America*, Drawn and Quarterly, 2007), a piece of historical fiction from the segregated era of Negro and Jewish baseball leagues. Each of these selections offers straightforward narrative, interesting characters, and information that may be of personal interest. The author and artist are a single individual in each of these cases, and the art is clear and accessible to most viewers.

As you read either of these, consider how the author moves you from concept to concept. How does she or he employ point of view in the images to communicate important information to you about events in the narrative? Spend time on a single page that has at least six panels and think about how you interpret what happens "off camera" as you move from the image in one panel to the image in the next. Are you able to pin down your own insertion of movement on the static page?

How do different styles of art fit different narratives in terms of content, mood, and theme? Move on to an anthology that offers you same-book access to a relatively large number of creators working on a similar topic or theme. Among good options for this are the collection *Postcards: True Stories That Never Happened* (Villard, 2007), edited by Jason Rodriguez, or a volume from editor Tom Pomplun's Graphic Classics series (Eureka Productions), such as *Twain, Jack London,* or *Gothic Classics.* Either of these options provides you with a relatively small volume that brings together more than a dozen different pieces.

As you read one of these, be generous with the time you take to flip back and forth to compare and contrast visual rendering styles, including techniques and moods evoked in the viewer. Do you find yourself attracted to, or wanting to take more time with, a particular visual style? By the time you have read the volume in its entirety, can you identify which parts of it attracted you more than others? Which parts put you off and why?

What's it like to give up text altogether and read a book that is composed entirely of images? Especially if you find yourself prone to skipping over visual content, or resistant to incorporating the reading of it into your attempts to understand how reading a graphic novel works, you may need to take this remedial break. I'd suggest you stick with a wordless book written for adult readers, rather than for children, because you are an adult reader and the point here is to tap the sophisticated reading experiences you already possess. If you are undertaking this short course on your own, you may want to find some reviews of the wordless book you select *after* you've read it, and see how your understanding squares with those of readers experienced in visual literacy. If you can, then have some coworkers read the same title you chose and discuss it.

For this endeavor, I'd suggest you read either Andy Hartzell's *Fox Bunny Funny* (Top Shelf, 2007) which, although disguised as a cute animal story, is actually a story about owning and asserting one's identity in the face of others' preconceptions; or Shinsuke Tanaka's *Wings* (Purple Bear, 2006), an all-ages story about friendship across a brief lifespan.

As you read either (or both) of these wordless books, what do you notice about the need to take the pages in order? What kinds of complexity seem to be present—that of ideas, emotions, narrative design? Do you ever become lost from the narrative thread? And if you do, how do you find your way again?

What's it like to take on a longer narrative and use your new skills with a book that may take multiple sittings to read through completely? Just as new readers of traditional texts move from books that can be completed in a single sitting to ones that require the ability to pause and then pick up where you stopped reading, you may need to practice reconnecting with the narrative thread of a graphic novel that you have put aside. For this exercise, I recommend that you choose a title that you know will be too long for you to complete in one or even two sittings. The point here is to consider how you carry what you've read across time (however brief) to the next point when you take up the same book. Depending on your personal genre tastes and the development of your graphic novel reading ease, you may want to try Kia Asamiya's *Batman: Child of Dreams* (DC Comics, 2003) from a superhero universe—or you may prefer the fairy tale riff to be found in the complete first volume of Linda Medley's *Castle Waiting* (Fantagraphics, 2006).

Your reading of either of these books, for this exercise, includes the time you aren't reading; that is, a consideration of how you bridge the time gap that occurs in your approaching the full narrative. Do you find that you are able to pick up the book where you left off in the same way—whatever that way is—as you do a traditional print text? At what points in the reading do you break? Does the creator offer you suggested breaking points, and are these useful to you?

Explore the use of sequential art as part of a narrative that also utilizes other formats in the telling of a single story. Sequential art may be part of a larger portfolio of presentation styles used by some authors to convey one connected narrative. Reading such works helps you to more fully grasp how sequential art provides both information and mood in contrast to and comparison with other formats. Try *The Magical Life of Long Tack Sam* (Riverhead, 2007), Ann Marie Fleming's biography of her ancestor, a man who lived the global life generations ahead of today's technology-enhanced capacities to network internationally, or Lucy Knisley's travel diary *French Milk* (Simon & Schuster, 2008).

How does the use of sequential art enhance the mood of the narrative? How is the sequential art approach sustained or expanded by other media used to recount the narrative? Would you prefer to read the same story in a different format? Would its presentation in a different format render the narrative into a different story in terms of information available to the reader, flow, or theme?

You've heard lots about manga, but have you tried it on for size? Because manga has become so popular as a library collection choice selected for American teens, some adults new to graphic novels are particularly resistant to sampling its aesthetics for themselves. And because of assertive marketing, it's important that the readers' advisor have a good feel for what makes manga both the same as and different from other graphic novel options. Manga and its cognates are now available from several countries other than Japan. And Japanese culture informs Japanese comics quite specifically. For this portion of your crash course then, you'll consider two titles, one a Japanese import that's been translated and the other manga produced in the West.

One of the perceived barriers to reading modern translations of Japanese manga is the editorial decision made by many translators in the past five or more years to present English text without translating the layout to conform to Western left-to-right reading standards. If you haven't tried reading a layout from right to left, this may make you feel anxious. That's fine, but try it anyway!

If you are feeling industrious, you might try one of the annual volumes of *The Mammoth Book of Best New Manga 3* (Running Press, 2008), an anthology edited by Ilya that will offer you dozens of short manga pieces in one place. If you are willing to try reading a book from right to left and want a manageable first effort, pick up the first volume of Natsuki Takaya's popular romantic comedy series Fruits Basket, but be sure it's the "unflipped" version (a language translation that maintains the panels and pages in Japanese order).

To get a firmer grasp on how manga transcends country or culture of origin, try a Western title that utilizes the aesthetic genre. You might try Russian-Canadian Svetlana Chmakova's Nightschool series (TokyoPop), a tale of discreet vampires, or the nonfiction biography *The 14th Dalai Lama* (Emotional Content, 2008) by Tetsu Saiwai.

What does a major award-winning graphic novel look like and read like? You'll want to sample some of the winners of specific awards for graphic novels and their creators to provide yourself with what experts judge as quality in the format. Pick up Printz winner and National Book Award shortlist-holder Gene Luen Yang's *American Born Chinese* (First Second Books, 2006), which weaves together three narrative strands into one compelling and literary novel, or Angoulême-honored creator Lewis Trondheim's *Little Nothings* (NBM, 2008), a collection of insightful and wry autobiographical admissions.

How does either of these titles compare to and contrast with other graphic novels you have read so far in this mini-course? Which specific attributes strike you as stellar? How would you compare one of these two titles to other literary award-winners like Pulitzer Prize–winning Harper Lee's *To Kill a Mockingbird*, or cinema winners like the Oscar-winning *Crash*? What aspects do exemplary graphic novels share with exemplary print literature? With film? With visual art?

Can a graphic novel give you information that standard news sources can't? Nonfiction sequential art, at its best, can provide the reader with a different perspective than a newspaper, website, or newsreel. I'd suggest you explore Joe Sacco's *Safe Area Gorazde* (Fantagraphics, 2000), a trained cartoon journalist's account of aspects of the Bosnian war of the early 1990s, or a volume from Rick Geary's series A Treasury of Victorian Murder (NBM).

How does the graphic novelist use point of view? How does his accuracy compare to and contrast with narrative accounts you have read of the event? What did you learn here that had escaped your understanding of the topic when you learned about it in previously read or viewed accounts? What's missing from the graphic novel that you believe is essential to understanding the topic?

As you do with any other area of literature for which you are responsible as an advisor, don't stop reading. Read new graphic novels, but also remember to go back and read ones that were published years ago and that have become classics. A readers' advisor's preparation for the job is always underway, and that is no less true for the graphic novel readers' advisor than for any other.

SOURCE: Francisca Goldsmith, *The Readers' Advisory Guide to Graphic Novels* (Chicago: American Library Association, 2010), 105–111.

GOVERNMENT INFORMATION

E-government services
by the ALA Public Library Funding and Technology Access Survey

LIBRARIES IN THE UNITED STATES always have had an important role in ensuring free and open access to the world's knowledge, including information documenting the work of our democracy and resources for connecting with government agencies at all levels. In the wake of the passage of the E-Government Act of 2002 and other state, local and federal government initiatives, public libraries have become more vital in communities nationwide—as online access points, as places for assistance learning to navigate computer and internet resources, and as trusted sources of information.

Public libraries are critical providers of employment and e-government services, resources, and support. Libraries report that they provide a number of resources and services to assist individuals seeking employment, applying for jobs, and interacting with government agencies. These service roles are in high demand as government agencies and employers increasingly require online interactions.

These services are related to the need to build patrons' digital-literacy skill levels. For example, an individual applying for e-government social services requires a continuum of computer and internet training services, as well as hands-on assistance, making the public library even more essential as the community's only free provider of public-access technologies, training, and professional assistance. In 2012, public libraries supported job-seekers in numerous ways:

- 92.2% provided access to jobs databases and other job opportunity resources, up from 90.9% in 2010–2011 and 88.2% in 2009–2010.
- 77.1% provided access to civil service examination materials, unchanged from 77.0% in 2010–2011 and up from 74.9% in 2009–2010.
- 77.5% provided software and other resources to help patrons create résumés and employment materials, up from 74.5% in 2010–2011 and 68.9% in 2009–2010.
- 76% provided patrons with assistance in completing online job applications, up from 72% in 2010–2011 and 67% in 2009–2010.

In providing these job-seeking services, nearly half of libraries (49.8%) reported the library did not have enough staff to help patrons effectively with their job-seeking needs. Further, 41.3% reported that library staff did not have the necessary expertise to meet patron job-seeking needs.

Almost all public libraries (96.6%) reported assisting patrons with applying for and accessing e-government services, an increase of almost 16% over the past year. Urban libraries reported the greatest increases: 97.3% provided this assistance, up significantly from 77.7% the previous year. The percentage of libraries that partner with government agencies and others to provide e-government services also continued to increase (30.9%, up from 25.1% the previous year).

Over 70% of libraries reported assisting patrons with completing government forms. Anecdotal reports indicate this percentage would be significantly higher were it not for privacy and liability issues that restrict the level of assistance.

Looking to the future

Libraries around the country are implementing various strategies to supply their communities with e-government services. There is a growing need for governments and public libraries to collaborate to meet community needs. By working together, agencies will improve their e-government services, libraries will be better able to meet patron needs, patrons will participate online more effectively, and communities will have successful e-government strategies in place.

SOURCE: *U.S. Public Libraries and E-Government Services* (Chicago: ALA Office for Research and Statistics, June 2010), ala.org/research/sites/ala.org.research/files/content/initiatives/plftas/issuesbriefs/IssuesBrief-Egov.pdf; *Libraries Connect Communities: Public Library Funding and Technology Access Study, 2011–2012* (Chicago: ALA Office for Research and Statistics, June 2012), ala.org/research/plftas/2011_2012; *Public Libraries and E-Government* (University of Maryland Information Policy and Access Center, 2012), www.plinternetsurvey.org/sites/default/images/Briefs/EgovBrief2012_31May2012.pdf.

Fixing the Federal Depository Library Program

by Patrick Ragains

IN APRIL 2009, the US Government Printing Office released its updated *Federal Depository Library Program Strategic Plan, 2009–2014* (www.fdlp.gov/home/about/237-strategicplan), which summarized the condition of the Federal Depository Library Program (FDLP) and posited a future for the program in which depository libraries will be significant providers of current and historical government information.

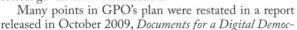

Many points in GPO's plan were restated in a report released in October 2009, *Documents for a Digital Democracy,* prepared by Ithaka S+R. The Ithaka report also addressed key service issues, among them digitization and discoverability of federal information and the future of tangible documents collections.

In the wake of those two crucial reports, I will try to clarify the key issues related to the future of depository libraries and emphasize practical steps in a transition to new models for collections and public service.

The FDLP's mission is to make federal government publications easily available in every congressional district (1,190 selective depositories and, in most states, a regional federal depository). The GPO identifies the following "Principles for Government Information" in its strategic plan:

- The public has the right of access to government information.
- Government has the obligation to disseminate and provide broad public access to its information.
- Government has an obligation to guarantee the authenticity and integrity of its information.
- Government has an obligation to preserve its information.
- Government information created or compiled by government employees or at government expense should remain in the public domain.

The plan also projects several characteristics of the FDLP through 2014:

- These Principles for Government Information will remain the FDLP's core ideology.
- Federal depository libraries will continue to facilitate access to the American public through traditional services as well as through enhanced or new services made possible by the digital age.
- GPO, working actively with depositories, will ensure accessibility, findability, and usability of government information dissemination products.
- The options for building federal depository collections will increase.
- Regional depositories will continue to have the responsibility for permanent public access for tangible publications that remain in their collections.
- GPO will ensure permanent public access to, provide version control of, and authenticate federal digital content. This does not rule out depository libraries providing redundancy.
- Communication will exist, and improve, between and among GPO, de-

pository libraries, other federal agencies, and the public and communities served by depository libraries.

• Consumers of federal information will be able to access it from wherever they are and whenever they need it.

Government information departments in many libraries have been downsized or eliminated. As this trend continues and more depositories leave the FDLP, many libraries will be unprepared to meet their users' needs for government information. Notwithstanding, the public, students, and researchers still need the full range of federal government information, from publications printed at the birth of the republic to those born digitally and posted on the internet.

Although libraries nationwide have partially bridged the digital divide by providing public access computers, these efforts do not ensure access to online government information. Disadvantaged segments of the public often lack internet access, making it harder for them to get tax forms, respond to proposed government regulations and actions, or find more elusive information such as federal reports not sent to depositories. If federal depository libraries are to have a significant future, they must effectively redefine both access and outreach. Failure to do so will distance populations from services they need and could further erode public support for libraries.

Meeting the public's needs

Regional depository libraries agree to receive all publications made available to federal depository libraries and retain them permanently. These libraries are intended to be an easily accessible safety net for meeting the public's needs for government information. The 47 regional depositories that exist in 2012 are somewhat redundant, due to the presence of holdings in multilibrary catalogs like WorldCat and availability of materials through regional and nationwide interlibrary loan networks. Even so, many libraries and their users rely on the relative permanence of regional library collections.

In contrast, selective depository libraries may receive only those publications they wish to add to their collections. Selectives may also reduce their collections by weeding (with approval from their regional library). A small but increasing number of selective depositories are leaving the FDLP, their directors citing the burden of processing publications that aren't used and the diminishing importance of maintaining tangible collections of government publications when most current federal publications are online.

The GPO and depository librarians see the national network of federal depositories as a safety net for public access to government information, but we can't presume they perform this function effectively for all of society. Many people in both urban and rural settings are isolated from libraries, such as those with mobility limitations or without convenient transportation. The safety net also misses a lot of information (including email messages, postings on social networking sites, presidential records, product safety and recall information, records and publications with a security classification, and federally funded research). Another threat to the safety net is the trend among libraries to reconsider their depository status, with some leaving the program altogether.

In our currently weak economy, depository status isn't too attractive if it entails staff costs for processing current paper and microfiche documents into collections, when virtually all of it is available online.

Fixing the safety net

In today's environment, what "safety net" roles can we propose for depository libraries and the US Government Printing Office? Congress can:

- Revise Title 44 of the United States Code to conform with current library and information service practices, specifically: allowing permanent online access to depository publications to replace tangible copies in all depository libraries; permitting establishment of interstate regional libraries and at least two comprehensive archival collections of federal government publications; and defining the scope and requirements for "digital deposit," whereby libraries would capture and locally host electronic copies of federal publications.

Selective depositories can:

- Affirm and strengthen their commitment to make government information easily available to their communities. They should do this with minimal reliance on tangible collections. The experiences of the University of Arizona and three new depositories (all in tribal college libraries), all of which have formally committed to emphasize online access, can guide other libraries moving in this direction.
- Meet community members in branch libraries and outside library buildings (shopping malls, schools, community centers) and bring popular government information to them in these locations. This will lessen the isolation of users from library services.
- Direct their public service staff's attention to government information–related training opportunities and provide support for them to participate.
- Include the *Catalog of US Government Publications* in a federated search or similar application with the local library catalog. This will lessen the library's workload for catalog maintenance and can be a cheap, satisfactory alternative to purchasing GPO bibliographic and item records from commercial services.
- Conduct zero-based reviews of publications they select from the GPO. Libraries should select only those items needed for 1) reference assistance, when a paper copy is more convenient than an online version; and 2) known user interests, which may include such things as maps and printed legal sources.
- Base continuing or relinquishing depository library status upon user needs rather than processing workload. Maintaining depository status will encourage valuable connections with other libraries and information providers and allow libraries to meet user needs better than if they exit the national program.

Regional depositories should adopt the first four points recommended above for selective libraries, plus the following:

- Conduct long-term outreach within their region (usually statewide) and provide needed staff training in both selective depositories and nondepositories. When training others, regional librarians should emphasize sources and search techniques. Good training will strengthen government-related reference and research services, even as selective depositories continue to leave the program.

- Join the Government Information Online reference service. GIO allows government information librarians to assist users and share their expertise nationally (membership is also open to selective depository libraries).
- Contribute to efforts to catalog pre-1976 U.S. government publications not already in OCLC and identify the best such records already in the database. GPO is currently creating brief records from its retrospective shelflist, but will need assistance from libraries to create complete MARC records.

The US Government Printing Office should:

- Comprehensively capture, archive, and disseminate born-digital federal government information. The GPO's FDSys program currently supplies authenticated files, including the *Congressional Record, Federal Register,* bills, and public laws. FDSys needs software that will scan the web for federal information not generated by GPO, then capture and authenticate it. Such harvested information must be organized for public access and archived for preservation, which requires periodic refreshing and migration to new formats.
- Provide bibliographic access to all known federal publications issued since 1789 by finishing the conversion of GPO's shelflist to MARC record format. Any records created or collected by this and other retrospective cataloging projects should be added to the online *Catalog of Government Publications.* GPO can collaborate with libraries by providing converted shelflist records, which participating libraries could check, revise, attach holdings to, and submit to OCLC.
- Create two tangible, national retrospective collections of U.S. government publications, to be housed separately in secure federal buildings. These would be archival collections from which tangible and electronic copies would be made for libraries and end users. Since the GPO has no library, collaboration with existing depositories will be necessary to establish and operate such collections.
- Create or sponsor an online retrospective collection of U.S. government publications, with both basic and advanced search interfaces. These electronic surrogates could be linked from the current *Catalog of Government Publications* interface, WorldCat, and local library catalogs. The need for coordinated standards and oversight makes GPO (or a contracting entity) the most logical organization to lead this effort. As public domain–based digitization of older federal documents progresses, each associated record in WorldCat and GPO's *Catalog of Government Publications* should include a hyperlink to a digital copy.
- Assist and consult with selective and regional libraries as they evaluate their depository status. The wide availability of federal government information online has eroded the value of building and maintaining tangible collections, and library directors are ever more reluctant to commit staff to traditional processing and maintenance routines. This forces selective and regional depository library directors to identify and protect services that their funding authorities will support.

James Madison wrote in 1822 that "a popular Government, without popular information, or the means of acquiring it, is but a Prologue to a Farce or a Tragedy; or, perhaps both . . . and a people who mean to be their own Governors, must arm themselves with the power which knowledge gives." The national library community should take Madison's warning to heart and use its expertise, infrastructure, and emerging technology to assure a strong and lasting presence for government information in library services.

SOURCE: Patrick Ragains, "Fixing the Federal Depository Library Program," *American Libraries* 41, no. 5 (May 2010): 36–38.

SPECIAL COLLECTIONS

Latin terms in early printed books

by Robert L. Maxwell, for the ACRL Rare Books and Manuscripts Section

4

THE FOLLOWING LATIN TERMS refer to information about the printer or seller of books published in the 15th to the 18th centuries. For the place of publication, Robert L. Maxwell has produced a Latin Place Names File, found at www.rbms.info/committees/bibliographic_standards/latin/index.html, that will identify such locations as Ratisbonae (Regensburg, Germany) and Caesaraugustae (Zaragoza, Spain).—*GME.*

Aedes, shop, printing establishment *In aedibus Aldi, et Andreae soceri* = [Printed] in the shop of Aldo [Manuzio] and of his father-in-law Andrea [Torresano].

Angulus, corner. *Ex officina Gulielmi Young, bibliopolae, no. 52 Secunda-Platea, angulo Castaneae-Plateae, M.DCC.XCIII* = From the shop of William Young, bookseller, 52 Second Street, on the corner of Castanea Street, 1793.

Annus, year. *Apud Io. Heruagium, mense Martio anno 1537* = At the shop of Johann Herwagen, in the month of March, the year 1537. *Anno Domini 1550* = In the year of our Lord 1550, i.e., A.D. 1550 or 1550 C.E.

Apud, at the shop of. *Apud Paulum Manutium* = At the shop of Paolo Manuzio.

> L V G D V N I,
> Apud Antonium Vincentium,
> M. D. LXIII.
> Cum priuilegio Regis.

Architypographia, head or main printing office or shop. *Ex architypographia Plantiniana* = From the main office of the Plantin Press.

Bibliopola, bookseller. *Ex officina Gulielmi Young, bibliopolae, no. 52 Secunda-Platea, angulo Castaneae-Plateae, M.DCC.XCIII* = From the shop of William Young, bookseller, 52 Second Street, on the corner of Castanea Street, 1793.

Castigator, proofreader. *Elaboratum est hoc Germaniae opus typis Thomae Anshelmi castigatoreq[ue] authore ipso* = This work was completed in Germany, with the type of Thomas Anshelmus, and with the author himself as proofreader.

Castigatus, corrected, proofread. *Impressum est & castigatum in aedibus Ascensianis* = Printed and proofread in the Ascensian shop.

Collegit/conlegit, collected, compiled, often in the phrase *collegit et edidit,* "compiled and edited."

Cura, care (often means "edited by"). *Cura et sumptibus Societatis Literatae* = By the care and expense of the Literary Society.

Emissio, edition. *Tertia emissio* = Third edition. *Secundam & castigatiorem emissionem* = Second and more correct edition.

Emissum, published. *Expletum est hoc opusculum & ex officina emissum in Parisiorum academia* = This little work was completed and published from the print shop in the Parisian academy.

Exarare, exarata, exaratum, exarantur, to print, printed (literally, "ploughed up"). *Gallica lingua, & deinde Latina exarata* = Printed in French, and then in Latin. *Evangelia characteribus Syriacis exarata* = The Gospels printed with Syriac type.

Excudebat, excudebant, excudebatur, excudebantur, excusa, excusae, excusum, printed, was printed. *Excudebat atque venebat Timotheus Green MDCCLI* = Timothy Green printed and sold [this book] in 1751. *Excudebatur Salmanticae in officina Andreae à Portonarijs* = [This book] was printed at Salamanca in the shop of Andreas à Portonariis. *Excusum Moguntiae* = Printed at Mainz. *Excusae Argentinae* = Printed at Strasbourg.

Excusor, printer. *Apud Antonium Bladum Pontificis Maximi excusorem* = In the office of Antonius Bladus, printer of the Pope.

Filius, son. *Ex Officina Plantiniana, apud viduam & filios Ioannis Moreti* = From the Plantin Press, in the shop of the widow and sons of Jan Moretus. *Sumptibus Matthei Rieger et filiorum* = At the expense of Matthew Rieger and his sons.

Frater, brother. *Apud Balthasarem et Ioannem Moretos fratres* = At the shop of Balthasar and Jan Moretus, brothers.

Haeredes, heredes, heirs. *Typis Ioannis Saurii, impensis heredum Petri Fischeri, M.D.IC.* = [Printed] with the type of Joannes Saur, at the expense of the heirs of Peter Fischer, 1599.

OXONIÆ,
E THEATRO SHELDONIANO,
Impensis *Thomæ Bennet*, ad Insigne Lunæ Falcatæ in Cœmeterio S.*Pauli*
LONDINI, Anno Domini MDCCII.

Impensa, expense. *Impensis Mathaei Carey* = At the expense of Matthew Carey.

Impressor, printer. *Timidi committere praelo non impressores audebant* = The frightened printers did not dare to commit [the book] to the press.

Impressum est, was printed. *Impressum est hoc opusculum per Ion. Antonium & fratres de Sabio* = This little work was printed by Giovanni Antonio da Sabbio and his brothers.

Imprimebat, printed. *Imprimebat Johannes Steinman* = Johannes Steinman printed [this book].

Insigne, sign. *Apud Martinum Iuuenem, via S. Ioannis Lateranensis, ad insigne Serpentis* = At the shop of Martin Le Jeune, Rue Sainct Jean de Latran, at the sign of the serpent. *Apud Ioan. Bellerum, sub insigni Falconis* = At the shop of Jean Beller, under the sign of the Falcon.

Mensis, month. *Apud Io. Heruagium, mense Martio anno 1537* = At the shop of Johann Herwagen, in the month of March, the year 1537.

Officina, shop, printing establishment. *Ex officina Gulielmi Young, bibliopolae, no. 52 Secunda-Platea, angulo Castaneae-Plateae, M.DCC.XCIII* = From the shop of William Young, bookseller, 52 Second Street, on the corner of Castanea Street, 1793. *In officina Sylvani Otmari* = [Printed] in the shop of Silvan Otmar.

Per, by/through. *Typis Academicis, per Leopoldum Berger* = [Printed] with the types belonging to the Academy, by Leopold Berger.

Platea, street. *Ex officina Gulielmi Young, bibliopolae, no. 52 Secunda-Platea, angulo Castaneae-Plateae, M.DCC.XCIII* = From the shop of William Young, bookseller, 52 Second Street, on the corner of Castanea Street, 1793.

Praelum, prelum, praelo, prelo, press. *Praelo Sheldoniano paratur* = Prepared at the Sheldonian press. *Timidi committere praelo non impressores audebant* = The frightened printers did not dare to commit [the book] to the press.

Prostat (venalis), prostant (venales), for sale. *Prostat venalis apud T. Payne et filium* = For sale at the shop of T. Payne and Son. *Vaenales prostant ex officina Henr. Knox* = For sale at the office of Henry Knox.

Recusa, printed. *Recusa Augustae Vindelicorum* = Printed at Augsburg.

Reimpressa, reprinted. *Reimpressa Pragae* = Reprinted at Prague.

Scutum, shield (i.e., sign). *Apud Ioannem Petit-Pas, via Iacobaea, sub scuto Venetiarum* = At the shop of Jean Petit-Pas, Rue St. Jacques, under the sign of the Venetians.

Signum, sign. *Apud Michaëlem de Roigny, in via Iacobæa, sub signo Quatuor Elementorum* = At the shop of Michel de Roigny, Rue St. Jacques, under the sign of the Four Elements.

Socius, associate, partner. *Apud Ioannem Variscum & socios* = In the shop of Giovanni Varisco and his partners.

Successores, successors. *Excudebant haeredes & successores Andreae Anderson* = The heirs and successors of Andreas Anderson printed [this book].

Sumptus, expense. *Sumptibus H. Maynardi* = [Published] at the expense of H. Maynard.

Typographia, typographeus, printing office/shop. *Ex Typographia Apostolica Vaticana* = From the Apostolic Vatican Printing Office. *E typographeo Clarendoniano* = At the Clarendon Press.

Typographus, printer. *Excudebat Joan. Hayes, celeberrimae Academiae typographus* = John Hayes, printer to the most famous Academy, printed [this book].

Typus, type. *E typis Thomae & Samuelis Green* = [Printed] from the type of Thomas and Samuel Green.

Venundatur, venundantur, sold. *Venundatur Parisiis in vico divi Iacobi sub Lilio Aureo* = Sold in Paris in the Rue St. Jacques under the [sign of] the Golden Lily.

Via, street. *Apud Martinum Iuuenem, via S. Ioannis Laterranensis, ad insigne Serpentis* = At the shop of Martin Le Jeune, Rue Sainct Jean de Latran, at the sign of the serpent.

Vidua, widow. *Ex Officina Plantiniana, apud viduam & filios Ioannis Moreti* = From the Plantin Press, in the shop of the widow and sons of Jan Moretus.

SOURCE: Robert L. Maxwell, *Glossary of Common Latin Terms Found in Imprints of Early Printed Books* (Chicago: ACRL Rare Books and Manuscripts Section, 1998), www.rbms.info/committees/bibliographic_standards/latin/glossary.html.

Access to research materials

by the ALA Association of College and Research Libraries and the Society of American Archivists

IN THIS 2009 JOINT STATEMENT on access to archives and special collections, the term "repository" is defined as an archive, special collections library, research center, museum, historical society, or any other institution responsible for keeping and providing access to research materials. It is used throughout to refer to any type of organization that holds documents—including business, institutional, and government archives; manuscript collections; libraries; museums; and historical societies. These documents can be in any form, including manuscripts, photographs, moving image and sound materials, and their electronic equivalents. "Research materials" are defined as archival or manuscript collections, individual manuscripts, fonds, or record groups found in repositories in any format, printed materials, photographs, artwork, and historical artifacts. "Access" is defined as permission to locate and consult materials within legally established restrictions of privacy, confidentiality, and security clearance.

Responsibility. It is the responsibility of a repository to make available original research materials in its possession on equal terms of access. Access to all research materials, irrespective of format, should be provided in accordance with a clearly defined and publicized institutional access policy, the *Code of Ethics for Archivists* (rev. 2012), the ACRL *Code of Ethics for Special Collections Librarians* (2003), and this joint statement. A repository should not deny any researcher access to materials, nor grant privileged or exclusive use of materials to any researcher, nor conceal the existence of any body of materials from any researcher, unless required to do so by law, institutional access policy, or donor or purchase stipulation.

Intellectual accessibility. A repository should inform researchers in a timely manner of the collections in its custody in accordance with institutional access policy and current professional practice. This may be accomplished through the assistance of staff members; entries in local, regional, or national catalogs; inventories and other documents describing a repository's holdings and created using nation-

ally recognized standards; published guides; repository websites; and other means, including announcements in appropriate print, electronic, and other media. The existence of original research materials should be reported, even if they are not fully accessible because they are not processed or because of restrictions.

Restrictions. Repositories must be committed to preserving research materials and to making them available for research as quickly as practicable following their acquisition. Nevertheless, a repository must fulfill legal and institutional obligations to protect confidentiality and physical security of its collections. Moreover, donors may wish to impose reasonable restrictions upon their papers for a defined period of time to protect privacy or confidentiality.

- Repositories must inform researchers of restrictions that apply to collections, and should be encouraged to make this information available.
- Repositories should discourage donors from imposing unreasonable restrictions, encourage a specific time limitation on restrictions that are imposed, and make the duration of the restriction known to its users.
- Repositories should periodically review and reevaluate restricted material and remove restrictions when they are no longer required.

Policies. To protect and ensure the continued accessibility of its holdings, repositories should require all patrons to use all research materials in accordance with published institutional policies. Each repository should publish, or otherwise make known to potential researchers, its policies governing access and use. Such policies should be applied and enforced equally, and may include provisions such as:

- To protect its collections, each repository may, in accordance with legal authority and institutional access policy, require acceptable identification of any individual wishing to use its materials, as well as a signature verifying the individual has agreed to abide by a statement defining the policies and regulations of the repository.

- Repositories should instruct researchers in proper handling of materials.
- Repositories may refuse access to an individual researcher who has violated the published policies and regulations of the repository.
- Repositories may limit the use of materials, but should try to provide suitable reproductions to researchers in lieu of the originals.
- Repositories may limit access to unprocessed materials, as long as the limitations are applied and enforced consistently and equally to all users.
- Repositories may, under special circumstances, lend or place on deposit with another repository part or all of a collection. When items are loaned, repositories have the responsibility to publicize this fact and the length of unavailability of the collections.

Fees and services. Repositories should strive to provide access to their holdings at no direct cost to the researcher. In situations where this is not possible, reasons for charging fees should be made publicly available. A repository should facilitate access to collections by providing reasonably priced reproduction services that are administered consistently in accordance with legal authority, including copyright law, institutional access policy, and repository regulations. These services may include electronic, paper, or photographic copies; microfilm; or other means of reproduction and should be clearly stated in a publicly accessible written policy. A repository is not obligated to provide reproductions or research services beyond those required by institutional access policy. Repositories may impose reasonable limits on requests for reproductions, but such limits should be clearly stated in the institutional access policy and should also be applied equally and consistently to all users.

Citations. Each repository should publish, or otherwise make available to researchers, a suggested form of concise citation crediting the repository and identifying items within its holdings for later reference. Citations to copies of materials in other repositories should include the location of the originals.

Copyright. It is the researcher's obligation to satisfy copyright law when copying or using materials found in collections. A repository should inform a researcher about materials for which it holds copyright.

Materials from the Helen Hunt Jackson Collection, Tutt Library Special Collections, Colorado College.

SOURCE: "ACRL/SAA Joint Statement on Access to Research Materials in Archives and Special Collections Libraries," *College and Research Libraries News* 70, no. 10 (November 2009): 590–592, ala.org/acrl/standards/jointstatement.

Digital cameras in special collections

by Lisa Miller, Steven K. Galbraith, and the RLG Partnership Working Group on Streamlining Photography and Scanning

DIGITAL CAMERAS ARE REVOLUTIONIZING special collections reading rooms and the research process, much as photocopy machines did for a previous generation. Reference routines focused on the photocopier are embedded in workflows of every repository; photocopying is accepted by repositories, tolerated by rights holders, and expected by researchers. Now technology is forcing repositories to confront change again. The ubiquity of digital cameras and other mobile capture devices has resulted in researchers desiring and expecting to use cameras in reading rooms. While some librarians and archivists have resisted digital cameras, others have embraced them—and rightfully so. The benefits to researchers, repositories, and collection materials are undeniable.

Benefits

Digital cameras are gentler on collection materials. Upending collection materials to position them on a photocopy machine, even when done with the utmost care, risks more damage to materials than photographing them in the reading room while they are face up and appropriately supported. The materials are not subjected to the intense light of a photocopier, but rather are usually easily photographed with ambient lighting.

Digital cameras facilitate use. Researchers with limited time can cover more collection materials during their visit by photographing relevant materials for in-depth study later. We preserve these materials so that they can be used. More use allows us to report higher reference figures and significant research use to our resource allocators.

Digital cameras increase researcher satisfaction. Researchers must take time from work and school to travel to our reading rooms during our limited business hours, often at great expense. Just as libraries and archives struggle with  tighter budgets in these challenging economic times, so, too, do researchers. Digital cameras maximize their precious time in the reading room and end their wait for copies. Depending on the nature of the repository's camera use policy, patrons may also save money and eliminate time spent on photocopy request paperwork. They may also make copies of a broader universe of materials, like oversize materials and bound volumes that are excluded from the photocopy policies of many repositories, and they can make color copies. Given a choice between two repositories, one that has more generous policies and one that does not, researchers may make choices accordingly.

Digital cameras reduce repository workload. Depending on the repository's photocopy and digital camera policies, allowing personal digital cameras outsources duplication tasks to the user, freeing staff to perform other work in these times of increased demands, expectations, and workloads. In addition, cameras may reduce photocopier maintenance and supplies.

Digital cameras enhance security and save reading room checkout time. Digital cameras decrease the number of photocopies leaving the reading room in the hands of researchers, reducing checkout time and the opportunity for theft. With 20th- and 21st-century collections, it is frequently difficult to distinguish between copies and originals.

Digital cameras save paper and photocopy toner. Photographing materials is an effortless way to reduce our environmental impact.

Repositories stay current and resolve an ongoing issue. Repositories remain largely analog outposts, in contrast to the 24/7 online world that most people live and work in. As much as we would like to deliver collection materials to all online, it is still beyond our grasp. Digital cameras are research tools that reach across this online/offline divide, one researcher at a time.

Digital cameras reduce liability for copyright infringement. Digital cameras lessen the repository's risk profile, especially if it maintains a "hands-off" approach towards the use of personal cameras. When a repository makes copies of copyrighted documents for users or provides equipment on which users can make their own copies, it runs the risk of engaging in direct and indirect copyright infringement.

Suggested practices for cameras in the reading room

To synthesize a core of suggested practices, the Research Libraries Group Partnership Working Group reviewed the current policies of 35 repositories comprised of academic libraries, independent research libraries, historical societies, government archives, and public libraries. Below are the most commonly shared elements, arranged in categories for administration and handling of materials.

Administration. Require camera users to complete and sign an application/policy/terms-of-use form agreeing that images of sensitive and copyrighted materials will only be used for study, teaching, or research purposes and will be used in compliance with copyright law. Some agreements also stipulate that the user cannot reproduce images without permission from the institution. A few forms require the user to list specifically what he or she is digitally reproducing. This allows the institution to keep statistics on what and how much is being digitized and to check whether any of the materials already exist in the institution's digital repository, though it increases liability for copyright infringement.

Staff reviews collection materials prior to photography. This ensures that items are not too fragile to be reproduced and allows staff to note any copyright or donor restrictions, though it also places the institution at greater risk of liability.

Limit the number of shots, when appropriate, to a quantity determined by institutional policy and/or in accordance with copyright policies.

Watermark digital reproductions by requiring that each item be photographed with a streamer, transparency, or card that identifies the item and its holding institution and, if applicable, displays a copyright notice. Patrons are responsible for properly citing their copies, but repositories may provide citation guidelines.

Digital photography must not disturb other users or staff. All audio functions on digital cameras must be turned off and users may not photograph other patrons, staff, or the reading room.

Handling collection materials. No flash photography. It is a distraction to other users. As with any method of duplication, camera use is considered only if it will not damage collection materials. Users are instructed on how to handle items during photography.

In an effort to monitor how users handle items during photography, several institutions designate specific work areas where items may be photographed or have a staff member present during shooting. Some provide or require use of an in-house camera stand. Some policies make a point of prohibiting users from bringing their own tripods or lighting equipment.

SOURCE: Lisa Miller, Steven K. Galbraith, and the RLG Partnership Working Group on Streamlining Photography and Scanning, "Capture and Release": Digital Cameras in the Reading Room (Dublin, Ohio: OCLC Research, 2010), www.oclc.org/research/publications/library/2010/2010-05.pdf. Reprinted with permission.

CHILDREN'S MATERIALS

Newbery Medal awards

THE NEWBERY MEDAL, named for 18th-century British bookseller John Newbery, is awarded annually by the ALA Association for Library Service to Children to the author of the most distinguished contribution to American literature for children. Here are the winners since the award's inception in 1922.

2013—Katherine Applegate, *The One and Only Ivan* (HarperCollins, 2012).
2012—Jack Gantos, *Dead End in Norvelt* (Farrar Straus Giroux, 2011).
2011—Clare Vanderpool, *Moon over Manifest* (Delacorte, 2010).
2010—Rebecca Stead, *When You Reach Me* (Wendy Lamb, 2009).
2009—Neil Gaiman, *The Graveyard Book* (HarperCollins, 2008).
2008—Laura Amy Schlitz, *Good Masters! Sweet Ladies! Voices from a Medieval Village* (Candlewick, 2007).
2007—Susan Patron, *The Higher Power of Lucky* (Atheneum, 2006).
2006—Lynne Rae Perkins, *Criss Cross* (Greenwillow, 2005).
2005—Cynthia Kadohata, *Kira-Kira* (Atheneum, 2004).
2004—Kate DiCamillo, *The Tale of Despereaux: Being the Story of a Mouse, a Princess, Some Soup, and a Spool of Thread* (Candlewick, 2003).
  2003—Avi, *Crispin: The Cross of Lead* (Hyperion, 2002).
  2002—Linda Sue Park, *A Single Shard* (Clarion, 2001).
  2001—Richard Peck, *A Year Down Yonder* (Dial, 2000).
  2000—Christopher Paul Curtis, *Bud, Not Buddy* (Delacorte, 1999).
  1999—Louis Sachar, *Holes* (Farrar, 1998).
  1998—Karen Hesse, *Out of the Dust* (Scholastic, 1997).
  1997—E. L. Konigsburg, *The View from Saturday* (Atheneum, 1996).
  1996—Karen Cushman, *The Midwife's Apprentice* (Clarion, 1995).
  1995—Sharon Creech, *Walk Two Moons* (HarperCollins, 1994).
  1994—Lois Lowry, *The Giver* (Houghton, 1993).
  1993—Cynthia Rylant, *Missing May* (Orchard, 1992).
1992—Phyllis Reynolds Naylor, *Shiloh* (Atheneum, 1991).
1991—Jerry Spinelli, *Maniac Magee* (Little, Brown, 1990).
1990—Lois Lowry, *Number the Stars* (Houghton, 1989).
1989—Paul Fleischman, *Joyful Noise: Poems for Two Voices* (Harper, 1988).
1988—Russell Freedman, *Lincoln: A Photobiography* (Clarion, 1987).
1987—Sid Fleischman, *The Whipping Boy* (Greenwillow, 1986).
1986—Patricia MacLachlan, *Sarah, Plain and Tall* (Harper, 1985).
1985—Robin McKinley, *The Hero and the Crown* (Greenwillow, 1984).
1984—Beverly Cleary, *Dear Mr. Henshaw* (Morrow, 1983).
1983—Cynthia Voigt, *Dicey's Song* (Atheneum, 1982).
1982—Nancy Willard, *A Visit to William Blake's Inn: Poems for Innocent and Experienced Travelers* (Harcourt, 1981).
1981—Katherine Paterson, *Jacob Have I Loved* (Crowell, 1980).
1980—Joan W. Blos, *A Gathering of Days: A New England Girl's Journal, 1830–32* (Scribner, 1979).

1979—Ellen Raskin, *The Westing Game* (Dutton, 1978).
1978—Katherine Paterson, *Bridge to Terabithia* (Crowell, 1977).
1977—Mildred D. Taylor, *Roll of Thunder, Hear My Cry* (Dial, 1976).
1976—Susan Cooper, *The Grey King* (McElderry/Atheneum, 1975).
1975—Virginia Hamilton, *M. C. Higgins, the Great* (Macmillan, 1974).
1974—Paula Fox, *The Slave Dancer* (Bradbury, 1973).
1973—Jean Craighead George, *Julie of the Wolves* (Harper, 1972).
1972—Robert C. O'Brien, *Mrs. Frisby and the Rats of NIMH* (Atheneum, 1971).
1971—Betsy Byars, *Summer of the Swans* (Viking, 1970).
1970—William H. Armstrong, *Sounder* (Harper, 1969).
1969—Lloyd Alexander, *The High King* (Holt, 1968).
1968—E. L. Konigsburg, *From the Mixed-Up Files of Mrs. Basil E. Frankweiler* (Atheneum, 1967).
1967—Irene Hunt, *Up a Road Slowly* (Follett, 1966).
1966—Elizabeth Borton de Treviño, *I, Juan de Pareja* (Farrar, 1965).
1965—Maia Wojciechowska, *Shadow of a Bull* (Atheneum, 1964).
1964—Emily Neville, *It's Like This, Cat* (Harper, 1963).
1963—Madeleine L'Engle, *A Wrinkle in Time* (Farrar, 1962).
1962—Elizabeth George Speare, *The Bronze Bow* (Houghton, 1961).
1961—Scott O'Dell, *Island of the Blue Dolphins* (Houghton, 1960).
1960—Joseph Krumgold, *Onion John* (Crowell, 1959).
1959—Elizabeth George Speare, *The Witch of Blackbird Pond* (Houghton, 1958).
1958—Harold Keith, *Rifles for Watie* (Crowell, 1957).
1957—Virginia Sorenson, *Miracles on Maple Hill* (Harcourt, 1956).
1956—Jean Lee Latham, *Carry On, Mr. Bowditch* (Houghton, 1955).
1955—Meindert De Jong, *The Wheel on the School* (Harper, 1954).
1954—Joseph Krumgold, *. . . And Now Miguel* (Crowell, 1953).
1953—Ann Nolan Clark, *Secret of the Andes* (Viking, 1952).
1952—Eleanor Estes, *Ginger Pye* (Harcourt, 1951).
1951—Elizabeth Yates, *Amos Fortune, Free Man* (Dutton, 1950).
1950—Marguerite de Angeli, *The Door in the Wall* (Doubleday, 1949).
1949—Marguerite Henry, *King of the Wind* (Rand McNally, 1948).
1948—William Pène Du Bois, *The Twenty-One Balloons* (Viking, 1947).
1947—Carolyn Sherwin Bailey, *Miss Hickory* (Viking, 1946).
1946—Lois Lenski, *Strawberry Girl* (Lippincott, 1945).
1945—Robert Lawson, *Rabbit Hill* (Viking, 1944).
1944—Esther Forbes, *Johnny Tremain* (Houghton, 1943).
1943—Elizabeth Janet Gray, *Adam of the Road* (Viking, 1942).
1942—Walter Edmonds, *The Matchlock Gun* (Dodd, 1941).
1941—Armstrong Sperry, *Call It Courage* (Macmillan, 1940).
1940—James Daugherty, *Daniel Boone* (Viking, 1939).
1939—Elizabeth Enright, *Thimble Summer* (Rinehart, 1938).
1938—Kate Seredy, *The White Stag* (Viking, 1937).
1937—Ruth Sawyer, *Roller Skates* (Viking, 1936).
1936—Carol Ryrie Brink, *Caddie Woodlawn* (Macmillan, 1935).
1935—Monica Shannon, *Dobry* (Viking, 1934).
1934—Cornelia Meigs, *Invincible Louisa: The Story of the Author of Little Women* (Little, Brown, 1933).
1933—Elizabeth Lewis, *Young Fu of the Upper Yangtze* (Winston, 1932).
1932—Laura Adams Armer, *Waterless Mountain* (Longmans, 1931).
1931—Elizabeth Coatsworth, *The Cat Who Went to Heaven* (Macmillan, 1930).

1930—Rachel Field, *Hitty, Her First Hundred Years* (Macmillan, 1929).
1929—Eric P. Kelly, *The Trumpeter of Krakow* (Macmillan, 1928).
1928—Dhan Gopal Mukerji, *Gay-Neck, the Story of a Pigeon* (Dutton, 1927).
1927—Will James, *Smoky, the Cowhorse* (Scribner, 1926).
1926—Arthur Bowie Chrisman, *Shen of the Sea* (Dutton, 1925).
1925—Charles Finger, *Tales from Silver Lands* (Doubleday, 1924).
1924—Charles Hawes, *The Dark Frigate* (Atlantic/Little, 1923).
1923—Hugh Lofting, *The Voyages of Doctor Dolittle* (Lippincott, 1922).
1922—Hendrik Willem van Loon, *The Story of Mankind* (Liveright, 1921).

SOURCE: ALA Association for Library Service to Children.

Caldecott Medal winners

THE CALDECOTT MEDAL, named in honor of 19th-century English illustrator Randolph Caldecott, is awarded annually by the ALA Association for Library Service to Children to the artist of the most distinguished American picture book for children. Here are the award winners since 1938.

2013—Jon Klassen, *This Is Not My Hat* (Candlewick, 2012).
2012—Chris Raschka, *A Ball for Daisy* (Schwartz and Wade, 2011).
2011—Philip C. Stead, *A Sick Day for Amos McGee* (Roaring Brook, 2010).
2010—Jerry Pinkney, *The Lion and the Mouse* (Little, Brown, 2009).
2009—Susan Marie Swanson, *The House in the Night* (Houghton Mifflin, 2008).
2008—Brian Selznick, *The Invention of Hugo Cabret* (Scholastic, 2007).
2007—David Wiesner, *Flotsam* (Clarion, 2006).
2006—Norman Juster, *The Hello, Goodbye Window* (Michael di Capua, 2005).
2005—Kevin Henkes, *Kitten's First Full Moon* (Greenwillow, 2004).
2004—Mordicai Gerstein, *The Man Who Walked between the Towers* (Roaring Brook, 2003).

Stop the presses
by Kathleen T. Horning

With all the care that goes into the production of children's books and all the scrutiny given to them by award committees, it is not often that mistakes slip by everyone involved in the process. But it has happened. The first printing of the first Caldecott winner, *Animals of the Bible,* illustrated by Dorothy P. Lathrop, features a Christ child with two left feet in an illustration of the peaceable kingdom. This was corrected in later printings.

A correction also had to be made to the 1979 Newbery winner *The Westing Game* after a young reader found an error in the intricately plotted puzzle mystery by Ellen Raskin. Nine-year-old Andrew Conner, after reading the book multiple times, found a misnumbered table and wrote the author to tell her. This mistake was minor, but in a novel that calls for careful reading in order to piece together clues to solve a mystery, it mattered enough to the author and her publisher that the error was corrected in subsequent printings.

SOURCE: The Newbery and Caldecott Awards: A Guide to the Medal and Honor Books (Chicago: ALA Association for Library Service to Children, 2009), 13–14.

2003—Eric Rohmann, *My Friend Rabbit* (Roaring Brook, 2002).

2002—David Wiesner, *The Three Pigs* (Clarion, 2001).

2001—Judith St. George, *So You Want to Be President?* (Philomel, 2000); illustrated by David Small.

2000—Simms Taback, *Joseph Had a Little Overcoat* (Viking, 1999).

1999—Jacqueline Briggs Martin, *Snowflake Bentley* (Houghton, 1998); illustrated by Mary Azarian.

1998—Paul O. Zelinsky, *Rapunzel* (Dutton, 1997).

1997—David Wisniewski, *Golem* (Clarion, 1996).

1996—Peggy Rathmann, *Officer Buckle and Gloria* (Putnam, 1995).

1995—Eve Bunting, *Smoky Night* (Harcourt, 1994); illustrated by David Diaz.

1994—Allen Say, *Grandfather's Journey* (Harcourt, 1993).

1993—Emily Arnold McCully, *Mirette on the High Wire* (Putnam, 1992).

1992—David Wiesner, *Tuesday* (Clarion, 1991).

1991—David Macaulay, *Black and White* (Houghton, 1990).

1990—Ed Young, *Lon Po Po: A Red-Riding Hood Story from China* (Philomel, 1989).

1989—Karen Ackerman, *Song and Dance Man* (Knopf, 1988); illustrated by Stephen Gammell.

1988—Jane Yolen, *Owl Moon* (Philomel, 1987); illustrated by John Schoenherr.

1987—Arthur Yorinks, *Hey, Al* (Farrar, 1986); illustrated by Richard Egielski.

1986—Chris Van Allsburg, *The Polar Express* (Houghton, 1985).

1985—Margaret Hodges, *Saint George and the Dragon* (Little, Brown, 1984); illustrated by Trina Schart Hyman.

1984—Alice and Martin Provensen, *The Glorious Flight: Across the Channel with Louis Bleriot* (Viking, 1983).

1983—Blaise Cendrars, *Shadow* (Scribner, 1982); illustrated by Marcia Brown.

1982—Chris Van Allsburg, *Jumanji* (Houghton, 1981).

1981—Arnold Lobel, *Fables* (Harper, 1980).

1980—Donald Hall, *Ox-Cart Man* (Viking, 1979); illustrated by Barbara Cooney.

1979—Paul Goble, *The Girl Who Loved Wild Horses* (Bradbury, 1978).

1978—Peter Spier, *Noah's Ark* (Doubleday, 1977).

1977—Margaret Musgrove, *Ashanti to Zulu: African Traditions* (Dial, 1976); illustrated by Leo and Diane Dillon.

1976—Verna Aardema, *Why Mosquitoes Buzz in People's Ears* (Dial, 1975); illustrated by Leo and Diane Dillon.

1975—Gerald McDermott, *Arrow to the Sun* (Viking, 1974).

1974—Harve Zemach, *Duffy and the Devil* (Farrar, 1973); illustrated by Margot Zemach.

1973—Lafcadio Hearn, retold by Arlene Mosel, *The Funny Little Woman* (Dutton, 1972); illustrated by Blair Lent.

1972—Nonny Hogrogian, *One Fine Day* (Macmillan, 1971).

1971—Gail E. Haley, *A Story A Story* (Atheneum, 1970).

1970—William Steig, *Sylvester and the Magic Pebble* (Windmill, 1969).

1969—Arthur Ransome, *The Fool of the World and the Flying Ship* (Farrar, 1968); illustrated by Uri Shulevitz.

1968—Barbara Emberley, *Drummer Hoff* (Prentice-Hall, 1967); illustrated by Ed Emberley.

1967—Evaline Ness, *Sam, Bangs & Moonshine* (Holt, 1966).

1966—Sorche Nic Leodhas, pseud. [Leclaire Alger], *Always Room for One More* (Holt, 1965); illustrated by Nonny Hogrogian.

1965—Beatrice Schenk de Regniers, *May I Bring a Friend?* (Atheneum, 1964); illustrated by Beni Montresor.

1964—Maurice Sendak, *Where the Wild Things Are* (Harper, 1963).

1963—Ezra Jack Keats, *The Snowy Day* (Viking, 1962).

1962—Marcia Brown, *Once a Mouse* (Scribner, 1961).

1961—Ruth Robbins, *Baboushka and the Three Kings* (Parnassus, 1960); illustrated by Nicolas Sidjakov.

1960—Marie Hall Ets and Aurora Labastida, *Nine Days to Christmas* (Viking, 1959); illustrated by Marie Hall Ets.

1959—Barbara Cooney, *Chanticleer and the Fox* (Crowell, 1958).

1958—Robert McCloskey, *Time of Wonder* (Viking, 1957).

1957—Janice Udry, *A Tree Is Nice* (Harper, 1956); illustrated by Marc Simont.

1956—John Langstaff, *Frog Went A-Courtin'* (Harcourt, 1955); illustrated by Feodor Rojankovsky.

1955— Charles Perrault, *Cinderella, or the Little Glass Slipper* (Scribner, 1954); illustrated by Marcia Brown.

1954—Ludwig Bemelmans, *Madeline's Rescue* (Viking, 1953).

1953—Lynd Ward, *The Biggest Bear* (Houghton, 1952).

1952—Will, pseud. [William Lipkind], *Finders Keepers* (Harcourt, 1951); illustrated by Nicolas, pseud. [Nicholas Mordvinoff].

1951—Katherine Milhous, *The Egg Tree* (Scribner, 1950).

1950—Leo Politi, *Song of the Swallows* (Scribner, 1949).

1949—Berta and Elmer Hader, *The Big Snow* (Macmillan, 1948).

Art media in the Caldecotts

ALA's Association for Library Service to Children, which is responsible for the Caldecott Medal and also the Newbery Medal, publishes a book every year that lists the winning titles, *The Newbery and Caldecott Awards: A Guide to the Medal and Honor Books.* Starting with the 1991 edition of the book, an article by Christine Behrmann appeared with the art media information for each Caldecott title, winners and honors. Titled "The Media Used in Caldecott Picture Books: Notes toward a Definitive List," the article had originally appeared in the Winter 1988 issue of the then-official ALSC publication, the *Journal of Youth Services in Libraries*, and was reprinted every year "with changes," updates, and any needed corrections to keep the list up-to-date and accurate. At the time, Behrmann was children's materials specialist in the Office of Children's Services at the New York Public Library.

The Newbery and Caldecott Awards: 2008 Edition was the last to reprint an updated version of Behrmann's original article. Starting with the 2009 edition, the art media information is incorporated into the text accompanying each entry.

For an entire list of the ALA and *Horn Book* publications with biographical sketches of the Newbery and Caldecott–winning authors and illustrators as well as the text of both the Newbery and Caldecott Medal acceptance speeches, see the Newbery and Caldecott Medal section of the ALA Professional Tips wiki, "Media Awards Acceptance Speeches," wikis.ala.org/professionaltips/index.php?title=Media_Awards_Acceptance_Speeches.

More detailed information is available in various publications; see Valerie Hawkins's list at the WorldCat.org library catalog, "Books with More Information on ALA's Literary Awards and Reading Lists," at www.worldcat.org/profiles/vhawkala97/lists/611529.

1948—Alvin Tresselt, *White Snow, Bright Snow* (Lothrop, 1947); illustrated by Roger Duvoisin.

1947—Golden MacDonald, pseud. [Margaret Wise Brown], *The Little Island* (Doubleday, 1946); illustrated by Leonard Weisgard.

1946—Maude and Miska Petersham, *The Rooster Crows* (Macmillan, 1945).

1945—Rachel Field, *Prayer for a Child* (Macmillan, 1944); illustrated by Elizabeth Orton Jones.

1944— James Thurber, *Many Moons* (Harcourt, 1943); illustrated by Louis Slobodkin.

1943—Virginia Lee Burton, *The Little House* (Houghton, 1942).

1942—Robert McCloskey, *Make Way for Ducklings* (Viking, 1941).

1941—Robert Lawson, *They Were Strong and Good* (Viking, 1940).

1940—Ingri and Edgar Parin d'Aulaire, *Abraham Lincoln* (Doubleday, 1939).

1939—Thomas Handforth, *Mei Li* (Doubleday, 1938).

1938—Helen Dean Fish, *Animals of the Bible: A Picture Book* (Lippincott, 1937); illustrated by Dorothy P. Lathrop.

SOURCE: ALA Association for Library Service to Children.

4

The children we serve

by Virginia A. Walter

IN *CHILDREN AND LIBRARIES: Getting It Right* (ALA Editions, 2001), I proposed three alternative visions for the children we would be serving as we moved into the 21st century: the original notion of the child reader, an idea that inspired and guided the founders of library service to children; the child of the information age; and the child in the community. It's now time to revisit those three concepts and look at two additional notions of childhood that might usefully inform our thinking today.

Each of these five concepts of the child leads to a different approach to library service. All are plausible, all are hopeful, and all are obtainable. They may not be mutually exclusive, but each is based on a different understanding of the child who will shape and claim the future of the 21st century.

The child as reader. The library for the child reader is the vision that offers the most continuity with the past. It builds on the core values and visions of the librarians who founded library services for children in this country. It is consistent with the niche that these services have traditionally occupied. It is therefore a conservative vision, in the sense that it conserves a cherished and valued tradition.

As we think about the future of library service to children, however, we must look at even our most cherished and valued traditions to see how they hold up against today's realities. Can we be sure that books and reading will continue to be valued by our society? Will parents, educators, and policymakers continue to believe that books and reading are essential to the healthy development of children? Will voters agree that providing books and promoting reading for children are appropriate functions for tax-supported public libraries?

I have previously written about our faith in a deeply held belief in the power of reading "good" books as a means of improving human nature and

behavior. However, the world we operate in now seems to require something more, and children's librarians have looked for research findings that bolster their claims of doing good work and providing meaningful service. One of the more significant initiatives has been "Every Child Ready to Read," a joint initiative by two ALA divisions, the Association for Library Service to Children and the

Public Library Association, to educate parents and caregivers in techniques they can use to transfer critical emergent literacy skills to their preschool children. Those responsible for the original program hired academics with impeccable credentials to design the workshop curricula and commissioned a study to determine whether the research-based curriculum achieved its desired learning and behavior outcomes. The study showed that parents of every age, educational background, income level, and ethnicity who attended the workshops significantly increased those behaviors that research has shown stimulate reading readiness in young children. The big lesson we learned is that we can't do this job alone; we need to enlist caregivers and parents as the child's first and best teachers.

The child of the information age. Children have claimed their right to computers and the internet. Never mind that they do not have all the rights that adult library patrons do; many, perhaps most, libraries use filtering software to screen content on computers in the children's room. Most young patrons probably don't care as much as we intellectual freedom advocates do; they are not there to access forbidden websites. They may not even want to access information sites at all. Mostly, they want to play games.

We children's librarians tend to be a little dismissive of gaming, unlike our colleagues in young adult services. Sometimes it seems that the best rationale we can offer for this activity is that we encourage reading for pleasure. Why not computing for pleasure? We should probably pay more attention to voices like that of Steven Johnson, who claimed in his book *Everything Bad Is Good for You* (Riverhead, 2005) that computer games place heavy cognitive demands on their players. In fact, much of these games' captivation is due to the challenges they place on individuals to persist in their efforts to solve complex challenges.

Some writers insist that the hours spent playing video games have given young people now entering the workforce some unique and badly needed skills: an ability to multitask and a willingness to take risks. Those 10-year-old boys clustered around a computer in your children's room arguing about the best strategy for knocking out an opponent's avatar may be engaged in the same kind of reasoning 20 years from now in some corporate boardroom.

However, access is only part of the problem. The other two issues that we need to think hard about are content and education for information literacy. And we also need to consider how we are going to integrate computers and digital resources into our services and collections.

The child in the community. Although the founders of library service to children designed their services to promote books and reading, they still understood the importance of their young patrons' environment. Librarians working in rural areas pondered schemes to bring books to children in remote farmhouses far from the nearest library. Urban librarians were concerned about crowded tenements and unsafe sweatshops where children labored for pennies. During home visits, librarians would gather a group of children from the neighborhood and talk about the books, read aloud, tell stories, and organize crafts such as sewing or basketry.

Outreach or social work? Librarians sometimes embrace the first activity and shun the second. Yet when they truly begin to plan and implement programs that take into account the communities in which children live, the lines tend to blur. Traditional library missions may expand when we go beyond superficial marketing studies or environmental scans and dig for insights into our communities.

We will rarely find those useful insights if we stay sequestered behind the walls of our library buildings. I understand the competing demands of reference desk schedules, storytimes, and staff meetings. In spite of those very real constraints, time must be found for walking in the footsteps of the children and families whom we serve.

The global child. The world feels more interconnected all the time. It is no longer unusual to find large urban school districts in cities that serve as ports of entry for new immigrants where the number of languages spoken in the homes of the students exceeds 50. In Los Angeles, these languages include the mostly oral dialects spoken by indigenous people from Central America as well as the more familiar Spanish, Korean, Mandarin, Thai, Filipino, and Armenian. For the children of these newcomer families, the country of origin remains an important influence. It is easy to see that the children whose families maintain their international connections are living in a global village. Other children are also residents in one global village. The ecological, economic, and geopolitical realities of the 21st century place them there. The library can help prepare them to be more competent and compassionate global citizens.

Books in languages other than English are most likely to be found in children's collections serving large immigrant populations. They are well used by children who haven't learned English yet and by families who hope to keep the mother tongue alive even as the children become fluent in English. I have found, however, that even monolingual American children are intrigued with books in other languages. They are especially fascinated by different alphabets. I'm not sure what an American child learns about Japan when she leafs through a Japanese picture book, but it can't hurt to be exposed to the notion that not everybody reads from left to right in the Roman alphabet.

If we begin to think of the American children we serve as citizens in the world republic of childhood who will grow up to be decision makers in an increasingly interconnected global village, we also add another critical dimension to our understanding of contemporary childhood.

The empowered child. Children have little legal power. They are dependent on their parents by law and in practice. They may depend on their parents to sign them up for soccer or to take them to the library. ALA in its Library Bill of Rights affirms the right and responsibility of parents to guide their own children's use of the library and its resources and services.

Given this legal and social reality, what is the justification for empowering children? Why should librarians be advocates for children's rights? In an essay in *Rethinking Childhood* (Rutgers, 2003), Barbara Woodhouse proposes that we recognize two categories of rights especially for children: needs-based rights and dignity-based rights.

Needs-based rights include positive rights to nurture, education, medical care, and other goods and services that children need to develop into productive adults. Dignity-based rights recognize that children are fully human from the time of their birth. They reflect both the inherent dependence and fragility of children and their developing capacity for participation in decisions that affect their lives. Woodhouse identifies five principles of human rights that could and should be applied to children:

- The equality principle: the right to equal opportunity
- The individualism principle: the right to be treated as a person, not an object
- The empowerment principle: the right to a voice and, sometimes, a choice
- The protection principle: the right of the weak to be protected from the strong
- The privacy principle: the right to protection of intimate relationships

This framework resolves much of the tension that has plagued the issue of children's rights. It acknowledges the child's right to protection as well as the child's right to autonomy. Librarians can contribute to this framework a principled defense of children's right to information and the active dissemination of the information that children need in order to exercise their other rights We can work even harder than we do now to ensure that the library advocates for the best interests of children.

One important document that deserves our attention is the United Nations Convention on the Rights of the Child as a framework for guiding their work. This document, adopted by the United Nations in 1989, has been ratified by ev-

ery country in the world except Somalia, South Sudan, and the United States. It is a remarkable international consensus on the civil, political, economic, social, and cultural rights of children. It covers just about every aspect of children's lives, and it emphasizes respect for children's dignity. It manages to avoid focus on either protection or self-determination for children, the usual opposing viewpoints, and instead promotes liberty, privacy, and nurturance.

The child as reader, the child of the information age, the child in the community, the global child, or the empowered child? Which child will we target as we plan and deliver library services in our communities? Can we strive to target them all?

SOURCE: Virginia A. Walter, "The Children We Serve," *American Libraries* 40, no. 10 (October 2009): 52–55.

Family storytime
by Rob Reid

I FIND MYSELF in front of dozens of family groups each year, entertaining them with stories and songs at libraries, schools, festivals, and literacy programs. I thoroughly enjoy audiences where young children are joined by older siblings, parents, grandparents, cousins, and friends.

This togetherness is in sharp contrast to my first introduction to public library story programs, in the early 1980s. I volunteered at my local library and was told, "Whatever you do, don't let the parents in!" The mind-set was that the parents were disruptive and the children needed to learn independence. I followed orders—for a while. Then I let one parent sneak in. I enjoyed her presence. She got into the stories and was able to interact in a positive literary manner with her

---

Reid's read-aloud tips

Know your audience. They may prefer a specific type of book. Some audiences may not be able to handle scary books, while another audience may clamor for more. Many younger groups can easily handle titles recommended for slightly older groups. I would not hesitate to read Kate DiCamillo's book *The Tale of Despereaux* to certain kindergartners even though the book is recommended for children in grades 2–5. Other groups of kindergarteners, on the other hand, may not be able to handle the book.

   Challenge your audience. Share a book that some kids may not normally choose on their own. Two great examples are Shannon Hale's books *The Goose Girl* and *Princess Academy.* The latter title was my favorite fantasy of 2005, the year I served on ALA's Newbery Award Committee. I knew boys would love both titles but wouldn't necessarily pick them up on their own because of the titles and jackets. Once the stories started, however, I found that both girls and boys were captivated by the exploits of Hale's lively, strong characters.

   Challenge older audiences to listen to younger material they may have missed when they were younger. There's no reason not to read a book such as *Elijah of Buxton,* by Christopher Paul Curtis, to high-schoolers, even though the book isn't marketed to this age group.

   Entertain your audience. Choose books you yourself have read and enjoyed. Your enthusiasm will carry over into your reading. Be prepared so you can handle vocabulary, names, and foreign phrases that are new to you. Don't read a book you haven't read in advance. Project your voice. Make sure the person in the back can hear your every word, even during the quiet, serious passages. Add variety to your vocalization. Trust the author's words.

SOURCE: "Reid's Read-Aloud Tips," *American Libraries* 40, no. 5 (May 2009): 45.

4

child. I let another parent in . . . and another. It was about this time that I got my first job as a youth services librarian, at Pueblo (Colo.) Library District. I created the library's first family story program. Two families attended. By the time I left Pueblo, two years later, we had crowds of 80 in attendance on a regular basis. I moved to Eau Claire, Wisconsin, and began a new series of family story programs there as well. Today, I can't imagine conducting a story program without adult family members in the audience.

   When parents and caregivers are present, the enjoyment and educational aspects of the story program are heightened. The adults become positive role models for the children for reading, reading-readiness activities, and becoming lifelong library users. Adults learn proper techniques for reading aloud. They learn stories, fingerplays, songs, and activities, remember them from their own childhood, and are thrilled to learn new ones.

   There is a growing pool of resources available to librarians for intergenerational story programs—from picture books to movement activities to songs to crafts—more varied than what is available for a traditional preschool storytime. Authors such as Doreen Cronin, Margie Palatini, Adam Rex, Jon Scieszka, and Mo Willems consciously speak to adults in their picture books. The child will enjoy the story at one level, older children will pick up some aspects the younger children will miss, and adults will catch all types of humor and sophistication not normally associated with children's fare.

   The last decade has been a rich period for both children's books and children's music. I've learned about many from my students at the University of Wisconsin at Eau Claire. Camp counselors have a wealth of musical and movement activities that can be altered to fit the different program themes. But I also encourage everyone to create their own original material or set new words to traditional songs.

To conduct successful storytime programs, I like having lists on hand to keep the overall program in mind. The list can include an opening song for each program theme. I like to play music as families enter the story program area.

I often find that an adult will walk up to learn the name of the artist. Once the program begins, I like to have a lively mix of picture books and supplemental activities, such as fingerplays, music, movement activities, and poetry. I also like to choose picture books that lend themselves to audience participation, usually with the audience members providing sound effects. I typically construct the program so that the more active stories and songs occur near the end of the program and the quieter, longer pieces are shared near the beginning. I encourage you to alter the programs to play to your strengths.

Storytime themes are timeless, and I like my programs to be noisy and active. I liken family storytimes to family reunions. Many families have busy schedules and are hard-pressed to have time together. By offering a family story program series, you will be a valuable partner creating many memories for many families.

SOURCE: Rob Reid, "Family Storytime," *American Libraries* 40, no. 5 (May 2009): 44–45.

Boys' literature
by Michael Sullivan

WHEN WE CONSIDER WHAT BOYS READ—and how they read, for that matter—there are some generalities to keep in mind. We should be careful not to use the terms *literature, fiction,* and *novel* as if they mean the same thing. Our literature for children includes both fiction and nonfiction, and fiction contains novels and the various genres. Boys tend to favor genre fiction, because it tends to be more plot-based than your basic novel, which is more character-based.

Boys' readings are often short, because they tend to read below grade level and shorter books seem to be less of a chore. Many boys are drawn to series books, again to limit the struggles associated with reading. The hardest 10 pages of any book are the first 10; that is when the reader must become accustomed to the writing style, setting, dialect, and a hundred other factors. With a series, the boy must go through that process only once and can then enjoy the rest of the series. Also, for boys who find little reading of interest, series give them the prospect of always having the next book when they do find something they like.

Boys are often attracted to edgy reading, in whatever format they find it. We all see it but maybe do not try hard enough to understand why this is. Too often we dismiss this tendency as acting out. Boys see the world as operating on rules, on limits. They want to explore as wide a world as they can find, and how do they

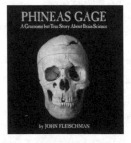

find out where the lines are if they do not dance over them every now and then? Boys often explore the extremes in many aspects of their lives; literature is one area where we can support that.

Bruce Coville observes that young boys are by nature mischievous and want to read about male characters who do naughty things. Is it hard to understand the appeal of the naughty? You are not supposed to understand it, because you are not the target audience. You are not a 12-year-old boy.

Nonfiction. When we talk about the types of reading that have boy appeal, we first and foremost need to speak of nonfiction. Teachers, librarians, and parents often see a boy with a nonfiction book in hand and respond, "That's fine, now get a book you can read." Boys often see nonfiction not as a vehicle for finding specific information but as a way to better understand the world around them, to acquire the rules and tools they so desire.

Ray Doiron of the University of Prince Edward Island observed 10,000 free-reading choices made by children in grades 1–6 from their classroom libraries. Boys, when given free range, found almost half their reading in nonfiction, despite the fact that there was scant nonfiction to choose from. This study should also caution us; the fact that these classroom libraries were more than 85% fiction tells us how easy it is for us adults to underestimate the value of nonfiction.

Many nonfiction books give boys back an important part of their reading, one that they lost early in their school years—illustrations. Pictures can be a powerful stimulant to a boy's brain, and because of differences in brain structure, boys benefit from stimuli in their environment when doing upper-level thinking, such as reading. Illustrations also help children read at a higher level by giving visual clues to aid comprehension. Boys rely more on these clues than girls do, partly because such clues stimulate the right side of the brain, which tends to be better developed in boys.

Visual fiction. If nonfiction is popular with boys partly because it gives them back their illustrations, it makes sense that boys would look to bring illustrations back into their fiction. There are various forms of visual fiction, such as Hudson Talbot's *Safari Journal: The Adventures in Africa of Carey Monroe* (Silver Whistle Books, 2003), which is laid out with words interspersed with photos, drawings, and comics. Big Guy Books, a small publisher from Carlsbad, California, has for some years produced the Time Soldiers series of chapter books, which mimics the picture book format but with photographs and computer-generated illustrations.

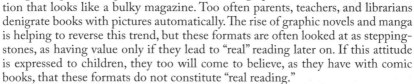

Today, boys have the graphic novel format, book-length stories told in comic book fashion. Even more popular is manga, a Japanese-inspired format of serialized graphic fiction that looks like a bulky magazine. Too often parents, teachers, and librarians denigrate books with pictures automatically. The rise of graphic novels and manga is helping to reverse this trend, but these formats are often looked at as stepping-stones, as having value only if they lead to "real" reading later on. If this attitude is expressed to children, they too will come to believe, as they have with comic books, that these formats do not constitute "real reading."

Humor. Humor is a powerful tool for reaching boys. Many boys understand that they do not read up to grade level or as well as their classmates. They often face the concern, or consternation, of adults who worry about their lack of reading and pressure them to change their ways. The stress involved seldom helps. Humor is a great release for boys, turning a chore into a pleasure. For this reason, they often seek out edgy humor, responding to the constriction of adults by seeking release in the forbidden. The fact that adults often despise their choice of reading materials only adds to its appeal.

Adults may sometimes enjoy humor for kids, but it is always suspect and we tend to shy away from offering it to children unless it is squeaky clean, and you can spell that boring. Jon Scieszka, the great boys' humorist, has said, "I can't think of a funny book that my kids ever had to read in school." When Jeffrey Wilhelm and Michael Smith surveyed 49 boys about their connection to reading, none of their respondents could remember reading anything funny in school.

Fantasy and science fiction. A friend of mine once called me over to discuss the reading habits of his son, whom he thought was in serious trouble. The father led me to his son's room and showed me a bookcase filled with paperback series

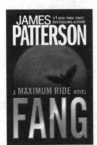

fantasy. My friend explained that his boy would read through the entire bookcase every couple of months, then go back and read it all again. He told me that we needed to get his son away from fantasy or he would never become a reader. Looking at that bookcase, I realized that the son in all likelihood read more than both his father and I did combined.

Adults often see fantasy as a stepping-stone, acceptable only if it leads to more serious reading. Science fiction tends to get even less respect. One researcher's son told her that some of his teachers treated sci-fi books like they were pornography. Why this indifference, and even hostility, to these forms? Educators tend to value the inward journey more than the outward, physical journey. We want children looking inward, to learn self-reflection and self-examination. Although these are noble goals, they are also in line with a typical female point of view. Girls tend to internalize, looking inward for their understanding of the world. Boys tend to look outward, placing themselves in a larger world.

In a study of boys choosing books on their own at a large bookstore, a researcher noted that "for all of the boys, the escapist qualities of imaginative fiction were strongly preferred over the immediate connections to their lives that young adult realistic fiction might provide." Science fiction and fantasy have great appeal to many boys because the basic structure is so much in opposition to the standard juvenile novel. These forms begin with the concept of an individual discovering a new world and journeying out to find a place in that world.

Sports, action, and adventure. Boys are active creatures, and they seek to connect their reading to what they like. They want to read about characters doing what they think they would enjoy doing. Sports and action/adventure stories are plot-driven, not character-driven. The action in the story takes precedence over characterization, character interaction, and character development. Many adults dismiss these stories because they are so external, so physical, and not inward or reflective.

Gothic horror. In this post-Columbine era, our society is very sensitive to the presence, or even the discussion of, violence around children. We believe that any exposure to violence increases the likelihood that children will engage in violence, especially if those children are male. What, then, are we to make of the fascination so many boys have with gothic horror and its graphic portrayals of violence? We need to step back and realize that violence is a fact in the world, and boys being external thinkers seek to understand the world around them.

Boys see violence in the media, in their communities, even in their homes. School librarian Alison Folios reports that in a single year an avid 13-year-old television watcher witnesses 7,000 screen murders. Violence is unavoidable, but it cannot remain unexplained. Boys can either face the fact of violence in the more visual media, to which language is ill-suited, or they can do it in books, where narration can give context and highlight consequences. Encountering violence in a narrative context may help boys learn to cope with violence rather than encourage them to engage in it. Sometimes we have to just get over it.

Coded language. Boys are often attracted to coded language—to riddles, puzzles, word games, and the like. Such reading is short and challenging to the mind, and often requires more thinking than actual reading. In addition, it turns language into a game. It also levels the playing field for boys who struggle with language. Boys may not understand coded language right off the bat, but neither does anyone else. For once, they are on an even footing.

No more dead dogs. What do all the aforementioned forms that appeal to boys have in common? Adults, especially educators, give them little respect. The disdain for the outward and physical over the inward and emotional, the fear of edginess and violence, and the denigration of humor all help to explain why so many educators look down at boys' favored reading material. Sports books, action/adventure, and gothic horror gain little respect from adults. How do we know this? How often do these traditionally boy-friendly formats find their way onto book award or school reading assignment lists?

Gordon Korman, a children's author who consistently produces books with high boy appeal, is fond of asking audiences to consider how many books there are on the Newbery Award list with an extremely slim plot element, namely, the death of a beloved dog, compared to truly funny books. Korman based an entire book on this concept, *No More Dead Dogs* (Hyperion, 2000). Most educators can name a handful of books considered to be among the best books for kids with this incredibly thin plot element. Consider *Sounder* by William H. Armstrong, a Newbery Medal winner in 1970; *Old Yeller* by Fred Gipson, a Newbery Honor Book in 1957; *Where the Red Fern Grows* by Wilson Rawls, which should count twice since two dogs meet their mortal end in that book; and more recently Sherman Alexie's *The Absolutely True Diary of a Part-Time Indian,* which won a National Book Award in 2008.

Conversely, there may be Newbery Award winners with humor, but there are none that are predominantly funny books. The same test can be applied to all boy-friendly forms. How many sports books carry the coveted gold seal? How many action/adventure stories? A quick check of the subject headings attached to the Newbery Medal winners in the 20 years from 1989 to 2008 shows no nonfiction at all. The last nonfiction title to win was *Lincoln: A Photobiography* by Russell Freedman, in 1988. Before that you have to go back to *Darnel Boone,* by James Daugherty, which won in 1940. In the past 20 years, no fantasy book has won the award, no book of gothic horror, and no action/adventure title. One science fiction title has won, but then again so have one fairy tale, one book of drama, and two books of poetry.

There are four books of medieval fiction among the last 20 Newbery Medal winners, three books on death, two about runaways, two about orphans, and three about depressions (the economic kind).

There is a definite bias toward the types of books that traditionally appeal to girls. This bias appears in other awards lists as well. The constant, cumulative reinforcement of this idea, that the types of books that appeal to boys are not good books, cannot help but affect the way boys see reading. The point is not that boys read bad books, it is that the books boys find value in thereby have value. The fact that you do not see the value is irrelevant; you are not the target audience. Boys' literature does exist, and it is a world we have to go out into and come to grips with if we are going to help boys become lifelong readers.

The nonfiction *Claudette Colvin: Twice Towards Justice,* by Phillip Hoose, was a 2010 Newbery Honor Book.

SOURCE: Michael Sullivan, *Connecting Boys with Books 2: Closing the Reading Gap* (Chicago: American Library Association, 2009), 61–68.

YOUNG ADULT MATERIALS

All I need to know I learned from young adult books

by Kate McNair

AH, VALENTINE'S DAY. I keenly remember the sweet pain of anticipation that each one brought. Waiting in home room at my high school for the coveted cans of soda to be delivered to their intended recipients bearing the note, "X has a crush on you!" And the agony of trying to decipher the intentions of the sender. Was the "crush" meant romantically or just in a friendly way? These questions would be discussed in the halls, at lunch, and in notes passed in class. Although my love life was a comedy of errors, I found solace in the romantic endeavors of my favorite characters. And so to celebrate relationships from fairy tale to failure, I offer up some favorite dating advice garnered from young adult books.

Read these books, learn these lessons

If the hottest guy in school acts like he hates you, but can't stop staring at you, it's probably because he's not quite human and your fates are intertwined.—Stephenie Meyer, *Twilight* (Little, Brown, 2005), and any number of other paranormal romances.

Never hypnotize a guy into being the friend you think you want at nine, because then he'll never develop into the guy you can date at 17.—Jennifer Jabaley, *Crush Control* (Penguin, 2011).

If you write your deepest emotions down in a "story" and you share it, eventually people are going to figure out what and *who* you are talking about—Jennifer Echols, *Love Story* (MTV, 2011).

You know that beautiful, witty, excentric girl that you have a crush on? Someday she will realize how amazing you are and take you on the adventure of a lifetime. Just be patient.—John Green, *Looking for Alaska* (Dutton, 2005) and *Paper Towns* (Dutton, 2008).

You have to ask yourself, "Is love worth starting a war over?"—Patrick Ness, Chaos Walking series (Walker, 2008–2010).

Never propose to a girl by insulting her parents.—Jane Austen, *Pride and Prejudice* (1813).

Stop thinking about the landing, because it's all about falling.— John Green and David Levithan, *Will Grayson, Will Grayson* (Dutton, 2012).

When a guy tells you that he is vampire royalty and the two of you have been betrothed since your birth, your best course of action is to stab him with a pitchfork and run like hell. He is obviously unhinged.—Beth Fantaskey, *Jessica's Guide to Dating on the Dark Side* (Harcourt, 2009).

Friedrich Nietzsche theorized that we are attracted to that which repels us. Applying this concept to dating, we should therefore treat those whom we like

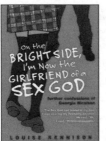

the most with disdain, and they will find themselves inexplicitly drawn to us.—Brent Crawford, *Carter Finally Gets It* (Hyperion, 2009).

Always apply more lipstick before seeing a boy. Like small monkeys, they are attracted to shiny things.—Louise Rennison, the Confessions of Georgia Nicolson series (HarperTeen, 1999–2009).

Don't mix up your grandfather's laxative with your protein powder. Ladies like confident and continent men.— Don Calame, *Swim the Fly* (Candlewick, 2009).

In any relationship, no matter how short, soundtrack is key.—Rachel Cohn and David Levithan, *Nick & Norah's Infinite Playlist* (Knopf, 2006).

If you like someone, tell them. You never know when it might be too late.—Jay Asher, *Thirteen Reasons Why* (Penguin, 2007).

If you look at your exes and see a theme emerging, maybe you need to examine your love life more closely.—John Green, *An Abundance of Katherines* (Dutton, 2006).

In a relationship, it is best to be honest up front.—Brian Katcher, *Almost Perfect* (Delacorte, 2009).

If you find yourself in a dystopian future, be prepared to make the difficult decision between dating a baker or a hunter. But either way, you have a chance of having enough to eat.—Suzanne Collins, *The Hunger Games* (Scholastic, 2008).

If you find the right guy, he'll still love you even if you drag him through a swamp at night and a monstrous creature chews off most of his arm.—Franny Billingsley, *Chime* (Dial, 2011).

Becoming undead? Totally worth it, because you wind up with the man of your dreams . . . *forever!*—Stephenie Meyer, *Twilight* (Little, Brown, 2005).

Playing ditsy and stupid will only get you boys who are stupider than you're pretending to be.—Neal Shusterman, *Bruiser* (HarperTeen, 2010).

Lessons from no place in particular

If you try to hide something from your boyfriend or girlfriend, they will find out, and it will eventually lead to you breaking up. If you have killed someone, have a secret identity, or have hidden super-powers, tell them *now* for the sake of your relationship.

If you're human, don't date a vampire, werewolf, or zombie. It never works out.

You know what they say about assumptions: If you are unsure how he feels, just ask.

Love doesn't solve the problem, but it sure makes things like the end of the world easier to deal with.

Treat every guy or gal you meet like a prince or princess. This will help you avoid awkward situations down the road when you have to apologize for yelling at the royal heir.

SOURCE: Kate McNair, "All I Need to Know I Learned from YA Books: Relationship Advice from Your Favorite Books," YALSA The Hub, February 14, 2012, www.yalsa.ala.org/thehub/.

The Printz Award, 2000–2012

by Michael Cart

HISTORY WAS MADE on January 17, 2000, when—at the ALA Midwinter Meeting in San Antonio, Texas—the first-ever winner of the Michael L. Printz Award was announced, along with three honor titles. Together the four books exemplified the newly literary, inventive, and diverse nature of young adult literature, which the award had been created to recognize.

Ever since 1989, when Francesca Lia Block, in her first novel *Weetzie Bat*, introduced magical realism and the verbal strategies of imagist poetry to YA literature, the field had become increasingly open to experiments in style, structure, and narrative form. Walter Dean Myers's *Monster*—the winner of the first Printz—is an excellent example. Originally conceived by the author as a screenplay, the resulting novel about Steve Harmon, an African-American teenager on trial for his life, is told in two different but interrelated dramatic forms: The first is a screenplay, written by the boy himself, who observes of his surreal experience, "I feel like I have walked into the middle of a movie"; the second is his journal (printed on gray paper and set in a handwriting-style font) in which he is able to record the more visceral reality of his interior life and emotional responses (of the prison he writes, "The best time to cry is at night when the lights are out and someone is being beaten up and screaming for help").

Reflecting the increasingly visual context of contemporary teens' internet-ridden lives, the book also includes a number of black-and-white, often digitally manipulated photographs—the work of Myers's gifted artist son, Christopher—that further ratchet up the reader's interest and engagement.

Though notable for its innovations, *Monster* is also very much of its time, rooted—as it is—in adult America's abiding fear and distrust of teenagers, especially those of color. The title of the book, in fact, is a reference to the prosecuting attorney's reference to Steve as being a monster.

Two of the three Printz honor books—Ellen Wittlinger's *Hard Love* and Laurie Halse Anderson's *Speak*—are also notable for their innovative formats and structures. The former, an ill-starred love story, includes pages from teen zines (self-designed, self-written, self-published magazines that captivated teen energies and imaginations in the late 1990s), along with such other anomalies as handwritten letters, poems, and pages from journals.

The latter is also notable for its nontraditional structure. Eschewing chapters, Anderson divides her debut novel into four sections that reflect a school year's traditional grading periods. The story is then presented in a series of short scenes told in the first-person voice of the protagonist (and outcast) Melinda, who brings a sense of imperative action to her almost-cinematic accounts by using the present tense and introducing scenes with headings ("Hard Labor," "Death by Algebra," "Lunch Doom") that recall title cards from silent films.

Though more traditional in its structure, David Almond's *Skellig*, the third honor title, is a departure in two other senses. First published in England, it evidences that young adult literature—born though it might have been in the United States—has become a global phenomenon. Second, the novel is a metaphysical exercise in ambiguity, raising—but never resolving—the central question of the identity of the eponymous Skellig while tacitly acknowledging the aesthetic and intellectual influence on its author of the British mystic William Blake. A staple of literary fiction, ambiguity had been largely absent from young adult literature, but it is an essential constituent of both *Skellig* and *Monster* (the question of Steve's guilt is essentially left to the reader to adjudicate), and its use is another herald of the coming of age of young adult literature.

The decade that has passed since the publication of these four landmark titles has only reinforced the validity of what I wrote about them in my "Carte Blanche" *Booklist* column of March 15, 2000: "Clearly, each of these books is extraordinary in its own individual way, but each has in common with the others innovation, creative courage, unimpeachable style, and, in sum, literary excellence."

Those words also serve to describe the Printz winners and honor titles in the years that have followed. Many of them also exemplify innovations and new trends that have characterized the literature's continued aesthetic evolution and, all in all, confirm one of the most exciting trends of the new decade: the emergence of the literary novel for young adults.

Printz winners

2013—Nick Lake, *In Darkness* (Bloomsbury, 2012).
2012—John Corey Whaley, *Where Things Come Back* (Atheneum, 2011).
2011—Paolo Bacigalupi, *Ship Breaker* (Little, Brown, 2010).
2010—Libba Bray, *Going Bovine* (Delacorte, 2009).
2009—Melina Marchetta, *Jellicoe Road* (HarperTeen, 2008).
2008—Geraldine McCaughrean, *The White Darkness* (HarperTempest, 2007).
2007—Gene Luen Yang, *American Born Chinese* (First Second, 2006).
2006—John Green, *Looking for Alaska* (Dutton, 2005).
2005—Meg Rosoff, *How I Live Now* (Wendy Lamb, 2004).
2004—Angela Johnson, *The First Part Last* (Simon & Schuster, 2003).
2003—Aidan Chambers, *Postcards from No Man's Land* (Dutton, 2002).
2002—An Na, *A Step from Heaven* (Front Street, 2001).
2001—David Almond, *Kit's Wilderness* (Delacorte, 2000).
2000—Walter Dean Myers, *Monster* (HarperCollins, 1999).

SOURCE: Michael Cart, *Young Adult Literature: From Romance to Realism* (Chicago: American Library Association, 2010), 75–77.

Top 10 best fiction for young adults, 2008–2012

EACH YEAR THE ALA Young Adult Library Services Association compiles a list of 10 fiction titles that have potential appeal to young adults and exhibit either high literary standards or technical accuracy. The following list encompasses 50 titles from 2008 to 2012.

Alexie, Sherman. *The Absolutely True Diary of a Part-time Indian* (Little, Brown, 2007).

Beah, Ishmael. *A Long Way Gone: Memoirs of a Boy Soldier* (Farrar, Straus & Giroux, 2007).

Bowman, Robin. *It's Complicated: The American Teenager* (Umbrage Editions, 2007).

Brennan, Sarah Rees. *Demon's Lexicon* (Margaret K. McElderry, 2009).

Carson, Rae. *The Girl of Fire and Thorns* (HarperCollins, 2011).

Cohen, Joshua C. *Leverage* (Dutton, 2011).

Collins, Suzanne. *The Hunger Games* (Scholastic, 2008).

Conner, Leslie. *Waiting for Normal* (HarperCollins, 2008).

de la Pena, Matt, *Mexican White Boy* (Delacorte, 2008).

Dowd, Siobhan, *Bog Child* (David Fickling Books, 2008).

Downham, Jenny. *Before I Die* (David Fickling, 2007).

Fletcher, Christine. *Ten Cents a Dance* (Bloomsbury, 2008).

Griffin, Paul. *The Orange Houses* (Dial Books, 2009).

Hemphill, Stephanie. *Your Own, Sylvia: A Verse Portrait of Sylvia Plath* (Knopf, 2007).

Herlong, M. H. *The Great Wide Sea* (Viking, 2008).

Jinks, Catherine. *The Reformed Vampire Support Group* (Houghton Mifflin Harcourt, 2009).

Jones, Lloyd. *Mister Pip* (Dial Press, 2007).

King, A. S. *Everybody Sees the Ants* (Little, Brown, 2011).

Landy, Derek. *Skulduggery Pleasant* (HarperCollins, 2007).

McCall, Guadalupe Garcia. *Under the Mesquite* (Lee & Low, 2011).

Monninger, Joseph. *Baby* (Boyd Mills Press, 2007).

Myracle, Lauren. *Shine* (Abrams, 2011).

Napoli, Donna Jo. *Alligator Bayou* (Knopf, 2009).

Ness, Patrick. *A Monster Calls* (Candlewick, 2011).

Peet, Mal. *Tamar: A Novel of Espionage, Passion, and Betrayal* (Candlewick, 2007).

Polly, Matthew. *American Shaolin: Flying Kicks, Buddhist Monks, and the Legend of Iron Crotch: An Odyssey in the New China* (Gotham Books, 2007).

Pratchett, Terry. *Nation* (HarperCollins, 2008).

Selznick, Brian. *The Invention of Hugo Cabret: A Novel* (Scholastic, 2007).

Sepetys, Ruta. *Between Shades of Gray* (Philomel, 2011).

Small, David. *Stitches: A Memoir* (Norton, 2009).

Stead, Rebecca. *When You Reach Me* (Wendy Lamb, 2009).

Stiefvater, Maggie. *The Scorpio Races* (Scholastic, 2011).

Stork, Francisco X. *Marcelo in the Real World* (Arthur A. Levine, 2009).

Tamaki, Mariko, and Jillian Tamaki. *Skim* (Groundwood Books, 2008).

Tan, Shaun. *The Arrival* (Arthur A. Levine, 2007).

Taylor, Laini. *Daughter of Smoke and Bone* (Little, Brown, 2011).

Taylor, Laini. *Lips Touch: Three Times* (Levine, 2009).

Voorhees, Coert. *The Brothers Torres* (Hyperion, 2008).

Walker, Sally M. *Written in Bone: Buried Lives of Jamestown and Colonial Maryland* (Carolrhoda, 2009).

Zarr, Sara. *How to Save a Life* (Little, Brown, 2011).

SOURCE: ALA Young Adult Library Services Association.

GAMES

Really? Study video games?

by Chad F. Boeninger

LIBRARIANS MAY WONDER why we would want to study video games when there are so many other technologies and media for us to attempt to master. The study of video games is a relatively new discipline, but it is beginning to gain prominence in academic circles. Authors such as James Gee (*What Video Games Have to Teach Us About Literacy and Learning*, 2004) and Mark Prensky (*Don't Bother Me Mom, I'm Learning!*, 2006) have written extensively on the topic, and they contend that video games have an important impact on those who play them. They also assert that by studying video games, educators, policy makers, and others can adapt game characteristics for the educational curriculum. As librarians, we can learn from Gee and Prensky (and from video games as well) in order to get a better idea about our users' backgrounds and preferences.

A primary job of the reference librarian is to help patrons find information about a particular topic in order to satisfy an information need. In helping them with this need, librarians teach patrons research and critical-thinking skills while helping them learn to adapt to a constantly changing information environment. Librarians understand that research can be a very difficult process that often results in high levels of anxiety, frustration, confusion, and even anger. Though many people consider them to be mindless entertainment, video games can be very complex and take a great deal of time and mastery to complete. As Steven Johnson explains in *Everything Bad Is Good for You* (Riverhead, 2006):

> The first and last thing that should be said about the experience of playing today's video games, the thing that you almost never hear about in the mainstream coverage, is that games are fiendishly, sometimes maddeningly, *hard*. The dirty little secret of gaming is how much time you spend not having fun. You may be confused, you may be disoriented, you may be stuck. When you put the game down and move back into the real world you may find yourself mentally working through the problem you've been wrestling with, as though you are worrying a loose tooth. If this is mindless escapism, it's a strangely masochistic version. Who wants to escape to a world that irritates you 90% of the time?

Johnson's description of the difficulty of video games draws upon some similar characteristics of information-seeking behavior. Both video game quests and research quests can be hard and frustrating and may lead to disorientation, confusion, and anger. However, gamers welcome the challenge of a difficult video game and often do their best to master a game. By studying the attraction of video games, librarians may understand this motivation and get patrons motivated in the same way about library research.

One of the difficulties that librarians face is the communication barrier between themselves and their patrons. When helping patrons at the reference desk, on the phone, or via instant message or chat, librarians generally provide better service when they avoid use of library jargon. However, it is not always easy to determine the most effective way to communicate with a particular patron, since professors, college students, retirees, international students, Millennials, and even gamers have different needs. Gamers may see things differently, as explained by John C. Beck and Mitchell Wade in *The Kids Are Alright* (Harvard Business School, 2006):

> This generation is literally growing up in the world of video games. That world is completely different from the one all of us grew up in. And growing up there is making this generation—our kids—visibly, measurably different. They can handle reality all right—in some ways better than we do. All those hours spent playing video games are teaching them important skills. But they don't see things the way nongamers do and they don't maneuver the same way. For their great new skills to work in our nongamer world, they need some help adapting.

With a better understanding of gamers, librarians can help them adapt to the information environment while adapting to gamers' information needs.

Many people assume that gamers are a small minority of the population that consists primarily of adolescent boys. If this assumption were true, it might not be worthwhile to spend time attempting to understand them. However, according to the Electronic Software Association, gaming is a great deal more prevalent than one would think. (See box below.)

Characteristics of video gamers

Video games are now a mass medium, widely enjoyed on a variety of platforms by a diverse audience. The Educational Software Association's 2012 *Essential Facts About the Computer and Video Game Industry* reveals interesting demographic facts about today's gamers and the games they play, including:

The average gamer is 30 years old and has been playing for 12 years. 68% of gamers are 18 years of age or older.

47% of all players are women, and women over 18 years of age are one of the industry's fastest growing demographics.

Today, adult women represent a greater portion of the game-playing population (30%) than boys age 17 or younger (18%).

62% of gamers play games with others, either in person or online. 78% of these gamers play with others at least one hour per week.

33% of gamers play social games.

Gamers play on-the-go: 33% play games on their smartphones, and 25% play on their handheld devices.

90% of the time parents are present when games are purchased or rented. 98% of parents feel the Entertainment Software Rating Board rating system is helpful in choosing games for their children. 73% of parents believe that the parental controls available in all new video game consoles are useful.

Parents also see several benefits of entertainment software, with 52% saying video games are a positive part of their child's life. 66% of parents believe that game play provides mental stimulation or education, 61% believe games encourage their family to spend time together, and 59% believe that game play helps their children connect with their friends.

SOURCE: "Game Player Data," Educational Software Association, accessed July 28, 2012, online at www.theesa.com/facts/gameplayer.asp.

Scholars have recognized the impact that video games have on popular culture and the economy while also studying the impact of games on education and learning. Prensky, Gee, and Johnson all offer their opinions and observations about what makes gaming so compelling to consumers. Each book is highly recommended for a more in-depth discussion of video games and learning. From these discussions about gaming and learning, one can see that there are common traits that libraries share with video games. In a sense, both video games and libraries attempt to immerse the player or patron, encourage learning by doing, and encourage exploration.

SOURCE: Chad F. Boeninger, "Get in the Game: Adapting Library Services to the Needs of Gamers," in Sarah K. Steiner and M. Leslie Madden, eds., *The Desk and Beyond: Next Generation Reference Services* (Chicago: ALA Association of College and Research Libraries, 2008), 106–119.

Modern designer games
by Brian Mayer and Christopher Harris

4

MODERN BOARD AND CARD GAMES are either directly descended from or inspired by a new wave of European imports. They bear little resemblance to the traditional American style of games involving rolling dice, moving a pawn, and seeing what happens on the square where you land. These new board games are called *designer games*. Unlike older games, modern board games usually feature the name of the designer on the box cover. Just like readers follow authors, gamers will follow game designers who may create games with multiple publishers.

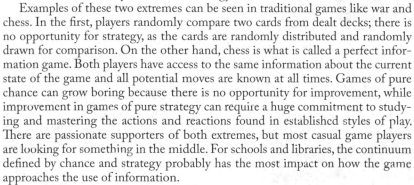

While risking everything on a roll of the dice can be exhilarating, it does not offer much in the way of long-term engagement and repeat play value. Recognizing this, modern game designers present a range of options spaced along a continuum defined on either end by chance and strategy.

Examples of these two extremes can be seen in traditional games like war and chess. In the first, players randomly compare two cards from dealt decks; there is no opportunity for strategy, as the cards are randomly distributed and randomly drawn for comparison. On the other hand, chess is what is called a perfect information game. Both players have access to the same information about the current state of the game and all potential moves are known at all times. Games of pure chance can grow boring because there is no opportunity for improvement, while improvement in games of pure strategy can require a huge commitment to studying and mastering the actions and reactions found in established styles of play. There are passionate supporters of both extremes, but most casual game players are looking for something in the middle. For schools and libraries, the continuum defined by chance and strategy probably has the most impact on how the game approaches the use of information.

The open nature of many designer games is one of the characteristics that makes them especially powerful in schools and libraries. When players are making complex decisions, they have to process more information and use higher-order thinking skills. This use of information literacy skills is the foundation upon which game/curriculum alignments can be developed.

Game mechanics

Given the complexity of many designer games, it helps that they often make use of common mechanics; this makes it easier for players to learn new games. Schools and libraries can use this as a scaffold to prepare students for more complex games.

Roll-and-move. Though certainly not as common as in traditional American board games, there are still designer games that use dice to control movement. The difference is that the designer games often give players a higher level of control over either the dice being rolled or what happens as a result of the roll. Based on the results on two regular six-sided dice, players in Enchanted Forest can move in any direction in any combination of the two results (four forward, complete an action, five backward, for example).

Open movement. Some games remove the dice completely in favor of movement points or action points that may be used to move or complete other actions. This gives the player a much higher level of control over his character in the game. This point is illustrated by comparing two different dungeon-crawling role-playing games: The traditional American game Talisman (below) has players roll a die, trying to get the one number needed to land on the spot that allows them to move forward in the game. Such a high level of chance introduces a great deal of frustration as players bounce back and forth around the one spot they need to hit. In contrast, Prophecy is a designer game that uses open movement to give

Talisman. Photo by Frecklefoot, used CC A-SA 3.0.

players control over the game. Players can move one space in either direction for free, pay coins for a horse to move two spaces, pay a few more coins to take a ship from one port to another, or even use coins to travel through portals.

Worker placement. Another common mechanic found in designer games is worker placement. For example, in Stone Age, a worker placement game that uses a strong element of chance to recreate the struggles of an early tribe to gather resources and thrive, players are not moving around a board. Instead, players are placing pawns into certain areas on the board to receive benefits during a resolution phase, thus the concept of worker placement. In this case, small wooden figures representing the members of a Stone Age tribe can be assigned to various gathering tasks that can result in food or other resources.

This style of game tends to focus on resource management. Not only must players plan ahead to receive maximum benefit from their limited supply of workers, but in most cases those workers are also producing goods that will be applied in various combinations for victory points. Stone Age's workers gather resources that can be turned in for special victory cards. At the same time, however, some workers will always need to be tasked with gathering the food required to sustain

RoboRally. Photo by Igor Polouchine, used CC A-SA 3.0.

the tribe each turn. Worker placement games also tend to feature higher requirements for time management. There are many more things in Stone Age that you will want or need to do than can be done in either a turn or the whole game. The placement of every worker ends up being more precious than expected.

Simultaneous action. RoboRally (left) is a chaotically fun game that teaches rudimentary programming as up to seven players simultaneously move their robots around the board. Games that use this mechanic are great for large groups, as it minimizes the downtime that comes with a player waiting for her next turn. In order to work, this mechanic also often requires a higher level of conversation between players. Not all games with this mechanic go to the extreme of RoboRally. Many designer games use some aspect of this by involving players in actions, reactions, and decisions during other players' turns.

Role selection. One way that some games implement simultaneous action is through the selection and resolution of roles. San Juan, a card game based on Puerto Rico, has players select roles in order to build, produce, or sell goods. Each round, every player has a chance to select a role from the available roles. All the players get to use that role, but the player who selected the role gets a bonus ability. This keeps everyone involved in simultaneous action but provides a more structured environment.

Games that use role selection can be more open-ended in their play style. Despite the openness, or perhaps because of it, in many games using this mechanic there will often be a mathematically best choice of role for each player in a round to take. Just as in the almost scripted play of very high-level chess, there can be a game choice that will maximize profit and opportunities for victory while minimizing benefits for other players. Mixing players of different skill levels for role selection games is a potential source of problems. More experienced players can become frustrated as new players make less-than-optimal choices of role.

Cooperative play. One way to accommodate players with different skill levels is to create a more casual, less competitive play environment using games that feature cooperative play. In this style of game, players are working together as a team against the game itself. Cooperative games range from very simple games for three-year-olds up to games that will provide a strong challenge for the most veteran players. This mechanic demands conversation, so don't plan to use cooperative games in a quiet space. On the other hand, the forced communication makes these games a great resource for speech therapy or English-language-learning classes.

Games for all

Designer games provide rich and engaging play experiences that easily match the level of complexity found in video games. With a variety of mechanics going well beyond the traditional roll-and-move, designer games force players to explore, inquire, interpret, and act upon information gathered from many sources. Perhaps more important for schools and libraries, these games provide a more social environment where players are interacting or collaborating as they play. Many of these games can be aligned with library and information literacy skills and state content standards. Through a combination of game mechanics that reinforce skills and themes that provide context for learning about content, designer games are valuable resources libraries can provide to support instruction.

Great games for school libraries

Knowing how to start building a game collection can be intimidating. Even when armed with well-developed selection criteria, finding gaming resources that are effective at engaging students and addressing the curriculum requires an experienced eye. To help you get started, this section features lists of 10 recommended games for each of the elementary, middle, and high school levels. (For a full description, see the complete text in our book *Libraries Got Game*.)

Top games for elementary school

Froggy Boogie (Blue Orange Games, 2007). Designed by Thierry Denoual. *Curricular area:* Math. *Number of players:* 2–6. *Playing time:* 15 minutes.

Gopher It! (Playroom Entertainment, 2003). Designed by Reinhard Staupe. *Curricular area:* Math. *Number of players:* 2–4. *Playing time:* 10 minutes.

In the Country (Habermaaß, 2006). Designed by Markus Nikisch. *Curricular area:* Science. *Number of players:* 2–4. *Playing time:* 20 minutes.

Incan Gold (FRED Distribution, 2006). Designed by Alan R. Moon and Bruno Faidutti. *Curricular area:* Math. *Number of players:* 3–8. *Playing time:* 20 minutes.

Max (Family Pastimes, 1986). Designed by Jim Deacove. *Curricular area:* English language arts and social studies. *Number of players:* 1–8. *Playing time:* 20 minutes.

Number Chase (Playroom Entertainment, 2006). Designed by Reinhold Staupe. *Curricular area:* Math. *Number of players:* 2–5. *Playing time:* 15 minutes.

Quiddler (Set Enterprises, 1998). Designed by Marsha Falco. *Curricular area:* English language arts. *Number of players:* 1–8. *Playing time:* 30 minutes.

7 Ate 9 (Out of the Box, 2009). Designed by Maureen Hiron. *Curricular area:* Math. *Number of players:* 2–4. *Playing time:* 5–10 minutes.

The Suitcase Detectives (Habermaaß, 2008). Designed by Guido Hoffmann. *Curricular area:* Science. *Number of players:* 2–4. *Playing time:* 15 minutes.

10 Days In... (Out of the Box, 2003). Designed by Aaron Weissblum and Alan R. Moon. *Curricular area:* Geography. *Number of players:* 2–4. *Playing time:* 30 minutes.

Top games for middle school

Amun-Re (Rio Grande Games, 2003). Designed by Reiner Knizia. *Curricular area:* World history. *Number of players:* 3–5. *Playing time:* 90 minutes.

Duck! Duck! Go! (APE Games, 2008). Designed by Kevin G. Munn. *Curricular area:* Math and technology. *Number of players:* 2–6. *Playing time:* 30 minutes.

LetterFlip (Out of the Box, 2004). Designed by Ruddell Designs. *Curricular area:* English language arts. *Number of players:* 2. *Playing time:* 30 minutes.

Nanofictionary (Looney Labs, 2002). Designed by Andrew Looney. *Curricular area:* English language arts. *Number of players:* 3–6. *Playing time:* 30 minutes.

Numbers League (Bent Castle Workshops, 2007). Designed by Chris Pallace and Ben Crenshaw. *Curricular area:* Math. *Number of players:* 2–4. *Playing time:* 30 minutes.

Oregon (Rio Grande Games, 2007). Designed by Henrik Berg and Ase Berg. *Curricular area:* Math. *Number of players:* 2–4. *Playing time:* 45 minutes.

Shadows over Camelot (Days of Wonder, 2005). Designed by Serge Laget and Bruno Cathala. *Curricular area:* English language arts. *Number of players:* 3–7. *Playing time:* 90 minutes.

Ticket to Ride (Days of Wonder, 2004). Designed by Alan R. Moon. *Curricular area:* Geography. *Number of players:* 2–5. *Playing time:* 45 minutes.

Tribune: Primus Inter Pares (Fantasy Flight Games, 2007). Designed by Karl-Heinz Schmiel. *Curricular area:* World history. *Number of players:* 2–5. *Playing time:* 60 minutes.

VisualEyes (Buffalo Games, 2003). Designed by Keith Dugald and Steve Pickering. *Curricular area:* English language arts. *Number of players:* 2–8. *Playing time:* 30 minutes.

Top games for high school

Antike (Rio Grande Games, 2005). Designed by Mac Gerdts. *Curricular area:* Global studies. *Number of players:* 2–6. *Playing time:* 120 minutes.

Battlestar Galactica (Fantasy Flight Games, 2008). Designed by Corey Konieczka. *Curricular area:* English language arts. *Number of players:* 3–6. *Playing time:* 120 minutes.

Bolide (Rio Grande Games, 2005). Designed by Alfredo Genovese. *Curricular area:* Science and math. *Number of players:* 2–8. *Playing time:* 120 minutes.

1960: The Making of the President (Z-Man Games, 2007). Designed by Christian Leonhard and Jason Matthews. *Curricular area:* Global studies and participation in government. *Number of players:* 2. *Playing time:* 180 minutes.

Once upon a Time (Atlas Games, 1993). Designed by Andrew Rilstone, James Wallis, and Richard Lambert. *Curricular area:* English language arts. *Number of players:* 2–6. *Playing time:* 30 minutes.

Pandemic (Z-Man Games, 2008). Designed by Matt Leacock. *Curricular area:* Science and geography. *Number of players:* 2–4. *Playing time:* 45 minutes.

Portrayal (Braincog, 2006). Designed by Amanda Kohout and William Jacobson. *Curricular area:* English language arts. *Number of players:* 3–10. *Playing time:* 45 minutes.

Power Grid (Rio Grande Games, 2004). Designed by Friedemann Friese. *Curricular area:* Science and economics. *Number of players:* 2–6. *Playing time:* 120 minutes.

Through the Ages (FRED Distribution, 2006). Designed by Vlaada Chvátil. *Curricular area:* Global studies. *Number of players:* 2–4. *Playing time:* 240 minutes.

Ultimate Werewolf: Ultimate Edition (Bézier Games, 2008). Designed by Ted Alspach. *Curricular area:* English language arts. *Number of players:* 5–68. *Playing time:* 15–45 minutes.

SOURCE: Brian Mayer and Christopher Harris, *Libraries Got Game: Aligned Learning through Modern Board Games* (Chicago: American Library Association, 2010), 3–10, 81–112.

What a librarian can learn from chess
by Kate Covintree

A FEW YEARS BACK I bought a chess board for our library, the kind with a magnetic board that makes it a bit portable, and one where I hoped students wouldn't lose pieces too easily. I placed it on a spare student-sized desk near the library's entrance with two nice chairs on either side. Teachers and students began sitting down or huddling deep into a game while waiting for a class to end or during a free period. I placed our few books about chess next to our game and hoped the board would help welcome in more library users. Then the school year ended.

When the new school year began, I put the chess board back on its desk. Three days into that school year, a handwritten notice was found under the board:

Collaborative Chess

- Look at the piece of paper to see which color's move it is.
- Make a legal move.
- Flip the card for the next passer-by.
- After moving put the paper under the piece you just moved.

- If you move a rook or a king mark it here so that we can know if we can legally castle.

Two pawns were moved into the center and under the black pawn was another scrap of paper reading "white's turn (flip over after moving)." In an upper corner was another paper stating "not check." (Check was written on the other side.)

Two seniors spearheaded this campaign and set it up without my knowledge. When I asked them about it, they explained to me that while they passed the board almost every day, they rarely had time to stop and play a whole game of chess. Making the game collaborative meant they could play when they were able, but didn't make them late to class. I thought it was a great student-driven solution, and only asked them to type up the instructions. From that day on, the game was always on. The board was open to every member of the school community every day of the school year.

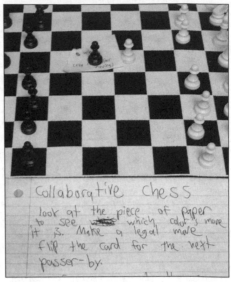

The players of these chess games varied in skill. Did I always know who played the game? No. Did every person who moved a piece on the board know the rules of the game? I know for a fact they did not, but they moved the pieces anyway. People contributed because they could. They took an interest in the collaborative chess game because what was being asked of them was manageable and easy.

There were times when a collaborative game would end in favor of two or more students wanting to dig deep into a full two-person-only game of chess. I liken those moments to times when we as information-gatherers decide to invest in an area of interest more fully, where depth of our own interest outweighs the collective breadth. At those times the needs of the immediate user who craves more supersedes those of the unknown user who could come later..

Our library chess board met students where they were in terms of skill and interest. There were a variety of entry points into the game with little to no consequence for mistakes. It brought students to the library who never found the time otherwise. And did I mention the best part? It was fun.

SOURCE: Kate Covintree, "What a Librarian Can Learn from Chess," YALSA Blog, February 19, 2010, yalsa.ala.org/blog/2010/02/19/chess-and-wikis/.

Operations

CHAPTER FIVE

See the Reference Librarian and the joys that appertain to her;
Who shall estimate the contents and the area of the brain to
    her?
See the people seeking wisdom from the four winds ever
    blown to her,
For they know there is no knowledge known to mortals but is
    known to her;
See this flower of perfect knowledge, blooming like a lush
    geranium,
All converging rays of wisdom focused just beneath her
    cranium;
She is stuffed with erudition as you'd stuff a leather cushion,
And her wisdom is her specialty—it's marketing her mission.
How they throng *to* her, all empty, groveling in their
    insufficience;
How they come *from* her, o'erflooded by the sea of her
    omniscience!
And they know she knows she knows things; while she drips
    her learned theses
The percentage of illiteracy perceptibly decreases.
Ah, they know she knows she knows things, and her look is
    education;
And to look at her is culture, and to know her is salvation.

—Sam Walter Foss, "The Reference Librarian" (1906)

BIBLIOGRAPHY

Preparing a bibliography

by the RUSA Collection Development Policies and Assessment Committee

THESE GUIDELINES originated as "Criteria for Evaluating a Bibliography," adopted by the ALA Reference Services Division board in 1971, and were revised in 1982, 1992, and 2008. They are intended for use by the entire library community. For purposes of these guidelines, a "bibliography" is a systematic list of bibliographic units within a subject. Bibliographies can exist either as stand-alone works or appear at the end of research documents. The author can choose a more common term to describe the final bibliography, such as "pathfinder," "finding aid," or "research guide."

Purpose. Ensure that the bibliography fills a significant need in order to justify its compilation. Fit the subject into the general scheme of available bibliographical sources without unnecessary duplication. If similar bibliographies exist, review them and then explicitly state the unique contribution of this new one. Clearly state the subject in the title and define the subject in a preliminary statement.

Scope. Clearly define the scope. Strive for completeness within the stated limitations (period, geographical area, medium, language, library holdings, quality, and intended audience). Identify and describe each different format appropriately.

Methodology. Provide sources consulted and information on the method of compilation. Include all available bibliographic units within the subject. A bibliographic unit is an entity in a bibliography: books, journal articles, reports, manuscripts, sound and video recordings, individual web pages and entire websites, computer programs or printouts, films, and charts. Identify all items not personally examined by the author(s).

Organization

Principles of organization. Organize the material suitably for both the subject and the targeted users. Arrange the material so it is possible to use the bibliography from at least one organizational approach without consulting supporting documentation such as an index.

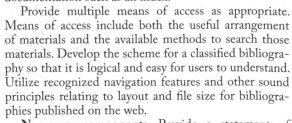

Provide multiple means of access as appropriate. Means of access include both the useful arrangement of materials and the available methods to search those materials. Develop the scheme for a classified bibliography so that it is logical and easy for users to understand. Utilize recognized navigation features and other sound principles relating to layout and file size for bibliographies published on the web.

Necessary components. Provide a statement of scope and purpose, an explanation of how to use the bibliography, a key to all abbreviations used, a table of contents, and an index or indexes. For an electronic version, include search engine or keyword searching capability. Describe indexes in sufficient detail to provide acceptable levels of recall and precision. Utilize terminology in the indexes that is appropriate to both the subject and the intended users. Provide cross-references adequate for normal reference purposes. Provide multiple indexes if required for complete access to the materials.

Desirable features. Consider utilizing entry numbers for bibliographic units. Consider including location of copies of bibliographical units, if not readily available. Include links to available full text in electronic bibliographies if there are no copyright issues.

Annotations and notes. Provide annotations or notes at one of the following three levels:

Informative. Use informative notes chiefly when the nature or reason for inclusion of a title is not clear. Limit use of this minimal level of description to those bibliographies that approach comprehensiveness for the area they are covering.

Annotated. For descriptive annotations, include enough of the contents to enable users to decide whether or not they want to view the original. Provide annotations at least at this level for any bibliography designated as "annotated."

Critical or evaluative. Have a knowledgeable person in the field write discriminating critical evaluations and ensure that the value of each item is assessed in relationship to other works in the area. Provide annotations at this level for any bibliography designated "critical" or "evaluative."

In each case, provide succinct and informative annotations or notes written on a level suitable for the intended users. If another source is drawn upon for the annotation, acknowledge the source appropriately.

Bibliographic form. Provide sufficient information to identify the bibliographic unit easily for the purpose of the bibliography and needs of the intended user. Consistently follow a recognized standard bibliographic form. Examples of these standards include, but are not limited to, those described in *The Chicago Manual of Style, The MLA Style Manual,* and *The Publication Manual of the American Psychological Association.*

Timeliness. Minimize the time lag between completion of a bibliography and its publication. In the introductory material, clearly state when the bibliography was completed. Issue bibliographies intended to be current as closely as possible after the publication of the bibliographical units listed. Periodically review the bibliography's life cycle and evaluate its current relevance.

Accuracy. Ensure that citations are correct and free from typographical errors. Ensure that information provided in annotations and elsewhere is factually accurate and grammatically correct. Consider provision for corrections after publication.

Format. Produce the bibliography with clear and appropriate format and typeface. Produce printed volumes sturdy enough to withstand anticipated use. Design the bibliography to keep its price within the means of potential users without sacrificing important features that facilitate its use.

Cumulation. Cumulate ongoing bibliographies whenever possible.

Distribution. Properly advertise and distribute published bibliographies in either print or electronic format as appropriate to the format, including notice to whatever standard national bibliography exists.

SOURCE: *Guidelines for the Preparation of a Bibliography* (Chicago: ALA Reference and User Services Association, 2010), ala.org/rusa/sites/ala.org.rusa/files/content/resources/guidelines/biblio-prep-guidelin.pdf.

ACQUISITIONS

Acquisitions options

by Peggy Johnson

MONOGRAPHIC MATERIALS may be ordered from wholesale book vendors, who handle new imprints from a variety of publishers. Book jobbers, as they are known, may specialize in disciplines or subject areas, publishers, or materials for types of libraries (public, school, or academic). Some types of materials, such as publications from small and alternative presses, may be available only by ordering directly from the publisher. Items that are ordered title by title are called *discretionary purchases* or *firm orders.* A firm order is an order for a specific title placed with a dealer or publisher that specifies a time limit for delivery and a price that must not be exceeded without the library's approval. Selecting individual titles is considered *micro selection.*

The alternative to micro selection is *macro selection,* which adds large quantities of materials to the library en bloc or en masse. Macro selection is managed through mass buying plans—standing orders, blanket orders, or approval plans—or the acquisition of large retrospective collections either through purchase or as a gift. Macro selection has been used more commonly by larger public and academic libraries, but it is increasingly found in smaller academic libraries and in public libraries of all sizes. Several authors have argued convincingly that approval plans are desirable in smaller libraries for the same reasons they are used in larger libraries—efficiency, cost-effectiveness, and well-rounded collections.

Photo by Nic McPhee, used CC BY-SA 2.0.

Macro selection does involve true selection. It typically uses a group of selectors who review a range of criteria that guide which titles are supplied. This may be through an RFP process, periodical review of approval plan profiles, or other analyses based on a range of criteria that are fundamentally the same as those used for micro selection. Macro selection programs may have substantial setup costs and do require time to establish, but costs of investing resources up front are offset by selector time savings once the macro selection plan is implemented.

Access to many electronic publications, e-journals, and ebooks is through macro selection—that is, acquiring access to an extensive package of titles from a single publisher or an aggregator. With this model, a package of titles from a single publisher often includes a clause that locks in the total price or caps the annual rate of price increase for a specified number of years. This is sometimes referred to as the "Big Deal," or journal bundling. Although this approach may offer differential pricing or a price discount and provide additional titles, it has disadvantages and has been viewed critically by some in the profession. Selectors can lose the ability to select and deselect individual titles. Tracking titles by discipline and budget line can be difficult. Libraries may be locked into keeping titles that are no longer relevant or of good value. On the other hand, Big Deal arrangements can offer a cost-effective approach to acquiring numerous titles for some institutions. Other advantages may include a single search interface for multiple titles, a single order and license agreement for multiple titles, and consistent presentation of usage statistics.

Serials can be acquired through subscription agents, directly from publishers (commercial publishers, scholarly associations), or e-journal aggregators. When possible, most libraries acquire as many serials as possible through one or a few subscription agents because of efficiencies gained. Instead of dozens or even thousands of individual invoices coming from multiple publishers, the agent provides a single invoice for all the titles it handles. Often the invoice is loaded directly into the library's automated system. Serial subscription agents usually offer centralized online ordering, claiming, renewal, cancellation, and reports and charge a service fee calculated as a percentage of the total cost of the serials being handled. The transition to e-journals is changing the role of serials agents, who are compensating for business lost to publishers' journal bundles by offering additional services (such as A-to-Z titles lists, contract negotiation, and management of contract access rights and license terms) and reports tailored to the digital environment.

Multipublisher packages and collections of articles from aggregators offer additional options for the acquisition of e-journals. Three examples of multipublisher packages are Project MUSE, BioOne, and JSTOR. Project MUSE (muse.jhu.edu) is a nonprofit collaboration among libraries and scholarly publishers.  Publishers joining the platform contribute the complete content of each journal as it is published, with articles available in HTML, PDF, or both formats. To supplement current issues, MUSE subscribers have access to a decade of back files for selected titles. The MUSE system provides a common search interface and allows libraries to subscribe to many titles through one transaction. This kind of collaboration offers small publishers many of the advantages large publishers obtain from economies of scale.

 BioOne (www.bioone.org) is another collaborative initiative, this one among scientific societies, libraries, academe, and the private sector; it offers a package of biological, ecological, and environmental science research journals. Most of BioOne's titles are published by small societies and other not-for-profit organizational publishers and, like Project MUSE, BioOne provides the latest issues and full journal content for titles in the BioOne collection.

JSTOR (www.jstor.org) is a nonprofit organization that provides a somewhat different kind of journal collection. It creates and maintains a trusted archive of important scholarly journals across many disciplines from many publishers and offers several packages of journal titles on a subscription basis. JSTOR creates scanned images of journal issues and pages as originally published and provides full-text searching of the journals based on optical character recognition. JSTOR does not offer access to current issues and employs a moving-wall approach, meaning that the most recently published journal issues are embargoed for one to five years, with only the older issues available. Some journals that participate in Project MUSE or BioOne for their current issues also work with JSTOR to provide access to their older issues.

Aggregator collections are developed by intermediaries that assemble e-journals from multiple publishers and offer them online through a common interface. Producers of many indexing and abstracting databases also offer aggregated article collections and build hypertext links between the full-text electronic documents and the index records, combining index searching with partial full-text access. Aggregators' agreements with journal publishers have been volatile, with publishers signing on with an aggregator and then withdrawing from the agreement. The description of EBSCO's Academic Search Premier makes this clear: "Publications included on this database are subject to change without notice due to contractual agreements with publishers." Aggregators rarely offer the full content of a journal up to the most current issues. They sometimes provide selected articles and may not include book reviews, editorials, or advertisements. Embargoes on current content from a few months to a few years are also the norm. Increasingly publishers contribute to multiple aggregator collections and also may offer separate e-journal subscriptions to libraries, which acquire the same content from multiple sources. Aggregator collections can be a convenient and cost-effective approach to providing access to a sizable set of journal articles, but they offer no long-term guarantee of access to the titles in the package.

Taking advantage of various macro selection options, a large academic library allocates anywhere from 65% to 90% of its acquisitions budget to nondiscretionary purchases. Relying on macro selection to supply significant amounts of materials can free selectors to focus their time on identifying and selecting more esoteric materials.

Approval plans

Monographic approval plans are business arrangements in which a wholesale dealer assumes responsibility for supplying, usually subject to return privileges, all new publications that match a library's collecting profile. Richard Abel is credited with the invention, in the early 1960s, of the approval plan as it is now employed. Approval plan vendors operate in many countries and provide books and services to libraries wherever they are located. An approval profile is defined by the library's collections librarians and specifies the subjects, collecting levels, formats, genres, prices, languages, publishers, and so on to be shipped. The supplier sends on a regular basis materials that fit the profile. Librarians review the items shipped and decide which to buy. Most vendors and libraries aim for a return rate of 2% or less. Some approval plans offer paper or online notification slips rather than the publications themselves, and some plans provide a combination of slips and books. Selectors refine and revise the profile as the library's goals, priorities, and budget change.

Order assistants at a university library review approval books from YBP Library Services.

A blanket order plan is an arrangement with an individual publisher or scholarly society to provide all its publications (or all publications below a specified price) each year, or with a vendor to provide a copy of every book published in a particular country within certain parameters. Blanket order plans do not, in most cases, include return privileges.

The variety of services and enhancements provided by both approval plan vendors and firm order suppliers has grown to include electronic data interchange through which digital order records and invoices can be loaded into a local library automated system, interactive access to the vendor or supplier online database, online order placement, cataloging records (which may be Library of Congress copy, CIP records, or original brief or full cataloging created by the vendor), and fully shelf-ready books. Shelf-ready books come to the library cataloged and processed with spine labels, book plates, and antitheft strips.

Thus, vendors are supplementing or replacing functions traditionally performed within libraries.

Gifts

Gifts may bring individual items or a collection of items to the library. A gift is transferred voluntarily without compensation. Gifts may be conveyed to the library through a deed of gift, a legal document that transfers title from the donor to the library without requiring payment. A deed of gift may contain conditions with which the library must comply. Generous donors expect careful stewardship of their gifts. No payment to the donor does not mean that the library has no costs associated with the gift. Costs arise when a gift is reviewed by the selector, cataloged and processed, shelved and reshelved, and repaired and preserved. Gift serial subscriptions have ongoing costs just as paid subscriptions do. Most selection decisions about gifts can be reduced to a trade-off between the cost of adding the item and its value to the library.

Donors must be considered as part of the selection process. Some gifts are not worth adding to the library precisely because of special conditions insisted on by the potential donor. Donors may offer gifts with conditions about use, housing, or special treatment. Even a library that does not have guidelines for the selection of gift materials may have guidelines that address acceptable and unacceptable donor restrictions. The selector should weigh the value of the gift (and possible future gifts) to the library against any donor restrictions.

5

Retrospective selection

Retrospective selection is the process of selecting materials that are old, rare, antiquarian, used, or out of print (OP). It includes seeking replacements for missing or damaged materials and older materials not previously acquired. Many librarians develop desiderata files of titles to be purchased when funding is available or the item is located. These materials may be needed to fill gaps in the collection or to support new academic programs or community interests. Retrospective selection is more common in larger research libraries. The usual sources for materials are OP dealers' catalogs, auctions, and personal negotiations with a private owner.

Out-of-print titles are those that can no longer be obtained from the original publishers. This can happen rapidly as a result of the limited number of copies printed in some fields. Many used and OP booksellers produce catalogs. These catalogs, either in print or online, usually list only single copies; therefore, the librarian must act quickly to ensure acquisition. Many OP dealers accept lists of titles the library is seeking. Dealers can be located through the *American Book Trade Directory*. Additional suppliers can be found through the Antiquarian Booksellers Association of America (abaa.org) and the International League of Antiquarian Booksellers (www.ilab.org). Many university press books no longer go out of print because of print on demand, a technology employed by publishers in which new copies of a book are not printed until an order has been received. Print on demand is also used by smaller presses and academic publishers to maintain an active backlist of short-run titles.

A specialized area within retrospective selection is filling gaps in serial runs and replacing missing issues. One source is the Duplicates Exchange Union (ala.org/

alcts/mgrps/ecoms/deu), sponsored by the ALA Association for Library Collections and Technical Services. Libraries prepare lists of periodical issues and books they are willing to supply to member libraries through a cooperative exchange of other duplicate materials. Libraries then check these available issues against their needs. Sometimes a publisher can provide missing issues for a price. Often the library is unable to locate replacement issues and borrows and photocopies issues needed to complete a serial run. The practice of assembling complete back runs of journals is often of less importance to libraries because of the increasing ability to access articles through online sources or interlibrary loan.

Microforms, reprints, and digital collections are viable alternatives in retrospective selection. If the item is too costly to replace in print, the OP title or issues cannot be located, or the item will not see heavy use, microform is a reasonable solution. Some titles are available in reprint editions, which are usually photoreproductions of the original and satisfy most users' needs. Librarians can purchase extensive microform sets of retrospective titles on specific topics, and several publishers and vendors are providing online access to important retrospective collections. *Early English Books Online* (eebo.chadwyck.com) is one example of the latter. The more than 125,000 titles published from 1475 to 1661 in this collection are also available in microfilm format.

SOURCE: Peggy Johnson, *Fundamentals of Collection Development and Management,* 2nd ed. (Chicago: American Library Association, 2009), 121–128.

Book ordering for school libraries
by Jacquie Henry

MANY BEGINNING LIBRARIANS are at sea about book ordering. Here is the gospel according to Henry. First, I would concentrate on just doing the best you can for your first year given the information you have. If you are not sure about nonfiction books, you could spend the year concentrating mostly on fiction and leisure reading books to encourage more reading for fun. That said, here is the process I follow.

1. I read tons of book reviews. I subscribe to *Booklist, School Library Journal,* and *Library Media Connection.* As I read them, I write what subject area I think they will be useful for on the top of the review. If there is a title that I am absolutely sure I want to order no matter what, I put a double check mark on it as well. Everything else gets a single check mark.
2. I cut up the book reviews and paste them onto 3×5 cards. That is the part that makes other librarians cringe. The reviews are in the back of *SLJ* and *LMC,* so I can cut them out and still retain the rest of the magazine. *Booklist* is nothing but reviews—so I just toss those when the reviews are all clipped out.
3. I sort the cards into a large shoe box. I have sections for all the subject areas. Fiction goes under English.
4. I generally order three times per year. I leave several orders in June that are sent out in July for the new fiscal year. Those orders are for reference sets—encyclopedias and subject reference books or sets. It

also includes my five subscriptions to Junior Library Guild. JLG books are mostly fiction books. I get five of them per month. It costs around $800 per year and keeps new fiction coming in on a regular basis. I use about a third of my book budget for these kinds of materials. I am cutting back on reference as more things get onto databases. The next order goes out in the fall and is for nonfiction additions and also replacements or updates based on the books I weeded in June. I generally spend another third of my budget on this nonfiction order. That leaves the last third for fiction. I order fiction the first of February after the Young Adult Library Services Association comes out with its final list of Best Fiction for Young Adults. Every year, I spend less money on nonfiction.

5. When I am ready to get an order together, I go through the cards and prioritize them into first choice and second choice. I then go to Baker & Taylor's website and start building an order. If I have $1,500 to spend on nonfiction, I set up an order that says "do not exceed" $1,500. I figure that the average nonfiction book, given the discount that B&T provides, will cost about $25. B&T recommends ordering about a third more books than you have money for so they can fill the "Do not exceed" order completely. So for a nonfiction order of $1,500 with an average price of $25 per book, I should aim for 60 books, plus an extra 20 titles just in case some of those books are out of stock. $15 per book seems to work well for fiction orders.

6. Why Baker & Taylor (or any other book jobber such as Follett and Mackin or Ingram) rather than individual publishers? Because they can find virtually any book that I want. By having one large order instead of multiple orders, I am able to look over all my book reviews and order the best of the best. If I ordered in little bits and pieces, I just don't feel that I would be getting the "cream of the crop" so to speak. B&T provides a 30-40% discount for trade bindings, and less of a discount for paperbacks and library bindings. Most  librarians use Follett, because of their great website and service. However, Follett generally only provides library bindings that cost way more and are discounted less. Buying trade bindings lets me stretch my budget. If the book is wildly popular and falls apart after a year, I send it out to be rebound. It basically costs $6 per book. In the long run most trade bindings hold up just fine. I have always been pleased with Baker & Taylor's service.

7. I always make sure that I order the books fully processed. This is another nice feature of book jobbers. You have your specs on file and they process the books with covers, spine labels, book pockets, barcodes—whatever you need, including MARC records to download. *Never* order unprocessed books unless there is no other choice. You and your assistant are just too busy to waste your time with this. Don't even look at what it costs. It is a bargain—pretty much no matter what they charge.

SOURCE: Jacquie Henry, "Book Ordering: Henry Style," Wanderings, November 9–10, 2009, wanderings.edublogs.org. Reprinted with permission.

SCHOLARLY COMMUNICATION

Recognizing opportunities

by Adrian K. Ho and Daniel R. Lee

LIBRARIANS IN THE MIDST of conversations with members of the campus community are often hesitant to bring up scholarly communication issues. Numerous online resources have been created in the past few years to help campuses address these issues, but some of us, whether or not we are familiar with these resources and are comfortable with the relevant concepts, aren't quite ready to talk about the resources and translate the concepts into practice. This article provides some scenarios for how such resources can come in handy during day-to-day interaction with faculty and students to help our campuses manage change and achieve an information-sharing environment that benefits everyone.

Opportune moments to discuss scholarly communication issues come up in a variety of settings. Librarians can often take advantage of these opportunities to increase awareness of scholarly communication issues and new developments in scholarly publishing. Discussions may then result in a faculty member's use of, and support for, new services created by the library's scholarly communication initiatives. Some faculty may even become advocates for introducing changes in the institution's strategies of disseminating research results.

The ACRL Scholarly Communication Toolkit (scholcomm.acrl.ala.org) includes a wide range of information and resources to help you understand these issues and support your work on campus. The following real-life questions present promising openings for you to take the information from the toolkit and other online resources to educate library users and create change on your campus.

Case 1: Limited journal access. Professor Jameson was trying to get online access to a journal article for her research through the library, but the library did not provide access to it. So she asked her subject librarian why.

Opportunity. The librarian could take the chance to talk about the access barrier created by the spiraling costs of journal subscriptions. She could also bring

up the concept of open access peer-reviewed journals. That would inform Jameson of the pricing practices of journal publishers and new scholarly publishing models that promote greater access at lower costs to readers.

This same discussion could follow questions surrounding journal cancellations. It would also be a prime opportunity to discuss what academic authors, editors, and reviewers can do to initiate change. For instance, authors can keep an eye on the pricing policies of journals in their fields and, where possible, choose to submit manuscripts to high-quality journals that have reasonable pricing practices. Faculty who serve as editors and reviewers can examine the journal's pricing practices and start an in-house discussion on pricing if appropriate.

Case 2: Efficient dissemination of research updates. Professor Tremblay and his colleagues recently founded a new research center on nanotechnology. To draw attention to their new effort, they are looking for a reliable channel to publish and disseminate updates of their research activities and findings efficiently.

Opportunity. The library can offer open access online publishing services to the research center if the library hosts its own publishing platform or participates in a consortial or collaborative online publishing initiative. Library publishing services can cover a variety of campus-based scholarly publications, such as peer-reviewed journals, faculty monographs, and technical reports. These services illuminate the library's changing role in the scholarly communication process and reinforce its status as a crucial partner in supporting learning and advancing scholarship.

Case 3: Student research reports. Professor Schulz teaches journalism at the graduate level. Her students have to conduct independent studies and write reports based on their investigations. She wants to make the students' reports widely available in order to highlight the value of student journalism, so she asks the librarian for ideas.

Opportunity. This is a great opportunity to call attention to open access digital repository services, both institutional and disciplinary. Local or shared repositories provide dissemination  and preservation services that enhance the visibility and accessibility of the institution's intellectual output. They also advance scholarship by expediting communication between different academic communities. Different types of digital repositories around the world can be found by using the Directory of Open Access Repositories (www.opendoar.org) and the Registry of Open Access Repositories (roar.eprints.org).

Digital repositories can serve as hosts for electronic theses and dissertations, student publications, survey and other data, photographic and manuscript archives, and previously published scholarly articles. Before depositing previously published journal articles in a digital repository, authors should check resources, such as RoMEO from the University of Nottingham (www.sherpa.ac.uk/romeo/), to confirm that posting the articles online will not violate the copyright policies of the journal publishers concerned.

For scholarly works yet to be published, authors and creators should retain the appropriate rights that will allow them to post their works in digital repositories. This can help authors, students, and faculty understand the benefits copyright holders can gain by managing their own publishing rights, enabling them to achieve the level of access they desire.

Case 4: Dissertation copyright. Michele Jackson is preparing to submit her dissertation and calls you to say she is confused by the option of paying an additional fee to have her copyright registered.

Opportunity. Now is a good time to explain some of the facts of copyright law, including the lack of a requirement to register a work for protection, as well as the additional value registration can bring. It is also an opportunity to explain the importance of authors holding on to their copyrights in order to control the ways readers can find and use their works. If Jackson had previously published any of her dissertation chapters as journal articles, this issue becomes an even greater concern. If she had retained the relevant rights when she signed her journal publishing agreements, she would have the necessary control over her own works to include them in this and any future works.

Case 5: National Institutes of Health (NIH) Public Access Policy. Professor Wilson from Biochemistry called saying he just heard from NIH that his recent grant report didn't comply with their Public Access Policy. They said he needed to include the PubMed Central ID Number for the articles he published as a result of the research his lab conducted under the grant. He asked if you could help him find the number and explain what these new rules were all about.

Opportunity. Working with researchers trying to comply with the NIH Public Access Policy (publicaccess.nih.gov) gives librarians an opportunity to address a number of important issues. One natural starting point is to address the availability of government-funded research findings to a wide readership, including taxpayers, health professionals, and other researchers. Broad readership increases impact. This conversation could also lead to a discussion of the common practice of journal publishers to require authors to transfer copyright of their articles.

To make their articles available in PubMed Central, authors need to be sure they retain rights that allow for deposit. Some publisher policies provide for this by default, and some even make the deposit to PubMed on behalf of their authors. For others, authors can attach formal addenda to journal publishing agreements in order to retain the rights to reuse the articles and post them online.

Case 6: Open educational resources. Dr. Akedoreva is a visiting scholar from a developing country. She is compiling a list of educational materials that are freely available online so that she can access and adapt them for local noncommercial use when she returns to her home country in three months. She plans to share the list with other educators there so that they all can benefit.

Opportunity. Akedoreva would be pleased to learn about open educational resources (OER) and OER collections such as MIT OpenCourseWare (ocw.

mit.edu), MERLOT (www.merlot.org), and Connexions (cnx.org). These collections provide materials for teaching and learning that are openly available for reuse and, often, adaption to users' local, specific needs. There is also DiscoverEd (wiki.creativecommons.org/DiscoverEd), a search engine for OER. Promoting these sites will drive home the benefits of open access and help avoid duplicating educators' efforts to create educational materials. A Creative Commons license (creativecommons.org) is sometimes appended to OER to explicitly specify the terms and conditions under which reuse and customization of the resources are allowed by the copyright owner. Akedoreva should be shown how to look for these licenses so that she will not infringe on the resource creator's copyright.

Case 7: Monograph purchases. Professor Balin, chair of the English Department, has recently returned from a professional conference where he heard several conversations about diminishing sales of scholarly monographs. He is concerned about how this may impact the junior faculty in his department and the difficulties this could cause for their tenure cases. He called to ask about the library's role in this trend.

Opportunity. Such a call opens a window into a wide-ranging conversation about the current state of scholarly publishing. It could start with a discussion of financial pressures on libraries brought about by years of flat or nearly flat collections budgets while journal prices have escalated steadily year after year. This has led many libraries to respond by cutting back on book purchases, including purchases specifically from university presses.

But the conversation needn't stop there. This is an excellent opportunity to talk about the emergence of new publishing models and how they can generate positive change in scholarly communication. For instance, open access publishing has been adopted by Open Humanities Press and Athabasca University Press to broaden the dissemination of their peer-reviewed monographs and to enhance knowledge sharing. Meanwhile, library-press partnership initiatives, such as University of California Publishing Services, the University of Michigan's Digital Culture Books, and Pennsylvania State University's Romance Studies series, demonstrate how different stakeholders in the scholarly communication process can collaborate to create a viable alternative avenue to traditional monograph publishing, where faculty can continue to share their research and scholarship with colleagues and other readers.

Conclusion

All of the cases discussed here are practical examples with suggested responses to openings given to you when faculty and student turn to their librarian for answers. But you can start your own conversations as well. Begin by asking your faculty and graduate students where they publish, how they raise the profile of their works, and what problems they are having in this realm. When they start telling you about their own experiences and what they would like to be different, you can help them reach their own scholarly publishing goals, working in the issues raised on the ACRL Scholarly Communication Toolkit.

SOURCE: Adrian K. Ho and Daniel R. Lee, "Recognizing Opportunities: Conversational Openings to Promote Positive Scholarly Communication Change," *College and Research Libraries News* 71, no. 2 (February 2010): 83–87, crln.acrl.org/content/71/2/83.full. An ACRL OnPoint chat on this topic appears at ala.org/acrl/conferences/onpoint/archives/2010-3-4.

5

Cataloging then, now, and tomorrow
by Elise (Yi-Ling) Wong

IF YOU THINK IT IS HARD to explain to nonlibrary users what a librarian does, try explaining the job of a cataloger. Not long ago (when I was still in library school), if someone had asked me what exactly a cataloger is, my answer would have been, "a guardian of the catalog." This still holds true today. However, cataloging is also a dynamic, ever-changing library field. Among the many useful and practical things I learned in library school, one idea stays fresh in my mind: The library world is changing faster than you think. Now that I have been a cataloger in a professional sense for almost two years, I can say that the world of cataloging is also changing rapidly.

Just as the function of libraries and the role of librarians are not the same as they used to be, the same is true of cataloging and catalogers. The *Cataloging Annual Report 2010–2011* by Hannah Thomas, head of cataloging and special collections at Saint Mary's College of California Library (SMCL), listed three trends in the changing landscape of cataloging: the increasing reliance on vendor-supplied records and services, the explosion of electronic resources, and the growing interrelatedness of local library catalogs with systems outside the library.

What do these trends mean, and how will they affect my responsibilities and workflow in cataloging and my role as a cataloger and a new librarian? While I ponder these questions, I find it helpful to draw a mind map representing the history of my cataloging experience—from my first exposure to cataloging to my broader responsibilities as a cataloging and reference librarian at SMCL.

Then: From card catalogs to ILSes

In 2002, I took my first cataloging course in a community college. For our final project, we were required to make a catalog card out of an actual 3x5-inch card or print one out with a word processor. Luckily, when I became a library technician in a university library I didn't need to manage a card catalog, since it was already automated on Innovative Millennium.

When I became a cataloger in 2009 at SMCL (also an Innovative library), I was surprised that some of the college's holdings still lacked online records and could only be located with a physical card catalog. Currently I am working on a retrospective conversion project to catalog all the materials we have in a remote storage facility, based solely on that catalog-card information. We estimate that the project will be completed in two years, and we are about halfway there. With the exception of the materials in storage, some microforms, the Lasallian special collection, and a small number of LPs, everything SMCL owns can be found in its online catalogs.

Now: From print to electronic

One statistic included in Thomas's *Cataloging Annual Report* showed a dramatic change in the percentage of the types of holdings in the library collections. In 2006–2007 we added a few electronic collections, such as Gale Virtual Reference Library, Oxford Reference Online, and Greenwood Press. Summer 2008 was the turning point for the overall proportion of print to electronic holdings: Our online collection surged dramatically following the major purchase of ebrary Academic Complete, which boosted our online collections by an additional 70,000 records. We also added nearly 30,000 online music files from Naxos Music Library.

As of 2010–2011, 39% of our collection is comprised of electronic resources, and the numbers will not stop there. Although our building reached its storage capacity 10 years ago, we have not stopped buying print books, journals, and DVDs. However, whenever our budget permits, our preferred formats are often ebooks, e-journals, online music/videos, streaming files, and other e-resources.

Tomorrow: From one to many

Library school cataloging courses taught me a great deal about cataloging materials of various formats. What they didn't focus on were the fundamental concepts of managing various integrated library systems. I acquired those skills on the job. At SMCL, most of what we do is copy cataloging. While some of our cataloging records are supplied by vendors and services like OCLC PromptCat (now WorldCat Cataloging Partners) and ebrary, the main source of our records is still OCLC Connexion.

Up until the early 2000s, libraries probably had only one catalog, hosted by an integrated library system. By 2011, most libraries had more than one catalog featured on their library website. There are many third-party information systems that work with library catalogs. Many library catalog interfaces are also powered by enhancement tools such as Encore, VuFind, or LibraryThing. In addition to the online public access catalog (Albert), SMCL also has Reference Universe, an electronic journal list (powered by Serial Solutions), and a few named special collections to facilitate access to some of our unique resources. We recently launched a new multisearch federated search engine with EBSCO Discovery Service.

Using power tools

Cataloging is no longer about knowing every card in the library catalog, or just about giving an individual touch to each record we download into an ILS. Today, catalogers need to know the various tricks of manipulating batches of records without having to edit them one by one. In addition to using OCLC to export records into library systems, catalogers often work with batches of records supplied by vendor and publisher packages.

Yes, we still embrace traditional cataloging duties: doing original cataloging, making enhancements to cataloging records, and managing other catalog maintenance work. However, it is essential that today's catalogers be trained to use power tools in their ILSes as well as other cataloging tools (such as MarcEdit) to do batch edits. At SMCL, we use OCLC Connexion client batch searches to export a few hundred records per week for our retrospective conversion cataloging project. Our weekly routine tasks include using "create list" and "data exchange" functions in Millennium to upload our holdings to OCLC and EBSCO Discovery Service. In fact, "Create Lists," "Global Update," and "Rapid Update" have become indispensable functions in our everyday catalog-record maintenance. Thomas's *Cataloging Annual Report* called this "the new normal" in cataloging.

Jacks of all trades

There's no question that the art of cataloging and the role of its practitioners are evolving. Where specialization is preferred, catalogers remain steadfastly the guardians of library catalogs to ensure their accuracy, currency, comprehensiveness, and user-friendliness. But catalogers are also mediators between libraries and other information organizations (museums and archives, for example), as they are charged with understanding the interoperability between the MARC standard and the different non-MARC metadata systems.

The notion of catalogers just being catalogers is gradually being replaced by a philosophy that all library staff be cross-trained and have hands-on experience working directly with library users. At SMCL, all librarians (including catalogers) take at least one reference shift. In collection development, we are subject selectors allocated funds to purchase materials in our subject areas. In addition, selectors are responsible for maintaining their subject pages on the library website. In library instruction sessions, we collaborate with faculty members in their teaching and research.

In short, there is more about being a cataloger than being an interpreter of cataloging rules or an expert on various formats of resources. Catalogers don't live in an isolated world anymore. We are proud to be managers of resources and library systems, but we are—and should be—capable of more.

SOURCE: Elise (Yi-Ling) Wong, "Cataloging Then, Now, and Tomorrow," *American Libraries* 43, no. 5/6 (May/June 2012): 52–54

RDA: An introduction

by Chris Oliver

RDA, RESOURCE DESCRIPTION AND ACCESS, is the new cataloging standard that replaces the Anglo-American Cataloguing Rules, 2nd edition (AACR2). Though it has strong links to AACR2, RDA is quite different because it is based on a theoretical framework, it is designed for the digital environment, and it has a broader scope than AACR2.

Like AACR, RDA consists of a set of practical instructions. However, RDA is based on a theoretical framework that defines the shape, structure, and content of the new standard. The key to understanding RDA is its alignment with the two conceptual models, Functional Requirements for Bibliographic Records (FRBR) and Functional Requirements for Authority Data (FRAD). FRAD is an extension of the FRBR model. The models are a way of understanding the bibliographic universe. They identify the tasks that users need to accomplish during the process of resource discovery and demonstrate how different types of bibliographic and authority data support the successful accomplishment of these tasks. FRBR and FRAD provide a theoretical and logically coherent basis on which to build an improved resource-discovery experience for the user.

The opening words of RDA state the overall purpose and scope as providing "a set of guidelines and instructions on formulating data to support resource discovery." The phrase "to support resource discovery" conveys a key message about the nature of RDA: This is a standard designed to focus attention on the user and on the tasks that the user carries out in the process of resource discovery. The purpose of recording data is to support the user tasks.

Every instruction in RDA relates back to the user and to the tasks that the user wishes to accomplish. These user tasks have their origin in the FRBR and FRAD models, and are introduced immediately, at the very beginning of RDA:

Tasks That Use Bibliographic Data	Tasks That Use Authority Data
find	find
identify	identify
select	clarify
obtain	understand

RDA takes as its starting point the theoretical framework expressed in the FRBR and FRAD models. This theoretical framework constitutes a new way of thinking about bibliographic and authority data. This change in approach is reflected throughout the standard, in the organization and structure of the instructions, and in the content of the instructions.

RDA's purpose is to support the production of robust data that can be managed using both current technologies and newly emerging database structures and technologies of the future. RDA is a content standard. RDA answers the question, "What data should I record and how should I record it?" RDA defines the elements required for description and access and gives instructions on formulating the data that is recorded in each element. Data is parsed or segmented into clearly defined elements. The elements may seem choppy after the paragraph style of the ISBDs, but each element is unambiguously defined and contains one particular kind of data. This way of recording data in a set of elements means that RDA is not tied to a single encoding schema or presentation style. RDA data can be encoded using existing schema, such as MARC 21, Dublin Core, or MODS, and can also be mapped to other schema, current or future ones. At first release,

RDA data can be encoded, stored, and transmitted using existing technology and databases, as MARC records in traditional library catalogs. However, RDA data is also designed for use in the networked environment of the web and in new types of database structures. RDA data can be used as the basis for a metadata element set that makes data visible and usable in a web environment.

RDA can be used for the description of both traditional and nontraditional resources, analog and digital, within and beyond the library. A key feature of RDA is the way it is designed to "provide a consistent, flexible, and extensible framework for both the technical and content description of all  types of resources and all types of content." It provides the principles and instructions to record data about resources that are currently known and resources that have yet to be developed. A major stumbling block for AACR2 was the description of new types of resources. AACR was originally developed as a cataloging code for print books and journals and other paper-based documents. Although rules for other media were grafted into the code, there was never a cohesive and logically consistent approach to the description of content, media, and carrier. This limitation made it difficult to extend AACR2 rules for the description of new types of resources, notably electronic resources. RDA provides an extensible framework for the description of all types of resources.

For the cataloging community, RDA marks a significant change because it is a standard designed to be used as a web tool. The standard is delivered primarily as a web document, within the RDA Toolkit. The content of RDA can be accessed in many ways, to suit different learning styles and different requirements. Some catalogers may choose to start by browsing RDA's table of contents because it provides a good sense of the intellectual organization of the standard and the way in which it is aligned with the FRBR and FRAD conceptual models. Others may prefer to start with the entity relationship diagram (ERD) that gives a visual outline of RDA's content. Others may want to start with one of the practical procedure documents, called workflows. Workflows focus on the instructions that relate to one specific procedure. The Toolkit also includes mappings that indicate how to encode RDA elements with different encoding schema. The workflows and mappings are tools that guide the cataloger in the application of the standard. Libraries can also share workflows and mappings, and customize them, incorporating their local policies and procedures and storing them as part of the Toolkit. The Toolkit includes multiple ways to access and use the instructions and includes tools that support the efficient integration of RDA into daily work. The Toolkit aims to support an efficient implementation of RDA.

We can think of RDA as the product of a thorough deconstruction of AACR2 and a rebuilding into a new standard around the framework of the FRBR and FRAD conceptual models. During the collective deconstruction of Part I of AACR2, the individual rules were taken out of their chapters. They were removed from the "class of material" structure that defined Part I of AACR2. A few rules or instructions were eliminated, some were changed, some were generalized, and new ones were added. A large number of the AACR2 rules were reworded to fit with RDA's vocabulary and were placed in a new location within RDA's structure, but were essentially kept the same. RDA uses many of the old building blocks, and rearranges them in a new structure built on the theoretical framework expressed in the FRBR and FRAD conceptual models. Thus, there are recognizable links to AACR2, and there are RDA instructions that are simply reworked

AACR2 rules, but the orientation of the standard as a whole has changed. In its alignment with the FRBR and FRAD conceptual models, RDA is built around a new, explicit, and logically sound theoretical framework.

SOURCE: Chris Oliver, *Introducing RDA* (Chicago: American Library Association, 2010), 1–5, 42–45.

Fun with RDA: Articles and prepositions in surnames

THE RESOURCE DESCRIPTION AND ACCESS (RDA) Toolkit has uses beyond the immediate needs of catalogers. You can turn to Chapter 9 or Appendix F to find out how non-English, historical, or compound personal names should be alphabetized in an index or bibliography. The rules for sacred scriptures and liturgical works (Chapter 6) and the appendices on capitalization, abbreviations, and initial articles are similarly instructive. Here is what RDA recommends for the placement of articles and prepositions in surnames.—*GME.*

9.2.2.11.1. If a surname includes an article or preposition, or a combination of the two, record as the first element the part most commonly used as the first element in alphabetically arranged directories, etc., in the person's language or country of residence or activity.

If such a name is listed in a nonstandard fashion in reference sources in the person's language or country of residence, record as the first element the part of the name used as the first element in those sources.

If a person has used two or more languages, record the name applying the instructions for the language of most of that person's works. In case of doubt, apply the instructions for the language preferred by the agency creating the data if that is one of the languages. Otherwise, if the person is known to have changed his or her country of residence, apply the instructions for the language of the adopted country. As a last resort, apply the instructions for the language of the name.

Record as a variant name a form using another part of the prefix or the part of the name following the prefix as the first element.

Afrikaans. Record the prefix as the first element.

De Wet, Reza
Du Toit, Stefanus Jacobus
Van der Post, C. W. H.
Von Breitenbach, Friedrich

Czech and Slovak. If the surname consists of a place name in the genitive case preceded by *z*, record the part following the prefix as the first element.

Žerotína, Karel z

Dutch and Flemish. If the surname is Dutch, record the part following the prefix as the first element unless the prefix is *ver.* In that case, record the prefix as the first element.

Aa, Pieter van der
Beeck, Jan op de
Beijerse, Jolande uit
Braak, Menno ter (right)
Brink, Jan ten
Driessche, André van
Duurstede, Wijk bij

Hertog, Gerard Cornelis den
Hoff, J. H. van 't
Reve, Gerard Kornelis van het
Wijngaert, Frank van den
Winter, Adriaan de
Ver Boven, Daisy

If the surname is not Dutch, record the part following the prefix as the first element for the name of a Netherlander and follow the instructions for the language of the name for the name of a Belgian.

Faille, J.-B. de la
  (*Netherlander*)
Long, Isaäc le
  (*Netherlander*)
Du Jardin, Thomas
  (*Belgian who wrote in Dutch; French name*)

English. Record the prefix as the first element.

À Beckett, Gilbert Abbott
D'Anvers, Knightley
De Morgan, Augustus
De la Mare, Walter
Du Maurier, Daphne
Le Gallienne, Richard
Van Buren, Martin (right)
Van der Post, Laurens
Von Braun, Wernher

French. If the prefix consists of an article or a contraction of an article and a preposition, record the prefix as the first element.

Le Rouge, Gustave
La Bruyère, René
Du Méril, Édélestand
Des Granges, Charles-Marc

Otherwise, record the part of the name following the preposition as the first element.

Aubigné, Agrippa d'
Musset, Alfred de
La Fontaine, Jean de

German. If the name is German and the prefix consists of an article or a contraction of an article and a preposition, record the prefix as the first element.

Am Acher, Paul
Aus'm Weerth, Ernst
Vom Ende, Erich A.
Zum Busch, J. P.
Zur Linde, Otto

Follow the same instruction for Dutch names with a prefix consisting of an article or a contraction of an article and a preposition.

De Boor, Hans Otto
  (*Name of Dutch origin*)
Ten Cate, Maria
  (*Name of Dutch origin*)

For other German and Dutch names, record the part of the name following the prefix as the first element.

Goethe, Johann Wolfgang von
Mayenberg, Wilhelm Anton Wolfgang von und zu
Mühll, Peter von der
For names that are neither German nor Dutch, follow the instructions for the language of the name.
Du Bois-Reymond, Emil Heinrich
Le Fort, Gertrud
Italian. For modern names, record the prefix as the first element.
A Prato, Giovanni
D'Arienzo, Nicola
Da Ponte, Lorenzo (right)
De Amicis, Vincenzo
Del Lungo, Isidoro
Della Volpaia, Eufrosino
Di Costanzo, Angelo
Li Gotti, Ettore
Lo Sapio, Francesco Paolo

For medieval and early modern names, consult reference sources about whether a prefix is part of a name. If a preposition is sometimes omitted from the name, record the part following the preposition as the first element. *De, de', degli, dei,* and *de li* occurring in names of the period are rarely part of the surname.
Alberti, Antonio degli
Anghiera, Pietro Martire d'
Medici, Lorenzo de'
Do not treat the preposition in an Italian title of nobility used as the first element as a prefix.
Portuguese. Record the part of the name following the prefix as the first element.
Canedo, Eneida Vieira da Silva Ostria de
Fonseca, Martinho da
Santos, João Antonio Correia dos
Romanian. Record the prefix as the first element unless it is *de.* In that case, record the part of the name following the prefix as the first element.
A Mariei, Vasile
Hurmuzaki, Eudoxiu de
Scandinavian (Danish, Norwegian, Swedish). Record the part of the name following the prefix as the first element if the prefix is of Scandinavian, German, or Dutch origin (except for the Dutch *de*). If the prefix is the Dutch *de* or is of another origin, record the prefix as the first element.
Hällström, Gunnar af
Linné, Carl von
De Geer, Gerard

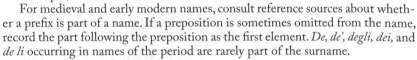

The first online cataloging

On August 26, 1971, the Alden Library at Ohio University in Athens cataloged 133 books online and made history as the first library in the world to do online cataloging. Within a year Ohio University increased the number of titles it cataloged by one third while reducing its cataloging staff by 17 positions. Fred Kilgour's vision, that OCLC would increase access to information while reducing costs, was beginning to be realized.

SOURCE: K. Wayne Smith, *OCLC, 1967–1997: Thirty Years of Furthering Access to the World's Information* (New York: Haworth, 1998), 56.

De la Gardie, Jakob
La Cour, Jørgen Karl
Spanish. If the prefix consists of an article only, record the article as the first element.
El Bravo, Pancho
La Torre Lagares, Elidio
Las Heras, José María
For all other Spanish names, record the part following the prefix as the first element.
Figueroa, Francisco de
Casas, Bartolomé de las (right)
Río, Antonio del

9.2.2.11.2. If the prefix is neither an article, nor a preposition, nor a combination of the two, record the prefix as the first element.
'Abd al-Hamīd Ahmad
Abū Zahrah, Muhammad
Āl Yāsīn, Muhammad Hasan
Ap Gwilym, Owain
Ben Harosh, Mosheh
Fitz Gerald, Gregory
Mac Murchaidh, Ciarán
Ó Faoláin, Dónal
Record as a variant name a form using the part of the name following the prefix as the first element.
9.2.2.12. Record a name containing a prefix hyphenated or combined with a surname applying the general guidelines on recording surnames. If the prefix is regularly or occasionally hyphenated or combined with the surname, record the prefix as the first element.
FitzGerald, Colin
MacDonald, William
Ter-Horst, Joannes Hermannus
Debure, Guillaume
Fon-Lampe, A. A.

SOURCE: RDA: Resource Description and Access Toolkit (Chicago: American Library Association, the Canadian Library Association, and CILIP: Chartered Institute of Library and Information Professionals, 2010).

CLASSIFICATION

Dewey Decimal Classification: The hundred divisions

MOST LIBRARY USERS KNOW the general structure of Melvil Dewey's decimal classification. First published in 1876, the Dewey Decimal Classification divides knowledge into 10 main classes, with further subdivisions. Here is an outline of its 100 major subdivisions.

000 Computer science, information, and general works

010 Bibliographies
020 Library and information sciences
030 General encyclopedic works
040 [not assigned]
050 General serial publications
060 Organizations and museums
070 News media, journalism, publishing
080 General collections
090 Manuscripts and rare books

100 Philosophy and psychology

110 Metaphysics
120 Epistemology, causation, humankind
130 Parapsychology and occultism
140 Philosophical schools of thought
150 Psychology
160 Logic
170 Ethics
180 Ancient, medieval, Eastern philosophy
190 Modern Western philosophy

200 Religion

210 Philosophy and theory of religion
220 The Bible
230 Christianity, Christian theology
240 Christian practice and observance
250 Christian pastoral practice and religious orders
260 Christian organization, social work, and worship
270 History of Christianity
280 Christian denominations
290 Other religions

300 Social sciences, sociology, anthropology

310 Statistics
320 Political science
330 Economics
340 Law
350 Public administration and military science
360 Social problems and social services
370 Education
380 Commerce, communications, transportation
390 Customs, etiquette, folklore

400 Language

410 Linguistics
420 English and Old English languages

430   German and related languages
440   French and related languages
450   Italian, Romanian, and related languages
460   Spanish and Portuguese languages
470   Latin and Italic languages
480   Classical and modern Greek languages
490   Other languages

500 Science

510   Mathematics
520   Astronomy
530   Physics
540   Chemistry
550   Earth sciences
560   Paleontology
570   Biology and life sciences
580   Plants (botany)
590   Animals (zoology)

600 Technology

610   Medicine and health
620   Engineering
630   Agriculture
640   Home and family management
650   Management and public relations
660   Chemical engineering
670   Manufacturing
680   Manufacturing specific products
690   Building and construction

5

700 Arts

710   Civic and landscape art
720   Architecture
730   Sculpture, ceramics, metalwork
740   Drawing and decorative arts
750   Painting
760   Graphic arts
770   Photography
780   Music
790   Sports, games, entertainment

800 Literature, rhetoric, and criticism

810   American literature in English
820   English and Old English literatures
830   German and related literatures
840   French and related literatures
850   Italian, Romanian, and related literatures

860 Spanish and Portuguese literatures
870 Latin and Italic literatures
880 Classical and modern Greek literatures
890 Other literatures

900 History

910 Geography and travel
920 Biography and genealogy
930 History of the ancient world (to ca. 499)
940 History of Europe
950 History of Asia
960 History of Africa
970 History of North America
980 History of South America
990 History of other areas

SOURCE: Summaries: DDC Dewey Decimal Classification (Dublin, Ohio: OCLC, 2005). Reprinted with permission of OCLC Online Computer Library Center, Inc.

LC classification outline

THE LC CLASSIFICATION was developed and used at the Library of Congress beginning in 1899. It has become the system of choice for many large research libraries. This list gives the scope for most one- or two-letter designators, which may serve as an aid in learning the classification schedules in more detail.

A (General works)

AC Collections, series, collected works
AE Encyclopedias
AG Dictionaries and other general reference books
AI Indexes
AM Museums, collectors, and collecting
AN Newspapers
AP Periodicals
AS Academies and learned societies
AY Yearbooks, almanacs, directories
AZ History of scholarship and learning, the humanities

B (Philosophy, psychology, religion)

B Philosophy (general)
BC Logic
BD Speculative philosophy, metaphysics, ontology
BF Psychology, parapsychology, occult sciences
BH Aesthetics
BJ Ethics, social usages, etiquette
BL Religions, mythology, rationalism
BM Judaism
BP Islam, Bahaism, theosophy
BQ Buddhism

BR Christianity
BS The Bible
BT Doctrinal theology, God, Christology
BV Practical and ecclesiastical theology
BX Christian denominations

C (Auxiliary sciences of history)

C Auxiliary sciences of history (general)
CB History of civilization
CC Archaeology
CD Diplomatics, archives, seals
CE Calendars, technical chronology
CJ Numismatics, coins, medals
CN Inscriptions, epigraphy
CR Heraldry, chivalry
CS Genealogy
CT Biography

D (History, general, and history of Europe)

D History (general)
DA Great Britain, Ireland
DAW Central Europe
DB Austria, Liechtenstein, Hungary, Czech Republic, Slovakia
DC France, Andorra, Monaco
DD Germany
DE The Greco-Roman world
DF Greece
DG Italy, Malta
DH Belgium, Luxembourg
DJ Netherlands
DJK Eastern Europe (general)
DK Russia, Soviet Union, former Soviet republics, Poland
DL Northern Europe, Scandinavia
DP Spain, Portugal
DQ Switzerland
DR Balkan Peninsula, Turkey
DS Asia
DT Africa
DU Australia, Oceania
DX Romanies

E–F (History, America)

E Indians, United States (general)
F U.S. local history, Canada, Mexico, Central and South America

G (Geography, anthropology, recreation)

G Geography (general), atlases, maps
GA Mathematical geography, cartography
GB Physical geography, hydrology
GC Oceanography

GE   Environmental sciences
GF   Human ecology, anthropogeography
GN   Anthropology, ethnology
GR   Folklore
GT   Manners and customs (general)
GV   Recreation, sports, games, leisure, physical education

H (Social sciences)

H   Social sciences (general)
HA   Statistics
HB   Economic theory, demography
HC   Economic history and conditions (by region or country)
HD   Industries, land use, labor
HE   Transportation and communications
HF   Commerce, business
HG   Finance, insurance
HJ   Public finance, taxation
HM   Sociology
HN   Social history, social problems, social reform
HQ   Sex, the family, marriage, women, life skills
HS   Societies, clubs
HT   Cities, communities, classes, races
HV   Social pathology, social and public welfare, criminology
HX   Socialism, communism, utopias, anarchism

J (Political science)

J   General legislative and executive papers
JA   Political science (general)
JC   Political theory
JF   Political institutions and
      public administration (general)
JJ   —North America
JK   —United States
JL   —Canada, Central and South America
JN   —Europe
JQ   —Asia, Africa, Australia, Oceania
JS   Local and municipal government
JV   Colonization, emigration, immigration, international migration
JX   International law (no longer used)
JZ   International relations

K (Law)

K   General law, jurisprudence, comparative law
KB   Religious law, legal research
KBM   Jewish law
KBP   Islamic law
KBR   History of canon law
KBU   Roman Catholic law
KD–KDK   United Kingdom and Ireland
KDZ   America

KE	Canada
KF	United States
KG	Mexico, Central America, Caribbean
KH	South America
KJ–KKZ	Europe
KL	Ancient Orient
KLA–KLW	Eurasia
KM–KPW	Middle East, Asia
KQ–KTZ	Africa
KU–KWW	Australasia, Oceania
KWX	Antarctica
KZ	Law of nations
KZA	Law of the sea
KZD	Space law

L (Education)

L	Education (general)
LA	History of education
LB	Theory, teaching, teacher training, higher education, school administration
LC	Forms, social aspects, types of education, special classes, adult education
LD	United States
LE	America, except United States
LF	Europe
LG	Asia, Africa, Oceania
LH	College and school magazines and newspapers
LJ	Student fraternities and societies
LT	Textbooks

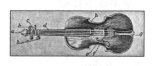

M (Music)

M	Music
ML	Literature on music
MT	Musical instruction and study

N (Fine arts)

N	Visual arts (general)
NA	Architecture
NB	Sculpture
NC	Drawing, design, illustration
ND	Painting
NE	Print media
NK	Decorative arts
NX	Arts in general, exhibitions

P (Language and literature)

P	Philology and linguistics
PA	Greek and Latin languages and literature
PB	Modern languages, Celtic
PC	Romance languages
PD	Scandinavian languages
PE	English language

PF   West Germanic languages
PG   Slavic, Baltic, Albanian languages
PH   Finnic, Hungarian, and Basque languages
PJ   Egyptian, Semitic, Arabic languages and literature
PK   Indo-Iranian languages and literature
PL   East Asian, African, Oceanic languages
PM   Inuit, American Indian, artificial languages
PN   Literary history, performing arts, journalism
PQ   Romance literatures
PR   English literature
PS   American literature
PT   Germanic and Scandinavian literature
PZ   Juvenile belles lettres

Q (Science)

Q   Science (general), information theory
QA   Mathematics
QB   Astronomy
QC   Physics
QD   Chemistry
QE   Geology, paleontology
QH   Natural history, biology
QK   Botany
QL   Zoology
QM   Human anatomy
QP   Physiology, animal biochemistry, experimental pharmacology
QR   Microbiology, immunology

R (Medicine)

R   Medicine (general)
RA   Regulation, public health, forensics
RB   Pathology
RC   Internal medicine, neurosciences
RD   Surgery
RE   Ophthalmology
RF   Otorhinolaryngology
RG   Gynecology and obstetrics
RJ   Pediatrics
RK   Dentistry
RL   Dermatology
RM   Therapeutics, pharmacology
RS   Pharmacy and materia medica
RT   Nursing
RV   Eclectic medicine
RX   Homeopathy
RZ   Alternative systems of medicine

"What's the verdict?"

Will you ignore the truth until it is too late? Many men and women do. And when maddening pain drives them to their dentist in search of relief they discover that neglect has taken high toll in precious health . . .

S (Agriculture)

S   Agriculture (general)
SB   Plant culture, gardening, pests and diseases

SD   Forestry
SF   Animal culture, pets, veterinary medicine
SH   Aquaculture, fisheries, angling
SK   Hunting, wildlife management

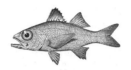

T (Technology)

T   Technology (general), industrial engineering, patents
TA   Engineering (general), civil engineering
TC   Hydraulic and ocean engineering
TD   Environmental technology, sanitary engineering
TE   Highway engineering, roads and pavements
TF   Railroad engineering and operation
TG   Bridge engineering
TH   Building construction
TJ   Mechanical engineering and machinery
TK   Electrical engineering, electronics, computers, nuclear power
TL   Motor vehicles, aircraft, astronautics
TN   Mining engineering, metallurgy
TP   Chemical technology
TR   Photography
TS   Manufactures
TT   Arts and crafts
TX   Home economics, hospitality industry

5

U (Military science)

U   Military science (general)
UA   Armies
UB   Military administration
UC   Maintenance and transportation
UD   Infantry
UE   Cavalry and armor
UF   Artillery
UG   Military engineering, air forces, space warfare
UH   Other military services

V (Naval science)

V   Naval science (general)
VA   Navies
VB   Naval administration
VC   Naval maintenance
VD   Naval seamen
VE   Marines
VF   Naval ordnance
VG   Minor services of navies
VK   Navigation, merchant marine
VM   Naval engineering, shipbuilding, diving

Z (Bibliography, library science)

Z   Books in general

Z 4–8	History of books and bookmaking
Z 40–115.5	Writing, manuscripts
Z 116–659	Printing, binding, the book trade, copyright, censorship
Z 662–1000.5	Libraries, library science, information science
Z 1001–8999	Bibliography
ZA	Information resources, electronic and media resources

SOURCE: Library of Congress Classification Outline, online at www.loc.gov/catdir/cpso/lcco/.

A history of classification
by Jean Weihs

IT IS OBVIOUS TO MOST OF US, and it was also obvious to early civilizations, that when a large number of books, tablets, or scrolls are acquired, some system must be devised to allow a particular item to be located and retrieved. This is the story of the long journey to the classification schemes that are used today.

The distant past

Archaeological expeditions have uncovered many ancient libraries, such as at Ebla, Nimrud, and Pergamon. Historians consider the first significant step toward cataloging and classification to have happened in Hattusa, capital of the Hittites (1600–1200 B.C.), when several lines of writing that identified a work were added to the text on the back surface of the tablets (this could be likened to the colophon). Each colophon began with the number of the tablet and information more or less the way it is found today on a title page. As the centuries passed, colophons ranged from a few words to a summary of the document's contents. By the 13th century B.C., the colophon also contained additional information, such as "they do not stand upright." In some places, colored markings were placed on tablets to aid classification.

During the second millennium B.C., Sumerian libraries classified hymns according to the musical instrument that was to accompany the hymn.

The earliest known cataloged library was in the palace of Ashurbanipal (685–627 B.C.) at Nineveh. The 30,000 tablets in the library were organized according

to shape and basic material for instant recognition and easy retrieval. These shapes were oval, round, pointed, or quadrangular and could be made of wood, clay, or stone. For example, four-sided tablets were for financial transactions, while round tablets recorded agricultural information. The cuneiform system used for administrative texts was different from the system used for literary works. The library was organized into sections: government records, historical chronicles, poetry, science, mythological and medical texts, royal decrees and grants, divinations, omens, and hymns to the gods. The tablets were placed in jars kept in orderly rows in many of the rooms in the palace. The rooms in which the jars were kept appear to have been arranged by subject; for example, there were separate rooms for astronomy, geography, government, history, and law. Each tablet bore an identification tag, indicating the jar, shelf, and room in which it was to be housed. Inscribed on the wall beside the door of each room was a list of works to be found in that room.

Aristotle (384–322 B.C.) created a large personal library that was considered to be the first of its kind, with a size and range that required a system of organization. Strabo (63 B.C.–24 A.D.), a Greek historian, geographer, and philosopher, wrote, "he was the first to have put together a collection of books and to have taught the kings in Egypt how to arrange a library." At this time another event took place that, while less important to the development of classification, was very important in the development of libraries. A serious problem in Greek and Roman times was that every copy of a book was made by hand and the possibility of a change of text in additional copies, either careless or willful, was a considerable concern. The Athenian government passed a decree in which an authoritative copy of the plays of important writers was to be kept on file.

No history of librarianship can be complete without a mention of the library at Alexandria, which was founded around 300 B.C. Ashurbanipal's library had been established for his use and specialized in materials for his particular needs. The library at Alexandria contained books of all sorts (ranging from epic poetry to cookbooks) from everywhere, and it was open to anyone with appropriate literary or scholarly qualifications. New acquisitions were housed in chests and on shelves in the groups in which they were acquired.

In 245 B.C., Callimachus of Cyrene (right) was appointed librarian, and during his tenure he created a subject catalog on 120,000 scrolls listing the library's holdings. The catalog's subject scheme followed Aristotle's divisions of knowledge. As far as scholars know, the Alexandrian library was the first to use alphabetical order as a mode of organization and shelving. However, at this time the alphabetization only went as far as the first letter of the author's name. Not until the second century A.D. was fuller alphabetization used in organizing library collections. How Callimachus handled authors who wrote works in different subject fields is unknown.

The *Pinakes* of Callimachus may be the first written work on library organization. Although Ashurbanipal's library is the best known of those in ancient Mesopotamia, there were other major libraries; palace, temple, and private libraries have been found ranging in age from 2000 to 500 B.C. Time and destruction have made it difficult to give a precise picture of the organization of these libraries. However, it appears that generally tablets were kept in a designated area, arranged in some manner, and supervised by competent staff members.

The great libraries of the ancient world were used by scholars, government officials, and other people of importance. Most of the information about smaller, local libraries is scattered and scanty. In Hellenistic times smaller libraries, frequently connected with a gymnasium, did exist in many communities. Part of a catalog has been found on the island of Rhodes that could be the work of a knowledgeable librarian. It is carved on a wall and lists authors in alphabetical order and under each author's name the title(s) of the work(s) of that author and the number of books in the work, each on an indented separate line.

Historians believe the first works of Latin literature appeared around 240 B.C. These were mostly translations or adaptations of Greek works. By the end of the century Rome had two types of private libraries: general collections of Greek classics owned by the wealthy, and comprehensive collections of Greek and Latin drama owned by theatre managers.

Rome's first public library was built by Gaius Asinius Pollio around 39 B.C. and, like most subsequent public libraries in the Roman Empire, its collection was bilingual with works in Greek and Latin housed in separate rooms. Books in Roman libraries were arranged according to general subjects with all works of a single author kept together under his major subject. The works about various schools of philosophy were separated, as were those of different religious groups. Each scroll bore a tag that indicated its contents. Bookcases were numbered and the appropriate number entered in the catalog beside a scroll's title. This only provided a general direction because each bookcase might hold several hundred scrolls piled on top of each other. If not conducted with care, a search for the appropriate scroll could result in damage to others in the bookcase. There were two types of catalogs, always divided first into Greek and Latin works: One was a sort of shelf list, the other arranged by author, which gave titles or first lines, length of works, and sometimes biographical information about the author. In contrast to Greek libraries, libraries in Rome were frequently attached to public baths.

The Dark Ages

In the 5th century Rome was occupied by invaders, its western empire crumbled, and a major fire in the capital of its eastern empire, Constantinople, burned down the imperial library. These events ushered in the period known as the Dark Ages (500–800 A.D.), during which cities and towns and their public libraries were destroyed and monasteries and churches became the main repositories of old books and the producers of new books. For the most part, these libraries were for the use of the monks. Around 550, the Roman writer Cassiodorus established a monastery he named Vivarium, which included a library and probably was the first in the western world to use classification symbols for organization.

Because the eastern empire was not invaded, the Byzantine emperors continued to build and maintain libraries up to the capture of Constantinople by the Ottoman Turks in 1453. My sources do not mention any development for the classification of library holdings during the Dark Ages. However, one of Rome's great contributions to learning and libraries did survive—the development of the codex format for books. (See pages 198–202.)

Classification in the Middle Ages

Most medieval libraries were found in religious establishments. Early monastic libraries were so small that they had no need for a classification of their materials.

Crediton Parish Church Library, Devon, England.

As libraries grew, it became obvious that some system must be found to locate a particular work. Many libraries had shelved their collection by accession number. In time, collections might be roughly classified by subject, first being divided between theological works and secular ones, then subdivided by works in Latin and those in other languages; and finally between textbooks and more serious works. Some libraries designated these divisions by letters of the alphabet.

University libraries in the medieval period devised local classification schemes, which usually were little more than a location symbol. One library used a bizarre classification system, arranging its inventory list by the first word on the second page of a book, whatever that word might be. Roger Bacon (1214?–1294) included a classification in his *Opus majus*, published in 1266.

In the Sorbonne Library catalog of 1289, books were arranged in major divisions, including those of the *trivium* (in medieval schools the lower division of a class of study comprising grammar, rhetoric, and logic) and the *quadrivium* (the higher group of the liberal arts, comprising arithmetic, geometry, astronomy, and music), plus theology, medicine, and law. The Sorbonne Library was the first in this period to list titles alphabetically under each subject area.

Classification in the Renaissance

The Renaissance began in Florence, Italy, in the 14th century and spread to the rest of Western Europe in the 15th and 16th centuries. Renaissance libraries were organized by the individuals in charge, some by the librarian's whim and some according to the educated knowledge of the individuals who were or acted as librarians. Some librarians arranged books by language, or by whether they were printed books or handwritten manuscripts. More scholarly attempts at organization used generally recognized categories such as astrology, Greek and Roman philosophers, mathematics, mythology, rhetoric, canon law, scriptures, the saints, and the writings of the Church Fathers.

The invention of the printing press in the 15th century had a profound effect on library collections. Many more books became available at an affordable cost and the need for a sensible arrangement of a library's growing collection was increasingly imperative.

People that contributed to the development of the classification of books in this period include Florian Trefler (1483–1565), Conrad Gessner (1516–1565), Sir Francis Bacon (1561–1626), and Gabriel Naudé (1600–1653). Trefler, a librarian at the Benediktbeuern Abbey in Upper Bavaria, wrote a treatise on library management titled *Methodus*, published in 1560, that included a scheme of library classification and call numbers. Gessner published *Bibliotheca universalis* in 1545, a bibliography of 10,000 titles that he arranged in subject order under 21 major classes with subdivisions.

In 1605, Bacon published a classification of the sciences, which divided them into agriculture, alchemy, astronomy (judicial and operative), medicine, perspective, the science of weight, and experimental science. He also divided other books into three categories: history, representing memory; poesy, representing imagination; and philosophy, representing reason. Each of these categories was subdivided into narrower subjects; for example, the subarrangements for history were natural, civil, ecclesiastical, and literary. Bacon proposed a system of classification in *The Advancement of Learning*, published in 1605, which influenced the classification systems of Thomas Jefferson and Melvil Dewey even though it was not intended for such use.

Some authorities believe Naudé (right), a French physician who became a librarian, to be the first important theoretician of modern library organization. His book, *Advis pour dresser une bibliothèque* (*Advice on Establishing a Library*), written in 1643 during his tenure as librarian of the Bibliothèque Mazarin in Paris, divided knowledge into what he considered best represented the known body of knowledge in the world: history, humanities, jurisprudence, mathematics, medicine, philosophy, and theology, with appropriate subdivisions. Naudé added other subject headings in later years.

Sir Robert Bruce Cotton (1571–1631) established the Cottonian Library at Westminster in London, which is now part of the British Library. He placed a bust of a famous Roman emperor or lady on the top of each of the 14 shelving areas. A book or a manuscript was located by the first letter of the name of the bust, for example, N for Nero, then the number of the shelf indicated by an Arabic numeral, followed by a roman numeral counting across the shelf from the left. Therefore, an item with the call number N.D.vi would be found on the shelf topped by the bust of Nero (N), on the fourth shelf down from the top (D), in the

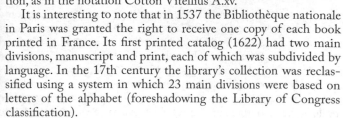

sixth position starting from the left (vi). The British Library still maintains this method of numbering in its special Cotton collection, as in the notation Cotton Vitellius A.xv.

It is interesting to note that in 1537 the Bibliothèque nationale in Paris was granted the right to receive one copy of each book printed in France. Its first printed catalog (1622) had two main divisions, manuscript and print, each of which was subdivided by language. In the 17th century the library's collection was reclassified using a system in which 23 main divisions were based on letters of the alphabet (foreshadowing the Library of Congress

Sir Robert Bruce Cotton classification).

Western Europe was not the only area where people were struggling with the establishment of an effective classification of their collections. Akbar (1542–1605), one of the greatest Mughal rulers of India, did much of the work in the classification of the books in his library. He established three main groupings: (1) poetry, medicine, astrology, and music; (2) philology, Sufism, astronomy, and geometry; and (3) commentaries on the Qur'an, general theology, and law. This classification grouping was similar to classification in most Muslim libraries of the era.

The Modern Era

17th-century attempts at classification had gone beyond the usual few categories of astrology, classical writings, law, and scriptures. As emerging subject fields—architecture, the arts, biography, commerce, economics, industry, linguistics, maps, mathematics, medicine, philosophy (divine and natural), sciences, and contemporary works in history and exploration—became part of library collections, librarians began to expand classification schemes. As the 17th century merged into the 18th century, some libraries began to be organized by an alphabetic-classed arrangement, a classified catalog arranged alphabetically by class and by author under the class. Examples of this type of organization were found in the Harvard Library (1790), the Baltimore Library (1809), and the Bowdoin College Library (1821).

The seeds of library classification used today in Western Europe and North America were planted in the period between the Renaissance and the middle of the 19th century. As the 19th century progressed, librarians strove to arrange their collections in a logical manner. In the 17th century, Ismael Boulliau had created a classification system for Paris booksellers. In his *Manual du libraire et de l'amateur de livres*, published in 1810, Jacques-Charles Brunet modified Boulliau's system. It had five main classes: history, jurisprudence, literature, science and arts, and theology, each with a number of subdivisions. Benjamin Peirce (1809–1880), mathematician and Harvard College librarian, was one of the first in the United States to use this system. This organization is still used in part today by the Bibliothèque nationale and some other French libraries, and an adaptation of this scheme is in use by the British Library.

Andreas August Ernst Schleiermacher (1787–1858), the court librarian at Darmstadt, designed the most detailed classification system of the 19th century. The scheme had 25 classes (the number of letters in the German alphabet) with some 13,000 subdivisions and a relative index.

James Duff Brown (1862–1914) wrote *An Adjustable Classification for Libraries* (1898) and *Subject Classification* (1906), in which the main classes are matter and force, life, mind, and record, with a mixed letter and number notation that does not permit an easy extension, although the Categorical Tables enable some subdivision. Each term in the tables is given a number (0 to 075). A point is added to these subject numbers as a separating device in any part of the classification, for example: .1 Bibliography, .33 Travel, .57 Museums. His work was one of the first to deal with synthesized notation. *Subject Classification* was designed for municipal libraries to encourage open-shelf access of books in the United Kingdom.

Jacob Schwartz (1846–1926), the chief librarian of the Apprentices' Library of the General Society of Mechanics and Tradesmen of the City of New York, was once considered an early rival to Melvil Dewey. He devised several classification schemes, the most notable of which was the one that he termed "the combined system," in use from 1871 and adopted in whole or in part by various librarians. In 1878 he published *A Mnemonic System of Classification*, in which 25 classes were denoted by A–Z, each class subdivided into nine classes, and each subdivision again subdivided into 25 classes (he ignored the "J" in his classification system). Within each subclass the books were arranged by a combined author/size system. For example, a particular book would be given a number according to its size. There were separate classification ranges for duodecimo, octavo, quarto, and folio sizes. In 1888 he increased the number of classes to 27.

In 1880, Stephen Buttrick Noyes (1833–1885) completed his catalogue of the Brooklyn Library, a modified alphabetical-classed arrangement without scientific basis. It was considered most usable by the general public and was widely praised by colleagues.

In 1894, William Isaac Fletcher (1844–1917, right) published *Library Classification*, in which he adopted 13 main classes using the letters, A–H, J–L, and R. These were further divided into numerical subdivisions, for example: 15. Philosophy and Study of History, 16. History of Civilizations. The class number E100-1 would be assigned to a book on travel (E) in Great Britain (100) that was the first received on that subject (1). The scheme was very elastic in order to allow it to be adapted by any library and was recommended to British librarians as an alternative to the more elaborate American systems of Melvil Dewey and Charles Cutter that required painstaking analytical classification. In 1899 Fletcher also devised a classification scheme for the U.S. Department of Agriculture.

Dewey Decimal Classification

The desire for an effective classification system did not originate with Melvil Dewey (1851–1931). Classification was an important concern for librarians in the latter part of the 19th century. It was apparent that the old system in which a book was assigned a permanent position on a shelf would no longer suffice for the emerging idea of collections on open shelves available to the general public. The need for a system that would allow the general public untrained in a classification scheme to browse the shelves for materials in a particular subject field became an imperative. The desire for such a scheme grew in the 19th century as many people tried to fashion a satisfactory classification for libraries.

Dewey superimposed a system of decimals on the structure of knowledge first devised by Sir Francis Bacon and later modified by William Torrey Harris (1835–1909). Among Harris's many accomplishments while a St. Louis school administrator (one of which was the establishment of the first permanent public

kindergarten in 1873) was developing the idea of classifying not the books but the knowledge they contained; such a system required a scheme of relative classification, in which books were found according to their relationship to one another. Harris used Bacon's tripartite theory of knowledge that assigned books first to the disciplines of history, poetry, and philosophy. These disciplines were then further analyzed into a structure of knowledge that would cover all works of the mind. Although such classification schemes had been known since the Middle Ages, they had rarely been applied to libraries. Dewey's innovation was to combine two systems, the knowledge contained in a work and its numerical position on a shelf.

DDC class. Photo: mdd, used CC BY-SA 3.0

The number assigned to a book would not just be part of a shelving system, but would also indicate its place in the field of knowledge. In addition, Dewey's system would accommodate all the books a library had and all the books that a library might acquire in the future.

Sources disagree on exactly when Dewey invented the Dewey Decimal Classification (DDC) system. Some say he invented DDC when he was 21 and was working as a student assistant in the library of Amherst College, while others say he invented it after he graduated in 1874, when Amherst College hired him to manage the library and reclassify the collections. The latter is probably wrong because Dewey worked on his scheme for two years and DDC was first used at Amherst College in 1873.

DDC was first published anonymously by Amherst College in 1876 in a pamphlet titled *A Classification and Subject Index for Cataloguing and Arranging the Books and Pamphlets of a Library*. In the same year Dewey copyrighted the "decimal classification." It was completely applied for the first time to a large library by Josephus Larned at the Buffalo Young Men's Association Library in 1877. It was not until 1930 that Dewey numbers appeared on Library of Congress printed catalog cards.

Universal Decimal Classification

The Universal Decimal Classification (UDC) is a faceted classification in which all possible components of a group of subjects are given and classification numbers are built by combining the appropriate components. UDC is used extensively in Europe. In North America UDC is found mainly in some scientific and technical libraries. Personally, I know of only two libraries in North America that use it: the Engineering Society Library in New York City and the library of a firm in Toronto whose head office is in Europe. This branch office is required to use UDC because all library resources of this global firm are amalgamated in one central catalog.

UDC is an elaborate expansion of the DDC that was begun by two Belgian lawyers Paul Otlet (1868–1944) and Henri La Fontaine (1854–1943) in 1885 and presented to the first International Conference of Librarians held in Brussels in 1895. It was based on DDC's fifth edition with Dewey's permission and expanded with many more detailed subdivisions. Symbols are used in addition to Arabic numerals to create longer notations, making it more flexible and precise than DDC and particularly suitable for specialized collections or collections where new fields of knowledge are likely to be added. The listed subdivisions in science and technology outweigh those of the arts and social sciences.

There have been editions in many languages as well as full, medium, and abridged editions. The first English full edition is the fourth international edition. The first complete edition was published in French between 1904 and 1907 as *Manuel du répertoire bibliographique universel.* The full edition has been discontinued and there have been three editions in English of what is now considered to be the Standard Edition, the equivalent to what was previously considered to be the medium edition. The Standard Edition is now considered the one from which all other editions are to be derived. The First Standard Edition was published in 1985, the second in 1993, and the third in 2005–2006. It is in two volumes and contains approximately 66,700 entries. UDC is now also in machine-readable form as a working file called the MRF (Master Reference File) and UDC Online for general use.

The system became the Universal Decimal Classification in 1927. UDC was managed by the Institut International de Bibliographie, now known as the International Federation for Information and Documentation. In 1992 the publishers of the Dutch, English, French, Japanese, and Spanish editions formed a new body, the UDC Consortium, to create a master file in an international database.

UDC is constantly under revision by an international group of experts. Published in many languages, it has been adopted by the International Organization for Standardization, which has recommended it for adoption by the national standards bodies that are members of ISO.

Expansive Classification

When Charles Ammi Cutter (1837–1903, right) began working at the Athenaeum Library in Boston in 1868, the library was using a fixed location for shelving its materials, not a satisfactory arrangement for the browsing of the materials on its open stacks. But it was not until 1879 that he started to devise his Boston Athenaeum Classification, which was first published in *Library Journal* that year. Originally this newly developed classification was tailored for the Athenaeum's collection of 100,000 titles and applied a numeric/alphabetic notation. The scheme was not broadly accepted, so in the late 1880s Cutter revised the Boston Athenaeum Classification and named it the Expansive Classification. It was a strictly alphabetic notation, which was applied to the collection of the Gary Library in Lexington, Massachusetts. When this proved successful, Cutter decided to create a classification system that would be suitable for any library.

The Expansive Classification consists of seven expansions with increasing levels of specificity. It was intended that the first expansion would be used by very small libraries and the seventh by the world's largest collections. Because each expansion was an outgrowth of the one before it, Cutter believed as a library's collection grew in size the library could move from one expansion to the next without needing to reclassify its older materials. (Some later writers disputed this claim, stating that moving from one expansion to a higher expansion required reclassification of some or many items.) The alphabetic notation used up to four letters per class, permitting a total of 367,280 possible subject areas. Within a given class, individual titles were distinguished from each other by alphanumeric author marks, which were arranged in tables. The development of these tables is familiar to today's catalogers as cutter numbers and cutter tables or Cutter-Sanborn tables. This is the only portion of the Expansive Classification that remains in general use.

Cutter published schedules for the first six expansions from 1891 through 1893. Portions of the seventh expansion were published from 1896 through 1911, but Cutter died before finishing work on it, including most notably the technology section. Some writers claim that Cutter did not actively promote his classification, while others claim he vigorously promoted it. What is certain is that he made no provisions for its continued revision and publication after his death.

I was not able to clearly establish the number of libraries that have been past and present users of the Expansive Classification. Robert L. Mowery in 1976 claimed 67 libraries, while R. Conrad Winke in 2004 expressed doubt about Mowery's number; he stated the number to be 57. Winke claimed that four libraries were still using the classification (Charleston Library Society in South Carolina; the Holyoke Public Library in Holyoke, Massachusetts; the Illinois State Historical Library in Springfield; and the Forbes Library in Northampton, Massachusetts, whose home page proudly proclaims that its books are arranged in the "Cutter Expansive Classification System, developed by Charles A. Cutter, the librarian at Forbes from 1894 to 1903").

Although adopted by comparatively few libraries, in its day the Expansive Classification was generally regarded as one of the most logical and scholarly of American classification schemes.

While Charles Cutter is not generally a recognized name outside the field of librarianship, his name is possibly second in familiarity to librarians, as all of us at one time were taught Cutter's functions of the catalog and know that cutter numbers can be part of a call number. He is one of the select number of people whose name has been celebrated by becoming a noun.

Library of Congress Classification

Although the Expansive Classification failed to become a standard for libraries, it did influence the Library of Congress classification (LCC), which was modeled after the Expansive Classification and was used to develop the library's "Class Z: Bibliography and Library Science," which served as the outline for the remaining schedules in that system.

After the Library of Congress was burned in the War of 1812, Thomas Jefferson sold his personal library to Congress. He had organized his library around the division of knowledge devised by Sir Francis Bacon. Jefferson expanded Bacon's categories of knowledge into 44 subject divisions. Jefferson's classification was a fixed-location scheme. This was the way in which the Library of Congress collection was classified for the next 100 years.

Thomas Jefferson's library catalog, 1815, Library of Congress.

By the late 19th century, librarians at the Library of Congress were finding their classification system hopelessly outdated. Melvil Dewey appealed to Congress concerning the reorganization of its library. He wanted it to be expanded into a national library serving as a center point to which other libraries could refer. LC staff extensively studied the Dewey Decimal Classification as the basis for an enlarged classification and engaged in long discussions with Dewey himself. They came to the conclusion that DDC was inappropriate for the Library of Congress because the collection was so large that many single DDC numbers would represent complete floors of books in LC.

LC then turned to Cutter's Expansive Classification, using his principles, but building its own classification scheme. The outline of the scheme was drawn up by Herbert Putnam (1861–1955, right) in 1897. The scheme was arbitrary and one of convenience, depending on the number of subtopics on a given topic. A logical progression from level to level of specificity was established. There were no rational shortcuts such as those found in the DDC. The scheme did not conform to the theoretical rules for classification and was designed for LC's particular needs. It was considered too detailed and complex for use in any but the largest libraries.

LCC schedules were published in pieces. Although Class Z had been the first schedule developed, it was the second schedule published (1904). The first schedule published was E–F in 1901. By June 1904, classes D, M, Q, R, S, T, and U had been completed. By 1948 all schedules except K were available.

The tedium of reclassification

5

The new classification scheme developed by LC for its collection meant that the whole collection had to be reclassified. This problem was also faced early in the 20th century by growing colleges and universities where whole libraries had to be better organized and arranged. In many cases the libraries had to be recataloged and new classification schemes employed. This was particularly urgent for those libraries purchasing the new catalog cards being sold by the Library of Congress. If a library wished to take full advantage of the savings presented by this purchase, it needed to switch its classification to LCC, because each card provided an LCC number. Dewey classification numbers were not included in these early days.

During my long career I have experienced reclassification in three libraries. There was a disastrous fire in 1890 in the University of Toronto Library and the collection had to be rebuilt. Hugh Hornby Langton, the chief librarian from 1892 to 1923, designed a classification system that, as far as I know, was not used 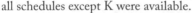 elsewhere. In the mid-1950s the library decided to discard Langton's scheme and adopt LCC. As I was hired as a bibliographer, I did not have direct involvement in the reclassification of the collection, but I well remember the fence placed in the stacks that separated the recataloged and the still-to-be-cataloged sections of the collection in order to control the possibility that someone would take a book from the uncataloged area and house it among the cataloged books.

A decade later I was directly involved in my second experience with reclassification. The Ontario Institute of Education Library wished to change its classification from the LCC to DDC because Ontario school libraries were classified by Dewey and it was thought that people using the institute's library would be confused by this strange LCC system. A library clerk would take a book from the shelf, remove the appropriate catalog cards from the public catalog and from the shelflist drawers in the work room, put them in the book, which she would then place on my desk. I assigned the new Dewey number and call letters and gave the book to the clerk, who would then proceed to "white out" the old call number, type the new number on all cards, and apply a new label to the book's spine. At the end of the day she would file the cards she had finished that day into the public catalog and shelflist drawers—always placing them above the rod. First thing next morning I would check the catalog drawers to ensure that the cards were filed correctly, then lower the cards into their proper places. Doesn't this description make you feel tired?

The third involvement happened in the 1970s when I was faced with recataloging the materials in all the school libraries in a suburb of Toronto. I came to the firm conclusion that nonbook materials needed to be housed on open shelving easily available to students. Some studies conducted by my colleagues and me convinced us that these materials were better used when they stood on the shelves with books on the same subject. This involved assigning DDC to a variety of media and sometimes required a new way of judging appropriate classification.

SOURCE: Jean Weihs, "A Brief History of Classification," *Technicalities* 30, no. 1 (January/February 2010): 14–16; (March/April 2010): 16–19; (May/June 2010): 15–18; (July/August 2010):

REFERENCE

Online reference service

by Carolyn M. Mulac

ONCE UPON A TIME the telephone was a new technology, and its introduction into reference services caused considerable discussion. When any new form of technology or new type of service is introduced in a library, the discussion usually includes questions such as "How will the staff be trained?" "Who will be eligible for this service?" "What are the limits of this service?" "Who will provide this service?" Online reference service, like reference service by telephone, extends reference service beyond the walls of the library's building. What is online reference service? Joan M. Reitz, who refers to it as "digital reference," defines it as

> reference services requested and provided over the internet, usually via email, instant messaging ("chat"), or web-based submission forms, usually answered by librarians in the reference department of a library. . . . Synonymous with *chat reference, e-reference, online reference,* and *virtual reference.*

The ALA Reference and User Services Association *Guidelines for Implementing and Maintaining Virtual Reference Services* includes this definition:

> Virtual reference is reference service initiated electronically where patrons employ computers or other technology to communicate with public services staff without being physically present. Communication channels used frequently in virtual reference include chat, videoconferencing, Voice-over-IP, cobrowsing, email, and instant messaging. (2.1)

So instead of asking a question in person at the library or on the telephone, the patron is usually somewhere else (but sometimes actually in the library) using some form of electronic communication. As you might imagine, these methods of communication have their own particular challenges as well as benefits when used to provide reference service.

I'd like to focus on the three most widely used forms of online reference: email, chat, and instant messaging (IM).

Email reference

Email reference is a service that has been offered by most libraries since the 1990s. Using a form on a library's website, a patron submits a question and an email address to which the response can be sent. Other details such as the patron's location, reason for the question (school assignment, personal interest, etc.), and sources already consulted are often requested on the form as well. An example of an email reference form can be found at www.ipl. org/div/askus/. This form has been carefully constructed to elicit as much information as possible from the patron (as in any good reference interview), and even explains why each bit of information is requested. For example, opposite the part of the form that asks "How will you use this information?" there is the explanation that "Understanding the context and scope of your information needs helps us to deliver an answer that you will find useful." Opposite "Sources already consulted" on the form is the comment that "Knowing where you've already looked will help us keep from sending you someplace you've already been." By now it should be obvious that asking such questions on an email request form takes the place of the "listening/inquiring" phase of the reference interview. The RUSA *Guidelines for Behavioral Performance of Reference and Information Services Providers* identify the five components of a successful reference transaction: approachability, interest, listening/inquiring, searching, and follow-up. They also expand each of these elements to include the remote forms of reference service (telephone, email, chat):

> Under "approachability" we find: "Should provide prominent, jargon-free links to all forms of reference service from the *home page* of the library's website, and throughout the site wherever research assistance may be sought out. The web should be used to make reference services easy to find and convenient." (1.8)

So that email request form should be as easy to locate as it is to use. To indicate "interest," the librarian "acknowledges user email questions in a timely manner" (2.7). An automatic message is often generated, such as "your request has been received and you will receive a response in [fill in the blank]." The "listening/inquiring" stage, as we've seen in the description of the Internet Public Library's email reference form, is carried out by the use of such a form (3.10). As for "searching," the recommendation is that the librarian "uses appropriate technology to help guide patrons through library resources when possible" (4.11). In the case of email reference, this might include providing links to sources or describing how such sources (say, a database) can be used. Finally, when it's time for the "follow-up" the librarian "suggests that the patrons visit or call the library when appropriate" (5.9). Sometimes the information requested cannot be relayed by email, and the patron will have to visit the library in person.

Some of the benefits of email reference are:

1. The patron can ask the question when it comes to mind (and a computer is available) and not have to deal with busy signals or stand in line.
2. The librarian can work on an email request at a more deliberate pace than what is possible with a queue of callers on the phone or in front of the reference desk.
3. The patron will have a written record of the answer (if he or she chooses to print it out) and won't have to decipher a hastily scribbled note made while calling or search for the call slip or printout handed out at the reference desk.
4. The librarian doesn't have to decipher an unfamiliar accent, listen to background noise, or keep an eye out for the next person in line.

Some of the challenges of providing email reference service are:

1. The patron sending the question may not be able to formulate a question clearly in writing.
2. The librarian may receive email requests that constitute research rather than reference questions.
3. The patron's own email service provider may block out the library's email response, or, if the response is received, the patron might accidentally delete it.
4. The librarian may have to send an additional email (or even two) to clarify what the patron (see no. 1) really needs.

Practitioners will tell you that email reference does indeed, as Karen G. Schneider puts it, require "a relatively small commitment of time and labor." In my experience in a public library, the majority of email requests received concern library policies and resources, local information, and death notices and obituaries, all of which can be easily and quickly located. The frequent thank-you messages sent by "e-patrons" bears out the impression that our answers, no matter how "easily and quickly located," are appreciated.

Chat reference

You might say that chat reference is to email reference what a telephone call is to a voice mail message. Chat, like a telephone call, is in real time. There is a person at the other end, and instead of talking to the librarian, she is typing. Unlike email reference, which, like a voice mail message, is static (the message is either written or a voice recording), chat is dynamic, with the give and take of a conversation. Chat requires the use of some special software, and once that is installed all that's left to do is train the staff and establish the hours of service.

As with email reference, chat reference has benefits and challenges. Some of the benefits of chat reference are:

1. Chat software programs offer transcripts of transactions, offering the patron a record of the information or website addresses provided. These transcripts can also be used for training purposes in the library.
2. Chat reference provides service at the time and place of need.
3. Chat reference allows patrons to ask questions they may feel uncomfortable posing in person.
4. Chat reference service can offer a teachable moment when the librarian is able to push a web page to the patron or cobrowse with them.

Some of the challenges of chat reference are:

1. A chat reference service needs to be answered live during the posted hours of service—there is no opportunity to let a question go to voice mail, or, in this case, email. The question will be lost if a response isn't made.
2. Practitioners report that there can be a variety of technical problems associated with chat software programs that can affect the service.
3. Fast, accurate typing is required of both patron and librarian for easily understood transactions.
4. As sometimes happens in telephone reference, patrons often disconnect in the middle of a reference transaction, leaving the librarian to wonder if it was a technical glitch or an unavoidable interruption at the other end.

Chat reference service has been offered by public and academic libraries for more than 10 years, and continues as another way to provide reference assistance (and sometimes instruction) to patrons.

IM reference

IM (instant messaging) uses free commercial networks, such as Yahoo! Messenger, MSN Instant Messenger, or Google Talk, and has been used for providing reference service for most of this decade. IM reference, or IMR, is a live service, like chat and telephone reference, and presents some of the same challenges in the reference interview. For example, there are no visual or nonverbal clues from either the librarian or the patron, only the words typed on the screen. As in chat, IM users often use a variety of abbreviations and shortcuts in what they type (LOL, BTW). Most professionals agree that the librarian should take cues from the patron in deciding how many of these shortcuts to use or how informal to be. The best course of action is to maintain some measure of decorum but, just as you might in an in-person encounter, use humor if appropriate.

IMR, like telephone, email, and chat reference, offers benefits and challenges. Some of the benefits of IMR are:

1. As its name indicates, IMR offers a patron instant access, no line to stand in, no busy signal to endure, or telephone tree to navigate.
2. Little staff training is needed, since the software used is not complicated.
3. IMR provides service at the time and point of need.
4. IMR allows patrons to ask questions they may feel uncomfortable posing in person.

Some of the challenges of IM reference are:

1. The absence of visual clues, like facial expressions, may make it difficult to determine if the patron understands the librarian's response.
2. Frequent updates may be needed, such as "I'm still looking" or "This may take a few minutes" to assure the patron that the librarian has not disconnected.
3. The nature of IM itself may lead patrons to expect an instantaneous, complete response before a reference interview can be conducted.
4. As sometimes happens in chat and telephone reference, patrons often

disconnect in the middle of a reference transaction, leaving the librarian to wonder if it was a technical glitch or an unavoidable interruption at the other end.

Whether the queries are coming in via email, chat, or IM, the goal is the same: to provide reference service. Offering reference service in a variety of formats allows us to reach patrons at their time and point of need and in the way in which they prefer to communicate. Once the technical aspects are dealt with, just remember that there is a *person* with a question at the other end and that goal will be reached.

SOURCE: Carolyn M. Mulac, *Fundamentals of Reference* (Chicago: American Library Association, 2012), 69–76.

Using LC subdivisions in reference

by Rebecca S. Kornegay, Heidi E. Buchanan, and Hildegard B. Morgan

LET'S START WITH A DEFINITION of subdivisions from Lois Chan in *Library of Congress Subject Headings: Principles and Application* (4th ed., 2005): "In the Library of Congress subject headings system, a main heading may be subdivided by one or more elements called *subdivisions*. . . . Subdivisions are used extensively to subarrange a large file or to bring out aspects of a topic." The first segment of a subject heading, called the main heading, tells what the book is about. The subdivisions follow the main heading, introduced by a dash, and add specificity. They tell which aspect of the main topic is treated; describe the format of the cataloged item; and, in some cases, state the geographic area or time period covered.

How subdivisions work

Detailed rules and specific definitions control the way subdivisions are assigned to a cataloged item. We'll use as an example the most common kind of rule, the "attached to" or "goes with" rule. Such rules tell which kind of main heading a particular subdivision may or may not be attached to. For example, a cataloger may not attach the subdivision —**Social life and customs** to the name of an individual. On the other hand, —**Social life and customs** does go with or may be attached to place names; —**Schooling** goes only with animals; —**Mood** is attached only to languages.

Those rules and definitions, based on scholarship, careful thought, and years of  fine work at the Library of Congress, are the foundation of the high-performance catalogs libraries are so proud of, yet reference librarians are unlikely to have the opportunity to learn them well. Guess what? They don't have to! In *Magic Search: Getting the Best Results from Your Catalog and Beyond* (2009), we tell you when rules are important and when you can ignore them, without having to consult the catalogers' best-kept secret, the *Subject Cataloging Manual: Subject Headings,* where all 3,500+ subdivisions are listed and defined. And we translate the definitions into front-of-the-house tools for searching so well that patrons will exclaim, "How did you find that?"

How can we be so nonchalant about the rules? Because in WorldCat and in most library catalogs, subdivisions perform beautifully in keyword searches, whether the searcher knows the rules or not. Keyword searches pull from all the subject headings assigned to a title. Here's an example of a keyword search that succeeds in spite of the "attached to" rule. **Shakespeare and social life and customs** finds:

> **Title:** Understanding Shakespeare's England
> **Subject headings:**
> Shakespeare, William, 1564–1616—Contemporary England
> England—Social life and customs—16th century
> England—Civilization—16th century

The conscientious cataloger, adhering to the rules, did not attach —**Social life and customs** to the main heading Shakespeare, but for the searcher it didn't matter. Shakespeare came from one subject heading; social life and customs from another. What did matter? That the searcher knew to use —**Social life and customs** in the first place. **Shakespeare and social life and customs** replaced the natural language inquiry, "How did people live and behave in Shakespeare's time?" and the search succeeded.

What knowledge must you bring to a search? Carefree keyword searching is the goal, but reality does intrude on occasion. Throughout our work, we tried to maintain a freewheeling search style and think like a "Googler." Usually it worked, but not always. So, when should a librarian bring out the tools of a professional searcher? And what does matter?

Precision matters. If the subdivision is singular, you'd better use the singular. If it's plural, use the plural. It's —**Influence,** not *influences,* —**Diaries** not *diary.*

Definitions matter. **Nurses—Attitudes** means how nurses feel about things, not the way people feel about nurses. If the precise definitions didn't matter, subdivisions would be useless.

Freewheeling searching means results will vary, so librarians must continue to use all of their professional search techniques. Keyword searches pull from more than just subdivisions, finding words from titles, contents notes, and more, so relevance may suffer. In some cases, educated browsing of subdivisions and their corresponding main headings works better than keyword searching, so we may caution you to browse display lists of subject headings and to choose the appropriate subdivision from the list. Finally, a keyword search on a subdivision that is a common word, like **History,** can lead to too many hits, so we suggest you perform a keyword-in-subject search.

In addition, librarians must know how their catalogs work:

- Does your library catalog allow keyword-in-subject searching? (Look for the advanced search option.)
- In a subject search, can you type in a main heading and then browse the accompanying subdivisions?
- Does a subject search in your catalog search each segment of the subject headings? This means that you can type a subdivision into the subject search box, without specifying a main heading.

Subdivisions at work

A few years ago some predicted that controlled vocabulary would go the way of the dodo. In fact, libraries are reaffirming the value of the Library of Congress subject heading system; catalogs and databases display controlled vocabulary more prominently than before; WorldCat is now freely available to the public; and a most unlikely player, Google, has bought into the system. These changes make searching with subdivisions relevant in settings old and new, large and small, local and international.

Facet-based searching. Library catalogs with faceted search capabilities alert the searcher to options that are available for any search at any time. These catalogs, often referred to as discovery tools, recommend that the searcher refocus the initial search by selecting from a list of system-suggested subjects, which include Library of Congress subdivisions. The searcher who knows subdivisions will be in a position to make good choices.

WorldCat. The OCLC database WorldCat.org is now available free of charge to everyone. WorldCat has millions and millions of records for 1.2 billion items— books, CDs, DVDs, websites—and most of those records include Library of Congress subject headings, complete with subdivisions. WorldCat searchers who replace the guesswork of natural language with the precision of subdivisions will find what they really want—even in this gargantuan wonder.

Google Book Search. An unexpected and exciting development for using subdivisions came via an OCLC news release. On May 19, 2008, OCLC announced an agreement with Google: "Under terms of the agreement, OCLC member libraries participating in the Google Book Search program, which makes the full text of more than one million books searchable, may share their World-Cat-derived MARC records with Google to better facilitate discovery of library collections through Google."

What does this mean for the subdivision savvy? Google Book Search users can now rely on library-style subject access to more than a million freely available full-text books—the best of both worlds!

SOURCE: Rebecca S. Kornegay, Heidi E. Buchanan, and Hildegard B. Morgan, *Magic Search: Getting the Best Results from Your Catalog and Beyond* (Chicago: American Library Association, 2009), v–ix.

Paraprofessionals at the reference desk
by Pamela J. Morgan

AS NEW LIBRARY SERVICES are added and old ones revamped, librarians must consider alternative staffing models. One model that is widely used is to utilize paraprofessionals (support staff, aides, associates, technicians) to assist with reference service, freeing professional librarians for other duties.

Arguments for using paraprofessionals

Redirect professional expertise. Even prior to the internet, both articles and presentations in the library science field indicated that many of the transactions at the reference desk did not require professional attention. A 1985 study estimated that as many as 80% of the questions asked at reference desks did not require professional attention. With the advent of internet search engines, the number of queries requiring professional attention further declined, especially ready reference questions—those that request brief, factual information that can be quickly answered utilizing one or two sources. What has increased is the complexity of reference queries. Patrons turn to the reference librarian after they feel they have exhausted their options, and these complex questions require a lengthier, one-on-one consultation.

These complex questions require careful thought in order to construct search strategies and research plans. With the reference desk serving as the place for directional questions and requests for computer and printing help, there is some question as to whether it is the appropriate location to handle such queries; a suggested alternative is a private office or consultation space. Carefully trained paraprofessionals could staff the reference desk to handle routine questions and tasks, freeing professional librarians for other duties and proper attention to more multifaceted queries.

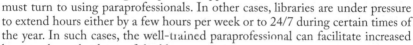

Cost savings. Sadly, many libraries are faced with stagnant or declining operating budgets and must explore new staffing models or cost savings. With ready reference decreasing, it might prove more cost-effective to hire paraprofessionals to staff the reference desk. Many libraries wish to hire professionals but simply cannot, due to a shortage of qualified applicants; these libraries must turn to using paraprofessionals. In other cases, libraries are under pressure to extend hours either by a few hours per week or to 24/7 during certain times of the year. In such cases, the well-trained paraprofessional can facilitate increased hours or keep the doors of the library open.

Combined service points. Due to shifting patterns in library use (reference transactions are in decline, patrons' greater use of self-check machines, etc.), many libraries are moving toward consolidating service points. A library's decision to combine service points is likely to result in paraprofessionals working alongside reference librarians to provide assistance with technology, circulation, interlibrary loan, and reserves. Regardless of what form the single service desk takes or why it exists, training is critical to the success of that service point. In order to maintain basic levels of service, staff at the combined service desk will need some form of cross-training. The paraprofessional's breadth and depth of reference expertise does not need to be that of the professional librarian, but some sort of competency should be required to maintain service levels. Cross-training benefits the patron in that there is a larger pool of staff available to answer a wide range of information questions.

Respond to changing patron needs. Many patrons expect different types of services and expertise from reference desks. One reason is the advent of computer workstations that provide access to a variety of tools: the library catalog and databases, word processing and spreadsheets, and communication software. Many users are often multitasking, searching for information as they create it. Patrons require help in a variety of areas and often do not distinguish between traditional library help and computer support; they might ask for in-depth assistance with spreadsheet formulas, complex headers and footers, uploading, downloading, transferring files, and digital imaging. A variety of expertise is needed. Paraprofessionals at a reference desk can help respond to the technology questions as well as answer basic reference questions. Their presence can also ensure that in-depth research questions are referred to professional librarians. Staff with a wide range of know-how at the reference desk ensure the following:

- Faster and more timely service (patrons are not shuttled between service points);
- Basic reference services and more hours;
- Efficient and flexible staffing solutions.

Arguments against using paraprofessionals

Value of professional education. Using paraprofessionals at reference desks is widespread. This has spawned the fear that the practice will devalue the library profession. The profession sends contradictory messages, "Come to the desk, where you'll be helped by professionals—experts in finding information." But we also say, "Well-trained paraprofessionals do a fine job at the reference desk. You won't be able to tell the difference between us." Another concern is that the practice robs patrons of the highest level of service to all library users. Ideally, paraprofessionals should be hired only to complement, not replace, professional librarians; unfortunately, this is not always the case. It is imperative that libraries that choose to use paraprofessionals at the reference desk provide adequate and ongoing training in order to maintain high service levels.

Inaccurate referrals. Some argue that paraprofessionals do not make referrals or do not realize when it is necessary to make a referral to a professional. There is concern that paraprofessionals feel, because they are asked, that they are required to provide assistance, even when it is not appropriate. The reluctance to refer patrons to a professional might also be a face-saving measure; staff fear appearing ignorant to the patron. In the case of cataloging and interlibrary loan work, the supervisor need not be immediately present to proof and correct. Reference service, however, is not always well suited to close supervision or correction. The immediate and individual nature of reference work makes it difficult to ensure that every question is answered correctly. If a professional librarian must be assigned to watch every transaction in which a paraprofessional is involved, no professional time has been gained. However, if the paraprofessional is allowed to answer questions without training, the quality of service may be lowered because of faulty reference interviewing, improper referrals, or incorrect answers.

Some libraries may choose to set up guidelines governing the use of paraprofessionals at reference desks. For example, policy may be written requiring that paraprofessionals always work with a librarian, or that the librarian receives all questions and then refers appropriate questions to the paraprofessional. Paraprofessionals may be allowed to answer only directional, ready reference, and "known item" queries, or they may be asked to get a patron started and then confer with a librarian to determine if the complete, correct answer was given.

Time to train and supervise. The decision not to use a paraprofessional might arise from a cost-benefit analysis. Is it worth the professional time to provide ongoing training and supervision? There is the issue of staff turnover; paraprofessionals, who may take a library position only until they can obtain higher-level jobs or work in the subject fields, may not remain long enough to justify their training. High turnover can greatly increase the time spent in the hiring and training process. In libraries where the paraprofessional staff is small and has a low rate of turnover, the hiring and training of paraprofessionals will be infrequent and less time-consuming. In libraries with larger staffs and high turnover, one librarian may need to devote some or all of his or her time to training and supervising paraprofessionals. Libraries with small staff and high turnover may need to have stricter guidelines about what paraprofessionals may answer.

Making the decision

Despite the arguments against the practice, many libraries realize that using paraprofessionals is an effective way of maximizing their services and better utilizing professional staff. Each library must make its own conclusions about using paraprofessionals at its reference desk. It can be helpful to ask the following questions when making the decision:

- How important is contact between a professional librarian and the public at the reference desk? Are there better places and methods for professional librarians to connect with patrons?
- What is the best way to ensure that a paraprofessional is capable of the reference interview?
- Are professionals wasting time answering directional and ready reference questions?
- Would the use of paraprofessionals inhibit patrons from asking for assistance because they feel support staff is incapable of answering a question?

Concerns about proper referrals and lack of familiarity with reference sources can be overcome if the library hires carefully, sets clear expectations for service provided by paraprofessionals, and follows up with thorough and ongoing training. It is important to realize, however, that these tasks require a considerable amount of planning and effort from the library's professional staff. The library must decide whether the benefits—realizing cost savings, adding new services, increasing hours, freeing its professional staff for other work, or some combination—are worth the professional time commitment to plan, train, and supervise the paraprofessional. Each library must also decide what type and level of questions are appropriate for paraprofessionals to answer and how much education the position should require. The question is usually not whether to use paraprofessionals at the reference desk, but how to use them.

Paraprofessionals cannot simply be given a manual and turned loose on the service desk. They need carefully planned training by professionals to orient them to the library, familiarize them with library philosophy, policies, and procedures, and guide them in using reference resources, answering questions, and making referrals. Only when this has occurred can libraries uphold the Code of Ethics of the American Library Association, which calls for "the highest level of service to all library users . . . and accurate, unbiased, and courteous responses to all requests."

SOURCE: Pamela J. Morgan, *Training Paraprofessionals for Reference Service,* 2nd ed. (New York: Neal-Schuman Publishers, 2009), 3–7.

Rethinking restroom questions
by Lorraine J. Pellack

EVERY LIBRARY THAT I HAVE WORKED IN over the last 20+ years has had at least one staff member grumbling about how often they have to give directions to the restroom. They grumble about patrons who need lessons in reading signs and architects who evilly plan library buildings with invisible restrooms or restrooms far from the entrance. My question is this: Why grumble? This is our chance to shine, to invite people in. While it's true that any trained monkey could point in the correct direction, I would like to believe that human beings aspire to be a bit more helpful than this. In the current economy, with declining numbers of reference transactions and dwindling budgets, every patron encounter is important. These are not just people in need; every one of them has potential. They are potential Nobel Prize winners, potential legislators, potential parents of eager readers, potential library enthusiasts, children with future academic potential—and maybe even future library supporters.

How to help students with assignments

Even if students have selected an appropriate resource, they often have difficulty constructing an effective search strategy. They may find too few or too many sources or fail to find sources that are relevant to their topic. This sidebar outlines some basic strategies faculty can suggest for overcoming some of the more commonly experienced problems.

Terms are too specific. Try alternative terms and ways of saying the same thing (capital punishment, death penalty). Be aware that some terms change over time or with context. *Example:* Blacks (1960s), African Americans (today).

Incorrect spelling or typing. Always check for misspellings and typographical errors. Alert students that some words have multiple spellings. *Example:* Brazil = Brasil.

Inappropriate resource. Suggest using a general resource to broaden a search or browse for ideas. Recommend a subject-specific resource to help students quickly focus on more relevant source materials.

Too broad or too narrow a topic or strategy. Suggest narrowing or broadening the search using different terms or limits. *Examples:* Subject vs. keyword searches; search restricted to peer-reviewed publications.

Unclear or unstated perspective. Emphasize the importance of clearly identifying the perspective from which a topic will be explored. *Example:* Teacher vs. student views of dress codes.

Use of noise words. Words like "of" and "what"—words that don't carry content—should generally not be included in a search unless they are part of a specific phrase. *Example:* History Paris; *A Tale of Two Cities*.

The following are just a few of the many ways in which librarians can help students optimize the time they spend working on assignments in the library.

Do

Be patient and listen carefully.

Ask to see a copy of the assignment.

Work with students to develop a list of resources, terms, and strategies that might be relevant to their topic.

Contact faculty members with questions and observations about their assignments.

Share a copy of each assignment with other librarians.

Generate a list of courses and professors likely to require research and contact them about scheduling library instruction and discussing their assignments before they are distributed.

Don't

Do not assume that students can clearly articulate their needs.

Do not expect students to know what they need or want.

Do not assume students know how to access library resources and construct effective search strategies.

Do not neglect problems with assignments when they occur.

Do not expect that other librarians will always know how to deal with assignment problems.

Do not wait for questions and problems to arise; try to identify and address potential stumbling blocks in advance.

SOURCE: Monty L. McAdoo, *Building Bridges: Connecting Faculty, Students, and the College Library* (Chicago: American Library Association, 2010), 127, 131.

Put yourself on the other side of the desk and rethink *why* someone might be asking a particular question. In the case of questions such as "where's the restroom?" most likely the person has never been in the building before. Yes, you've answered the question a bazillion times, but most people only ask the question on their *first* visit. Despite many efforts to the contrary, we are still fighting librarian stereotypes of cantankerous old ladies who shush people. Here is a golden opportunity to make a positive first impression, be welcoming, and influence a new person about the helpfulness of library staff. These interactions, in turn, affect the eagerness of visitors to return in the future.

Patrons frequently ask for directions even when the person they are asking is standing right next to a sign that gives the answer. Clearly, some people prefer to ask a human being rather than take the time to read building signs. Habits of people in a new environment often include asking directional questions first because they are less threatening. If they do okay, and feel comfortable, they work their way up to more complicated questions later on. Directional questions may seem mundane, but they can be the first step toward answering future needs and instilling confidence in the person asking the question.

Have you ever noticed that patrons working at computers near public service desks often overhear conversations? If you watch, you will occasionally see a nearby person looking up and smiling after a joke someone made at the desk. They might even raise an eyebrow after being startled by a particular comment. Have you ever wondered if that person sitting near the desk is too shy, or too embarrassed, to ask a question? Could it be they asked a simple question in the past and were affronted by a less than enthusiastic staff member? Remember, all patrons are important—even ones that are just asking directional questions. They are the reason we are here.

Library desk staff regularly can and do affect visitors' first impressions. Try coming through the front door of your library and pretending you are a first-time visitor. Go visit a nearby library and see what reaction you get when you ask a few simple questions. Which library staffers make you feel at home and why? Do any of them annoy you enough to not ask questions in future? Why? Use this information to rethink how patrons may feel as they enter your library and have a question.

SOURCE: Lorraine J. Pellack, "First Impressions and Rethinking Restroom Questions," *RUSQ* 49, no. 1 (2009): 4–6.

Stupid reference questions

by Will Manley

WE KNOW THAT THE MACHINES in our libraries are getting smarter, but how about our patrons?

In the past when people would ask me if libraries have a future my response was always, "Yes, because patrons bring a never-ending stream of cluelessness to the reference desk. They need our help." I wonder if that still holds true. Judging from all the bright yellow books that are being written for dummies and the bright orange books that are being written for idiots, I have to assume that it is still true that the human race needs us to point them the way to wisdom, knowledge, and information. Has much changed since I retired in 2008?

When I was a working librarian, one of my favorite activities was writing down stupid reference questions. Remember David Letterman's "Stupid Pet Tricks" routine? Well, I developed a stupid reference question routine. Here are some of my favorites:

Patron: Does this library have any information on King Malcolm the Tenth?
Reference Librarian: You mean the king from the play *Macbeth*?
P: No I mean the civil rights leader.
RL: Oh, you mean Malcolm X.

P: I need to interview a schizophrenic. Can you refer me to one?
RL: Maybe you should see a psychiatrist.

P: Do you have a videotape of Abraham Lincoln giving the Gettysburg address?
RL: No, we don't.
P: You should get it. You have Bush on tape, and Lincoln was a greater president.
RL: Thanks for that historical analysis.

P: Do you have a good English translation of *Hamlet*?
RL: Yes, it's by a man named William Shakespeare . . . very close to the original.

P: Who invented the time machine?
RL: H. G. Wells.

P: I need information on the car BMW. How do you spell it?
RL: Go to the head of the class . . . you just did.

P: Why were so many Civil War battles fought in national parks?
RL: Trees provided great protection from bullets.

P: Do you have an audiotape of live dinosaur sounds?
RL: No, but you might want to try the zoo.

P: I need information on the woman named Rosetta Stone.
RL: Good luck. Let me know when you find it.

P: I need books on youth in Africa.
RL: You need books on young people in Africa?
P: No, I need books about killing old people and vegetables.
RL: Oh, you have the wrong continent. That's youth in Asia.

P: Is the correct term Swiss or Swedish?
RL: Yes.

P: I want to get the Gutenberg Bible on interlibrary loan.
RL: That depends. Will you pay the shipping costs?

P: Do you have a copy of the Jerusalem newspaper for the day Jesus was born?
RL: No, but it might be on microfiche.

P: I need a book on impudence.
RL: Can you be more specific?
P: My husband can't sustain an erection.

P: I need a cookbook for preparing dog food.
RL: You mean like Kibbles 'n Bits?
P: No for preparing a roast dachshund.

P: Is this library a government suppository?
RL: Sometimes it seems like it is.

P: I need all the books in this bibliography by the man named Ibid.
RL: You must be a rocket scientist.

SOURCE: Will Manley, "Are Patrons Getting Smarter?" Will Unwound, April 21, 2010, online at willmanley.com. Reprinted with permission.

USAGE

How Americans use online sources and their libraries
by the OCLC staff

5

AS AMERICANS BECOME more familiar, maybe even expert, with a wide range of online services, excitement with and overall impressions of information resources have declined. Information consumers are just less impressed with information sources in 2010 than they were in 2005.

Email (94%) and search engines (92%) still lead as the most widely used online resources, with usage rates for both services jumping up almost 30% when compared to our 2005 study results. Most use email and search engines daily. Half of Americans report using email alerts as a primary means of receiving news and information. Email and search engines have achieved near-ubiquitous status among online Americans, and social networking and social media are quickly catching up.

More than half of social networking users log on daily (55%), with 80% visiting at least once a week. While social media site use (YouTube, Flickr) led the use of social networking sites (MySpace, Facebook, and LinkedIn) in 2007, the distinction between social media and networking sites has quickly blurred. Social media users now log on to these sites less often than social networking users do—15% daily and 47% weekly—but more of the traditional social networking sites now offer media and content exchange as part of the service.

Social sites were used predominantly by teens (ages 14–17) and young adults (ages 18–24) in 2007 when OCLC released its *Sharing, Privacy, and Trust in Our Networked World* report. Since then, there has been triple-digit growth in the use of social sites among Americans age 25 and older. Americans ages 25–45 are now using social sites at rates similar to young adults, and even exceed teens in their use of social networking.

2010 survey results reveal that Americans who have experienced a negative job impact are using social networking sites at even higher rates than Americans not impacted (80% vs. 64%), and they are also more likely to use social media sites (71% vs. 66%).

Information searches

We asked information consumers in 2005 where they were most likely to start their search for information. 82% reported that they began their information search on a search engine, while 1% indicated that they started their search for information on a library website. When we surveyed information consumers in 2010, they were just as strongly tied to search engines as the starting point for information, with 84% beginning on a search engine. Not a single survey respondent began an information search on a library website.

While we did not inquire about the use of Wikipedia as a starting point for an information search in 2005, 3% of information seekers began their information searches on Wikipedia in 2010.

Although not the starting point for online information searches, library websites are used by a third of Americans. Use of the library website has remained relatively steady (33% in 2010 from 31% in 2005). Use of online databases has also held steady, at about 16% in both 2005 and 2010.

We surveyed information consumers about their overall impressions of search engines, libraries, and online libraries related to the availability of six types of information: educational materials, recreation and leisure materials, self-help materials, healthcare materials, financial and money management information, and job and career information. Search engines garnered the highest favorability ratings for each except for educational materials, where libraries and search engines nearly tie. Despite the higher ratings for search engines, information consumers recognized the critical role libraries play. Nearly half or more of Americans attribute favorable ratings related to the availability of self-help materials (57%), recreation and leisure materials (57%), and healthcare materials (48%) at the library. Two-fifths view the library as favorable for financial and money-management information (40%) and job and career information (38%).

Americans who experienced a negative job impact provide even higher favorability ratings for both search engines and libraries. Three-fourths view the library as favorable for educational materials (79%) and recreation and leisure materials (75%). More than half attribute favorable ratings to job and career information (51%), financial/money management information (51%), healthcare materials (60%), and self-help materials (68%) at the library. Search engines again were rated higher than libraries.

Ask-an-expert sites

One of the most significant changes noted from the 2005 study was the marked increase in the use of online reference or "ask-an-expert" services. Ask-an-expert sites (question-and-answer sites) have experienced a tremendous increase in use, nearly tripling since 2005. Today, 43% of information consumers report using an ask-an-expert site, up from just 15% in 2005.

Young adults showed the largest growth in demand, with use up 350%. Today, 40% of teens are monthly users of online "ask-an-expert" services.

Respondents indicated that they used online librarian question sites "as needed," but the popularity of ask-a-librarian sites has not seen the same spike in use as ask-an-expert sites. In fact, ask-a-librarian sites have increased only slightly since 2005 (5% to 7%) and remain relatively unused or undiscovered. Availability of ask-a-librarian sites has increased since 2005, with an estimated 58% of libraries now providing such services.

Wikipedia, Skype, and Twitter

Wikipedia is now used by 73% of Americans, with half of these users visiting the site at least once a month. This usage rate rivals both search engines and social sites, making Wikipedia an information staple for online Americans.

We asked about the use of two new social services that did not exist when we polled users in 2005: Skype and Twitter. Per Wikipedia, Skype is a software application that allows users to make voice and video calls over the internet. In 2010, two in ten Americans (20%) indicated in our survey that they had used Skype. A recent version of the Skype software offers linking to Facebook.

Per Wikipedia, Twitter is a social networking and microblogging service that enables its users to send and read messages called "tweets," text-based posts of up to 140 characters that can be displayed on a user's profile page. It launched in 2006. In 2010, two in 10 Americans we surveyed (18%) had used Twitter.

Reading

The most popular activities among library users continue to be borrowing books and leisure reading. Two-fifths of these Americans go to the library at least annually for leisure reading (45%). Books continue to hold the top spot with 28% of Americans borrowing them monthly and 59% borrowing at least once a year.

A significant number of Americans are borrowing books even more often—a 23% bump in monthly borrowers and 11% increase in annual borrowers. Two in 10 Americans also come to the library annually to read magazines (27%) and newspapers (19%).

Beyond reading, borrowing DVDs and videos also increased. A third of Americans (36%) borrow DVDs and videos annually. A quarter of Americans use technology provided by the library, such as computers (27%) and the internet (28%), at least once a year.

Library services are used even more by Americans impacted by the recession. Americans impacted by job loss are using the library at greater rates and are using a full range of library services, in addition to reading. Twice as many economically impacted Americans regularly borrow DVDs and videos (20% vs. 11% monthly). More than a third of economically impacted Americans use the computers (35%) and access the internet for free (35%) annually at the library.

Research activity is down. Fewer Americans report conducting research activities at the library compared to five years ago. While over a third of Americans continue to conduct research at the library at least once a year, use of library research services has declined.

Use of reference books is down 21% from 2005, now at 38%. Fewer Americans are asking for assistance with research at the library; 28% of users ask for help annually compared to 39% annually in 2005, a decrease of 28%.

Impressions decline

Americans are just not as impressed with their information resources as they were in 2005. While almost all information resources saw marked increases in use over 2005, favorability ratings of both online and offline information resources have declined since 2005. Favorable ratings have declined for search engines, physical libraries, online bookstores, and physical bookstores.

Our findings suggest that as online resources become more commonplace, the shine has likely dulled. Information consumers are also likely to increase their expectations of all online resources as more features are added and new and more alternatives are introduced. And finally, the impact of the struggling U.S. economic environment is likely another factor lowering overall optimism and favorability.

Information consumers surveyed in 2005 accurately predicted future library use. The majority (61%) predicted that their use would remain steady in the next three to five years. The 2010 survey results reveal that half of users (52%) indicated their library use had remained the same in the previous year. Almost a quarter of 2005 respondents thought they would increase their library use; indeed, a similar proportion of 2010 information consumers reported growth (27%).

Top reasons cited for increases in library use are:

- to save money (borrowing instead of purchasing) (75%);
- my children enjoy visiting the library (27%);
- homework or school demands (25%);
- more available time (25%).

Information consumers also accurately predicted decreases in library use. 18% of Americans predicted that their library use would decline, and 21% of the 2010 respondents reported a drop in library use.

The top reasons for decreased library use include:

- less available time (33%);
- no need since leaving school/college (28%);
- unable to get to library because homebound or disabled (20%);
- prefer to purchase materials (16%);
- library has an outdated collection (13%).

SOURCE: *Perceptions of Libraries, 2010: Context and Community, a Report to the OCLC Membership* (Dublin, Ohio: OCLC, 2011), 30–37. Reprinted with permission.

Got signs?

by June Paynter

BACK IN TIMES NOW LONG GONE, the primary sign in most libraries seemed to be a seldom-followed warning that prohibited any kind of conversation. Despite the failure of many of these signs to accomplish their desired end, signs in libraries remain vitally important.

Good signs can make visitors to your library feel at home—and empowered.

We live in a self-service culture, and people are often more comfortable when they can take care of things themselves, should they wish. Where should they look if they want to find a book on divorce, grief, or sexuality? Where should they look if they want to explore a biography of an unusual someone who is personally important to them? Good signs can take the mystery out of your collection.

COMPUTERS Second Floor

Take a critical look at your library's signs. Do they support visitor self-sufficiency? Can people find their own way to the most common answers? Can they readily find materials without asking for help? If your answer to all of these questions is "yes," then congratulations. Your library signs are doing their job.

However, when you look closely at your library, do you see dog-eared, handwritten signs taped to doors and machines? Are there ragged paper notes glued on shelving or pinned anywhere there was once a bare spot? Do your computer-generated signs display a dizzying array of bizarre and decorative fonts? Is your library missing markers providing needed information on how your materials are arranged or grouped? If so, improvements should be made.

Sign experts suggest a brief user survey to supplement your own observations and reveal some of the needs. The survey need not be complicated. You could create a simple sheet like this for library visitors to complete and leave behind:

How many times do you visit the library per month? **1–2 3–10 11–20 20+**
Which are you? **Adult Child Teen**
Which are you? **Female Male**
Which are you? **Member Visitor**
Do you sometimes need help to find what you're looking for? **Yes No**
Are there enough signs so that you can easily find what you need? **Yes No**
Without asking a library worker, can you readily find any audio or video materials that you want to borrow? **Yes No**
Can you find the children's materials in the library? **Yes No**
Is it easy to see what hours the library is open? **Yes No**
Are there signs that you think the library should add? **If so, please list them.**

In addition to what the survey tells you, keep track of questions you are frequently asked. These may reveal signage opportunities.

Before developing a new and improved signage plan, create an inventory of your current signs. Make a complete list: location, text, size, material, color/font, priority, type (see below), and status (keep or replace). To aid in planning, you might even want to print out digital photos of each of your signs.

Classify your existing signs by type. Here are five common categories:

Directional (or arrow) signs tell visitors where to go. These are especially important if your library has hidden areas, turns, different levels, or different rooms.

Identification signs let people know when they have entered a major area of your collection, such as fiction, children's books, DVDs, or reference materials.

The Fallbrook branch of the San Diego County (Calif.) Public Library lets everyone know what it is.

Instructional signs provide "how to" help for visitors, walking people through use of your online catalog, internet connection, or your Dewey Decimal classifications.

Regulation signs tell visitors what is permitted or prohibited. Ideally, these should use a positive tone, even when discussing prohibitions. For example, in place of the usual "Quiet" sign, you might say, "Please respect the needs of others reading in this area."

Current awareness signs are changeable signs for upcoming events, special programs, and other time-sensitive announcements. These are often computer-produced and displayed in professional sign holders or on changeable message signboards.

When your building was constructed, many of the major sign choices may have been made with care by the architect or designer but probably with little regard for the specific needs of library patrons.

As a librarian, you might want to be more creative in your use of signs than an architect might, but remember that even smaller, nonarchitectural signs represent an investment of time and money. You should plan carefully before ordering or creating your signs. Remember, also, that there is a balance between adequate signage and visual clutter. Here are some factors to consider:

Size. One-inch letters can be seen up to 24 feet. Four-inch letters can be seen up to 150 feet. Six-inch letters can be seen up to 200 feet.

Color. White type on a dark background gives the best visibility. Black letters, if used, should be on a white or very light background.

Font. Helvetica or a similar sans serif face provides maximum clarity. Designer styles can add playfulness or pizzazz to special areas but should be used *very* sparingly.

Color coding. In a large space, color coding your signs can help identify particular areas in your collection. Spine labels can use the same color.

Given your own desire to welcome as many people as possible to your library, you should probably pay attention to Americans with Disabilities Act guidelines in developing your signs. These guidelines, which seek to make facilities as accommodating as possible for people with disabilities, are mandatory for public spaces and optional for private facilities.

In lay terms, here are the primary guidelines as they apply to signs. Many of the guidelines are helpful to people without disabilities as well:

- Characters must be raised 1/32 of an inch.
- Characters must be upper case and either sans serif or simple serif.
- Characters must be accompanied by Grade 2 Braille.
- Raised letters must be a minimum of 5/8 of an inch and a maximum of 2 inches in height.
- If you use a pictogram with an equivalent written description, the written description must be placed directly below the pictogram.
- Pictograms can be raised 1/32 of an inch, but they are not required to be raised.
- The characters and background of all signs must have an eggshell, matte, or other non-glare finish.
- Characters must have at least 70% contrast with the background (light on dark or dark on light).
- Signs near a door must be mounted on the wall adjacent to the latch side of the door.
- Signs near a door must be mounted so that a person can approach within 3 inches of the sign and still avoid the door swing and any protruding objects.
- The center line of all signs should be 60 inches from the floor.

Once you've done your inventory and gathered some ideas from a survey and from your own observations, make a list of the signs you want to add or replace. If you are pleased with a previous sign supplier, contact that supplier for a quote on the additional signs you'll need. (If money is tight, you may need to purchase a few at a time.)

If you decide to replace most or all of your signs, consider consulting a sign professional. Signs in a library make a subtle but powerful statement. The choice of materials, type styles, sign frames, and colors used can make a big difference in your library's appeal and appearance.

Many sign companies offer websites showing huge varieties of signs and appropriate uses. Some will make complimentary visits and recommendations. Catalog companies will supply free samples as you try to decide the best materials to use.

Make it a point to look at signs in retail, bookstore, and other establishments to get ideas of what you like. Remember that consistency in some of the common elements gives a more planned look.

Of course, a signage plan is never done. So now and then follow the oldest library sign of all—"Quiet"—and in that quiet, listen carefully for clues about any changes or additions that may be needed. Good luck!

SOURCE: June Paynter, "Got Signs?" *Congregational Libraries Today,* July/August 2008, pp. 1–3. Reprinted with permission.

Programming on a shoestring
by Colleen Leddy

HERE'S SOME ADVICE that works for us in planning successful low-cost programs for our tiny library (Stair Public Library in Morenci, Michigan).

- **Keep your ears and eyes open** to program ideas, especially on discussion lists. I found out about "Ultimate Cheapskate" author Jeff Yeager when a librarian in California raved about him on the ALA Public Programs Forum list.
- **Apply for grants** that you stand a chance of getting and that don't require a lot of time to write. Lobby your state humanities council to offer a quick grant program if they don't already have one.
- **Don't be afraid to ask** anyone you'd like to host, even if they're famous.
- **Use what you've got.** We're lucky. We have a former director with amazing culinary skills, but you probably have someone similar in your community. Find her.
- **If you can't get what you want,** find the next best thing. Hosting an author in person is great, but speakerphone chats are pretty wonderful, too. Skype, of course, would be even better.
- **Convey your enthusiasm** in requests, but be genuine.
- **Be selfish.** Don't hesitate to plan programs that intrigue and interest you personally. At the same time you're striving to appeal to the interests of a wide variety of your community members, you're also being a little self-centered: Planning a program is like planning a party, and you're running the show. It's special and fun; you want to offer your guests a good time, and you're thinking about what they might like. But you're also cooking up foods *you* enjoy, and decorating to please *your* tastes—and your guests are going to love it. So, don't hesitate to pursue program ideas for which you

Author Elizabeth Berg reduced her fee in return for sticky toffee pudding and other delicacies.

5

have a lot of excitement and enthusiasm. It will bubble over to others.
- **Provide food!** In addition to a meal we provided one author, we served refreshments to the audience afterwards. Find a way to provide good and special refreshments that make it worth a person's while to attend the event. Literally, leave them with a good taste in their mouths.

Low-cost programming ideas

Enthusiasm and ingenuity can result in a wonderful program on a shoestring budget. Programs we've hosted include these no-cost, very-low-cost, or can-be-modified-to-be-very-low-cost ideas:

- **Book discussion group:** Interloan books (choose titles that are not currently in high demand); meet monthly; rotate discussion leaders or seek out volunteers.
- **Speakerphone chats:** Find authors on their websites, Facebook, your state Center for the Book, or the Book Club Cookbook (www.bookclubcookbook.com). You only need a speakerphone (print a headshot of the author to put in plastic display frame near phone) or Skype.
- **"Talk @ Two" discussion group:** Meets every Thursday afternoon at 2 to discuss issues, from local to international, from abortion to religion.
- **Art exhibits from schools:** Partner with art teachers at local schools to create art that relates to programs you are planning or just to showcase student talent. Teachers like that their students' work gets a different audience; parents come to the library to see the work and attend related programs. Use tops of bookshelves and any wall space (you can attach lightweight art with blue painter's tape).
- **Human Library** (humanlibrary.org): Get sponsors for shirts, donations for refreshments.
- **Magnetic Poetry Jam/Slam:** Buy magnetic poetry sets, allow time for patrons to come up with poems, and then recite them.
- **How-to programs:** make a fruit cascade, knit; give people what they want to know or what you are excited about.
- **Fantasy Village:** Create cardboard gingerbread houses in advance and ask the community to donate stale crackers, cereal, pretzels, old Halloween candy, etc. Spread royal icing on the houses and decorate with donated items.
- **Ask a Lawyer, Ask a Financial Planner:** A professional gives an overview of what they offer, and patrons can ask any kind of questions. Strictly informational, no promotion or sales.

The community cleans out its cupboards to supply building materials for gingerbread houses.

Some long, fancy shoestring programs are worth every penny. If your budget doesn't allow for special programs, look for grants, ask for donations, or talk to your Friends group to sponsor them.

Not only does live entertainment inspire and enrich lives, but along with its intellectual and cultural value, it provides economic value to communities as well. People come from all over to hear the Paul Keller Jazz Trio and then go out to dinner at the Pizza Box afterward. Or maybe they'll see our town has a really cool theater and come back with the kids another day.

Stimulating special programs also offer a real sense of community for those attending. Participants linger over refreshments, neighbors visit with neighbors, and friends are made. Hosting an author on a topic such as the University of Michigan/Ohio State football rivalry brings in a whole new crowd; reaching out to all segments of the community keeps your library vibrant and relevant.

Inspiration

To find ideas and inspiration for programs, check out these websites:

- **Your state library.**
- **Your state humanities council.** If your state's council is weak, look at what other states offer. You'll find ideas galore.
- **The American Library Association Public Programs Office.** Subscribe to the pubprgrms and ppogrants lists.
- **Programming Librarian** (www.programminglibrarian.org). An incredible wealth of information on this site.
- **National Endowment for the Humanities** (www.neh.gov). We the People Bookshelf offers endless ideas for programs. The Picturing America grants are over, but see if a school or library near you (picturingamerica.neh.gov/public_awards.php) has a set you could borrow. We have an amazing art teacher at the high school who uses the Picturing America art posters to inspire her students to create art that we display.

5

Collaboration

- **Schools:** Make friends with teachers and administrators; promote programs for kids in the elementary school weekly newsletter.
- **Churches:** Ask to have programs mentioned in the church bulletin. (We limit requests to major programs of broad appeal.)
- **Local organizations:** Approach the Chamber of Commerce, Kiwanis and other service clubs, garden clubs, 4-H groups, or senior centers.

Planning pointers

- **Scheduling:** Contact schools about a date on which you are planning an event to avoid conflicts; you can check an online school calendar and confirm with the school secretary. Sports are hard to compete with, and major events that involve a wide range of ages such as band performances will really cut down on your audience.
- **Volunteers:** Approach Friends group, VolunTeens, and high school volunteer clubs; print a notice in the newspaper for whatever is needed; or offer sign-up sheets in the library.
- **Space issues:** Consider moving furniture around to create open space. Put furnishings on wheels or gliders to facilitate. Enlist teen volunteers to help set up before and clean up afterward. Have your local Department of Public Works move big items out temporarily. Borrow chairs if necessary.

It's worth seeking grants for some costlier programs, such as storyteller La'Ron Williams.

- **Sound system:** A small, cordless, portable one is nice, especially for older people with hearing problems.
- **Don't forget the little details:** Water for the speaker, extra toilet paper and paper towels in bathrooms, a table set up to sell books.
- **Flexibility:** Try to work in time to take advantage of programs that come up suddenly. Last-minute or close-to-event planning keeps things fresh and interesting. Plan too far in advance, and a million other things get scheduled on the event date that hadn't been on anybody's calendar when you did the planning.

Publicity and promotion

- **Use in-house signs** on doors, bulletin boards. Simple bookmarks created in-house on colored paper, four to a page, are easy to pass out in the library and local stores and schools. Hang simple posters around town. Place notices in school newsletters and in church bulletins. Give flyers for distribution to friendly businesses, especially pizzerias, hardware stores, laundromats—any high-traffic store. Ask local grocery stores to stuff flyers in bags.
- **Target your anticipated audience:** For whatever program you are hosting, consider who would enjoy it the most and reach out to that group. We get a class count list from the elementary school and count out the number of flyers needed for each classroom, labeled with teacher's name. For the senior center, we deliver bookmark flyers on the day they're having the best meal.
- **Make an email contact group** for media and email announcements, and make follow-up calls on important events.
- **Make contact groups** for the Friends group, patrons who regularly attend events, etc. Remind all groups a day or two before events.
- **Call regular patrons** the day of event to remind them to attend.
- **Place a banner** outside the library, if budget allows.
- **Post** on your website, Facebook, and Twitter.

Program enhancements

- **Refreshments**—serve good ones. Ask patrons or your Friends group for donations of baked goods, cut-up veggies, fruits. Have a wide variety of easy-to-eat finger foods: Offer good things so people linger and visit with each other while munching. Use cloth tablecloths and nice serving dishes.
- **Designate** a hearing-impaired section with reserved seats.
- **Treat the presenter** as an honored guest. Provide snacks or a meal and water at the podium, anticipate their needs, and sell their books.

There is a wide universe of program ideas out there. Consider what your community might like, but also follow your passions. Then watch that strategy result in interesting, innovative, creative programming that doesn't have to cost $5,000 a speaker.

SOURCE: Colleen Leddy, "Programming on a (Long, Colorful) Shoestring," Programming Librarian, May 2011, online at www.programminglibrarian.org/library/planning/programming-on-a-long-colorful-shoestring.html.

INTERLIBRARY LOAN

Interlibrary loans
by the ALA Library

AS DEFINED BY the Interlibrary Loan Code for the United States, "Interlibrary loan is the process by which a library requests material from, or supplies material to, another library. The purpose of interlibrary loan as defined by this code is to obtain, upon request of a library user, material not available in the user's local library."

Interlibrary loan in the United States

Libraries should follow the Interlibrary Loan Code for the United States, which was prepared by the ALA Reference and User Services Association's Interlibrary Loan Committee in 1994, revised in 2001, and revised again by the Sharing and Transforming Access to Resources Section of RUSA in 2008. The full text of the 2008 Interlibrary Loan Code for the United States statement appears online at ala.org/rusa/resources/guidelines/interlibrary.

The May 2008 Explanatory Supplement of the U.S. Interlibrary Loan Code also appears online at ala.org/rusa/resources/guidelines/interlibraryloancode.

Most state and regional library networks and consortia and state library agencies have interlibrary loan procedures, and libraries in their service areas should be familiar with these procedures.

Interlibrary loan form

Libraries normally transmit requests either electronically (through OCLC or other networks) or using ALA-approved interlibrary loan forms. The interlibrary loan form, sometimes called "the ALA form," can be accessed as a PDF file (ala.org/rusa/sites/ala.org.rusa/files/content/resources/guidelines/illformprint.pdf) as well as a Microsoft Word file (ala.org/rusa/files/resources/guidelines/illformprint.doc), which can be edited. The form can also be purchased in bulk from library supply houses. A list of directories of library product suppliers is available on ALA Library Fact Sheet 9, Library Products, Services, and Consultants.

Interlibrary loan information resources

For more information on interlibrary loan, you may want to consult the following.

Guidelines for Interlibrary Loan Operations Management (Chicago: Reference and Adult Services Association, 2012), online at ala.org/rusa/sites/ala.org.rusa/files/content/stars-guidelines-for-ILL.pdf.

Cherié L. Weible and Karen L. Janke, *Interlibrary Loan Practices Handbook*, 3rd ed. (Chicago: American Library Association, 2011).

Guidelines for Resource-Sharing Response to Natural and Man-made Disasters (Chicago: Reference and Adult Services Association, 2010), online at ala.org/rusa/sites/ala.org.rusa/files/content/resources/guidelines/disasterguidelines.pdf.

Emily Knox, *Document Delivery and Interlibrary Loan on a Shoestring* (New York: Neal-Schuman, 2010).

Valerie Horton and Bruce Smith, eds. *Moving Materials: Physical Delivery in Libraries* (Chicago: American Library Association, 2010).

Anne K. Beaubien. "ARL White Paper on Interlibrary Loan." (Washington, D.C.: Association of Research Libraries, June 2007), online at www.arl.org/bm~doc/ARL_white_paper_ILL_june07.pdf.

Leslie R. Morris, ed. *Interlibrary Loan Policies Directory,* 7th ed. (New York: Neal-Schuman, 2002).

Interlibrary loan in Canada

Loans to Canada are conducted on much the same basis as domestic loans, with slightly different mailing procedures (many Canadian libraries are part of OCLC or other networks).

For more information on ILL in Canada contact Library and Archives Canada, 395 Wellington Street, Ottawa, Ontario, Canada K1A 0N4; (613) 996-7527; illservicespeb@lac-bac.gc.ca (for general messages only). LAC ended its own ILL service in December 2012 (www.collectionscanada.gc.ca/ill/index-e.html).

International interlibrary borrowing

Any library may participate in international interlibrary loan activities. When seeking a loan from a library outside North America, follow the guidelines set forth by the Document Delivery and Resource Sharing Section of IFLA:

Guidelines for Best Practice in Interlibrary Loan and Document Delivery (The Hague, Neth.: International Federation of Library Associations and Institutions, October 15, 2007), online at www.ifla.org/files/docdel/documents/guidelines-best-practice-ill-dd-en.pdf. IFLA loan/photocopy request form, online at www.ifla.org/en/node/5402.

IFLA voucher scheme, a payment system for international interlibrary transactions, online at www.ifla.org/en/voucher-scheme. Do you have a question about document delivery and/or interlending? Send your question to the information coordinator for the IFLA Section on Document Delivery and Resource Sharing (gillet@inist.fr), who will either reply directly or refer your question to an appropriate person for response. While the service is intended particularly for questions related to IFLA documents and services, questions related to international document delivery and interlending are also welcome.

International Lending and Document Delivery: Principles and Guidelines for Procedure (The Hague, Neth: International Federation of Library Associations and Institutions, 2001), online at www.ifla.org/files/docdel/documents/international-lending-en.pdf.

Model National Interlibrary Loan Code (The Hague, Neth: International Federation of Library Associations and Institutions, 2000), online at archive.ifla.org/VI/2/p3/model.htm.

SOURCE: ALA Library Fact Sheet Number 8: Interlibrary Loans, ala.org/tools/libfactsheets/alalibraryfactsheet08.

Interlibrary loan systems

by Tina Baich and Erin Silva Fisher

THANKS TO TECHNOLOGY, interlibrary loan practitioners are able to move away from the stacks of paper that once surrounded them. Several software applications are available from which to choose. This section provides background on each to help in your decision-making process.

OCLC systems

Although some libraries choose to manage their ILL operations using home-grown systems, many libraries use vendor-based products. One of the major providers of ILL management systems is OCLC. Libraries can choose to subscribe to OCLC WorldCat Resource Sharing (WCRS) or license OCLC ILLiad. The internal management capabilities of ILLiad are far greater than those of WCRS, which is primarily a request platform. Although designed to work in conjunction with OCLC WCRS, ILLiad can be used to manage requests outside the OCLC system and, in theory, could be used completely independently of OCLC. According to OCLC, over 10,000 OCLC member libraries use WCRS, while over 1,000 libraries and other institutions use ILLiad.

WorldCat Resource Sharing is a web-based platform accessible through the OCLC FirstSearch interface. Subscribers are able to search for requested items in the WorldCat database, view and select potential lenders, and send requests. From the main Resource Sharing screen, ILL staff can view how many requests are in each OCLC status, such as Request Pending, Shipped, Received, and Returned. Benefits of this product include Direct Request, Custom Holdings, and Constant Data profiles, all of which save large amounts of staff time when implemented as they increase automation of routine tasks.

Direct request allows for the unmediated sending of requests into the OCLC ILL system. You can create a direct request profile to specify the types of requests you want sent automatically, including limiting by format. Direct requests must include either an OCLC or ISBN/ISSN number in order for OCLC to identify the item. Before choosing a lender string and submitting the request, the system checks the item against your own holdings as well as any other library groups you identify in the profile. In order for WCRS to choose the most appropriate lender string, it is helpful if you also create custom holdings groups.

Custom holdings are groups of potential lending libraries defined by the borrowing library. A borrowing library can use a number of criteria to establish these groups, including geographic proximity of the potential lending library, preferred delivery method, and lending fees that may be incurred in the transaction. In addition to working in conjunction with direct request, library holdings are displayed in these customized groups when processing a request

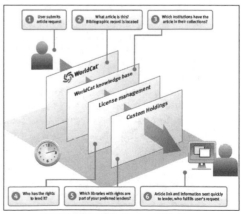

OCLC WorldCat Resource Sharing.

manually. Creating groups of preferred lenders has the potential to save both time and money by reducing turnaround times (geographic proximity groups) and fees paid (reciprocal library groups).

Constant Data profiles are another useful WCRS tool. You can establish multiple profiles as needed that automatically populate request forms with information regarding your library, including address information, preferred delivery methods, and the maximum cost you are willing to pay for borrowing an item. You will have one default Constant Data profile, but you can choose another profile at the point of request processing.

OCLC ILLiad screen.

ILLiad, or Interlibrary Loan Internet Accessible Database, is a software package that provides increased automation of ILL procedures over what is possible in WCRS. Developed in the interlibrary loan department of Virginia Tech University Libraries, ILLiad was launched in phases from 1997 to 1999. Since 2000, it has been a product of Atlas Systems and licensed by OCLC. ILLiad uses a web-based patron interface that allows users to directly submit and track ILL requests without staff mediation. Requests are stored in the database and are accessible to library staff through a separate interface, or client.

Transactions are divided into three modules—Borrowing, Document Delivery, and Lending—within the client. The ILLiad Client allows staff to search and order on OCLC as well as track requests that fall outside the OCLC workflow. ILLiad also has an integrated scanning utility called Odyssey, which will be discussed later. Standard ILL practices can be automated and managed through the use of several companion pieces, including Odyssey Helper, Web Circulation, and the Staff, Billing, Database, and Customization Managers.

Odyssey Helper, released with ILLiad 7.3 in 2008, imports TIFF and PDF images from a specified networked folder and sends and auto-updates article requests in ILLiad as well as external services such as OCLC or DOCLINE. This capability allows ILL staff to use scanners and software outside the department to create electronic files and batch send them at a later time. Odyssey Helper works with Document Delivery and Lending requests.

Web Circulation, also released with ILLiad 7.3, is a web-based interface that allows access to ILLiad's circulation functions without requiring access to the client. The abilities to check out, mark in transit, check in, and renew can all be controlled through settings in the Customization Manager. Web Circulation users can also search for and retrieve basic request information to respond to patron queries.

The Staff Manager, previously the User Manager, is used to create staff user accounts and set permissions for each staff member. An ILL supervisor can grant access to each of the other ILLiad managers and to specific modules within the client. Although the use of other companion pieces is largely optional, the Staff Manager must be used to configure staff users before they can use the client.

The Billing Manager allows you to generate and print invoices and track payments. Like the ILLiad Client, it is divided into Borrowing, Document Delivery, and Lending modules. A library can choose to use any combination of these modules depending on its fee policies.

The Database Manager is a powerful tool that should be used with caution as its purpose is to delete information from your ILLiad database. There are four tabs within the Database Manager: Transactions, Patrons, Other, and Billing Manager Test Mode. There are three keys in the Customization Manager to help protect transaction data from being deleted based on status and date of request. Patrons can only be deleted if there are no transactions associated with them. A variety of nontransaction and nonpatron information can be deleted using the Other tab. The Billing Manager Test Mode allows you to delete any data created during the testing phase of Billing Manager setup.

The ILLiad system is highly customizable, and most of this is accomplished using the Customization Manager. There are numerous keys that allow you to configure your own settings, including the definition of file names for the various print and email templates used by ILLiad and date-sensitive tasks such as the number of days before sending overdue notices. The Customization Manager is also where Web Circulation options are set. There are also tables for Reasons for Cancellation, Email Routing, and Custom Queues, among others, all of which are customizable.

All of the WCRS features are also available in ILLiad. Added benefits to using ILLiad include custom web pages, print templates, emails, and request queues. The custom email and queue features allow for custom integration of non-OCLC requests into ILLiad. Virtually all requests can be tracked within the system, often with the aid of customizable routing and request queues. For instance, you can create a custom email for frequent suppliers who do not use OCLC such as the National Library of Medicine or for international requests, which also are regularly outside the OCLC workflow. These requests can be routed to a custom queue such as "Awaiting Email Response from Lender" as a reminder to follow up at a later date. More information about ILLiad customization can be found at the Atlas Systems website. ILLiad is also compatible with DOCLINE and RapidILL.

Other systems. Clio is another ILL management system that operates similarly to ILLiad, working to automate and track interlibrary loan tasks. Clio Software is a family-owned business that has provided interlibrary loan software in the United States since 1994. Clio is completely compatible with WCRS and the National Library of Medicine's DOCLINE system. The software has two versions, ClioBasic and the Clio System. ClioBasic is a solution primarily for staff to manage requests, while the Clio System allows for patron request submission and interaction with an online interface as well as interaction with Ariel and Odyssey electronic delivery methods.

Another popular provider of ILL management products is Relais International. Relais ILL also works to electronically manage interlibrary loan requests with capabilities similar to ILLiad and Clio. For increased productivity, Relais also offers integrated scanning and electronic delivery components.

Scanning technologies

Interlibrary loan operations vastly improved with the creation of scanning hardware and software. Scanners transform printed documents into electronic files that can be sent to lending libraries via a variety of electronic delivery methods. Scanning capabilities have aided in the automation of interlibrary loan operations, improved the speed of delivery, and provided new conveniences for patrons.

Types of scanners. The three most common scanning devices within interlibrary loan are flatbed scanners, feeder scanners, and overhead scanners. The construction of each varies, but all three types work similarly to create a digital rendering of a physical document. To use a flatbed scanner, place items face down on the glass component of the machine. Users manually turn pages and repeat the process to scan multipage documents. A feeder scanner, which can be included as a component of a flatbed scanner, automatically feeds loose pages through the machine. Overhead scanners are sometimes referred to as book scanners. With this method, items are placed face up, reducing the impact on the books or other bound items that are being scanned. Overhead scanning also requires less time and effort than flatbed scanning because it is not necessary to remove the book from the scanner in order to turn pages.

Specialized scanning software. Scanners work to digitally render analog data, but additional components are necessary to create usable files. A scanner driver serves as the communication link between a scanner and scanning software application to facilitate the creation and manipulation of digital files. Various drivers exist to interface between scanner hardware and software, and both the software and the hardware must be compatible with the same driver to operate correctly.

Once a digital file has been imported into the designated software application, it is ready to be manipulated according to your needs. For example, pages can be split, rotated, inserted, or deleted.

A variety of scanning software applications have been developed specifically for interlibrary loan. Ariel and Odyssey are the two most common examples; however, new software options to streamline interlibrary loan even more are constantly in development. Ariel and Odyssey products offer both file-editing options and mechanisms for electronic delivery through an internet connection. Ariel, managed by Infotrieve, is a stand-alone product. Odyssey, developed by Atlas Systems, is a component of OCLC ILLiad and can also be used as a stand-alone product.

The Ariel software allows you to scan and send documents to the Ariel workstations of other libraries, or the files can be directly sent to a patron's email address. Documents can also be received from lending libraries using Ariel. The software converts the files from Tagged Image File Format (TIFF) to Portable Document Format (PDF). The PDF file format is preferable for various reasons. TIFF files are typically very large, whereas PDFs are compressed and thus easier to transfer. Additionally, PDF viewing platforms are prevalent. As mentioned, Ariel is a stand-alone product, but various ILL management systems have incorporated Ariel into the workflow of their products.

If you are interested in learning more about Ariel, Infotrieve maintains an in-depth user's manual, which can be downloaded from the Ariel Information Center web page at www.infotrieve.com/ariel-interlibrary-loan-software.

The Odyssey software operates similarly to Ariel, allowing you to scan and send documents to borrowing libraries that are using the same protocol. Documents can also be received from lending libraries that use Odyssey. For libraries using ILLiad, electronic documents received through Ariel or Odyssey are imported into ILLiad, converted to PDFs, and posted to a web server. The OCLC record is automatically updated at this point, if appropriate. An email notification is then generated alerting patrons that their requested article is available. To access the file, patrons simply log on to their online ILLiad account where the file can be accessed.

The free Odyssey standalone product does not provide the full range of capa-

ODYSSEY

bilities mentioned earlier, but it does allow you to edit scanned images, send files between libraries using Odyssey, and convert file formats. Both Ariel and Odyssey products also include an address book component to manage contact information for other libraries. These contacts are usually in the form of IP or email addresses.

File conversion

When dealing with the delivery of electronic documents, you may find it necessary to convert files from one type to another. Ariel and Odyssey, for instance, both use TIFF files for delivery. You may want to convert PDFs to TIFFs to be delivered, or you may need to convert TIFFs to PDFs in the course of troubleshooting. Converting PDFs to TIFFs saves paper and time by eliminating printing and rescanning of articles. There is also the possibility of locating a requested item on a web page, which would require conversion in order to be deliverable.

The National Library of Medicine offers two free file-conversion options, Doc-Morph and MyMorph. DocMorph is a web-based tool that requires no local installation. It is capable of converting over 50 file types into PDF, TIFF, or text files, but it can only convert one file at a time. If you plan to regularly convert a number of files, MyMorph is the better option. This downloadable program is similar to DocMorph, but it allows conversion of multiple files at the same time.

Printing documents to another file type is also a file conversion option. If your Microsoft Office suite includes the Document Imaging program, you can use the Document Image Writer to instantly convert electronic files when needed. The Document Image Writer is a virtual printer that can be used to convert any printable document to a TIFF file. Adobe offers a free PDF Printer Driver plug-in, which also acts as a virtual printer. After downloading, you can convert any printable document to a PDF file. Another option is to install a browser add-on for converting web pages to PDFs.

5

SOURCE: Tina Baich and Erin Silva Fisher, "Technology and Web 2.0," in Cherié Weible and Karen Janke, eds., *Interlibrary Loan Practices Handbook,* 3rd ed. (Chicago: American Library Association, 2011), 93–107.

PRESERVATION AND DISASTERS

Conservation training programs

THE FOLLOWING INSTITUTIONS offer educational programs in document conservation and materials preservation. For graduate programs in historic preservation, see the listing by the National Council for Historic Preservation at www.ncpe.us/chart.html.

American Institute for Conservation of Historic and Artistic Works, 1156 15th Street NW, Suite 320, Washington, DC 20005; (202) 452-9545. *Website:* www.conservation-us.org. Regional workshops and online courses.

American Library Association, Association for Library Collections and Technical Services. *Website:* ala.org/alcts/. Webinars and web courses.

Amigos Library Services, Imaging and Preservation, 14400 Midway Rd., Dallas, TX 75244-3509; (972) 851-8000, (800) 843-8482. *Website:* www.amigos.

org. Regional and online workshops.

Balboa Art Conservation Center, P.O. Box 3755, San Diego, CA 92163-1755; (619) 236-9702; info@bacc.org. *Website:* www.bacc.org. Workshops and graduate internships.

Buffalo State College, Art Conservation Department, 1300 Elmwood Avenue, Rockwell Hall 230, Buffalo, NY 14222-1095; (716) 878-5025; artcon@buffalostate.edu. *Website:* artconservation.buffalostate.edu/. Graduate degree.

Campbell Center for Historic Preservation Studies, 203 East Seminary, Mount Carroll, IL 61053; (815) 244-1173; registrations@campbellcenter.org. *Website:* www.campbellcenter.org. Courses and certificate program.

Canadian Bookbinders and Book Artists Guild, Suite 112, 60 Atlantic Avenue, Toronto, Ontario, Canada M6K 1X9; (416) 581-1071; cbbag@cbbag.ca. *Website:* www.cbbag.ca. Workshops.

Canadian Conservation Institute, 1030 Innes Road, Ottawa, Ontario, Canada K1B 4S7; (613) 998-3721; cci-icc_edu@pch.gc.ca. *Website:* www.cci-icc.gc.ca. Workshops, internships, and fellowships.

Columbia University, Historic Preservation Program, Graduate School of Architecture, Planning, and Preservation, 400 Avery Hall, 1172 Amsterdam Avenue, New York, NY 10027; (212) 854-3518. *Website:* www.arch.columbia.edu/programs/historic-preservation/. Graduate degree.

Conservation Center for Art and Historic Artifacts, 264 South 23rd Street, Philadelphia, PA 19103; (215) 545-0613; ccaha@ccaha.org. *Website:* www.ccaha.org. Workshops.

Cornell University Library, Department of Preservation and Collection Maintenance, Ithaca, NY 14853; conservation@cornell.edu. *Website:* www.library.cornell.edu/preservation/. Workshops and internships.

Getty Foundation, Getty Conservation Institute, 1200 Getty Center Drive, Suite 700, Los Angeles, CA 90049-1684; (310) 440-7325. *Website:* www.getty.edu/conservation/our_projects/education/index.html. Graduate internships.

Harvard University, Straus Center for Conservation and Technical Studies, Harvard University Art Museums, 32 Quincy Street, Cambridge, MA 02138-3383; (617) 495-2392; am_straus@harvard.edu. *Website:* www.harvardartmuseums.org/study-research/straus. Graduate internships.

Intermuseum Conservation Association, 2915 Detroit Avenue, Cleveland, OH 44113; (216) 658-8700; info@ica-artconservation.org. *Website:* www.ica-artconservation.org. Workshops.

Iowa State University, Gladys and Grover Hertzberg Conservation Internship, 441 Parks Library, Ames, IA 50011-

Preserving the Declaration of Independence.

2140; hseo@iastate.edu. *Website:* www.lib.iastate.edu/narrative-menu/3032/4010. Internship program.

Johns Hopkins University, Department of Materials Science and Engineering, Room 102, Maryland Hall, 3400 North Charles Street, Baltimore, MD 21218; (410) 516-8145; materials@jhu.edu. *Website:* materials.jhu.edu/index.php/grad/. Graduate degree.

Lyrasis, Digital and Preservation Services. *Website:* www.lyrasis.org/Products-

and-Services/Digital-and-Preservation-Services.aspx. Online classes.

Midwest Art Conservation Center, 2400 Third Avenue South, Minneapolis, MN 55404; (612) 870-3120; info@preserveart.org. *Website:* www.preserveart.org. Workshops.

New York University Institute of Fine Arts, Conservation Center, The Stephen Chan House, 14 East 78th Street, New York, NY 10075; (212) 992-5848; conservation.program@nyu.edu. *Website:* www.nyu.edu/gsas/dept/fineart/conservation/. Graduate degree, workshops.

Northeast Document Conservation Center, 100 Brickstone Square, Andover, MA 01810-1494; (978) 470-1010. *Website:* www.nedcc.org. Webinars, workshops, and e-courses.

Northern States Conservation Center, P.O. Box 8081, St. Paul, MN 55108; (651) 659-9420; helen@collectioncare.org. *Website:* www.collectioncare.org. Online courses, certificate program.

Queens University, Art Conservation Program, Department of Art, Art Centre Extension, 15 Bader Lane, Queen's University, Kingston, Ontario, Canada K7L 3N6; (613) 533-6000, ext. 77776; artcon@queensu.ca. *Website:* www.queensu.ca/art/artconservation/courses.html. Graduate degree.

Simmons College, Graduate School of Library and Information Science, Preservation Management, 300 The Fenway, Boston, MA 02115-5898; (617) 521-2800. *Website:* www.simmons.edu/gslis/academics/programs/preservation.php. Graduate degree.

Smithsonian Museum Conservation Institute, Conservation and Technical Studies, Museum Support Center, 4210 Silver Hill Road, Suitland, MD 20746; (301) 238-1240; mciweb@si.edu. *Website:* www.si.edu/mci/. Graduate internships and fellowships.

Society of American Archivists, 17 N. State St., Suite 1425, Chicago, IL 60602-3315; (312) 606-0722, (866) 722-7858; info@archivists.org. *Website:* www2.archivists.org/prof-education/course-catalog. Hosted courses.

University of Arizona, Heritage Conservation Materials and Technologies, Department of Materials Science and Engineering, Mines Building, P.O. Box 210012, University of Arizona, Tucson, AZ 85721-0012; (520) 621-6070. *Website:* www.mse.arizona.edu. Graduate degree.

University of California, Los Angeles, Cotsen Institute of Archaeology, 308 Charles E. Young Drive North, A210 Fowler Building, Box 951510, Los Angeles, CA 90095-1510; (310) 206-8934. *Website:* www.ioa.ucla.edu/conservation-program/. Graduate degree.

University of Pennsylvania, School of Design, Graduate Program in Historic Preservation, 210 South 34th Street, 115 Meyerson Hall, Philadelphia PA 19104-6311; (215) 898-3169; pennhspv@design.upenn.edu. *Website:* www.design.upenn.edu/historic-preservation. Graduate degree.

University of Texas at Austin, Historic Preservation, School of Architecture, 1 University Station B7500, Austin, TX 78712; (512) 471-3792; holleran@mail.utexas.edu. *Website:* soa.utexas.edu/hp/intro/. Graduate degree.

University of Texas at Austin, Preservation Studies, School of Information, 1616 Guadalupe Suite #5.202, Austin, TX 78701-1213; (512) 471-3821; info@ischool.utexas.edu. *Website:* www.ischool.utexas.edu/programs/specializations/#Preservation. Graduate degree.

Winterthur/University of Delaware, Department of Art Conservation, 303 Old College, University of Delaware, Newark, DE 19716-2515; (302) 831-3489; art-conservation@udel.edu. *Website:* www.artcons.udel.edu. Graduate degree.

Disaster supplies

by Frances C. Wilkinson, Linda K. Lewis, and Nancy K. Dennis

YOUR LIBRARY DISASTER PLAN should include an inventory of all disaster-related supplies, where they are located, and a timeline for reviewing and refreshing them. Lists of recommended supplies for libraries abound in the literature and on the internet, including the Federal Emergency Management Agency and Homeland Security websites. The exact supplies required will vary by library depending on size, type, geographic location, and environment. Larger libraries will need greater numbers of supplies and specialized libraries will need more-focused supplies. Supplies needed for unique materials can be found on the Library of Congress and National Archives websites. Depending on the environment where the library is located, having additional or supplemental supplies on hand such as plastic or poly sheeting (like Visqueen) in areas where water leaks or flooding are more prevalent, may be advisable.

Regardless of the type of library or its location, having basic supplies readily available in multiple locations can ameliorate the impact of small emergencies like roof or water leaks. Emergency supply kits such as the Rescubes and its slightly larger counterpart ReactPaks (both from ProText at www.protext.net) are convenient and designed to be compact and easily portable. They can be purchased from various library supply vendors. These kits are a good, basic start to ensuring that supplies are readily available when and where they are needed. As a matter of basic safety, supplies like first-aid kits and flashlights should be provided to all public service areas.

Having a more extensive selection of supplies available centrally at one library branch on campus can significantly reduce damage in even a moderate disaster. Store supplies in containers that are portable, such as in large, clean plastic trash containers with wheels, or provide fold-up cubes on wheels to make transporting them easier. Where feasible, several libraries may enter into a collaborative arrangement and agree to store a cache of supplies in a central area where they can be shared. This arrangement can prove especially advantageous for smaller libraries that are geographically near one another such as those in a major metropolitan area. In a larger or more widespread disaster, appropriate supplies are useful to rescue workers once they are allowed back in the building after a fire, major flood, or earthquake.

The plan should also include locations to obtain additional or specialized supplies and equipment. Some larger or expensive equipment such as industrial fans, large humidifiers or dehumidifiers, portable generators, water pumps, or forklifts may be housed offsite or be provided by a campus department such as the physical plant. Be sure to determine which emergency equipment is available on campus, as well as which equipment can be rented or provided by local vendors, and include that information in the disaster plan. In the event of a major disaster, the library may hire—or have precontracted with—a large national commercial disaster recovery company that will arrange for nearly all supplies from latex gloves to forklifts.

All supplies should be labeled with the date they were purchased, and they should be checked on a regular basis, preferably quarterly but at least annually, and refreshed as needed. When storing supplies, consider arranging them into more frequently and less frequently used categories and labeling and storing accordingly. For example, paper towels are likely to be used more often than plastic sheeting.

As part of the supply inventory in the disaster preparedness, response, and recovery plan, the library should include a timeline for checking supplies to determine if supplies are still viable and specify a replacement plan. In the event of an emergency, ensure that batteries for flashlights are not expired, rubber gloves and booties are not crumbling from age, and plastic sheeting to shield books from water is not used up from a previous water leak. Staff need to know where the supplies are located and have access to them. All efforts should be made to avoid stumbling around searching for a flashlight when the lights go out or discovering that the locked supply closet key is assigned to someone who is not available.

Core supplies that most libraries should have consist of command center supplies, general supplies, first aid supplies, safety supplies, and specialized supplies for major disasters. Some duplication of supplies within the categories may be needed. For example, the command center may be located at a considerable distance from the location where the safety supplies are located. Core supplies include:

Command Center supplies

- Identification—badges and/or badge holders, brightly colored vests
- Communication and safety devices—cellphones, walkie-talkies, megaphone or bullhorn, whistles, air horns, caution tape
- Documentation—tape or digital recorders, disposable digital cameras, camcorders and supplies, portable flash drives
- Technology support—regular and heavy-duty extension cords in various lengths, surge protectors
- Miscellaneous—folding chairs, blankets, emergency snacks and bottled water, cash or credit card access

General supplies

- Paper and writing implements—clipboards with paper, larger paper for signs, poster board, pens, pencils, markers
- Tape—transparent tape, duct tape, masking tape, caution tape
- Cleaning and sanitary supplies—paper towels (without dyes that can leave stains), white towels, rags, sponges, mops, brooms, buckets, garbage bags, all-purpose cleaners, antimicrobial soap, alcohol-based hand cleaner, eye wash, toilet paper, disposable wipes, wet-dry shop vacuum
- Scissors, utility knives with extra blades
- Tools such as screwdrivers, hammers, nails, crowbar
- Plastic crates, folding wheeled carts, wheeled garbage cans
- First aid supplies, per ANSI Z308.1-2003
- Adhesive tape
- Adhesive bandages and sterile scissors
- Antiseptic
- Burn treatment
- Gloves
- Sterile pads
- Absorbent compresses
- Bandages in a variety of sizes
- Eye covering that can be attached, eyewash, cold packs, rolled bandages

Safety supplies

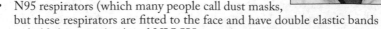

- Lighting—flashlights with extra batteries, small temporary hanging lights
- Protective clothing (in various sizes)—rubber or nitrile rubber gloves, disposable latex gloves, booties to cover shoes in various sizes, safety-toed boots, protective coats and smocks, disposable overalls, plastic aprons, hard hats, protective safety glasses, and eye covering
- N95 respirators (which many people call dust masks, but these respirators are fitted to the face and have double elastic bands to hold them in place) and NIOSH-compliant respirators
- Object protection, drying, packing, and salvage—plastic sheeting in large rolls, unprinted newspaper to protect surfaces and wrap materials, blotting paper, waxed paper, transparent tape, packing tape, scissors, clothesline and pins, cardboard sheets and boxes, plywood

Moderate to major disaster supplies are typically not stored in the library (supplied by recovery and salvage vendors or available through campus physical plant or other campus areas):

- Generator, industrial fans, large humidifier or dehumidifier, large water pumps, portable devices that measure moisture in solid objects such as Aqua Boy, pallets, forklift, crane, freezer space, extensive temporary emergency lighting, sandbags.

SOURCE: Frances C. Wilkinson, Linda K. Lewis, and Nancy K. Dennis, *Comprehensive Guide to Emergency Preparedness and Disaster Recovery* (Chicago: ALA Association of College and Research Libraries, 2010), 21–23.

Library fires timeline

330 B.C.—The Zoroastrian library and archives at Persepolis in Persia are burned by Alexander the Great.

475—The Imperial Library in Constantinople is completely incinerated in a city fire. Housed in a basilica, the library holds some 120,000 volumes, including a huge parchment scroll on which is inscribed Homer's *Iliad* and *Odyssey* in golden letters.

870—The 250-year-old library of the Patriarch of Constantinople burns down.

1666, September 6—St. Paul's Cathedral and its ecclesiastical library are gutted in the Great Fire of London.

1728, October 31—A city-wide fire rages for nearly three days in Copenhagen, Denmark, and burns up the university library housed in the Trinitatis church.

1731, October 23—A fire in Ashburnham House in Westminster, London, destroys or damages about 25% of the Cottonian Library, a private collection donated to the people of Great Britain. Librarian Richard Bentley escapes with the 5th-century Codex Alexandrinus in his arms.

1764, January 24—Harvard College Library loses most of its collection to a fire that starts in Harvard Hall after the General Court of Massachusetts holds a meeting in the building. Students are away on winter break. The books that survive are either on loan or stored in shipping crates from a recent delivery. The disaster inspires the college to take precautions against fire in a new building, which is built of brick, stone, and slate. New library laws enacted in 1765 prohibit patrons from bringing candles or lamps into the library.

1812, August 15–18—Moscow State University Library is destroyed by fire as Napoleon's army enters the city.

1814, August 24—British troops under General Robert Ross briefly capture Washington, D.C. American troops and government officials have fled the city and Ross can find no one with whom to negotiate a capitulation. To cause confusion during his withdrawal, he orders all public buildings burned including the Capitol, which houses a small congressional library of some 3,000 volumes in the Senate wing. A State Department clerk named Stephen Pleasonton manages to rescue some irreplaceable documents, including the Declaration of Independence, and transports them to Leesburg,  Virginia. Former President Thomas Jefferson offers to sell his personal library to Congress as a replacement for the loss. The legislature purchases his collection for $23,950 in 1815, forming the basis of a new Library of Congress.

1827, September 4—The Royal Academy Library in Turku (modern Åbo), Finland, is destroyed by a fire that engulfs the city. Of the 40,000 books in the collection, only 800 that are out on loan survive. These form the basis of a library at a new university in Helsinki.

1851, December 24—Fire ravages the Library of Congress and destroys about two-thirds of its 55,000 volumes, including most of Thomas Jefferson's personal library. Congress responds quickly and generously to the disaster, and within a few years a majority of the lost books are replaced.

1871, October 7–10—The Chicago Library Association, a fee-based subscription library, loses almost all of its collection of 30,000 books in the Great Chicago Fire. Many other small private libraries are also consumed. When news of the tragedy reaches Great Britain, A. H. Burgess and Thomas Hughes respond by collecting and donating books to establish a free public library in Chicago.

1879, January 11—The central library in Birmingham, England, sustains considerable damage during the building of an addition. The fire starts when a workman tries to thaw out a frozen gas pipe that illuminates a chandelier and he ignites some wood shavings. Library patrons and staff try to contain the flames, but they are hampered by the water buckets being stored too high in order to prevent theft. Some 50,000 reference books are lost.

1895, October 27—A fire caused by faulty electrical wiring starts in the annex of the University of Virginia Rotunda, a structure designed by Thomas Jefferson to be the centerpiece of the campus and house its library. Before it can be brought under control, the annex, dome, and interior of the Rotunda are destroyed, leaving only the charred, circular brick walls. Students are able to rescue a portion of the library collection, including the Lee Family papers.

1897, June 19—A lightning strike on a chimney at the University of Iowa Library in Iowa City causes a fire that destroys some 25,000 of its 33,600 volumes and 15,000 pamphlets, along with the shelflist and 40,000 catalog cards.

1900, June 24—The collections of the Hanlin Academy in Beijing are severely damaged during the siege of the foreign legations during the Boxer Rebellion. Among the treasures lost in the fire is a copy of the 15th-century *Yongle Encyclopedia*.

1911, March 29—A fire in the Assembly Chamber of the New York State Capi-

5

tol in Albany, where the New York State Library is located, destroys approximately 450,000 books and 270,000 manuscripts, including historical records that document New York's early Dutch and colonial history. The fire strikes as the overcrowded library is four months away from moving into new, spacious quarters across the street.

1914, August 25—The library of the Catholic University of Leuven, Belgium, is purposely set on fire by German troops occupying the city. Some 300,000 books and irreplaceable manuscripts are lost.

1962, June 7—The OAS, a French right-wing underground group opposed to Algerian independence, sets fire to the University of Algiers library (right), destroying its 60,000 volumes in one of the culminating terrorist acts of the Algerian War.

1966, April 18—A fire rages for nine hours in the library tower of the Jewish Theological Seminary at Broadway and 122nd Street in New York City. Firefighters have difficulty extinguishing the blaze in the narrow confines of the steel stacks, where there is only one entrance and stairwell from the bottom and limited window access.

1981, May 31–June 2—Sinhalese police and thugs on a rampage set fire to the Jaffna Public Library during the Sri Lankan Civil War. The library has been a repository of Tamil literature since 1933. By the time of the fire, it houses nearly 100,000 Tamil books and rare manuscripts, some written on dried palm leaves and stored in sandalwood boxes.

1986, April 29—An arson fire in the crowded, closed stacks of the landmark Los Angeles Central Library destroys some 400,000 volumes—20% of the library's holdings—with water and smoke damaging many of the surviving works. It takes 350 firefighters and more than 80 emergency vehicles working for over seven hours to extinguish. The staff and 1,500 volunteers mount an around-the-clock salvage operation to move the 700,000 remaining water-soaked volumes to cold storage.

1986, September 3—A second fire at the Los Angeles Central Library destroys the Music Department Reading Room.

1988, February 14–15—The worst library fire of the 20th century begins in the newspaper room of the Library of the Russian Academy of Sciences in Leningrad (modern St. Petersburg). By the time it is extinguished the next day, it has destroyed 400,000 of the 12 million books housed in the building; 3.6 million more are damaged by water. Director Valerii Leonov and his staff commandeer every commercial freezer in the city and spend the next four years, with the help of the Getty Conservation Institute and the Library of Congress, carefully drying out and repairing the damaged materials. Leonov believes that three separate fires were set by arsonists who placed incendiary devices inside hollowed-out books in the stacks.

1992, August 25—Serbian incendiary shells during the Siege of Sarajevo cause the near-complete destruction by fire of the National and University Library of Bosnia and Herzegovina. Among the losses were about 700 manuscripts and incunabula and a unique collection of Bosnian serials, some from the 19th-century Bosnian cultural revival. Locals manage to save around 100,000 volumes.

1994, August 1—A fire at Norwich Central Library in England is caused by an explosion triggered by faulty wiring in an illuminated bookshelf. Some

200,000 books, newspapers, and recordings are destroyed, along with the valuable Norfolk Studies collection. All that survives of the U.S. Army Air Force 2nd Air Division Memorial Library (recording American contributions to World War II) inside the building is one flak jacket.

2003, April 10–13—Fires are set in the Iraq National Library and Archive by Saddam Hussein loyalists intent on destroying the records of the Ba'athist regime between the years 1958 and 1979 and court proceedings detailing the trials and charges against party opponents.

2003, July 23—An arson fire breaks out in the second floor annex of the University of Georgia Main Library in Athens housing government documents.

2004, September 2—A fire at the Duchess Anna Amalia Library (right) in Weimar, Germany, destroys some 50,000 volumes. Among the major losses are the library's collection of original musical scores by the Duchess Anna Amalia, who established the library in 1766. Some 6,000 historical works are saved, including a 1534 Lutheran Bible and a collection of Alexander von Humboldt's papers, by being passed hand-over-hand out of the building. An additional 62,000 burned or waterlogged books are taken to the Center for Book Preservation in Leipzig for deep-freezing.

Photo by PatrickD, used CC BY-SA 3.0

2006, April 30—A possible arson fire starts in the basement of the Zimmerman Library at the University of New Mexico in Albuquerque, shutting down all library operations. Approximately 30,000 volumes—bound periodicals in history, Latin American, Hispanic, Native American, and African American studies—are a total loss.

2007, April 30—A three-alarm fire damages the two-story, Georgian Revival, Georgetown branch of the District of Columbia Public Library, including its Peabody Room, which houses precious oil paintings, leather-bound maps, photos, and files on neighborhood properties. Workers pitch hundreds of irreplaceable items into boxes and load them into a freezer truck to be hauled to a restoration company in Texas for freeze-drying. Although much of the circulating collection is lost, only about 20% of the historical collections require repair or replacement. The branch reopens in October 2010.

2008, February 2—A late-night blaze causes nearly $2 million in damage to the Cathedral City branch of the Riverside County (Calif.) Library System.

2008, July 24—The historic Swan's Island (Maine) Library burns to the ground after it is hit by lightning during an early morning thunderstorm. In addition to more than 10,000 volumes, the library holds irreplaceable local-history materials, including genealogical records, historic photographs, archives from local quarries, weather data, and ferry logs. The collection has been housed for the past 10 years in the Atlantic Schoolhouse, a century-old, two-story structure that served as a village school from 1903 to 1954.

2010, April 25—Thousands of books and historical documents are lost when the Twiggs County Public Library in Jeffersonville, Georgia, goes up in flames, possibly due to a lightning strike. More than 15,000 books are burned and the building destroyed.

2010, May 8—A fire causes $1.5 million in damage to the G. Allen Fleece Library at Columbia International University in South Carolina. The blaze is caused by an electrical problem around a fluorescent light fixture in the 42-year-old building. As many as 15,000 books, many of them scarce theo-

5

logical volumes, are affected by heat, smoke, or fire damage.

2011, February 24—An early-morning fire consumes the Cosmos (Minn.) Public Library, destroying a building that originally housed a bank. The 9,000-volume collection, which includes scrapbooks with old newspaper clippings and other items unique to the town, is a total loss.

2011, December 17—The 200,000-volume collection of the Egyptian Scientific Institute, established by Napoleon Bonaparte in 1789, is burned down during a wave of protests in Cairo.

Fire! The San Diego County Library responds

by Pat Downs

A FEW DAYS INTO the weeklong siege of wildfires that ravaged San Diego County, California, in October 2007, a customer came into one of the dozens of San Diego County Library branches that remained open. She wanted to report that after several decades, she had just made her final mortgage payment. Staff rejoiced with her.

She then solemnly reported that she would not be returning two books—one about household organization—because her house had burned the day before and she had lost everything. Staff turned from congratulating to consoling her. And so it played out in community libraries throughout the county, the heart-wrenching stories of loss and luck, triumph and tragedy.

San Diego County officials and emergency responders garnered national praise for their prudent planning and efficient use of resources as they served the more than 3 million residents affected by the wildfires that devastated southern California that fall. San Diego County took the hardest hit, with multiple fires that burned 368,000 acres, destroyed 1,750 homes and businesses, killed 10 people and sparked the evacuation of more than a half million people. A total of 12,361 San Diego County families and business owners ultimately registered for assistance with FEMA.

San Diego County Library staff responded to and recovered alongside their fellow citizens. In the process we learned valuable lessons for handling the aftermath of future calamities. We were also able to affirm those among our disaster preparations that worked well—practices worth consideration by other library systems as they, too, consider how they hope to respond to catastrophic events.

Before the fire

Preparedness. SDCL's Site Emergency Response Plan, created in the aftermath of the September 11 attacks, is a fine-tuned version of an earlier emergency manual. It is a go-to guide in case of earthquake, fire, bomb threat, flood, power outage, or break-in. Stored in a three-ring notebook—making it easier to update—each SERF manual is branch-specific because logistics and resources vary greatly throughout the county. Most important is the listing of each Emergency Response Team—the staff on call as first responders. Supervisors as well as staff local to the branch are placed on the ERT. During emergencies, mobility can be a major challenge. Having staff who can actually get to buildings is key.

During the fire

Interagency coordination. The County of San Diego Office of Emergency Services, charged with coordinating plans and programs designed to protect life and property, is headquartered in the same central complex as SDCL administration offices and other county departments. This turned out to be a great advantage to the library. Phone service was unreliable, and phone lines to emergency services were overloaded. So when we needed portable toilets and potable water so we could reopen the Ramona branch, Director José Aponte simply walked a few blocks to the headquarters of the Department of General Services to ask for them.

Many County of San Diego employees are trained in CPR and first aid. All are issued staff badges that read, "Employee identified by this card has an emergency response assignment. Please allow passage through roadblocks and into affected areas." Staff at several threatened SDCL branches were able to use their badges to navigate roads closed to everyone else, assessing damage firsthand.

Teamwork and collaboration. With displaced staff stepping in to run branches, the importance of cross-training and standardizing procedures came into clear focus. All SDCL staff are encouraged to cross-train in frontline functions, including basic circulation and reference services—our service priorities during the crisis.

The Office of Emergency Services established Local Assistance Centers as bases for fire victims to meet with FEMA representatives and begin the recovery process. Bilingual library staff provided critical translation services while Youth Services staff worked as lead childcare experts, providing crafts, read-alouds, music, and comfort to many displaced children.

And that interagency collaboration reached a crucial climax at the Potrero branch as the wildfires approached. When firefighters asked Branch Manager Candy Bonner if they could set up shop in the parking lot there, she added that if they saved the building, they could use it as a command post. Result? "They saved our library! The firefighters put up a stand right here and saved the building." And Bonner has photos to prove it. The branch, located in the same complex as a school, suffered burnt landscaping as well as interior ash and debris. But the adjacent preschool building and a storage shed directly behind the library were completely destroyed by the fires.

Although only one San Diego County Library branch, Borrego Springs, was designated an official evacuation center, many displaced citizens used their libraries as

The 2007 Harris Fire damage outside the Potrero branch library.

shelters during service hours, finding them more comfortable, less chaotic, and offering more resources than official evacuation centers.

Just as in Potrero, citizens around the county rediscovered firsthand just how vital their local public library is, especially during a disaster.

What we learned

- Listen. Many people simply wanted to talk about their experiences and came to their public library to do so. Provide the library as a living room where residents can share their stories. No other community space offers this important venue for neighbors to talk to neighbors.

- If possible, offer your library as an alternative evacuation center, noting capacity and other limitations. Evacuated Valley Center branch staff used their building for shelter several nights during the fires. The Campo–Morena Village branch in rural San Diego County served as a headquarters of sorts for residents seeking assistance throughout the crisis. Separately keyed entrances for community rooms make them much more flexible for use during emergencies, mitigating risks of major damages or materials loss.
- Convert as many computers as possible to public internet access to facilitate customers' urgent online needs. Limit use to 15–30 minutes.
- Provide office supplies, fax service, and free copies for emergency-related documents. Sell stamps if you have them. Designate one or several workstations as word processors or computers where customers can complete lengthy online paperwork. "This was especially important to customers several days into the crisis, as they began to work with FEMA and insurance agents," said Doris Adam-Hillert, manager at the Fletcher Hills branch.
- Print and distribute emergency services info and disaster updates for those who can't get on computers. Post them next to telephones so staff can answer phone queries.
- Waive late fees and show leniency for items lost in the fires, forgiving replacement costs or charging a nominal fee. Circulation Manager Bertha Huertero worked with administration to quickly communicate to staff that SDCL intended to waive fines during the fires. "Staff appreciated being able to offer some immediate relief to customers," she said.
- Open as early as possible but close before dark. Curfews and power outages are common during disasters, so take advantage of daylight.
- Provide constant television news access by positioning a television centrally in the adult browsing area, with volume low or muted, closed-captioned. Consider installing satellite dishes at remote branches, where cable service is not available. A computer may be used for the same purpose, with streaming video available via many local stations.
- Use outdoor bulletin boards and/or marquees to communicate with the public. The high-profile marquee at the Del Mar branch proclaimed "Open!" "Customers were so grateful for our efforts to let them know we were open during the fires," said librarian Gretchen Schmidt.
- Most schools cancelled classes for a week during the wildfires, leaving public libraries as the only free indoor gathering spot for students and their families. Staff put out playing cards, board games, puzzles, coloring sheets, and crafts as diversions for evacuated families. Public-performance rights videos and DVDs were popular pastimes for fatigued customers. Most SDCL branches have public performance licenses (via Movie Licensing USA) so they can regularly show feature films.
- Allow customers to use electric outlets to recharge cellphones.
- Customers were oftentimes the source for the best local information— which roads and gas stations were open or which stores still had masks. By the same token, local branch staff sometimes had the most recent information, providing administrators timely and invaluable updates.
- To communicate up-to-date information to customers, SDCL Online

staff structured the immediate development and launch of a wildfires-related website. For several weeks it was linked to a large rotating web banner featured on SDCL's home page.

- SDCL's RSS feed broadcast up-to-date information for customers.
- If possible, send bulk email to customers. Use this as a means to send service updates, as well as other advisories, including late return fee waivers and other accommodations due to emergency circumstances.
- Staff needs a voice of authority amidst the chaos. Administration needs to issue regular updates, even if the facts haven't changed since the last update. Besides basic information like closures, it's important to let staff know which branches don't have phone or internet services. Director Aponte sent daily systemwide email updates. He and Assistant Director Betty Waz nis kept in constant phone contact with Emergency Operations Center officials and local branch staff to make informed decisions about service hours, staffing, damages, and community needs.

Harris Fire burning down Mount Miguel in San Diego County on Oct. 23, 2007. Photo by David S. Roberts, used CC BY-SA 3.0.

- Staff should know how to change telephone answering messages remotely. Systems using a centralized phone number for all branches may face extra technological difficulties, but citizens want local service updates and don't want to have to navigate complex telephone maneuvers to get the information.
- Provide a sample script, accessible remotely, for updating phone messages in an emergency.
- Because not all staff have access to email during emergencies, an internal emergency phone line is crucial. Administrators and public information officers should update messages as often as needed, including date and time of updates so that staff know how recent the information is. The phone line should also accept incoming messages so that staff who don't have other options can ask questions/give information. Designated staff should monitor and respond promptly.
- Community room reservations may need to be cancelled if libraries are evacuated or closed, so take the calendar and contact info if you are not able to make copies before vacating the building.
- Realizing that frontline staff might not be able to access their email to get updates on branch closures, status of mobile library services in affected areas, and alternative work sites for staff in the event of these closures, SDCL Online staff created a library Twitter account for real-time, quick information.
- Some SDCL branches established backup group email accounts (Yahoo, Hotmail) to share info during the crisis.

After the storm

When the smoke cleared, literally, and operations returned to normal, San Diego County Library administrators were able to assess a number of unexpected positive outcomes of the crisis. Polly Cipparrone, SDCL's web services manager, had been training staff to use Web 2.0 applications when the firestorms necessitated jumping right in, taking coworkers with her. Besides the Twitter account, she created a library staff blog.

Recognizing that staff and customers might want to share photos in the aftermath of the wildfires, Cipparrone's staff created a library Flickr account. Dozens of photos were posted from the far corners of the county. SDCL administrators, moreover, used this site to convey wildfire-related information to answer inquiries from county departments and other library-related organizations. Going forward, it serves as a useful tool for centralized image storage.

In an effort to maximize open hours during the fires, many branches opened earlier than usual. When assessing capacity and community needs in the days following the crisis, the library administration determined that branch staffing could support earlier opening hours on a regular basis—a goal for the near future that had now been fast forwarded in response to community needs.

After any emergency, administrators are compelled to ask the critical question: How can we be better prepared next time? Solicit input from not only staff but customers, community partners, and cooperating city/county agencies. San Diego County Library held extensive staff debriefings resulting in improved emergency preparedness. Bottom line: In times of crisis, we want to be a key resource to all county residents, not just those who are able to walk through our doors.

Keep a record

Accounts of just how vital public libraries are on so many levels emerge variously but constantly in post-disaster dialogue. Gather the stories and document the variety of services provided—virtually, as well as via bricks-and-mortar facilities. Therein we find the common, central charge expressed by a guiding principle of public libraries: Be responsive to the needs of the community—in times of crisis as well as calm.

SOURCE: Pat Downs, "Fire! The San Diego County Library Responds," *Clarion* 4, no. 1 (April 2008): 6–10. Reprinted with permission.

Ten flood lessons learned

by Jo Ann Calzonetti and Victor Fleischer

ON A BITTERLY COLD SUNDAY AFTERNOON in January 2011, personnel from the University of Akron Libraries were called from their warm homes to the chilly and wet environment of the university's Science and Technology Library. Earlier that day, an unwrapped fire suppression pipe burst, sending thousands of gallons of water gushing through the library. Luckily UAL had recently finalized an updated disaster preparedness and recovery plan.

The plan included creation of a disaster action team (DAT) whose members were charged with specific emergency-response duties. Disaster supplies were delivered to all campus libraries just two weeks prior to the incident. Although these essential components were in place, the plan had not been tested and we had not conducted response and recovery exercises. This unexpected disaster was a real-world test of our plan and an uninvited opportunity to acquire on-the-job training.

While we passed the test with flying colors, this experience taught us valuable lessons that helped us improve our plan and that, we hope, will benefit others.

Ten lessons learned

1. **Have your disaster preparedness plan up-to-date and conduct regular training exercises.** This seems obvious; however, we all know that in the press of day-to-day activities planning and practicing, recovery exercises for events that might never take place get postponed. As this incident proved to us, you never know when the unexpected will occur.

2. **Have a security plan in place.** During the response efforts, DAT members noticed patrons entering the building and roaming the library. This is both a security risk and a liability. Emergency personnel initially secured all entrances, but later unlocked all entries to facilitate entry in and out of the building by the recovery team. This allowed patrons unfettered access as well. DAT personnel should have posted signs on all entrances to alert patrons that the library was closed and posted personnel at all unsecured entrances to monitor people entering the building.

Plastic sheeting protects books from water damage.

3. **Make sure collections- and equipment-salvage priorities are clearly identified on your floor plans and physically marked on shelving units.** While S&T Library personnel knew the location of their collection- and equipment-salvage priorities, DAT members had trouble locating some of these materials. The salvage priorities were marked on the floor plans in the disaster plan. Most DAT members were not familiar with the layout of the library and had difficulty deciphering the floor plans. Labeling shelving units that house priority collections and equipment with color-coded signs would have helped DAT members locate these priority items. The libraries' forthcoming training program will include a visit by DAT to each library to see where priority collections and equipment are located.

4. **Ensure that a list of each library's disaster supplies and their location is in your disaster plan.** While S&T Library personnel knew the location of their disaster supplies, no one outside of their unit was aware of their location. Because the supplies were delivered only two weeks prior to the disaster, their location had not been added to the plan. Personnel from other university libraries arrived on the scene first and had trouble locating the supplies. In addition, only the members of DAT knew the contents of the disaster packs. One of the most frequent complaints of response workers was cold and wet feet. These individuals would have benefitted from the rubber boots and gloves included in the disaster packs.

5. **Try to prevent disasters before they take place.** This incident could have been prevented if the fire suppression pipes were insulated. A comprehensive internal and external hazards survey was conducted during the disaster planning, but the unwrapped pipes went unnoticed. Particular attention should be paid to such issues during facilities

5

surveys, and maintenance staff should be made aware of them so they can be remedied. Fire and police need to be aware of all pipes that run through your libraries. Emergency personnel did not shut the fire pump down until 35 to 40 minutes after the pipe burst, as they saw steam and thought it was a steam pipe issue, but steam pipes do not run through this building. If they had been aware of this, the water damage would have been minimized.

6. **Communicate with emergency personnel before a disaster occurs.** Throughout the response efforts, communications between university libraries staff and university facilities emergency response personnel were minimal and not effective in part because personnel from the disparate units were not very familiar with one another. This led to several problems. For example, maintenance personnel kept turning up the heat in the building to increase the efficiency of the dehumidifiers in drying carpet and furnishings. Library personnel kept turning the heat down because higher temperatures encourage mold growth on paper-based materials. Meeting before a disaster to outline our needs and requirements may have prevented such situations and eliminated a lot of confusion, misunderstanding, and miscommunication.

7. **Test all emergency contact information for accuracy and completeness before a disaster happens.** While most of the contact information in the disaster plan was checked for accuracy and completeness, a few contacts were added later and were never tested. The campus extension for one of our most important contacts, the director of university food services, who offered freezer space for wet books, was inaccurate. In addition, his home phone and cellphone numbers were not included in the plan, nor was information for a backup contact. Although we were eventually able to obtain his cellphone number, this oversight cost us valuable time.

8. **Pack books flat, not on their tails.** Our disaster plan recommended packing wet books on their tails in a fanned position to facilitate drying. This method was recommended by a conservation lab when the plan was being created. Working in haste, our pack team placed most of the books flat. This turned out to be fortuitous inasmuch as after the damaged items were removed from the freezer we learned that books packed flat had a better survival rate. On the other hand, those that were packed upright, especially paperbacks, tended to swell and distort.

9. **Prepare for the worst.** Almost every person who arrived on the scene stated that the disaster was worse than they anticipated. This caused  some individuals to panic, which can lead to poor decision-making. Imagine the worst possible scenario and prepare mentally before you arrive on the scene. This will help to create a calm demeanor, which will facilitate better decision making. During the planning process, no one anticipated a disaster of this magnitude. As a result, there was an inadequate amount of plastic sheeting to cover the bookshelves. A trip to the hardware store remedied the situation, but valuable time and energy were lost and books were damaged unnecessarily.

10. **Do not store valuable items on the floor.** This is one of the biggest lessons learned from this experience, and it was learned the hard way. Since there was up to four inches of standing water in many areas of the library, everything stored or left on the floor was damaged beyond repair. This included several important and valuable library resources that were left on the floor by library personnel. These materials can be replaced, but at a great cost to the library.

The flood in the S&T Library was a real disaster. The entire facility was flooded and thousands of materials were affected. The library was closed for two days, temporarily suspending important services to the campus and the community. While a disaster plan, supplies, and a response team were in place, the plan was untested and training and recovery exercises had not taken place. Despite lack of training and practice we had an up-to-date plan and most of the supplies we needed to respond to and recover from the incident quickly and efficiently. Hard work and commitment of personnel from the libraries and the university's physical facilities staff were critically important.

We were lucky. Two weeks earlier and there would have been no disaster supplies in place. Three months earlier and our disaster plan would have been woefully incomplete and inadequate. Luckily the library was open and our student employees knew to take immediate action evacuating the building and activating our disaster plan. We learned many valuable lessons from this traumatic real world experience. One of the most important is that you should not rely on luck and can never be too prepared.

SOURCE: Jo Ann Calzonetti and Victor Fleischer, "Don't Count on Luck: Be Prepared," *College and Research Libraries News* 72, no. 2 (February 2011): 82–85.

Book donation programs

THE AMERICAN LIBRARY ASSOCIATION does not accept or distribute donations of books or any other materials. This section provides information on some of the groups and organizations that *do* handle book donations—including donations of used books.

Book donations in the United States

Most public libraries in the United States accept gift books with the proviso that the library is free to decide whether to keep the book in the library's collection, put it in a book sale to raise funds for the library, or discard it. Persons seeking to donate books to libraries are encouraged to contact their local library and ask about donating books to it.

First contact your state library for local suggestions. Other groups that distribute book donations primarily within the United States include the following:

Books for Kids (formerly known as Books for Kids Foundation). Books for Kids creates and furnishes libraries within existing children's centers. 240 West 37th Street, Suite 309, New York, NY 10018; (212) 760-2665; info@booksforkids.org. *Website:* www.booksforkids.org. *Facebook:* /booksforkidsorg. *Twitter:* @booksforkidsorg.

First Book. First Book distributes new books to children in need. It accepts monetary donations and large-scale donations of new books from publishers.

1319 F Street NW, Suite 1000, Washington, DC 20004. *Website:* www.firstbook. org. *Facebook:* /FirstBook. *Twitter:* @FirstBook.

Judith's Reading Room. This cornerstone project of the Leiber Family Foundation provides fully stocked, custom-designed mobile bookcarts to nonprofit organizations that serve people who are not mobile. The program is named after Judith Krug, founding director of the ALA Office for Intellectual Freedom. Leiber Family Foundation, P.O. Box 20711, Lehigh Valley, PA 18002-0711; (484) 661-6151; info@judithsreadingroom.org. *Website:* www.judithsreadingroom.org. *Facebook:* /JudithsReadingRoom. *Twitter:* @JReadingRm.

Libri Foundation. The Libri Foundation is a nationwide nonprofit 501(c)(3) organization that donates new, quality, hardcover children's books to small, rural public libraries in the United States through its Books for Children program. P.O. Box 10246, Eugene, OR 97440-2246; (541) 747-9655; libri@librifoundation.org. *Website:* www.librifoundation.org.

Roads to Reading Initiative. The Books for All Kids Program is designed to provide books for nonprofits, after-school programs, and childcare centers at no charge for the books. P.O. Box 960154, Boston, MA 02196; (651) 515-7084; director@pwirtr.org. *Website:* www.pwirtr.org/booksforkids.html.

Book donations overseas

If you are interested in donating books to countries overseas, there are several organizations that distribute books to other countries. Many of these organizations distribute books overseas at no cost to the donating person or library other than shipping costs to the U.S. facility.

Be aware that most organizations only accept new books or books in good condition; these are not places to dump unwanted literature. Books that are outdated, damaged, and worthless will be just as useless abroad. Make sure that the information will be useful to the schools or people receiving them and that the information is in a language that they can read and understand. Finally, the materials must be culturally appropriate for the audience that will receive them.

Here is a list of organizations that distribute books to other countries. It is important to contact these groups beforehand, to find out what kind of books they need and are hoping to receive for distribution.

Asia Foundation, Books for Asia Program. This organization puts one million new books into the hands of students, educators, and local and national leaders in 18 countries annually. 2490 Verna Court, San Leandro, CA 94577; (510) 667-6480; wrockett@asiafound.org. *Website:* asiafoundation.org/program/overview/books-for-asia. *Facebook:* /AsiaFoundation. *Twitter:* @Asia_Foundation.

Better World Books. This online bookstore supports book drives and collects used books and textbooks through a network of more than 2,300 college campuses and partnerships with more than 3,000 libraries nationwide. It has donated 5 million books to partner programs around the world, primarily Books for Africa, Room to Read, Worldfund, the National Center for Family Literacy, and Invisible Children. 11560 Great Oaks Way, Alpharetta, GA 30022; 11@betterworldbooks. com. *Website:* www.betterworldbooks.com/Info-Discards-Donations-Program-m-4.aspx. *Facebook:* /betterworldbooks. *Twitter:* @BWBooks.

Book Aid International increases access to books and supports literacy, education, and development in sub-Saharan Africa. 39-41 Coldharbour Lane, Camberwell, London SE5 9NR; +44 (20) 7733-3577; info@bookaid.org. *Website:* www.bookaid.org. *Facebook:* /bookaid. *Twitter:* @Book_Aid.

Bookfriends International, NFP provides textbooks and library books to secondary school children in Africa. 1000 Rand Road, #206, Wauconda, IL 60084; (847) 726-8776, (877) 726-8777. *Website:* bookfriends.org/default.aspx. *Facebook:* /pages/Bookfriends-International-NFP/172340207690.

Books For Africa collects, sorts, ships, and distributes books to children in Africa. 253 East 4th Street, Suite 200, St. Paul, MN 55101; (651) 602-9844; bfa@booksforafrica.org. *Website:* www.booksforafrica.org. *Facebook:* /pages/Books-For-Africa/27933548445. *Twitter:* @BooksForAfrica.

Bridge to Asia receives books from used book wholesalers, publishers, college bookstores, faculty, students, and the reading public and ships them to 1,000 universities in China. 665 Grant Avenue, San Francisco, CA 94108-2430; (415) 678-2990; asianet@bridge.org. *Website:* www.bridge.org.

Brother's Brother Foundation promotes international health and education through the effective distribution of donated medical supplies, textbooks, seeds, food, and other resources. 1200 Galveston Avenue, Pittsburgh, PA 15233-1604; (412) 321-3160; mail@brothersbrother.org. *Website:* www.brothersbrother.org. *Facebook:* /pages/Brothers-Brother-Foundation/141763585250.

Darien Book Aid Plan sends books in response to specific requests from Peace Corps volunteers, libraries, and schools all over the world. Books are also donated to libraries, prisons, hospitals, and Native American and Appalachian groups in the United States. 1926 Post Road, Darien, CT 06820; (203) 655-2777; darienbookaid@yahoo.com. *Website:* www.darienbookaid.org. *Facebook:* /groups/44290269199/.

Hester J. Hodgdon Libraries for All Program supports the San Juan del Sur Biblioteca in Nicaragua and promotes other lending libraries in Central America. 1716 Del Norte Boulevard, Loveland, CO 80538; (970) 227-9278; janem101@aol.com. *Website:* www.librariesforall.org.

International Book Bank donates books and other educational materials to Africa, Asia, Eastern Europe, the Caribbean, and Central and South America. 4000 Buena Vista Avenue, Baltimore, MD 21211; (410) 685-2665; info@internationalbookbank.org. *Website:* www.internationalbookbank.org. *Facebook:* /pages/International-Book-Bank/101080883287201. *Twitter:* @IntlBookBank.

Pearson Foundation. The We Give Books initiative enables anyone with internet access to put books in the hands of children who don't have them, both in the United States and overseas. Readers select a literacy group, then they choose a children's book or books to read. For each book read online, the foundation donates a book to the group. wegivebooks@pearsonfoundation.org. *Website:* www.wegivebooks.org. *Facebook:* /WeGiveBooks. *Twitter:* @WeGiveBooks.

Sabre Foundation, Book Donation Program. The foundation provides books and other educational materials to partner institutions in Africa, Asia, Europe, the Middle East, and Latin America. 872 Massachusetts Avenue, Suite 2-1, Cambridge, MA 02139; (617) 868-3510; inquiries@sabre.org. *Website:* sabre.org/programs/books/index.php.

The University at Buffalo Health Sciences Library maintains a comprehensive list of organizations that coordinate international book donations, specifying types of books and periodicals, at libweb.lib.buffalo.edu/dokuwiki/hslwiki/doku.php?id=book_donations.

SOURCES: ALA Library Fact Sheet 12: Sending Books to Needy Libraries, ala.org/tools/libfactsheets/alalibraryfactsheet12; ALA International Relations Office, International Donation and Shipment of Books, ala.org/offices/iro/iroactivities/intlbookdonations.

SECURITY

Responding to a theft

by the ACRL Rare Books and Manuscripts Section

LIKE A DISASTER PLAN, an institutional plan for dealing with a theft will ensure a quick and well-organized response. The Library Security Officer (LSO), in concert with appropriate administrators, public relations personnel, security personnel, law enforcement (local, state, and federal, if necessary), and legal counsel, should formulate a course of action that includes:

- Establishment of good working relations with law enforcement agencies—institutional, local, state, and/or federal—and determination of which agency has original jurisdiction over the institution (in-house security, local or state police) and under which circumstances they should be called. The institution should maintain a list of contacts in each level of law enforcement and discuss the plan of action with each. The FBI, as well as U.S. Customs or Interpol, might become involved if stolen items are suspected of being smuggled into or out of the country.
- Notification of appropriate stolen and missing books databases and other appropriate networks.
- Notification of local and regional booksellers and appropriate specialist sellers.
- Transfer of vulnerable items to a more secure location.
- Arrangement of appraisals upon discovery of missing items.
- Questioning of staff regarding any suspicious behavior by users or other persons.
- Preparation of regular communications to staff about progress in the case, consistent with the investigation's integrity.
- Preparation of news releases and responses by authorized institutional representatives to questions posed by the news media; all staff should be instructed to refer inquiries to the authorized spokesperson.
- Maintenance of internal record of actions taken during the case's progress, from its discovery to its final disposition.

Response to a theft in progress

If suspicions are sufficiently aroused, both a witness and the LSO should immediately be summoned and if possible the subject's actions captured on a security camera. After this point, it is necessary to follow institutional policies and applicable state laws concerning the incident. Because of wide vagaries in both those variables, more specific recommendations about potential courses of action in this situation are problematic. Whereas some actions, such as summoning security or the police may seem logical, they may in fact be counter to institutional policies.

If there is probable cause that a theft has occurred, the appropriate library staff should request that the police officer place the suspect under arrest. (Laws regarding grounds for arrest vary from state to state, and library staff should know the relevant state laws.) If there is evidence of theft (such as materials hidden on the suspect's person), one should not agree to the suspect's release in return for the suspect's assurances that he or she will return to face charges. If the officer will not make an arrest, attempt to persuade the officer to detain the suspect until the officer can verify his/her identity and place of residence.

At the first opportunity, each person involved should describe in writing the suspect's physical appearance and obtain written accounts of the entire event from witnesses involved. This document may be needed later, especially if the case is prosecuted. Any materials the suspect has already turned back in should be immediately retrieved and inspected for loss or damage.

Subsequent response

Gather evidence. The LSO will notify administrative officers and institutional security personnel, as well as appropriate law enforcement personnel, and will compile a list of missing items. (This does not mean that the entire collection needs to be inventoried.) Other units and local repositories should be alerted. However, after the immediate steps listed below have been taken, it is suggested that works similar to those that have been stolen be inventoried. In consultation with the personnel previously notified, one should gather all available evidence of theft (such as those items listed below), which must not be altered in any way:

- Detailed, copy-specific descriptions of missing materials.
- Any relevant video files or electronic security system logs.
- Chain of custody documentation for missing materials (including call slips or copies of electronic records).
- Indications of unauthorized physical access to restricted areas.
- Report of any missing cataloging or circulation records and database tampering.
- Indications of systematic patterns of loss of materials.

Report to appropriate organizations and agencies. The library should inform local booksellers of the institution's collecting areas and establish a procedure for quickly informing them of any theft that has occurred in the repository. Thieves sometimes try to sell stolen property quickly, and sellers with knowledge of the collections can recognize, or at least be suspicious of, these genres of materials when they are offered.

Thefts or missing items that are believed to have been stolen should be immediately reported to appropriate electronic mailing lists and national stolen and missing book databases. A search of auction sales records may be advisable if there is reason to believe the stolen material reached the market.

Assist with prosecution. After the perpetrator is apprehended and brought to trial, the institution should establish lines of communication with the prosecution throughout the process of adjudication. This is particularly important if a plea bargain and restitution are involved, since the institution may need to submit an account of damages. It is advisable for a representative to be present during the trial and especially during the sentencing phase, at which point the institution may wish to make a statement. This statement should refer to the seriousness of the crime, the damage to the cultural record, and its impact on the institution and its users. Such statements have been known to influence judges to impose harsher punishments.

Arrange for the return of located materials. Once stolen materials are identified, it is necessary to confirm that they indeed belong to the institution; this process is facilitated by recommended record-keeping recommendations.

If the stolen materials reached the market and are in the hands of a new owner, recovery may be a difficult and time-consuming process. This is especially true if the materials are in a foreign country, where different legal systems and laws of title regarding the transfer of stolen goods are involved. Law enforcement and legal counsel will be able to provide advice on these issues. If a bookseller or auction house sold the items, its assistance should be enlisted in the recovery effort.

While in some cases authorities may be able to seize stolen items, in many cases this is not possible. Negotiation may be required, and it may prove necessary to compensate the current owner to obtain the timely return of the items. Depending on the circumstances, a bookseller or auction house should be requested to participate in the compensation, though this cannot be enforced.

Careful records of the stolen and returned items and all other aspects of the theft should be kept in perpetuity.

SOURCE: ACRL Rare Book and Manuscript Section, *Guidelines Regarding Security and Theft in Special Collections* (Chicago: ALA Association of College and Research Libraries, September 2009), ala.org/acrl/standards/security_theft.

BUDGETING

Eight ways to deal with tough times

by James LaRue

MANY PUBLIC LIBRARIES—in Colorado, the United States, and even worldwide—are facing significant financial troubles. We are part of a larger economic system, and this is a dip in the cycle. Such dips are inevitable over the course of one's career.

The purpose of this article is to provide an overview of some strategies for reining in expenditures without compromising the long-term integrity of our institutions. Making cuts isn't unusual. Businesses do it. Homeowners do it. In libraries, I believe there are eight basic approaches. Not all of them are good ones.

1. **Make across-the-board cuts.** Just make every department in a large organization absorb a uniform percentage of reductions. Such an exercise may well help root out frivolous expenses, or discover more cost-effective alternatives. The problem is, some items—like utilities or insurance—aren't discretionary. Some library programs and practices are more essential to our mission than others.

This is the "nickel-and-dime" approach. It is easy, but not strategic. It is the path most taken, and one that most often leads to general decline.

2. **Reduce the number (or cost) of library staff.** For every public library, this is the key cost, ranging from at least 51% upwards to 80% of the annual budget. To reduce costs without losing people, some libraries freeze salaries and shift a higher percentage of the cost of benefits to the employee. When that isn't enough, libraries seek to reduce head count. The continuum from gentle to drastic looks like this: Buy people out, freeze hiring and wait for attrition, reduce hours, force days off (furlough), or lay people off.

Most institutions move by stages along this continuum. But this isn't necessarily strategic, either. The people who leave aren't always the ones you want to leave, and may be the ones doing the jobs you consider most vital. The good news: Recent jumps in technology (RFID, self-check, automated materials handling) may allow us to provide better service with fewer staff. The not-so-good news: That technology has a cost, too, and capital money may be hard to come by in a crisis.

3. **Gut the materials budget.** In an effort to save jobs, many libraries look to their second-largest category of spending to balance the budget: the acquisitions budget. I have concluded that this strategy is among the most dangerous. It's easy to lose collection relevance. It's very, very hard to get it back again. On the other hand, this might be the time to look at some benchmarks of use: How many times should an item have to be checked out to be retained? Maybe we need to buy more copies of fewer titles.

4. **Reduce the number of library facilities.** Buildings drive most library expenditures: staff, materials, IT, and maintenance. But be prepared: Closing a library will stir up strong emotions in almost any community. That might mean the birth of political will to raise necessary funds. It may also expose a common dilemma: People tend to demand services that they are unwilling to pay for. If that's the case, we need to say so, or commit slow suicide by our silence.

In general, the argument for closure must be buttressed by a clear presentation of the financial facts, as well as other service standards (cost of circulation per item, distance between locations, staffing costs per use, etc.). This strategy—reducing the number of buildings—may well allow the library as a whole to continue to provide a high level of service, but at fewer locations.

5. **Reduce the hours of library operations.** The fewer hours a library is open, the less it costs to run it. Most libraries have a predictable bell curve of use. A 20% reduction in hours might preserve 95% of the use—or all of it, if library users simply shift their schedules. Note that this really only saves money if it is also accompanied by a reduction in work force.

6. **Raise fines and fees.** Inevitably, helpful members of the public suggest that all our financial problems are easily solved. All we have to do is charge for services we now provide for "free": Boost our fines, charge for meeting rooms, rent out internet use, assess a fee for reserves, or even charge for library cards or checkouts.

In my experience, however, most of these don't generate a lot of money. What they do is reduce use. But some hike in these transaction fees may make sense anyhow, both for public relations effect ("You told us to raise our fees, and we did") and to deliberately refocus efforts from one area to another.

7. **Seek private funding,** whether in dollars, in-kind services, or volunteer labor. On the one hand, the more layoffs there are, the larger is the pool of potential volunteers. On the other hand, there's less private money available. But the message of donations to a public institution whose use goes up but funding does not may well resonate with a community that now depends on the library more heavily.

8. **Stop doing something you know you shouldn't be doing anyhow.** Now is the time to shake the organization out of its complacency. In all of our organizations, we're doing something that isn't best practice, doesn't meet basic benchmarks of service, and costs a lot and serves few. This is the time to use the perfectly graspable explanation of "tight times" to demonstrate courageous management.

The importance of tone

There seem to be two basic philosophies about cuts: Make them invisible, or make them clear. I belong to the second camp.

When conscientious librarians try to absorb budget cuts without any fuss or disruption, they provide a disservice to their community. They hide the real costs of operation and suggest that there is no consequence for inadequate funding. Most people have no idea how libraries are funded, or what is necessary to keep them open. Public institutions should present as clear a case as possible about what they do, and what it takes to do it well. That's what transparency is about.

So making budget reductions clear means this: Mount a public campaign to say just where the money comes from, and how much. Let people know that you track the success of your programs, and you won't support those that aren't used. There is a sprinkling of good Return on Investment studies out there now. Libraries consistently return to their communities between $4 and $8 for every tax dollar received, a statistic that is particularly impressive in today's business environment, provided anybody hears us talk about it.

When you need to make cuts, tell people why, in simple and direct language. Say what you might cut. Invite the public to weigh in, but keep the costs of your services on the table. If something is saved, then what is supposed to take its place to ensure the sustainability of the institution? And when you decide what is going to be cut, give that a lot of publicity, too. Say when it's going to happen, and when it happens, remind them why.

Setting the stage for the future

Today's crisis will pass. At that time, libraries will return to the larger crisis: the plain fact that most citizens have no idea what libraries cost, that—as OCLC's 2008 report *From Awareness to Funding* shows us—there is no relationship between use and support, that the actual expenditures on libraries are a fraction of the costs for many other services that have far less significance on our lives and communities, and that fewer libraries are making it to the ballot, or winning when they do.

A financial downturn has predictable results: Libraries all across the country are seeing an upsurge in use as people borrow what they cannot buy, attend programs that don't require an outlay of cash, retool for a new career, hunt for new jobs, or simply hang out in a friendly place.

This gives us an opportunity not only to demonstrate our value to the public, but to be emboldened to talk about it, to point out our long history of remarkably cost-effective service delivery, and the vital significance of our institution to the infrastructure of our shared lives.

We are there for our communities when they most need us, and if that becomes part of our message, maybe we can help them learn to be there for us, too.

SOURCE: James LaRue, "Tough Times and Eight Ways to Deal with Them," *American Libraries* 41, no. 1/2 (January/February 2010): 16–17.

Figures and finances

by Elisabeth Doucett

FIGURES AND FINANCES will be part of your life as a librarian. This article identifies some of the basic methods of quantification and measurement that you will work with and offers some simple ways to manage that information without fear.

Data. You hate working with numbers, but you can't live without the information they provide. Measurement and standards are an integral part of every librarian's life today because they are how you track your resources, and they give you an objective form of evaluation for spending that you can then use to rationalize why your library should receive continued financial support. In today's world you need to demonstrate that what you do has value, and quantification is the best way to do that.

The heart of the matter

If you are like the majority of librarians, you don't like numbers, you aren't particularly intrigued by statistics, you see data as the Great Satan, and your sincere hope was that by becoming a librarian you would never have to see another number in your life. In the past, that might have been a possibility. Sadly for those of us who are numberphobes, data is an important part of our jobs as librarians today. The objective isn't to teach you to love budgeting, numbers, statistics, data, and other quantified information, but rather to demonstrate how to use them effectively and accurately when necessary in your job, and to help you lose your fear and avoidance. The following are my basic "facts and figures for librarians" tools.

Tool 1: Learn how to use Microsoft Excel. There is no way around this one. You have to at least be able to find your way around a spreadsheet, even if you don't become an expert at it. You will use Excel to track the number of people who use your library, to track book buying, to track spending on book buying, to track the number of interlibrary loans. The list goes on and on. If you don't feel your Excel skills are adequate, ask to take a class as soon as you start your new job. If there is no funding for staff development, see if your state library association provides access to WebJunction, an online learning site for librarians where

you will be able to take basic classes in Excel. If that doesn't work, check *Excel for Dummies* out of the library and practice on your own. There are also several online resources that provide basic classes in Excel. These classes are a good way of learning Excel, because they allow you to move at your own speed. Bottom line: Find a way to learn how to manage a basic spreadsheet, so that when someone in your library asks you to track the circulation of mystery books over a period of six months, you have a simple, effective way of doing that.

Tool 2: Learn how to calculate "percentage difference." One of the measures most frequently tracked by libraries (of all types) is the percentage increase or decrease from one period to another (month to month, year to year, week to week) in library traffic, library lending, or spending. It is a very simple calculation and if you can learn it right here and now, you will be happy you did. These examples will show you how to calculate percentage change.

> lending volume for 2008
> − lending volume for 2007
> ÷ by lending volume 2007
> = percentage change in lending volume between 2008 and 2007
> 100,000 − 90,000 = 10,000 ÷ 90,000
> = +11.1%

In 2008 your library spent $1,120,000 on materials. In 2007 the library spent $1,700,000. How much did the budget change from year to year?

> Answer: 1,120,000 − 1,700,000 = −580,000 ÷ 1,700,000 = −34.1%

In January your library circulated 47,000 items. In February your library circulated 53,400 items. How much did circulation change?

> Answer: 53,400 − 47,000 = 6,400 ÷ 47,000 = +13.6%

There are a few things to remember about this calculation:

- It works for any measure to be evaluated: volume, number of patrons, dollars spent, etc.
- You are trying to determine how much increase or decrease there has been in a specific measurement over a period of time. So always start with the most recent time period measurement and subtract from that the starting time period (2008 minus 2007). You might get a negative number if the number decreased between the first and second period. Divide the resulting number by the starting time period (in this case 2007).

This isn't a difficult calculation, but it is a very important one that you should be able to do quickly. You'll find that if you are comfortable with this calculation, it will become one of the most used tools that you will employ in your job.

Tool 3: Measurements of use. Libraries vary tremendously in the degree to which they track and evaluate their performance. The following list identifies some of the most basic measures that every library should track. Upon starting a new position, you might want to ask to see your library's performance measurements and, if they do not exist, offer to track them yourself. Nothing speaks more loudly about the positive

The STORY of PERCENTAGE

value of what a library provides to its community than clear and definitive numbers.

How many people walk through your door every month and every year? The best way to collect this information is to have an electronic counter on all doors into your building and track the numbers on a weekly basis. If your library can't afford to purchase an electronic counter, then the next best step is to have a staff member count the number of people that walk through the library doors for busy, moderate, and slow times of the day and extrapolate a number for the year. The average number of visitors to your library is a critical measurement tool to have. It tells your funding authorities the extent to which the community is using the library and, as you track the number from year to year, if that usage is increasing or decreasing.

Here is an example of how to do this:

- Identify a slow, average, and very busy hour in your library.
- During each of those three time periods, count the number of visitors coming into your library.
- Find the average of those three numbers. For example, 20 during a slow period, 40 during an average period, 75 during a busy period. In this case, the average would be 45 people per hour.
- Multiply that number times the number of hours you are open each week (45 people times 50 hours per week = 2,250 people through the library doors per week). Now, multiply by the number of weeks you are open in a year and you have an average number of visitors per year (2,250 people x 52 weeks = 117,000 people per year).
- Of course this number isn't exact, but it does give you a rough estimate of the number of visitors to your library per year. What is most important is to keep your calculation consistent from year to year. This means to get your average visitors by evaluating the same time periods in the same months every year. This will allow you to understand if your average usage is going up or down.

How many materials are circulated at your library? Circulation measurements are tricky. They are only useful as a tool of measurement in comparison to something else. For example, if you tell someone that your library circulated 100,000 books last year, there is no way to understand if that number is good, bad, or indifferent because there is nothing to which to compare it. However, if you say that the number of books circulated at your library has increased 50% every year for each of the past five years, then you can understand that this library's circulation is growing at a good rate. Or, if your library's circulation is 100,000 and all other similar-sized libraries in your state circulate approximately 50,000 items, then you know your library is being well used, because you have a point of comparison.

Tracking circulation is something that every library does, whether by hand or via a computerized system. However, not all libraries define key points of comparison for their circulation. Some ideas for doing this include picking two to three other libraries in your state or system that are of roughly the same size and comparing your library's circulation to theirs; tracking your library's circulation over six-month periods and comparing them to the same periods in prior years to understand if your usage is trending up or down; and tracking your circulation in particular after you've done a specific program at your library to see if the number of items increases as a direct result of the program execution.

How many programs do we have and how many people attend them? This measurement of use is simple. You count the number of attendees at programs and the number of programs each month at your library. This number is much like the circulation number—it doesn't mean much except in comparison to something else. So you might want to compare the number of attendees to a program this year, versus the number of attendees to the same program last year. Or you might evaluate the total number of programs at your library this year versus last year. What caused the increases or declines? Again, the number itself isn't as important as the comparison that you do with it.

How many reference questions do we answer? When we track reference questions, we divide them into two types of questions: real reference questions ("I need a medical resource so I can understand the impact of diabetes on my spouse") versus what we call directional reference questions ("Where is the bathroom?" or "Where do I find this book?"). It helps to know if there is a specific time of the year when library users ask more reference questions (you might get more medical reference questions in the winter, when people tend to get sick more) to meet staffing needs at the reference desk. It is also helpful to track the number of question from year to year to see how effective a reference department is in maintaining its relevance to an increasingly internet-oriented customer.

How many cardholders do we have? At public libraries the number of cardholders is a critical measurement of use. Library funding groups expect the number of cardholders to increase or at least stay even from year to year. If this doesn't happen, then you need to understand why.

How much money do we spend on the library collection? The amount of money spent on your collection is a measurement of the health of your library. By itself, the amount doesn't tell you anything. However, if you compare your spending with other, similar libraries and find that you are spending far less (or in some rare instances, far more), then you need to understand why. It also provides a compelling piece of data to be able to go to your funding authorities and demonstrate with data how your library's spending doesn't measure up to your competitors.

Tool 4: Learn the basics of your library's budget. If your first job as a new librarian is in a large library, it is unlikely that you will have to see or worry about

the library's budget. However, if your first job is in a small library, it is very likely that you will be involved with the yearly budget development in some capacity, and in fact you may end up having to manage the budget yourself. In any case, it is always helpful to a library director to have staff members who understand how a budget is put together and managed, so it is never a bad thing to gain a basic understanding of budgeting.

At its simplest level, a budget defines what expenses in a library will require funding over a fiscal year. At a more theoretical level, a budget defines the expectations of an organization from a financial perspective. Most libraries are nonprofit organizations of one type or another, so their budgets generally balance out income and expenses to zero. However, their status as nonprofits does not make a budget any less important to them. It is still critical to have a budget so that expectations are established as to how spending will occur throughout a fiscal year. Clear definition of anticipated spending patterns will ensure that all those involved in running a library are in agreement as to how money will be spent.

A budget is established before the beginning of a fiscal year. (A fiscal year is the defined period of time, most often July 1 through June 30, during which budgets are managed.) A library's yearly operating budget defines how much money will be needed by a library to keep the doors open, the lights on, and staffing in place over the course of a year. The operating budget will generally identify fixed and variable costs. *Fixed costs* are any expenses that are the same regardless of use. An example might be what your library pays for interlibrary loan delivery. If the cost is the same regardless of how often you use the delivery service, then it is a fixed cost. If the cost changes depending on how often you use the service, then it is a *variable cost*. Utility costs are another example of variable costs. They change depending on how much electricity or oil or gas your building uses.

During the course of a fiscal year, spending may match the budget expectations or expenses may fluctuate depending on what is going on in the library. Your budget does not change in accordance with those fluctuations. (Remember: once established, a budget never changes.) What changes is your *budget update*. Libraries do budget updates over different periods of time. In my library I see weekly budget updates, but I generally share that information with the library's board of directors once a month. Budget updates help you understand if your spending is on track against the expectations defined in the budget.

A budget and the budget updates can be laid out in many different ways. The basic format for an operating budget is to identify first your income and then your expenses. Each of your expenses will fall into a specific category of expense such as "personnel expenses." These would cover anything to do with library staffing, such as salaries or benefits. The category of expense is called a *line item*.

Some libraries have the flexibility to manage their operating budgets more aggressively than others. One library may be able to manage the budget at the *bottom line*. This means that at the end of the year, the library director is only responsible for ensuring that the library does not overspend its total budget. In this situation the director has the option of moving money between line items, depending on changing priorities. In other libraries, there may be rules that funds can be moved only within a line item. In that situation, a director might be able to move money within the personnel line item from salaries to staff development. However, the director cannot move money from personnel to equipment purchasing. One type of budget management is not better or worse than the other. They simply indicate different levels of control.

The more time you spend looking at and reviewing budgets and budget updates, the more comfortable you'll be with the process of budgeting. If you would like experience with budgets, ask your manager if you can establish a budget for a program that you are developing. The principle of budgeting is the same for a program or for the library's operating budget. By managing a budget at a project level, you'll get a good understanding of how your library's operating budget is managed at a larger level.

Tool 5: Understand a profit and loss statement. A profit and loss (P&L) statement is exactly what it sounds like. It defines how much revenue is expected by an organization over the course of a year and how many expenses will be incurred to drive that revenue. The net result of income minus expenses will result in the operating profit of the organization. A P&L is used to evaluate the day-to-day or immediate operations of the library. It does not consider the *capital expenses* of the library. Capital items can be thought of as anything that will affect the library across multiple years. A good example of a capital item is the library building or the library collection. See the discussion under Tool 6 for further discussion about capital items. Profit and loss statements are typically generated monthly throughout a fiscal year so an organization can see how it is progressing against its goals for achieving profit. If an organization is not achieving its goals, an organizational manager can *manage* the P&L to try to reach its goals. Managing a P&L means that the manager may try to increase revenue or cut expenses to reach the desired profit level. Generally, as long as a library balances out revenue and expenses, it has met its goals. Because most libraries are nonprofit organizations, they frequently do not concern themselves with a profit and loss statement. However, it is still a useful concept to understand, since some libraries do use P&Ls as a way of evaluating their performance over the course of a year.

Tool 6: Learn to read a balance sheet. A P&L defines the yearly or short-term financial expectations of where a library will get revenue and where it will spend money. In comparison, a balance sheet is a one-time snapshot of an organization's complete financial situation. It includes any money in bank accounts or in the library's endowment. It includes property owned by the library. A balance sheet defines the overall health (or illness) of an instituion by putting all of its financial assets (positive cash flow) and liabilities (negative cash flow) in one place. A balance sheet is really an accounting tool in that it provides information—but it is not information that you would or could generally act upon (unless you plan to sell your library building). A balance sheet is important, because it helps keep track if you are dipping into long-term savings for short-term benefit. For example, you might look at a balance sheet and see that your library's checking account for day-to-day operational expenses has been tapped out. That means that you might have to transfer funds from your library's endowment to cover the shortage in cash in your checking account. Essentially, you are taking money from long-term savings and putting those funds against a short-term expense. This may be a necessity, but it also indicates the need for a strategic discussion with your library governing body. A balance sheet is useful for identifying issues of this type and provoking discussion.

SOURCE: Elisabeth Doucett, *What They Don't Teach You in Library School* (Chicago: American Library Association, 2011), 133–141.

USERS

CHAPTER SIX

There is no frigate like a book, and no harbor like a library, where those who love books but can't afford their own complete collections, or those who need a computer, or kids who need a safe place to read after school, or moms with toddlers who want their babies to learn to read, can all come together and share in a great community resource.

—Detective fiction author Sara Paretsky, urging residents of Chicago, and everywhere library hours and staff are threatened, to advocate for their public libraries, Sara Paretsky's blog, October 30, 2011

USER EXPERIENCE

Bringing in new users and nonusers
by Jan LaRoche

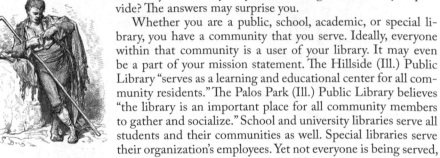

YOU PROBABLY KNOW A LOT about the people using your library. But what do you know about the people who aren't using your library? Do you know who they are or why they are not using the services you provide? The answers may surprise you.

Whether you are a public, school, academic, or special library, you have a community that you serve. Ideally, everyone within that community is a user of your library. It may even be a part of your mission statement. The Hillside (Ill.) Public Library "serves as a learning and educational center for all community residents." The Palos Park (Ill.) Public Library believes "the library is an important place for all community members to gather and socialize." School and university libraries serve all students and their communities as well. Special libraries serve their organization's employees. Yet not everyone is being served, or being served equally.

Identifying nonusers is not as easy as it may sound. First one must determine what a nonuser is. Many libraries define a nonuser as a person who lives within their service area who does not have a library card. But does simply having a library card make a resident a user? Barb Coward of the Cortland (Ill.) Community Library says, "Community members who get a card but never take advantage of the library's services are a true puzzle. We try to make Cortland Library an inviting and useful destination . . . but some people just don't make time for libraries in their lives."

What of those residents who don't have a card but use the library for other resources? Carolyn Mesick of the Moline (Ill.) School District defines a nonuser as "someone who comes to the library with the class and only takes out books to fulfill classroom requirements." In a public library a nonuser could be a patron who uses the internet but does not check out materials.

Special libraries may fulfill research needs but find their patrons are not taking advantage of the many other services they offer. Once you have determined what a nonuser is, you need to find out who your nonusers are. If you define a nonuser as someone who does not have a library card, demographics can help. Manhattan-Elwood (Ill.) Public Library District Director Judith Pet uses data from the U.S. Census and current cardholders to determine how many residents do not have library cards. However, finding those people who have a library card but simply do not use the library can be trickier, particularly in a larger community. Shirley Carney, director of the Western District Library in Orion, Illinois, works in a small library, "so we know most of the users." Even in larger libraries, observation is the first step. Once you know who your users are, you will have a better idea of who is not being served.

The next step is to determine what is preventing these nonusers from becoming users. Reaching out to nonusers, of course, requires more work than reaching the people already coming through your doors. You have to reach out to them. Community-wide surveys are one option. If you have observed a particular group is being underserved, invite them to a focus group. Partnering with a community organization that serves your nonusers can be a big help. In Moline, Illinois, a partnership with the Mexican cultural center Casa Guanajuato has improved awareness of the needs of the Hispanic population, resulting in an increase in service and use to the community.

Now it is time to set goals. Your ultimate goal may be to serve everyone in your community to the fullest extent possible, but it is virtually impossible to appeal to everyone in the same way. Intermediate goals, with a specific target population and objective, should be based on your definition of a nonuser and the results of your studies of nonusers.

Manhattan-Elwood Public Library District has a goal of getting everyone in the community a library card. Knowing that families with small children were underserved, it made a cooperative agreement with local schools to send registration cards home with K–1 students. As a result, their primary school  applicants increased by 100% in fall 2009. Next they plan to have an online application available to target an increase in adult applicants.

With no video store in town, the Cortland Community Library's collection of more than 2,000 movies offers the best selection around. The library uses this to appeal to nonusers and nontraditional users. Barb Coward believes "the fact that some residents use the library only as a video store may have been a factor in our passing a 2007 referendum to increase our operating budget," which doubled the library fund and allowed the library to increase its hours.

The Malta Township (Ill.) Public Library tripled the number of individuals using the library from 2004 to 2007. Prior to that time, the only programming offered was preschool story hour and summer reading for preschool to fifth grade. They now have more than 16 regular programs and a summer reading program that covers all patrons, newborn through adult.

Turning nonusers into users is a long-term process, one that is never fully accomplished. However, by having a clear idea of the needs of your community and a plan to meet those needs group by group, you can always be one step closer to your goal.

SOURCE: Jan LaRoche, "Bringing in New Users and Nonusers," *Illinois Library Association Reporter* 28, no. 2 (April 2010): 4–7. Reprinted with permission.

From gatekeepers to gate-openers

by Steven J. Bell

DO YOU WANT TO BE A GATEKEEPER or a gate-opener? Library workers have long held the position of gatekeeper, historically determining what books, media, and other materials to acquire, and then creating the structures that allow our community members to access them. In more recent times we design websites that allow those same users to choose from an array of resources and services, but as gatekeepers we decide the what, where, and how of presentation. How well or poorly we accomplish the gatekeeping task determines end users' success or failure in achieving their learning or research outcomes.

As gatekeepers, we can aspire to only a limited professional role: making information accessible. But in today's crowded information-provider landscape, that role fails to distinguish the many great assets libraries bring to their communities. Our future may depend on our ability to differentiate what libraries offer and what library workers contribute to communities. The library profession should consider an alternate vision for our future: the library worker as gate-opener. In that role we shift from a focus on creating access to resources to creating meaningful relationships with community members—both those who use and those who don't use our libraries. One way to differentiate ourselves while building these relationships is by designing great library user experiences.

In 2008, I attended a presentation to librarians by author and entrepreneur Seth Godin, a leading authority on nontraditional marketing methods. One thing Godin said stood out in my mind as a critical piece of advice for library workers: "You need to stop being gatekeepers and start being gate-openers." He gave examples of profit and nonprofit organizations that created loyal and dedicated followers, groups he described as "tribes" that emerged as these organizations transformed their core purpose from gatekeeping to gate-opening.

Godin explained that people join tribes, whether as leader or follower, because it offers them something in their lives that provides meaning. In other words, they seek and find a unique experience. Likewise, Godin urged the audience of librarians to better understand what their community members need to accomplish, and to then open up the gates in order to deliver the resources they need for their learning, their research, their lifestyle, and their well-being, and to invite them to discover meaning through personalized relationships with library workers.

Delivering

Our lives are a series of experiences. Some are memorable, others not so much. Think about your own experiences. In my workshops on user experience, librarians' personal examples include great dining experiences, shopping at retail establishments that make them feel special, and visits to resort settings such as Disneyland. Great experiences are memorable, special, and make us want to return for more.

What you might not know is that many of these great experiences are not left to chance or random possibilities. Organizations with reputations for delivering great experiences succeed at it because of significant investments in experience design. But some experiences grow out of a confluence of circumstances such as location and a unique activity; then it is up to organizations to capitalize and build the experience. Think of the Pike Place Fish Market in Seattle, where the vendors wildly toss the fish that customers have purchased. How can the mundane act of buying fish be made into an experience so great that people from around the globe want to bask in the good feeling? When I encourage library workers to think about the design of a great library experience they express doubt or cynicism about the possibility. How can libraries deliver an experience? Well, if a fish market can do it, why can't a library?

If Fish Markets Can Do It, So Can We: Designing Memorable Library Experiences for Students and Faculty

What would constitute a great library experience? The obvious answer is great customer service. People like being treated well. When they get poor customer service, they will likely go elsewhere.

You know your library offers great reference desk service or access services. Patrons tell you so. But what aren't they telling you? A great experience reaches beyond one or two desks and extends to each and every touchpoint in the library organization. That means anyplace where community members come into contact with your library—service stacks, the website, the OPAC, and even that student worker in the stacks.

Information is available from too many sources, and to the casual user all information is the same in terms of quality. That's why differentiating the library is a critical part of user-experience design. If users perceive all information sources as the same then it really doesn't matter where they go for it. Experiences can be created around differentiation. That's largely how Starbucks achieved its incredible success. Pre-Starbucks there was no coffee experience; most retailers sold nearly identical or indistinguishable coffee products at a similar price. Starbucks created an entirely different approach to selling coffee that focused on the quality of the beverage and the ambience of the location. Certainly offering new coffee drinks to the American public created some differentiation, but the crucial factor was the experience of the Starbucks store: It was about more than just buying coffee.

Vive la différence

Now here's the hard part. How can libraries achieve differentiation? In what ways can libraries offer a uniquely different information experience? That's where meaning comes into play. Libraries have always been about providing meaning to people, and now people in search of meaning could be looking to libraries to find a different information experience. In *Making Meaning: How Successful Businesses Deliver Meaningful Customer Experiences* (New Riders Press, 2005), authors Steve Diller, Nathan Shedroff, and Darrel Rhea describe 15 dimensions of meaning based on interviews with thousands of individuals who shared what matters to them, what they most value, and what is memorable. The list certainly will resonate with any library worker because libraries are all about delivering these types of meaning, among them:

6

Accomplishment. Library workers help students and others achieve academic success, they help community members develop new skills and talents, and the act of reading a book is itself an accomplishment.

Beauty. Libraries are places where community members can indulge in the appreciation of the arts.

Creation. Libraries provide the raw materials that stimulate creativity, but unlike other information providers they offer real people with whom creative individuals can establish relationships.

The list goes on, encompassing Community, Freedom, Enlightenment, and Truth. It's clear that libraries can offer meaning across the entire spectrum of what is important to people. That is the answer to the "How can libraries design a differentiated user experience" question. Begin by designing a library user experience that focuses on creating meaning for people, and deliver it through personalized relationships and across all of the library's touchpoints.

Just as there is no single user experience for retailers, resorts, or cafés, each library's user experience will be as different as its history, community, and culture is from all other libraries. The library's workers, in defining their gate-opener role, must identify what will make its user experience unique. As with all new ventures, the hardest part is getting started. The first step is to be clear about what business the library is in. We need to think less about the goods, services, and content libraries provide, and focus instead on the value that our user communities derive from the services and content.

Consider a staff exercise in which the question is framed as "The library isn't in the business of connecting people with information, the library is ————." What comes next helps to define the library's true business. And we can look to business for some examples. Harley-Davidson isn't in the business of selling motorcycles; it sells the concept of freedom to middle-aged men. Black and Decker doesn't sell drills; it sells holes in the wall. Again, focus on the value delivered, not the product or service.

As technology-based organizations, libraries may be particularly susceptible to disruptive technologies that hasten obsolescence. You've heard such statements as "They thought they were in the telegraph business, but they were really in the communication business" to describe companies that became obsolete because they poorly understood the nature of their business. It's up to us to prevent libraries from becoming one more example of an industry that was disrupted by new technologies because it thought it was in the information business but failed to understand what people really valued about its services. So start with the people in your community. Ask them why they use the library. Ask those who don't use it why they don't. Consider just observing how your community members use what the library offers. It should provide new insights into your library's real business, and ideas for a truly gate-opening library experience.

In his closing remarks, Godin said that there was little any of us could do to convince those who thought they no longer needed libraries that they were wrong. Instead, he advised, we needed to humanize the library, to get out into the community and make the library not about the resources and the technology but about us. We needed to open the gates to ourselves. That, he stressed, lays the foundation for relationships to develop; then the community, even the naysayers, would seek us out. The library worker as gate-opener, I believe, is the essence of the 21st-century library user experience.

SOURCE: Steven J. Bell, "From Gatekeepers to Gate-Openers," *American Libraries* 40, no. 8/9 (August/September 2009): 50–53.

JOB SEEKERS

Helping the job seeker
by Jane Jerrard

OFFERING RELEVANT GUIDANCE AND TRAINING for job seekers is one of the biggest challenges faced by today's public libraries. Of course, many libraries have been offering some type of computer classes for a long time, and today, according to *Job-Seeking in US Public Libraries,* nearly three-quarters of libraries offer information technology training for library patrons.

Though your computer classes traditionally may have been taken by curious senior citizens, they are now more likely to be jammed with job seekers—former workers who don't have the skills to search and apply for a position on the internet or who need a refresher course on today's job market. Depending on the state of the community you serve, your library can be overwhelmed with these customers, who seek a crash course that can ultimately help them pay the rent and buy groceries. The Nashville (Tenn.) Public Library has offered basic computer skills classes for years; its public education and web development administrator, Pam Reese, reported that demand for classes has almost doubled as a result of the influx of job seekers.

Teaching basic computer skills is time-intensive; walking a novice computer user through setting up an email account, for example, takes careful attention from an instructor and some time to navigate through the process. Your training issues can be compounded if you have customers with limited fluency in English or only basic literacy skills. Instructors may end up sitting down with such a customer and reading them a job application, and even typing in the answers.

Staff up for training

Devoting extensive time to individual customers may seem impossible, given limited staff, but there are options to increase your number of instructors or guides.

Cultivate in-house trainers. Consider which staff members are able and available to help with training job seekers. Depending on the format and curriculum of the training, you might enlist general staff and put them on a rotating schedule for classroom or computer lab instruction, or for one-on-one computer help. Or you might dedicate a specialized team who could become well versed in job search advice. Consider involving your library system's business staff, particularly human resources, to share their expertise on writing and formatting résumés, professional conduct, and related matters for a few hours each week.

Enlist an army of volunteers. Supplement your staff with more volunteers. "There are a ton of people who are out of work and looking to keep their skills fresh and put something on their résumé," said Joe Yersavich, manager of the Hilltop branch library in Columbus, Ohio. Find those best suited to teaching and guiding job seekers: retirees and laid-off workers who can offer one-on-one help; teachers and college students who can teach basic computer skills; and current or former human resources professionals and other experienced businesspeople who can coach résumé writing and interviewing skills. These people can lead workshops, train library staff, or aid instructors in a computer lab.

Include family and friends. Another simple way to cut back on staff time spent helping individual job seekers on the computers is to recommend that customers coming in to look for a job, fill out an application, or file for unemployment bring a friend or family member along to help them. This gives the customer devoted help, speeds their time on the computer, and reduces demand on staff.

Partner up

Many towns and communities have local government and nonprofit agencies devoted to helping people find employment; many of these agencies are willing to partner with the local library to share resources. Their employees may be available to conduct workshops or classes at your facility, and they can provide valuable information targeted to local job seekers. If your local agency is stretched too thin for this, perhaps it can offer a training module for your staff, who can then share their knowledge with library customers.

Training modules for information literacy

Consider the best ways to offer training in those skills essential to job seekers. Ideally, you will be able to find the resources—staff and volunteers, computers, and physical space—to offer an open computer lab where instructors are available to help with whatever job seekers need, from setting up an email account to formatting a résumé. When the Fresno County (Calif.) Public Library began offering free basic computer classes, attendees had to preregister—but many who registered didn't show up. Each class had empty chairs, although the registration numbers indicated the classes should be full. So in 2007, the library dropped the preregistration requirement and now holds regular weekly classes that are first-come, first-served. For reasons like this, many libraries find an open-lab model to be best. When working with job seekers, encourage them to keep a list of the following:

- Different passwords and login information for sites that require signing on. (It's probably best to use the same login name and password for all.)
- Details of each job applied for, along with the employer/company, the open position, and the date of application. Beginning job seekers may not realize that they may have a hard time remembering what they've applied for, particularly if they send multiple applications to the same corporation over time.

Additional training modules

Don't forget the job seekers at the other end of the spectrum—those who know their way around a computer and are able to craft their own résumé and conduct an online job search. This segment of your customer base will appreciate any training or guidance you can provide on networking, both in-person and electronic. Effective use of networking sites such as LinkedIn and Facebook are proven methods for making connections that lead to jobs. There are many other topics for classes, workshops, and hands-on help that job seekers and the unemployed can benefit from. Here are a few.

Unemployment claims. If you haven't been inundated with customers asking for help navigating online unemployment claims, this may seem like a strange topic to cover in training. But instructions and forms may be difficult to understand or answer correctly, which can cause serious problems for those filing and may result in multiple questions for librarians.

The steps for filing for unemployment compensation vary from state to state. Some states require online filing; others offer options for filing in person, by mail, or online. If you notice an influx of customers seeking help to file their unemployment compensation claims online, consider setting up one-on-one attention or classes to help ensure that they apply and file correctly. Be sure to consider these points:

- Staff involved in helping filers should be familiar with the necessary forms, processes, and deadlines. If possible, partner with your state or local employment office to ensure that you get updated information.
- Create a checklist of information needed for first-time filers and make it available in a handout and on your website. It may include Social Security number, dates of last employment, and contact information for that employer.
- Recommend that beginning computer users, non–English speakers, and

others who may need intensive help bring a friend or family member with them. This built-in support can provide help that your staff may not be able to (such as translating into another language), frees up staff to help others, and enhances privacy.

- If you are aware of problem areas on your state's form, highlight them in training or in a handout. This helps avoid mistakes that may cost filers a week's compensation or more.

Job skills. As with basic computer skills, classes in GED preparation and other job skills have been offered in public libraries for quite some time. Consider adding to your current class offerings, particularly if you can find willing volunteer instructors to teach regular classes in writing skills, basic math, Spanish or another foreign language (or English as a second language), or whatever is deemed marketable for your service community. Look for partnerships with literacy groups that have experience with these issues. Free education in these areas may help job seekers broaden their range of employment possibilities.

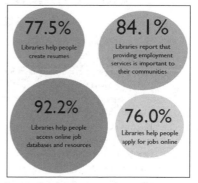

77.5%
Libraries help people create resumes

84.1%
Libraries report that providing employment services is important to their communities

92.2%
Libraries help people access online job databases and resources

76.0%
Libraries help people apply for jobs online

Résumés. "The biggest thing that libraries can do is get people to understand how important the right résumé is," says Barb Vlk, business librarian at Arlington Heights (Ill.) Memorial Library. The art of crafting an effective résumé has changed; résumés submitted electronically are often scanned by software searching for specific key words. The way a résumé is formatted, and how it is submitted, must be correct or a human will never even look at it.

There are several options for helping job seekers create appropriate résumés, from hands-on computer classes in basic set-up and formatting; to expert guidance in words, phrases, and information to include; to one-on-one critiques of résumés. If your staff does not have the expertise or qualifications to help with one or more of these, you have several options:

- Enlist your business staff such as human resources personnel to help.
- Find volunteers in the community or business world.
- Ask for staff volunteers to train on résumés.

Interview skills. Free and accessible training on interview skills can be of immeasurable value to job seekers. As with résumé creation, you can find volunteers or staff to lead a group training session on the interview process. Consider breaking this down into separate steps, possibly over several classes, including tips for first and second interviews, how to dress for success, and negotiating your pay and benefits. Ideally the class will include a chance to practice interview skills one-on-one. The Public Library of Cincinnati and Hamilton County has partnered with local nonprofit Superjobs to offer classes on "Tough Questions" in job interviews, "Résumé 101," and "8 Steps to Successful Employment."

Emotional impact of unemployment. If you have the space and a knowledgeable trainer or moderator (staff or volunteer), it can be helpful to offer a workshop or regular support group to help unemployed people cope with their new status. The financial anxiety and stress, along with loss of identity and self-esteem, can lead to feelings of isolation and depression.

SOURCE: Jane Jerrard, *Crisis in Employment: A Librarian's Guide to Helping Job Seekers* (Chicago: American Library Association, 2009), 13–19.

ETHNIC GROUPS

Collection development for Spanish-speaking users

by the RUSA Library Services to the Spanish-Speaking Committee

LIBRARY SERVICES TO SPANISH-SPEAKING USERS can be complex: Nationality, regional differences, and culture provide myriad combinations within that community. As an example, there are significant linguistic and cultural differences reflected in the varieties of Spanish spoken by Mexicans, Puerto Ricans, Cubans, and other Spanish-speaking groups. To recognize and respond correctly to these differences is a major theme within these guidelines. Although the RUSA Library Services to the Spanish-Speaking Committee is aware of numerous terms for this target population, it has chosen to use the term "Spanish-speaking" in order to encompass the many users that make up this diverse community instead of the outdated and limiting term of Hispanic.

Spanish-speaking communities in the US have varying language skills and competencies in English and Spanish. The members of these communities have diverse needs and are entitled to access to materials that meet those needs. Use standard criteria to aid in the selection of library materials. In order to best carry out a systematic focus for collection development for these communities, develop and regularly update a Spanish Language Collection Development Policy.

Relevance. Library materials for Spanish-speaking library users should meet the educational and recreational needs of the communities served. Libraries should provide appropriate and culturally relevant materials at a level that meets the needs and interests of the various user groups represented in the communities.

Language. The collection should also contain bilingual materials. Emphasize titles from publishers in the countries represented by the major user groups in these communities. The collection should also contain standard Spanish-language titles from Spanish-speaking communities and countries. When purchasing translated works, carefully examine the languages used to insure accuracy and faithfulness to the original work.

Bibliographic access. Bibliographic access to the library's collection should include Spanish-language subject headings in the public catalog to facilitate the location of Spanish-language and bilingual materials. Also provide any locally produced access and identification aids, including lists, bibliographies, and point-of-use bibliographic instructional materials in Spanish.

Formats. Collect all formats, including both print and nonprint materials. Include all reading levels, whether educational or recreational. Supplement traditional print and audiovisual materials with electronic resources available on the internet.

Georgina Gaytan (right) and her daughter Paulina in the El Paso (Tex.) Public Library bookmobile.

Selection. Selection of Spanish-language materials should follow the established procedures for collection development. Consult general and specialized evaluation tools. In addition to Spanish review publications and popular Spanish periodicals, regularly review Spanish-language resources, discussion lists, websites, and other internet resources to identify potential materials to include in the collection.

Vendors. Carefully select and evaluate vendors that supply Spanish-language materials. Take into consideration the country of origin and communities served. As part of the process for acquiring Spanish-language materials, develop good professional relationships with vendors and continually explore different options and services. Support local Spanish-language bookstores and consider them important sources of information and materials. Select and evaluate bookstores and their services on an ongoing basis.

Gifts and donations. Work with local community groups in selecting, acquiring, evaluating, and weeding Spanish-language collections. Encourage local support through gifts, exchanges, and donations to the collection. When evaluating these items, consider the formally established criteria included in a gifts and donations policy statement. Apply normal selection criteria when determining whether to add gifts and donations to the collections. Include those materials not appropriate for the collection in book sales, exchanges or donations to other libraries or organizations that serve Spanish-speaking communities.

Evaluation. Criteria used in evaluating Spanish-language collections should be consistent with review and maintenance policies of the library.

SOURCE: *Guidelines for Library Services to Spanish-Speaking Library Users* (Chicago: ALA Reference and User Services Association, January 2007), ala.org/rusa/resources/guidelines/guidespanish.

Misconceptions about Latinos and library use

by Rose Zertuche Treviño

SOME PEOPLE HAVE MISCONCEPTIONS that Latinos do not use the library, that Latinos do not check out books, and that Latinos don't ask for help if they do come into the library.

Myth: Latinos do not use the library. It is very important to establish trust with all customers. This is even more important with Latinos. There are several factors to consider. Some Latinos often see libraries as being for the educated, as costing money to use, or as being only for the elite. In many Latin American countries, there are no public libraries. Libraries are for research purposes, and one must pay to use the library. For many families, a library experience is not part of their background. The grandparents did not have a library, so this was not something that they would have passed on to their children. Those children, now adults, did not grow up with libraries, and the cycle is ready to continue. Unless those adults be-

Athens-Clarke County (Ga.) Library created "Read" posters for its Latino patrons.

gin to understand how important books and reading are to their child's success, they may continue to pass up the opportunities at the library. This is where the librarian steps in and begins establishing trust, promoting library services, and developing programs of interest to Latinos.

Myth: Latinos do not check out books. Many libraries have a look about them that says "government entity." Signage that says "welcome" and "bienvenidos" will catch the attention of those whose preferred language is Spanish. The library card application should be simple and easy to fill out and should be available in Spanish and English. There should always be a welcome smile on the face of the first person a customer will encounter, and that person should make the effort to assist in any way possible, even helping fill out the library card application. Some Latinos may be immigrant families who fear the government. They may or may not be in the country legally, and they may or may not know someone who has entered the country illegally. Fear of immigration, or *la migra,* will prevent them from filling out a library card application because then they will be "on record." Keep your collection current and in good condition. Make sure it is visible. Weed regularly. Your Spanish-language collection should be just as important as any other collection in your library.

Myth: Latinos don't ask for help if they do come into the library. Latinos generally do not want to put anyone out. Asking for help means interruption, and this is something that is difficult for some Latinos. Once again, there should always be a welcome smile on the face of the first person a customer will encounter entering the library, and that person should make the effort to assist in any way possible. Make an effort to approach customers as they enter the library. Welcome them and offer to help them find books, DVDs, the computer, and more. Be sure to take them to someone on staff who speaks Spanish if you are unable to communicate with them; however, that first welcoming effort is very important.

SOURCE: Rose Zertuche Treviño, *Read Me a Rhyme in Spanish and English: Léame una rima en español e ingles* (Chicago: American Library Association, 2009), 5–6.

Asian-language speakers: Cultural considerations

edited by Shelly G. Keller

AS HUMAN BEINGS, we share many commonalities, and yet we live in different ways. Among Asian cultures, there are also many commonalities as well as differences. All of us have the ability to live in any culture, but most of us live our lives knowing only one. Culture is a survival mechanism, consisting of plans and recipes for handling the world. Culture can guide how we see and think, how we relate, what makes us laugh or cry, and how we eat and dress, as well as how we are born and how we die. Culture allows the individual to survive within the strength of the group with whom he or she shares a homeland, ancestry, and environment.

When presenting information specific to cultural groups, one must guard against inadvertent stereotyping. In learning about Asian cultures, it is important to remember that each individual is unique, and that there is enormous diversity and complexity in humans, regardless of their cultures. In learning about the commonalities and differences among Asian cultures, there are several influences that should be recognized. These include:

- historical and cultural backgrounds;
- generations, immigration, and length of U.S. residency;
- social class structure and region of original or ancestral country;
- family and children;
- language;
- religion and spirituality;
- manners, customs, etiquette, gestures, and taboos;
- cultural ideals; and
- social interaction and relationships.

While many Asian cultures value family, education, and cultural and linguistic retention, most Asian cultures express those hopes and expectations in different ways. And while some Asian cultures share a common language and culture that crosses geographic boundaries, one's homeland or nation is equally important. The homeland and its political history also contribute to the uniqueness and distinct differences from culture to culture. Each Asian culture is distinct and should be valued and recognized as such.

With regard to Asian languages, Chinese is to Asian languages what Latin is to the Romance languages (Spanish, Italian, French, Portuguese, and Romanian). Japanese and Korean languages, for example, are so deeply indebted to Chinese that the two languages still use many Chinese characters in writing along with their own alphabets or vernacular scripts. The Chinese characters often retain the same or similar meanings, although they are pronounced differently.

Vietnamese written language was originally based on Chinese characters, but the influence of the French during their occupation of Vietnam resulted in the language being romanized as it is today. Publications from mainland China are often written in the simplified Chinese characters, a shorthand that was promulgated during Communist rule to expand literacy in the Chinese population. These simplified Chinese characters and other intricacies of Asian languages can pose problems for Chinese-language collection development.

The spoken language—dialects and word order—also differ greatly from one Asian culture to another.

Influences of other cultures are also reflected in interpretation and meaning in each Asian language. Within Asian cultures, there are not only different languages, but different dialects within each language. Such language regionalisms can make it difficult for people from the same culture to understand other dialects, as is the case with the Chinese language.

Recommendations

1. When developing a collection of video and audio resources, try to balance the collection to meet the specific language needs of the library's service area population. When you have patrons who speak different dialects (for example, Mandarin and Cantonese), try to provide resources for each.
2. Expect a wide range in paper and binding quality when purchasing Asian-language materials because place of publication often impacts both language and production quality. For example, Chinese-language resources published in Hong Kong will have a decidedly British influence in terms of product quality (binding, paper), while resources

published in Taiwan will deliver high quality in both language and product. As for Korean-language materials, almost all now available are published in South Korea. Publications from South Korea far exceed those from North Korea in paper quality, printing, and binding.

3. The belief that all Asian cultures are the same can interfere with the library's ability to provide effective service to individuals. Asian cultures are distinct and unique. To provide effective library service, it is helpful when the staff members attempt to understand the differences between Asian cultures and are respectful of those differences.

4. When serving Asian-language speakers, the staff must be flexible. Ask tactful questions. Learn the distinctions between cultures. Do not insist on applying English, American, or Western cultural standards when serving Asian-language-speaking patrons. For example, inserting Asian-language magazines into plastic magazine covers so that the back cover is displayed demonstrates the library's disregard for the fact that many Asian-language publications are read from right to left, with the binding on the right, not the left.

5. Remember, no culture is monolithic with everyone in that culture behaving in exactly the same way or believing exactly the same thing. The best approach is to deliver library service with the individual in mind. Try to understand that people within each Asian culture have many different views, experiences, values, feelings, and beliefs, regardless of sharing a common culture or language.

6. It is best not to make assumptions. Do not assume someone is of a particular culture. It is better to ascertain the person's language preferences. For example, a Korean raised in Japan, or in Korea before the end of World War II when Korea was under Japanese rule, can speak Japanese and may enjoy Japanese-language materials.

7. Keep in mind the political, economic, and social differences within the homeland region of an Asian-language speaker. People of all cultures bring those political, economic, and social differences—and their feelings about them—with them when they emigrate to another country.

8. Be sensitive to political issues when planning programs, outreach activities, and collection development. Avoid cultural symbols, such as flags, which can carry too much political meaning for some people. Instead, consider using maps of the Asian countries that are the homelands of the Asian-language-speaking groups the library serves.

9. Learn to rely on the library's cultural community to verify the accuracy and appropriateness of language use or other cultural issues. When you act without help from someone in the key culture, you can make mistakes.

10. Videos on learning Chinese refer to learning Mandarin unless they specify Cantonese. One must determine whether the patron wants Mandarin, Cantonese, or another dialect when helping them to check out videos.

11. Many Asians are family-oriented, so library programs designed for parents and children are likely to attract more participants than programs designed just for children or just for adults. Consider providing programs both inside the library and in locations convenient to the targeted audience.

12. Many Asians are highly motivated about obtaining a high-quality

education for their children. Enhance their awareness of the public library as an educational institution where children can develop reading skills at an early age.

Misconceptions about Asian cultures

When trust has been established between a library staff person and an Asian patron, the patron develops the expectation of having a face-saving experience. This trust requires that management empower library staff to be flexible regarding library rules and policies, such as how overdue fines are charged. Remember that once an Asian patron loses face or reputation, that patron may never return to that library or any other.

Library service to all patrons should be fair and equitable, but it also should be delivered within the patron's own cultural context. California's public libraries serve people of many cultures. Staff members need flexibility to serve diverse patrons with equanimity without pitting people of different cultures against one another. Keep this in mind when resolving problems between patrons of different cultures over issues that may arise in the library setting.

Some misconceptions about Asians include:

1. "Asians are the 'model minority.'" This implies Asians are without problems. This belief can detract staff members from providing the type and level of library service to Asian-language-speaking individuals that would be most effective.

2. "Asians are shy, quiet, and not expressive." This misconception affects how service is provided and can cause the level of service to decline. When an Asian person is outgoing or assertive, some people misinterpret those actions as misbehavior. In many Asian families, children are raised to be respectful, modest, and humble, with the purpose of creating a harmonious or cooperative relationship within the family and community. Because Western culture values individuality and competitiveness, this modesty and humility can be viewed as weakness or as being submissive.

3. Asians are often stereotyped as having a high socioeconomic status, especially when they have large, extended families. Asian merchants and retailers are also perceived as being more affluent than other immigrants, bringing more money with them, having better access to funds to start businesses, making more money than other immigrants, excelling in both education and work. These are stereotypes and are not true of all Asians.

4. Additional misconceptions about Asians include the belief that all Asians are smart, wealthy, hard-working, frugal, highly educated, highly technically skilled, good at science and math, and successful. While these qualities may be highly desirable, they are not always accurately applied. Many Asian immigrants, like immigrants from other countries, are frugal and hard-working in order to survive in their new country.

SOURCE: Shelly G. Keller, ed., *Harmony in Diversity: Recommendations for Effective Library Service to Asian Language Speakers* (Sacramento: California Library Association, 1998), 13–16. Reprinted with permission.

USERS WITH DISABILITIES

Twenty years of assistive technologies

by Barbara T. Mates

ON JULY 26, 2010, THOUSANDS OF PEOPLE applauded the 20th anniversary of the signing of the Americans with Disabilities Act, which mandated that disabled individuals be accorded the same rights as persons without disabilities. The celebration stimulated reflection and debate on the effectiveness of the law. No consensus about success has been reached, but most people agree that despite slow and steady progress, much still remains to be done—especially if we are to achieve true parity in the workplace.

Approximately half of this country's disabled workforce is unemployed, and higher education for many disabled individuals is still just a dream. Much of this can be traced to a lack of funds to purchase technologies and to make accommodations, but some roadblocks stem from insufficient knowledge about disabilities and what disabled individuals can accomplish if given the opportunity.

People with disabilities are the most diverse of all minority groups; they may be young or old, rich or poor, male or female. Ensuring that library staff knows how to work with them is one of the most critical components in creating an accessible environment. Such interactions are made one patron at a time, and most disabled individuals will respond positively if they sense that someone is trying to do the right thing.

To ensure that staff has a rudimentary knowledge of how to work with persons with disabilities, ALA's Association of Specialized and Cooperative Library Agencies (ASCLA) has developed a helpful toolkit of etiquette tip sheets. The sheets, which can be read and assimilated relatively quickly, suggest appropriate behaviors for staff working with persons who have specific disabilities, and identify materials and assistive technologies that will help disabled individuals use the library more successfully. The toolkit will be a useful supplement to training organized by a library's human resources department. Tip sheets are available on ASCLA's website. In the meantime, you'll find a few simple suggestions below:

- Talk directly to the disabled individual whenever possible.
- Don't raise your voice when speaking to a person who is hard-of-hearing or deaf. Look directly at the person, preferably in a properly lit area, giving a clear view of your face and lips.
- Be precise when giving directions to a blind person.
- Autistic children who don't want to participate in activities during story or craft time should be allowed to opt out. Don't continue to coax a child who really prefers to stay on the sidelines.

Screen readers. Screen-reading software enables persons with severe visual impairments or blindness, learning disabilities, or cognitive disorders to use computers to access the web and electronic information. Unfortunately, many disabled people find the price of such technology prohibitive. Having access to public usage computers with these technologies can be a great equalizer, helping individuals find employment, improve their job skills, connect with friends and relatives, locate valuable social services information, or simply have fun.

Screen-reading software, including products such as JAWS (Freedom Scientific), Window-Eyes (GW Micro), and Hal (Dolphin), scans the text being presented, then reads it aloud using a speech synthesizer. JAWS is the most popular program in North America, but Window-Eyes, which originated in the U.K., is less expensive and has a growing following in North America. The program that a library purchases should dovetail with what is most popular in the surrounding geographic area. Contact rehabilitation centers, schools, consumer organizations, and vendors of assistive technology in your area before making a choice.

Enlarging software. Screen-enlarging software allows persons with low vision to read email and documents displayed in standard type, visit social networking websites, and more easily do other text-based tasks. Patrons can adjust the size of the text and change attributes such as background color. Some software packages permit users to remove all color. The products are easy to install and work in harmony with most operating systems. Currently the two most popular programs in North America are ZoomText from AI Squared and MAGic for Windows from Freedom Scientific. Dolphin's Lunar and SuperNova have strong followings in other parts of the world. All allow the user to change the size of the display, including menus, toolbars, and icons, with a few keystrokes.

Hardware, workstations, and monitors. Most assistive technology hardware is manufactured to suit particular needs, but all patrons will appreciate an accessible workstation. Such workstations permit patrons to adjust the height of the worktable. They include a moveable arm for mounting the monitor so the user can tilt the display as needed. An ergonomic keyboard tray and an oversize monitor (20 inches or larger) should also be part of the workstation. The larger monitor allows patrons using screen-enlarging software to see more of the displayed text as they move through documents. When text is enlarged on a standard monitor, the user can read only a limited portion at a time and his or her train of thought can easily be lost.

6

More to keep in mind. Much is made of access to electronic communications, but the library must also build collections with disabled patrons in mind. Consider storyboards for families with members who have autism spectrum disorders, recorded books for people who cannot read print, and large-print books for those with limited vision. Patrons who read Braille will appreciate Braille magazines. Braille-and-print children's books, which feature Braille pages bound into the original print publication, are also available.

Libraries without funds to develop an audio or Braille collection can connect with a cooperating member of the Library of Congress's National Library for the Blind and Physically Handicapped to learn about digital playback equipment and program downloads and to determine if they are eligible for a depository collection of books.

Communication. It is important that all patrons be able to contact the library and communicate their needs. For persons who are deaf or hard-of-hearing, this is a challenge—unless the library has video relay service equipment, such as that offered by Sorenson Communications, in place. The system uses a video phone to enable individuals who use sign language to communicate with those who cannot, and vice versa. Sorenson offers the system free of charge to entities like libraries. Face-to-face communication can be enhanced simply by typing back and forth, using a word processor, writing notes, or using a cellphone display.

Websites and electronic databases. Technological advances have enabled people with a wide range of disabilities to use computers and the internet, but some standards are needed. Librarians can refer to guidelines established by the World Wide Web Consortium (W3C). The concept to keep in mind is that technologies have limitations. For example, if an important graphic on a web page is not sufficiently described within the text, a blind user may miss the entire point of the page. Screen readers cannot yet interpret graphics. It doesn't cost more to design a universally accessible website; it simply requires care, adherence to design, and the ability to resist the temptation of new applets. ASCLA has devised an "Internet and Web-Based Content Accessibility Checklist" (online at ala.org/ascla/asclaprotools/thinkaccessible/internetwebguidelines) that can be used to assess websites for access and usability. The list may not ensure 100% compliance with the W3C, but it is a very good start.

It is also important to ensure that databases purchased by the library are usable by all patrons. Despite the ADA, misinformation remains a problem, and some database providers do not yet accept "access for all" as an issue they must resolve. It is always prudent to check a database before purchase to determine if it will fully fit patron needs. No librarian wants to have to explain why the disabled son or mother of a library trustee or local politician can't use a database that cost $10,000. Here again ASCLA can help; a useful toolkit on database evaluation, "Think Accessible before You Buy: Questions to Ask to Ensure That the Electronic Resources Your Library Plans to Purchase Are Accessible," is online at ala. org/ascla/asclaprotools/thinkaccessible/default.

It may not be immediately possible to purchase, update, and maintain the assistive technologies needed to serve all your patrons. Purchase and implementation can, however, be done gradually. At the very least be aware of the accessibility options available through the Microsoft and Apple software packages already owned by your library. Both manufacturers provide features such as text enlargement, screen reading, online keyboard, voice recognition for inputting data, and screen alerts for users unable to hear. Although this isn't the best solution, it does provide some access, and it is a start toward ensuring equitable service for all.

SOURCE: Barbara T. Mates, "Twenty Years of Assistive Technologies," *American Libraries* 41, no. 10 (October 2010): 40–42.

Mouse emulators

by Barbara T. Mates

CERTAIN INDIVIDUALS have mobility disabilities that prevent them from using any type of mouse, although they may be able to grasp other items and manipulate them. They do not benefit from software that simulates mouse actions. This group of people needs a device that will emulate mouse actions. A variety of items work well and will help individuals to exploit their personal abilities to their fullest advantage.

Trackballs

Sometimes called an upside-down mouse, trackballs can be found in mainstream technology as well as in specialized assistive-technology arenas. The sophistication and applications vary. If the library's budget is limited, information technology staff may be able to find a usable trackball from one of the library's suppliers.

Wave Wireless Switch-Adapted Trackball. A product of AbleNet, the Wave Wireless Switch-Adapted Trackball (right), also called the Wireless Wave, acts as a mouse emulator and a switch interface. It is a plug-and-play device that works with most computers. It is designed for users with limited hand control, motor skill difficulty, hand-eye coordination challenges, and involuntary muscle spasms. The Wireless Wave features an oversize trackball that will activate with the lightest of touches.

BIGtrack. For patrons with little or no fine motor control, there is a three-inch trackball device called BIGtrack, made by Infogrip. The trackball is sturdy; it is a bright yellow color that is easily seen; and it can withstand use in a public environment. In addition to being a trackball device, it has left-click, right-click, and drag-lock features for those able to use these functions.

Kensington Expert trackball. Kensington Computer Products Group is a longtime fixture in the trackball community. The company continues to produce quality products and does not rest on its laurels. It continues to improve its products, and in doing so, it wins awards for innovation. The ball of the Kensington trackball is the largest available. The product has a unique design, as it incorporates a scroll ring, which enables people to move the ring with their fingertips.

L-Trac high-performance trackball. The L-Trac high-performance laser optical trackball, a product of Clearly Superior Technologies, has a natural contour shape that enables the user to grip it and control its actions. The device is based on laser navigation technology, and as a result, it produces a predictable, quick, and precise motion that becomes intuitive in a few minutes of use. It is well designed and is used in gaming as well, making it a good option for the rigors of public use.

6

Joysticks

Joysticks are an essential tool for gamers and have been for a generation. The technology allows easier maneuverability. Often, all that is needed is a tip of the stick to the left or right, and movement is made. This technology enables some with limited physical strength to move the cursor and input commands.

SAM-Trackball and Joystick. The SAM (Switch-Adapted Mouse) Trackball, distributed by RJ Cooper and Associates, was designed to be used with personal switches and will help users access computers. The device enables persons with gross-motor hand control or fine-motor head control to move the mouse, click, and doubleclick with whichever part of their body can be controlled.

The same technology used for the SAM-Trackball is also available as a joystick. When the user pushes the stick, the cursor does not fly off; rather, it moves in the direction pushed and at a given speed. Joysticks have worked well with users who do not have defined motor skills.

Both SAM technologies are "plug and use," but it is more than likely that the person requesting a SAM-Trackball would be highly technologically literate.

Roller II Joystick. The Roller II Joystick (right), which is also available as a roller ball, is a product of Traxsys Input

Products, a manufacturer of assistive and mainstream input devices. The Roller II Joystick allows users with severe motor impairments to locate and input information. It comes in either a large 2.5-inch trackball or a 3-inch joystick. Each has separate buttons for left click, right click, and drag lock, with color-corresponding switch ports on the back of the units. A flashing light indicates the drag button has been activated. The Roller II products include a key guard to help users isolate the buttons. The joystick comes with two alternative handles—T-Bar and Soft Sponge Ball—to accommodate different input needs. The joystick can be outfitted with several handles to allow users a more comfortable and usable fit.

Unique mice

Although someone with a disability may not be able to use a conventional mouse, he or she may be able to use a mouse that was developed for targeted audiences.

Senior Mouse. The Senior Mouse (left) was designed by the German company INCAP and is shaped to fit the curvature of the entire hand to ensure a secure grip. Should the user have trembling in his or her hand, the motion is counterbalanced so that uncontrollable movements do not affect the mouse. This is especially useful for individuals with upper-extremity disabilities, neurological disabilities, arthritis, cerebral palsy, multiple sclerosis, muscular dystrophy, and carpal tunnel syndrome. This is an important device to consider if there is a large senior population using the library's computers in addition to those with disabilities.

Zero Pressure Finger Mouse. The Zero Pressure Finger Mouse, by Special Needs Computer Solutions, is 100% optical, with no moving parts. The device has arrows for cursor positioning, left and right buttons, and a separate key for one-touch double clicking, as well as a Fast key for quicker traversing. If the library is looking for a unique product that will come with boasting rights, while being low-cost and easy to install, this device may be it.

Zero Tension Mouse. The Zero Tension Mouse was developed to help prevent injuries and to help those who have disabilities caused by factors like carpal tunnel syndrome to use computers pain-free. The mouse allows the user to relax the hand, shoulder, and neck. The mouse is a mainstream item, and it is relatively low-cost. Its one drawback is also its strong suit: One size does not fit all users, and it is available in several sizes. The product is available from a multitude of vendors of ergonomic products as well as mainstream resources such as Amazon.com.

Touch pads

With laptops, PDAs, and netbooks being a part of both our office and home lives, there are many touch pads in the mainstream technology area. Many of these may be able to work for patrons with disabilities. When looking for such a product, determine how much control is ceded to the user. For example: Can users use a light tap to enter commands? Can they run a finger across the pad for input simulation?

Cirque Easy Cat (left), Cirque Smart Cat, Smart Cat PRO. Cirque Corporation was developing innovative technology long before PDAs and laptops were in vogue. The three touch pad versions by Cirque Corporation are available to give people unable to use a mouse a device that will yield total mouse emulation. The user slides his or her finger across the pad, then gently taps on the pad or clicks one of the buttons to perform all mouse functions. Hot links are provided to perform repetitive functions. The touch pads vary in price and utilities.

Jelly Bean switches. Jelly Beans (right), by AbleNet, are 2.5-inch brightly colored flat discs that can be used to emulate mouse clicks. These are switches; a switch is a broad term used for a myriad of assistive devices that replace a keyboard or replace the mouse's left click and right click. The Jelly Beans are inexpensive and useful for people who can only press downward on an object. They also work well for those with cognitive disabilities who can more easily understand that depressing the red jelly bean will let you cut, paste, copy, change the font, and so forth. The switches are low cost, are widely available, and can be used within a Wi-Fi environment.

SOURCE: Barbara T. Mates, *Assistive Technologies in the Library* (Chicago: American Library Association, 2012), 88–92.

OLDER ADULTS

Guidelines for library services to older adults

by the RUSA Library Services to an Aging Population Committee

6

THE AMERICAN LIBRARY ASSOCIATION has a longstanding record of promoting library and information services to older adults. These guidelines, first developed in the 1970s, have been updated to respond to the changing demographics of an aging U.S. population and reflect a basic principle in library services to older adults that recognizes their diversity and discourages stereotyping in planning collections, programs, and services for this growing population.

For purposes of these guidelines, an "older adult" is defined as a person at least 55 years old.

Acquire current data about the older population and incorporate it into planning and budgeting. Conduct surveys on a regular basis of the older population and their service providers in the community, including their numbers, demographic characteristics, and other information, such as their location and housing; educational, socioeconomic, and ethnic background; religious organizations and other groups to which they belong; agencies that serve them; and the local media that targets older adults in the community.

Supplement surveys with focus groups and user studies among the community's older population to determine their needs and interests and to gauge how services, collections, and programs might be made more appropriate and relevant to this population.

Collect data on the specific and varied information needs of older adults due to language, culture, education, income, internet skills and access, gender identity/expression, sexual orientation, and age.

Utilize the above data in combination with the more general informational needs basic to older adults in their everyday lives. Such subjects include health, health care, Social Security, financial planning, housing, independent living, elder law, caregiving (including grandparenting), lifelong learning (including adult literacy and computer skills), community service, civic engagement, and volunteering. The library's collections, programs, and informational services should reflect the diverse interests and needs of older adults.

Ensure that any services that target older adults are an integral and ongoing part of the library's operations and budget. Additional funding may be required

 for collections, accessibility equipment/software, and the time expended by library staff in services to older adults and community. If a special grant or external funding is sought to support a pilot or demonstration program, consider how the program will be integrated into the library's regular budget and services at the end of the grant.

Involve older adults in the library's planning process by establishing an advisory committee. This committee might include older adults who are regular library users; library volunteers, staff, board members, or members of the library's Friends group; and leaders of organizations of older adults and other community organizations.

Ensure that the special needs and interests of older adults in your community are reflected in the library's collections, programs, and services. Appoint a librarian to act as a coordinator of services to older adults, ensuring that there is at least one designated staff member monitoring and developing the library's collections and services with older adults in mind.

Consider how the library can be made more visible, more welcoming, and more relevant to older-adult users.

Advertise the library's services and website in local newspapers, magazines, radio or television programs that target older adults, and in senior centers, nutrition programs, and residential housing.

Offer to speak to organizations of older adults about the library's services on a regular basis.

Establish an ongoing liaison with agencies that serve older adults (especially senior centers that employ activity coordinators) to explore cooperative programming, recruit volunteers or friends of the library, and seek suggestions for programs or services that would encourage library use.

Work with state library agencies that may provide staff training and development and information resources for older adults.

Make the library's collections and physical facilities safe, comfortable, and inviting for all older adults. Evaluate your library's accessibility by older adults with physical, visual, aural, reading, and other disabilities, according to the Accessibility Guidelines for Buildings and Facilities of the Americans with Disabilities Act.

Consider providing at least one wheelchair in the library for public use.

Accommodate users for whom prolonged standing is difficult by placing chairs or stools near stacks, information desks, checkout areas, computer terminals, and other areas. If possible, create a Senior Space using easy chairs gathered in an area adjacent to books and magazines of interest to older adults.

Consider placing materials frequently used by older adults on easily accessible shelves.

Place paperbacks, clearly labeled and well spaced, in areas of the library that are especially well lit, accommodating older adults who prefer paperbacks over heavier and more cumbersome hardback books.

Assure that spacing between shelving accommodates users in wheelchairs.

Ensure that signage is clear, Brailled (where appropriate), and readily visible to all, including users in wheelchairs. Library brochures should be in at least 14-point font type.

Provide at least one computer station prominently labeled and installed with large-type software for older adults with low vision. If needs warrant and resources are available, acquire other assistive technology such as a stand-alone Reading Machine, which speaks the book's text to a blind reader; speech synthesizer and related software; low-tech magnification and other devices.

Provide TTY access, closed-captioned videos, and assistive listening systems to older adults with hearing disabilities.

Acquire and make available books and periodicals in large print.

Make the library a focal point for information services to older adults. Cooperate with local Area Agencies on Aging, senior nutrition programs, senior volunteer programs, and others in the aging service provider network by advertising their services and making their publications and other information more readily accessible. The library can provide an invaluable service by organizing and consolidating information about government and community programs and services available to older adults.

Consider developing or expanding the library's website to provide links to the sites of organizations of older adults, government departments and agencies serving older adults, newspapers, and other websites whose focus is older adults.

Ensure that the library's collection includes materials that are pertinent for caregivers of older adults, for their children or other family members, and for professional caregivers in the community.

Target the older population in library programming. Incorporate adequate funding for programs, materials, and services for older adults in the library's operating budget, and actively seek supplemental funding through partnerships with other agencies, organizations, and foundations interested in serving older adults.

Plan programs each year that specifically target older adults and enhance their ability to remain independent and skillful library users. Publicizing such programs can heighten the library's visibility among the older population.

Select themes for programs that deal with specific interests of older adults identified through user surveys, focus groups, or circulation statistics reflecting borrowing patterns by older adults.

Plan programs for specific age groups or generations within the older population, being aware that interests and information needs vary greatly. Include intergenerational programs and participate in intergenerational projects sponsored by others in the community. Consider partnerships with local schools, daycare facilities, or community organizations.

Pursue other opportunities for cooperative programming with partners such as community and senior centers, Area Agencies on Aging and other community agencies, and educational institutions offering continuing educational programs for older adults. Cooperative efforts might involve active participation in planning and delivering programs, assistance in advertising programs, or providing book displays and booklists in conjunction with the library's programs.

Consider providing computer and internet courses specifically designed for older adults to accommodate a slower pace of instruction, provide sufficient time to develop mousing skills, and allow for the possibility that some older adults may have visual, physical, or hearing disabilities. If possible, include individual tutoring provided by peers or others.

Explore opportunities to provide library services and programming to older adults outside the library, such as in senior or community centers, nursing homes, and senior housing units. Consider offering computer and internet training in these locations. Use library displays to combat ageism or the stereotypes in our society about older adults. Provide opportunities for older adults to volunteer in the library. Create opportunities for lifelong learning programs.

Reach out to older adults in the community who are unable to travel to the library. Survey community needs and consider library budget planning to accommodate possible increases in demand for outreach services, such as delivery of library materials by mail and mobile library services. Analyze community demographics, population forecasts, and housing trends to plan to meet this need effectively.

Offer the library's services to assistive living and alternative housing sites, senior day care, congregate meals sites, senior community centers, nursing homes

---

10 tips for teaching computer skills to older adults

by Abby Stokes

There are unique obstacles to teaching technology to a generation of adults who not only weren't born with a computer mouse in their hands, but who clearly remember when telephones were rotary dial. There are three motivating factors that inspire most silver surfers to take on the challenge of the computer—the internet, email, and a desire to not be left behind. Keeping those three objectives in mind, here are my 10 tips on how to bring the computer-fearful onboard successfully and enjoy the experiences the computer and internet have to offer:

1. **Watch your language.** You probably shouldn't cuss at the computer or your student, but that's not what I mean. Be aware of the words you chose. You'll lose someone in the first five minutes if you speak computer jargon. They don't need to know computer terms in order to use the computer, so avoid tech talk unless absolutely necessary.

2. **What turns them on?** Before sitting down in front of the computer, ask your students what interests them. You want to be able to dazzle them with what the internet has to offer specific to their needs and interests. What questions would they like answered? What are their hobbies? What is their family into that they would like to know more about?

3. **Slow and steady wins the race.** Most seniors are not in a rush; you shouldn't be either. Assume that you are always going too fast. Take your cues not from the agenda you've set for the lesson, but from the look in the eyes of your student. Eyebrows raised in surprise are good. A furrowed brow and a glazed look are bad. When you see the latter, you need to back up and figure out where you lost your student and start again from there.

4. **Shake it up.** Before you even turn on the computer, have your student put both hands on the monitor and shake it a little. Take the mouse in your hand and swing it by its tail. It reassures the fearful to know that the computer is just a big plastic box and nothing more. A little levity, with the intimidated, goes a long way.

5. **Play wingman.** Your student should start in the driver's seat from the get-go. They do all the hands-on controlling of the experience starting with turning the computer on. Think basic, basic, basic and assume they don't know anything, but can learn everything.

and senior residential or care homes in the community. Also offer assistance to older adults who are confined to private residences or who are unable to carry library materials home. Advertise the library's services through local media, public health agencies, and other agencies that work with older adults.

Eliminate waiting lists for library services through innovative approaches to delivery of materials, a redistribution of personnel, or establishment of a volunteer delivery system. Partner with Regional Libraries for the Blind and Physically Handicapped to expand available services.

Train the library's staff to serve older adults with courtesy and respect. Provide sensitivity training to staff at all levels to make them aware of difficulties older adults may have in using the library, and how to make the library a more welcoming and comfortable place for older adults. Train staff to recognize and combat ageism and stereotypes about older adults.

Ensure that all staff are aware of any special services the library offers that may be of interest to older adults, such as home delivery service, a talking books collection, a service to retrieve materials from the stacks, reading aids, or waiving of fines or fees. Promote the employment of older adults as professional and support staff members.

SOURCE: *Guidelines for Library and Information Services to Older Adults* (Chicago: ALA Reference and User Services Association, 2008), ala.org/rusa/resources/guidelines/libraryservices.

---

6. Conquer the mouse. Any activity on the computer can be broken down into step-by-step instructions to be practiced until the steps become habitual. But until the mouse is conquered, a newbie can't practice the steps. Your first teaching session may just be about hand position, single-clicking, double-clicking, and clicking and dragging. The best way to practice all of these skills is by playing solitaire. (I kid you not.) Be patient and reassuring, and sing their praises when they get it right.

7. Take a break. There's a limit to how much anyone can absorb. No matter how far you've gotten, stop after 45 minutes. Use a 15-minute break to talk about the importance of good posture while on the computer, what websites you find fun, or chat about the weather. You'll know you can return to the lesson as you see your student relax.

8. A three-step method. Repetition helps us remember. Do everything three times. The first time they do it is hands-on. The second time they do it is to take notes. The third time they do it is to follow their notes to be sure the notes are clear without you guiding them. For example, to access the internet and visit a new website: With their hand on the mouse you instruct them to 1) double-click on the icon to access the internet. Next have them 2) single click in the website address box to highlight, and 3) type in a website address. Finally they should 4) depress and release the enter/return key. Four simple steps: Do it, write it, and do it again.

9. It's not their fault. When the time comes (and it will) that a website is hard to navigate, place blame where it belongs. Shame on web designers and computer manufacturers. This could all be much easier if those who designed the computer and the Internet took into consideration user issues. Relieve your student from feeling inadequate by pointing out the flaws in design and usability.

10. Give homework. Inspire your student to get on the computer for just 15 minutes a day to practice what you've worked on together. It is through short, daily visits to the computer that they will be able to conquer the beast.

SOURCE: Abby Stokes, "Ten Tips for Teaching Computer Skills to Older Adults," OLOS Columns, February 8, 2010, olos.ala.org/columns/?p=148.

YOUNG ADULTS

Customer service for teen users

by Kimberly Bolan

CUSTOMER SERVICE PLAYS a huge role in teen services best practices. First-rate customer service for all ages should be part of a library's mission, vision, and planning process. San José (Calif.) Public Library has the motto "Everyone Services Youth." This is a reminder that no matter what age the customer is, they are valued and their use of the library is just as important as anyone else's.

Rather than shushing them, staff at the Evansville Vanderburgh (Ind.) Public Library welcome teens. Movable chairs that can be easily rearranged are a big hit as the teens can rearrange the seating into clusters for socializing.

The Seward (Nebr.) Memorial Library has after-hours for 9th–12th graders on Thursday evenings from 8:00 to 9:30. No registration is required for the evenings, which offer 25-cent cans of soda, free food once a month, and various activities. Teens can also be the first to see new books added to the collection. From positive staff interaction with teens to incorporating simple tools such as an online suggestion box for gathering teen input on collections, programs, and facilities, strong customer service is fundamental in making teen space successful.

Changing attitudes. How many times have teens been treated poorly just because they're teenagers? We want teens to help libraries increase our statistics and be future library supporters, yet we continue to treat them badly. Quite clearly, this attitude tells teens that we don't want their business. Many library workers

---

Customer service tips

Here are a few customer service tips for adults working with teens:
Smile.
Be proactive—go to them, don't wait for them to come to you.
Don't try to be one of them—be friendly and be yourself.
Show leadership and supervision, but don't be dictatorial and condescending.
Greet teen customers, even briefly.
Don't stare or give the evil eye.
Don't have Velcro butt—come out from behind the desk.
Make eye contact and use positive body language when speaking to teens.
Really listen—show interest in what teens are saying.
Don't interrupt.
Be approachable and nonjudgmental.
Encourage teens to come to you if they have questions.
Be aware of teens' different learning styles and cultural differences, if possible. This is very helpful when working directly with them, creating signage, instruction, and more.
Get customer service training as well as training on adolescent development and teen needs and behaviors.
Treat all patrons the same—no double standards.
Work to change negative librarian stereotypes.
Remember to smile!

admit that they want teens to use the library but that teen behavior and attention level drives them crazy; consequently, these workers are turned off to helping teens. Others struggle with being liked versus letting teens walk all over them.

No doubt these are tough issues, but they're not as hopeless as you might think. Staff members who are trained to understand the developmental needs and behaviors of teens are better able to cope and respond positively to difficult situations. Everyone needs to clearly understand that customer service means consistently treating all customers equally and with respect. Teens can recognize good service as quickly as anyone else, and it's this good service (and an occasional smile) that will keep them coming back.

When the Peabody Institute Library in Peabody, Massachusetts, had behavioral issues with teens, instead of banning them, the staff started a young adult drop-in program. By providing teens with computer access, a place to hang out, casual homework assistance, after-school snacks, daily crafts, and games, they changed the atmosphere of the entire library. When teens were asked to comment on the newly redesigned YA Drop-In space (right) and the program as a whole, teens responded, "I love the YA Drop-In" and "YA Drop-In rocks!" Because this  successful program is one of the only free after-school programs in Peabody, local business partners now provide the library with additional funds for extra programs and new computers each year as part of an effort to prevent teen drug use.

The Campbell County (Wyo.) Public Library System has a window that allows staff to see into the bathroom and water fountain areas without leaving the teen room. That was an afterthought when they had problems in the hallway and there was concern about noise and behavior problems. The window solved their problem fast and opened up the feel of the room too—without affecting customer service.

First and foremost, dedicated, enthusiastic, and open-minded employees are key to good customer service. All staff members (not just youth staff) are important. Providing great customer service consists of knowing the customer and applying the golden rule: Treat others as you would like to be treated. To begin the process of evaluating and developing a customer service plan, have all staff rate themselves from one to five on the following points, with one as the lowest score. Staff should ask themselves how the last three teen customers they worked would have rated them.

- I like what I do.
- I believe the library is a great asset to teenagers.
- I like people.
- I like working with *all the users* of the library.
- I'm a great person to work with.
- I have a good sense of humor.
- I am patient.
- I really listen when others are talking.

Scores:

8–23 might indicate a need to work a bit on self-image and learn more about the value of the library.

24–31 would indicate that you are above average. Keep smiling and do your best.

32 and above reflects a great attitude.

40 would indicate that you are perfect (and therefore probably very annoying!).

Use these questions and the results as a point of discussion to further discuss customer service practices and goals.

Customer service training. Regular, ongoing customer service evaluation and training are essential. For more customer service information and a sample training program, visit the Houston (Tex.) Area Library System's online training site at www.hals.lib.tx.us/cust123/index.html. Modules include a basic practices and skills overview, overcoming barriers in difficult situations, cultural diversity, basic skills of frontline public services, working with teens, web and email, telephone, and challenging situations.

As part of a library merchandising initiative in 2004 called Trading Spaces, the Mount Laurel (N.J.) Public Library staff members were trained in new merchandising and customer service techniques. Even though this project was librarywide (not solely a teen project), the general idea behind the process is essential. Staff were involved throughout the entire project, which promoted buy-in to making the project work. As with teen services, there were uncertainties and unfamiliarity with what, at the time, were new techniques and practices. With perseverance and teamwork, the project was a success. Now every staff member is a marketer, a passionate public speaker, and knowledgeable about big-picture policies and procedures.

Beginning in 2004 with the support of the Wallace Foundation, the New York Public Library, in cooperation with the Brooklyn Public Library and Queens Library, has offered a workshop titled "Everyone Serves Youth," which encourages staff to reach out to children and teenagers as library customers. Teen librarians are encouraged to participate on community youth councils to increase public awareness of the library and services to teenagers. As a result, service is booming at New York's Bronx Library Center for Teens, which opened in January 2006. A statistical comparison between July 2005 through June 2006 and July 2006 through June 2007 showed that teen circulation increased 56%, attendance at programs increased 41%, and the number of teen-related information requests increased 128%.

SOURCE: Kimberly Bolan, *Teen Spaces: The Step-by-Step Library Makeover,* 2nd ed. (Chicago: American Library Association, 2009), 140–42.

Serving urban teens

by Denise E. Agosto

PUBLIC LIBRARIANS SHOULD REMEMBER that teens in urban areas use libraries for many reasons beyond just schoolwork and leisure reading. There are seven major areas in which teens seek development: the social self, the emotional self, the reflective self, the physical self, the creative self, the cognitive self, and the sexual self. The traditional view of the public library as an information resource clearly supports the development of the cognitive self, and it supports development of most of the other selves in part as well. But to support all seven areas of teen development to the fullest extent possible, librarians must broaden their views of public libraries beyond just that of information providers. We should think of our libraries as combined information gateways, social interaction and entertainment spaces, and beneficial physical environments. And we should think of them as important resources for supporting the broad range of teens' developmental needs, needs that extend beyond just schoolwork and leisure reading.

Public librarians who would like to support the fuller range of urban teens' developmental needs but are not sure how to go about it can use the model presented here as a guide for planning and delivering library services and programs. The next sections offer programming and service examples for each of the areas in the following model.

The role of the public library in teens' lives

The library as information gateway
  information for unspecified needs
  information for personal interests or needs
  information for schoolwork needs
The library as social interaction and entertainment space
  organized entertainment
  interaction with peers
  unorganized entertainment
  interaction with library staff
The library as beneficial physical environment
  refuge
  community improvement
  personal improvement
  financial support

The library as information gateway. Urban teens' use of the library as an information gateway reminds us that we must continue to make information and literacy services a cornerstone of public library service. Just like teens in any other situation, urban teens need and deserve access to high-quality information resources and services.

In addition to developing and maintaining high-quality collections of books, magazines, DVDs, audio materials, databases, and other computer resources, we should also provide literacy support services for teens. Examples of these services include read-alouds and readers' theater programs, tutoring help, hi-lo reading materials, and computer literacy classes.

Keep in mind that when creating and maintaining library collections for urban teens it is also important to include a wealth of culturally relevant information resources. This is especially crucial in urban areas with significant foreign-born populations, especially those with language difficulties. Teens from other cultures can find interpreting materials representing the predominant US culture difficult. As Sandra Hughes-Hassell and I wrote in 2007: "The most responsive collections include not only multicultural books, but a wide range of materials including newspapers from the students' countries of birth, bilingual books and videos, music, English-language translations of stories from students' countries/cultures of birth, and links to websites that are culturally relevant and, if available, written in their native languages."

A diverse collection is also important for teaching all teens about our diverse world and for promoting tolerance of diversity. Diversity of materials applies to both fiction and nonfiction items, and to all media formats as well. The web is an easily accessible, fertile source of authentic information representing all types of cultures. Librarians can create pathfinders that link to sets of resources from different cultures to bolster the multicultural offerings within their collections, and they can link these pathfinders to the library's website for easy access.

Urban librarians should also check their websites to make sure that they offer links to resources in all three of the information gateway subcategories: information for unspecified needs, information for personal interests or needs, and information for schoolwork needs. A web page offering access to resources related to information for unspecified needs might include basic information about library policies and procedures of special interest to teens, such as how to get a library card and whether parents or guardians can look at teens' library records.

To create a web page linking to resources relating to information for personal interests or needs, librarians can distribute short surveys within the library asking teens about their hobbies and interests. A simple three-question survey that asks, "What kinds of things do you like to do?" "What kinds of materials do you like to read?" and "What kinds of topics do you like to learn about at the library?" can produce a wealth of information about teens' personal interests. Librarians can then search for high-quality books, magazines, websites, and other resources related to these topics and create links to them on the library's website.

Even better is to create pathfinders on popular topics. Pathfinders are annotated bibliographies that briefly introduce a topic, such as skateboarding or science fiction, and then provide tips for searching for information related to the topic and suggest books, magazines, and websites on the topic. They offer those interested in learning about a topic a place to start and guidance in investigating that topic.

Finally, careful collection maintenance and frequent weeding are crucial for increasing teen use of the library as an information gateway. Out-of-date, torn magazines and books and dead links on the library's website are turn-offs not just to teens but to library patrons of all ages.

The library as social interaction and entertainment space. The heavy use of the library as a social interaction and entertainment space by the teens in this study tells us that librarians should promote and support the social and entertainment roles of their organizations if they want provide the full range of services teens want and need from their public libraries.

Fulfilling teens' social and entertainment needs is not just fun or frivolous. Teens need social and entertainment opportunities for self-expression, to develop social skills, and to support their healthy development into adulthood. Providing book clubs, computer clubs, gaming clubs, and movie viewings can create badly needed opportunities for teens' healthy social and emotional development. Public libraries can provide these important social and entertainment opportunities for urban teens who lack transportation to other venues or who lack the funds to pay for activities such as movies, summer camps, and social clubs.

Teen models take a photo break from the runway during the Back 2 School Fashion Show at Newport News (Va.) Public Library's Grissom branch.

The greatest number of responses under the social interaction/entertainment category described teens visiting their libraries to attend organized entertainment events. Teens mentioned everything from movie showings to manga club meetings to fencing club practice as drawing them into their libraries. Many US public libraries do provide organized events for teens, but most could expand these offerings. One of the best ways of starting new library programs is to learn about successful programs at other libraries. The fifth edition of the Young Adult Library Services Association's *Excellence in Library Service to Young Adults* (2008) provides planning, staffing, funding, and materials details for a wealth of successful YA programs and can serve as a guide for increasing your library's organized teen activities. The chapter "Services under $100" is especially helpful for libraries with limited programming budgets.

If providing a range of programs other than literacy-related services seems beyond your area of expertise, there is no need to worry. This is where collaboration can really help librarians meet teens' needs. For example, if you learned from teens at your library that they are interested in sketching, you could contact your local museum to ask if a museum employee or volunteer would be willing to visit your library to offer sketching classes. You would provide the space and the access to the teens. The museum would provide the sketching knowledge. And you could work together to plan the program, find program funds, and advertise, increasing the staffing power and visibility of both your library and the museum.

Organized library programs provide teens with the chance to interact with their peers, but equally important is providing unstructured socialization time. This is why it is so important that teens have a space of their own in public libraries. Ideally, that space is a closed-off room where teens can play music, eat, play games, and interact without disturbing the rest of the library. But if physical space limitations preclude a separate room, then blocking off a corner of the library and placing a few comfortable chairs there can serve as a substitute for a separate teen space. Or, if the library insurance policy permits it, creating a teen garden space on the library grounds might serve as a pleasant substitute.

Unorganized entertainment is probably best supported by the library, again, by a space dedicated to teen use. Providing a teen space shows adolescents that they are welcome and gives them a sense of ownership. Yet, sadly, even though almost all US public libraries provide space dedicated to adult services and to children's services, many fewer have spaces dedicated to serving adolescents.

Teens in this study visited their libraries because they liked their librarians and felt personal connections to them. It follows that another way to bring more urban teens into public libraries is to work to change their unfavorable perceptions of librarians. Both of the libraries in the study reported here had highly active YA librarians in place, librarians who were successful at connecting to their teen communities. As a result, their teen programming was generally well attended, and they had built up groups of regulars who frequented the libraries not just to use their services but also to visit their favorite librarians.

The library as beneficial physical environment. Recall that teens in this study who used their libraries as beneficial environments had gone there seeking refuge, community improvement, personal improvement, and financial support. Support for this last major role of the public library in urban teens' lives can be done at several levels, from evaluating the safety of the library environment to creating targeted programming related to safety issues and increasing teen volunteering opportunities.

To bolster the library as a refuge for teens, librarians in urban areas should keep in mind that although no public library is a completely safe place, it may be the safest place for some urban teens after

Chicago Public Library's YouMedia space. Photo by Jenny Levine.

6

school and on weekends. Library staff might look into ways to make the library building safer and more welcoming. Or they might team up with the local police department and use the physical space of the library as a place where teens can learn about personal-safety issues.

The most logical method of supporting the library as a place where teens can engage in community improvement is by creating an active teen volunteer program. Several teens in this study were eager to volunteer at their libraries. Teen volunteer programs help teens (by enabling them to improve their communities and by giving them important early work experiences) as well as libraries (by providing inexpensive labor and by increasing teens' sense of ownership in their libraries). Teens can be instrumental in providing homework and technology assistance to children, in supervising children's programs, in organizing and running teen advisory boards, and in many more ways. Teen volunteers can be valuable library website maintenance assistants and help with link checking and other maintenance tasks. This kind of technical work can also provide teens with valuable work experience.

In another *School Library Journal* article in December 2007, Tricia Suellentrop noted a "recent explosion of teens seeking to volunteer at libraries." She suggested that a teen volunteer program include a variety of volunteer roles and counseled librarians to match teens' talents with their tasks:

> Not every task fits every teen. Help teens discover their talents by offering them a wide array of possibilities. Outgoing teens can hand out programs, welcome patrons to an event, or help visitors with computer questions. Artistic teens would love reading to children, assisting with storytime, or designing programs and displays. Shy teens can make name tags, as well as develop scavenger hunts and word puzzles for younger children. Those who are more detail oriented can help with inventory supplies, labeling, making sure periodicals are in order, and preparing summer reading packets.

Providing volunteer opportunities is also a method of supporting urban teens' use of the library for personal improvement. However, most teens in the survey who had visited their libraries for personal improvement were seeking educational opportunities. Librarians can support these interests by providing high-quality, teen-friendly reference services and by developing and maintaining high-quality collections. Though most public libraries that target YA services work hard to develop and maintain their YA collections, many fewer have an information desk located within the YA area. This omission leaves teens to choose between the children's department and the adult department to ask for help. A desk dedicated to serving teens sends the message that teens' reference questions and other requests for help are important and valued, and it goes a long way toward making young adults feel included in library services.

Finally, teens' use of the library as a source of financial support tells us that librarians should hire teens from their communities when feasible to work in positions such as library pages and other part-time roles. Again both the libraries and the teens benefit. Teens can find valuable part-time work and early work experience, which can be difficult to acquire, and libraries can gain energetic new employees who know the library community from an insider's perspective.

SOURCE: Denise E. Agosto, "Urban Teens and Their Use of Public Libraries," in Denise E. Agosto and Sandra Hughes-Hassell, eds., *Urban Teens in the Library* (Chicago: American Library Association, 2010), 93–98.

INCARCERATED PERSONS

Reaching out to incarcerated youths
by Patrick Jones

THE TERM "OUTREACH" is used to describe library services that take place outside of the library setting. Outreach normally refers to either a community relations function (promoting services) or actual service delivery. The decision to deliver a service outside of the library depends upon a variety of circumstances for both the library and the customer. For the library, the call is usually based on the belief that the delivery of service directly to patrons in their homes, schools, or other locations is a more cost-effective way of reaching customers.

For the customer, outreach is an answer when there are obstacles to physically visiting a library. For all teens, there are plenty of obstacles, such as transportation, blocking their path to a library. For a small group of teens, often ones in desperate need of reading materials and information, the obstacles are the bars on their jail cell.

Despite the ever-increasing number of teens serving time behind bars, few public libraries provide services to teens in juvenile correctional facilities (JCFs). A literature search revealed that 44 public libraries were identified as providing some level of service to jailed teens. In the fall of 2003, these libraries were surveyed, and 16 libraries (36%) responded to questions about the history of their services, the range of services offered, and restrictions on materials. The goal of the survey was to identify the "state of the art" for this type of service, with a particular focus on collection development issues. Intellectual freedom is always an issue in dealing with materials for teens; and in the correctional setting, it is perhaps the single largest concern facing any library serving JCFs.

While our professional values embrace intellectual freedom, there is the reality of working with the correctional system. Any person in a correctional facility is deprived of certain liberties. So a teen in corrections finds the facility acting *in loco parentis* and determining which materials are appropriate to be read. When libraries partner with correctional facilities, we must understand the need to support the goals of that institution, even if they may conflict with our values. Our values don't trump their values. When a correctional facility allows a library to provide a service, we are bound by the regulations of the facility.

The survey revealed a wide range of services and history of providing service, with some libraries just getting into the business while others, such as Hennepin County (Minn.) Library, have more than a decade of experience. The facilities also differ greatly, ranging from 25 to 800 prisoners, with an average of 200. The one constant was that the large majority of these prisoners were male. The ratio of ethnicities and races varied widely, from 75% white at one program to primarily Latino at another. The range of African-American populations ranged from 10% to 50%. While the demographics and economics vary, an incarcerated teen is an at-risk teen lacking in developmental assets.

6

The vast majority of services to JCFs operate without a written service agreement, collection policy, or materials reconsideration procedure. Even though the majority of libraries embrace the Library Bill of Rights, all but two programs leave the final decision on removing materials with the JCF. Almost all of the services consist of more than dropping off materials and allow for interaction with residents. Most of the services have funding (an average of $6,000) for materials, but most also make use of donations and weeded materials. The one common element that every library surveyed providing services to teens in JCFs faces limitations on materials.

Format restrictions prevent almost half of libraries from providing magazines. Staples in magazines, as well as spiral-bound books, could be used as a weapon against correctional officers and other residents, or used as an instrument of self-injury. Only a few libraries reported not being able to supply hardback books (again, safety concerns), but every single library surveyed reported restrictions on materials due to content.

The materials most commonly prohibited were:

- *Anarchist Cookbook* or similar
- *High Times* magazine or similar
- Donald Goines and Iceberg Slim street-life novels
- *Vibe, Source*, or similar magazines
- Sex instruction books
- *Body Art Book, Tattoo* magazine, or similar
- *Low Rider* or similar magazines
- *The Godfather* and other Mafia books
- *Helter Skelter* and other true crime
- Martial arts instruction or similar
- *Monster, Do or Die, My Bloody Life,* and other gang stories

While the survey did not pose the question, anecdotally we learned that most libraries also don't provide erotica or sexually explicit materials.

Even those libraries that on paper face few restrictions find the reality quite different. One librarian noted that "there is a guard from the facility who accompanies the patrons, and the guard (usually) examines each item and denies those that they don't feel are appropriate." Another commented that "we have had several instances in which a resident will request a book, we bring it, and it is taken from the resident by a staff member who personally disagrees with the material."

Almost all of the survey respondents expressed similar frustration in working with correctional officers whose worldview is so different. Librarians are paid to provide free access to information; correctional officers are paid to work in an environment where freedom is limited.

So, is it worth it? The experience of the Hennepin County Library certainly proves that the payoffs far outweigh the frustration and professional compromises. The library has a long history of outreach to correctional facilities, all of which were combined into an Outreach Department in 1974. In the late 1980s, however, budget issues forced the libraries to eliminate a full-time juvenile correctional librarian. Despite that, services to teens in corrections remained strong, utilizing other outreach staff to include biweekly visits by staff to the library created at the 87-bed Juvenile Detention Center. The library also provides library materials ("cottage collections") to teens incarcerated at the County Home School. CHS is a correctional treatment facility for boys and girls from the ages of 12 to 18. Both facilities are units of the county's Community Corrections Department.

In early 2002, the library obtained grant funds to further the award-winning Great Transitions program already in place at CHS. Great Transitions is a collaborative project of Hennepin County Library in cooperation with Hennepin County Home School, Epsilon School, and Minneapolis Public Library. Using these grant funds, the library was able to offer students at CHS:

- A Born to Read program for teen mothers and fathers
- A creative writing workshop
- An author visit (YA writer Will Weaver)
- Book discussion groups
- Monthly booktalks held in classrooms
- Creation of a 5,000-item library and regular visits by library staff
- Information literacy instruction
- Library card sign-up and fine waiver
- Publication of a literary magazine (*Diverse City*)

"Best books" read by students at County Home School

Dickinson, Peter. *The Rope Maker.* When the magic that protects their valley starts to fail, Tilja and her companions journey into the evil Empire to find the ancient magician Faheel, who originally cast those spells.

Draper, Sharon. *Romiette and Julio.* An African American girl and a Latino boy fall in love after meeting on the internet, but they are harassed by a gang that objects to their interracial dating.

Homer. *The Odyssey.* Classic Greek epic poem recounts the tale of a hero's journey home.

LaHaye, Tim. *Left Behind.* This fictional account of life after the Rapture delivers an urgent call to today's readers to prepare their own hearts and minister to others.

Moore, Yani. *Triple Take.* Jonathan "JC" Cole is about to get out of the joint, and he has one thing on his mind—revenge against the three men who betrayed him to save their own skins.

Mosley, Walter. *Bad Boy Brawly Brown.* Easy Rawlins is out of the investigation business, but when an old friend gets in enough trouble to ask for Easy's help, he finds he can't refuse.

Myers, Walter Dean. *Slam.* Seventeen-year-old "Slam" Harris is counting on his basketball talents to get him out of the inner city and give him a chance to succeed in life, but his coach sees things differently.

Pelzer, David. *A Child Called It.* Dave Pelzer shares his unforgettable story of the many abuses he suffered at the hands of his alcoholic mother and the averted eyes of his neglectful father.

Roberts, Katherine. *Spellfall.* Natalie and her friends are caught up in a sorcerer's attempt to cross an invisible boundary in order to invade another world.

Rock, Chris. *Rock This.* Chris Rock confronts all the hot-button issues, such as finding a black leader, addiction to bubble wrap, why white folks can't say the n-word, the dirty socks rule, marriage, Bill Clinton, sexual harassment, and more.

Sachar, Louis. *Holes.* Stanley Yelnats is sent to a hellish correctional camp in the Texas desert where he finds his first real friend, a treasure, and a new sense of himself.

Sapphire. *Push.* This is a self-portrait of an unloved black teenage girl with a father who rapes her and a jealous mother who screams abuse.

Shaukur, Tupac. *Rose That Grew From Concrete.* This collection of more than 100 poems honestly and artfully confronts topics ranging from poverty and motherhood to Van Gogh and Mandela.

Souljah, Sister. *The Coldest Winter Ever.* After a black drug dealer goes to jail in Brooklyn, his ruthless 17-year-old daughter takes over his empire.

6

Many of these programs had been offered in the past at CHS, but these grant funds allowed them to be planned, implemented, and evaluated as a total package.

Residents also readily supplied information about the best books (see sidebar on page 377) they have obtained from the library and read during their stay at CHS. While teens at CHS indicated they would continue reading upon release, we don't have any way to measure the lasting effect of our work with these challenged young people.

If we look at outreach from the viewpoint of old-school library statistical measures, services to kids in corrections don't make a great deal of sense. The loss rate for materials is high, the time spent setting up services is great, and the return on the circulation bottom line is low. But if we think about outcomes rather than outputs, then programs like these are an obvious choice for any library actively engaging in building community. These programs also represent a new direction in teen services where the focus is not only on what services libraries provide young adults but, just as importantly, on the outcomes of those services. Our focus needs to be on assets—not library resources, but on a positive youth development approach. For more on this, see also Angela Craig, "High Impact Partnership: Serving Youth Offenders," *Young Adult Library Services* 9, no. 1 (Fall 2010): 20–22.

Focusing on positive youth development represents a vision of looking outside of the walls of the library, not only for the usual suspects of collaboration or outreach, but looking at what value our services have in the lives of teenagers. The question no longer asks what a young adult does in a library or as part of an outreach, but also asks what happens to that young adult as a result of checking out a book, attending a book discussion program, having their creativity tapped, or learning how to locate information on the internet. Librarians want incarcerated teens, such as this young man from the County Home School, to discover that:

> I never knew reading could be so fun. When I was out, I never did read a book. But now that you showed me how fun it can be, I'm going to read every book I can, not just 'cause of you. But because I really like reading and like to learn new things. Things I never knew."

SOURCE: Patrick Jones, "Reaching Out to Young Adults in Jail," *Young Adult Library Services* 3, no. 1(Fall 2004): 14–17.

Prisoners' right to read

THE AMERICAN LIBRARY ASSOCIATION asserts a compelling public interest in the preservation of intellectual freedom for individuals of any age held in jails, prisons, detention facilities, juvenile facilities, immigration facilities, prison work camps, and segregated units within any facility. As Supreme Court Justice Thurgood Marshall wrote in *Procunier v. Martinez* (416 US 428 (1974)):

> When the prison gates slam behind an inmate, he does not lose his human quality; his mind does not become closed to ideas; his intellect does not cease to feed on a free and open interchange of opinions; his yearning for self-respect does not end; nor is his quest for self-realization concluded. If anything, the needs for identity and self-respect are more compelling in the dehumanizing prison environment.

Participation in a democratic society requires unfettered access to current social, political, economic, cultural, scientific, and religious information. Information and ideas available outside the prison are essential to prisoners for a successful transition to freedom. Learning to be free requires access to a wide range of knowledge, and suppression of ideas does not prepare the incarcerated of any age for life in a free society. Even those individuals that a lawful society chooses to imprison permanently deserve access to information, to literature, and to a window on the world. Censorship is a process of exclusion by which authority rejects specific points of view. That material contains unpopular views or even repugnant content does not provide justification for censorship. Unlike censorship, selection is a process of inclusion that involves the search for materials, regardless of format, that represent diversity and a broad spectrum of ideas. The correctional library collection should reflect the needs of its community.

Libraries and librarians serving individuals in correctional facilities may be required by federal, state, or local laws; administrative rules of parent agencies; or court decisions to prohibit material that instructs, incites, or advocates criminal action or bodily harm or is a violation of the law. Only those items that present an actual compelling and imminent risk to safety and security should be restricted. Although these limits restrict the range of material available, the extent of limitation should be minimized by adherence to the Library Bill of Rights and its Interpretations.

These principles should guide all library services provided to prisoners:

- Collection management should be governed by written policy, mutually agreed upon by librarians and correctional agency administrators, in accordance with the Library Bill of Rights, its Interpretations, and other ALA intellectual freedom documents.
- Correctional libraries should have written procedures for addressing challenges to library materials, including a policy-based description of the disqualifying features, in accordance with "Challenged Materials" and other relevant intellectual freedom documents.
- Correctional librarians should select materials that reflect the demographic composition, information needs, interests, and diverse cultural values of the confined communities they serve.
- Correctional librarians should be allowed to purchase materials that meet written selection criteria and provide for the multifaceted needs of their populations without prior correctional agency review. They should be allowed to acquire materials from a wide range of sources in order to ensure a broad and diverse collection. Correctional librarians should not be limited to purchasing from a list of approved materials.
- Age is not a reason for censorship. Incarcerated children and youth should have access to a wide range of fiction and nonfiction, as stated in "Free Access to Libraries for Minors."
- Correctional librarians should make all reasonable efforts to provide sufficient materials to meet the information and recreational needs of prisoners who speak languages other than English.
- Equitable access to information should be provided for persons with disabilities as outlined in "Services to People with Disabilities."
- Media or materials with nontraditional bindings should not be prohibited unless they present an actual compelling and imminent risk to safety and security.
- Material with sexual content should not be banned unless it violates state and federal law.

6

- Correctional libraries should provide access to computers and the internet.

When free people, through judicial procedure, segregate some of their own, they incur the responsibility to provide humane treatment and essential rights. Among these is the right to read. The right to choose what to read is deeply important, and the suppression of ideas is fatal to a democratic society. The denial of the right to read, to write, and to think—to intellectual freedom—diminishes the human spirit of those segregated from society. Those who cherish their full freedom and rights should work to guarantee that the right to intellectual freedom is extended to all incarcerated individuals.

SOURCE: Prisoners' Right to Read: An Interpretation of the Library Bill of Rights, adopted June 29, 2010, by the ALA Council, www.ifmanual.org/prisoners.

ALA policy on library services to the poor
by the ALA Social Responsibilities Round Table

THE AMERICAN LIBRARY ASSOCIATION promotes equal access to information for all persons and recognizes the urgent need to respond to the increasing number of poor children, adults, and families in America. These people are affected by a combination of limitations, including illiteracy, illness, social isolation, homelessness, hunger, and discrimination, which hamper the effectiveness of traditional library services. Therefore it is crucial that libraries recognize their role in enabling poor people to participate fully in a democratic society, by utilizing a wide variety of available resources and strategies. Concrete programs of training and development are needed to sensitize and prepare library staff to identify poor people's needs and deliver relevant services. And within the American Library Association the coordinating mechanisms of programs and activities dealing with poor people in various divisions, offices, and units should be strengthened, and support for low-income liaison activities should be enhanced.

Policy objectives

ALA shall implement these objectives by:

1. Promoting the removal of all barriers to library and information services, particularly fees and overdue charges.
2. Promoting the publication, production, purchase, and ready accessibility of print and nonprint materials that honestly address the issues of poverty and homelessness, that deal with poor people in a respectful way, and that are of practical use to low-income patrons.
3. Promoting full, stable, and ongoing funding for existing legislative programs in support to flow income services and for proactive library programs that reach beyond traditional service sites to poor children, adults, and families.

4. Promoting training opportunities for librarians, in order to teach effective techniques for generating public funding to upgrade library services to poor people.
5. Promoting the incorporation of low-income programs and services into regular library budgets in all types of libraries, rather than the tendency to support these projects solely with soft money like private or federal grants.
6. Promoting equity in funding adequate library services for poor people in terms of materials, facilities, and equipment.
7. Promoting supplemental support for library resources for and about low-income populations by urging local, state, and federal governments and the private sector to provide adequate funding.
8. Promoting increased public awareness through programs, displays, bibliographies, and publicity of the importance of poverty-related library resources and services in all segments of society.
9. Promoting the determination of output measures through the encouragement of community needs assessments, giving special emphasis to assessing the needs of low-income people, and involving both antipoverty advocates and poor people themselves in such assessments.
10. Promoting direct representation of poor people and antipoverty advocates through appointment to local boards and creation of local advisory committees on service to low-income people, such appointments to include library paid transportation and stipends.
11. Promoting training to sensitize library staff to issues affecting poor people and to attitudinal and other barriers that hinder poor people's use of libraries.
12. Promoting networking and cooperation between libraries and other agencies, organizations, and advocacy groups in order to develop programs and services that effectively reach poor people.
13. Promoting the implementation of an expanded federal low-income housing program, national health insurance, full-employment policy, living minimum wage and welfare payments, affordable day care, and programs likely to reduce, if not eliminate, poverty itself.
14. Promoting among library staff the collection of food and clothing donations, volunteering personal time to antipoverty activities and contributing money to direct-aid organizations.
15. Promoting related efforts concerning minorities and women, since these groups are disproportionately represented among poor people.

SOURCE: American Library Association Policy Manual, chapter 61, ala.org/ala/aboutala/governance/policymanual/updatedpolicymanual/section2/61svctopoor.

What poor people want from library computers

by Leslie Edmonds Holt and Glen E. Holt

BEGINNING IN 1994, St. Louis Public Library undertook an extensive set of focus groups with users. Over 10 years, the library and its contractor organized more than 100 meetings with constituents, asking for their help in the design of new branches and the remodeling of old branches. One message came through over and over: Our poorest constituents wanted "rooms full of computers," not so much for themselves as for their children. The adults regarded the computers as an entrance into the educated, literate, good-job world of middle-class families.

This desire was especially seen in poor African Americans and more recently in immigrants who came poor to their new nation. Why, we asked? What did they expect from computers? Their reply in summary was "access to a world of education and better jobs." As one person told us, "When your schools are bad, if kids can use computers at the library, they can educate themselves."

People came to use library public access computers (PACs) for many reasons.

For kids, the PACs represent an opportunity to catch up with their friends (email) and find out things they want to know about their school assignments (how to do homework successfully and faster), the social mores of their culture (Facebook), and entrance into the adult world (how to get a driver's license).

Young employed people come to use PACs to look for a different job and to do research because their low status at work gives them only slow computers without access to all websites.

Seniors come to do their family email and trade pictures of their travel for the newest cute shots of the grandkids.

For immigrants, PACs represent a connection with the former homeland and relatives (email, international news), with the employment world (job ads), and with citizenship (for example, the American Place at Hartford Public Library).

For the homeless, PACs represent an opportunity to connect with friends and family in a social setting in which the person can protect as much about himself or herself as desired, find shelter, and get information on how to obtain free medical care.

For the job changer or the unemployed person, PACs are an opportunity to get help writing a résumé, obtain education or training for a new job, or find job listings. Increasingly, online communication is the only way that prospective employers will accept résumés and applications.

For the rural person, PACs are an information source about other people, employment, and living conditions in cities, other states, and other nations; a chance to get a degree or certification via distance education; a venue in which to meet other people with similar interests; and an opportunity to learn about and purchase products and services not available in the nearby community.

The list goes on and on. Each person without access to an internet-connected computer in the home, school, or office uses the library computer to construct or fill out her or his social, cultural, and economic universe without being bothered by human intermediaries. In a nation that values privacy, individualism, and upward mobility, people—especially poor people—find free PACs convenient, time-saving, and personally helpful.

Consequently, individuals who want library PACs believe that, like books on library shelves, computers should be used for whatever the person wants and needs. They want help when they want it and of a type they believe they need.

Even though the digital divide is contextual and debatable, the popularity of PACs in libraries is an ongoing testament that the internet machines represent what Enoch Pratt Library Director Carla Hayden calls "leveling" and what we have come to call one of the library's "equity functions." In each case, individuals used their personal time (their most valuable commodity other than their money) to come to the library to use library PACs.

SOURCE: Leslie Edmonds Holt and Glen E. Holt, *Public Library Services for the Poor: Doing All We Can* (Chicago: American Library Association, 2010), 92–94.

ADVOCACY

CHAPTER SEVEN

Cuts to libraries during a recession are like cuts to
hospitals during a plague.

—Eleanor Crumblehulme, technical services library assistant at the
University of British Columbia Law Library, in a tweet to
author Neil Gaiman, April 12, 2010.

MARKETING

Marketing best practices

by Nancy Dowd, Mary Evangeliste, and Jonathan Silberman

LET'S SAY YOU HAVE DECIDED that you would like to increase teen participation in after-school programs at the library. What are teens thinking about? Who do they look up to? What kind of music do they like? Movies? What else? This is the time for you to do some market research! Market research is any research that you do to understand the buying habits of a particular audience.

Observe the group members in their natural habitat—in this case, the mall. If you can look at and listen to this group without your own biases, you will create a teen program that will really appeal to them. Also look at how others market to your age group—as you can imagine, for-profit marketing always has a bigger budget than nonprofit marketing like libraries, so take the time to analyze the marketing targeted to the age group you are interested in.

- What color palettes are used? Hey, those companies just spent millions of dollars figuring that out. Take advantage so you don't have to spend that money.
- Who are the influencers or spokespeople (Miley Cyrus or major sports figures)?
- What is the language being used? This is a very slippery one. There is nothing worse than a person who is outside a particular age group using slang inappropriately, so do so sparingly.

Marketing and design are everywhere:

- Don't just watch TV; analyze it. What ads play at what time? What ads appeal to what values? What colors, spokespeople, and themes are dominant?
- Look at magazines. If you are a woman, look at men's health magazines. If you are a man, look at women's fashion magazines. Look at magazines for teens, for tweens, for young adults, and so on. In these, what colors, spokespeople, and themes are dominant?
- When you are in stores, ask yourself the same questions about colors, spokespeople, and themes.

Assessment. One of the easiest ways to get honest opinions about your library is to run some focus groups. Often you can entice certain populations to engage in a focus group by buying them lunch—this works well with students. Another way to encourage people to attend focus groups is to give each member a gift card from locally owned businesses. This helps the library build relationships with the community by assuring local businesses that you support the local community and not a faceless global chain.

Advisory group. If you think running a focus group is complicated, you can instead start with an advisory committee. This is an informal group brought together to tell you the truth from their personal point of view. You can start by asking a club that already exists, such as student government, the parent-teacher association, or service clubs. Some caveats to keep in mind:

- You have to be ready to hear negative things.
- Some things people ask for will be too expensive.
- You have to learn to listen to users with a nonjudgmental ear.
- This is a one-way conversation, one of those rare occasions where you are not there to talk them into loving the library.
- You should only ask questions, not talk at the group.

Usability testing. You can also engage in usability testing, which is when you ask patrons very specific questions about finding things on your website and observe the path that they take to get there.

The similarity between all these different forms of feedback is that you must listen without inserting your opinion or leading the conversation in any way. You want the patrons to tell you exactly what they think about your resources, services, or whatever you are asking them about.

Sometimes this information is hard to hear and even harder to understand. So it is very important to find someone who can ask the questions impartially without becoming emotionally invested in the answers. Also, you must ask a lot of clarification questions without leading.

You can also use groups that already exist, such as a teen group, a book group, or another regularly meeting group. You probably want to ask them no more than three questions. On a college campus, you might work with the student government or a student group.

Although it is very difficult to do so, you should try to find ways to reach nonusers of the library, because you want to try to find out what the obstacles are that these groups face and how to remove them.

Assessment can come in many different forms. Creating a culture of assessment requires the organization to always think about what it wants to measure. For example:

- Number of attendees at programs such as story times, classes, workshops, musical events, or lectures
- Number of resources used: books checked out, database searches, or digital collection views

Corporate sponsorship

Getting corporate sponsorship for your library events is easy if you follow a few simple steps.

1. Define the type of sponsor you want to go after: you always want to make sure that a business knows that you picked it for a specific reason. For example, you might call a sporting-goods store to sponsor a video game night at the library. You explain to the store that you chose it because your target audience is teenage boys ages 12 to 17. Obviously, this age group frequents sporting-goods stores and wears sports attire. You can tell the store that it seems great for them to sponsor a library event and that you would like to provide your target audience with some gifts.

2. Write up a sample sponsor letter. Each store or organization that sponsors you usually needs to show or have proof that they are giving away goods to someone legitimate. In the letter, write a one-line description of the event, the rationale for having the event, and one goal of the event. Always make sure to tell the sponsor how many attendees you expect. Then tailor each letter to the sponsor.

3. Be tenacious. Sometimes you have to call your contact several times to secure sponsorship. Remember that these people are as busy as you are, so until they say no, continue to call and write. Keep track of each time you make contact so that you do not call them too little or too much.

4. Ask the sponsor for a camera-ready logo to put on your posters. Explain to sponsors when and how you will use their logos and how many people will be exposed to the logo. This is great for the sponsor's public image, so it is a win-win situation.

5. Follow up with thank-you cards and details of how the event went. If you want to continue building a list or all possible sponsors for different events, make sure to follow up and thank them.

Internal marketing

Marketing is relatively new to libraries. Before the widespread use of the internet, people who wanted to research a specific topic had limited choices. Two of the most-used sources were to go to a bookstore and buy a book, magazine, or newspaper or to go to the library and borrow a book and/or copy a magazine or newspaper. Obviously, the choices for finding information have multiplied and exploded in the past 15 years, and libraries no longer have a monopoly on information. In other words, we are no longer the gatekeepers of information. In marketing terms, we need to reposition our brand. We need to find ways to raise awareness of our vital role in our communities and articulate the role that libraries play in the new information landscape.

But before we create external marketing for our libraries, we have to get the internal organization comfortable with marketing. We have to introduce people to many different concepts of marketing, such as branding, visual consistency, communication vehicles, and channels. Most of these marketing concepts may be new to employees who have worked in educational organizations or nonprofits for most of their careers. Internal marketing is the communication you have with the members of your organization about marketing and their role in it.

Internal marketing ideas

Create a publication wall:

1. Gather all of your current publications.
2. Put them all up in a place where they can be viewed together.
3. Are there many different looks and treatments in the publications?
4. Are there different colors, fonts, and designs used in publications?
5. Are there too many publications going out? Could some of the publications be combined?
6. Does this exercise make it clear that library publications need a more consistent look?

Top 11 marketing tips for collaboration
by Peggy L. Barry

1. Limited staff and funds generally make it necessary to take time, in advance, to plan out what you want to do and how to proceed. Assess the costs and benefits of potential collaborations and partnerships. Establish policies, guidelines, and evaluative mechanisms as might be needed to select and follow the best direction for your library over time.

2. Partner with other local governmental entities to benefit the mutual taxpayers you serve. It may be your municipal, township, or county government or the park district in your area. You have a lot in common with all of these agencies that are also tax-based and are seeking to be fiscally responsible. Whether in areas of programming, staffing, promotion, or community involvement, you may find that shared costs and efforts prove beneficial to all parties, especially the taxpayers.

3. Partner with local arts organizations, high schools, colleges, cultural centers, art leagues, public art groups, park districts, and other performing or visual arts agencies to develop and present exhibits and/or programming at your library, using combined resources.

4. Become an active participant or member of community-wide committees where the goal and target audiences overlap with your own. Examples might be a local literary fair hosted by a bookstore; a Born to Read program with local physicians; a One City, One Book program; a new-mother gathering at the hospital; or a community heritage celebration.

5. Collaborate with local nonprofits and organizations that cater to special needs audiences who may be physically or mentally disabled. You might work towards special training for your staff so they can better serve a specific population, collaborate on unique programming for special audiences, or pursue a donation of special software that better accommodates a targeted audience group.

6. Partner with your local school districts to collaborate on special programs and challenges such as reserving meeting room spaces for students during finals week, working with teachers on homework alerts, making sure all local textbooks are part of your reference collection, confirming you have the books from the school's reading lists available in your collection, or inviting the theater or choral students to perform at your library.

7. Join or initiate a communications roundtable in your community, inviting the marketing personnel for local agencies and organizations to meet on a regular basis to discuss common issues, solutions, and challenges. You may even discover a variety of cross-promotional opportunities available. You might invite the school district, park district, city government, nearby college or university, historical society, public art commission, YMCA/YWCA, homeowner's confederation, chamber of commerce, tourism office, economic development group, and others, depending on the makeup of your service area.

8. Become active in your chamber of commerce. Many partnerships, sponsorships, and other collaborative opportunities can be found in the chamber. Assign members of your management staff, or others, to become active members of an appropriate chamber committee. For example, the head of your IT department could join the technology committee, while a business librarian would be a good fit with the small business group. Seek to participate in their expos, after-hours gatherings, luncheons, speakers bureau, and publications.

9. Enter into a partnership with local welcome wagons, greeter groups, and real estate agents to include the library's print publications in packets distributed to new residents.

10. Pursue a relationship with your local print and electronic media to provide interviews, stories, and photographs. They, too, have been hard hit by the economy and even more so by the changing face of communications, especially print media.

11. Arrange to set up an information table at sidewalk sales, farmers markets, school orientations, festivals, fairs, and other special events.

SOURCE: Peggy L. Barry, "Top Eleven Marketing Tips for Collaboration and Partnerships," *Illinois Library Association Reporter* 27, no. 4 (Aug. 2009): 10–11. Reprinted with permission.

7

Hold an open house. Once you are far enough along in your campaign—after you and your team have created key messages and are beginning to think about the look and design—create mock-ups and hold an open house to see what library staff think about your direction.

Find different ways for staff to provide feedback during open houses. Some examples include the following:

- Note cards for employees' comments.
- Members of the marketing committee talking with and recording feedback from staff.
- A sign-up sheet for departments, teams, or committees to use if they want the marketing team to come to their meetings.
- A follow-up time for staff to come and speak to the marketing committee.

Keep employees informed. Update employees through appropriate communication channels available in your organization. Remember that updating does not mean boring people with too much detail.

- Use staff meetings to update employees and ask for feedback.
- Talk informally and individually with employees.
- Send out executive summaries of the marketing committee's work via email.
- Create a marketing portfolio with all of the designs you have created with the corresponding style sheet—you can do this in hard copy or invite people to electronically view the information and comment.

SOURCE: Nancy Dowd, Mary Evangeliste, and Jonathan Silberman, *Bite-Sized Marketing: Realistic Solution for the Overworked* (Chicago: American Library Association, 2010), 126–136.

Writing grant proposals
by Herbert B. Landau

A GRANT PROPOSAL IS A FAIRLY STYLIZED piece of marketing literature that may be characterized as a cross between a technical report and a sales brochure. The grant-seeking institution is selling its credentials and its project's value to a grantor who has funds to support good works. If the grant process is competitive, the grant proposal must also convince the reviewers that the grant-requesting institution and its proposed project are more worthy of the grant than those of other competing institutions. Your grant proposal is often all the review panel will employ to make their award decisions, so it must tell your whole story in a clear, concise, and convincing manner.

Style tips. You should recognize that your grant proposal is a marketing document. You are competitively selling your institution, its needs, and its qualifications to one or more grant reviewers. Since the best salespeople are those who empathize with their customers, write your proposal with the needs of the reviewers in mind. You can facilitate the review of your proposal by giving it a straightforward, logical format; labeling all sections; writing in a clear, concise, simple style; and avoiding jargon. You want your proposal to convince the reviewer that awarding your institution a grant will yield a highly successful project that will reflect positively on both the grantor and grantee. The style pointers below will help you to write a proposal to accomplish this result.

Keep it simple. The first and foremost thing to keep in mind is the KIS principle, "Keep It Simple." Use short paragraphs and strong topical sentences. Use bullet points to list important facts. Explain anything that is not obvious. Do not assume that reviewers are familiar with your organization, service area, or the needs of your community. Sarah Collins, an experienced grant reviewer, warns against proposal complexity when she states that "an idiosyncratic proposal format signaled [to the reviewer] larger problems with a nonprofit applicant." Collins also cautions against being too rigid in responding to an RFP and advises flexibility in choosing the best way to sell your program to the funder.

The sheer volume of proposals that most foundations receive means that your proposal will initially be read quickly. Simple sentence structures, short paragraphs beginning with strong topical sentences, and important facts broken out in bullet points will best reveal the proposal's main points and help advance it to a more in-depth reading by the reviewer.

I am not suggesting that you dumb down the proposal or define every technical term. What I do recommend is that you write your proposals on a level that shows respect for your audience and your ability to communicate your case to a lay audience. The experts will be impressed, not put off, by your ability to explain complex issues in simple terms. The lawyer portrayed by Denzel Washington in the movie *Philadelphia* was fond of saying: "Explain it to me like I'm a six-year-old." You don't have to go that far, but it's a good phrase to remember. When I started my career as a young research librarian at AT&T's Bell Labs, I was instructed to follow Robert Gunning's principles of clear writing in my business and technical writing. "Gunning's fog index" is a test designed to measure a document's readability. The fog index number indicates the number of years of formal education that a person requires in order to easily understand the text on the first reading. If a passage has a fog index of 12, it has the reading level of a 12th-grade U.S. high school senior. The fog index is generally used by people who want their writing to be read easily by a large segment of the population. Texts that are designed for a wide audience generally require a fog index of less than 12. Texts that require a close-to-universal understanding generally require an index of eight or less. Since I do not know who will actually be reading the proposals I write, I strive to keep the fog index at level eight.

Develop catchy project and goal titles. It is both good writing and good marketing technique to come up with a descriptive and catchy title for your grant project that will appeal to reviewers and make them want to read your proposal. An interesting title will also be handy to use in press releases and reports after you win the grant. It is also good style to apply this rule to the titles of your stated project goals and individual tasks. For example, instead of naming your project "Computer Courses for Senior Citizens," why not term it "Computer Skills for Technologically Challenged Older Adults"?

Use simple, declarative, positive sentences. When you write, concentrate on producing simple, clear, declarative sentences. Do not obfuscate. Leave out emotion and hype. Be precise. I have found that a proposal's narrative comes across better if written as short precise statements in a positive, forceful, and declarative mode. Use action verbs such as *will* and *shall* in first-person plural, future tense. Examples are statements such as, "In month one we (or the XYZ Library) will perform the following tasks," "Phase one shall be the implementation of," or "In this task we will define (or investigate, or create, or evaluate)." Remember, faint heart never won fair grant. Write with confidence, as if you are certain the proposed project will be successful. Avoid such iffy qualifying phrases as "we hope," "hopefully," "with luck," "maybe," or "if possible." A proposal that exudes uncertainty or a lack of confidence will not likely be a winner.

Avoid your own jargon. You should always make an effort to avoid jargon. That includes not only your library's in-house jargon but also the jargon common to your field. You cannot be certain that your proposal's reviewers are experts in your field, and you want them to understand what you are proposing to do. For example, I have stopped using the phrase "my library's collections" because I found that non-librarians thought I was discussing fundraising (I now say "my library's collection of books").

Some advisors on grant writing suggest that you should eschew even the jargon used by the funder in the RFP and translate RFP jargon into plain language. I disagree on this point. I believe that by employing the funder's language in your proposal, you demonstrate both that you have read the guidelines and that you will be a responsive and adaptive grantee. My marketing sense tells me that if you want to use the grantor's money, then you must play by the grantor's rules and use his language.

Be consistent and complete. Make sure the information and wording in each table, chart, and attachment is consistent with the proposal narrative and the information in other tables. Your budget line items should reflect back to the proposed activities. All required forms should be filled in accurately and completely. Use consistent language when describing things or processes. For example, while textual variety is nice for creative or literary writing, calling the people who visit your library by differing names in different parts of your proposal (patrons, customers, users, readers, clientele) may serve only to confuse reviewers.

Write for your audience. When writing, just as when speaking, address your audience. "Audience" does not just mean the program officer who will first read your proposal or the peer reviewer panel that will rank it. It means everyone who will read it, possibly including foundation management and trustees. Therefore, write for a wider audience than just program officers and technical reviewers alone. Chances are that the executives who are ultimate decision-makers are going to read at least some of your proposal.

Strive for a conversational tone. A conversational tone automatically eliminates long, winding sentences and excessive jargon. You do not speak that way, so there is no reason to write that way. I suggest that proposal writers imagine they are explaining the what, why, and how of the proposed project to a friend or relative (a favorite uncle or aunt). A conversational tone helps establish the sense of personal contact with the reader. Individuals, not faceless institutions, make grants, and connecting person-to-person is critical in making a persuasive case for funding. Read the entire proposal aloud, sentence by sentence. If it does not sound right or you cannot finish a sentence on one breath, more work is needed to simplify and shorten. If possible, read your proposal aloud to a friend outside the profession, gauge her reactions, and revise your proposal accordingly. Alternately, have someone from outside your organization read your proposal to make sure it holds the reader's interest and that your message is clear.

Be brief. In *Hamlet* Shakespeare has Polonius profess, "Brevity is the soul of wit." I think that grant proposal reviewers appreciate this advice. They have many words to review, and more is not better in this context.

Use proper physical format. Unless otherwise specified, use large type (12-point), double-spaced; use one side of 20-pound white paper; provide reasonable margins; number the pages and employ an easy-to-use removable binding (binder clips). Section divider tabs are not commonly used.

Use graphics to strengthen your case. If graphics are allowed in the proposal, you can effectively use statistical tables, charts, graphs, photos, news clippings, and organization charts to illustrate and support your case. These are useful and can reduce verbiage in the text, but they must be relevant, labeled, and cited in the appropriate section of the text. Color is nice (if it really adds something), but use caution when including graphics in an e-proposal. Too much graphics and color can complicate transmission, storage, display, and printing for both you and the reviewers.

Miscellaneous style pointers. Here are some other suggestions that I have found to be useful guidelines in writing proposals:

- Maintain reader interest by starting with a question and then answering it.
- Use language familiar to the funder; repeat back the language of the RFP.
- Be logical and linear in approach.
- Observe page and section limitations (especially in e-proposals).
- Reviewers can consider only the information in the application, so make no assumptions about what they do and don't know.
- If you're unable to provide any required information, be honest about the reasons for the omission.

SOURCE: Herbert B. Landau, *Winning Library Grants: A Game Plan* (Chicago: American Library Association, 2011), 88–93.

Keeping our message simple
by James LaRue

A FEW YEARS AGO, our library lost two local bond issues in a row. I was so surprised and so concerned about the future of my organization that I started reading much more widely and deeply. Many of the books were about brain research. Most focused on how and why we come to believe things, both as individuals and as communities. A couple of those books dug into how difficult it is for us to admit we've been wrong—and to change our views.

The problem is plain: Over the past 10–15 years, even before the recession and our current funding crisis, fewer libraries made it to the ballot, or won when they did. This is in sharp opposition to the long trend of rising library use.

I do not contend that every library, in every community, is worthy of increased funding. Some cases are better than others, and some communities may justly conclude that their libraries are not the current priority. I do contend that our social environment at this moment in history works against all libraries. We need to change that. And we can.

Brutal facts

It is time for the library profession to come to grips with some harsh realities. The first is that use has nothing to do with support. The storytime mom who checks out 40 books a week and loves her library doesn't necessarily vote for it. Why? Because she thinks her taxes are too high. The 84-year-old man who drags his friends to his public library once a week to brag about its marvels may not even have a library card. But he votes for the library in every election, because he thinks a community that doesn't support libraries is pathetic.

The second reality further underscores the first: Demographics have nothing to do with library support. It simply isn't the case that we can reliably predict that moms, or senior citizens, or the poor, or the wealthy will vote either for or against us. We can't solve our funding dilemmas by promoting our services or marketing more vigorously to our traditional demographics.

I'll pose a third, and even more brutal hypothesis: Library *performance* has nothing to do with fiscal support. I've seen very poor-performing libraries get consistently strong local financial support, and I know some very good ones (including mine) that are consistently punished at the polls. It's not about who we are or what we do. It's about what our communities feel and believe about us.

So what generates library support? I believe there are three essential factors:

1. The frame.
2. The story.
3. The repeated message.

The frame is something well articulated by George Lakoff (*Don't Think of an Elephant*) and appears again in the work of Dan Ariely (*Predictably Irrational*). Humans make meaning; they strive constantly to make sense of the world, to predict the future from the past. If it rains the first two times you visit Chicago, you think, "It always rains in Chicago!" Once you think that, you don't notice that the sun was shining the last three times you were there. You've got a frame, and you simply don't see what doesn't fit.

The frame that most affects library funding today is the result of 50 long years of conservative framing. It can be summed up in two words: "tax burden."

If you accept that frame, then any investment in your social infrastructure isn't seen as what it is—a cooperative purchasing agreement, often brilliantly cost-effective—but as a terrible weight, barely to be borne. There is only "tax burden" and "tax relief."

Frames are quickly established and, once adopted, prove very hard to break out of. I did an exercise with a room full of elected county officials. I asked them to write on a note card no more than three to five phrases that captured what they thought their neighbors felt about local government. It wasn't flattering.

I gathered the words and dropped them into Wordle to make it clear what a word cloud looks like. The big words (the most frequently repeated) were as follows: Taxes. Bloated. Inefficient. Bureaucratic. Parasitical.

Then I asked those officials to flip over the note card and write three to five more phrases that captured why they had run for office. This time, the big words were different: Community. Giving back. Quality of life. Pride. Sustainability.

Pointing to the first exercise, I said, "Use these words and you undercut everything you hoped to accomplish." Then I pointed to the second word cloud and told them: "Use these words." I can't say that it worked, at least not for more than a day or two. It doesn't even work reliably with librarians.

Far too often, we are complicit in our own demise. When we adopt the words, the language, the frames of those who seek to destroy us, there is little difference to be perceived between us.

The story is something librarians really ought to understand—but don't. In 2010, I worked with a cadre of passionate librarians around Colorado to launch what we called "BHAG: The Colorado Public Library Advocacy Initiative." BHAG, of course, stands for Big Hairy Audacious Goal. We were fighting a trio of state ballot issues that would have gutted the funding of libraries (and most other public-sector institutions).

The idea of BHAG was simple: All of our communities have good speakers, well respected and well connected. Why not find them, arm them with a short, compelling, even powerful little talk, and send them out into the community on our behalf?

There have been many library advocacy efforts over the years. Often, they begin with the attempt to train librarians to speak up. They are based on the premise that librarians advocating for increased use will result in increased support. OCLC's 2008 study *From Awareness to Funding* disproved that premise.

Not all librarians are good speakers. Nor are they all well respected or connected. Nor, even if they are, will simple promotion of library services build a community that is willing to pay for them.

Let me be blunt: Library advocacy as we have done it for the past 20 years doesn't work. We need a fundamentally different approach.

The BHAG approach was this: Let's just give a vivid script to passionate library supporters who already love to talk to their community, and whose communities are liable to listen. Let's book these speakers for five talks apiece to different kinds of groups (business, faith-based, nonprofit, civic, etc.). And let's have them talk not about services, but about value.

This effort didn't really cost anything. The script, the methodology, even YouTube training videos, were all right there on our project website. The talk itself, which was designed to take about 12 minutes, is a template for statewide and even national library advocacy. Use of this talk is freely offered to all. You have only two responsibilities: Use it, and make it better.

I won't go into great detail here about what you can find on our website, but the talk has four main components—and should have had one more.

A gimmick. The talk begins by asking for $1 from the audience "for the library." Why becomes clear later.

A cost-setting exercise. The speaker asks the audience how much they pay per month for internet access at home, satellite or cable TV, cellphones, and Netflix.

It asks why people pay for those things, and what good they do the community. Then it contrasts those costs with the average monthly cost for libraries. The idea is to reset the mental frame regarding both the cost and the value of libraries.

Stories. This, I think, is the heart of the talk. A successful library story follows a simple narrative structure.

Who: "Caiden was a smart three-year-old boy."

The Problem: "Like a lot of smart little boys, he started to stutter."

Library Intervention: "Our Read to Dogs program marked a tipping point for him."

Happy Ending: "Caiden doesn't stutter anymore."

Moral: "Libraries change lives."

The talk had three stories, each with a distinct final message. While the stories changed—each library was encouraged to come up with a local story of its own—the messages did not.

A close. That $1 bill was returned to the first donor. Then that person got $4 more, each accompanied by a little illustration demonstrating the return on investment of libraries.

What was missing? We should have had a stronger call to action. Not "Vote for the library," because that pitch tends to happen only in election years and appears blatantly self-serving. Rather, it should have been something like, "So the next time you hear someone say, 'My taxes are too high,' remember Caiden. Libraries change lives. Stand up for the library!"

Repetition of a concise message is something librarians have trouble with. We can't just tell people three things and leave. We have to give them six brochures, nine bookmarks, four fliers, describe three new services, and highlight one research study. We overwhelm people with information and communicate nothing.

We need to keep things simple. We should have no more than four stories and messages, we should make them human and memorable, and we should keep saying them, over and over and over and over, not just in Colorado, but all around the country, and for years. Just like the folks who speak against public-sector funding.

What next?

I'm pleased to report that the three ballot measures were soundly defeated in Colorado. Over 3,000 people heard our talks, and about 20% of our public libraries "got it." That's not bad for the first year. We made many important new allies.

I can't emphasize enough that advocacy is not the work of a season. It is the duty of a generation of librarians. Turning our situation around cannot be fixed by librarians talking to each other. We need to recruit and position nonlibrarians to talk to other nonlibrarians, presenting the smartest and most compelling thinking and presentations our research and experience can assemble.

Now would be a good time to start. The four messages of the Colorado Public Library Advocacy Initiative were these:

1. Libraries change lives.
2. Libraries mean business.
3. Libraries build community.
4. Libraries are a smart investment.

The longest message has only five words.

SOURCE: James LaRue, "Keeping Our Message Simple," *American Libraries Online*, May 31, 2011, americanlibrariesmagazine.org/features/06082011/keeping-our-message-simple.

From awareness to funding

by Anita S. Duckor

MINNEAPOLIS PUBLIC LIBRARY AND the suburban Hennepin County Library made history in January 2008 when they merged, creating a single system serving 1.1 million with a collection of more than 5 million items. The unprecedented measure, which required the approval of three elected bodies plus the state legislature and governor, was precipitated by a financial crisis that crippled MPL, and an outpouring of support wasn't enough to save it. Shortcomings in the Minneapolis experience demonstrate that public awareness can only lead to funding when that leap is made with robust advocacy tactics based on strategic alliances and political pressure points and by empowering supporters with more than awareness.

The Minneapolis Central Library, completed in 2006. Photo by Michael Hardy, used CC BY-SA 3.0.

Largely stable funding since MPL's foundation in 1885 created an excellent library system renowned for a historic collection, high circulation, and strong public support. Tides began to turn in the 1990s when public funds floundered. The final blow came in 2003 when the state of Minnesota made drastic cuts in aid to cities. The funding formula for MPL depended more on local government aid than on the ever-increasing property tax base of the same period. Thus, we underfunded collections, building maintenance, and technology—a sadly common scenario across the country.

The rigid city-funding formula meant that MPL suffered more than other city departments; city revenues increased by 3.6% between 2003 and 2007, while the library's revenues essentially remained stagnant, falling by 0.4%. Like all libraries, ours experienced a time of rising staff, collection-development, and subscription expenses. To meet the budget limitations, the MPL trustees were forced to cut 30% of staff members in 2004, reduce hours, and close three community libraries in 2007. Further cuts were on the horizon.

Action was needed. City and state government needed to restore funding and correct several structural problems contributing to the crisis. An outpouring of community support was easily found at library board and city council meetings. Media attention was at times significant. Ultimately, the efforts of library supporters in Minneapolis, some of whom were interviewed in OCLC's *From Awareness to Funding* report in 2008, failed to win enough votes on the city council to save MPL.

Libraries are the most local form of local government—each library's unique circumstances reflect this. Yet the broader lessons learned in the battle for MPL call for an advocacy strategy beyond awareness to be imported by any library community:

Lesson 1: Filling the room is not enough. Library advocates must show their support in quality as well as quantity. They should be aware of the stakes at hand yet also understand the background, counterarguments, and the political allegiances of each policymaker. Impressive numbers of library supporters in Minneapolis frequently filled public hearings, but it wasn't enough because MPL hadn't made a solid case for a long-term financial solution.

Lesson 2: Active advocacy is never out of season. Libraries can't wait to mo-

7

bilize direct advocacy efforts until funds are threatened. Effective advocacy must be built on a solid business case articulating the community's investment in addressing community issues such as graduation rates, unemployment, homelessness, immigrant integration, school readiness, a skilled workforce, juvenile crime, and library funding. In Minneapolis, an insular mentality held on too long, and subsequent efforts to mobilize were hindered by other demands on staff time and a business case built too late.

Lesson 3: Turn competing priorities into common causes. When justifying a decision, politicians too often use the classic either/or argument. It's often a false choice. Building ongoing outside-the-box alliances strengthens community relations and makes nearly every vote a vote pertinent to the library's wider societal roles. One Minneapolis city council member justified his vote against library funding by saying, "Books don't stop bullets." The truth is, libraries prevent bullets. Establishing that with community partners and this council member may have prevented the closing of libraries.

Lesson 4: Constantly communicate value and consequences. Libraries sell themselves short when they only promote circulation, cardholders, and other traditional measures of output. The ways libraries truly improve lives, although difficult to quantify, are critical when competing for public dollars. It is important for libraries to articulate their contribution in making a community a vibrant place to live, work, and own a business. MPL failed to market its intrinsic value soon enough or broadly enough with all key stakeholders.

Taking care of business

2.8 million
times every month

COME IN, WE'RE OPEN

business owners and employees use resources at public libraries to support their small businesses.

Source: OCLC, 2010, primary research.

Lesson 5: Demand transparency. Minneapolis's confusing arrangement of library governance and funding structures handicapped our ability to understand the problem before it hit us. Multilayered library governance is a problem across the country; part of library advocacy must include the insistence on the greatest possible transparency. Transparency leads to political accountability. Advocates must enlist any help they need to develop a list of factors likely to affect both short- and long-term funding, and must monitor these factors with vigilance.

Lesson 6: Call out your supporters and the opposition by name. Successful campaigns at capitals across the country share a common tactic: Organizers publicly thank, by name, those officials supporting their cause and broadly publicize their gratitude. Equally, successful campaigns name their opposition. Too often, libraries think they need to play it safe through blanket messaging. This is politically ineffective and risks alienating allies. So instead of "Ask the county board to fund libraries," messaging should feel like: "Thank Commissioners X and Y for their support and tell Commissioner Z to vote yes on resolution 42." And never mention political affiliations—support for libraries is a nonpartisan issue and so too must be our advocates.

Lesson 7: Make use of your Friends. Policymakers expect to hear from library directors and trustees. Hearing from constituents makes more of an impact. A strong library Friends organization must be encouraged. As community members, they can lobby with much greater political latitude than library professionals. In Minneapolis, our impressive Friends organization wasn't able to maximize its advocacy effectiveness—in part because of a concurrent capital campaign.

Lesson 8: Invest in advocacy. The library administration must have a solid stakeholder-relations plan and work closely with the Friends in developing long-term advocacy. Library staff and supporters must join community and business groups, such as the chamber of commerce, neighborhood organizations, arts council, or service club. It requires an investment of time and money.

MPL didn't survive as a standalone institution, but the outpouring of support did create the political will to merge the two library systems in Hennepin County—with the successful outcome of libraries staying open and with more hours. But had we been aware of the true impact of the long-term underfunding and made a better business case with elected officials, we might have remained independent.

SOURCE: Anita S. Duckor, "From Awareness to Funding," *American Libraries* 40, no. 1/2 (January/February 2009): 45–47.

What to do when the media calls
by the ALA Public Information Office

THESE TIPS AND TALKING POINTS are suggestions on how best to answer questions from radio, TV, print, and online journalists when they call to ask about news or events at your library. Some of these suggestions will also apply if you are appearing on a podcast or televised panel discussion.

General tips

1. **Ask questions.** Determine the name of the publication or media outlet. Find out the story's theme, the reporter's angle, and the deadline. If you do not feel qualified to address the question or are uncomfortable with the approach, say so. Help the reporter find another source.
2. **Be clear about whose position you are representing**—yourself, your library, or the American Library Association.
3. **Be prepared to answer the standard questions** of who, what, when, where, why, and how. Have supporting facts and examples on hand.
4. **Pause before answering** to think about what you want to say and the best way to say it. Keep your comments positive and to the point. If you must say something negative, only say it once; never repeat.
5. **Keep your answers simple and brief.** Too much information can overwhelm the reporter or the audience—and it may keep you from being quoted.
6. **Don't be afraid to admit you don't know.** Reporters do not want incorrect information. Tell them you'll get the information and call back.
7. **Never say "No comment."** Acceptable alternatives are "I'm sorry, I can't answer that" or "I'll let you know as soon as I know."
8. **Know your audience** (teens, seniors, business owners) and what their concerns are. Ask your interviewer if you aren't sure.
9. **Know your key message.** What is the most important point you want the reporter to convey to the audience? Deliver it at the first opportunity and try to repeat it at least twice. Check the ALA website for a policy statement or fact sheet on a variety of topics.

7

10. **Talk, don't speak.** Use simple language. Avoid acronyms, jargon, and technical language.
11. **Limit yourself to three talking points.** In an interview, less is more. Keep your answers short, to the point, about 25 words or fewer (12 seconds). Let the interviewer ask the questions.
12. **Use statistics sparingly.** People don't remember them.
13. **Tell stories and use real examples** to illustrate key points. Audiences remember good stories.
14. **Let your enthusiasm show.** Deliver your message in a way that makes people feel—not just think—that libraries are important.

Stay in control

15. **Anticipate the questions** you will most likely be asked and have answers ready.
16. **Ask the interviewer in advance** what questions you will be asked. Although many will not provide specifics, they will at least give you a general outline.
17. **Speak deliberately.** Pause after you answer. It lends you authority and allows the interviewer time to react.
18. **Never answer a question you don't fully understand.** Say, "I'm not sure I understand the question, are you asking. . . . ?"
19. **Beware of manipulation.** Some reporters may ask leading questions, such as "So, you are saying that . . ." followed by an idea for your agreement. Make your own statement and use your own words.
20. **There is no such thing as "off the record."** Don't let a reporter trick you into saying more than you want to say.
21. **Focus the interviewer** by going back to your primary message: "The real issue is. . . ."
22. **Buy yourself time to think** by saying, "That's an excellent question," or, "Let me think about that and come back to it."
23. **Flag key thoughts** with words and phrases like "The most important point I want to make is. . . ." or "This issue is critical because. . . ."
24. **Bridge to the positive.** When asked a negative question, answer briefly without repeating any charged or negative words. Then bridge to a positive message. For example: Q. "Isn't it true that librarians allow children to watch pornography on the internet?" A. "Absolutely not. Our role is to help children learn to use the internet wisely and to help guide them to all the great sites that are out there."
25. **Listen to your interviewer.** Watch for the wandering eye, the bored look. Make adjustments. Change your pacing. Pause. Raise and lower your voice.

Especially for radio and TV

26. **Use lots of expression**—highs and lows, enthusiasm. It's all in the voice. Use simple, colorful language that paints a picture for the listener. Tell stories, but keep them brief and to the point.
27. **Brevity is even more important** with broadcast media. You may have less than 20 seconds to answer one question.
28. **How you look on TV is as important as what you say.** Keep an open

face with eyebrows raised, maintain good posture, use hand gestures, and vary your vocal expression. All this helps establish you as a credible and enthusiastic spokesperson. Props—a book, poster, or large photo—can add interest.

29. **Look at the interviewer,** not the camera or the audience, unless you are doing an interview by remote or the interviewer is behind the camera.

30. **Practice active listening.** In a panel discussion, look at whoever is speaking. The camera may still be on you.

31. **Picture who your audience is** and speak directly to them—from your heart as well as your mind. Use stories and examples listeners can relate to.

32. **Wear more makeup than usual.** Heavier lipstick and blush counteracts the harshness of the lights and still looks natural. Powder helps minimize shine. Some stations provide professional makeup assistance for both men and women.

33. **Avoid harsh colors** like black, navy, white, or bright red. Rich colors— bright blue, rust, wine, or purple—work well for most women, as does charcoal gray or brown for men. Dress as you would for a business meeting. A blouse and suit with an open collar is flattering for most women.

34. **Keep jewelry simple.** Medium-sized earrings or a pin helps focus attention on the face. Avoid dangling earrings or necklaces that move or glitter when you talk; they distract from what you are saying.

35. **Use glasses with nonreflective lenses,** if possible.

SOURCE: The ALA Public Information Office.

How to communicate with legislators
by the ALA Office for Library Advocacy

WHETHER YOU DO IT IN PERSON, by phone, email, or letter, communication is necessary for good relations with public officials—not just when your library's funding comes up for a vote, but on a regular basis so the lawmaker can become familiar with library issues and trends. The first step should be a face-to-face meeting if at all possible. Keeping legislators informed about library concerns, trends, and successes is the best way to turn them into supporters and even library champions. Invite them to participate in National Library Week and other special events. Send letters or emails to alert them to library issues you are concerned about. Send the library newsletter and other publicity materials. Send a letter highlighting library resources of special interest to a legislator and expressing your desire to be of service. Include a business card with the library's address and telephone number, website, and email. Be sure to thank legislators for their ongoing support.

Although many people are intimidated or put off by having to compete for the time and attention of legislators, lobbying or advocating for a particular cause is the American way. Politicians are busy people, but they welcome their constituents' input, both as a way of gauging community opinion and learning about issues with which they may not be familiar.

7

The American Library Association maintains an Office for Government Relations and an Office for Information Technology Policy in Washington, D.C., to help educate legislators and to monitor issues that relate to libraries and information access, such as copyright, government information and publications, censorship, the internet, and electronic information.

Tips

- **Start with legislators** you know support libraries. Keep them informed as your issue or legislation moves forward.
- **Recognize** that public officials can't be experts on everything. Be prepared to provide them with information or referral sources.
- **Stick to one issue.** Decision makers do not want to listen to a laundry list of issues.
- **Do your homework.** Find out what you can about an official. Link the library message to something you know that relates to their special interest or cause.
- **Develop relationships** with federal, state, and local lawmakers. A growing number of federal policy issues have a direct impact on libraries and their users.
- **Get to know staff.** Legislative staff members can be very powerful. If convinced about your issue, they can become important allies. Staff members change frequently. Be sure to stay current. Offer to brief new staff on library issues.
- **Don't give misinformation.** If you don't know the answer or have the information at your fingertips, promise to get back to the lawmaker as soon as possible.
- **Be personal.** Share your own real-world stories about your library.
- **Seal the deal.** Be direct about what you want and try to get a commitment.

Know your legislator

The more you know about a legislator or official, the more effective you can be in communicating the library message and ensuring a successful outcome from your advocacy efforts.

Sen. Jack Reed (D-R.I.) addresses library advocates during the 2010 ALA Annual Conference in Washington. Photo by Jennifer Henderson.

Some legislators are more important than others because they control more votes, sit on important committees, are members of the governing body's power structure or leadership, or are considered experts in a particular area. When deciding which legislators to approach, always ask yourself who can make or break this piece of legislation.

Policymakers who hold appointments on critical committees should be targeted first. After all, if your bill doesn't make it out of committee, it will never be voted on. Committees that often consider issues that affect libraries include Ways and Means, Appropriations, Education, Urban Affairs, Judicial, and Commerce.

Shaping the message

To be effective, your message should show how the proposed legislation or policy benefits or harms the lawmaker's constituents. Be clear about what you are asking (vote for or against a particular measure, persuade other committee members to support your side, cosponsor a bill, or sign on to a Dear Colleague letter).

Who can be most effective?

Selecting the best person to deliver your message can make the difference as to whether you are successful. Smart legislative advocates know which legislators are most influential on any given issue. They also know the names of those who are in a position to influence the legislator. The most important person to any elected official is a voting constituent.

Other important people are:

- Campaign donors
- Local civic and business leaders
- Editors of local media who shape editorial opinions and news coverage
- Potential candidates who may oppose lawmakers in future elections
- Individuals who have had a positive impact on his or her life

Libraries have just about every kind of person imaginable as users and supporters. Just as politicians rank the importance of certain constituency groups in terms of their value, we need to do the same in order to know who can best champion our cause.

Ways to communicate

There are many ways to communicate with legislators. These include:

Personal visits. A face-to-face visit with the lawmaker is the most effective means of communication. It is essential to establish a comfortable working relationship with your elected officials. Schedule a meeting when the governing body is not in session, so there is less competition for the legislator's time and attention. Call the local office to make an appointment, if possible at the library so you can highlight what's happening in your operation. Always call ahead to reconfirm your appointment.

Telephone calls. Once you have established a relationship, telephone calls are appropriate and easy. Regular contact with staff is possible and desirable. When should you call? Call to ask support before a hearing or floor vote. You also may make an annual call or visit to keep the legislator and his or her staff informed of trends and problems that have surfaced during the year.

Letters. Letters are the fuel that powers the legislative process. They are read. Letters elicit responses. They represent votes. Each letter-writer is deemed to represent several like-minded, if less highly motivated, constituents. Letters may be formal or informal, typed or handwritten. They should be composed by you, giving reasons for your position and how it will make a difference for the lawmaker's constituents.

It is now preferable to fax letters to congressional offices rather than sending through the US mail because new security procedures keep the US Postal Service from delivering mail in a timely manner.

Email. Email is a good option, particularly when time is of the essence.

7

In general, the best option is to call the official's office and ask which method of communication is preferred. It's a good idea to call in advance and keep a list of names and numbers handy for quick action.

Tips for effective letters

Whether you send a letter or email, legislators want to hear from their constituents. A well-written letter lets them know you care and can provide valuable facts and feedback that help the official take a well-reasoned stand.

- **Use the correct form** of address.
- **Identify yourself.** If you are writing as a member of your library's board of trustees, as a school librarian, officer of the Friends, or college administrator, say so.
- **State why** you are coming forward.

Let your elected officials know you believe all types of libraries are central to our democracy and that you are counting on them to make sure that all libraries—public, school, and academic—have adequate funds and resources.

Be specific. Cite a bill number or other identifying information. Give examples. If budget cuts have forced your library to cut book and journal budgets or students are graduating without necessary information literacy skills, say so.

Write from the heart. Avoid clichés. Form letters that look like they're a part of an organized pressure campaign don't have as much impact as a personal letter.

Focus on the people who depend on library services. Include real-life stories or examples of how the library makes a difference in the lives of constituents.

Be brief. A one-page communication is easier to read—and more likely to be read.

Be sure to include your name, mailing address, and telephone number in the letter, not just on the envelope. If the letter gets separated from the envelope, the legislator may not be able to respond.

Extend your communication's impact by sending copies to city councilors, other members of Congress, and relevant state and local officials. Be sure to send a copy to your library's advocacy coordinator, the ALA Office for Library Advocacy, and ALA Washington Office if appropriate. Also let them know any response you receive.

Be strategic. Know the budget cycles for various governing bodies. Send letters early to maximize their impact. ALA and many state associations will issue action alerts on timely issues.

SOURCE: ALA Office for Library Advocacy, *Library Advocate's Handbook,* 3rd ed. (Chicago: American Library Association, 2008), 25–31.

Technology

CHAPTER EIGHT

Download me another ebook, madame,
For they are the best in the land.
I need another hit
Mystery or wit
To be a satisfied ebook readin' man.

The librarian brought me a print book;
I thanked her but set it right aside.
She went back to her desk
While I did the rest
And logged right on into OverDrive.

—David Tyckoson, "Ebook Reading Man" (2012)

LOW TECHNOLOGY

The library embossing stamp
by Melvil Dewey

THIS IS NEEDED TO MARK the name and place of the library on the title pages and all plates, maps, and inserts not printed on the regular forms and therefore liable to be removed. If the stamp is properly made, it is impossible to iron out its impression so that it cannot be detected if the sheet is held up to the light and the broken fibers examined. A rubber stamp used to mark titles and plates is apt to stain, blot, or offset; or if an ink that acts like a paint instead of a dye is used, after many years it can be removed with an ordinary eraser. Safety and neat appearance both require the raised letters of the seal press.

The best form of seal for embossing is the simple name of the library with its location in plain, gothic letters. Fancy types are less legible and the fine lines wear out and break quicker. The gothic letter will wear better than any other. A very common outline is an oval about 2x3 cm, but the words alone without the borderline are still neater. The town and (except for very prominent cities) the state should be given, for books get carried long distances in family movings and find their way home in time if it is clearly indicated.

Library embossing stamp. Photo by Larry T. Nix.

If the letters are cut on a globe in bas relief, the fibers of the paper are pressed into a new shape more difficult to iron out, but it is safe to avoid all designs and alleged ornaments. A borderline round the oval, if cut in the ordinary way as for a notary's seal, is very apt in the hands of beginners to act like a punch and cut out the paper, sometimes leaving the space open when the lever is raised but oftener cutting the fiber so that the center drops out after a little handling.

The impression should never be made with a quick stroke, such as is used with a dating stamp, but, especially with old or tender paper, with a slower, steady pressure that forms the paper into the new shape without cutting it out. An illustration of the principle may be seen in pressing a die on hard wax. If done too suddenly it simply shatters it, but a firm, slow push gives a perfect outline. A careful embosser will soon learn just how fast he can work his machine safely by examining closely the result on different kinds of paper.

The die should be set to read in the line of the lever, so that standing before it with the right hand on the lever and the book in the left, the impression will read straight on the page. A press made to stamp envelopes is set at right angles to the lever so as to seal the other corner.

For ordinary books, the press should be secured firmly to a table corner, or better, to the left end of the top of the taller-sized library steps [*Ed.:* stepladder]. This has all the advantages of the table and in addition, can be readily moved wherever it may be wanted. In embossing books already on the shelves, the step can be set in front of the tier and each book replaced as soon as done, thus saving much handling.

An ordinary book is held in the left hand and the title, or the page to be embossed, is held out from the rest by the little finger, leaving the right hand free for the lever. For books too large to be held in one hand, two persons are required, or the press is unscrewed and a piece of felt glued on the bottom to prevent injury to the book from the rough edges of the iron frame. Then the large book being opened on a table, the press is set on the leaves below that to be marked, thus enabling one person to emboss each plate neatly without assistance. It is of course much cheaper, when there are many large books, to have a duplicate press with felt bottom instead of unscrewing from the steps each time it is wanted.

We recently bought from the Library Bureau their new treadle embossing machine, which allows of much quicker work, and one person can handle all but the largest folios alone. This is the regular press with a hole through the end of lever where a wire is connected and dropped through the top of the step to a treadle. A spring below completes the machine. The foot gives the firm pressure, and both hands are free to handle the book. With this there is less chance of the book slipping from the hand and tearing or crumpling the leaf.

Libraries also formerly used perforating stamps, which produced ownership marks like this one.

The impression is best put in the right-hand upper section of the page, and as the purpose of this stamp is to make theft impossible, it must not be so far in the margin as to allow its being cut off without taking any of the print. The rule is to let the stamp touch some of the print, but young embossers should be

Library book trucks

by Larry T. Nix

The Library Bureau's *Classified Illustrated Catalog* of 1886 described the library book truck as "The most useful single device ever made for an active library." An image of the Library Bureau's book truck, item 21a in the catalog, is shown on the right. Starting with the Library Bureau, book trucks (also called book carts) were sold and continue to be sold by most library supply companies. Gaylord Brothers included "The Truck Beautiful" (left) in its 1933 catalog of Library Furniture and Supplies. My introduction to book trucks came as a page at the Public Library of Nashville (Tenn.) and Davidson County way back in 1963. I'm sure I shelved tens of thousands of books using these handy devices. Nowadays, we also have book cart drill teams and tricked-out book cart contests. There are thousands of images of book trucks/book carts on the web that can be found by searching Google or Flickr. If your library has one of the early wood book trucks, consider yourself very fortunate.

SOURCE: Larry T. Nix, "Library Book Trucks," Library History Buff Blog, July 12, 2011, libraryhistorybuff.blogspot.com. Reprinted with permission.

8

cautioned against disfiguring portraits or any special feature of a plate. Where a book has many plates, the first should be stamped at the top, the next the width of the stamp lower, and so on until the bottom is reached, then repeating the distribution, and thus avoiding swelling the top corner from having all the raised letters in the same portion of the book.

SOURCE: Melvil Dewey, "Embossing Stamp," *Library Notes* 1, no. 1 (June 1886): 26–27.

INTERNET SERVICES

Public computers in libraries

by Jeannette Woodward

WHATEVER THE SPECIFIC COMPONENTS of your technology plan, the internet should be a primary focus. In the last few years we have witnessed one resource after another becoming available on the internet. Library catalogs are internet-accessible, allowing users to dial in from home. Indexes and full-text journals are also available, as are cataloging and acquisitions utilities. These developments simplify your planning in some respects, but they also make greater technical demands on a library. Libraries have unique requirements when it comes to meeting the information needs of their users. Here, for example, is a description of a sophisticated library emphasizing its broad access to information resources on the internet:

Public computers at Burley (Idaho) Public Library.

- Technology is designed to support and facilitate both casual information-seeking and the research process.
- Desks and carrels are equipped with desktop computers or with power outlets to accommodate laptop computers.
- All library-owned and personal laptop computers can connect to the internet from any area in the library.
- The network offers a variety of information resources, including local and regional materials, productivity software, graphics, and statistical software packages.
- Scanners, fax machines, laser printers, and other hardware serve the needs of library users and staff.
- From a single library-designed web browser menu, users can connect to a wealth of networked utilities.
- Wireless technology facilitates the digital transmission of data, graphics, audio, and video resources, and the library provides whatever peripheral equipment (headphones or graphic tablets) is needed to make effective use of this digital delivery system.

- In academic libraries, the library is an extension of the campus information network and ably supports electronic scholarship. Information technology is a natural, fully integrated part of the public library environment.
- In public libraries, the library is an extension of local government and other community services, offering residents the opportunity to be fully informed of local resources.
- Comfortable furniture encourages users to spend extended periods of time studying, researching, and writing.
- Carpeting incorporates antistatic properties that safeguard computers, and it also creates an aesthetically pleasing environment.
- Sophisticated daylighting technology permits exterior vistas and natural daylight without interfering with the visibility of projected images or posing a hazard to paper resources.
- HVAC systems offer zone control, providing comfort for human users and adequate cooling for heat-generating computer servers.
- Noise is controlled with an appropriate level of comfort-inducing "white noise" to facilitate viewing, reading, and study.
- Spacious instruction rooms are equipped with up-to-date equipment to teach groups how to use online resources safely and effectively.
- Collaborative or teaching spaces are wired to accommodate multiple workstations with access to the library network. High-quality, easy-to-operate projection equipment is mounted to the ceiling with controls adjacent to the team leaders workstation.
- Contracts with database suppliers permit enough simultaneous connections to accommodate large numbers of users.
- One or more firewalls separate public and library functions; protect against viruses; and routinely monitor, adjust, and redirect system traffic.
- Hardware or software solutions prevent changes from being made to computer settings, or they return computers to their original condition at the end of each user's session.

SOURCE: Jeannette Woodward, *Countdown to a New Library: Managing the Building Project*, 2d ed. (Chicago: American Library Association, 2010), 170–171.

Open source public workstations

by John Houser

8

PRIOR TO 1999, mentions of any open source operating system in mainstream library literature were rare. No one was writing about using Linux and other open source solutions for desktop computing in a public setting. By 2000 Linux was making headway as a server operating system in libraries. Roy Tennant kicked off the year writing about open source software *in Library Journal.* By mid-decade, discussion of Linux and open source technology in libraries was commonplace.

Three approaches. There are three distinct approaches to using open source software for public workstations. The first approach is simply to replace the Windows operating system with a Linux distribution on every PC. The second method is to utilize a multiuser configuration, based on Linux, that supports two to six users on a workstation. The third recommendation is to use the Linux Terminal Server Project (LTSP) software to run a terminal session for every user from a central server or set of servers. This thin-client effort can support a large number of users connected to one server—50 or more, if the server is configured appropriately. It can significantly simplify system administration because the server administers all functions. This approach requires greater technical knowledge but may also result in greater hardware savings, reduced power consumption, and reduced air-conditioning costs.

Organizations using these models report mixed results, but their experimenting with open source public workstations is overwhelmingly positive. They have proven effective in cutting cost and environmental impact.

Two future trends. Two trends that will continue to impact libraries are also likely to help facilitate the introduction of more open source workstations. First, funding issues, particularly in light of the current economic climate, will make it imperative that libraries find ways to spend their technology budgets more efficiently. That alone will continue to encourage interest in low-cost, open source computing solutions.

Second, we can expect to see the continued development of web-based applications for office productivity and other common functions. Cloud computing utilities, such as those offered by Amazon, Google, Sun, and others, make it possible for application developers to utilize a software-as-a-service (SaaS) model without having to create the infrastructure and middleware necessary for such systems. The result is speedier development of scalable web-based applications and more options for consumers.

Growth potential. Open source public workstations are an excellent option for libraries looking for cost-effective alternatives to proprietary software. Any systems decision in a library is extremely important, so it is vital for decision makers to consider all angles before making a choice. Still, with growing popularity and a growing number of options available, open source workstations are an increasingly important part of the library technology world.

SOURCE: John Houser, "Open Source Public Workstations," *American Libraries* 40, no. 5 (May 2009): 35.

EBOOKS

Warning: You are about to enter the ebook zone

by Robert C. Maier and Carrie Russell

WELCOME TO THE WORLD of constant change. Every week sees a new twist in the world of public libraries and ebooks, and if you are feeling bewildered, you're not alone. What happened to the physical-book world that we knew so well? It's still here, but since 2010 a newcomer has started to shake things up. Hello, ebooks.

Ebooks have been running along in the background for some time now, but with the development of good-quality readers (Kindle, Nook, iPad, and many more) and the ability of consumers to acquire ebooks instantly, the game has changed. Just as libraries have always re- sponded to the consumer market and the demands of our users, we now need to meet the demand for ebooks.

We have made ourselves experts in the world of physical books. We have review media. We have jobbers to purchase from. We have automated systems to manage our collections and our relationship with bor- rowers. We have systems that support inter- library borrowing. And we can retire books and turn them into revenue through book sales. If we want to retain books for the long run, we know how to preserve them for fu- ture generations.

Nearly every aspect of this comfortable business proposition is turned on its head with ebooks. We've got work to do.

And to do that work we need to focus on a relationship we haven't had to pay much attention to in a long time—our dealings with publishers. If anything, this new ebook market is even more challenging to publishers than it is to libraries, and that's why we face such turbulence. Like libraries, publishers had it all fig ured out in the traditional book world. They knew how to work with authors and agents to secure the rights to publish books, and they had all the pieces in place with editors, reviewers, designers, printers, and distributors (our jobbers). They also understood how to structure the economics of book publishing to make a profit.

In the ebook world nearly all of these factors have changed and continue to change, generating an obvious and serious concern for publishers' ability to re- main financially viable. The lessons learned by the music industry regarding illegal copying play very heavily in this new equation, both for publishers and libraries, and it presents significant threats for libraries, such as maintaining reader privacy and ensuring continued access for readers with print impairments and other dis- abilities.

Get your ebooks here—for a price

We've been saying for 20 years that the internet would make everyone a pub- lisher, and now that prediction is a reality. Not only is self-publishing providing competition for traditional publishing companies, but giant distributors such as Amazon and Apple have become ebook publishers and are looking to take big- name authors away from the traditional publishing houses. Amazon is drawing the largest crowd to the Kindle format through low ebook prices, which custom- ers have begun to expect. Libraries are facing competition as well, as these same distributors also offer ebook lending.

So how are we to sort this out? Let's consider the major trade publishers and how they are dealing with libraries so far. There are six major publishers that are referred to as the Big Six: Hachette, HarperCollins, Macmillan, Penguin, Ran- dom House, and Simon & Schuster. Together they publish the work of such familiar authors as Laura Lippman, Jonathan Kellerman, James Patterson, Anita Shreve, and Ruth Ozeki. As of this writing, just *two* of the Big Six offer their ebooks to libraries—HarperCollins and Random House. Libraries can't buy newer ebook titles from the others, foreclosing the opportunity to lend such authors as Jonathan Franzen, Sue Grafton, Walter Mosley, Jodi Picoult, and Tina Fey. This is bread and butter for public libraries, but these publishers refuse to sell ebooks to libraries or to distributors like OverDrive, 3M, Ingram, and Baker & Taylor, our traditional sources.

In February 2011, HarperCollins changed its terms of service for library lending of ebooks, slapping a 26-loan limit on all its titles. After 26 loans, the library could rebuy the ebook at a discounted price. As librarians cried foul over any limit on the number of loans, they began to understand that libraries may not even own these books.

More recently, Random House changed its pricing policy for selling ebooks to libraries, increasing the price by factors of two to three times the list price of a hardcover copy of the same book, though libraries still retain perpetual access to their ebook purchases. Also, the ebooks will be available to libraries simultaneously with the print book release. This may be good for the publisher's bottom line, but how are libraries to afford these ebooks? We're caught between tight budgets and huge public demand.

Another model for your consideration: *the metering model,* or pay-per-use. Unlike the other models, libraries only pay for what is used. Freading, the ebook platform of the music-download service Freegal, offers this model, allowing publishers to establish a point system to vary loan fees for bestsellers vs. backlist titles. For publishers, making the most of the backlist brings in new revenue from books that were only previously available in print. The used-bookstore model of reselling books was vexing for publishers, because they were unable to monetize repeated sales of the same book. Pay-by-the-download solves that problem.

For libraries, this is a risky budget arrangement, requiring them to forecast use, and the cost of that use can change at any time. Say a backlist title has a second resurgence after being adapted into a film. No problem for publishers: Just start charging more per use for that title.

For larger public libraries that typically buy numerous copies of a bestseller only to weed the majority of the copies at a later date, the *simultaneous-access model* may be preferred. To meet user demand, these libraries may buy access to numerous copies of an ebook, recognizing that after its popularity wanes, they can reduce the number of copies dramatically, freeing up money that can be spent on new ebooks. Smaller libraries might opt for paying a higher fee for an ebook at the front end, if they pay only once and can keep the book in perpetuity. Pure metering might be an option for a library that has some flexibility in managing the budget throughout the year.

Some lesser-known business models are also on the table. The *rent-to-own model* would require that libraries continue to pay for a book over a certain amount of time or number of loans. On the bright side, libraries that want to own their ebooks eventually could, but how long would the rental period last? Would the time or use limit be the same for all titles? Could publishers modify the rental terms as they wished without notice? How much money must one pay for the same book before the ownership goal kicks in?

Consider subscription plans. One already in use by some publishers and vendors is the *bookshelf model.* The library would subscribe and pay an annual fee for a set of ebooks, their selection likely in the hands of publishers or distributors. The following year, the bookshelf disappears. Libraries that continue to pay their annual fee receive another, different set of ebooks. In this model, ownership of the content is off the table. The library can't build a collection but would pay for access to a temporary collection of ebooks that might include some that they do not want. Moreover, publishers could use this system to hold back the bestsellers until sales for these books begin to wane.

Media librarians may be familiar with the *embargo model*, in which DVDs cannot be purchased for the collection until after a particular period of time following general consumer release. In this model, rights holders believe the loan and rental markets cut into retail sales of DVDs of first-run films. A positive aspect of this approach is that libraries, if they are patient, can build collections. A negative aspect is that library users will be unhappy and the library is relegated to lending yesterday's goods and becoming holder of the hand-me-downs.

How bad can it get?

Worse scenarios have been proposed. Examples include library users paying for access to ebooks; users having to come to the library to download; and users paying an annual fee for their library cards. For publishers, making no-fee lending less desirable to potential ebook buyers is often articulated as a priority. This line of thinking is that "friction"—for example, either making it next to impossible to successfully download a book, or imposing difficulty by requiring a user to physically go to the library, stand in line to check out books, place a hold on a book that is checked out, and return a book to the library—will turn book borrowers into book buyers. People would eventually get fed up and buy the book online.

While there is no evidence that library lending negatively affects sales, we do know that book borrowers are also book buyers. According to an April 2012 study by the Pew Research Center's Internet and American Society Project, ebook enthusiasts read more books than the average print-book reader and prefer to purchase what they want to read, although some start their search for reading material at their library. People discover books at the library. With the demise of the local bookstore, the library becomes a welcome spot where book borrowers and buyers can browse. They can also be a point of sale for borrowers who are also buyers. Libraries are starting to offer a purchase option right in their catalogs in return for a share of the revenue. And why not? It's time for libraries to claim more credit for the work we do promoting books and authors.

Douglas County (Colo.) Libraries did just that, by establishing a do-it-yourself ebook lending service through the purchase of its own Adobe Content Server software to self-host some of its copy-protected ebook content, bypassing the vendor intermediary (and the costs involved). One of DCL's innovations is an agreement with the Colorado Independent Publishers Association to both loan its ebooks and offer them for sale.

Problem solved? It's a beginning. The reality is that most libraries are accustomed to working through a distributor to obtain ebooks. OverDrive, one of the first distributors to offer ebooks and content services to libraries, is the big player on the block, with more than 1,500 library customers. Since 2002, OverDrive has been negotiating with publishers to obtain the rights to sell ebooks to libraries. New entrants in the field include 3M, Baker & Taylor, and Follett. Each offers multiple kinds of service features for libraries, such as one ebook file/one loan, library-catalog links that direct users to stores where ebooks can be purchased (such as OverDrive's "buy it now" option), patron-driven acquisitions where an additional copy of an ebook is automatically acquired by the library once a certain number of patron holds are placed on the title, and so on. Especially for public

8

libraries just dipping their toes in the ebook water rapids, it is difficult to know what distributor to choose, what business models to select, and what percentage of your meager collections budget to devote to ebooks.

One thing is sure: Library ownership of content is completely different than licensing access to it. Some argue that it is possible to own ebooks, but the legal language confuses us. Libraries can obtain a license for perpetual access to the ebook content purchased, allowing them to retain or move content to another provider or server continuously—that is, if the license agreement says so. Some business models are clearly rentals, such as the bookshelf model in which the library acquires a new but different set of ebook titles on an annual subscription basis. Rental or pay-per-use models may be preferable to some; but bear in mind that even with perpetual access you still have to negotiate for other rights, such as lending and preservation.

Publishers, distributors, and libraries must accept that new models of lending will not look like the old print model. There will be missteps. There will be controversy. Librarians will have to hang in there.

We are not just trying to solve a library lending problem, although that is the current emergency. What we do today may very well shape the future of public libraries. Where do libraries want to be in the coming decades? As *Twilight Zone* narrator Rod Serling said, "You're moving into a land of both shadow and substance, of things and ideas." That's the signpost up ahead: Your next stop—the Ebook Zone.

SOURCE: Robert C. Maier and Carrie Russell, "Warning: You Are About to Enter the Ebook Zone," *American Libraries*, E-Content Digital Supplement, May/June 2012, www.americanlibrariesmagazine.org/features/05222012/warning-you-are-about-enter-ebook-zone.

A guide to ebook purchasing
by Sue Polanka

FOR THOSE LIBRARIES LOOKING to purchase ebooks, you are not alone. According to the *Library Journal* 2011 survey of ebook penetration and use in libraries, 95% of academic, 82% of public, and 44% of school libraries are already offering ebooks, and many more are considering it. For anyone contemplating purchasing ebooks, asking why is the most important question. What are the primary goals of purchasing ebooks in your library or your consortium? Is it to expand the collection or to increase the buying power of a group of libraries? Is it to replace existing print collections, offer new services, or experiment with new business models in the hope of saving money? Whatever the reason, it is imperative to keep one's goals in mind throughout the process. Buying ebooks is a complicated process. To do it effectively is an even greater challenge due to the many ways to procure ebooks.

Print to digital. Buying a print book is relatively easy. With the introduction of library ebooks in 1999, however, the once-straightforward process of buying books took on many complexities. First, for purchasing and accessing ebook content, vendors require license agreements. These agreements contain terms of use and restrictions on access. Second, ebooks are priced differently from print. Instead of the traditional print list price (or list price with a discount), the price of an ebook is generally the list price plus a percentage. The final price is determined by the business model selected, the number of people who will use the book, or the size of a library's user group. Third, new business models were developed—and continue to be developed—to fit the diverse needs of libraries and vendors. Many of these models are very different from traditional print purchase models. Fourth, the notion of ownership has come into question with ebooks. Do libraries actually own the content, or is it leased? Libraries must circle back to the license agreement to determine the answer to this question.

Business models. There are a variety of business models available for purchasing ebooks. (See pp. 414–417 for the latest information.) Some vendors, such as OverDrive, calculate annual fees based on existing collection use data. Libraries that choose not to pay the access fees could lose the content. Therefore, it is imperative that librarians carefully read the license agreement to determine if ebook content can be used when access fees are withheld.

Publishers, aggregators, and wholesalers. Ebooks can be purchased directly from publishers, through aggregators (vendors that distribute content from multiple publishers), or wholesalers (vendors that distribute print and electronic content from publishers and aggregators). Keeping their prime directive in mind, libraries should investigate the opportunities and challenges of purchasing ebooks from all vendor types. When buying directly from publishers, libraries have more room for price negotiation since there is no intermediary. Publishers may be the only vendor for top-producing or backlist titles, providing a larger title list from which to choose content. Furthermore, publishers that offer book, journal, or multimedia content may provide access to all formats through a single interface. Because the interface concentrates on one publisher, unique features may be available to augment the content.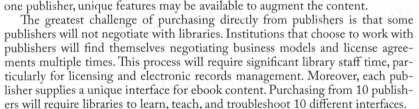

The greatest challenge of purchasing directly from publishers is that some publishers will not negotiate with libraries. Institutions that choose to work with publishers will find themselves negotiating business models and license agreements multiple times. This process will require significant library staff time, particularly for licensing and electronic records management. Moreover, each publisher supplies a unique interface for ebook content. Purchasing from 10 publishers will require libraries to learn, teach, and troubleshoot 10 different interfaces.

Buying through consortia. Libraries that are members of consortia will discover many benefits in operating as a group when purchasing ebooks. First, libraries can increase their buying power and access larger collections by negotiating as a group. In other words, 20 libraries with $5,000 each will acquire far more content than a single library with a $5,000 budget. Second, the ebooks can be shared across a consortium. This loosens the limitations of interlibrary loan—a primary library service that is excluded in most ebook license agreements. Third, libraries in the consortium have equal and consistent access to content. For example, a liberal arts college with fewer than 2,000 students can access the same content as a state university with 25,000 students. Finally, the licensing and technical work can be centralized, saving individual libraries staff time and money.

Despite all these advantages, there are some drawbacks to buying ebooks through a consortium. Determining the content, vendors, business models, and level of access is difficult for one library. Within a consortium, however, this problem is exacerbated by the number of libraries involved. As a result, the unique needs of libraries may not be met by group purchases. Once the best mix of content is finalized, the consortium must negotiate with vendors to determine the price of the ebook collections. The purchasing history of member libraries comes into play in negotiations. Vendors determine how many consortium members have already purchased their titles, and from this they determine a multiplier. The multiplier is the number of times the list price will be paid to provide unlimited simultaneous access to the consortium members. For instance, a consortium with 34 members may negotiate a multiplier of six times the list price. A title with a $100 list price will cost the consortium $600. Some consortia say that negotiations among members take as much effort as negotiations with vendors.

Evaluating vendors. No ebook should be selected, no money exchanged, and no license signed without properly evaluating vendors. Libraries should again visit their prime directive and determine the criteria most important to their purchase decision. Once criteria or questions are determined, the easiest way to conduct the evaluation is by tracking data through a matrix or spreadsheet. There are several good examples online that can be adapted by libraries. Equally as important, ebook publishers and aggregators have existing clients. Find them. Ask them questions. Solicit their advice.

Transitioning to ebook purchases in libraries offers many opportunities and challenges. These challenges, however, are not insurmountable. New business models continue to emerge. Changes and improvements are occurring in the industry every day. These changes will continue as publishers, libraries, and vendors experiment with the growing market of ebooks. The most important thing that librarians must do in this changing environment is to articulate clear ebook purchasing goals. With these goals in mind, libraries need to find the content they desire, seek the best price possible, determine sustainable business models, analyze license agreements, and evaluate vendors to effectively purchase ebooks.

It's a complex labyrinth. But one day, it will be easy.

SOURCE: Sue Polanka, "A Guide to Ebook Purchasing," *American Libraries* 42, no. 11/12 (November/ December 2011): 30, americanlibrariesmagazine.org/columns/dispatches-field/guide-ebook-purchasing.

Ebook business models
by the ALA Digital Content and Libraries Working Group

IN RESPONSE TO urgent member concerns, the ALA Digital Content and Libraries Working Group has focused on influencing the largest ("Big 6") trade publishers to sell ebooks to libraries on reasonable terms. The working group has developed considerable knowledge about the ebook market, publishers, and the new challenges posed by library ebook lending to inform its discussions with publishers and distributors. However, it is well aware that information about this topic is highly sought in the library community generally, and so this report was prepared to share some of what we have learned.

Ebook publishing is expanding and evolving rapidly, and the terms under which ebooks are made available to libraries show wide variation and frequent change. Some major trade publishers will not sell ebooks to libraries under any terms; others do so only at inflated prices or with severe restrictions. Some publishers have scaled back their initial offerings, but are beginning to explore new business models under pilot programs of limited duration or in selected regions. Other publishers seem to be making little or no headway in dealing with libraries.

In this volatile period of experimentation, no single business model will offer the best terms for all libraries or be adopted by all publishers or distributors.

This report describes model terms libraries should look for in their dealings with ebook publishers and distributors, as well as conditions libraries should avoid. While business models will continue to evolve, models that are explored in 2013 may well pave the way to the models of the future. It is therefore important that libraries negotiate aggressively for the most favorable and flexible terms possible.

General features and attributes

Replicating the print model. Unlike a printed book, a single copy of an ebook could potentially be read by many users simultaneously, from any location. Thus, a major concern of publishers is that ebook borrowing from libraries will be so easy as to erode consumer sales. To counter this opinion, many publishers insist on terms that replicate aspects of print book lending. Some of these terms may be necessary and tolerable, at least temporarily, to offset what publishers perceive as risks in selling ebooks to libraries. Others are onerous, such as requiring patrons to come to the library to check out ebooks; this alone contradicts a fundamental benefit of ebook technology and damages patron perceptions of library service. In any case, innovative models that test new and alternative potentials offered by ebooks should be encouraged, rather than slavishly imposing restrictions based on the characteristics of print.

Trade-offs. Many publishers offer ebooks to libraries only under conditions less favorable than those for print. For example, new publications may be offered only after an embargo period, or the number of circulations may be limited. In such cases, when libraries are asked to give up some rights they have always had, it is reasonable and fair to expect some other benefit in return. Possible benefits include discounted prices for certain titles, a share of the revenues generated from book purchases patrons make through the library's website, and limited free access to selected titles.

Essential features. Three basic attributes are beneficial to libraries under any business model for ebooks. While it may not be feasible to realize all of these immediately, and a library may elect to do without one or more in return for more favorable terms in other areas, at least temporarily, these features are ultimately essential to the library's public role:

- *Inclusion of all titles.* All ebook titles available for sale to the public should also be available to libraries for lending. Libraries may choose not to purchase some titles if restrictions or prices are deemed unacceptable, but withholding titles under any terms removes the library's ability to provide the services its patrons need and expect.
- *Enduring rights.* Libraries should have an option to effectively own the ebooks they purchase, including the right to transfer them to another delivery platform and to continue to lend them indefinitely. Libraries may choose more limited options for some titles or copies, or in return for lower pricing, but they should have some option that allows for permanent, enduring access.
- *Integration.* Libraries try to provide coherent access across all of the services they offer. To do this effectively, they need access to metadata and management tools provided by publishers or distributors to enhance the discovery of ebooks. Separate, stand-alone offerings of ebooks are likely to be marginalized, or to diminish awareness of other library offerings. Mechanisms that allow ebooks to be discovered within the

8

library's catalog and checked out or reserved without undue complexity are basic needs.

Business model constraints and restrictions

To enable library and retail distribution channels for ebooks to coexist, most business models currently offered to libraries include constraints on how ebooks can be used.

Single user. By replicating the print model, loans are limited to one user at a time for each ebook license purchased. This constraint often results in long waiting lists for popular titles, and is currently found in almost all publisher models.

While the single-user constraint is generally accepted, alternatives might be considered and sought: e.g., the ability to allow two or more simultaneous users for a higher price; the ability to combine multiple simultaneous users with a limited-number-of-loans model.

Limited number of loans. The library must repurchase the same title after a defined number or loans. (In theory, this is to offset the fact that ebooks don't wear out, get lost or stolen, or have coffee spilled on them.) While this model violates the principle of ownership, it may be an acceptable way of achieving lower pricing if the defined number of loans is high enough.

Ideally, this model could be combined with a sunset provision, providing for permanent ownership after a period of years. At minimum, the library should have permanent access if the ebook title is no longer offered for sale when the loan limit is reached.

Paying a set price for a limited number of loans is, in effect, a rental. Librarians may seek to apply a similar fee to current titles: a cost-per-circulation that replaces or augments purchased titles. Under this model, the library will never have enduring access to the title, unless the fee schedule is maintained. A lease-to-own arrangement may be more prudent. Another option might be to seek the right to sell at a discount to the community those materials that did not circulate well. In this case, the library might share some percentage of the sale with the publisher.

Variable pricing. Ebook prices for libraries vary widely, with some titles well above the print price and others offered at a discount. While libraries will always want to seek the best terms possible, the maximum price that is considered acceptable depends on other terms of the sale. One example of this might be a "platform" fee—a merging of a sale with database-like annual subscriptions.

Delayed sale. Publishers may delay sales of ebooks to libraries for a period after the title is released for public sale. This embargo period or "window" may last anywhere from a few weeks to several months or more. While any delayed sale violates the principle of inclusion of all titles, a brief delay may be acceptable, especially if titles are then offered at a discount. Embargoed titles are less valuable, and their price should reflect that. Conversely, libraries may be willing to pay a premium for immediate access to the most popular titles.

In-library check-out. Publishers may insist that patrons come to the library in order to check out ebooks. Although this is often seen as a way of adding "friction" to the transaction, it is also presented as a guard against "shopping" for library privileges in desirable areas, or to counter the perceived risk that patrons will forego buying ebooks while traveling if borrowing is simpler. In the absence of hard evidence that these risks are real, few libraries will find this model acceptable. The requirement for in-library check-out will make no sense to users, but be seen as a barrier needlessly imposed by the library.

If unavoidable, an alternative may be to allow check-out only by patrons who are physically present within the geographic boundaries of the library's service area.

Restrictions on consortial or interlibrary loans. Publishers may attempt to forbid, through license agreements, the sharing of titles among more than one institution. In essence, this is no different than a library restricting circulation to some subset of its branches. With the one-use-at-a-time model, libraries and publishers should not need to employ such restrictions.

Digital-native business models. Libraries will need to consider business models that take advantage of the digital nature of ebooks to go beyond what has existed for print. These models will have unique advantages and drawbacks that libraries should carefully consider. For example, subscription models may provide unlimited or metered access to broad collections. Open-access models, in which access to content is unrestricted, can provide global benefits when libraries act together to provide funding. Finally, libraries should give more emphasis to the use of public domain and open license ebooks.

Advantages to publishers

Because of the fundamental shift facing trade publishing, including the entry of retail companies that currently dominate the ebook market, publishers and authors have much to gain from enabling libraries to distribute ebooks. There is compelling evidence that during periods of technological, social and economic change, people use libraries more. With many bricks-and-mortar bookstores closing, publishers need new ways to "showroom" their titles. Publishers may be willing to offer more favorable terms and lower prices in exchange for specific accommodations.

Enhanced discovery. Library users are also heavy book buyers, and publishers value the role libraries play in connecting readers with authors. Libraries might offer to provide access to a publisher's entire catalog (including books not yet purchased) as a way of connecting readers with additional offerings which they may buy or request the library purchase. This would also enhance integration. (In addition, by refusing to load titles excluded from library sales, libraries may gain leverage in reducing or eliminating embargoes.)

Sales channel. By adding a "buy it" link in the library catalog, libraries can generate additional sales for the publisher. In return, libraries could negotiate for a share of the revenues generated through this channel, either as a direct payment or as a discount on future purchases.

Readers advisory. Librarians stimulate interest in books through their recommendations. By expanding this service in the ebook realm, libraries will strengthen their role of connecting readers with authors and books they might otherwise miss. Libraries may also enhance publisher offerings through reader and staff reviews incorporated into the catalog, and/or local recommendation engines.

With today's rapidly changing business environment for ebooks, the choices that libraries make today can have a profound impact on the direction taken by the entire reading ecosystem. It is thus of utmost importance that these choices be made with careful consideration of the needs of both present and future users. Decisions are best made in the context of an informed community and never in isolation or with passivity.

SOURCE: ALA Digital Content and Libraries Working Group, *EBook Business Models for Public Libraries* (Washington, D.C.: American Library Association, August 8, 2012).

DIGITAL RESOURCES

12 misconceptions about license agreements

by Lesley Ellen Harris

LICENSING INFORMATION such as an electronic journal or a database involves entering into a legally binding contract with a rights holder. Although license agreements may appear daunting, they are becoming a fact of life for many who work in libraries. A license agreement merely sets out the terms and conditions for use of specified content and should reflect what the parties have agreed to during their discussions.

The following 12 common misconceptions regarding license agreements will hopefully guide you toward better licenses and less daunting experiences.

1. **A license means permanent ownership.** This is false. When you license a DVD or a book from a publisher, the publisher is merely allowing you to use the content for a specific purpose. The publisher is not assigning copyright or permanent ownership of the content to you. It is a license to use content, not a transfer of ownership.

2. **Lawyers always negotiate licenses.** Not long ago, a librarian was responsible for providing access to information. However, with the proliferation of electronic content, librarians are often called upon to negotiate licenses. Licensing has now become a part of the job for many librarians, as well as for those working in archives and museums. In many situations, librarians are more experienced than lawyers in licensing, as they often deal with licensing on a daily and practical basis. Librarians are also often responsible for ensuring compliance with licenses, and again, are forced to understand their complexities.

3. **Renegotiating each year is a necessity.** It is not necessary to renegotiate your licenses on a yearly basis. Negotiating with a content owner is time-consuming and costly. If both you and the content owner are happy with the license, why should you reopen negotiations? If an automatic renewal clause does not exist in the license, suggest one that would allow the license to automatically renew on the same terms and conditions for a further year, upon notice of such automatic renewal by either party; for example, within 90 days of the expiration of the license.

4. **Librarians have no choice but to fight with content owners over licenses.** It is best to work with content owners and rights holders who are fair and reasonable with the terms and conditions they offer you in their licenses. If a content owner is not flexible enough to be open to your needs, then consider licensing from other content owners. If you cannot obtain the access you need for your patrons, then the electronic product loses much of its value to you. For example, if you are licensing a DVD on medicinal plants for your library and the content owner will

only allow library staff (and not the public) to use the DVD, you may want to work with another content owner.

5. **Content owners all charge the same way.** All content owners do not charge the same way. For example, some content owners are willing to charge on a per-use basis. As long as your university or institution can effectively count the number of people accessing or printing the content, you may be able to negotiate payment per use. In other cases, payment may be based on estimates of the number of users, or based on which print subscriptions you also receive. Some content owners may charge one fee for those with a print and electronic subscription, and a different fee for electronic subscriptions only. How much you pay and the method of payment will depend upon what works for the parties involved. There are no set rules or standards. Choose a method that works the best for your organization and for the content owner.

6. **The term "user" is always defined by the content owner.** A user refers to who can use the content you are licensing. In a university library, you would want students and professors to be able to use content for their courses. Although the term is often defined by the content owner, the library may need to redefine this term according to its own needs. Users must be defined in each particular case according to who is actually accessing the content being licensed. Is it the public or members only, or perhaps students and professors? It is important that the definition be broad enough to encompass all individuals who require access to the content.

7. **The library is responsible for its users.** Although this may be stated in a license, it is not necessarily the case. The content owner may request that the library be responsible for ensuring that all of its users abide by the license agreements. The content owner may also want you to keep statistics regarding content usage. A librarian is not a police officer. Do not allow the content owner to define the terms of what is suitable enforcement, and do not allow him to hold you liable for patron abuses. At most, agree to a clause that obligates you to notify the content owner should you see any possible violation of copyright in relation to the content. However, you should not have to take positive steps to police the use of licensed content. Always keep in mind that just because the content owner presents you with a license, you do not have to agree to everything in that license, and in certain areas you should insist that unreasonable obligations on your part be deleted from the license.

8. **Licenses do not allow for protection of user privacy.** This is not necessarily true. You may be asked to track usage of the licensed content by your patrons, which could raise a question of privacy. Monitoring how and when your patrons use materials may be considered an invasion of user privacy. If you are concerned with protecting user privacy, you should not agree to track usage by your patrons. If you do agree to track usage of the content, it is a good idea to inform your patrons about this practice and allow them to determine whether or not they choose to use the materials.

9. **Licenses and interlibrary loan are not related.** Interlibrary loan is a component of many license negotiations. One of the main functions of

libraries is to share information, and ILL or sharing information with other libraries is a big part of that. You should be ready to negotiate with the content owner as to how you want ILL to operate. Content owners have very different expectations in this area, from no ILL at all to allowing the host institution to print and send copies to other libraries. You must be careful that you do not overcomplicate your ILL process by having too many standards among your different content owners and licenses; this can lead to unexpected costs and issues.

10. **Electronic journals are cheaper than paper ones.** Electronic journals are not necessarily cheaper than traditional paper journals. Not only will new staff be required to manage the collection (such as negotiating licenses, monitoring licenses, or managing computers), but the library is also paying for the technology needed to access this information. This may involve purchasing new computers, software, or servers. In addition, patrons may also be paying part of the costs when they access the information and then print it.

11. **You have no control over the format of delivery or storage.** You do have control over what format the content is being delivered to you and how it is stored. It is important that the content is provided to you in a format that is acceptable to your institution and fits with your technology. Determine in what format the information will be provided to you, when it will be provided to you, and if there will be any technical support provided to you if there are problems accessing the information. For example, if you are licensing an electronic journal from a publisher, will the journal be provided to you in DVD format or will you need to access the information from the publisher's server? What if there are defects in the DVD? Keep in mind how you would like these problems to be addressed and set it out in your license.

12. **Fair use or fair dealing do not apply to the electronic environment.** The concept of fair use or fair dealing by users applies to content in the electronic environment. Many libraries and organizations negotiate a clause that specifically states that fair use and fair dealing are available in relation to licensed content. This is a clause you may want to add to your license, if appropriate, and if it does not already appear there.

Note that your patrons are not a party to the license agreement. As a result, they are not bound by the license agreement that you make with the content owner. Thus, even if you and the content owner agree to limit the fair use or fair dealing portions of the applicable copyright act in your license agreement, fair use and fair dealing are still available to the library's patrons.

SOURCE: Lesley Ellen Harris, *Licensing Digital Content: A Practical Guide for Librarians* (Chicago: American Library Association, 2009), 30–34.

The case for CLOCKSS

by Vic Elliott

NOT SO MANY YEARS AGO when the digital world first beckoned, when we were working hard to encourage our academic communities to accept and start using electronic resources, one of their first demands was an assurance that such resources would not disappear, that they were not being offered attractive but insubstantial riches. They trusted print—all those journal back runs sitting on library shelves gave them the reassurance they sought. They saw no such reassurance in a digital environment, happy though they were to use electronic resources on a day-to-day basis.

Today, I think, that concern is not so widespread among our users. Most university libraries have electronic-only policies in the case of journals. Most, but not all. And our academic communities have not risen up in protest. The concern about continued access, about electronic archiving, lies now with the profession, with us. And it is a responsibility that I believe we cannot shirk or attempt to offload on to others.

The rapid transition from an exclusively physical collection environment to a largely digital equivalent has radically changed the way in which information resources are managed within academic libraries. Put simply, whereas we once owned all our collections, we now merely rent most of the digital resources we make available to our users. And what is more, whereas in a physical world we exercised sole responsibility for curating the books and journals we acquired and made available, in a digital world the resources we rent do not reside within our libraries but are largely served from and curated within remote facilities controlled by the content providers.

Such a situation implies real risk. The assurance of continuing access to key scholarly information resources that we could blithely give to our communities in a physical world no longer applies in a digital environment of this kind. Given that the digital resources we make available are not under our control, and certainly not subject to our stewardship, access may be cut at any time, not simply temporarily but conceivably forever. Clearly, one way or another, we must seek a mechanism to address this challenge, to mitigate this risk, and ensure continuing access to these resources over time, just as, at present, we do with conventional physical materials.

In seeking a way forward, it may be useful to look outside our usual frame of reference, to H. L. Mencken and Jacques Derrida (right):

> ". . . for there is always an easy solution to every human problem—neat, plausible, and wrong." (H. L. Mencken, "The Divine Afflatus," *A Mencken Chrestomathy*. New York: Alfred A. Knopf, 1953, 443).
>
> "There is no archive without a place of consignation, without a technique of repetition, and without a certain exteriority. No archive without outside." (Jacques Derrida, *Archive Fever: A Freudian Impression*, trans. by Eric Prenowitz. Chicago: University of Chicago Press, 1996, 11).

In quoting from Mencken and Derrida, I am not trying to add a spurious authority to dubious contentions. If that was my intention, I would seek different authorities, different authors. The Mencken essay is now quite dated, viewed from an early 21st-century vantage point. It is the aphorism, taken out of its original context, that is instructive. And the Derrida book is really a discussion of the tension between the personal, the private, and their public manifestation, viewed from a psychoanalytic, mostly Freudian, perspective. But the quotation is useful, I think, in the context of the CLOCKSS (Controlled LOCKSS) archiving option, in terms of aspiration, technique, and method.

Mencken suggests that in addressing human problems we should not be looking for neat, easy solutions. There is rarely a simple answer, let alone a solution.

What we are usually left with is, rather, a variety of different approaches. And the advice is apposite in this case of electronic archiving. Offering and employing a range of options is not indicative of uncertainty or indecision. It is a perfectly acceptable risk-mitigation strategy that we should welcome and applaud.

Derrida, on the other hand, reminds us that there is no archive, viewed broadly, without an act of gathering together, of iteration, and of making public. And this, of course, is the CLOCKSS (and LOCKSS) approach. The mantra, after all, is that "lots of copies keep stuff safe."

LOCKSS

LOCKSS provides the software platform for CLOCKSS and may be seen as a precursor system. It was designed to give institutions the capability to manage their digital resources in the same way as their physical collections by allowing libraries, easily and inexpensively, to collect, store, preserve, and give access to their own local copy of licensed, authorized content. Although, perhaps inevitably, the emphasis has been on archiving subscribed proprietary content, the system may also be used locally to capture other web content, such as websites, electronic theses and dissertations, archival and image collections, and government documents.

Operated and controlled at the local level, the action to open up the archive, to make content available, is taken by the individual institution when, for whatever reason, content is deemed no longer available from the publisher.

CLOCKSS

The CLOCKSS mission is simple and unsurprising. Ensuring access to published scholarly content over time; a community-governed partnership of publishers and libraries working to achieve a sustainable and globally distributed archive.

In focusing on the criticality of ensuring access to published scholarly content, the mission addresses the identified primary risk. What is interesting is the emphasis on the "how," the corporate mechanism, the community-governed partnership of publishers and libraries, and the establishment of a globally distributed archive. Sustainability in a very practical sense is achieved through the choice of host libraries or archive nodes on geopolitical grounds. It is clearly in the interest of the sustainability of the network to place CLOCKSS servers strategically across the world in secure computing environments with uninterrupted power and network connectivity.

CLOCKSS is a private LOCKSS network. And in one sense, CLOCKSS may be seen as a publisher, rather than a library, initiative. The standard LOCKSS application is not really a dark archive. Given that the decision on when to open up content lies with individual institutions, it is more in the nature of a bright archive. Understandably, some publishers became a little nervous about the highly distributed character of the LOCKSS system and the consequent lack of control over decisions on access. In short, they were concerned about content leakage.

A closed network was seen to provide the necessary level of security and reassurance, and accordingly a new small partnership of publishers and libraries was formed in 2006 to develop the concept. LOCKSS remains the software platform at the core of the network, but the business model is quite different in several important respects.

CLOCKSS is indisputably a dark archive. Decisions on whether to provide access to archival content, to open up part of the archive, are taken not by individual institutions but by the CLOCKSS board itself. Such decisions will be prompted by major trigger events such as the corporate failure of a publisher, the catastrophic and sustained failure of a publisher's delivery platform, the cessation of publication of a particular title, or a publisher's decision no longer to offer back issues. And when access is opened to endangered content, that access is not limited to CLOCKSS participants or to current or former subscribers to that licensed content, but to everyone throughout the world. In effect, the content is made available under open-access conditions.

The first of two such trigger events occurred in late 2007. It arose from the intention of Sage Publications to discontinue the provision of online access to the journal *Graft: Organ and Cell Transplantation*. Following a decision by the CLOCKSS board, the three volumes of *Graft* published by Sage were copied from the seven archive nodes or servers within the pilot system and in early 2008 made available to the world free of charge through two hosting platforms at Stanford and Edinburgh Universities. Although the hosting platforms are strategically positioned, in the United States and Europe, access is available worldwide to either platform. The *Graft* (and subsequent *Auto/Biography*) experience is a good example of what can happen  in the world of proprietary digital resources and a timely demonstration of the ability of e-archiving systems like CLOCKSS to respond effectively.

It would be wrong to see CLOCKSS as a successor to LOCKSS, as somehow superseding a precursor system. In fact, they are complementary systems. It is a matter of focus, a concentration in the case of LOCKSS on the local community and in the case of CLOCKSS on the global community. A reliance on CLOCKSS as the global archive of last resort does not preclude working with LOCKSS to meet local community-archiving needs.

Why CLOCKSS?

The question whether or not to choose CLOCKSS is in some ways redundant. You don't choose CLOCKSS. It chooses you. For whether you support the initiative or not, it will be there to support you, should a trigger event occur and access to subscribed (or unsubscribed) scholarly content be denied. That this is so is evidenced by the *Graft* example or experience.

Perhaps I should try to answer a different question—why is my university willing to act as a host library, to operate a CLOCKSS box and seek to attract Australian and New Zealand content into the CLOCKSS dark archive?

The argument is philosophical and professional. In moving to a digital environment, libraries have largely outsourced the management and curation of electronic information resources to the content providers. The archiving of these same electronic resources offers us an opportunity to reclaim that role, not alone but in partnership with publishers. I for one am not willing to outsource that role again, to spurn the chance to exercise stewardship over critical information resources in the interests of our academic community. I didn't join the profession to be a retailer, a purveyor of commodities. And it does not appear to me to be in the interest of libraries in these professionally perilous times to abdicate the stewardship role when it lies there for the taking.

It seemed to me CLOCKSS offered us that rare chance, that unusual opportunity. It is a community-governed partnership in which libraries and publishers together determine strategy and policies within a transparent governance structure. We decide our own future—it is not decided for us.

The technology is proven. The risk management strategy is robust, and acceptable to both partner communities, libraries and publishers. And the geographical spread of host institutions ensures that the CLOCKSS archive will be representative of global scholarly output, not simply that of Europe and North America.

I can't resist adding that for someone like me, who after all these years remains uncomfortable with the idea that scholarly information should be traded as a commodity, the CLOCKSS policy that after a trigger event endangered content should be released to everyone, not simply current or former subscribers, is a return to reason and sane public policy.

It is evident that the case for CLOCKSS is rapidly gaining acceptance. In addition to the decision of the Australian National University to act as a CLOCKSS archive node, seven university libraries in Australia and three in New Zealand have signed supporting library agreements. Given that collaborative electronic archiving within a community-governed partnership remains novel to many, this is an encouraging result. CLOCKSS is just one approach to electronic archiving, but it is the approach to which my university is committed. For us, the case is conclusive.

SOURCE: Vic Elliott, "Triumphing over Chance: The Case for CLOCKSS," *Against the Grain,* February 2009, 18–19. Reprinted with permission.

Social media: A guide for academic librarians

by Andy Burkhardt

SOCIAL MEDIA IS A POWERFUL new form of communication. The number of users on popular social media sites is growing at exponential rates. Facebook has more than 750 million active users in 2011, about one-ninth of the world's population. In October 2010, Twitter had 165 million users. Millions of people are using these tools as part of their everyday lives for both work and play.

Because of the ubiquity of social media use, academic libraries can leverage these communication tools to interact with faculty, staff, and students in new ways. It is often difficult in academic libraries to spread the word about different events or services that the library is offering. Social media provides another method to market new library products or initiatives.

In addition to marketing, the simple act of having conversations and creating relationships with patrons is immensely useful. Through conversations on social media, libraries can gain insights into what their users want and need and ultimately understand their users better.

Many libraries are already experimenting with different social media services like Twitter or Facebook to interact and connect with their patrons, yet there are still a number of questions that come up: "How do I get started?" "What sorts of things should I post?" "How can I grow our social media presence and gain more fans or followers?"

This article seeks to be a practical guide for launching and sustaining a successful social media presence.

Why use social media?

When starting out, the first thing libraries should always do is ask, "Why are we doing this, and what do we hope to gain from it?" There are plenty of great reasons, but you will have to find the ones specific to your library. Framing your new endeavor in these terms gives the project focus and is important whether you are trying out social media, redesigning your website, or deciding to replace the furniture in the library.

Asking questions like this will eventually inform what tools you choose and how you use them. Once you under-  stand your reasons for implementing a social media presence, the next step is to come up with concrete goals. A goal can be something as simple as, "After one year we will have 100 fans." The goals you set may eventually evolve into something different as you start using the tools and interacting with patrons, but having goals allows you to know whether you are succeeding.

Not everyone may be keen on something new, though. This is where coming up with reasons for why you should be using these tools comes in handy. Write a brief, well-thought-out proposal using the reasons you chose. Also include other important information, such as who will monitor and post to your social media account. Showing that you have given this idea significant consideration goes a long way. It also may help to offer this idea as a pilot project that you could revisit in a year's time. This allows you to revisit your goals to see if you're meeting them.

Prep work

When setting up a social media account it is important to personalize it. No matter which social media service your library decides on, there are a few things that your account should include. Foremost, a link to your library website is necessary. Patrons should be able to easily get to your website, where they can learn more or begin their research. Almost all social media profiles have a section for a bio or description. Always fill this out. Make it succinct and friendly. This is social media, not your mission statement. Create a welcoming and informal description of the library. There are also always options for customization. Work with these options until you find something that fits your library. You can change colors and backgrounds in Twitter. You can add custom tabs and boxes in Facebook. Take some time to make your library profile unique.

What to post?

After all the preparatory work, you must begin creating content and posting things on a regular basis. This can be one of the more difficult things for anyone starting an institutional social media presence. "What should I post?" "How professional should I be?" Here are a few ideas of things you could post to your social media account:

- **Library news and events.** If you are going to host a gaming night in the library, social media is the perfect place to tell people about it. If your website is going to be down for repairs, let people know via your social media accounts. Social media is great for updating people on what is going on.
- **New additions to your collection.** Got some new books or a new bibliographic-citation management tool? People might not know about additions to your collection unless you tell them. Social media can be helpful for informing patrons about new resources.

- **Links to articles and videos.** If you come across web content that would be relevant or helpful to your patrons, post it. Not everything you post has to be directly related to your library. Do not lose sight of why you started using this tool in the first place, but a variety of postings keeps things fresh.
- **Community information.** You can also pass along information of significance to your community via your social media channels. The library is the heart of a college campus. It is natural that it should be a place where people go to get information about the community.
- **Solicit feedback.** Social networking is built for conversations, so feel free to ask questions of your fans or followers. Questions also often get the most response. Ask interesting things that you actually want to know, such as, "Why do you use the library?" When people answer, continue the conversation with your patrons.
- **Respond to people.** Acknowledge compliments to your library gracefully. Reply to negative feedback by addressing the problem people are having and staying positive. For example, if someone complains via Twitter that the library is too loud, perhaps a response could be, "Who do we need to come shush? Also, we have some great private study rooms in the basement that are quiet as it gets." Using humor, staying positive, and trying to help with the problem are good strategies to use when trying to change people's minds. You have power online to influence conversations about your library, and the worst thing you can do is ignore people.
- **Pictures.** Both Twitter and Facebook allow you, without much hassle, to post or link to pictures. Text can get boring after a while. Enhance your posts by including a picture. For example, if you have an event where an author is on campus, include a picture of him talking to students and tell people to stop by.
- **Anything else.** Get creative with your posts. Do not limit yourself to this list. You know your community. Ask yourself, "What would be interesting or useful to them?" and then post that.

When posting content to a social media account like Twitter or Facebook, it is important to remember to be both social and human. Being social means responding to people when they comment on your Facebook wall or @reply to you in Twitter. It means having conversations. Being human involves humor and a personal touch. Not every post has to be strictly library-related or in perfectly punctuated English. Be authentic when you are tweeting and let the human behind the post shine through. Users are going to connect with and respond to a human. They'll likely ignore a robotic institution.

How to market your presence

Having interesting, useful content to post is important, but how do you let users know about your social media presence? Just like any new library resource or initiative it is necessary to promote it. "Build it and they will come" is not a viable strategy. "Market it and they may take a look" is much more realistic. Then, if you have interesting content and are engaging they may stick around. The following are several strategies for how to market your social media presence.

- **Link wherever possible.** Have a link to your social media account on your library homepage. If you're on multiple social networks, mention one on the other. Put links to them in your email signature. Links are good. Use them generously.
- **Talk to people.** Word of mouth is one of the most powerful forms of marketing, so mention it to friends, people at the reference desk, and people in your community.
- **Instruction sessions.** When you're in the classroom, feel free to mention your social media presence to students. Let them know that you're trying to make it as easy as possible to connect with the library. They just might appreciate it.
- **Print advertising.** Post fliers around your library and around campus, especially next to computers. You could even take out an ad in your local or school newspaper. There's still a place for print.
- **Web ads.** On Facebook you have the ability to purchase ads targeted to your community. They are fairly inexpensive and some libraries, Stanford being one, have had success with them.
- **Build a contingent of friends.** There are probably people already in your community whom you are friends with on a social network. On Facebook you can "suggest a page to friends." Ask people who are your friends to follow/fan the library. You can also mention your social media presence to student workers. They are often some of the first students to follow or fan the library on a social network.
- **Follow and be followed in return.** On Twitter, find people in your community and start following them. Chances are most of them will follow you back. This one is important because the goal of social media is not simply to gain followers. Social media is about sharing, learning, conversations, and giving. Following others shows that you are interested in them and care about what they have to say.
- **Give it time.** Set small goals for yourself and meet them. Then set larger goals. You likely will not attract a thousand followers the first day. Social media requires time and attention, but slowly your presence will grow.

Maintain communication

Having a social media presence is a commitment. It is much like maintaining a friendship. Friendships require constant attention and communication to remain strong. Social media is no different. Much like in real life, if you talk only about yourself, people will soon become bored. If you ignore your fans and followers when they are talking to you or post to your profile, they will not continue to talk to you. Constant communication in both directions is crucial to social media success.

When you are just starting out, you may not always get it right. It is okay if things begin slowly or you make a few mistakes. It takes time to learn what sorts of things get reactions from people or how to keep the conversation going. Feel free to experiment from time to time with different or unorthodox posts, but, as with any experiment, remember to note results. See which posts get responses and attempt to replicate them.

Social media, like any other technology, takes a bit of time and play to learn. Once you do get the hang of it, though, you will see a growing, active community begin to emerge. This community can be a powerful thing, and the benefits to both your library and patrons will become clear.

SOURCE: Andy Burkhardt, "Social Media: A Guide for College and University Libraries," *College and Research Libraries News* 71, no. 1 (January 2010): 10–12, 24.

Five tips for successful webinars
by Peter Bromberg

GOOD WEBINARS DON'T JUST HAPPEN. Beyond having a relevant topic and a great presenter, there are a number of factors that affect the end result. Whether you are scheduling and producing webinars, or creating and presenting them, these tips will help you deliver a great webinar experience for everyone.

Write for the medium. Regardless of the platform you use, tailor the lesson plan to the webinar environment. Most webinars consist of an audio feed, a chat space, and a space that allows the presenter to share a slideshow, and possibly share their desktop or a whiteboard. The webinar environment doesn't allow for the useful visual cues that body language and eye contact provide in a face-to-face (F2F) environment, and may not even provide audio feedback for the presenter. For these reasons, well-designed lessons that work like a charm in a F2F environment might fail to engage the audience and hold their attention in a webinar.

You can mitigate these issues and engage the audience by building in more questions and taking advantage of whatever interactive features are offered in your platform. Does your platform offer polling? Use it. Shared whiteboard? Use it. Hand-raising or yes/no capability for participants? Use them.

I like to start webinars by posting a map of the state (or country) and asking participants to use the arrow tool in Wimba (now Blackboard Collaborate) to point to where they are on the map. This communicates to the participants early on that the webinar will not be a passive experience for them—they are going to be involved. I also work with trainers/presenters to build in slides/questions that can be drawn on (literally) during the webinar, and encourage presenters to include these types of interactive activities throughout the presentation. At a minimum, plan on using more questions, and using them early, to mentally engage participants and create the expectation that they will not be passive observers.

Know your platform. There are many good webinar platforms out there, including Adobe Connect, Blackboard Collaborate, iLinc, Cisco WebEx, and Citrix GoToTraining. Each platform has its own benefits and its own limitations. You wouldn't go into a F2F training without knowing the room layout and the availability of training tools such as chartpads, markers, laptop, AV, projectors, and screen; so don't go into your webinar environment without knowing the layout, the tools available, and how to use them. Most webinar platforms offer some great screenshot-heavy help files and/or recorded screencasts you can use to learn the layout and the tools. Find them and use them, once you know your platform.

Test, test, test. The most common reason a webinar tanks is technology failure. Wait, let me rephrase that. The failure is not the technology, but the failure of the webinar producer, presenter, and participants to account for the platform's limitations, and prepare and test their computers. Each platform has its own requirements regarding browsers, operating systems, necessary bandwidth, and downloads or plugins that are recommended or required. Each platform generally offers a simple link that can be clicked to set-up/test the user's computer. Every person involved in the webinar must click the setup link prior to the webinar and make certain their computer is set up, tested, and ready to go. Send this information out early and often to the participants. And make sure the presenter has tested and set up the computer he will use, and make sure it is a wired, not wireless, connection.

Let everyone know the preferred method of audio participation. Nothing beats a good noise-canceling headset. If you're offering dial-in access, send or post the number or PIN. If participants are going to use laptop or desktop speakers, make sure they know to mute their microphones. Nothing ruins a webinar faster than feedback (which is why you also need to know how to mute participants individually or en masse—it's a lifesaver).

Practice, practice, practice. Whether you are the webinar producer, presenter, or both (not recommended), it is imperative that you log some practice time in the webinar environment. I highly recommend that there is at least one producer in the webinar (someone other than the presenter who knows the webinar platform cold.) The more experienced the producer, the less time the presenter has to practice, but the presenter *always* has to practice. At minimum, the presenter should know how to advance slides (if used), and how to log out and log back in again, in case of a network interruption. Desktop application sharing, a vital part of some webinars, adds a higher level of complication, and usually requires the presenter to master the application-sharing mechanism—something that is not always simple or intuitive. The producer needs to know everything else: how to advance slides, how to mute participants, how to expand/limit control of various room features (whiteboards, control of microphone), how to toggle between various features (polls, whiteboards, slides.)

The actual event. So the presenter has written a great lesson, you've learned your platform inside and out, and everything has been set-up and tested. Now there's just the little matter of actually having the webinar. Here are a few tips that I've found will greatly reduce problems and add to the overall quality on the day of the event:

- *Arrive early.* Both the presenter and producer should arrive at least 15 minutes early to get logged in and do a final test to make sure the tech-

8

nology is working, and do one final review of the tools and features to be used.

Example of a webinar. Photo by TopRank Blog, used CC BY 3.0

- *Webinar environment review.* Before the presenter begins the lesson or presentation, spend five minutes doing a brief review of the webinar environment with participants. Walk them through playing with the features that they will be using during the webinar (writing tools and pointing tools).
- *Have a wingman (or wingwoman).* In webinar parlance, the wingman is the producer's assistant. The wingman ideally knows the webinar platform inside and out, and is available to help participants with any tech or audio issues and keep an eye on chat for questions or problems.
- *Recording.* Yeah, it's a newbie mistake, but it happens to everyone. Don't forget to hit "record." (I put this right into my script in 24-point bold type. But then again, I need notes to myself to remember to leave the house with my pants on in the morning. Whatever works for you.)
- *Take notes during the webinar.* During the course of the webinar many useful resources or URLs may be mentioned by the presenter or by the participants in chat. It's a great value-added service if you can capture these resources and post them with the recording and other handouts (the presenter's slideshow or supporting documents) after the webinar.
- *Save the chat.* Before logging out, copy and paste everything in the chat into a Word document and save that document. Besides being a good backup for the recording, having a text copy of the chat to share with participants after the webinar can help them quickly find useful pieces of information that may have been shared in chat. I treat the chat transcript as semi-confidential and I don't post it—but depending on the webinar I will send copies directly to those who participated.
- *Extend the learning by posting the recording, notes, handouts.* Finally, spend some time in post-production (the specifics vary with each webinar platform) and get the recording posted to a website along with related documents and the presenter's presentation, if available.

SOURCE: Peter Bromberg, "Five Tips for Successful Webinars," ALA Learning, March 15, 2010, alalearning.org/2010/03/15/five-tips-for-successful-webinars/.

Selling new technology

by Meredith Farkas

I'M SURE YOU'VE HEARD THIS story before; maybe it's even happened to you. A librarian comes back from a conference all excited about a new technology she learned about. She thinks it would be a perfect fit for her library and presents her idea to her colleagues.

Unfortunately, colleagues don't share her enthusiasm and can't really see the value of this technology. Their initial resistance discourages the librarian and she abandons the idea altogether.

Regardless of whether your idea is the best thing since sliced bread, the way you promote an idea to library staff and administration can mean the difference between buy-in and rejection. Here are some tips for selling a new technology to staff and administrators at your library.

Tie the technology to strategic goals. Most libraries develop long- and short-term goals that define what staff should be working toward. If you can show how the technology you want to implement would help further one or more of those goals, you'll be much more likely to get the support of administration and staff.

Have plenty of hard data. While some libraries do like to be trailblazers, with limited resources most library staff will want to see some evidence of a new technology's utility. Before you present an idea, scan the library literature to see if any studies exist supporting the effectiveness of the technology you want to implement. If no literature exists, you may want to show how many libraries are already doing what you want to do and what the results have been. You could even interview some of the librarians who have implemented it at other libraries.

Develop a prototype. It can be difficult to envision the usefulness of a new technology based on someone's description, and staff may need to see it to believe it. That's why it's helpful to develop a prototype that will concretely demonstrate what it is you hope to accomplish. If another library has already done exactly what you want to do, you might be able to show staff what they did instead.

Get colleagues to use the technology. For staff members who are not technologically adept, any new technology can be a bit intimidating. No matter how easy you think the technology is, staff may not buy in until they've tried it out themselves. Offer training on this new technology that gives all staff the opportunity to try it out with the help of a knowledgeable facilitator—you!

Know your stuff. Just because you immediately saw the great potential of this new technology doesn't mean your colleagues will. They may have lots of questions about your idea, and you need to have enough knowledge about the technology to answer them. Your preparation also indicates to others that you're serious about the project.

Find champions. There are probably a few people at your library whose opinions on any topic tend to influence others. Seek out those individuals and try to sell them on your idea. If you have an influential champion on your side, your chances for securing buy-in will be much greater.

Be patient. It may take patience and persistence to get staff members on board with your ideas. While a technology may be easy to use, it can take time and effort to build use of these tools into staff workflows. Don't give up so easily on a technology you think will benefit staff or patrons. Try to understand your staff's resistance and don't simply write them off as being against change.

If your idea has value for the long-term future of your library, it will keep while you continue to promote it.

SOURCE: Meredith Farkas, "Selling a New Technology," *American Libraries* 40, no. 1/2 (January/ February 2009), 36.

Ten technology ideas for your library
by Ellyssa Kroski

SOCIAL MEDIA WEBSITES such as Facebook and Twitter enable librarians to converse, communicate, and collaborate with patrons as never before, because they are increasingly a part of people's everyday lives. A brochure that describes your library with a few pictures is great, but a video tour that people can watch on your website or blog is immeasurably better. Enabling patrons to save their catalog searches is important, but offering the ability to notify patrons via email and text messaging when new acquisitions arrive presents a fresh way to connect with users.

Librarians who are still becoming comfortable with the web are often reticent to begin using new technologies in their day-to-day work because the learning curve often takes more time than they have at hand. When I begin teaching people about Web 2.0, mobile, and emerging technologies, I try to answer three questions:

- What is it?
- Why is it important?
- How can it help me better serve my users tomorrow?

Here are 10 ideas you can use to start creating, collaborating, connecting, and communicating through cutting-edge tools and techniques.

Create a library video tour to welcome people 24 hours a day, seven days a week from any location. With today's technology, even inexperienced video producers can create a video tour and put it on the library's website for little time and money. The tools of the trade are: a camera, microphone, lights, computer, video and audio editing software, tripod for the camera, microphone stand, a portable lighting structure, and headphones. It seems like a lot, but with some bargain-hunting you should be able to get everything you need for a webcam setup from about $100.

Library video tours aren't just about the facility and its features; they're a way to invite nonusers to come and visit. It's about the warm welcome and the friendly service they will receive when they do come. It's about the pride you feel being part of the community. It's much more than just a tour!

The secret is to pretend that you have never been to the library and are discovering it for the very first time. The tour should begin from the moment potential users decide that they are coming to the library. So the first thing you want to do is welcome them, introduce yourself, and tell them the hours you are open. Then introduce them to any library feature or service that you'd like, from information about travel, parking, and restrooms to instructions for getting a library card or visiting the reference desk.

Use SMS to send patron alerts and notifications. SMS (short message service, aka texting) is ideal for broadcast services. If your library sends out notices to its patrons, having the ability to send SMS alerts is a nice alternative to email, and much more useful for most younger patrons. Research has shown that the current generation of students sees email as old and outdated; they rely almost exclusively on texting to communicate with each other. There are ILS systems that provide a direct SMS gateway option and natively send texts out to patrons. But even if an ILS doesn't have SMS capabilities built in, it probably has email, and with a little effort you can give most patrons the option of receiving info via an email SMS gateway.

Most cellular carriers have a gateway that allows email to be transmitted to a mobile phone via SMS. If your ILS can send out alerts via email, you just need to give it the equivalent email address for a patron's cell phone, and it should work transparently. SMS has a 160-character limit for transmitting text, so if your emails tend to be very wordy or have extraneous text (signatures and such), you will need to pare them down before implementing SMS in your ILS.

Feed your library's blog posts into Twitter without doing any more work. Twitter is immensely popular right now, and it's a great way of letting your community members know what's happening at the library. Is today's storytime canceled? Let patrons know automatically. You can begin using Twitter by posting tweets yourself, but there are ways to automate Twitter so that it instantly posts content that other parts of your organization—from public programs to children's services—originally creates. This can help to both reduce your workload and improve your library's communication with patrons.

One of the easiest ways to start getting content into a Twitter account is to set up a blog feed to post to your Twitter account automatically. You don't have to use a blog; any application that can give information in RSS format (such as many online calendars or other social networking sites like Facebook) can be used as seed content for a fledgling Twitter account. All you have to do is find the RSS feed; once you've got the address for the feed, you can then use a third-party service such as TwitterFeed to have all posts automatically added to your library's Twitter stream.

Improve customer service by developing a technology skills list for your staff. A technology skills list is an easy and efficient way to organize an ongoing technology-training program at your library. Technology skills or competencies are the technology-related abilities, qualities, strengths, and skills required for the success of the employee and the organization. As you might imagine, these skills have increased in number with the advent of personal computers, the internet, and Web 2.0. Technology skills are crucial for the success of any organization, but critically important for successful customer service in libraries.

Many of us in libraries are acting as first-line, de facto tech support. If we do not have a handle on the technology tools that we use, the technology gets in the way of our service to our users and things don't run smoothly. We want everyone on our staff to be able to help our users equally. Our technology skills need to be so second nature to each of us that they come as naturally as breathing. By getting everyone on the same page with their technology skills, the library creates a frontline force with technology know-how, expertise, and ability, each one ready to step in and solve whatever problem or question comes up—right then and there. No more shuffling a user from one person to another or making the user wait minutes, even days, for an answer.

Create a special-event wiki. A wiki can be a good solution if you are creating a website for a special event but do not want to bother your webmaster with the regular updates you are planning to make. If you choose to host the wiki yourself, you will need to work with a webmaster in setting it up. Once the webmaster has set up the backend, or you have used a third-party site to meet your requirements, you are ready to start adding content.

Like any upcoming-event site, your wiki should be designed to include relevant information for the participants you are targeting. If you are planning a lecture series, you will want to include when, where, and who will be speaking. Your audience will find it useful if you include an image of the speaker and a biography; you might also consider embedding video footage of the speaker at another event. If you are planning a workshop or conference, you might start the wiki with just an announcement. As you figure out more about what is going to happen at the conference, what hotel will offer a discount, who the keynote speaker will be, and all the other conference details, you will want to add this information.

Help your catalog evolve with personalization. A website can offer many additional features to users willing to register and sign in. Traditional library catalogs have offered such services to patrons as the ability to view the materials currently checked out, make renewal requests, place requests to be notified when items become available, make interlibrary loan requests, pay fines, and many other actions that might otherwise require a visit to the library. Self-service through the website has become increasingly expected.

Personalization also enables the use of customized settings related to search and retrieval. Users might want to save search results for future consultation, bookmark specific items, or establish preferences regarding narrowing searches to their favorite databases or disciplines. Notification services also tie in to personalization, such as the ability to set up alerts to be notified by email when the library obtains new materials in a specific area of interest.

Put together a Guitar Hero tournament that will attract a wide range of nonusers to your library for the very first time. Guitar Hero is a very popular video game. Its controllers resemble musical instruments allowing players to "play music" by pressing the appropriate key as it scrolls across the screen. One of the reasons for Guitar Hero's success is its popularity among both male and female gamers; another is that it can be played on almost every console (as well as mobile phones).

The first thing you should do is determine what age level to target for your tournament. While the majority of your programs might group similar ages together, keep in mind that video game skills often can transcend the age of the player. It's important to be clear about what age range your tournament is open to so that people don't feel the rules are being changed midway through the registration period.

Use Facebook for chat reference. Many libraries have expanded into digital reference service by providing chat or instant messaging service to their users. Libraries use a variety of programs to provide chat service to library users. Facebook, as a social environment, is a perfect place to distribute chat reference service. In some cases, applications are already available for Facebook users. Services such as MeeboMe and AIM Wimzi can be added to librarian profiles as a way for users to ask for help.

In addition to these applications, Facebook also has its own chat service available to users. As librarians add library users to their Friends lists, they should not be surprised if they get the occasional question or comment about the library from Facebook Chat.

Collaborate and communicate with internal blogs. Several types of internal blogs exist. Especially for libraries serving members of a specific organization, some blog types may be visible only to those inside the organization, such as subject-specific or subject specialist blogs.

Other internal blogs are meant for use by the library staff for communication with one another. Some types of blogs you might consider to boost your internal communication:

- A weeding blog discussing what has been removed from the library shelves and why.
- A training blog discussing what is being taught in library-run seminars and the related resources and logistics, giving you a place to discuss new ideas before trying them out.
- An acquisitions blog explaining buying decisions and reasons for purchase delays.
- A professional development blog where staff share what they learned at conferences, seminars, and courses or in their own reading.
- Blogs from each of your departments or teams discussing the work they are doing and their latest projects.

The larger your staff, the more value they will see in these kinds of blogs as they will not have time to talk with everyone and learn what they are doing. Blogs discussing department work help keep everyone up to speed on what is happening in other departments, and invite a spirit of collaboration.

Hold a themed unconference to tackle important issues. Of course, any library unconference already has a theme—libraries. But some unconferences, or library camps, are also built around a more specific theme. Technology-related themes are popular, but they're not the only kinds of themed unconferences that have been successful.

An unconference at the 2010 American Library Association Annual Conference discusses such topics as nextgen catalogs and the digital divide.

- The L2 Unconference in Melbourne and Library 2.0 on the Loose in Perth were two Australian unconferences in 2007 that took Library 2.0 as a theme.
- RepoCamp was an unconference held at the Library of Congress in 2008 for people who are "interested in managing and creating digital repository software."
- Mashed Libraries UK 2008 was devoted to library applications of "mashups," the programming practice of bringing data together from multiple online sources to create a new service.
- The Radical Reference group hosted an unconference as an unofficial preconference to the 2009 Association of College and Research Libraries meeting in Seattle. The meeting focused on "social justice and alternative and radical collections and programs in academic libraries."

Many good things can come out of having a theme for your unconference. Rather than having sessions that range widely from high-tech topics to community and personnel issues, a themed camp will keep participants talking about issues around a single agreed-upon topic, offering participants a more focused

8

experience. There will also be more carry-over from one session to another, and participants may feel comfortable with less uncertainty about what they'll be talking about that day.

These are just a few ideas for ways that libraries can start implementing these new technologies right now to enhance public services, communicate with staff, and facilitate remote collaboration. What makes these 10 tools and techniques particularly appealing is that most can be utilized to create cutting-edge programs and services with just a little investment of time and resources and a low learning curve. These simple suggestions can get you started creating innovative programs and initiatives using today's hottest technologies as soon as next week.

SOURCE: Ellyssa Kroski, "10 Technology Ideas Your Library Can Implement Next Week," *American Libraries* 41, no. 3 (March 2010): 30–33.

ISSUES

CHAPTER NINE

I have often thought that nothing would do more extensive good at small expense than the establishment of a small circulating library in every county, to consist of a few well-chosen books, to be lent to the people of the country under regulations as would secure their safe return in due time.

—Thomas Jefferson, letter to John Wyche, May 19, 1809

CORE VALUES

Core values of librarianship

THE FOUNDATION OF MODERN LIBRARIANSHIP rests on an essential set of core values that define, inform, and guide our professional practice. These values reflect the history and ongoing development of the profession and have been advanced, expanded, and refined by numerous policy statements of the American Library Association.

It would be difficult, if not impossible, to express our values more eloquently than ALA already has in the Freedom to Read statement, the Library Bill of Rights, the ALA Mission Statement, Libraries: an American Value, and other documents. These policies have been carefully thought out, articulated, debated, and approved by the ALA Council. They are interpreted, revised, or expanded when necessary. Over time, the values embodied in these policies have been embraced by the majority of librarians as the foundations of their practice.

The following are some representative excerpts from ALA policy expressing the values listed above. These selections are direct quotes from the *ALA Policy Manual*. Many of these statements express the interrelationship of these values.

Access. All information resources that are provided directly or indirectly by the library, regardless of technology, format, or methods of delivery, should be readily, equally, and equitably accessible to all library users. *ALA Policy Manual* 53.1.14 (Free Access to Information).

Confidentiality and privacy. Protecting user privacy and confidentiality is necessary for intellectual freedom and fundamental to the ethics and practice of librarianship. *ALA Policy Manual* 53.1.16 (Library Bill of Rights).

Democracy. A democracy presupposes an informed citizenry. The First Amendment mandates the right of all persons to free expression, and the corollary right to receive the constitutionally protected expression of others. The publicly supported library provides free and equal access to information for all people of the community the library serves. Interpretations of the Library Bill of Rights: Economic Barriers to Information Access.

Diversity. We value our nation's diversity and strive to reflect that diversity by providing a full spectrum of resources and services to the communities we serve. *ALA Policy Manual* 53.8 (Libraries: An American Value).

Education and lifelong learning. ALA promotes the creation, maintenance, and enhancement of a learning society, encouraging its members to work with educators, government officials, and organizations in coalitions to initiate and support comprehensive efforts to ensure that school, public, academic, and special libraries in every community cooperate to provide lifelong learning services to all. *ALA Policy Manual* 1.1 (Mission, Priority Areas, Goals).

Intellectual freedom. We uphold the principles of intellectual freedom and resist all efforts to censor library resources. *ALA Policy Manual* 54.16 (ALA Code of Ethics, Article II).

The public good. ALA reaffirms the following fundamental values of libraries in the context of discussing outsourcing and privatization of library services. These values include that libraries are an essential public good and are fundamental institutions in democratic societies. 1998–1999 ALA Council Document #24.1, Motion #1.

Preservation. The Association supports the preservation of information published in all media and formats. The Association affirms that the preservation of information resources is central to libraries and librarianship. *ALA Policy Manual* 52.2.1 (Preservation Policy).

Professionalism. The American Library Association supports the provision of library services by professionally qualified personnel who have been educated in graduate programs within institutions of higher education. It is of vital importance that there be professional education available to meet the social needs and goals of library services. *ALA Policy Manual* 56.1 (Graduate Programs in Library Education).

Service. We provide the highest level of service to all library users. We strive for excellence in the profession by maintaining and enhancing our own knowledge and skills, by encouraging the professional development of coworkers, and by fostering the aspirations of potential members of the profession. *ALA Policy Manual* 54.16 (Statement of Professional Ethics).

Social responsibility. ALA recognizes its broad social responsibilities, defined in terms of the contribution that librarianship can make in ameliorating or solving the critical problems of society; support for efforts to help inform and educate the people of the United States on these problems and to encourage them to examine the many views on and the facts regarding each problem; and the willingness of ALA to take a position on current critical issues with the relationship to libraries and library service set forth in the position statement. *ALA Policy Manual* 1.1 (Mission, Priority Areas, Goals).

SOURCE: ALA Core Values of Librarianship, ala.org/offices/oif/statementspols/corevaluesstatement/corevalues/.

COPYRIGHT

Copyright basics

COPYRIGHT IS A FORM OF PROTECTION provided by the laws of the United States (Title 17, U.S. Code) to the authors of "original works of authorship," including literary, dramatic, musical, artistic, and certain other intellectual works. This protection is available to both published and unpublished works. Section 106 of the 1976 Copyright Act generally gives the owner of copyright the exclusive right to do and to authorize others to:

- reproduce the work;
- prepare derivative works;
- distribute copies of the work to the public;
- display or perform the work publicly.

9

It is illegal for anyone to violate any of the rights provided by the copyright law to the owner of copyright. These rights, however, are not unlimited.

One major limitation is the doctrine of "fair use," which is given a statutory basis in Section 107 of the act. In other instances, the limitation takes the form of a "compulsory license" under which certain limited uses of copyrighted works are permitted upon payment of specified royalties and compliance with statutory conditions.

Who can claim copyright?

Copyright protection subsists from the time the work is created in fixed form. The copyright in the work of authorship *immediately* becomes the property of the author who created the work. Only the author or those deriving their rights through the author can rightfully claim copyright. In the case of works made for hire, the employer and not the employee is considered to be the author. The authors of a joint work are co-owners of the copyright in the work, unless there is an agreement to the contrary.

Copyright in each separate contribution to a periodical or other collective work is distinct from copyright in the collective work as a whole and vests initially with the author of the contribution.

Mere ownership of a book, manuscript, painting, or any other copy or phonorecord does not give the possessor the copyright. The law provides that transfer of ownership of any material object that embodies a protected work does not of itself convey any rights in the copyright.

What works are protected?

Copyrightable works include the following categories:

1. literary works;
2. musical works, including any accompanying words;
3. dramatic works, including any accompanying music;
4. pantomimes and choreographic works;
5. pictorial, graphic, and sculptural works;
6. motion pictures and other audiovisual works;
7. sound recordings; and
8. architectural works.

These categories should be viewed broadly. For example, computer programs and most compilations may be registered as literary works; maps and architectural plans may be registered as pictorial, graphic, and sculptural works.

What is not protected by copyright

Several categories of material are generally not eligible for federal copyright protection. These include among others:

1. Works that have *not* been fixed in a tangible form of expression; for example, choreographic works that have not been notated or recorded, or improvisational speeches or performances that have not been written or recorded.
2. Titles, names, short phrases, and slogans; familiar symbols or designs; mere variations of typographic ornamentation, lettering, or coloring;

mere listings of ingredients or contents.

3. Ideas, procedures, methods, systems, processes, concepts, principles, discoveries, or devices, as distinguished from a description, explanation, or illustration.

4. Works consisting *entirely* of information that is common property and containing no original authorship; for example, standard calendars, height-and-weight charts, tape measures and rulers, and lists or tables taken from public documents or other common sources.

How to secure a copyright

No publication or registration or other action in the Copyright Office is required to secure copyright. There are, however, certain definite advantages to registration.

Copyright is secured *automatically* when the work is created, and a work is created when it is fixed in a copy or phonorecord for the first time. Thus, for example, a song can be fixed in sheet music (copies) or in phonograph disks (phonorecords), or both. If a work is prepared over a period of time, the part of the work that is fixed on a particular date constitutes the created work as of that date.

The use of a copyright notice is no longer required under U. S. law, although it is often beneficial. Because prior law did contain such a requirement, however, the use of notice is still relevant to the copyright status of older works. Notice was required under the 1976 Copyright Act. This requirement was eliminated when the United States adhered to the Berne Convention, effective March 1, 1989.

How long copyright protection endures

Works originally created on or after January 1, 1978, are automatically protected from the moment of creation and are ordinarily given a term enduring for the author's life plus an additional 70 years after the author's death. In the case of joint works, the term lasts for 70 years after the last surviving author's death. For works made for hire, and for anonymous and pseudonymous works, the duration of copyright is 95 years from publication or 120 years from creation, whichever is shorter.

Works originally created before January 1, 1978, but not published or registered by that date, are computed in the same way. In no case will the term of copyright for works in this category expire before December 31, 2002; for works published on or before December 31, 2002, the term of copyright will not expire before December 31, 2047.

Works originally created and published or registered before January 1, 1978. Under the law in effect before 1978, copyright endured for a first term of 28 years from the date it was secured. During the 28th year of the first term, the copyright was eligible for renewal. The Copyright Act of 1976 extended the renewal term to 47 years for copyrights that were subsisting on January 1, 1978, making these works eligible for a total term of protection of 75 years. The Sonny Bono Copyright Term Extension Act, enacted on October 27, 1998, further extended the renewal term of copyrights still subsisting on that date by an additional 20 years, providing for a renewal term of 67 years and a total term of protection of 95 years.

The Copyright Amendments Act of 1992 provides for automatic renewal of the term of copyrights secured between January 1, 1964, and December 31, 1977, and makes renewal registration optional. Thus, filing for renewal registration is no longer required in order to extend the original 28-year copyright term to the full 95 years.

Mandatory deposit

Although a copyright registration is not required, the 1976 Copyright Act established a mandatory deposit requirement for works published in the United States. In general, the owner of copyright or the owner of the exclusive right of publication in the work has a legal obligation to deposit in the Copyright Office, within three months of publication in the United States, two copies (or two phonorecords) for the use of the Library of Congress. Failure to make the deposit can result in fines and other penalties but does not affect copyright protection.

For general information about copyright matters, contact the Library of Congress, Copyright Office, 101 Independence Ave. SE, Washington, DC 20559-6304; (202) 707-3000. All copyright application forms are available from the Copyright Office website at www.copyright.gov.

SOURCE: U.S. Copyright Office, www.copyright.gov/circs/circ01.pdf.

Copyright in a nutshell
by Carrie Russell

YOU MAY HAVE WONDERED whether you hold the copyright to work you've put many hours into creating on the job. Who holds the copyright to works created by teachers or librarians? Short answer: In general, when employees create works as a condition of employment, the copyright holder is the employer.

As a school librarian or teacher, you create works all the time—lesson plans, finding tools, and so on—fairly independently, without specific conditions established by the school. If you are developing a syllabus, the school generally does not specify what to write or how long or detailed the syllabus should be, as would be the case in a "work for hire" situation (see box on next page). Nonetheless, you are being paid by the school to do a particular job, so the rights for materials you create are held by the school.

The employer holds the copyright when you create the works on the job, using school resources and technology, and receive a regular paycheck with Social Security and insurance deductions. These conditions point to an extended and anticipated ongoing relationship with your employer. Understandably, a school librarian may believe she holds the copyright to her recently completed lesson plan. But if she used school resources and created the lesson on "company time," the school likely holds the copyright.

Use of your work outside of school

If the school holds the copyright to your works, are you allowed to use those works outside of the school—at a conference or in a training session? Can you lend your lesson plans to other teachers in another district without asking for permission? The answer depends on how restrictive your school policy is about works created on the job. For the most part, members of an educational community tend

---

US Copyright Law

The creator or author of an original work holds the copyright to the work. However, rights of copyright can be transferred, as stated in 17 U.S.C.§ 201(d): The ownership of a copyright may be transferred in whole or in part by any means of conveyance or by operation of law, and may be bequeathed by will or pass as personal property by the applicable laws of intestate succession.

Any of the exclusive rights comprised in a copyright, including any subdivision of any of the rights specified by section 106, may be transferred as provided by clause (1) and owned separately. The owner of any particular exclusive right is entitled, to the extent of that right, to all of the protection and remedies accorded to the copyright owner by this title.

Example: A researcher writes a paper that is later published in an academic journal. The researcher holds the copyright to his work, but under a contract with the publisher, transfers an exclusive right or more (the right of reproduction, the right of distribution) to the publisher. The publisher can then exercise an exclusive right that originally was held by the researcher to publish and sell the article to the public.

Transfers of copyrights can be "exclusive" or "nonexclusive." An exclusive transfer means that only one publisher (as in the example above) is assigned those particular rights. Nonexclusive means that the rights holder may transfer the same right to other individuals or entities. Naturally, a publisher would negotiate for exclusive rights to eliminate any potential competitors.

Work for hire. A work for hire is one that is commissioned by an employer or other person. In a work-for-hire situation, the employer is hiring an individual to create a work for the employer under a written contract. The copyright is held by the employer unless the contract says otherwise.

As stated in 17 U.S.C.§ 201(b): In the case of a work made for hire, the employer or other person for whom the work was prepared is considered the author for purposes of this title, and, unless the parties have expressly agreed otherwise in a written instrument signed by them, owns all of the rights comprised in the copyright.

---

to have a more open view about sharing works with colleagues because of their collective commitment to advance learning. In addition, unlike other creators, we do not make our living selling the works we create on the job.

Many schools do not have a policy addressing the "ownership" of librarian- and teacher-created content, and you may want to pursue establishing such a policy. Alternatively, forgo a strict policy, which allows the flexibility of determining the best course of action on a case-by-case basis—whether to use a created work at a professional conference, for instance. In many cases, use of works outside of the classroom will be "fair use," which does not require permission from the copyright holder.

Using the copyrighted work of others

Copyrights can be transferred and those transfers can be "exclusive," "nonexclusive," or "time-based." In an example of a time-based transfer, say a librarian wants to establish movie night at the library. Showing movies to the public is a right held by the rights holder (in this case, the motion picture company). The librarian would—if the rights holder agreed—license the right to publicly perform a work on the date of the movie screening only. This is also an example of a nonexclusive contract, because the rights holder can transfer the right to publicly perform to anyone as many times as the rights holder desires.

9

SOURCE: Carrie Russell, "Copyright for Librarians and Teachers, in a Nutshell," *American Libraries* 43, no. 5/6 (May/June 2012): 56–58.

Introducing Creative Commons

by Molly Kleinman

THESE ARE DIFFICULT TIMES when it comes to copyright on campus. Big music companies are suing fans, publishers are suing librarians, and the principle of fair use is under siege everywhere. Litigation-happy content holders have fostered a climate of fear in which every student is a music pirate and every professor a book thief. While I don't doubt that there is some copyright infringement happening on university campuses, the bigger problem by far is the chilling effect of all these lawsuits and "copyright awareness campaigns."

Eugène Delacroix *La liberté guidant lepeuple,* derivative work by Ju, used CC BY-SA 3.0.

Scholars and students are afraid to do the one thing that copyright law has intended from the beginning: "Promote the progress of science and the useful arts" by creating new works and building on the works of those who came before. Every academic librarian knows at least one sad story about a professor who couldn't include necessary illustrations in her book because her publisher was worried about a copyright lawsuit, or a digitization project that couldn't get approved because the copyright status of the materials was uncertain.

Additional problems result from major changes to copyright law over the last 40 years. Now, every new work is copyrighted—lecture notes, emails, snapshots, doodles, presentation slides. And where once copyright lasted for 14 years, with the option to renew for another 14, now copyright lasts for the lifetime of the author, plus an additional 70 years after the author's death, for an average duration of more than a century. That's a very long time, and it leaves thousands of works orphaned—under copyright but without a locatable copyright holder. Between the fear and the orphans, life is hard for an ordinary academic who just wants some pictures to liven up her classroom presentations, or the student who would like to add a soundtrack to his final project.

Enter Creative Commons

Creative Commons is a nonprofit organization that created a set of simple, easy-to-understand copyright licenses. These licenses do two things: They allow creators to share their work easily, and they allow everyone to find work that is free to use without permission. The value of those two things is enormous. Before Creative Commons licenses, there was no easy way a creator could say, "Hey world! Go ahead and use my photographs, as long as you give me attribution."

Similarly, there was no place for members of the public to go to find new works that they were free to reuse and remix without paying fees. Creative Commons changed all that. As it says on its website, "Creative Commons defines the spectrum of possibilities between full copyright—all rights reserved—and the public domain—no rights reserved. Our licenses help you keep your copyright while inviting certain uses of your work—a 'some rights reserved' copyright."

The licenses come in three languages: Human Readable, which is a very brief and easy-to-understand summary of what is permitted and under what conditions; Lawyer Readable, which is a legally binding three-page deed; and Machine Readable, which is the metadata, a little snippet of code that makes it possible for search engines like Google to search by Creative Commons license, and return only those works that are free to reuse.

There are six major Creative Commons licenses that all include different combinations of four basic requirements:

Attribution (BY): You let others copy, distribute, display, and perform your copyrighted work—and derivative works based upon it—but only if they give you credit the way you request. This element is a part of all six licenses.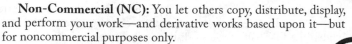

Non-Commercial (NC): You let others copy, distribute, display, and perform your work—and derivative works based upon it—but for noncommercial purposes only.

No Derivatives (ND): You let others copy, distribute, display, and perform only exact copies of your work, not derivative works based upon it.

Share Alike (SA): You allow others to distribute derivative works only under a license identical to the license that governs your work.

Founded by a group of intellectual property and technology experts in 2001, Creative Commons has emerged as a major player in the growing movement to provide an alternative to "All Rights Reserved." Their goal is "to build a layer of reasonable, flexible copyright in the face of increasingly restrictive default rules." They appear to be succeeding. As of this writing, Creative Commons licenses are available in 44 countries, with 9 more on the way. There are more than 60 million photographs available under Creative Commons licenses on the popular photo-sharing website Flickr; nearly 10,000 sound clips, samples, and remixes on the music site ccMixter; and materials from 1,800 undergraduate and graduate level MIT courses in the MIT OpenCourseWare program.

Benefits

The most immediate benefit of Creative Commons licenses to academia is the wealth of new works that are available for use without permissions or fees. Instructors, librarians, and students no longer have to rely on the public domain for materials that they can repurpose without risk of copyright infringement. In the time it takes to do a Google search, members of our community can find Creative Commons–licensed photographs, illustrations, music, video, and educational resources, *and they're all free.*

Creative Commons answers one of the most common copyright questions librarians get: "Is it okay for me to use this photograph/article/figure/etc. in my classroom/article/website/etc.?" If the photograph/article/figure is Creative Commons–licensed, the answer is always "Yes." At the University of Michigan Library, we decided we wanted to get the word out to our faculty and librarians to encourage them to take advantage of the incredible resources available through Creative Commons, and to contribute to those resources by licensing their own work.

9

Teaching Creative Commons

It may be easy to see the appeal of 60 million free photos, or 10,000 free songs, but it can be hard to understand exactly what Creative Commons is without some context. At the University of Michigan Library, we have included Creative

Commons in a larger copyright outreach campaign that began in May 2007. The campaign targets university faculty, researchers, students, staff and librarians, and aims to raise community members' awareness of their rights as authors and creators, improve their understanding of fair use, and promote a balanced approach to copyright. It has involved the redesign of the university's copyright website, outreach to academic departments through their subject specialists, and a series of copyright workshops offered in the library.

We structured the workshops around the assumption that a person has to understand at least a little bit about copyright, and the flaws in the current copyright system, in order to comprehend and appreciate the Creative Commons licensing model. The first half of the workshop is dedicated to laying that foundation, and to explaining what Creative Commons is. We begin with a showing of the video

Get Creative!, which uses appealing animation and real world examples to explain why Creative Commons was founded and how it works.

Participants repeatedly mentioned the video as one of their favorite parts of the workshop. We have found that it is a very effective way to communicate the power of Creative Commons and to get the class engaged so that they will listen to the dry, copyright-related parts that come next.

After the video, the presenter explains the key facts about copyright that are integral to the functioning of Creative Commons:

- Copyright happens automatically and lasts for the life of the author plus 70 years.
- Copyright is a bundle of rights; you can sign them away exclusively or grant nonexclusive licenses that give multiple people permission to use a work.
- Most everything is copyrighted, but creators may not want or need all those rights.

This section of the presentation is not intended to be a comprehensive introduction to copyright law. The purpose is to help the class understand why Creative Commons is important and the major ways that Creative Commons licenses differ from regular copyright.

We follow the copyright overview with an examination of the four license elements and a look at all six licenses. We explain what each license permits and doesn't permit, and emphasize that most academic uses are considered noncommercial. We also show examples of the three different kinds of language that make up a Creative Commons deed (Human Readable, Lawyer Readable, and Machine Readable). The aim here is to help get the class comfortable with the icons and terms used to represent aspects of Creative Commons licenses so that when participants encounter Creative Commons–licensed work in the future, they will be able to identify it and use it appropriately.

The second half of the workshop is comprised mainly of a series of live web demonstrations that show off the rich deposits of Creative Commons–licensed work available on the web. The presenter walks the participants through searches on Flickr for photos, ccMixter for music, and MIT OpenCourseWare for class materials. At this point, the class gets really excited. We

suggest potential uses for these resources, but participants have no trouble coming up with their own ideas.

One librarian who works with the Communications Studies department regularly fields questions about whether students can use popular music in their multimedia projects, and he couldn't wait to show them all the music that was available on ccMixter. A professor who likes to include a lot of images in her conference presentations was thrilled to learn about all the photographs that she could use without worrying about copyright when she posts those presentations online. The range and quality of Creative Commons–licensed material is inspiring.

Before opening up the workshop to questions, we always demonstrate how to apply a Creative Commons license to a website or photograph. We show them how to choose a license and where to get the code from the Creative Commons website. By now the participants have seen what a wonderful resource Creative Commons has provided, and we hope that they will begin using it to license their own work.

SOURCE: Molly Kleinman, "The Beauty of 'Some Rights Reserved,'" *College and Research Libraries News* 69 (Nov. 2008): 594–597.

The fair use statute
by Kenneth D. Crews

FAIR USE IS THE SUBJECT of numerous misconceptions and myths. The best place to begin a clear understanding of fair use is the statute itself—the real source of fair use law in the United States. The fair use statute takes hardly a minute to read and is remarkably simple and clear compared to many other federal statutes:

> Notwithstanding the provisions of sections 106 and 106A, the fair use of a copyrighted work, including such use by reproduction in copies or phonorecords or by any other means specified by that section, for purposes such as criticism, comment, news reporting, teaching (including multiple copies for classroom use), scholarship, or research, is not an infringement of copyright. In determining whether the use made of a work in any particular case is a fair use the factors to be considered shall include—
>
> (1) the purpose and character of the use, including whether such use is of a commercial nature or is for nonprofit educational purposes;
>
> (2) the nature of the copyrighted work;
>
> (3) the amount and substantiality of the portion used in relation to the copyrighted work as a whole; and
>
> (4) the effect of the use upon the potential market for or value of the copyrighted work.
>
> The fact that a work is unpublished shall not itself bar a finding of fair use if such finding is made upon consideration of all the above factors.

The statute establishes the framework for answering the extensive variety of questions you might have about clipping materials for websites, quoting from articles, making handouts for teaching, or sampling and remixing a sound recording. Numerous court cases apply that framework to the facts at issue in order to determine whether an activity is fair use or infringement.

A closer look at the statute

Of course, the law is never so simple. Fair use is the subject of numerous books, thousands of articles, and a growing cascade of court opinions. Understanding fair use in any particular setting best begins with an overview of the language from Congress. The words of the statute may be relatively simple, but they are rich with meaning.

Working with fair use

Always keep in mind these practical principles for working with this important copyright doctrine.

Fair use is a balancing test. You need to evaluate and apply the four factors, but you do not need to satisfy all of them for a use to be fair. The pivotal question is whether the factors overall lean in favor of or against fair use.

Fair use is highly fact-sensitive. The meaning and application of the factors will depend on the specific facts of each situation. Each time you face a new or changed situation, you need to evaluate the factors anew.

FAIR USE: IT'S THE LAW

EXERCISE YOUR COPYRIGHT RIGHTS IN THE CLASSROOM

Graphic by Timothy Vollmer, used CC BY 3.0.

Don't reach hasty conclusions. The question of fair use requires evaluation of all four factors. Do not conclude that you are within fair use merely because your use is for nonprofit education or has important scholarly objectives. You have three more factors to evaluate. Similarly, a commercial use can be within fair use after examining all factors.

If your use is not "fair," don't forget the other statutory exceptions to the rights of owners. Fair use and the other exceptions apply independently of one another. You need to comply with only one of them to make your use lawful.

If your use is not within any of the exceptions, permission from the copyright owner is an important option. Indeed, unless you change your planned use of the copyrighted work, you might have little choice but to seek permission.

Fair use is relevant only if the work is protected by copyright. Do not overlook the possibility that the work you want to use may be in the public domain; if it is not protected by copyright, you do not have to worry about fair use. Similarly, if your use is not within the legal rights of the copyright owner, you are not an infringer, and you also do not have to consider fair use.

SOURCE: Kenneth D. Crews, *Copyright Law for Librarians and Educators,* 3rd ed. (Chicago: American Library Association, 2012), 55–56.

INTELLECTUAL FREEDOM

The Library Bill of Rights

THE AMERICAN LIBRARY ASSOCIATION affirms that all libraries are forums for information and ideas, and that the following basic policies should guide their services.

1. Books and other library resources should be provided for the interest, information, and enlightenment of all people of the community the library serves. Materials should not be excluded because of the origin, background, or views of those contributing to their creation.
2. Libraries should provide materials and information presenting all points of view on current and historical issues. Materials should not be proscribed or removed because of partisan or doctrinal disapproval.
3. Libraries should challenge censorship in the fulfillment of their responsibility to provide information and enlightenment.
4. Libraries should cooperate with all persons and groups concerned with resisting abridgment of free expression and free access to ideas.
5. A person's right to use a library should not be denied or abridged because of origin, age, background, or views.
6. Libraries which make exhibit spaces and meeting rooms available to the public they serve should make such facilities available on an equitable basis, regardless of the beliefs or affiliations of individuals or groups requesting their use.

Since 1948, when the Library Bill of Rights was first adopted, ALA Council has affirmed 22 interpretations that elaborate its provisions:

Access for children and young adults to nonprint materials. Adopted 1989; amended 2004.
Access to digital information, services, and networks. Adopted 1996; amended 2005 and 2009.
Access to library resources and services regardless of sex, gender identity, gender expression, or sexual orientation. Adopted 1993; amended 2000, 2004, and 2008.
Access to resources and services in the school library media program. Adopted 1986; amended 1990, 2000, 2005, and 2008.
Challenged materials. Adopted 1971; amended 1981, 1990, and 2009.
Diversity in collection development. Adopted 1982; amended 1990 and 2008.
Economic barriers to information access. Adopted 1993.
Evaluating library collections. Adopted 1973; amended 1981 and 2008.
Exhibit spaces and bulletin boards. Adopted 1991; amended 2004.
Expurgation of library materials. Adopted 1973; amended 1981, 1990, and 2008.
Free access to libraries for minors. Adopted 1972; amended 1981, 1991, 2004, and 2008.
Importance of education to intellectual freedom. Adopted 2009.

9

Intellectual freedom principles for academic libraries. Adopted 2000.

Labeling and rating systems. Adopted 1951; amended 1971, 1981, 1990, 2005, and 2009.

Library-initiated programs as a resource. Adopted 1982; amended 1990 and 2000.

Meeting rooms. Adopted 1991.

Minors and internet interactivity. Adopted 2009.

Prisoners' right to read. Adopted 2010.

Privacy. Adopted 2002.

Restricted access to library materials. Adopted 1973; amended 1981, 1991, 2000, 2004, and 2009.

Services to persons with disabilities. Adopted 2009.

The universal right to free expression. Adopted 1991.

SOURCE: ALA Office for Intellectual Freedom, www.ifmanual.org/part2.

Minors and internet interactivity

THE DIGITAL ENVIRONMENT offers opportunities for accessing, creating, and sharing information. The rights of minors to retrieve, interact with, and create information posted on the internet in schools and libraries are extensions of their First Amendment rights. (See also other interpretations of the Library Bill of Rights, including Access to Digital Information, Services, and Networks; Free Access to Libraries for Minors; and Access for Children and Young Adults to Nonprint Materials.)

Academic pursuits of minors can be strengthened with the use of interactive web tools, allowing young people to create documents and share them online; upload pictures, videos, and graphic material; revise public documents; and add tags to online content to classify and organize information. Instances of inappropriate use of such academic tools should be addressed as individual behavior issues, not as justification for restricting or banning access to interactive technology. Schools and libraries should ensure that institutional environments offer opportunities for students to use interactive web tools constructively in their academic pursuits, as the benefits of shared learning are well documented.

Personal interactions of minors can be enhanced by social tools available through the internet. Social networking websites allow the creation of online communities that feature an open exchange of information in various forms, such as images, videos, blog posts, and discussions about common interests. Interactive web tools help children and young adults learn about and organize social, civic, and extracurricular activities. Many interactive sites invite users to establish online identities, share personal information, create web content, and join social networks. Parents and guardians play a critical role in preparing their children for participation in online activity by communicating their personal family values and by monitoring their children's use of the internet. Parents and guardians are responsible for what their children—and only their children—access on the internet in libraries.

The use of interactive web tools poses two competing intellectual freedom issues—the protection of minors' privacy and the right of free speech. Some have expressed concerns regarding what they perceive is an increased vulnerability of young people in the online environment when they use interactive sites to post personally identifiable information. In an effort to protect minors' privacy, adults sometimes restrict access to interactive web environments. Filters, for example, are sometimes used to restrict access by youth to interactive social networking tools, but at the same time deny minors' rights to free expression on the internet. Prohibiting children and young adults from using social networking sites does not teach safe behavior and leaves youth without the necessary knowledge and skills to protect their privacy or engage in responsible speech. Instead of restricting or denying access to the internet, librarians and teachers should educate minors to participate responsibly, ethically, and safely.

The First Amendment applies to speech created by minors on interactive sites. Usage of these social networking sites in a school or library allows minors to access and create resources that fulfill their interests and needs for information, for social connection with peers, and for participation in a community of learners. Restricting expression and access to interactive websites because the sites provide tools for sharing information with others violates the tenets of the Library Bill of Rights. It is the responsibility of librarians and educators to monitor threats to the intellectual freedom of minors and to advocate for extending access to interactive applications on the internet.

As defenders of intellectual freedom and the First Amendment, libraries and librarians have a responsibility to offer unrestricted access to internet interactivity in accordance with local, state, and federal laws and to advocate for greater access where it is abridged. School and library professionals should work closely with young people to help them learn skills and attitudes that will prepare them to be responsible, effective, and productive communicators in a free society.

SOURCE: Minors and Internet Interactivity: An Interpretation of the Library Bill of Rights, adopted July 15, 2009, by the ALA Council, www.ifmanual.org/minorsinteractivity.

The freedom to read

THE FREEDOM TO READ is essential to our democracy. It is continuously under attack. Private groups and public authorities in various parts of the country are working to remove or limit access to reading materials, to censor content in schools, to label "controversial" views, to distribute lists of "objectionable" books or authors, and to purge libraries. These actions apparently rise from a view that our national tradition of free expression is no longer valid; that censorship and suppression are needed to counter threats to safety or national security, as well as to avoid the subversion of politics and the corruption of morals. We, as individuals devoted to reading and as librarians and publishers responsible for disseminating ideas, wish to assert the public interest in the preservation of the freedom to read.

Most attempts at suppression rest on a denial of the fundamental premise of democracy: that the ordinary individual, by exercising critical judgment, will select the good and reject the bad. We trust Americans to recognize propaganda and misinformation, and to make their own decisions about what they read and believe. We do not believe they are prepared to sacrifice their heritage of a free press in order to be "protected" against what others think may be bad for them. We believe they still favor free enterprise in ideas and expression.

These efforts at suppression are related to a larger pattern of pressures being brought against education, the press, art and images, films, broadcast media, and the internet. The problem is not only one of actual censorship. The shadow of fear

9

cast by these pressures leads, we suspect, to an even larger voluntary curtailment of expression by those who seek to avoid controversy or unwelcome scrutiny by government officials.

Such pressure toward conformity is perhaps natural to a time of accelerated change. And yet suppression is never more dangerous than in such a time of social tension. Freedom has given the United States the elasticity to endure strain. Freedom keeps open the path of novel and creative solutions, and enables change to come by choice. Every silencing of a heresy, every enforcement of an orthodoxy, diminishes the toughness and resilience of our society and leaves it the less able to deal with controversy and difference.

Now, as always in our history, reading is among our greatest freedoms. The freedom to read and write is almost the only means for making generally available ideas or manners of expression that can initially command only a small audience. The written word is the natural medium for the new idea and the untried voice from which come the original contributions to social growth. It is essential to the extended discussion that serious thought requires, and to the accumulation of knowledge and ideas into organized collections.

We believe that free communication is essential to the preservation of a free society and a creative culture. We believe that these pressures toward conformity present the danger of limiting the range and variety of inquiry and expression on which our democracy and our culture depend. We believe that every American community must jealously guard the freedom to publish and to circulate, in order to preserve its own freedom to read. We believe that publishers and librarians have a profound responsibility to give validity to that freedom to read by making it possible for the readers to choose freely from a variety of offerings.

The freedom to read is guaranteed by the Constitution. Those with faith in free people will stand firm on these constitutional guarantees of essential rights and will exercise the responsibilities that accompany these rights.

We therefore affirm these propositions:

1. It is in the public interest for publishers and librarians to make available the widest diversity of views and expressions, including those which are unorthodox, unpopular, or considered dangerous by the majority.

2. Publishers, librarians, and booksellers do not need to endorse every idea or presentation they make available. It would conflict with the public interest for them to establish their own political, moral, or aesthetic views as a standard for determining what books should be published or circulated.

3. It is contrary to the public interest for publishers or librarians to bar access to writings on the basis of the personal history or political affiliations of the author.

4. There is no place in our society for efforts to coerce the taste of others, to confine adults to the reading matter deemed suitable for adolescents, or to inhibit the efforts of writers to achieve artistic expression.

5. It is not in the public interest to force a reader to accept the prejudgment of a label characterizing any expression or its author as subversive or dangerous.

6. It is the responsibility of publishers and librarians, as guardians of the people's freedom to read, to contest encroachments upon that freedom by individuals or groups seeking to impose their own standards or tastes upon the community

at large; and by the government whenever it seeks to reduce or deny public access to public information.

7. It is the responsibility of publishers and librarians to give full meaning to the freedom to read by providing books that enrich the quality and diversity of thought and expression. By the exercise of this affirmative responsibility, they can demonstrate that the answer to a "bad" book is a good one, the answer to a "bad" idea is a good one.

We state these propositions neither lightly nor as easy generalizations. We here stake out a lofty claim for the value of the written word. We do so because we believe that it is possessed of enormous variety and usefulness, worthy of cherishing and keeping free. We realize that the application of these propositions may mean the dissemination of ideas and manners of expression that are repugnant to many persons. We do not state these propositions in the comfortable belief that what people read is unimportant. We believe rather that what people read is deeply important; that ideas can be dangerous; but that the suppression of ideas is fatal to a democratic society. Freedom itself is a dangerous way of life, but it is ours.

SOURCE· ALA Office for Intellectual Freedom. Adopted 1953; revised 1972, 1991, 2000, and 2004 by the ALA Council and the Association of American Publishers Freedom to Read Committee; www.ifmanual.org/ftrstatement

Judith Krug, 1940–2009:
The freedom to read

by Leonard Kniffel

JUDITH KRUG BELIEVED that no one has the right to tell other people what they can or cannot read. When asked where libraries should draw the line when it comes to stocking controversial material, she always had one answer: "The law." She understood that we are a nation living under the rule of law, and that creating, enforcing, or overturning the laws of the land is the single most important way to safeguard the freedom to read for all Americans.

In establishing the Freedom to Read Foundation in 1969, Krug based the organization's mission firmly in the First Amendment: "Congress shall make no

law respecting an establishment of religion, or prohibiting the free exercise thereof; or abridging the freedom of speech, or of the press; or the right of the people peaceably to assemble, and to petition the Government for a redress of grievances."

When Congress did try to make laws "abridging the freedom of speech," her tenacious involvement in court battles was the stuff of legend. From the triumphant Supreme Court decision that overturned the Communications Decency Act in 1997 to the court's stubborn upholding of the Children's Internet Protection Act in 2003, Krug never gave up the fight. Many disagreed with her, but none disrespected her.

Judith Krug, 1960s

9

On April 11, 2009, after a long and courageous battle with stomach cancer, Krug died as she had lived for 40 years, as the proud director of the American Library Association's Office for Intellectual Freedom, still leading the charge, still presiding over Banned Books Week as she had done since founding it in 1982.

Krug often said that when ALA established OIF in 1967 and put her in charge, then–Executive Director David H. Clift sat her down and told her to

Guidelines for responding to complaints
by Candace Morgan

The goal is to respond to the complaint in a way that will:
  Acknowledge the right to complain.
  Show an effort to respond to the patron's needs.
  Consider alternatives.
  Stay within library policy.
  Uphold the First Amendment rights of all library users.

Be prepared

Know and understand the US and state constitutional principles involved.
Know your library's policies.
Know what your responsibility is.
Know whom to refer to (the appropriate forms, etc.).
Remember that having a book (or other material) in the collection, or accessible through the internet or interlibrary loan, does not mean that you or the library endorses it.
Seek to understand why people complain about library materials or services.
Seek to acknowledge what is offensive to ourselves and prepare ourselves to deal with it.

Things to do (if appropriate and possible)

Listen carefully to the complaint.
Establish a common ground.
Demonstrate respect for the patron's values, beliefs, opinions.
Treat the complaint seriously.
Be polite—even in response to rudeness or attack.
Offer assistance in finding something that will meet the patron's needs.
Suggest the consequences of granting government (the library) the right to censor (complainers have rarely considered that someone who would censor what they want to read may take control).
Explain the library's complaint policy, procedure, and process.
Thank the person for expressing interest in the library or for being involved with their child's reading and use of the library.
Provide information about next step available if not satisfactorily resolved.

Things to avoid

Attack, intimidation, escalation.
Defensiveness (words or body language).
Overreaction.
Philosophical debate.
Defense of literary quality (defend place in collection).
Quoting policy as the only response.
Compromising library policy or the principles of intellectual freedom upon which this country is based.

SOURCE: Guidelines for Responding to Complaints, September 2009, www.ifmanual.org/guidelinecomplaint.

"put that office on the map." Rallying her BA from the University of Pittsburgh (1961), her master's in library science from the University of Chicago (1964), and her natural gifts as a writer, speaker, and progressive thinker, she set about to do just that.

Judith Krug with her friend, author Judy Blume, 2008.

"From time to time, and especially in periods of great stress or social upheaval, a variety of real or imagined evils have been attributed to the reading of obscene and pornographic works," she wrote in the April 1968 issue of *American Libraries* (then called *ALA Bulletin)*. "The words 'obscenity' and 'pornography,' which in themselves cause considerable emotion, are often applied indiscriminately to materials containing ideas, acts, and words which one or another group may find reprehensible," she added, setting the stage for placing ALA often on the same side of the censorship battle with the likes of *Hustler* magazine's Larry Flynt and *Playboy* mogul Hugh Hefner.

A suburban Chicago mom in her private life, Judith Krug was no prude, and she understood ALA's obligation to defend the right of Americans to publish and read what she personally thought of as "sleaze," a word she used to describe Madonna's 1992 book *Sex*, which many libraries refused to purchase. Call it sleaze she did, but with the caveat that it should be available in every public library. Krug understood that people have the right to make up their own minds, without librarians exercising a kind of prior restraint by refusing to buy controversial materials.

Frequently attacked by would-be censors, Krug defended what they often called her liberal agenda. She said in an interview in the September 1995 issue of *American Libraries*, "If I have an agenda, it is protection of the First Amendment. Libraries in this country cannot operate unless we can stand foursquare on the First Amendment. And if that becomes a partisan position, well, OK, I guess if I have to be partisan I will be partisan on behalf of the First Amendment."

Although she was a liberal Democrat in her personal political leanings, Krug was well aware that, as she put it in the same *AL* interview, "Our threats come from across the spectrum of social and political thought. . . . We have gone through periods where our biggest threats have been from the left of center, where people have wanted to remove materials that did not portray, for instance, minority groups in the way that they thought minority groups should be portrayed." She also believed it was the librarian's responsibility to listen respectfully to those complaints.

She was speaking from experience. One of her greatest challenges as OIF director came in 1977, when she and ALA's Intellectual Freedom Committee produced a film titled *The Speaker*, tackling censorship by telling the story of a library's decision to allow a racist to speak. Designed to serve as a focal point for library discussions about the First Amendment, the film ironically became a divisive issue at the 1977 ALA Annual Conference in Detroit, denounced by some librarians who called it "insulting in its characterization of black people." Then–ALA Executive Director Robert Wedgeworth, her boss at the time, calls the moment one of the Association's most dramatic. "It split ALA wide open," he said, and "there was a lot of pressure for me to fire Judith."

Whatever the arguments in favor of censorship were, Krug had the rebuttal.

9

"She was always ready for confrontation," Wedgeworth recalled, "and she was such a good debater she could win almost any argument."

Cooler heads prevailed in the case of *The Speaker,* said Wedgeworth, "but we had underestimated the fact that discussion of race was the one issue that people could not accept with respect to the First Amendment." He noted that "true to her convictions, Judith stuck by the film."

Handling controversy was an innate talent that Krug possessed. "She invented what they now call media training," said Art Plotnik, former editor of *American Libraries.*

Krug debated the Equal Rights Amendment in Kentucky with conservative activist Phyllis Schlafly in 1990, drawing cheers from a Berea College crowd for articulating "the librarians' view," while Schlafly inspired booing.

Krug refined her communications skills to yet another level when dealing with the media frenzy over sexually explicit material online, a furor that erupted as internet access began becoming available in public libraries.

For Krug, one of the greatest triumphs of her career was the Supreme Court ruling that overturned the Communications Decency Act. Under her leadership, ALA filed suit in 1996, challenging the CDA, a provision of the Telecommunications Act that President Clinton had signed into law, as an unconstitutional violation of the free speech rights of adults while failing to accomplish its intended purpose of protecting children from inappropriate online content.

Perhaps her greatest disappointment was the 2003 Supreme Court ruling that the Children's Internet Protection Act was constitutional, ending a battle over internet filtering that cost ALA over a million dollars. Adults, the court decided, could ask that filters be turned off for unrestricted access and Congress could require libraries to install filtering in exchange for funding. It was a decision that Krug had fought hard.

"She was a purist, uncompromising," said Plotnik. "Anyone else would have caved with the exceptions people would throw at her." He recalled working many a late night across the hall from Krug. "I never remember her turning away a cold call from a librarian who needed help," he said. "She would stay long hours to give the most elaborate advice to people calling from the field."

Krug believed that it was ALA's role to help libraries set standards and create policies. "If I've done nothing else in my career but convince people that they have to have policy and then help them develop good policy, I will have considered my career a success," she said.

Judith Krug famously attributed her open-mindedness to her unflappable mother, revealing that at the age of 12 she had obtained a sex-education book and was reading it under the bed covers with a flashlight when her mother suddenly threw back the covers and asked what she was doing. Young Judith shyly held up the book. "For God's sake," her mother said, "turn on your bedroom light so you don't hurt your eyes."

But Judith Krug wasn't doing her job just for librarians; she was doing it for her country, and for the rights and privileges her children and grandchildren enjoy as Americans. From the beginning of her career as a librarian, she thought big, and she inspired countless librarians to do likewise. She shattered the image of libraries as the benign sanctuary of the meek, and she forever altered the image of librarians, from bespectacled guardians of the respectable to articulate and unyielding defenders of the freedom to read.

SOURCE: Leonard Kniffel, "Judith Krug: The Freedom to Read," *American Libraries* 40, no. 5 (May 2009): 40–43.

Privacy: An interpretation of the Library Bill of Rights

PRIVACY IS ESSENTIAL to the exercise of free speech, free thought, and free association. The courts have established a First Amendment right to receive information in a publicly funded library. Further, the courts have upheld the right to privacy based on the Bill of Rights of the US Constitution. Many states provide guarantees of privacy in their constitutions and statute law. Numerous decisions in case law have defined and extended rights to privacy.

In a library (physical or virtual), the right to privacy is the right to open inquiry without having the subject of one's interest examined or scrutinized by others. Confidentiality exists when a library is in possession of personally identifiable information about users and keeps that information private on their behalf.

FREEDOM FROM SURVEILLANCE

CHOOSE PRIVACY
PRIVACYREVOLUTION.ORG

Protecting user privacy and confidentiality has long been an integral part of the mission of libraries. The ALA has affirmed a right to privacy since 1939. Existing ALA policies affirm that confidentiality is crucial to freedom of inquiry. Rights to privacy and confidentiality also are implicit in the Library Bill of Rights' guarantee of free access to library resources for all users.

Rights of library users

The Library Bill of Rights affirms the ethical imperative to provide unrestricted access to information and to guard against impediments to open inquiry. Article IV states: "Libraries should cooperate with all persons and groups concerned with resisting abridgement of free expression and free access to ideas." When users recognize or fear that their privacy or confidentiality is compromised, true freedom of inquiry no longer exists.

In all areas of librarianship, best practice leaves the user in control of as many choices as possible. These include decisions about the selection of, access to, and use of information. Lack of privacy and confidentiality has a chilling effect on users' choices. All users have a right to be free from any unreasonable intrusion into or surveillance of their lawful library use.

Users have the right to be informed what policies and procedures govern the amount and retention of personally identifiable information, why that information is necessary for the library, and what the user can do to maintain his or her privacy. Library users expect and in many places have a legal right to have their information protected and kept private and confidential by anyone with direct or indirect access to that information. In addition, Article V of the Library Bill of Rights states: "A person's right to use a library should not be denied or abridged

9

because of origin, age, background, or views." This article precludes the use of profiling as a basis for any breach of privacy rights. Users have the right to use a library without any abridgement of privacy that may result from equating the subject of their inquiry with behavior.

Responsibilities in libraries

The library profession has a long-standing commitment to an ethic of facilitating, not monitoring, access to information. This commitment is implemented locally through development, adoption, and adherence to privacy policies that are consistent with applicable federal, state, and local law. Everyone (paid or unpaid) who provides governance, administration, or service in libraries has a responsibility to maintain an environment respectful and protective of the privacy of all users. Users have the responsibility to respect each others' privacy.

For administrative purposes, librarians may establish appropriate time, place, and manner restrictions on the use of library resources. In keeping with this principle, the collection of personally identifiable information should only be a matter of routine or policy when necessary for the fulfillment of the mission of the library. Regardless of the technology used, everyone who collects or accesses personally identifiable information in any format has a legal and ethical obligation to protect confidentiality.

The American Library Association affirms that rights of privacy are necessary for intellectual freedom and are fundamental to the ethics and practice of librarianship.

SOURCE: Privacy: An Interpretation of the Library Bill of Rights, adopted June 19, 2002, by the ALA Council, www.ifmanual.org/privacyinterp.

Q&A about state privacy laws
by Theresa Chmara

DOES EVERY STATE PROVIDE protection for library circulation records through a state statute? With the exception of Hawaii and Kentucky, every state provides some protection for library circulation records through a state statute. In Hawaii and Kentucky, Attorney General Opinion Letters provide direction to libraries and take the position that library patrons have a privacy interest in their library circulation records. Whether through statute or attorney general opinion, the extent to which protection is provided for such records varies in each state.

Even if a state provides that records are confidential, is the library required to provide parents with the records of their minor children? Most state statutes do not differentiate between adults and minors. If a state statute generally provides protection for library circulation records, then that protection should apply to minors as well. If a state has a general privacy protection for patron records, the library should not divulge patron information to anyone other than the patron. Several states, including Alabama, Alaska, Louisiana, South Dakota, Utah, West Virginia, Wisconsin, and Wyoming, currently provide libraries with an explicit directive to allow parents access to minors' records. In Colorado, parents can access their child's records if they have the minor's account number. In New Mexico, the state legislature has provided that parents can access the school library records of their children but has not extended that access to public library records. Florida permits a library to disclose a minor's circulation record to a parent in order to collect a fine.

What if the parent needs to see the record to pay an outstanding fine for overdue books? In a state that does not give parents explicit access to their minors' records, the library should not disclose that information to anyone other than the minor patron. Libraries should use their regular method of pursuing compensation for overdue materials, such as sending an overdue notice to the home of the patron. The parent will need to coordinate with the minor to pay the outstanding fine.

If the confidentiality statute in my state provides that the library may disclose patron record information in response to a subpoena, is my library obligated to disclose that material? No. Some statutes provide that the library "may" disclose information in response to a subpoena, but they do not compel the library to disclose such information. If the library has a confidentiality policy related to patron records, then it should contact an attorney to review the subpoena and determine whether the records should be produced. A subpoena is not a court order. It is simply a request from a law enforcement official or attorney in a private matter seeking such information in relation to a court case or investigation. The subpoena may be overbroad and violate the confidentiality provision of the library.

What is the difference between a subpoena and a search warrant? A search warrant is a court order directing law enforcement personnel to search a particular place for particular information. The person or entity to which a search warrant is directed cannot refuse to comply with the warrant. A subpoena is merely a request for records, not a court order to produce records.

If a law enforcement officer comes to my library with a search warrant, must I let him search information about patron records? Yes. You can ask the officer to wait until you have called an attorney, but the officer does not have to comply with that request. You should nonetheless call your attorney and ask her to arrive as soon as possible. An attorney can review the warrant for legality and can ensure that it is executed as required by the court. If the law enforcement officer will not wait for an attorney, then review the warrant carefully and observe the search to ensure that the officer searches only the records permitted by the court. If, for example, the warrant only allows the search of one computer, be sure that only one computer is searched.

If a law enforcement officer comes to my library with a subpoena, must I disclose the requested information? No. A subpoena is not a court order and has not been reviewed by a judge. A subpoena is merely a request for records. The law enforcement officer should be informed that the library attorney will be notified of the request and will respond to the officer's request. The library should, however, at this point ensure that the requested information is retained even if it would have been destroyed in the ordinary course of business.

Is there any situation in which a law enforcement officer could seize information without a search warrant or subpoena? Yes. There are two instances in which law enforcement officers could seize information without a warrant and without making a subpoena request. First, an officer may seize evidence without a warrant in "exigent circumstances," where the officer believes that failing to seize the evidence will result in physical harm to someone or destruction of the evidence and it is impossible to obtain a warrant before such harm results. If such a seizure is challenged in court, the judge will consider whether a reasonable person

9

would have acted in the same manner. Second, an officer may seize evidence that is in "plain view." If, for example, an officer saw a crime being committed and saw evidence of the crime without a search, then the evidence could be seized.

Should a library disclose records to law enforcement if the crime has been committed at the library? In all instances in which a request for patron records has been made, the library attorney must be consulted. If a patron has engaged in theft or vandalism, witnesses can assist law enforcement in apprehending the right individual without the need to disclose circulation records or other records whose disclosure would impact First Amendment rights. Only the state of Louisiana provides an exemption to the confidentiality provisions for actual crimes witnessed by a librarian or patron and reported in a specified manner to law enforcement.

Are surveillance cameras at the library subject to the restrictions imposed by confidentiality statutes? A library may need to use surveillance cameras to prevent theft, vandalism, or crimes against other patrons on the premises. The library must, however, ensure that the placement of the cameras does not reveal the reading or library material choices of patrons. For example, surveillance cameras should not be placed behind the circulation desk if they would reveal the books that patrons are borrowing or behind computers in a manner that would reveal the sites visited by a patron.

If library circulation information is disclosed in violation of a state confidentiality statute, will the librarian face any consequences? In some states, disclosure of confidential information can lead to criminal fines or civil penalties. Criminal fines can be imposed in Arizona, Colorado, the District of Columbia, Montana, Rhode Island, and South Carolina. Some states, such as Michigan, Montana, New Mexico, and Rhode Island, permit the person whose record was disclosed to file a civil suit for penalties.

If the library receives a request for patron information, should the patron be informed of the request? In most cases, the person to whom a request for records was directed will also be asked to refrain from revealing the request to prevent criminal obstruction by the target of the investigation. These types of requests commonly are referred to as "gag orders." An attorney should be consulted prior to any publication of the request. Only the District of Columbia explicitly requires that patrons be informed if their records are requested. The District of Columbia statute has a specific notice procedure that must be followed if a request for patron information is received by the library.

Should libraries have record destruction policies? Yes. Libraries should have a record destruction policy in place to purge records that are not needed. Personally identifiable information about patrons should be destroyed as soon as the library no longer needs that information for the efficient operation of the library. For example, many libraries have a system in place that retains information pertaining to the materials borrowed by a patron only until those materials are returned. The library has no need to know that a particular patron borrowed a particular book once the book has been returned. The library system could, however, retain the information that a particular book was borrowed 10 times in the last year without retaining the names of the person who borrowed the materials. Statistical information about the number of times a book was borrowed that does not reveal personally identifiable information about patrons can be useful to the efficient operation of the library and resource allocation decisions.

SOURCE: Theresa Chmara, *Privacy and Confidentiality Issues: A Guide for Libraries and Their Lawyers* (Chicago: American Library Association, 2009), 44–47.

PATRON BEHAVIOR

Problem patrons in the library
by Elisabeth Doucett

THERE ARE ALWAYS PEOPLE who create problems in libraries. I don't say this from cynicism but from experience. There might be a few more in public than academic libraries because public libraries are open and accessible to all. But from my conversations with different types of librarians, I've learned that they can be found everywhere. So just make up your mind that the odds are very, very good that you will encounter "problem patrons" (as they say in the world of public libraries) at some point in your career, and for whatever reason you will be the only one in that place at that moment who can deal with the problem. You won't always be able to depend on more senior librarians or the folks in administration to take care of the problem. It will be immediate and in your face, and you'll do a whole lot better if you put a few tools in place before this happens to address the problem.

Tool 1: Be respectful. The first and most powerful tool is to approach all users of your library with respect, regardless of their circumstances or behavior. Assume that no one got up this morning and decided to be a problem for you personally. Also assume that everyone has worth and value. This doesn't mean that you allow bad behavior. It does mean that you treat everyone the same, recognizing that they are part of your community, and that they believe they have a perfectly good reason for the behavior

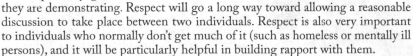

they are demonstrating. Respect will go a long way toward allowing a reasonable discussion to take place between two individuals. Respect is also very important to individuals who normally don't get much of it (such as homeless or mentally ill persons), and it will be particularly helpful in building rapport with them.

Tool 2: Be informed. When you start on your new job, make a point of asking more experienced staff members to tell you about the type of problems they encounter on a regular basis with library users and how they deal with those problems.

You'll probably have to sit through many war stories, but you'll be able to glean two things: where issues generally come from among your library's users, and what tools more experienced staff use to deal with those problem users effectively. At a college it might be students who ignore the library's "no gambling on computers" rule. Or it might be individuals who regularly sneak into the library to steal unguarded computers. In a public library it might be homeless individuals from a local shelter who use the library as their living room. Or it might be local gang members who try to use the library for drug dealing. Whatever the story is, it is good to have some sense of the cause of problems, the seriousness of those problems (gangbangers or seniors arguing over bridge games), and how the prob-

9

lems have been addressed in the past. You may choose not to deal with issues the same way others have, but it can't hurt to have a sense of what has been effective and what hasn't. This type of research will also help you be prepared for the first time a problem occurs.

Tool 3: Be involved. Make a point of watching the more experienced librarians manage difficult situations. Don't hide in the stacks when there is a problem and hope that it will go away. Your goal here is the same as with tool number two: to learn what works and doesn't work in your library. Many libraries today have a policy that if there is a problem in the facility, librarians address the problem in teams to ensure the safety of all involved. Offer to be backup for other librarians when it is appropriate, so that you can see firsthand how situations are managed in your library. An added benefit of doing this is that these encounters help you get over any initial fear you might have about this type of problem solving. Immersion therapy does work in this particular situation.

Tool 4: Be aware. This is a difficult tool to develop. In any library it is likely that you will have a great deal of work to do and not enough time to do it. It becomes very easy to put your head down and crank away on your work, only looking up to address library users who have questions or issues. However, being oblivious to who is in the library can be a real issue. You need to be aware of who walks into your library, what they look like, and your intuition about that individual. If you get nervous over someone walking around the library, trust your instincts. Pay attention to that individual. Be aware of what she looks like (height, hair color, clothes). If it happens naturally, say hello and make her aware that you know she is there. (People who want to cause problems frequently want to stay unnoticed.) Keep your eyes open. All of this will help you if there is a problem, and it may avert a problem before it occurs. Also, it is a great way of building your customer-service skills and making sure that your library is a welcoming, comfortable environment.

Tool 5: Be objective. When you observe people in your library, actively work to monitor your internal dialogue about each individual. If you find that you start automatically categorizing people by their looks (that person is obviously homeless, so he is going to be a problem), you've lost your objectivity and your corresponding ability to identify and assess potential problems. Problems can come from anywhere, not just from certain categories of people. What you need to be aware of are behaviors, not how someone looks. So if you say to yourself "that person is jittery and talking to himself and getting more and more agitated," and he is dressed like a banker, then you have maintained your objectivity. To use a librarian analogy, you are looking beyond the cover of the book to the contents—and that is what is important when you are identifying problems. Be aware of this internal dialogue and correct yourself when you find you are losing your objectivity.

Tool 6: Be calm. Everyone says this about difficult situations in the library and no one ever tells you how hard it is to do. Here are a couple of very basic things you can do to help maintain your calm:

Breathe deeply. A little oxygen goes a long way in counteracting the adrenaline pumping through your system in a difficult situation.

Stop and think. You can't always stop and take a moment to collect yourself. Sometimes events just move too quickly. However, if possible, stop and consider what you are going to say before you open your mouth.

Take a partner with you if you are going to deal with a difficult situation. It always helps to have backup, and after the situation is over, a partner can provide helpful input about what you did well and areas where you might improve.

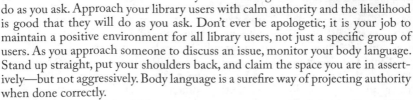

When you need to give direction, do it with authority. Assume that the individual with whom you are talking will do as you ask. Approach your library users with calm authority and the likelihood is good that they will do as you ask. Don't ever be apologetic; it is your job to maintain a positive environment for all library users, not just a specific group of users. As you approach someone to discuss an issue, monitor your body language. Stand up straight, put your shoulders back, and claim the space you are in assertively—but not aggressively. Body language is a surefire way of projecting authority when done correctly.

Have a mantra with which you can encourage yourself, along the lines of "be calm, be strong." Say this to yourself if you start to feel your emotions getting the best of you. Always keep in mind that you are doing the best you can and that is all anyone can expect from you.

Practice. Put together a script that you can use for common situations and use it with fellow librarians. If you say something enough times, eventually you'll be able to be calm no matter the situation. Practice does make perfect.

Trust yourself. Believe that you can deal with any situation, and you will be able to deal with any situation.

Tool 7: Be careful. When you approach an individual in your library to address an issue, always think about your own safety first. There are a lot of ways to deal with problem patrons in your library, but I use the old command we were taught when we were kids and learning to cross the street: Stop, look, and listen.

Stop. Before you talk to the individual with the problem, stop for a second when possible, take a deep breath, and collect your thoughts. Don't be frazzled before you even begin a conversation. If one of your library patrons is mentally ill, then the last thing she needs to deal with is an upset librarian. This will only amplify and exacerbate her issues. Rather, a calm, quiet, collected approach will be much more helpful.

Look. Assess the physical situation that you are entering. You never want to end up physically cornered, and you don't want to corner the individual with the problem. Make sure you know how you can get away and that there is an avenue of escape for the other person. Again, if you feel uncomfortable, trust your intuition. Keep a distance between you and the person you are addressing so you both feel more comfortable. When possible, take another staff member with you. I always ask my backup to stay in the background and remain unobtrusive so that the person with whom I am talking doesn't feel overwhelmed by attention.

Listen. Start by listening to the person with the problem. Don't formulate answers before the person is done talking. Really listen to what they are saying. Frequently, the fact that someone is truly listening and giving them time diffuses the anger of a lot of individuals, particularly the homeless and mentally ill. However, at the same time that you are listening to that person, listen to your own intuition and pay attention. Do you feel unsafe or uncomfortable in this person's presence? If so, there is probably a good reason even if you can't put your finger on it. Don't put yourself in a place (like an office) where you will be alone. If you feel like someone is about to explode and lose it, pay attention to that feeling. Get

9

the police involved. I always tell the staff at my library that if calling the police ever crosses their minds for a particular issue, then call the police. Their intuition is telling them something important.

Tool 8: Be able to laugh. Don't take the world, your job, or yourself too seriously. Whenever it is appropriate, I try to bring humor into difficult situations because I find it can do a tremendous amount to diffuse tension. I also find it is a wonderful way of getting past a problem that has occurred and been addressed. It is also tremendously helpful to be able to laugh at yourself when you are dealing with teens and young adults. However, be careful about using humor inappropriately. When someone is really upset or is having a mental health issue, he wants to be taken seriously, and if you attempt to diffuse the situation with humor, he may feel slighted. Gauge the situation carefully before bringing out the jokes.

Tool 9: Be thorough. When you are addressing a problem patron, be willing to invest the time necessary to identify the real issue. If the issue is not something you can personally address in the moment, you will have to tell the patron that you will talk to your manager about the problem and that either you or the manager will get back to the patron. If this is the situation, you will need to make sure you have all the correct facts in hand before discussing the issue with your manager. This is will ensure that an appropriate decision can be made.

Tool 10: Be finished. Sometimes you will have an issue with a regular library user. It may be someone having a bad day, or a student who is unhappy with a policy. In any case, it is someone you know and with whom you have regular interactions. Once you've dealt with whatever the issue is, be prepared to let it all go. Don't hold grudges and don't assume behavior on one day will predicate specific behavior on another day. Accept that the past is past and assume that in the future all interactions with that particular individual will be fine.

SOURCE: Elisabeth Doucett, *What They Don't Teach You in Library School* (Chicago: American Library Association, 2011), 53–59.

Make your library safer

by Warren Graham

NEVER, AND I MEAN NEVER, count money in view of patrons. Make up your deposits and balance the register or cash drawer before you open or after you close. Gone is the day you can run your library like Sam Drucker's general store in Hooterville (I'm really dating myself with that one). I've seen staff hurry in at five minutes before opening. They cut on the lights and maybe do a personal thing or two and open the doors to the public. Then they get out the cash and make sure it is counted properly, right in front of patrons. It looks like they are running some wheel of fortune game in Vegas. But that's okay, right? Because, after all, you've "never had a problem before."

You open with, say, only $50, so you think that doesn't offer a robber enough. Well, the robber doesn't know how much you have. All a thief sees is the green you are handling. People are hurt for much less, and $50 is a lot of money to a destitute person.

Whether you have money drawers or cash registers, make sure they stay locked when you are away from the circulation desk. Countless libraries are ripped off because there is no one at the desk and the drawer is not locked. If you are working up front and it's busy, it is acceptable to have it unlocked, but at any other time, lock up. And please, locking the drawer and leaving the key in the lock is not really securing it, is it?

Circulation staff can have a key to the drawer that they carry with them. Don't have a key at the front desk on a huge dowel marked "cash drawer" or "register." I would laugh along with you, but I have actually seen that one so much it's depressing.

Keep library keys with you at all times, and don't leave them lying around. Put them on one of those little coil gizmos that fits around your wrist or on a lanyard. Belt clips work too. If you have so many keys that they weigh you down, it is way past the time to rekey the building.

Be very careful in handling your deposits. There is no such thing as a night deposit. Always take money to the bank during regular business hours. Break up the times you go as best you can. Don't always go, for example, every Tuesday and Thursday at high noon.

I will never forget what I saw during a visit to the Midwest, when arriving at a library with my host. We saw the branch manager going across the lot with a bank bag with the bank's name clearly marked on the side. He waved at us with the bag and shouted from across the lot, "I didn't know you guys would be here so soon. I always go to the bank about one o'clock."

Never leave your pocketbook or briefcase where it can be seen by patrons. I know this can be inconvenient at times, but if you are ever ripped off, it makes for a dangerous environment because the thief now thinks your library is an easy mark, and he will return. And if you, a fellow employee, or a patron catch him in the act, he could assault someone. Always secure these items.

Staff areas should be locked at all times. Staff areas should be locked at all times. Staff areas should be locked at all times. No, this is not a misprint. Staff areas should be locked at all times. You never want to walk into back rooms or offices and find someone who is not supposed to be there.

Double-check all bathrooms, stacks, study rooms, and the rest of the public areas to make sure all patrons are out before you close. You do not want to be alone with some unknown individual after closing. If you think you might have trouble with someone at closing, call the police well before you start closing procedures so you won't be by yourself with the potential problem.

Never let anyone other than authorized library staff or service contractors into the building before opening or after closing. If you have not been advised that Billy Bob's Carpet Cleaning is coming, don't let them in. The same goes for the telephone guy here to "check the phone lines." He had better have some ID, and you had better ask him for it.

Working alone in the library building is one of the most dangerous things you can do. Take a look at scheduling to see if there is anything you can do to avoid being there by yourself. Maybe you can get a part-time page or ask for a volunteer to be there with you. When alone, keep your phone use and duties to an absolute minimum. The standard rule is: The less staff on hand, the more your awareness goes up. I know this is difficult, because you still have a library to operate, but pay as much attention to who is in the building and what they are doing as you possibly can.

9

Never admit to being alone to a patron you don't really know. If a patron asks you if you are by yourself, say something like, "No, Jeff is in the back, but he's also busy. One of us will be with you in a moment." Although such an inquiry is usually innocent, there is no point in exposing your vulnerability.

These points are the main short-term things you need to consider. I would bet that you recognize something in this list that you can change. Let me just warn you that old habits die hard, and some employees are often negative about changing their ways, even if it is for their own safety. And of the staff members who are already safety-minded, there are even fewer who will readily go along with new procedures if they are seemingly inconvenient to them. But as the saying goes, "The only thing that doesn't change is change," so it is part of staff members' jobs to adapt and help make the workplace safer for everyone.

SOURCE: Warren Graham, *The Black Belt Librarian: Real-World Safety and Security* (Chicago: American Library Association, 2012), 47–49.

ALA Code of Ethics

AS MEMBERS OF THE AMERICAN LIBRARY ASSOCIATION, we recognize the importance of codifying and making known to the profession and to the general public the ethical principles that guide the work of librarians, other professionals providing information services, library trustees, and library staffs.

Ethical dilemmas occur when values are in conflict. The American Library Association Code of Ethics states the values to which we are committed, and embodies the ethical responsibilities of the profession in this changing information environment.

We significantly influence or control the selection, organization, preservation, and dissemination of information. In a political system grounded in an informed citizenry, we are members of a profession explicitly committed to intellectual freedom and the freedom of access to information. We have a special obligation to ensure the free flow of information and ideas to present and future generations.

The principles of this code are expressed in broad statements to guide ethical decision making. These statements provide a framework; they cannot and do not dictate conduct to cover particular situations.

1. We provide the highest level of service to all library users through appropriate and usefully organized resources; equitable service policies; equitable access; and accurate, unbiased, and courteous responses to all requests.
2. We uphold the principles of intellectual freedom and resist all efforts to censor library resources.
3. We protect each library user's right to privacy and confidentiality with respect to information sought or received and resources consulted, borrowed, acquired, or transmitted.
4. We respect intellectual property rights and advocate balance between the interests of information users and rights holders.

5. We treat coworkers and other colleagues with respect, fairness, and good faith, and advocate conditions of employment that safeguard the rights and welfare of all employees of our institutions.
6. We do not advance private interests at the expense of library users, colleagues, or our employing institutions.
7. We distinguish between our personal convictions and professional duties and do not allow our personal beliefs to interfere with fair representation of the aims of our institutions or the provision of access to their information resources.
8. We strive for excellence in the profession by maintaining and enhancing our own knowledge and skills, by encouraging the professional development of coworkers, and by fostering the aspirations of potential members of the profession.

Adopted at the 1939 Midwinter Meeting by the ALA Council; amended June 30, 1981; June 28, 1995; and January 22, 2008.

SOURCE: Code of Ethics of the American Library Association, ala.org/advocacy/proethics/codeofethics/codeethics.

INFORMATION LITERACY

Defining moments in information literacy

by Monty L. McAdoo

STARTING WITH THE FIRST RECOGNIZED use of the term *information literacy*, the following list highlights some of the key moments in the evolution of the understanding and interpretation of IL.

Pre-1980s. Technology is seen primarily as a tool to complete tasks, especially within the workplace.

Post-1980s. Networked technologies enable anyone to create, store, and access information anywhere in the world, thereby expanding perceptions about computer technologies.

1974. Paul G. Zurkowski, president of the Information Industry Association, is credited with coining the term *information literacy* in a National Commission on Libraries and Information Science paper titled "The Information Service Environment: Relationships and Priorities" (ED100391).

1976. Lee G. Burchinal is among the first to link IL to emergent information technologies and networks in a paper presented at the Texas A&M University Library.

1979. Institute for Scientific Information President Eugene Garfield expands the definition beyond the workplace in "2001: An Information Society?" *Journal of Information Science: Principles and Practices* 1 (1979): 209–215.

1982. The microcomputer is chosen as Machine of the Year by *Time* magazine, focusing attention on using computers to accomplish tasks and perform specific functions.

9

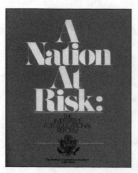

1983. *A Nation at Risk,* the report of President Ronald Reagan's National Commission on Excellence in Education, talks about information in education and the workplace in the knowledge society. Information consultant Forest Woody Horton discusses the distinction between computer literacy and information literacy in the *Bulletin of the American Society for Information Science,* laying the groundwork for modern definitions of information literacy.

1986. William Demo, librarian at Tompkins Cortland Community College in New York, discusses emergent communication technologies (such as email) and the fact that information is no longer the sole province of libraries and librarians (information literacy is important beyond the library).

The Carnegie Foundation Report on Colleges is one of a growing number of publications discussing concerns about graduating students' ability to succeed in the new age.

1987. A national symposium, "Libraries and the Search for Academic Excellence," is held in New York to discuss the role of academic libraries in the reform movement, pushing IL to the forefront of general education agenda.

1989. The ALA Presidential Committee on Information Literacy is formed to define IL, design a model, and determine implications; it provides a list of requisite skills (ala.org/acrl/publications/whitepapers/presidential) that have since become the foundation of most current understandings and definitions of IL.

The National Forum on Information Literacy (infolit.org) is formed to identify trends in information literacy and to bring various groups together.

The American Council on Education publishes *Information Literacy: Revolution in the Library* by Patricia Senn Breivik and E. Gordon Gee. It talks about the role of librarians in the teaching and learning process (particularly with respect to information literacy) and observes that the education of information-literate graduates is a joint responsibility to be shared by everyone—librarians, faculty, and administrators alike.

1990. The Secretary of Labor's Commission on Achieving Necessary Skills (SCANS) is formed to study the skills that contemporary workers need to succeed; its 1991 report closely parallels the final report of ALA's Presidential Committee on Information Literacy.

Mike Eisenberg and Bob Berkowitz develop the Big6 Skills Model (www.big6.com), a process model of IL that focuses on how people solve information problems.

1992. Christina S. Doyle expands the definition of IL (ERIC Document 351033) based on responses from more than 100 librarians and other information professionals noted for their work in or contributions to IL.

1997. Christine Bruce publishes *The Seven Faces of Information Literacy* (Auslib Press), which presents a relational model of IL that acknowledges individual interpretations of what is meant by the term; her model not only articulates seven characterizations of IL but also examines how individuals relate to information itself.

Pre-2000. The trend emerges of interpreting IL as an inclusive term that encompasses other literacies (business, computer, health).

2000 to present. The ALA definition of IL evolves into a series of standards that are subsequently reviewed and approved by the ACRL board of directors on January 1, 2000 (ala.org/acrl/standards/informationliteracycompetency).

In 2002, the Educational Testing Service convenes the International Information and Communication Technology (ICT) Literacy Panel to better understand and assess IL, to better understand how people think about information while using technology (especially when communicating information), and to address perceived shortcomings of existing IL models and definitions. It articulates seven proficiencies and descriptions as part of its ICT literacy model.

SOURCE: Monty L. McAdoo, *Building Bridges: Connecting Faculty, Students, and the College Library* (Chicago: American Library Association, 2010), 143–145.

Library instruction in a postmodern world

by Elizabeth M. Williams

POSTMODERNISM IN RELATION TO LIBRARIES and library instruction is a topic of interest. Melody Burton (right), in a 1995 article in *The Reference Librarian*, discusses the barriers that libraries impose on student research and proposes an instructional method that uses critical pedagogy, and an active learning and teaching method to empower the researcher. She suggests that the traditional research path has changed; description and interpretation are more difficult for the postmodern student. Reality to them is subjective, and knowledge is no longer the prerogative of the teacher, as

Melody Burton

there can be more than one answer to a research question. Accuracy and authenticity of texts can be questionable because textual sources can be customized. First editions online can have no resemblance to the print item. Burton felt compelled by the information explosion and the reality of postmodern students to revise her instruction to include more active classroom strategies.

Robert H. Kieft offers some rules or assumptions for librarians:

- Students do not want to learn how to use a library. They want to get their work done.
- Librarians are not in the business of teaching students how to use a library. Rather, they are in the business of teaching them how to think critically about research problems and papers.
- Students have difficulty abstracting from experience with one research project to others.
- Students tend to cast all their relationships in the mode of social relationships. What adults think of as working relationships (responsibility, accountability) are mostly foreign to them.
- Students do not receive enough, let alone systematic, instruction in information literacy to go about doing the work assigned to them. Very little in US culture does much to encourage them to seek such training.
- Academic librarians are not nor have they ever been major players in the information game. Most people find what they want or what they are willing to settle for without the direct intervention of most of the people who work in libraries.

Kieft suggests that librarians are in the education business, not the information business: "Librarians should look to functions other than those of gathering, stor-

9

ing, or delivering information as their true functions." As educators, they should be achieving other goals. They should be more interested in "enhancing human capacity" than in providing students with information or technological skills.

Taylor Hubbard agrees. He advocates focusing on educating about knowledge rather than how to find information. In a 1995 article in *Library Trends* he suggests that libraries should be learning laboratories to study information in the context of the literature of an academic discipline, making the process a discovery experience, not information-gathering. To do this effectively, library instruction should be integrated into the curriculum. We keep track of our gate-counts and the number of books circulated, but when asked how these numbers support the academic disciplines, we have no evidence.

Hubbard sees the internet as the working model of postmodernism, demolishing physical and textural dimensions: "If all knowledge is local, should not our instructional focus be on those who create it rather than the subsequent acts of other who publish, collect, and organize it?" Our traditional bibliographic instruction is modernistic: We legitimize our organized collections and discourage students from questioning the authority of established literary works. Students should be encouraged to be conscious of the role they play in information creation, for knowing about knowledge implies knowing how and why it is created and used.

Teaching the postmodern student

What, then, can we offer postmodern students? We can show them the easiest and quickest ways to get to the best resources. We know how to do that. We can help them develop their ideas and point out that the subjects they are researching have most certainly been written about before, that their dilemmas are the themes of great literature. Thomas Hardy's Tess was at the mercy of nature and fate. The brothers Karamazov were psychological case studies. Hamlet, after all, was the quintessential postmodernist, questioning everything.

In the introductory classes we can concentrate on the basics: researching one topic for one assignment. First-year students need to be guided in the right direction. That is about all that can be absorbed. When students have chosen majors and have settled into a discipline, we can collaborate with departmental faculty to teach them the best resources for literature, linguistics, or literary theory—online and in print. Even more importantly, we can teach them how their discipline interacts with others, such as science in literature, psychology in literature, education in literature, and so on. We can encourage English departments to include advanced information literacy instruction in their curriculum and give them reasons why they should.

Postmodern students like to see the connection, the reason for what they are doing. Partnering with faculty helps make that connection between library instruction and classroom teaching. We should be maximizing the library's role in their lives—in college and out. Catherine Lee makes suggestions for the design of instruction sessions, which include presenting short sessions using hands-on, active learning, and using their skills and interest in technology. Focus on an assignment they are working on, so they will know they can use what they are learning. We should try to stimulate and entertain them and encourage questions and comments. We need to keep handouts to a minimum, as students think paper guides are dull. Making a web page for their class is helpful, if appropriate, and we should show them library electronic subject guides.

Teaching with technology

Articles about teaching with technology are helpful to those trying to reach computer-dependent students. Educause (www.educause.edu) provides excellent information on "transforming education through information technologies," including numerous resources for working with Millennials and technology. In a 1997 article, Brent Wilson discusses both postmodernism versus modernism and instructional theory versus practice of design. He provides a set of useful guidelines for postmodern instructional design:

- Be willing to break the rules.
- Place principles above procedures, and people above principles.
- Allow instruction and learning goals to emerge during instruction.
- Don't sacrifice educational goals for technical training.
- Emphasize problem solving.
- Present content in multiple ways to accommodate different learning styles.
- Appreciate the value-ladenness of all analysis.
- Distinguish between instructional goals and learners' goals; support learners in pursuing their own goals.
- Think of instruction as providing tools that teachers and students can use for learning; make these tools user-friendly.
- Consider strategies that provide multiple perspectives that encourage the learner to exercise responsibility.
- Allow for the teaching moment.

Wilson also suggests that assessment should be incorporated into the learning experience and that informal assessments such as observing student reaction can be useful.

In his preface to the *Literary Text in the Digital Age* (1996), Richard Finneran discusses the revolution resulting from the access that computers can give to the study, creation, and preservation of literary texts. Although electronic texts can never replace the printed word, there is no denying the future, and there is much to gain from embracing the new technology: "If the achievement that we have come to value is to remain a viable part of our cultural inheritance, it needs to be made accessible to future generations in the form that they will understand as the standard way of interacting with 'monuments of magnificence.'"

SOURCE: Elizabeth M. Williams, "The Printing Press and the Web: Modernists Teaching Postmodernists," in Kathleen A. Johnson and Steven R. Harris, *Teaching Literary Research: Challenges in a Changing Environment* (Chicago: ALA Association of College and Research Libraries, 2009), 66–74.

Visual literacy competency
by the ALA Association of College and Research Libraries

9

VISUAL LITERACY IS A SET OF ABILITIES that enables an individual to effectively find, interpret, evaluate, use, and create images and visual media. Visual literacy skills equip a learner to understand and analyze the contextual, cultural, ethical, aesthetic, intellectual, and technical components involved in the production and use of visual materials. A visually literate individual is both a critical consumer of visual media and a competent contributor to a body of shared knowledge and culture.

The Visual Literacy Competency Standards for Higher Education were adopted by the Association of College and Research Libraries in 2011. Standard 3 is reprinted here. For the full set of standards, visit the ACRL website.

Visual literacy competency standard 3. The visually literate student interprets and analyzes the meanings of images and visual media. Performance indicators:

The visually literate student identifies information relevant to an image's meaning:

- Looks carefully at an image and observes content and physical details.
- Reads captions, metadata, and accompanying text to learn about an image.
- Identifies the subject of an image.
- Examines the relationships of images to each other and uses related images to inform interpretation.
- Recognizes when more information about an image is needed, develops questions for further research, and conducts additional research as appropriate.

The visually literate student situates an image in its cultural, social, and historical contexts:

- Describes cultural and historical factors relevant to the production of an image (time period, geography, economic conditions, political structures, social practices).
- Examines the purposes and meanings of an image in its original context.
- Explores choices made in the production of an image to construct meaning or influence interpretation (framing, composition, included or excluded elements, staging).
- Describes the intended audience for an image.
- Explores representations of gender, ethnicity, and other cultural or social identifiers in images.
- Investigates how the audience, context, and interpretation of an image may have changed over time.

The visually literate student identifies the physical, technical, and design components of an image:

- Describes pictorial, graphic, and aesthetic elements of an image (color, composition, line, shape, contrast, repetition, style).
- Identifies techniques, technologies, or materials used in the production of an image.
- Determines whether an image is an original or a reproduction.
- Examines an image for signs of editing, alteration, or manipulation (cropping, color correction, image enhancements).

The visually literate student validates interpretation and analysis of images through discourse with others:

- Participates in classroom and other discussions about images.
- Seeks expert and scholarly opinion about images, including information and analysis found in reference sources and scholarly publications.
- Informs analysis with discipline-specific perspectives and approaches.

SOURCE: Visual Literacy Competency Standards for Higher Education (Chicago: ALA Association of College and Research Libraries, October 2011), ala.org/acrl/standards/visualliteracy.

LIBRARIANA

CHAPTER TEN

The dispositions of mind displayed by these librarians
are wide as the poles asunder. Some of them babble
like babies, others are evidently austere scholars; some
are gravely bent on the best methods of classifying
catalogues, economizing space, and sorting borrowers'
cards; others, scorning such mechanical details, bid
us regard libraries, and consequently librarians, as the
primary factors in human evolution.

—Augustine Birrell, "Librarians at Play,"
In the Name of the Bodleian and Other Essays (London, 1906)

WORDS

25 library quotes

1. "A librarian should be as unwilling to allow an inquirer to leave the library with his question unanswered as a shop-keeper is to have a customer go out of his store without making a purchase."—Samuel Swett Green, "Personal Relations Between Librarians and Readers," *Library Journal* 1, no. 2 (Sept. 1876): 74–81.

2. "To the librarian himself one may say: Be punctual; be attentive; help develop enthusiasm in your assistants; be neat and consistent in your manner. Be careful in your contracts; be square with your board; be concise and technical; be accurate; be courageous and self-reliant; be careful about acknowledgments; be not worshipful of your work; be careful of your health. Last of all, be yourself."—John Cotton Dana (right), *The Library Primer* (New York: Library Bureau, 1899), 22.

3. "What an opportunity presents itself for some millionaire citizen to come forward with one of his useless, embarrassing, and retarding millions and link his name forever with this great community."—Andrew Carnegie, on investing $5.2 million into the New York Public Library, *New York Times,* March 17, 1901.

4. "The librarian must have all of the qualifications of a good routine worker: quickness, accuracy, and neatness. Even the girl who can never become more than a thoroughly reliable routine worker will find here an unusually pleasant workroom, good associates, and reasonable pay; and her services will be in demand more and more as the work of the library becomes more completely specialized."—Eli Witwer Weaver, "Librarianship," *Profitable Vocations for Girls* (New York: A. S. Barnes, 1915), 138.

5. "If most people were asked what qualifications are necessary for a librarian, probably most of them would say a soft voice with which to say 'Shhh.'"—Priscilla Hendryx, *Pittsburgh (Pa.) Post-Gazette,* September 15, 1948.

6. "In early days, I tried not to give librarians any trouble, which was where I made my primary mistake. Librarians like to be given trouble; they exist for it, they are geared to it. For the location of a mislaid volume, an uncatalogued item, your good librarian has a ferret's nose. Give her a scent and she jumps the leash, her eye bright with battle."—Catherine Drinke Bowen, "Salute to Librarians," Chapter 9 of *Adventures of a Biographer* (Boston: Little, Brown, 1959).

7. "How *dare* you and the rest of your barbarians set fire to my library? Play conqueror all you want, Mighty Caesar! Rape, murder, pillage thousands, even millions of human beings! But neither you nor any

other barbarian has the right to destroy one human thought!"—Elizabeth Taylor (Cleopatra) castigating Rex Harrison (Julius Caesar) for torching the Library of Alexandria, in the movie *Cleopatra* (1963).

8. "A library is a good place to go when you feel unhappy, for there, in a book, you may find encouragement and comfort. A library is a good place to go when you feel bewildered or undecided, for there, in a book, you may have your question answered. Books are good company, in sad times and happy times, for books are people—people who have managed to stay alive by hiding between the covers of a book."—E. B. White, in a letter to the children of Troy, Michigan, on the benefits of a library, April 14, 1971.

9. "[The library is] one of the very few institutions on earth where any soul may walk through its doors free, and depart enriched."—Diane Asséo Griliches, *Library: The Drama Within* (Albuquerque: University of New Mexico, 1996), vii.

10. "If there is a heaven . . . I'd want a big library. The biggest library you've ever seen. One that's opened all the time, not just half days. That's what I hope heaven's like."—Cassandra King (right), *Making Waves* (New York: Hyperion, 2004), 93.

11. "If television's a babysitter, the internet's a drunk librarian who won't shut up."—Dorothy Gambrill, Cat and Girl cartoon, August 26, 2005.

12. "The Library of Doom is dark. The stairways are silent. Cobwebs hang across the doors. The Library's gardens are filled with weeds and creeping vines. Floors are covered with broken glass. Somewhere, boots crunch on the broken glass. A shadow walks through the hallways. It is the Librarian."—Michael Dahl, *The Beast Beneath the Stairs* (Minneapolis: Stone Arch Books, 2007), 5–6.

13. "If anything could dampen the excitement of going on a treasure hunt, it was having to do it with the town librarian."—Eric Berlin, *The Puzzling World of Winston Breen* (New York: G. P. Putnam's Sons, 2007), 86.

14. "Now you may have gotten the impression that there are absolutely no uses for Librarians. I'm sorry if I implied that. Librarians are very useful. For instance, they are useful if you are fishing for sharks and need some bait. They're also useful for throwing out windows to test the effects of concrete impact on horn-rimmed glasses. If you have enough Librarians, you can build bridges out of them. (Just like witches.) And, unfortunately, they are *also* useful for organizing things."—Brandon Sanderson, *Alcatraz Versus the Knights of Crystalia* (New York: Scholastic, 2009), 187.

15. "You can take the girl out of the library, but you can't take the neurotic, compulsively curious librarian out of the girl."—Molly Harper, *Nice Girls Don't Have Fangs* (New York: Pocket Star, 2009), 118.

16. "Pimps make the best librarians."—Avi Steinberg, first line of *Running the Books: The Adventures of an Accidental Prison Librarian* (New York: Nan A. Talese, 2010).

17. "You're pretty cocky for someone whose job is obsolete because of the internet."—Amy Poehler as *Parks and Recreation* Deputy Director Leslie Knope, responding to a Pawnee (Ind.) Public Library staffer's wisecrack, February 4, 2010.

10

18. "How do you tell when the person addressing a group of librarians is not a librarian? Easy. He or she will, as surely as day follows night, make a reference to the Library of Alexandria." —Stephen Ramsey, associate professor of English at the University of Nebraska–Lincoln, October 8, 2010.

19. "Hey, times are tough, especially when your mansion isn't worth what it once was. But before fighting taxes became the only American principle that mattered, all kinds of people, wealthy and not, recognized the public library as one of the inspiring ideas that makes us American."—Laura Berman, columnist, *Detroit Times,* October 23, 2010.

20. "Fredo, you're my older brother, and I love you. But don't ever take sides with anyone against the library again. Ever."—@LibrarianJP, #jerseylibrarians hashtag on Twitter, February 17–18, 2011.

21. "Closing libraries is the behaviour of a debased culture. Libraries are not just a source of books. Many of us feel that they symbolise something more, that Britain is a civilised place. And when part of our civilisation is being destroyed, we have to stand up against the barbarians."—Philip Pullman, author of the His Dark Materials trilogy, on efforts by British councils to close their libraries, *Daily Telegraph,* July 20, 2011.

22. "The internet is an accumulation; a library is order. I have nothing against the electronic library, it's just not a replacement for the library of ink and paper."—Alberto Manguel, Argentine-born Canadian writer, *Ottawa (Ont.) Citizen,* November 20, 2011.

23. "The library, to me, is the second most sacred physical space on the planet."—Nikky Finney, winner of the 2012 National Book Award for poetry, March 22, 2012.

24. "I was raised by librarians. It's like being raised by wolves, but wilder."—Dan Yashinsky, founder of the Toronto Festival of Storytelling, *Toronto Globe and Mail,* May 21, 2012.

25. "I do this for the money, prestige, and power. Said no librarian ever."—Bobbi Newman, someecards.com, June 30, 2012.

I'm tired of LOL

by Will Manley

I'M TIRED OF LOL, LMAO, WTF.
It's time for some new internet lingo. Here are my nominees:
YYY...Yada, yada, yada.
RUOOYFM...Are you out of your freaking mind?
TYGA...There you go again.
HSDUTIM...How stupid do you think I am?
VVV...Vini, vidi, vici.
RUN...Are you nuts?
IIABDFI...If it ain't broke don't fix it.
ICRS...I can't remember shit.
OMDB...Over my dead body.
MTRRTMU...May the road rise to meet you.
WPONDYU....What part of no don't you understand?

ARWTW…All's right with the world.
WADITW…We've always done it this way.
MCCBUYMDS…My cataloger can beat up your metadata specialist.
YTS….Your timing sucks.
BRHMF…Boat rockers have more fun.
DBMUWTABB…Don't beat me up with the aluminum baseball bat.

SOURCE: Will Manley, "Tired of LOL," Will Unwound, June 3, 2011.

BOOKS

Famous librarians' favorite books

WHAT DO PROMINENT LIBRARIANS have to say about their favorite books? In previous editions of *The Whole Library Handbook*, library leaders have identified the publications that have given them great enjoyment or have significantly affected their professional or personal lives and philosophies. This edition adds the fond favorites of nine new individuals to the reading list. I defined the term "book" as loosely as possible, to allow them to select anything from ancient codices to magazines, websites, or databases.—*GME*.

STEVEN J. BELL, associate university librarian for research and instruction, Temple University, Philadelphia: "My reading interests could be described as having gone through three stages (up to now). First, great books read in college. Second, post-college discoveries in leisure reading. Three, career-oriented reading."
College reading:
1. Joseph Heller, *Catch-22* (1961). On the first reading, it's a war novel. After multiple readings, it's the quintessential story of the basic human struggle to survive overwhelming conditions. I've read this book again and again, and there are new insights each time—and the stories never grow dull. This is what great novels are supposed to be.
2. Ken Kesey, *One Flew over the Cuckoo's Nest* (1962). Who doesn't wish they were Randle Patrick McMurphy, being a rebel and fighting the system? Beyond all the symbolism (RPM, Nurse Ratched/rachet, etc.), it's a good reminder to stand up for yourself and that life is about living.
3. James T. Farrell, *Studs Lonigan* (the trilogy, 1932–1935). This book opened me up to another world. Beyond just enjoying the stories and situations into which Studs got himself, it impressed upon me, at an early age, the importance of doing more than just drifting through life—and not just growing older but growing up.
Post-college reading:
4. Dashiell Hammett, *The Continental Op* (1945). I discovered this on the leisure reading shelf of the library where I was attending my library science program. I guess after years of mostly academic reading I was taken by the sheer grittiness of Hammett's pulp fiction. It wasn't so much that I liked mystery fiction, I just like the characters, situations, and dialogue.

10

5. John D. MacDonald, *Bright Orange for the Shroud* (1965). The Travis Mc-Gee novels are the only other mystery/detective books I've read—and I've read all of them, all the colors. McGee is a great character, and all the stories are fun reading. It's hard to pick one. I guess this one is my favorite because it's among the grittiest of them, McGee has a worthy opponent and it has all the elements of a great McGee novel. If I had three wishes, I'd use one of them to ask for one more Travis McGee novel.

6. Dr. Seuss, *Thidwick the Big-Hearted Moose* (1948). Any parent goes through those years where it seems the only books you read are of the children's variety. In my house Dr. Seuss ruled. Of all the ones I read (out loud), Thidwick was always my favorite. It was great getting to the part where the antlers fall off. Dr. Seuss came up with a great escape clause that allowed the moose to solve his problem without really confronting it. Sometimes, not often, life just works out that way.

Contemporary career reading:

7. Tom Kelley, *The Art of Innovation: Lessons in Creativity from IDEO, America's Leading Design Firm* (2001). When I first started getting interested in design, this is the first book I read that really made a difference for me. It tremendously impacted my work as I developed a passion for learning about design thinking, innovation, and creativity. It has influenced my professional work over the last few years, as evidenced by my practice, writing, and presentations.

8. Dan Heath and Chip Heath, *Made to Stick: Why Some Ideas Survive and Others Die* (2007), and Dan Roam, *The Back of the Napkin: Solving Problems and Selling Ideas with Pictures* (2008). I'm counting these two books as one because both have influenced and improved my thinking about how to communicate ideas. *Made to Stick* emphasizes the importance of creating messages with which audiences can emotionally connect and the importance of creating compelling stories. *The Back of the Napkin* encouraged me to take risks with visual communication techniques. When I craft messages based on the lessons of these books they sometimes fail, but I believe they are always challenging me to be unique and different. I think that is more important than succeeding with what everyone else is doing.

9. Simon Sinek, *Start with Why: How Great Leaders Inspire Everyone to Take Action* (2009). Reading about leadership consumes a fair amount of my time. I'm always looking for ideas to help me improve. I'm still contemplating this book, but Sinek's Golden Circle framework is so simple yet complex and it intrigues me. Of course you have to understand the "why" behind your motivations. Yet it's much harder than it sounds. Leaders who achieve it are inspirational.

10. George D. Kuh and Elizabeth J. Whitt, *Invisible Tapestry: Culture in American Colleges and Universities* (1988). I'd be remiss if I failed to include at least one higher education reading on this list. I've read many of the great books on higher education, but this one rises to the top for me because it helps you to understand the importance of culture at our institutions. It communicates the necessity of working within the culture to create change. Those who miss this lesson are doomed to failure.

RICHARD M. DOUGHERTY, president of Dougherty & Associates, who served as ALA president in 1990–1991.

1. Ayn Rand, *The Fountainhead* (1943). This the first book that made a lasting impression on me. I read it twice and I'm sure that Howard Roark's refusal to

compromise his principles influenced me in later life. I tried Rand's *Atlas Shrugged* (1957), but I never finished it.

2. Allen Drury's *Advise and Consent* (1959) was another book that influenced me early on. Although Drury was a conservative, he told a fascinating story. As a result, I became much more interested in the machinations of politics. An understanding of politics became particularly valuable as I became involved more deeply in academic politics.

3. Warren Bennis's *Managing People Is Like Herding Cats* (1999) also influenced my thinking about library management. Leadership became one of my core professional interests. It bothers me that too few librarians are willing to take risks in the exercise of leadership.

4. James Clavell's *Shōgun* (1975) was another title that influenced my thinking. It was an epic tale that made me realize how important it was to compartmentalize conflict. Lawyers traditionally have been good at such compartmentalization, whereas we as librarians, along with many other academics, get personal when conflict arises.

5. The last 10 years of my professional life were dominated by my interest in change management. Again it was the influence of people rather than books that sparked my interest and enthusiasm. However, a book written by Lawrence L. Lippitt titled *Preferred Futuring* (1998) helped to shape my thinking.

6. The book I wish I had written is *Our Iceberg Is Melting* (2006) by John Kotter. To use penguins to explain the hows and whys of organizational change was a stroke of genius. It is better than Spencer Johnson's *Who Moved My Cheese?* (1998). That is saying something, because Johnson's book was a great hit.

7. Over the years I particularly enjoyed Bruce Catton's books about the Civil War. I read all of them.

8. Herman Wouk's *The Caine Mutiny* (1951), *The Winds of War* (1971), and its companion volume *War and Remembrance* (1978) are three of my favorites.

9. If reading a book twice is a measure, then James Jones's *From Here to Eternity* (1951) ranks high on my list.

10. Finally, one recent title made a big impression on me was *The Help* (2009) by Kathryn Stockett. Her moving tale of life among black housemaids in Jackson, Mississippi, brought back memories of my own childhood as I was raised in part by a black woman, Elmina Talbert. Elmina became an important part of our family, because both of my parents had to work full-time throughout World War II.

GEORGE M. EBERHART, editor of *American Libraries Direct*.

1. Charles Fort, *The Books of Charles Fort* (1940). I learned about critical thinking, intellectual freedom, and research skills from this bulky tome, which I purchased in high school. Fort's nimble skewering of the positivist 19th- and early 20th-century debunking of scientific anomalies was instructive, as were his alternative hypotheses, which had to be taken with a large grain of salt. My father secretly took the book from me and asked a local Catholic priest (ironically, his name was Fr. Fortkamp) whether it was safe for me to read, since Fort was described on the dust jacket as "iconoclastic" (think Eastern Orthodox icons). When it came back with a cautious approval, my uncle recommended that I check all the author's sources, which I proceeded to do at the Ohio State University libraries, nearly every Saturday in my junior and senior years. I drew from the experience a B.S.-equivalent degree (interpret the abbreviation any way you want) in

alternative science and history that has kept me both open-minded and healthily skeptical ever since.

2. Ambrose Bierce, *Collected Works* (1909). The aforementioned Fr. Fortkamp was my Latin teacher in high school, and every Friday, instead of reading Caesar's *Gallic Wars*, he would introduce us to literary works that were not part of our English curriculum. He called it "culture hour." One week he read Bierce's sardonic short story "Oil of Dog" (1911). This prompted me to explore everything Bierce had ever written, including *The Devil's Dictionary* (1911), his poetry, and Civil War stories. Bierce's satire as a newspaper columnist in San Francisco is best reported in Ernest Jerome Hopkins's *The Ambrose Bierce Satanic Reader* (1968), which recounts his triumph in 1897 over the Central Pacific Railroad "robber barons" who were attempting to delay for another 80 years their debt obligations to the US treasury. This ultimately led me to decide on a journalism major in college.

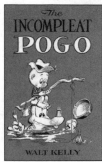

3. Walt Kelly, *Pogo* (comic strip, 1948–1975). One of my earliest memories is of my father reading to me from Dr. Seuss books and the book-length compilations of the daily *Pogo* comic, particularly *The Incompleat Pogo* (1954). Kelly's politics were liberal, and the denizens of the Okefenokee Swamp (Pogo Possum, Albert Alligator, "Churchy" La Femme the mud turtle) reflected the opinions of the Common Man (in pseudo-Southern "swamp speak" dialect) versus the 1950s collectivist Organization Man and the military-industrial complex that Eisenhower warned us about. Not only did Kelly identify the dangers of McCarthyism, gimmicky and intrusive marketing schemes, and environmental deterioration ("We have met the enemy and he is us"), the books were funny! Albert: "I is maintainin' an aloof, noble, dignified, kindly, courteous, wounded, and secret silence as a gentle reproof to the management, which is a goggle-eyed, knock-kneed burglar and bum" (*G.O. Fizzickle Pogo*, 1958).

4. Marcello Craveri's *The Life of Jesus* (1966) gave me the historical and philosophical background necessary to reject traditional Christianity and instead see Jesus of Nazareth as an "individual born into a clearly defined society at a clearly defined point in history, and ... to understand his life, his ideas, his behavior as the product of a particular culture and unique historical circumstances."

5. Mika Waltari's *The Egyptian* (1945) opened a window into ancient history at a time when I was struggling with typical problems of youthful rebellion and political and religious beliefs. The backdrop of Egypt's New Kingdom provided me with insights into the follies of war, the malaise of monotheism, the manipulations of sexuality, the ambiguities of idealism, and the corruption of power that remain relevant today.

6. *Fate* magazine (1948–   ). I bought my first issue of this treasure trove of "true stories of the strange and unknown" in December 1963 and have been a subscriber ever since. With articles titled "The Great Sky Procession of 1913" (a famous meteor procession), "The Dutch Put Psi to Work" (the research of Dutch parapsychologist Wilhelm H. C. Tenhaeff), "Ghosts That Pursued a Ship" (the supposed photo of two dead sailors taken on the oil tanker *SS Watertown* in 1925, now seen as a probable hoax), "Dowsing in Swampscott, Mass." (when the town discovered a lost water supply in 1962 through divining rods), "The Cursed Poltergeist of Baldoon, Ontario" (a "noisy ghost" case of 1829–1831 that took place near modern Wallaceburg and featured outbreaks of fire, phantom footsteps, and stone-throwing), and "Taped Voices of the Dead" (the 1959 tape recordings of

mysterious voices by Swedish artist Friedrich Jürgenson), I became instantly hooked. Now eclipsed by the much more rigorous, whimsical, and skeptical British magazine *Fortean Times, Fate* still adheres to its original winning formula of psychics, saucers, and sasquatch stories.

7. Bernard Heuvelmans, *On the Track of Unknown Animals* (1958). This was the first book on cryptozoology I ever read, which led to a life-long interest in yetis, surviving African dinosaurs, Australian bunyips, and even stranger crypto-fauna. The topic desperately needed a field guide, which I finally wrote in 2002 as *Mysterious Creatures: A Guide to Cryptozoology.*

8. Wikipedia (2001–   ). I can't imagine reading another book, especially nonfiction, without having this comprehensive people's encyclopedia on hand to identify obscure references, locate photos of people and places, plumb the unknown depths of popular culture, and uncover the many details that authors omit from their novels and histories.

NANCY EVERHART, former president of the American Association of School Librarians and associate professor at the Florida State University School of Library and Information Studies.

1. John Irving, *The World According to Garp* (1978). My introduction to Irving was with this work that draws you in and wraps around you with stories within stories within stories. A close second is *The Cider House Rules* (1985). As a librarian, I don't purchase a lot of books, but I have owned all of Irving's works.

2. Pat Conroy, *The Prince of Tides* (1986). Conroy is another excellent storyteller whom I enjoy immensely. His works are tinged with a bit of pain, often based on his difficult childhood, and always in Southern settings.

3. Loretta Lynn, *Coal Miner's Daughter* (1976). This honest portrayal of Lynn's life is great reading and it resonates with me, having grown up in the coal regions of Pennsylvania and marrying young.

4. Steven Levy, *Insanely Great: The Life and Times of Macintosh, the Computer That Changed Everything* (1994). Reading about the history of the Apple computer is totally fascinating to me, as are any biographies of visionaries.

5. Astrid Lindgren, *Pippi Longstocking* (1945). Pippi was the first liberated woman!

6. Carolyn Keene (pseud.), Nancy Drew Mystery Stories (1930–2003). I read *The Secret of the Old Clock* (1930) in fourth grade and could not get enough of Nancy Drew for many years to come.

LOIDA GARCIA-FEBO, international librarian, consultant, and president of Information New Wave in Brooklyn, New York.

1. Louisa May Alcott, *Little Women* (1868–1869). I read this book in elementary school and since then it has been one of my all-time favorites. I thought Jo was such a spectacular example of a strong woman determined to write her own story against all odds.

2. Sherman Alexie, *The Lone Ranger and Tonto Fistfight in Heaven* (1993). I couldn't stop reading this book. Its short stories showed me a meaningful insight into the varied experiences of indigenous people. This story was turned into a movie that I also watched, *Smoke Signals.*

3. Gabriel García-Márquez, *Love in the Time of Cholera (El amor en los tiempos del cólera)* (1985). This is the ultimate magical realism novel. I have read many of García-Márquez's works, but this one is special. It narrates Florentino and Fer-

10

mina's love story spanning 53 years of distance, letters, and waiting time. Impossible love to the max!

4. Rómulo Gallegos, *Doña Bárbara* (1929). Doña Bárbara knows what she wants and how to obtain it. She is one of the most beloved women in Latin American literature. She is probably my favorite.

5. Jhumpa Lahiri, *The Namesake* (2003). I loved the beautiful way Lahiri portrayed the deep conflicting layers of the lives of those with links in two cultures, traditions, and religions.

6. Nelson Mandela, *Long Walk to Freedom* (1994). This is the most powerful memoir I have ever read. It is 751 pages of pure heart, courage, and passion.

7. Jorge Ramos, *The Other Face of America: Chronicles of the Immigrants Shaping Our Future (La otra cara de América)* (2002). Ramos, a renowned journalist for Univision News, put into words many sentiments experienced by Latino Americans.

8. Rory Stewart, *The Places in Between* (2006). I was impressed by this insightful memoir of a man who walked across Afghanistan, dealt with hectic conditions at various levels, and acquired high regional responsibilities, all before turning 30. Hats off to Rory for taking time to share his adventure.

9. Mario Vargas Llosa, *Aunt Julia and the Scriptwriter (La tía Julia y el escribidor)* (1977). I devoured this novel that includes many autobiographical sketches from Vargas Llosa. The Nobel Prize–winner captivates with his writing technique.

LORI GOETSCH, dean of libraries at Kansas State University in Manhattan.

1. Mary Field Belenky, Blythe McVicker Clinchy, Nancy Rule Goldberger, and Jill Mattuck Tarulet, *Women's Ways of Knowing* (1986). This book opened my eyes and mind to how women receive and communicate knowledge through our own lenses and voices.

2. Gabriel García-Márquez, *One Hundred Years of Solitude (Cien años de soledad)* (1967). I read this book in college and have reread it more than once since then. I love its epic nature, multiple points of view, and magical realism.

3. George Eliot, *Middlemarch* (1874). I wrote my master's thesis on this novel, so it has a soft spot in my heart—great Victorian characters and storytelling. For those who were forced to read *Silas Marner*, this is Eliot at her best. Give it a chance!

4. Jane Austen, *Pride and Prejudice* (1813). What's not to love about this wonderful story with its lively characters and plot twists? It transcends its time period and remains a favorite of so many readers.

5. Michael Chabon, *The Amazing Adventures of Kavalier and Clay* (2000). I devoured this book! I was immediately drawn into the lives of the characters as immigrants, as comic book creators, and as flawed superheroes in their own right.

6. J. K. Rowling, the Harry Potter series (1997–2007). While I love the magical nature and classic themes of the Potter books, I think I enjoyed them most as coming-of-age stories.

7. Suzanne Collins, *The Hunger Games* trilogy (2008–2010). This series is strong stuff for the young adult reader but offers a thought-provoking, dystopian view that takes reality television to a frightening level.

8. Margaret Atwood, *The Handmaid's Tale* (1985). Another dystopian world, particularly for women, is presented in this wonderful story that, as with the Collins trilogy, can seem just plausible enough to give me chills each time I read it.

JASON GRIFFEY, head of library information technology at the University of Tennessee at Chattanooga.

1. William Gibson, The Sprawl Trilogy: *Neuromancer* (1984), *Count Zero* (1986), and *Mona Lisa Overdrive* (1988). Reading *Neuromancer* the first time was like the first time I tasted curry, or the first time I saw a Piet Mondrian painting. I wasn't sure at all what to think, but I knew that nothing was ever really going to be the same.

2. E. E. Cummings, *is 5* (1926). A set of poems that showed me what power words can have when treated sparsely and uniquely.

3. Neal Gaiman, *The Sandman* (1989–1996) redefined what a comic book could be and created a robust mythology that spoke directly to its time. Gaiman has become famous for his novels by now, and he wrote other comics, but this is the one that made him famous—and for a very good reason.

4. Michael Ende, *The Neverending Story* (*Die unendliche Geschichte: Von A bis Z*) (1979). The book that introduced me to metafiction, although I wouldn't understand the term for another decade. For a young, nerdy, somewhat awkward eight-year-old boy, this was exactly the right book to give me permission to dream.

5. Douglas Adams, *The Hitchhiker's Guide to the Galaxy* (1979). This is the book that showed me that humor and great books aren't incompatible.

6. Laozi, *Tao Te Ching* (6th century B.C.). This taught me to be calm, to be thoughtful, to be the water and not the stone. A beautiful book in so many ways, and a revelation after my childhood in eastern Kentucky.

7. Dave Eggers, *A Heartbreaking Work of Staggering Genius* (2000). I wish that I could say that the title is false advertising, but it's not. Should have won the Pulitzer the year it was published.

8. Gary Gygax, Advanced Dungeons & Dragons (*Player's Handbook, Dungeon Master's Guide,* and *Monster Manual*) (1977). Just when you think this list couldn't possibly get any geekier, here's the mother lode of fantasy geekdom. These books showed me how stories are created, how narrative should work, how to create meaningful characters, and much more.

9. Neal Stephenson, *Snow Crash* (1992). The beginning of the second wave of cyberpunk fiction that redefined sci-fi for the 1990s.

10. Charles Darwin, *On the Origin of Species* (1859). Way up at the top of my list of most important books ever written. Methodical and precise, but beautiful all the same, Darwin knew exactly what this book would do, and he wrote it anyway. There is no better example of the power of the book.

BARBARA JONES, director of the ALA Office for Intellectual Freedom in Chicago.

1. The fiction of Chimamanda Ngozi Adichie, especially *Half of a Yellow Sun* (2006) and *Purple Hibiscus* (2003). Her writing leaves me breathless. I was fortunate to meet her at Wesleyan University and to visit many of the places she talks about in Nigeria, one of my favorite countries. *Half of a Yellow Sun* is about the Biafran War—Nigeria's civil war of 1967–1970—and the impact on twin sisters and their family. She should get the Nobel Prize for Literature.

2. Herman Melville, *Moby-Dick* (1851). I try to read it every year starting in November—as Ishmael states, during the "deep November of my soul." The quintessential US novel.

3. Miguel de Cervantes, *Don Quixote* (1605–1615). Someday I hope to be

10

able to read it in its original Spanish! This book covers all aspects of the human condition—the way Shakespeare does—and reminds me that there is basically nothing new under the sun.

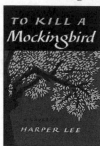

4. Harper Lee, *To Kill a Mockingbird* (1960). This is one of the books that led to my activism in the US civil rights movement in the 1960s. It is also one of my favorite "banned books," and I use it to demonstrate the short-sightedness and tragedy of censorship.

5. Richard Kluger, *Simple Justice* (1975). A powerful story of the work of Thurgood Marshall that led to *Brown v. Board of Education of Topeka*, 347 U.S. 483 (1954). The desegregation battles still continue.

6. Shmuel Yosef Agnon, *Only Yesterday* (1945). A big fat novel about the emigration of Jews to Palestine around the time of WWI. Good historical context, but really great writing, too.

7. James Jones (no relation), *From Here to Eternity* (1951). I love big fat war books, and also books about Midwesterners (he's from Robinson, Illinois). In fact, I love all his books.

8. F. Scott Fitzgerald, *Tender is the Night* (1934). I did my bachelor's thesis on this book and I continue to love it. There are two versions (the second was published in 1951), and it is fun to read both and see which order of events you prefer.

9. James Ellroy, *My Dark Places: An L.A. Crime Memoir* (1996). A heartbreaking autobiography by a man still haunted by his mother's brutal and still unsolved murder. I was delighted to finally meet him at an ALA conference, and he was so gracious when I told him how much I admired his courage to write this.

10. Larry Heinemann, *Paco's Story* (1986). I collect Vietnam War novels and wrote my PhD dissertation about PTSD, so it was hard to choose just one. Larry is a Chicagoan and has often returned to Vietnam to help restore Buddhist monuments destroyed during the conflict, so I admire him and his writing a great deal.

LARRY ROMANS, head of government information and media services at Vanderbilt University Central Library in Nashville, Tennessee.

My favorite books vary over time, but these have remained among my favorites for many years. I read fiction almost exclusively. These choices are mostly Southern, although I sneaked in a novel set in South Boston and another set in Los Angeles and Nebraska. My choices also include four novels with gay major characters. I have chosen works that I think are underappreciated. So I didn't include *The Lord of the Rings* or the Harry Potter series, both of which I love. Carson McCullers, Flannery O'Conner, Truman Capote, and William Faulkner are also among my favorite writers. I haven't read some of these in a while, so I looked at the website of a major online bookseller and a major online reference source to remind me of details. Any mistakes in my summaries are their fault.

1. Ann Patchett, *The Magician's Assistant* (1997). After 20 years as his assistant, Sabine marries Parsifal, a magician who is gay and whose lover has just died. When Parsifal dies, Sabine uncovers his unknown early life in Nebraska and visits his relatives to understand the man she thought she knew. Patchett is a Nashville writer.

2. Clyde Edgerton, *Walking Across Egypt* (1987). Mattie, age 78, longs for grandchildren. She picks up two strays, a mutt and Wesley, who was reared in an orphanage and ended up in reform school. Despite the disapproval of Mattie's children and friends, she and Wesley realize that they need each other. A somewhat comic novel set in North Carolina.

3. Dori Sanders, *Clover* (1990). Clover is a 10-year-old black girl whose father dies in an automobile accident just hours after he weds Sara Kate, a white woman not liked by Clover's family. Clover and her family have to adjust to change and each other. Sanders's family owned a vegetable stand near the property of a librarian I worked with. I've talked with her at ALA conferences as she regaled me with stories of my friend and the stand.

4. Ellen Gilchrist, *Victory over Japan* (1984). I normally don't like short stories, but this book of stories about strong and willful women is an exception. I lived in New Orleans shortly before this book was published.

5. Harry Crews, *A Childhood: The Biography of a Place* (1978). This memoir covers the early life of the novelist, who grew up in poverty in southern Georgia during the Depression. He shares his memories of the lives of tenant farmers, relatives, and friends, including his black friend Willalee Bookatee. Crews describes his bout with polio and his near-fatal scalding in a vat of boiling water. He gives great readings and savors his writing. He has the tattoo of a hinge on the crook of his arm, which I found fascinating and no doubt contributes greatly to his writing.

6. J. G. Hayes, *A Map of the Harbor Islands* (2006). Petey is a golden boy in South Boston who excels at school and baseball. A wild pitch puts Petey in a coma, after which he has a bad stammer and is decidedly peculiar. His "bestest" friend gradually pulls away from Petey. Hayes was charming on the phone when I called about getting copies of his books for our gay book group. All of his books are currently out of print because his publisher was bought out by a group who weren't interested in publishing GLBT books.

7. Jim Grimsley, *Comfort and Joy* (1999). This is my favorite book by my favorite author. Danny Crell, a plain HIV-positive hospital staffer with an abusive working-class background, develops a relationship with handsome, old-moneyed Dr. Ford McKinney. When Ford's parents refuse to invite Danny for Christmas, the two go home to visit Danny's family instead. A sequel to *Winter Birds*.

8. Jim Grimsley, *Dream Boy* (1995). Nathan's alcoholic, bible-reading father abuses him sexually. He and his next-door high-school classmate have a relationship that ends in tragedy because of jealousy and homophobia. The ambiguous ending allows some hope for the future. Grimsley has signed books at a number of ALA conferences. I've coerced friends into stopping by the Algonquin Books booth to get signed copies of his latest galley or book.

9. John Kennedy Toole, *A Confederacy of Dunces* (1980). Ignatius J. Reilly is almost arrested as a vagrant in New Orleans and gets into a car accident with his tipsy mother behind the wheel. He sells Lucky Dogs from a hot-dog shaped cart in the French Quarter and then becomes a filing clerk at a pants company. There are wonderful secondary characters, my favorite being Miss Trixie, who in her 70s keeps trying to retire. I was living in New Orleans when this book was published and remember laughing out loud as I read this book on the "Freret Jet" city bus in trips from the Tulane library to the French Quarter.

10. Lee Smith, *Oral History* (1983). As part of an assignment for a college class, Jennifer returns to her mother's childhood home with a notebook and tape recorder to document three generations of the cursed Cantrell family. The stories are told through many voices and in mountain dialect. I heard Smith read a number of times, most memorably when I sat in on a Vanderbilt Maymester course in which each week two Southern writers would give readings, after which we would have sandwiches and then ask questions of the author.

10

MEDIA

Libraries and librarians in film and TV, 2004–2012

by George M. Eberhart and Jennifer Henderson

THIS LIST INCLUDES FILMS from 2004 and later not included in previous editions. *The Whole Library Handbook 4* offered a list of films from 1999 to 2005, while *The Whole Library Handbook 3* included a list through 1998. For a massively expanded, corrected, and comprehensive list that goes back to the earliest movie with a librarian (1912), visit www.alaeditions.org/webextras.—*GME.*

The Adjustment Bureau (2011). The Rose Reading Room of the New York Public Library serves as the library setting for the mysterious Adjustment Bureau. (The book retrieval section was green-screened out and the reference books were covered by wooden paneling.) Director George Nolfi liked the leather-paneled swinging doors of the Art and Architecture Collection, so they serve as a portal to the Bureau Office throughout the film. Other scenes show the first-floor Grand Hallway, the steps leading to the second floor from Astor Hall, and other hallways.

Admissions (2004). Lauren Ambrose as Evie Brighton works in a library; Jennifer Schweickert plays the librarian.

After Sex (2007). Mila Kunis as Nikki and Zoe Saldana as Kat talk about oral sex and make out in an academic library.

After Twilight (2005). Rather than remove banned books from the library shelf, Christine M. Auten as young librarian Jen Frazier becomes a freedom fighter against a theocratic regime occupying the state of Texas. She carries a mysterious package to the underground resistance and becomes a hunted fugitive.

The Age of Stupid (2009, UK). An archivist (Pete Postlethwaite) in the post apocalyptic year of 2055 looks back on footage from the early 21st century to try to understand why no one did anything about runaway climate change.

Agnes and His Brothers [Agnes und seine Brüder] (2004, Germany). This is the story of three brothers and their search for happiness. One brother, Moritz Bleibtreu as Hans-Jörg Tschirner, is an oedipal, sex-addicted academic librarian who is interested in young students. Several times he follows a girl into the library restroom so he can spy on her through a peephole in an adjoining stall.

Agora (2009, Spain). Rachel Weisz plays Neoplatonist philosopher and teacher Hypatia, the daughter of Theon (Michael Lonsdale), who is the director of the Musaeum (a center for scholarship) in Alexandria, Egypt. In 391, she and other pagans are trapped by a Christian mob in the library of the Serapeum (not the Great Library), from which they manage to save some valuable scrolls before the building is destroyed.

Alexandria . . . New York (2004, Egypt/France). Egyptian student Yehia meets his American girlfriend Ginger in the library of the Institute of Dramatic Art in California.

Alice (2009, UK/Canada, TV miniseries). Andrew Lee Potts as the Hatter escorts Caterina Scorsone as Alice into the city of Wonderland and brings her to a Great Library, filled with books and information rescued by the resistance movement when the Queen of Hearts seized power. A librarian is armed with a shotgun.

All About Evil (2010). Natasha Lyonne plays nerdy San Francisco librarian Deborah Tennis. She has a secret life as a psychotic killer who films her murders and screens them to audiences at a movie theater she inherited from her father. Mink Stole as Evelyn is a library coworker who becomes one of her victims.

Alone [Allein] (2004, Germany). Lavinia Wilson as Maria works at a university library in Essen, Germany, but she has borderline personality disorder.

The Amazing Spider-Man (2012). Marvel Comics creator Stan Lee has a cameo as a school librarian who is stamping books and listening to music on headphones, unaware of an epic battle going on in the library between Spider-Man (Andrew Garfield) and The Lizard (Rhys Ifans).

American Horror Story (November 9, 2011, TV series), "Piggy Piggy." Evan Peters as Tate Langdon stages a Columbine-style massacre in the Westfield High School in 1994. He murders 15 students, five of them in the library, and permanently disables a teacher (possibly the librarian), Mr. Carmichael (Tom Gallop).

American Pie Presents: The Book of Love (2009). One night, Bug Hall as Rob accidentally sets fire to the school library and finds the bible (or book of love), the creation of Mr. Levenstein (Eugene Levy), nearly ruined. The book has incomplete advice and sends them on a hopeless journey to lose their virginity.

American Pie Presents: The Naked Mile (2006, Canada/US). In the high school library, Jessy Schram as student Tracy Sterling tells her boyfriend Erik Stifler (John White) that she is just not ready to have sex yet.

Amhurst (2008). Mickey Mello plays a librarian.

Angels & Demons (2009). Tom Hanks as Harvard symbologist Robert Langdon and Ayelet Zurer as Vittoria Vetra look for clues to the kidnapping of cardinals in ancient manuscripts in the Vatican Library. The filming actually took place in the Biblioteca Angelica in Rome.

Anna M. (2007, France). Lonely Anna M. (played by Isabelle Carré), who works at the conservation department of the Bibliothèque Nationale in Paris, tries to kill herself and winds up in the hospital, where she develops an unhealthy fixation on her doctor.

Antarctica (2008, Israel). Tomer Ilan as Omer works in a library in Tel Aviv. He is shy, turning 30, and looking for a stable gay relationship.

Archangel (2005, UK, made for TV). Daniel Craig as Russian history professor Fluke Kelso goes to the Lenin Library in Moscow to research a clue about the death of Stalin. One librarian (Elena Butenko) refuses to help, but Kseniya Entelis as younger librarian Yelena gets him the materials he needs. Later, he travels to a Communist Party archives in Arkhangelsk to find more evidence.

Ask the Dust (2006, US/Germany). Natasha Staples is a librarian in 1930s Denver.

10

Atonement (2007, UK/US/France). James McAvoy as Robbie and Keira Knightley as Cecilia get lusty against the bookshelves in a private library in the 1930s until young Briony (Saoirse Ronan) walks in on them.

Avatar: The Last Airbender (July 14, 2006, animated TV series), "The Library." In a Spirit Library hidden in the desert, Sokka (voiced by Jack DeSena) discovers crucial information on a solar eclipse that could end a war. But the library's owl spirit, Wan Shi Tong (Hector Elizondo), sinks the library into the sand and traps him. In M. Night Shyamalan's 2010 film, *The Last Airbender,* the Great Library is frequently mentioned but never shown.

Back When We Were Grownups (2004, made for TV). Lynette DuPree plays a librarian.

Barbara Wood: Lockruf der Vergangenheit (2004, Germany, made for TV). Hamish Hamilton plays a British library employee in 1923.

Barney: The Land of Make Believe (2005). Jennifer Skidmore as Lily the Librarian comes outside and shushes three kids and Barney the Dinosaur as they sing a song about the wonders found in libraries. They enter the Land of Make Believe through the library doors.

Be Kind Rewind (2008, US/UK). In Passaic, New Jersey, Jack Black as Jerry Gerber and Mos Def as Mike dress up as Ghostbusters and attempt to reshoot the library sequence from that film in order to replace a damaged tape. A woman shelving books shushes them. Elizabeth Berkley is allegedly one of the uncredited library patrons. The children's reading room is used to recreate the hotel scene where Mike gets slimed.

The Beaver (2011, US/United Arab Emirates). Anton Yelchin as Porter Black meets with other students in the high school library to sell them his term-paper–writing services.

Because of Winn-Dixie (2005). Eva Marie Saint plays Miss Franny Block, a lonely spinster librarian in Naomi, Florida, who loves books and tells interesting stories, such as the time she fended off a bear in the library by throwing *War and Peace* at it.

Becoming Jane (2007, UK/Ireland). Anne Hathaway as budding author Jane Austen accidentally encounters brash Irishman Tom Lefroy (James McAvoy) in a friend's private library in 1795. He flirts with her, hands her a copy of Henry Fielding's *Tom Jones,* and tells her to read it if she wants to become a novelist.

Beginners (2010). Ewan McGregor as graphic artist Oliver Fields romances Mélanie Laurent as French actress Anna. They read together in the public library. Stills showing people and events from the 1950s came from the Library of Congress photograph collection.

Being Flynn (2012). Robert De Niro as homeless writer Jonathan Flynn spends the day in the library and on snowy nights uses the outside steam vents that release the excess heat from the building so that he has a warm place to sleep.

Beyond the Mat (2013). Sabrina Guyll plays a high school librarian.

Bibliotekstjuven [Library Thief] (2011, Sweden, TV miniseries). Gustaf Skarsgård as John Manneus is a manuscripts librarian at the National Library of Sweden whose salary does not allow the lifestyle he wants to lead. He takes to stealing rare materials from the library and selling them to auction houses. Based on the real-life case of a librarian/thief, who committed suicide after he was apprehended by police in 2004.

A Bird of the Air (2011). Rachel Nichols plays the assertive Fiona, a Santa Fe college librarian who helps Lyman (Jackson Hurst), an introverted courtesy patrolman, find the owner of a runaway, talkative green parrot. The two consult library books (such as the DK encyclopedia *Bird*) and investigate phrases the parrot uses to search for clues. Fiona leaves free books around town in little handmade dioramas and at one point impersonates a blind person so she can bring her dog into a library. Carrie Fleming is a reference librarian.

Black Gold (2011, France/Italy/Qatar/Tunisia). Tahar Rahim as Auda is an Arabian prince who serves as a bookish scholar or librarian for the Emir Nesib (Antonio Banderas) in the 1930s. When a Texas oil prospector comes looking for oil in a disputed zone, Nesib sells out but Auda emerges as an anti-Western warrior.

Blame It on Fidel [La faute à Fidel!] (2006, France/Italy). In Paris in the early 1970s, Anna de la Mesa (played by Nina Kervel-Bey) takes her brother Fernando (Stefano Accorsi) to a library to avoid hearing their activist parents arguing. She researches Chile and reads aloud to Fernando.

The Book of Eli (2010). In the postapocalyptic world of 2043, the wanderer Eli (Denzel Washington) arrives at Alcatraz, where he recites his memorized Bible to Lombardi (Malcolm McDowell), a curator of sorts who is collecting anything that remains of prewar culture. He writes it all down verbatim and places the text in his library between a Qu'ran and the Torah.

Booky's Crush (2009, Canada, made for TV). Sarah White plays Willa Thomson, a part-time librarian in 1930s Toronto, who is attracted to Russell (Marc Bendavid), a medical student she meets in the library. Lisa Berry is another librarian.

The Box (2009). In 1976, James Marsden as Arthur Lewis is followed by slack-jawed zombies in the creepy Richmond (Va.) Public Library (actually filmed in the Boston Public Library). He approaches Clymene Steward (Deborah Rush), who leads him to a room with three "gateways" (identical floating water coffins) and gives him a damnation-or-salvation choice.

Brain Zapped (2006, short, made for TV). When booklover and all-around supergirl Emily Grace Garcia (played by Selena Gomez) hears about strange happenings at the local library, she decides to investigate and brings her best friend Kingston (Lewis Parry) to help. Things seem normal until they witness electric holograms popping out of books and mysterious glowing bookshelves.

Breaking Dawn (2004). Marilyn McIntyre plays an academic librarian.

Brick (2005). Joseph Gordon-Levitt as Brendan meets with Matt O'Leary as The Brain in the high school library.

Brutal Massacre: A Comedy (2007). In *El Libro del Muertes*, a horror film that some of the characters watch on TV, Francine Bianco Tax plays a librarian who throws books at zombies who can only be stopped this way because they are compelled to read every word.

Burning Annie (2004). Teresa Gillmor plays a librarian. Filmed at John Deaver Drinko Library, Marshall University, Huntington, West Virginia.

Cabin Fever 2: Spring Fever (2009). Disease-tainted bottled water infects a high school. When Rusty Kelley as student Alex becomes infected, he goes to the school library and discovers that the disease is incurable necrotizing fasciitis (flesh-eating disease).

Casino Royale (2006, UK/Czech/US/Germany/Bahamas). The library of the

10

Strahov Monastery in Prague serves as the setting for London's House of Commons.

Centochiodi (2007, Italy). An intruder desecrates a research library at the University of Bologna by pulling 100 books from the shelves, opening them, and nailing them to the floor with iron spikes. The guilty party is a philosophy of religion professor (played by Raz Degan) who has renounced his identity ("All the books in the world aren't nearly as valuable as a single cup of coffee with a friend"), left his BMW near a bridge, and feigned suicide by throwing his car keys and wallet into the water.

Chainsaw Sally (2004). Drab Porterville librarian Sally Diamon (played by April Monique Burril) turns into an insane, cannibalistic, chainsaw-slinging, goth vigilante at night, dealing death to those who threaten her or her cross-dressing brother. She offs one male patron in the library men's room for being noisy, and brutally executes Tina in the woods for not returning the overdue *Atkins for Life* diet book. Kit Batman is a library assistant.

Chemical Wedding (2008, UK). Lucy Cudden as varsity journalist Lia Robinson researches poet and occultist Aleister Crowley at the Cambridge University library.

Cirque du Freak: The Vampire's Assistant (2009). Michael Cerveris as Mr. Tiny spends some time in the Council library messing around with *The Book of Souls*.

Clapham Junction (2007, UK, made for TV). Luke Treadaway as Theo cruises Joseph Mawle as Tim in the Clapham Library in South London, picking up a pen that he has left behind.

Coach Carter (2005, US/Germany). Samuel L. Jackson as Coach Ken Carter gives the basketball team a pep talk in the Richmond (Calif.) High School library.

Cold Weather (2010). Cris Lankenau as Doug goes to the Branford P. Millar Library at Portland (Oreg.) State University to look at books on code-breaking. He makes his sister Gail (played by Trieste Kelly Dunn) steal a reference book on baseball statistics. Aubrey Dean plays a librarian.

Collateral (2004). Tom Cruise as hitman Vincent stalks a victim (Jada Pinkett Smith as Annie) late at night in a corporate law library.

The Colour of Magic (2008, UK, made for TV). Nicholas Tennant is the head librarian at Discworld's Unseen University, who turns into an orangutan. The library owns the *Octavo,* a powerful spell book.

Coming Up Easy (2004). Ellis Williams as the homeless Alfred and Anya Profumo as Lily Garcia meet in a library—an original Carnegie library in Portland, Oregon, that now houses the Multnomah County Library's bookstore. They exchange a piece of origami that was actually folded by a bookstore volunteer. Rod Richards has a part as a librarian.

Community (February 10, 2011, TV series), "Early 21st Century Romanticism." Troy Barnes (Donald Glover) and Abed Nadir (Danny Pudi) attempt to catch the eye of sexy librarian Mariah (Maite Schwartz) by yelling "Books!" across the room.

Community College (2009). Robert Boileau plays a community college librarian.

Conspiracy (2008). Jennifer Esposito as Joanna is in charge of the lending library in a small town in the Southwest where the evil megacorporation Halicorp is in control.

Conviction (2010). Hilary Swank as Betty Anne Waters spends time in an academic library looking up legal information on DNA testing in books and online.

Copacabana (2010, France/Belgium). Isabelle Huppert as aging hippie Babou visits the library in Tourcoing, France, with her boyfriend Patrice (Luis Rego) to look for cookbooks containing recipes to use for a meal of reconciliation with her daughter Esméralda (Lolita Chammah).

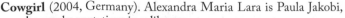

Cowgirl (2004, Germany). Alexandra Maria Lara is Paula Jakobi, who works part-time in a library.

Credo (2008, UK). MyAnna Buring as London psychology student Alice is studying in a library when staffer Chris Courtenay comes in to tell her the library is closing.

Crime Scene: The Bobby Ray Summers Story (2008). A comedy about a maladjusted janitor who abducts sexy librarians.

Cry_Wolf (2005). Marty Terry plays a librarian at Westlake Prep boarding school who tells a necking couple in the stacks to try the German philosophy section because no one will bother them there. Library scenes were filmed at the Union Theological Seminary in Richmond, Virginia.

Cthulhu (2007). Hilary H. J. Specht has an uncredited part as a librarian. The library scene was shot at the Masonic Retirement Center in Des Moines, Washington.

The Cursed (2010). Brad Thornton as writer Denny White comes to McMinnville, Tennessee, to investigate some unsolved murders. He visits the Warren County Library, where librarian Sara Belmont (Francesca Cecil) gives him books on Southern history that fulfill his research needs.

Cyber Seduction: His Secret Life (2005, made for TV). Jeremy Sumpter as popular high school sophomore Justin Petersen develops an addiction to internet porn. When his parents disconnect the internet at home, he finds it on the high school library computer. But he gets caught.

The Da Vinci Code (2006). After being shown a dead body, Tom Hanks as Harvard symbologist Robert Langdon says, "I've got to get to a library . . . fast!"

The Dark (2005, Germany/UK). Maria Bello as Adèlle visits a Welsh library to research the town records (on microfilm) on a mysterious girl named Ebrill. Gwenyth Petty plays the librarian.

Dark Remains (2005). Patricia French is the stern, cardigan-clad librarian at Kingspike (Ga.) Public Library who shows Allen Pyke (Greg Thompson) where the newspaper archives are stored but is otherwise not too helpful.

The Darkest Hour (2011). During an alien invasion, the Russian army encamps in the Lenin Library in Moscow.

The Day after Tomorrow (2004). After an ecodisaster, some teenagers take refuge in the New York Public Library, where they must burn books to keep warm. They have a debate about which books to burn and decide to torch the "whole section on tax law." One librarian (Tom Rooney) saves the Gutenberg Bible because, even though he is an atheist, it symbolizes "mankind's greatest achievement," the printed word. Another librarian (Sheila McCarthy) diagnoses the condition of a girl who develops an infection when she cuts her leg.

Dear Frankie (2004, UK). Elaine M. Ellis is a librarian at a lending library in Greenock, Scotland. She doesn't realize at first that Jack McElhone as Frankie is deaf and calls him a "cheeky wee devil." She apologizes after he puts in his hearing aid and lets him check out an armload of books.

Death Defying Acts (2007, US/Australia). Catherine Zeta-Jones as Scottish

10

psychic Mary McGarvie goes to a library to research news items about the dupes she is scamming in London in 1926. An "oily librarian" played by Anthony O'Donnell leers at her as she climbs a ladder for a book and makes inappropriate comments. She coughs and tears out a page about Houdini from a bound newspaper when the librarian turns the other way.

Deep Gold 3D (2011, Philippines). A bad guy attacks Amy Sanchez (model Bebe Pham) in a library. José Ch. Alvarez plays a librarian.

Demons and Doors (2012, UK). Kyri Saphiris plays Lenny the Librarian.

Demoted (2011). The Southfield (Mich.) Public Library board room serves as the setting for the office of Reilly Auto Parts.

The Disappearance of Haruhi Suzumiya [Suzumiya Haruhi no shôshitsu] (2010, Japan). After the credits roll, Yuki Nagato (voiced by Minori Chihara) is seen in a public library watching a boy helping a girl get a library card. After they leave, Yuki covers her mouth with the book, possibly hiding a smile, as she remembers how she first met Kyon.

Doctor Who (May 31, 2008, UK, TV series), "Silence in the Library" (right). Doctor Who (David Tennant) and Donna Noble (Catherine Tate) probe the secrets of a seemingly uninhabited, planet-sized, 51st-century book repository called "The Library." Some scenes were filmed in the Old Swansea Central Library in Wales.

Dolphins (2007, UK). Gary Blair is a librarian in Brighton.

Don't Be Afraid of the Dark (2010, US/Australia/Mexico). Katie Holmes as Kim goes to a public library to research the creepy Rhode Island house she now lives in with her boyfriend and his daughter. James Mackay is the librarian who explains to her all about the former owner's art, his life, his apparent madness, and the fairies who live in the basement.

Dracula 3D (2012, Italy/France/Spain). Unax Ugalde as Jonathan Harker journeys from England to Castle Dracula in the Carpathians. His mission is to catalogue the huge library owned by the count (Thomas Kretschmann).

Dread (2009, US/UK). Jackson Rathbone as film student Stephen Grace and Laura Donnelly as Abby work an English college library. They participate in a senior-thesis research project that records people talking about their innermost fears.

Dreams for Life (2004, Australia). Kylie Foster plays a librarian.

Edmond (2005). William H. Macy as down-and-out Edmond Burke is sentenced to life for first-degree murder. He spends much of his time in the prison library writing about his misspent life.

The Education of Charlie Banks (2007). Mick (Jason Ritter) tags with an orange marker a pillar in the college library with his and Mary's (Eva Amurri Martino) names as Charlie (Jesse Eisenberg) watches.

Einstein and Eddington (2008, UK/US, made for TV). Lucy Briers is a librarian.

Ella Enchanted (2004, US/Ireland/UK). In this reinvention of the Cinderella story, Anne Hathaway as Ella of Frell and Hugh Dancy as Prince Charmont visit the palace Hall of Records to track down the fairy Lucinda. Merrina Millsapp is a records attendant.

The Face of Jizo [Chichi to kuraseba] (2004, Japan). A young Hiroshima librarian and atomic bomb survivor (Rie Miyazawa as Mitsue) and a shy, bespectacled library researcher (Tadanobu Asano as Kinoshita) explore guilt and love in 1948.

The Fantastic Flying Books of Mr. Morris Lessmore (2011). A short, poignant, humorous allegory about the curative powers of books that tells the story of Morris Lessmore, who discovers a library full of living, flying books after his city is destroyed by a hurricane.

Fat Albert (2004). Dumb Donald (played by Marques Houston) jumps out of a TV along with other cast members of the *Fat Albert and the Cosby Kids* show. He goes to a school library to read African American history and removes his pink ski mask.

Faut que ça danse! (2007, France). Valeria Bruni Tedeschi as Sarah Bellinsky has an emergency birth on a reading table in a library.

Flipped (2010). In 1957, Juli Baker (Madeline Carroll) is in the library when she overhears Bryce Loski (Callan McAuliffe) and Garrett (Israel Broussard) talking about her mentally disabled uncle.

The Fog (2005). Maggie Grace as Elizabeth Williams visits an Oregon museum library to research some mysterious symbols and consult with local history expert Mr. Latham (Robert Harper).

Footloose (2011). A student hands a joint to transfer student Ren McCormack (Kenny Wormold), who is studying in the Bomont (Ga.) High School library. The librarian sees it and chases Ren down the hall.

Footnote (2011, Israel). Shlomo Bar-Aba plays Eliezer Shkolnik, a philologist and Talmudic scholar who does research every day in the basement of the library of the Hebrew University of Jerusalem.

The Forgotten (2004). Katie Cooper is a library clerk who helps Telly Paretta (Julianne Moore) with a microfiche reader and confirms that newspaper articles no longer exist about the airplane crash that killed her only son.

Frankenstein (2004, made for TV). Sandra Dorsey as Orleans Parish (La.) Public Library Director Nancy Whistler throws up when she discovers the mutilated corpse of a night security guard after she opens up in the morning. Apparently the killer had come in to consult a book on abnormal psychology.

Fraternity Massacre at Hell Island (2007). Kaleo Quenzer as Felix University student Tommy would rather come out as gay than be known for studying in the library. He manages to find a book using what he calls the "Donald Duck" (Dewey Decimal) system.

Freedom Writers (2007, US/Germany). Hilary Swank as teacher Erin Gruwell works with an integrated population of students at Woodrow Wilson High School in Long Beach, California, in 1994 (though filmed at Hamilton High School in Los Angeles). She has them read and discuss *The Diary of Anne Frank*, then she invites Miep Gies (played by Pat Carroll), the woman who hid the Frank family, to visit her class in the school library.

Fright Flick (2011). An unseen person leaves an envelope addressed to a film production crew on the desk at a branch of a Dallas-area library. The librarian (Melissa McCurley) passes it on to Gill (Adam Kitchen), who uses a library computer to follow up on a murder clue.

Fright Night (2011). Viola Valdez has an uncredited part as a librarian.

From Prada to Nada (2011, Mexico/US). Tina French plays an old librarian.

Fulgazi (2004). Someone credited only as Mary has a small part as a librarian.

Ghost Lake (2004). Tatum Adair as Rebecca Haster uses a public library news-

10

paper archive to research mysterious accidents at Rushford Lake in western New York. She has an encounter there with a mysterious little girl (played by Azure Sky Decker) that no one else can see. Mary Ann Layman is the librarian.

The Girl Next Door (2004). At the end of this campy teen film, Emile Hirsch as Matthew Kidman breaks into a high school library to shoot a porn video.

The Girl with the Dragon Tattoo [Män som hatar kvinnor] (2009, Sweden/Denmark/Germany/Norway). Noomi Rapace as Lisbeth Salander studies newspaper records in the archives of the Vanger Group.

The Girl with the Dragon Tattoo (2011, US/Sweden/Norway). Rooney Mara as tattooed goth hacker Lisbeth Salander studies records in the archives of the Vanger Industries, looking for locations of all the company's factories and offices from 1949 to 1966 and disgruntling Anne-Li Norberg as archives librarian Lindgren. Later, Daniel Craig as Mikael Blomkvist visits the *Hedestads Kuriren* newspaper office to look at photo archives, assisted by Sandra Andreis as the photo editor.

The Golden Compass (2007, US/UK). John Franklyn-Robbins plays a librarian.

The Good Shepherd (2006). Matt Damon as Yale University student Edward Wilson meets a deaf student named Laura (Tammy Blanchard) at the library in 1939. The library scenes were actually filmed at the Gould Memorial Library at Bronx (N.Y.) Community College.

Goodbye Bafana (2007, Germany/France/Belgium/Italy/UK/Luxembourg/South Africa). Joseph Fiennes plays prison guard Sgt. James Gregory whose job is to censor the mail at Robben Island prison in Cape Town, South Africa, where Nelson Mandela is held. Another guard tells him that the Freedom Charter of the African National Congress calls for the extermination of whites, but he decides to read it for himself. He goes to the restricted section of a public library in Cape Town and tricks the librarians (Paula Pursch and Michele Belknap) into letting him see it. He steals it for more careful scrutiny later.

Gracie Rose (2008). One segment was filmed at the Haysville (Kans.) Public Library.

Graduation (2007). Minda Fisher is a high school librarian.

Grave Misconduct (2008, made for TV). Crystal Bernard as librarian and novelist Julia London steals a recently deceased author's manuscript and gets it published as her own. Her supervisor is Fran Bennett as Mrs. Crutch.

Half Light (2006, Germany/UK). Demi Moore as Rachel Carlson discovers that newspaper records about a murder-suicide are mysteriously missing from the library. The library scene was filmed at the Prichard Jones Institute, Newborough, Anglesey, Wales. Polly Frame plays the librarian.

Harold & Kumar Escape from Guantanamo Bay (2008). Kal Penn as Kumar meets Danneel Harris as Vanessa for the first time in a college library as he is writing a poem. They wind up making out in the stacks.

Harry Potter and the Goblet of Fire (2005, US/UK). In the richly vaulted Divinity School of Oxford University's Bodleian Library, Professor Minerva McGonagall (Maggie Smith) teaches a deeply embarrassed Ron Weasley (Rupert Grint) to waltz.

Harry Potter and the Half-Blood Prince (2009, US/UK). Harry Potter (Daniel Radcliffe) and Hermione Granger (Emma Watson) are in the Hogwarts library talking about going to Slughorn's Christmas Party, as student Romilda Vane (Anna Shaffer) ogles Harry from afar.

The Haunting of Molly Hartley (2008). Haley Bennett as Molly Hartley is in a school library looking at a book (with several bad misspellings) when her friend Joseph Young (Chace Crawford) gives her a scare.

He's on My Mind (2009). Read MacGuirtose plays a cranky librarian.

Heartbreak Library [Keu namjaui chaek 198jjeuk] (2008, South Korea). Librarian Eun-soo Jo (Yoo-jin Kim) discovers a tall young man dressed in a black suit ripping the pages out of books and calls him a criminal. Joon-oh Kim (Dong-wook Lee) tears out page 198 from each book and explains that his former girlfriend left him a note saying to check page 198 but did not mention the title of the book. Eun-soo sympathizes with him and determines to help him find the right book.

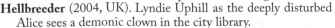

Hellbreeder (2004, UK). Lyndie Uphill as the deeply disturbed Alice sees a demonic clown in the city library.

Herb & Dorothy (2008). A documentary about Herbert Vogel and his wife Dorothy (a librarian) who became world-class art collectors on their limited salaries.

The Hideout (2007, Italy/US). Jesse Nagel is an assistant librarian in Davenport, Iowa.

High School Musical (2006, made for TV). Joyce Cohen plays East High School librarian Mrs. Falstaff, who constantly reminds student Chad Danforth (Corbin Bleu) to keep quiet in the library.

The History Boys (2006, UK). A montage early in the film features the library at Cutlers' Grammar School in England. At least two books visible in the scene were published after 1983–1984, when the film was set.

The Hollywood Librarian: A Look at Librarians through Film (2007). A documentary by Ann Seidl on librarians, both in their depictions in movies and their work in real life, that premiered at the 2007 ALA Annual Conference.

Home by Christmas (2006, made for TV). Donna White is a librarian.

Hooking Up (2009). Three students spend all their time in the high school library talking about sex instead of studying.

The Howling: Reborn (2011). Landon Liboiron as Will Kidman gets it on with Eliana Wynter (Lindsey Shaw) while he is tied up on the floor of a college library as he tests his limits turning into a werewolf.

Hugo (2011). In Paris in 1931, orphan Hugo Cabret (played by Asa Butterfield) and his friend Isabelle (Chloë Grace Moretz) discover the book *Inventer le rêve: L'Histoire des premiers films,* a book on early cinema history, at the Film Academy Library and a montage of historical films flashes by. With the help of its author, film historian René Tabard (Michael Stuhlbarg), they discover that Isabelle's godfather Papa Georges is really French film pioneer Georges Méliès (Ben Kingsley).

I Love You, Beth Cooper (2009, Canada/US). Natalie von Rotsburg is the librarian at Buffalo Glenn High School.

I Love You Phillip Morris (2009, US/France). Jim Carrey as insurance-fraud criminal Steven Russell meets Ewan McGregor as Phillip Morris (serving time for auto theft) in the prison library and arranges for them to be cellmates. Filmed at Orleans Parish (La.) Prison.

Idiocracy (2006). Luke Wilson is Private Joe Bauers, an underachieving Army librarian who supposedly has no outstanding attributes or glaring flaws, thus

10

making him perfect for a one-year cryogenic experiment. But he is forgotten and wakes up 500 years later.

The Imaginarium of Dr. Parnassus (2009, UK/Canada/France). Christopher Plummer as Doctor Parnassus is reduced to begging outside a shopping mall, which is actually the Vancouver (B.C.) Public Library.

In God's Country (2007, Canada, made for TV). Agi Gallus plays a librarian.

In My Life (2009, Philippines). Vilma Santos as Filipino librarian Shirley Templo heads to New York to reunite with her openly gay son, Luis Manzano as Mark Salvacion.

In Plain Sight (2004). Susie Goldberg is a librarian.

The Incredible Hulk (2008). Edward Norton as Dr. Bruce Banner ducks into a library to avoid the bad guys chasing him.

Indiana Jones and the Kingdom of the Crystal Skull (2008). In 1957, Harrison Ford as Indiana Jones and his sidekick Mutt Williams (Shia LeBeouf) escape from KGB agents by riding a motorcycle through Marshall College library (actually filmed in Yale University's Commons, while the entrance is that of Sterling Memorial Library). A student (Chet Hanks) asks Jones for help on an assignment; he replies, "You want to be a good archaeologist, you've got to get out of the library."

The Initiation of Sarah (2006, made for TV). The Temple Hill University library (filmed at Centenary College in Shreveport, Louisiana) serves as the backdrop for a confrontation between two rival occult sororities of witches. Sarah Goodwin (Mika Boorem) and her sister Lindsey (Summer Glau) are conflicted about which to pledge. Esme (Tessa Thompson) from the evil Alpha Nu Gamma magically traps Sarah in the stacks and threatens her.

Inside (2006). Nicholas D'Agosto as Alex Wells is a recently orphaned young man who works in a public library. He notices that a married couple checks out the same book every month. He begins watching them in the library, then he decides to secretly follow them home and spy on them to see what their lives are like.

Intimate Strangers [Confidences trop intimes] (2004, France). Anne Brochet plays a librarian named Jeanne who helps her ex-lover, Fabrice Luchini as tax accountant William, through an emotional crisis. The student who asks a question in the library is played by Aurore Auteuil.

Into the Darkness (2006, UK, short). Christopher Dane as the Archangel Michael helps Jennie Fox as Abigail keep an ancient book from falling into the hands of the devil. Carl Homer plays a librarian.

J. Edgar (2011). Department of Justice official J. Edgar Hoover (played by Leonardo DiCaprio) brings his attractive date (Naomi Watts as Helen Gandy) to the Library of Congress Main Reading Room in 1918 in order to demonstrate to her the efficiency of the card catalog system that he claims to have developed. Gandy times how long it takes Hoover to use the catalog to find a book. Hoover proposes marriage to her on bended knee in Alcove 6, an offer that she rejects. But she does accept his offer to work as his secretary.

The Jane Austen Book Club (2007). Five women form a book club to discuss the six novels written by Jane Austen. One is a library staffer (Amy Brenneman as Sylvia) who plans a fundraising dinner in the library. As the months progress, their lives seem to parallel those of Austen's characters. Emily Blunt as high school French teacher Prudie watches Trey (Kevin Zegers) and another student make out in the library stacks.

The Jealous God (2005, UK). In an industrial town in Yorkshire during the mid-1960s, Jason Merrells as Roman Catholic schoolmaster Vincent Dungarven visits the library and encounters Laura (Mairead Carty), a new librarian. He asks her out and soon falls in love with her, although she is a Protestant. Annie Lavelle plays another librarian.

Jumper (2008, US/Canada). Hayden Christensen as high school student David Rice discovers that he can teleport himself instantaneously to anywhere on earth. The first time, when he is drowning in a pond, he teleports to the Ann Arbor (Mich.) Regional Library and causes the stacks to flood with water. The scene was actually filmed at the Peterborough (Ont.) Public Library.

Kill List (2011, UK). Mark Kempner plays a librarian (and child porn distributor) marked for murder. Neil Maskell as Jay, a former soldier and hitman, brutally breaks his hands and bashes his head in with a hammer.

Kill Switch (2008, US/Canada). Steven Seagal as police detective Jacob King visits the Memphis (Tenn.) Public Library to research the zodiac symbols left by a serial killer. Anna Mae Routledge as a goth-outfitted librarian rudely refers him to the occult section. It turns out she knows a rock band that uses the same symbolism in their lyrics. She is killed by another Memphis murderer.

Killer Movie (2008). Mary Murphy plays a North Dakota school librarian. She orders reality-TV director Jake Tanner (Paul Wesley) out of the library after his production assistant complains about the lack of internet connectivity.

Kit Kittredge: An American Girl (2008). Joan Cusack as Miss Bond plays a mobile librarian in Cincinnati in 1934. She drives the bookmobile (a panel truck with shelves on the outside and the inside) a bit too fast and she encourages children to read.

Knock Knock (2007). Ilene Kristen plays a Glass County public librarian who reads a newspaper story aloud to retired detective Mike Soato (Antonio Mastrantonio) because he left his glasses at home and flirts with him.

Labou (2008). Monica May plays a Louisiana public librarian who helps three youngsters—Emily Ryan (Marissa Cuevas), Gavin (Darnell Hamilton), and Toddster (Bryan James Kitto)—find a map of bayous where they suspect a pirate treasure ship is hidden. Emily steals the library map and tears it into three sections, giving two to her schoolmates.

The Lady of Names (2011, Canada). A beautiful librarian named Sorrow, voiced by Eleonora Barna, discovers the power of magic when an ill-conceived wish catapults her into the world of fairy tales.

Lage Raho Munna Bhai (2006, India). Sanjay Dutt as Munna Bhai poses as a history professor specializing in the life of Mahatma Gandhi. He visits the Gandhi Library and studies there. After three days of tedious research, he begins to see a hallucination of Gandhi himself (played by Dilip Prabhavalkar) who gives him advice on nonviolent strategies to life's problems.

Late Afternoon of the Living Dead (2007). A Chicago librarian named Chris (played by Chris Hutson) awakens in an abandoned attic after a near-fatal zombie attack. He turns into a zombie-slaying machine and wanders the streets with Shelton (Jason Huls), a wisecracking ghost, looking for a cure to the plague.

Layer Cake (2004, UK). Daniel Craig plays an unnamed cocaine dealer who impresses Eddie Temple (Michael Gambon) at a meeting in the library of the

10

Athenaeum Club in London.

The Legend of Lucy Keyes (2006). Julie Delpy as Jeanne Cooley researches a ghost legend in the Princeton, Massachusetts, library (filmed in the Princeton Center building). Elizabeth Duff is the librarian.

Legend of the Guardians: The Owls of Ga'Hoole (2010, US/Australia). Grimble is a boreal owl warrior (voiced by Hugo Weaving) with a library.

A Legend Told [Kammaren] (2007, Sweden). Olof S. Larsson plays a librarian. The scenes in the library's second room were shot in the Karlstad municipal library.

The Librarian (2006, short). Amy Jean Page as lonely Prescott, Arizona, librarian Henrietta Fink becomes entangled in a deadly game of cat and mouse with two professional killers on Valentine's Day.

The Librarian: Curse of the Judas Chalice (2008, made for TV). Noah Wyle as Flynn Carsen has a breakdown at the Metropolitan Public Library, so his bosses Judson (Bob Newhart) and Charlene (Jane Curtin) suggest he take a vacation to New Orleans. His girlfriend Katie (Beth Burvant) says: "Maybe some women are okay with the wild and unpredictable lifestyle of dating a librarian, but I'm not." The exterior of the museum/library where Carsen works is the New Orleans Museum of Art.

The Librarian: Quest for the Spear (2004, US/Germany, made for TV). Noah Wyle as Flynn Carsen is hired as the librarian of the Metropolitan Public Library, which houses rare books and such artifacts as the Ark of the Covenant, Pandora's Box, and Excalibur. Someone breaks through the elaborate security and steals a section of the spear that pierced the side of Christ (the Spear of Destiny). Carsen is charged to find the spear and return it to the library. He joins forces with Nicole Noone (Sonya Walger), who also works for the library, and his boss Judson (Bob Newhart). Kyle MacLachlan plays former librarian Edward Wilde.

The Librarian: Return to King Solomon's Mines (2006, made for TV). Flynn Carsen only spends a few moments in the library, trying to avoid Poseidon's trident.

The Librarians (2007–2010, Australia, TV series). Frances O'Brien (played by series cocreator Robyn Butler), a devout Catholic and panic-disorder sufferer, runs a tight ship as head librarian at the Middleton Interactive Learning Centre, a suburban public library, in this comedy series. Her life unravels when she is forced to hire her ex–best friend, Christine Grimwood (Roz Hammond)—facing criminal drug charges—as the children's librarian. The series does not shy away from unusual topics, including multicultural tensions, dyslexia, a paraplegic staff member, and even an accreditation hearing.

The Living Wake (2007). Mike O'Connell as eccentric writer K. Roth Binew has a terminal disease, so he is planning to host his own wake. He and his biographer Mills Joaquin (Jesse Eisenberg) go to the public library to donate a set of his self-published children's books, but the librarian (Ann Dowd) deems them unfit for reading.

Long Weekend [Długi Weekend] (2004, Poland, made for TV). Bogdan Lewicki (Krzysztof Globisz), a shy, middle-aged man, chooses Girl No. 3, Marta Walkowska (Joanna Zólkowska), in the TV show *Blind Date*. The winning couple is to spend a long weekend in a luxurious hotel by the lake, but they do not seem suited to each other at all. Marta, a library supervisor, is a former opposition activist; and Bogdan is a professional soldier. Elzbieta Jarosik plays another librarian.

The Longest Yard (2005). Nelly as Megget is harassed in the prison library by guards who hope he will strike one of them, thus disqualifying him for the football team.

Love in Another Language [Başka dílde aşk] (2009, Turkey). Onur (played by Mert Firat) is a young deaf man who works as a librarian in Istanbul. Yonca Erturk is the library manager.

Love Life [Liebesleben] (2007, Israel/Germany). Zeruya Shalev, the author of the novel that this movie portrays, plays a librarian.

Love My Life (2006, Japan). Several scenes take place in an academic library; in one, the librarian shushes students for talking too loudly.

Loverboy (2005). Kyra Sedgwick as Emily has casual sex with a man (played by Nick Gregory) in the stacks of an Albuquerque public library where the Flaubert novels are shelved.

The Magic of Ordinary Days (2005, US/Canada, made for TV). Colorado farmer Skeet Ulrich as Ray Singleton goes into a public library to check out a book on the ancient city of Troy. The librarian, played by Kira Bradley, helps him spell Heinrich Schliemann.

Maid of Honor (2006, Canada, made for TV). Linda Purl as Laci Collins goes to the Lakeview (N.J.) Public Library to look at newspapers on microfiche.

Main, Meri Patni . . . Aur Woh! (2005, India). Rajpal Yadav plays Mithilesh Shukla, a bachelor librarian in Lucknow University's Tagore Library, who has a severe inferiority complex.

Main Street (2010). Orlando Bloom as Durham, North Carolina, police officer Harris Parker visits a library to look up a toxic-waste processing company on the computer. Nadya Simpson plays Kate, the library staffer.

Make Believe (2010, US/Japan/South Africa). One of the competitors in the Teen World Championship at the World Magic Seminar in Las Vegas is Krystyn Lambert, who volunteers at the Malibu (Calif.) High School library. William Goodwin, librarian at the Magic Castle in Hollywood, California, is also interviewed in this documentary.

The Manchurian Candidate (2004). Denzel Washington as Desert Storm veteran Captain Marco researches the politically powerful and corrupt Manchurian Global corporation at the New York Public Library. Using the internet, microfilm, and the copy machine, he compiles damning evidence against the company.

A Mão e a Luva: The Story of a Book Trafficker (2010, Italy). In this documentary, an ordinary young man named Kcal (aka Ricardo Gomes Ferraz) decides to open a library for children in Recife, Brazil, one of the poorest regions on earth. Using his limited savings, he buys used books and invites kids to have a look for a few hours a day. Referring to himself as a "book trafficker," his library becomes a meeting place for hundreds of children and adults. Thanks to Ricardo's work, the Brazilian Ministry of Culture has funded more than 500 small libraries throughout the favelas.

Margot at the Wedding (2007). Ciarán Hinds as Dick Koosman interviews author Margot (Nicole Kidman) at a book signing in the public library.

10

Marple: The Body in the Library (2004, US/UK, made for TV). A young woman's corpse is dumped in the library of Gossington Hall and Agatha Christie's octogenarian detective Miss Marple (Geraldine McEwan) is asked to solve the crime.

The Matchmaker [Pa'am Hayiti] (2010, Israel). In Haifa in 1968, Arik (played by Tuval Shafir) goes to a library to research the Holocaust, where he befriends Meir the librarian (Dror Keren). Meir turns to Yankele Bride (Adir Miller), a matchmaker and Holocaust survivor, for help finding a partner.

May the Best Man Win (2009). Victoria Chiaro and Marcia White play librarians.

The Memory Thief (2007). Mark Webber as Lukas gets a job at a Holocaust Archive in Los Angeles transcribing tapes and interviewing Holocaust survivors. Peter Jacobson is Mr. Freeman, the archivist.

Micky McGee Hates to Read! (2010). Dean E. Mehling as Dr. Meanandevil wants to destroy books in the public library and replace them with his own. But first he must find one child who refuses to read. Reluctant reader Micky McGee (Colin Arians) is transported to the library, where he meets four famous authors. Stephen Howard is the spirit of the library and Michael Patton is a librarian.

The Middle (May 19, 2010, TV series), "Average Rules." Betty White plays a stereotypical school librarian (Mrs. Nethercott, complete with pink cardigan, I Heart Books pin, and reading glasses on a necklace) who threatens to hold back from the third grade Brick (Atticus Shaffer), an intelligent but absent-minded boy who loves to read, because he has 31 books overdue.

MirrorMask (2005, US/UK). Teenage circus worker Helena (Stephanie Leonidas) becomes trapped in an imaginary world of her own making. In her quest to return home, she searches for a "useful book" in a library where the librarian (Stephen Fry) is part human and part puppet. He insists that patrons use a net to catch information, because the books literally fly off the shelf, and he gives her *A Really Useful Book* that continues to provide advice to deal with whatever situation she is in.

Mother of Tears [La terza madre] (2007, Italy/US). Asia Argento as assistant art museum curator Sarah Mandy consults Roman libraries to uncover legends about the returning Mater Lacrimarum, who seems determined to destroy the city with an army of demons.

My Afternoons with Margueritte [La tête en friche] (2010, France). A village librarian (Hélène Coulon) helps Germain Chazes (Gérard Depardieu) find some good reading material.

My Week with Marilyn (2011, UK/US). Derek Jacobi plays Sir Owen Morshead, the royal librarian at Windsor Castle. He gives Colin Clark (Eddie Redmayne) and Marilyn Monroe (Michelle Williams) a tour. Monroe says, "Gee, I'd sure like to read all these books."

Mysterious Skin (2004, US/Netherlands). Brady Corbet as Brian thinks he was abducted by aliens during a Little League game, so he spends much of his time in the library researching the incident.

N (Io e Napoleone) (2006, Italy/Spain/France). Elio Germano as young Martino Papucci gets a job as librarian/secretary to Napoleon (Daniel Auteuil) in exile on Elba in 1814–1815. He hates Napoleon, but begins to respect him when he starts recording the emperor's memoirs.

Naked in the 21st Century (2004). This quasi-documentary features nudist librarian Douglas Dunning.

The Namesake (2006, US/India). A Bengali family settles in New York City and struggles to become assimilated while retaining their traditions and cultural identity. Ashima, the mother (played by Tabu), takes a job in a library. The library scene was filmed at the Nyack (N.Y.) Public Library.

National Treasure (2004). Two thieves (Nicolas Cage as Benjamin Franklin Gates and Justin Bartha as Riley Poole) do some research in the Library of Congress, trying to find a way to break into the National Archives so they can steal the Declaration of Independence. Diane Kruger plays Abigail Chase, the US Archivist (with a foreign accent) who helps them.

National Treasure: Book of Secrets (2007). Treasure hunters Nicolas Cage as Benjamin Franklin Gates and Justin Bartha as Riley Poole find the *Book of Secrets*, which contains the handwriting of every president from Washington to Clinton, in the Library of Congress.

The New World (2005, US/UK). Oxford University's Bodleian Library serves as the entrance to the British royal court in the early 17th century.

Night at the Museum (2006, US/UK). Ben Stiller as Museum of Natural History night security guard Larry Daley goes to a library to read about Attila the Hun and other characters who come to life in the museum at night.

Night of the Sinner (2009, Italy/Spain). Ivana Miño as young rare-books librarian Rebecca flies to Italy to assess the collection of a prince (Robert Englund) for insurance purposes. She discovers a mysterious diary written by another librarian named Lara (Olga Shuvalova) and decides to unravel its secrets.

9 (2009). After all human life disappears from earth, a group of rag dolls comes to life in this animated feature and fights for survival against machines intent on their destruction. The mute twin dolls 3 and 4 live in an old library. They devise an ingenious system for cataloging and retrieving information: They fill a book with pictures and scraps of articles, then connect the page with a string that leads to the information on the shelf. Conveniently, they have projectors for eyes so they can replay audiovisual information.

Notre musique (2004, France/Switzerland). An off-screen narrator recites the Charles Baudelaire poem "Correspondences" as the camera pans through the ruined Bosnian National Library in Sarajevo. Spanish novelist Juan Goytisolo wanders through the ruins and recites a poem about the better fate of the dead. Jean-Luc Godard is in Sarajevo to attend a European Literary Encounters conference; he comments to another attendee, "Humane people don't start revolutions, they start libraries. And cemeteries."

Obselidia (2010). A lonely librarian (Michael Piccirilli as George Ruben) believes love is obsolete. In his spare time at home he is writing *An Encyclopedia of Obsolete Things* on a typewriter, but he doesn't include libraries as obsolete because home computers are not yet ubiquitous. A road trip to Death Valley with a beguiling cinema projectionist (Gaynor Howe as Sophie Fitzpatrick) gives him a new outlook. Linda Walton is a library coworker. Scenes were filmed at Santa Monica (Calif.) Public Library.

The Off Season (2004). Christina Campanella as Kathryn Bennett gets a temporary job as a library assistant in a small Maine public library. A dream ghost

10

hits her in the eye with a library book and knocks her out for a week. The librarians are played by Francine Pado as Claudette and Noah DeFilippis. Filmed in Old Orchard Beach, Maine.

The Old Guys (July 9, 2010, UK, TV series), "Quiz." Aging housemates Tom Finnan (Roger Lloyd-Pack) and Roy Bowden (Clive Swift) are determined to win a pub quiz to prove that their minds are still agile. They visit a library where Tom tries to impress Barbara the librarian (Cherie Lunghi) with his knowledge of literature.

Older Than America (2008). Barbara Kingsley is a librarian at the Penmore County (Minn.) Historical Society. She brings out 1955 editions of the *Pine Knot* newspaper for Bradley Cooper as government geologist Luke Peterson, who is investigating an earthquake that occurred that year on the Fond du Lac Indian Reservation. He also looks at old photos of a government-run Indian boarding school. She makes him wear archival gloves for the newspapers, but not for the photos. The scenes were actually filmed at the Carlton County Historical Society in Cloquet, Minnesota.

Oliver Sherman (2010, Canada). Garret Dillahunt as combat veteran Sherman Oliver spends much of his time in the North Bay (Ont.) Public Library researching war.

On a Clear Day (2005, UK). Peter Mullan as laid-off shipworker Frank Redmond stumbles on fish-and-chips shop owner Chan (Benedict Wong) in the library and they seem to have a connection. Chan agrees to do some library research for Frank's attempted English Channel swim.

Once Beautiful Past (2008, short). In 1980, Henry Hall (Robin Calvert) is a reclusive librarian in Berkeley, California, who discovers that he has Alzheimer's disease on the eve of his second marriage.

Ondine (2009, Ireland/US). Alison Barry as Annie goes to the library and checks out all the books she can find on selkies. Norma Sheahan plays a librarian.

One Missed Call (2008, Japan/US/Germany). Azura Skye as Leann is studying in the university library at closing time. She phones her friend and says, "I just got sprung from the stacks; my brain was mushing out." Her friend Beth (Shannyn Sossamon) is in the library researching a mysterious hospital fire when she starts seeing some weird things. An uncredited librarian has a brief scene behind a desk. The library scenes were filmed at the Georgia Institute of Technology in Atlanta.

1001 Inventions and the Library of Secrets (2010, UK, short). Three teenagers are assigned by their teacher to research the impact of the Middle Ages on the modern world. In the library they meet a librarian (Ben Kingsley) who transforms himself into the 12th-century scholar Al-Jazari and  enlightens them on the scientific and technological discoveries of the golden age of Muslim civilization.

Oranges and Sunshine (2010, UK/Australia). In 1986, Emily Watson as social worker Margaret Humphreys digs through records at libraries and archives looking for evidence of the UK government's enforced deportation of children to Australia in the 1950s and 1960s. John Robinson is a library researcher.

The Oxford Murders (2008, Spain/UK/France). Martin (Elijah Wood) and Beth (Julie Cox) have an argument at Oxford University's Bodleian Library.

ParaNorman (2012). Bridget Hoffman is the voice of the librarian.

Parks and Recreation (November 5, 2009, TV series), "Ron and Tammy." Amy Poehler as Leslie Knope and the rest of the parks department express hatred for the Pawnee (Ind.) Public Library, which Leslie declares a "diabolical, ruthless bunch of bureaucrats." Tammy Swanson (Megan Mullally) is the new library deputy director, who seems sweet at first but acts crazy when she gets together with her ex-husband Ron Swanson (Nick Offerman).

Parks and Recreation (February 10, 2011, TV series), "Ron and Tammy: Part Two." Ron Swanson (Nick Offerman) and his ex-wife Tammy—the psychopathic director of the Pawnee (Ind.) Public Library (played by Offerman's actual wife, guest star Megan Mullally)—continue their hilarious, insane relationship. Tammy sexily slaps herself in the face with a piece of beef jerky, and Ron and Tammy do some dirty dancing.

The Party Never Stops: Diary of a Binge Drinker (2007, Canada/US, made for TV). Insecure University of Victoria freshman student Sara Paxton as Jessie Brenner sits at a library table with girlfriends and asks, "Does anyone actually study in the library?" However, she goes there repeatedly. Scenes include an uncredited older librarian pushing a "stack maintenance" bookcart and Jessie blaming the library for her stolen phone.

The Path of Evil (2005). Rod Richards plays a librarian in Devil's Lake, Oregon.

Pirate Kids II: The Search for the Silver Skull (2006). Betty Ann Austin plays a librarian.

Pizza: The Movie (2004). Craig Wisniewski as high-school graduate Kevin Miller works in a library for a horny, matronly supervisor.

Poison Friends [Les amitiés maléfiques] (2006, France). Natacha Régnier as Marguerite is a popular-literature student who works as a clerk at the Sorbonne Nouvelle university library in Paris. She discovers a love letter from another student tucked into a book.

Portlandia (January 21, 2011, TV series), "Hide and Seek" sketch. Two rival teams in Portland's Adult Hide-and-Seek League, the Sherlock Holmies and the Punky Bruisers, play a match in the reading room of the Portland Community College library.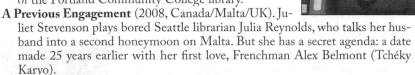

A Previous Engagement (2008, Canada/Malta/UK). Juliet Stevenson plays bored Seattle librarian Julia Reynolds, who talks her husband into a second honeymoon on Malta. But she has a secret agenda: a date made 25 years earlier with her first love, Frenchman Alex Belmont (Tchéky Karyo).

Primer (2004). Aaron (Shane Carruth) and Abe (David Sullivan) use the Richardson (Tex.) Public Library to research stock market trades.

The Prince and Me (2004, US/Czech). Julia Stiles as farm girl Paige Morgan and Luke Mably as foreign exchange student Eddie make out in the stacks of a library at the University of Wisconsin. Scenes were filmed at the University of Toronto's E. J. Pratt Library.

Princess Protection Program (2009, made for TV). Samantha Droke as Brooke asks the librarian in her high school library in Lake Monroe, Louisiana, for some easy reading in Spanish. In an issue of ¡Estilo! Magazine, she discovers that her classmate Rosie Gonzalez (Demi Lovato) is actually the relocated Princess of Costa Luna, Rosalinda Montoya, in hiding from an attempted coup.

Prism (2007). Stephanie Vukadinovich and Judy Lee Watts play librarians.

10

Prometheus (2012, US/UK). Charlize Theron as Meredith Vickers, mission director of the spacecraft *USS Prometheus,* has a library in her quarters in which the book spines face inwards.

Psych (December 1, 2010, TV series), "Dual Spires." Sherilyn Fenn plays an enigmatic librarian, Maudette Hornsby, in a satiric tribute to David Lynch's *Twin Peaks.* A close look at the Dual Spires Public Library shelves reveals a mix of Dewey and LC class numbers as well as extremely poor volume arrangement.

Psychoville (May 5, 2011, UK, TV series), "Survivors." Reece Shearsmith is Jeremy Goode, a librarian who is obsessed with the return of the overdue book *50 Great Coastal Walks of the British Isles,* vol. 2, by a woman who claims she lost it. When angry or paranoid, he sees a figure he calls the Silent Singer, a jagged-toothed man dressed in braided pigtails who pretends to sing into a cane.

Pulse (2006). Josh (Jonathan Tucker) enters a university library in Ohio intending to meet his friend Douglas Zeiglar (Kel O'Neill). He rides the elevator down to a lower level and is attacked in the dimly lit stacks by a half-seen spirit that sucks the life force out of him.

Rabbit Hole (2010). Nicole Kidman as Becca is following high school student Jason (Miles Teller) whom she recognizes as the driver of the car that hit her four-year-old son months earlier. She unexpectedly meets up with him in the library, where he confronts her. She checks out the book Jason had been reading, *Parallel Universes.* Marylouise Burke plays a librarian.

Racing Daylight (2007). Melissa Leo as librarian Sadie Stokes returns to her hometown to care for her ailing grandmother, but she soon begins to have hallucinations about her Civil War ancestor.

Rampart (2011). Woody Harrelson as corrupt cop David Douglas Brown meets with retired cop Hartshorn (Ned Beatty) in the Los Angeles Law Library. When he slams the table, a patron shushes him.

Rare Books and Manuscripts (2005, UK, short). In the reading room of the British Library, Jess (Neve McIntosh) falls in love with the gorgeous Heinz (Ian Mosby). Too shy to talk to him, she starts sending him books spelling out her feelings for him. But she starts receiving books in return—and they are not from Heinz.

The Reader (2008, US/Germany). Kate Winslet as Hanna Schmitz is sent to prison for murders she was held responsible for as an SS guard 20 years earlier. She learns to read in the prison library, where Carmen-Maja Antoni is the librarian.

The Reading Room (2005, made for TV). James Earl Jones plays affluent suburbanite widower William Campbell, who honors his wife's dying wish by opening up a reading room in a gang-dominated inner city neighborhood and donating his extensive library.

RED (2010). Ex–CIA agent Frank Moses (Bruce Willis) recognizes the mysterious numbers on a postcard as the Harvard-Yenching call number of a book in the Bobst Library at New York University. He goes to the library (filmed at Toronto Public Library) and finds the book, which contains a list of agents involved in a dirty war in Guatemala in the 1980s.

Reincarnation [Rinne] (2005, Japan). Ghostly, blue-hued hands reach out from the college library bookshelves to attack Nagisa Sugiura (Yûka) and drag her away.

Remember Me (2010). Tyler Hawkins (Robert Pattinson) is a student worker in the New York University library. He falls off a library ladder during an argument.

Robot & Frank (2012). Susan Sarandon (right) plays Jennifer, a small-town public librarian in the "near future" whose library is replacing its books with ebooks, thanks to a smarmy businessman named Jake (Jeremy Strong). She bonds with old codger Frank (Frank Langella), an ex–jewel thief who has a robot caretaker that helps him carry out heists, the first of which is saving a rare printed edition of *Don Quixote* before the library discards it.

Rocket Science (2007). Jonah Hill plays the Junior Philosopher, a teen whom Hal Hefner (Reece Thompson) meets in the high school library while studying for a policy debate with Ginny Ryerson (Anna Kendrick).

The Roommate (2011). An unhinged college student (Leighton Meester as Rebecca) stalks Stephen (Cam Gigandet) in the library stacks of a Los Angeles university. Stacy Barnhisel plays a librarian.

Rounding First (2005). Jo Mercer plays a librarian at the Allentown (Pa.) Public Library.

Roxy Hunter and the Mystery of the Moody Ghost (2007, made for TV). Julian Richings plays Serenity Falls librarian Mr. Tibers.

Salvage (2006). Lauren Currie Lewis as convenience store clerk Claire Parker goes to the library to look at newspapers on microfiche. Georgine A. Timko is a librarian.

Scott Pilgrim vs. the World (2010, US/UK/Canada). Michael Cera as Scott Pilgrim is helping his girlfriend Knives Chau (Ellen Wong) pick out some calculus books at a public library. He sees the mysterious pink-haired Ramona Flowers (Mary Elizabeth Winstead) dropping off a package at the circulation desk.

The Secret [Si j'étais toi] (2007, France). David Duchovny as Dr. Benjamin Marris goes to the library to look up "scientific research" on the web.

Sex and the City (2008). Sarah Jessica Parker as Carrie Bradshaw returns a book (volume 1 of *Love Letters of Great Men*) to the New York Public Library (although the Research Library had not circulated books for decades), sees that a wedding is taking place in the McGraw Rotunda, and decides to hold her own wedding there as well. But when the date arrives, Mr. Big (Chris Noth) calls her cellphone while she is standing in the Astor Hall area and says he won't go through with it.

Sex Is Zero 2 [Saekjeuk shigong ssizeun 2] (2007, South Korea). Good-hearted Eun-sik (Chang Jung Lim) is a law student who is preoccupied with checking out female legs in the library.

Shadow Man (2006). Steven Seagal as former CIA agent Jack Foster agrees to exchange data on a killer virus for his daughter at the Romanian central library in Bucharest and winds up destroying it.

Shake It Up (March 25, 2012, TV series), "Parent Trap It Up." Tyra Banks appears in a cameo as Miss Burke, a school librarian with pencils in her hair, oversized glasses, and a cardigan. She helps Rocky Blue (Zendaya) and CeCe Jones (Bella Thorne) come up with a plan to create the right circumstances for CeCe's father to propose marriage again to her mother.

Shameless (2010–2011, UK, Season 7–8, TV series). Pauline McLynn plays Libby Croker, a librarian who spends time in jail for protesting the library closing and falls for the drunken slacker Frank Gallagher (David Threlfall).

10

Shelf Life (2005). Betsy Brandt as goth slacker Nikki Reynolds gets a job as a shelver in a small-town public library as part of her drug-recovery program. She immediately faces off with huffy Library Director Betty Bonhauser (Elisa Bocanegra), who brags of having librarians in her family tree for four generations but yells at children to pay attention during storytime. When Betty accuses Nikki of stealing a dictionary, Assistant Librarian Ronald (Joe Smith) takes Nikki's side. Ray the Mumbler (Richard Ankrom) teaches Nikki to shelve books.

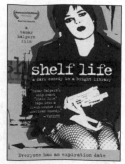

SideFX (2005). Amanda Phillips as Tuesday is in a Dallas university library studying when she sees a creepy old man watching her.

Silent Library (2008–2011, TV series). A team of six players sits at a table on a set that looks like a public library in this MTV game show. Whoever draws a skull-and-crossbones card must endure a punishment challenge. The entire team must endure each challenge silently (without laughing or crying out) to win four rounds of the game. The show was based on a segment of the Japanese variety show *Downtown no gake no tsukai ya arahende!!*

The Skulls III (2004, Canada). Clare Kramer as Taylor Brooks researches the law on campus gender equity so she can be admitted to an all-male secret fraternity. Later she and some friends use the library computer to hack into the university server and read archived emails. They leave without turning the computer off. Irene Dale plays a librarian.

Sky High (2005). An amusing romp about a high school for superheroes. Exteriors of the school were filmed at the Delmar T. Oviatt Library building, California State University, Northridge.

Sleep Furiously (2008, UK). The stories of villagers in Trefeurig, Wales, are framed in this documentary by scenes showing the yellow mobile library van on its monthly tour driven by kindly librarian John Jones, who talks to patrons about books and the town.

The Smile Behind the Mirror (2010). Evangeline Joy Galliford is Eleanor, a librarian who seeks to make her mark on history with the help of a friend's time-machine computer.

Solitary Man (2009). Michael Douglas as car dealership magnate Ben Kalmen was a major donor to his alma mater, an East Coast college, and the library is named after him.

Something Borrowed (2011). Rachel (Ginnifer Goodwin) and Dex (Colin Egglesfield) goof around while studying torts in the New York University Law School Library and get shushed by another student (Noel Davis Poyner).

Somewhere in Between (2005, short). Adapted from Paul Gitschner's short play *The Diary Library*, this is the story of Dawn (Franceska Lynne), a confused young woman who wanders into a strange, cluttered library. She meets Lib (Erica Engelhardt), a quirky librarian charged with collecting and filing the diaries of all the library's previous visitors.

The Squid and the Whale (2005). Owen Kline as preteen Frank Berkman rubs up against library shelves to masturbate as an act of defiance against his divorcing parents. Shot in Midwood High School library in Brooklyn, New York.

Star Wars: The Clone Wars (October 2, 2009, TV series), "Holocron Heist." Flo Di Re appears in this and two later episodes as librarian/archivist Jocasta Nu.

State of Play (2009, US/UK/France). The scene in which Anne Collins (Robin Wright) makes a statement to the press was shot at the Library of Congress in Washington, D.C.

Stay (2005). One scene shows the Gould Memorial Library dome at Bronx (N.Y.) Community College.

Stay until Tomorrow (2004). Barney Cheng as Providence (R.I.) Public Library worker Jim likes to read the books while he is shelving them, even though the rule is that at work "librarians are only supposed to read book reviews." He lets his childhood pal Nina (Eleanor Hutchins) stay at his place for a while. She tries to learn Italian at the library for her next job, but manages to have flings with a security guard and a high school student on the library roof. Seven librarians are credited in the film, including Cynthia M. Reed.

Stellina Blue (2009). Shawn M. Richardz plays a librarian.

Strip Mind (2007, Germany). Jodie Ahlborn as clinical psychiatry student Samantha spends extra time studying in the library. Barrett Jones plays a crazed library assistant in Munich.

Suburban Girl (2007). Sarah Michelle Gellar as assistant editor Brett Eisenberg and Maggie Grace as Chloe go to a literary lecture in a library (filmed at the New-York Historical Society). Geoffrey Cantor is a library curator.

Super (2010). Rainn Wilson as hapless short-order cook Frank D'Arbo decides to turn his life around by becoming a superhero, The Crimson Bolt. He poses as a student with a fake beard, goes to the college library to read comics about superheros, and asks the librarian (played by Laurel Whitsett) where he can find information on recent crimes. She locates abundant drug dealing on the internet and tells him the worst activity is on Euclid Street.

Sydney White (2007). Amanda Bynes as Southern Atlantic University freshman student Sydney White falls asleep studying in the library. She almost misses a debate, but her boyfriend Tyler (Matt Long) kisses her awake in time. Phyllis Fludd White plays a librarian.

Szerafina (2007, Hungary, short). Mari Nagy is a librarian.

Take Shelter (2011). Disturbed by apocalyptic visions, Curtis (Michael Shannon) checks out a book on mental illness from the Elyria (Ohio) Public Library.

The Tale of Despereaux (2008, UK/US). The bold and daring mouse Despereaux (voiced by Matthew Broderick) is taken to the library of the Castle of the Kingdom of Door to learn to eat paper, but he reads a fairy tale about a princess instead.

Tambourine, Drum [Buben, baraban] (2009, Russia). Depressed librarian Katya (Natalya Negoda) steals books from the library and sells them on trains.

The Ten (2007). Gretchen Mol plays uptight librarian Gloria Jennings, who goes on vacation to Mexico and has a torrid affair with a mysterious man named Jesus H. Christ. Other librarians are Oliver (A. D. Miles) and Tony (Jason Sudeikis).

Ten Inch Hero (2007). Julia (Adair Tishler) goes to the Santz Cruz (Calif.) Public Library with her father and surprises art student Piper (Elisabeth Harnois), whom she persuades to give her drawing lessons.

These Amazing Shadows: The Movies That Make America (2011). Librarian of Congress James Billington appears in this documentary showcase of films selected since 1989 by the National Film Preservation Board for preservation in the National Film Registry of the Library of Congress.

10

13 Going on 30 (2004). Jennifer Garner as Jenna Rink and Mark Ruffalo as Matt Flamhaff stage their *Poise* magazine photo shoot on the front steps of the New York Public Library.

Thor (2011). After his laptop is stolen, Stellan Skarsgård as scientist Erik Selvig uses a public computer at a New Mexico library to email a colleague. While he is there, he happens upon a book of Norse mythology.

A Thousand Years of Good Prayers (2007). Retired Beijing widower Mr. Shi (Henry O) decides to visit his divorced daughter Yilan (Faye Yu), who works as a librarian at Gonzaga University's Chastek Law Library in Spokane, Washington.

Time of Her Life (2005, UK). Gemma Robinson is a library assistant.

The Time Traveler's Wife (2009). Special Collections Li-brarian Henry DeTamble (Eric Bana), who works at the Newberry Library in Chicago, has a genetic disorder that causes him to involuntarily travel through time. He occasionally returns to work nude from a time trip. He is approached by 20-year-old Clare Abshire (Rachel McAdams) who knows and loves him since she met him at age six. Carly Street is a librarian, and Bart Bedford is a library researcher.

Tinker Tailor Soldier Spy (2011, France/UK/Germany). Benedict Cumberbatch as Peter Guillam goes to the MI6 Secret Intelligence Service archive in the early 1970s to look at (and snitch) a critical document. Sal the archival clerk (Laura Carmichael) lets him into the closed stacks with the information: "Corridor D, the 2-8's are halfway on your right. The 3-1's the next alcove down."

Tiny Furniture (2010). Lena Dunham as Aura moves back home to Brooklyn after graduating from college in Ohio. She is depressed and calls her friend Frankie (Merritt Wever), who happens to be sitting on the floor of the college library stacks. Later, Aura meets up with Jed (Alex Karpovsky), a YouTube video artist, and asks him what people without money do; he suggests that they "loiter at libraries."

Tokyo Sonata (2008, Japan/Netherlands/Hong Kong). Ryûhei Sasaki (played by Teruyuki Kagawa) loses his job after 46 years and tries to hide it from his family, going to the public library instead.

Toronto Stories (2008, Canada). In "The Brazilian" segment, Sook-Yin Lee as Willia goes to the public library to look up what "Polkaroo" means, a name that her reserved friend Boris (Tygh Runyan) has been calling himself.

Toy Story 3 (2010). The Bookworm (voiced by Richard Kind) is a green worm flashlight toy with glasses who maintains a library of instruction manuals in a closet.

Transformers: Revenge of the Fallen (2009). Isabel Lucas plays Alice, a Decepticon Pretender, who chases Sam (Shia LeBeouf), Leo (Ramon Rodriguez), and Mikaela (Megan Fox) into a Princeton library and destroys it, crashing through walls and knocking over bookshelves and tables. Scenes were filmed outside the Firestone Library at Princeton and at the Free Library of Philadelphia.

29 Reasons to Run (2006). Renee Waits plays a librarian.

Two:Thirteen (2009). Jo Steele plays a librarian who brings Police Detective Russell Spivey (Mark Thompson) the complete works of William Shakespeare.

The Ultimate Gift (2006). Spoiled kid Jason Stevens (Drew Fuller), in order to claim an inheritance after the death of his billionaire grandfather (James Garner as Howard "Red" Stevens), must complete a series of tasks designed to teach him the value of money. One is to work for a month in a nearly bookless rural library (Stevens Biblioteca) that his grandfather established in Ecuador. Rose Bianco plays Bella, the Ecuadorian librarian.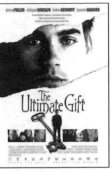

Universal Signs (2008). Sabrina Lloyd is Mary, an academic librarian who befriends a deaf artist named Andrew (Anthony Natale). Susan Wilder plays another librarian.

Vampiros (2004, Puerto Rico). Vampire-bite victim Jonathan (played by Jorge Dieppa) goes to a public library to research the undead, but a library staffer refers him to books by Anne Rice and Bram Stoker.

Vault of Darkness (2009). The "Its Hour Come Round" segment features Christina Cupo as Alma, a librarian who has some terrifying moments.

Vicky Cristina Barcelona (2008, Spain/US). Rebecca Hall as Vicky is on vacation in Barcelona, but she spends time in local libraries researching Catalan culture.

Wanted (2008, US/Germany). Several scenes take place in the headquarters library of a secret Fraternity of assassins.

A Way of Life (2004, UK). Stephanie James as teenage mother Leigh-Anne Williams, accompanied by her brother and two friends, has a confrontation with a Turkish man in a Welsh library. Siriol Jenkins plays a librarian.

Welcome Home (2004, Austria). Stephanie Commings plays a librarian.

Welcome to Mooseport (2004, US/Germany). Gene Hackman as former US President Monroe Cole has retired to his vacation home in Mooseport, Maine, where he plans to build his massive presidential library. The library architect, Izuki Nami (Dennis Akayama), describes it as "European rationalism interwoven with American modernism, a metaphor of organic growth, a man-made mountain over which soars the eagle."

What's Your Number? (2011). Anna Faris as Ally Darling tries to spy on ex-boyfriend Tom Piper (Anthony Mackie) in the "Adams Library" in Washington, D.C., by asking patrons to move a study table so she can see him better. The courtyard of the Boston Public Library was transformed into a romantic restaurant for another scene.

When a Man Falls (2007, Germany/Canada/US). Dylan Baker as agoraphobic janitor Bill compulsively rearranges the audiocassette collection at a public library until he finds a self-help tape on lucid dreaming.

The Wives He Forgot (2006, Canada, made for TV). Teri Philips plays a librarian.

Wulf (2009, UK, short). A librarian works overtime to get the books ready for the opening of a new corporate headquarters. But there is a rogue werewolf prowling the corridors.

Yalp (2004, France/Germany, short). In a library where the cast moves forward but the scenes are recorded in backward action, only books written in reverse writing are available. Marianne Döring is the librarian.

You, Me, and Dupree (2006). Molly (Kate Hudson) and Carl (Matt Dillon) try to get rid of their unwelcome house guest Dupree (Owen Wilson) by setting him up with an elementary school librarian named Mandy (uncredited). How-

10

ever, it turns out she has a reputation as a slut.

Zhou Yu's Train (2004, China/Hong Kong). Chen Qing (Tony Leung Ka Fai) is a shy poet who works in a library in Chongyang.

Zodiac (2007). *San Francisco Chronicle* cartoonist Robert Graysmith (Jake Gyllenhaal) and crime reporter Paul Avery (Robert Downey Jr.) use an archive to consult back issues of the *Modesto Bee* in their quest to find the Zodiac Killer in 1969–1970. Graysmith soon becomes obsessed with the case, bringing home armfuls of library books on psychology and cryptography.

SOURCES: Martin Raish, Librarians in the Movies: An Annotated Filmography, emp.byui.edu/raishm/films/introduction.html; Antoinette Graham, Movie Librarians, movielibrarians.com; Jennifer Snoek-Brown, Reel Librarians, reel-librarians.com; Notorious BIB, notoriousbib.wordpress.com; Libraries at the Movies, librariesatthemovies.blogspot.com; Internet Movie Database, www.imdb.com.

COLLECTIONS

Larry Nix's 10 favorite library postcards
by Larry T. Nix

MY APPROACH TO LIBRARY POSTCARD COLLECTING has been a targeted one. I collect postcards that feature Wisconsin libraries, military library service, state libraries, and bookmobiles. I also collect postcards that contain a library-related message in the message portion of the postcard and postcards that have been part of another person's collection. I acquire other library postcards because of the unusual nature of their topic. My 10 favorite library postcards reflect those interests.

Sault Ste. Marie Carnegie Library, Ontario, Canada. I acquired this postcard as part of the Anna E. Felt library postcard collection. Felt was a trustee and benefactor of the Galena (Ill.) Public Library, and an avid collector of library postcards in the first two decades of the 20th century. The postcard depicts the city hall, Carnegie library, municipal building, and fire hall of Sault Ste. Marie, Ontario.

City Hall, Carnegie Library, Municipal Building, Fire Hall.

The message on the front of the postcard, which was mailed to Felt on September 5, 1906, reads: "I understand that you have the 'library habit' so send you this delightful combination which certainly is unusual." The Carnegie library was completed in 1904 and destroyed by fire in 1907. Ironically, the library was uninsured because of its location next to a fire station. Fortunately, after some difficult persuasion, Sault Ste. Marie was able to obtain a second Carnegie grant for a new library.

Williams Free Library, Beaver Dam, Wisconsin. There are a number of postcard views of this library that was built in 1890–1891. I like this one that shows people waiting for the train at the adjacent railroad depot. The library was named for John J. Williams (1820–1896), who donated $25,000 to build the library. It is an outstanding example of the Romanesque Revival architectural style inspired by American architect Henry Hobson Richardson (1838–1886). The building currently houses the Dodge County Historical Society. This is a "real photo" postcard, a card that is a true photograph produced from a film negative and printed onto photographic paper.

Nashville (Tenn.) Carnegie Library. This library was razed in 1963 to make way for a new building on the same site. I should know. I started my library career in this Carnegie building as a part-time page in that same year. Although I spent most of my two-and-a-half-year stint at the Nashville library in temporary quarters while the new building was under construction, I have some especially fond

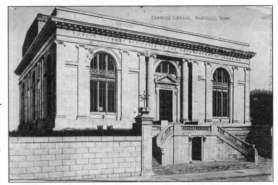

memories of my time in this old Carnegie. Across the top of the library is the statement: "Public library dedicated to the advancement of learning." Carnegie's name is over the front door.

Carpenter Memorial Library, Manchester, New Hampshire. I find postcards depicting the interiors of libraries particularly appealing, especially when library users are shown. This interior view of the Carpenter Memorial Library includes an unusually large number of library users. They are probably

10

part of a school class visiting the library. The building still serves as the main library of the Manchester City Library. It was dedicated as the Elenora Blood Carpenter Building in 1914, in memory of the wife of Frank Pierce Carpenter, who funded its construction.

California County Libraries. This postcard was used to promote county library service in California. First published in 1915, the card has been updated by typewriter to show that 33 county libraries were established up to that point. The California State Library, under the overall leadership of James Gillis (state librarian from 1899 to 1917), took on the task of organizing county libraries throughout the state. Harriet Gertrude Eddy joined the staff of the California State Library in 1909 and was the person responsible for organizing county library service in 40 of California's 58 counties in the next nine years.

Kentucky Bookmobile Service. The Friends of Kentucky Libraries created this postcard to promote bookmobile service. A printed message on the back of the card says in part: "One of Kentucky's 98 bookmobiles which give service to young and old in remote corners of the state." The postcard was mailed by a resident of Elizabethtown, in Hardin County, Kentucky, on November 1, 1958, to a friend in California. The card has been stamped on the back with a message in support of a referendum to establish a free public library in an election on November 4. A handwritten message says: "Our county will vote on this next Tue. Hope we can get it." The Hardin County Public Library was founded in 1958, so the referendum must have passed.

Ohio State Library's Traveling Library Service. This is one of several postcards that the Ohio State Library in Columbus created to promote its traveling library service. Traveling libraries were small, rotating collections of books that were used to extend public library services in rural areas. Melvil Dewey implemented

the traveling library concept in New York in 1892 and many other states followed. Ohio's traveling libraries began in 1896 and grew to be one of the largest systems in the nation. Traveling libraries were usually delivered to their various locations in wooden boxes by express companies, as illustrated on this postcard.

Redwood Library and Athenaeum, Newport, Rhode Island. Membership libraries, which usually required readers to pay an annual fee, preceded free public libraries. Most of these libraries, which went by a variety of names, have long since disappeared. An exception is the Redwood Library and Athenaeum of Newport, Rhode Island, established in 1747 and shown on this postcard. The building is the oldest continuously occupied library building in the United States. The postcard was produced by the prolific British postcard publisher Raphael Tuck & Sons, which began publishing postcards in 1899. Tuck commissioned its own artwork for most of its postcards, including this one showing an attractive scene with people strolling in front of the library.

American Library Association Camp Library, Camp Sherman, Ohio. ALA used postcards to promote its Library War Service during World War I. Although these colorless postcards are of poor quality, they are definitely among my favorites. This one shows the interior of the Camp Sherman Library near Chillicothe, Ohio. The librarian and two assistants are shown near the circulation desk. I'm pretty sure the librarian who is depicted standing in front of the circulation desk is Burton E. Stevenson (1872–1962), who served as the first camp librarian. Stevenson took a leave from his job as director of the Chillicothe Public Library to play a leadership role in the Library War Service. He is also the author of many romance and mystery novels. The Camp Sherman Library building, one of over 40 constructed by ALA during WWI, may be the only one still in existence. It has been transformed into a farm building for the Ohio Department of Rehabilitation and Correction Institutions but is no longer recognizable as a library.

10

American Library Association Hospital Service, U.S. Debarkation Hospital No. 5, New York City. I couldn't resist choosing a second postcard produced by the ALA Library War Service during World War I. The description of the view on the postcard reads: "With her book truck, the librarian brings to the men's bed the book he wants. The A.L.A. has placed libraries in 208 hospitals." This postcard also promotes a service of the US Post Office that allowed anyone to place a one-cent stamp on a magazine and drop it into a mailbox. The magazines were then delivered to ALA and other organizations for use by soldiers and sailors in camps and hospitals.

Collecting the Newts

by Karel Čapek

SO IT WAS THAT MISTER POVONDRA started his collection of newspaper clippings about the Newts. Without his passion as a collector, much of the material we now have would otherwise have been lost. He cut out and saved everything written about the Newts that he could find; it should even be said that after some initial fumblings he learned to plunder the newspapers in his favorite café wherever there was mention of the Newts and even developed an unusual, almost magical, virtuosity in tearing the appropriate article out of the paper and putting it in his pocket right under the nose of the head waiter. It is well known that all collectors are willing to steal and murder if that is what's needed to add a certain item to their collection, but that is not in any way a stain on their moral character.

His life was now the life of a collector, and that gave it meaning. Evening after evening he would count and arrange his clippings under the indulgent eyes of Mrs. Povondra, who knew that every man is partly mad and partly a little child; it was better for him to play with his clippings than to go out drinking and playing cards. She even made some space in the scullery for all the boxes he had made himself for his collection; could anything more be asked of a wife?

Even Mister Bondy was surprised at Mister Povondra's encyclopaedic knowledge of everything concerning the Newts, which he showed at every opportunity. With some embarrassment, Mister Povondra admitted that he collected everything printed about the Salamanders and let Mister Bondy see his boxes. G. H. Bondy kindly praised him for his collection; what does it matter that only great men can be so generous and only powerful people can give pleasure without it costing them a penny? It's all right for those who are great. Mister Bondy, for instance, told the office of the Salamander Syndicate to send Mister Povondra all the clippings to do with the Newts that they did not need to keep in their archives, and lucky Mister Povondra, somewhat dismayed, received whole parcels of documents in all the languages of the world every day. And for documents in the Cyrillic alphabet, Greek, Hebrew, Arabic, Chinese script, Bengali, Tamil, Javanese, Burmese, or Nasta'līq he was especially grateful. "When I think," he said about it all, "without me it would never have happened!"

As we have already said, Mister Povondra's collection saved much historic material concerning the whole story of the Newts; but that, of course, does not mean to say it was enough to satisfy a scientific historian.

Firstly, Mister Povondra had never received a specialist education as assistant in historic or archival methods, and he made no indication on his cuttings of the source, or the date, so that we do not know when or where each document was published.

And secondly, faced with so much material piling up around him, Mister Povondra kept mainly the longest articles, which he considered must be the most important, while the shorter reports were simply thrown into the coal scuttle; as a result, through all this period, remarkably few facts and reports were conserved by him.

Thirdly, the hand of Mrs. Povondra played a considerable part in the matter; when she carefully filled up one of Mister Povondra's boxes, she would quietly and secretly pull out some of the cuttings and burn them, which took place several times a year. The only ones she spared were the ones that did not grow in number very fast, such as the cuttings printed in the Malayalam, Tibetan, or Coptic scripts; these remained more or less complete, although for certain gaps in our body of knowledge they are not of great value. This means that the material we have available concerning the history of the Newts is very fragmented, like the land records of the 8th century A.D., or the selected writings of the poetess Sappho; but some documents, here and there, did happen to survive about this phase of the great history of the world, and despite all the gaps we will do our best to summarize them under the title *The Rise of Civilization*.

SOURCE: Karel Čapek, *War with the Newts*, book 2, chapter 1, originally published in Prague in 1936. This selection translated by David Wyllie, 2002, for Project Gutenberg Australia, used CC BY-SA.

Things librarians fancy
by Travis Jonker

HAVE YOU EVER WANTED to delve into the unexplored world of librarian culture? If you just said "no," I can't hear you. If you just said "yes," then today, my friend, is your lucky day. Cribbing heavily and blatantly from another website, I bring you Things Librarians Fancy. I am guilty of many, many (okay pretty much all) of the items listed below.

Carts. Be it book, A/V or other, librarians love all things multishelved and four-wheeled. The tech-savvy may gush about how they put together "the perfect document camera setup," the bookish may encourage you to check out their drill cart team at ALA Annual Conferences—either way, librarians rely heavily on these contraptions for their identity. *Fast fact:* Librarians are known to keep their cart wheels free of oil, so that the screeching sound may announce their arrival in advance.

Sensible lunches in brown paper bags. When it comes to lunch, librarians completely refrain from warm food in favor of items that can be pulled out of the refrigerator and eaten at once. Raw vegetables, various cheeses, whole-grain crackers, granola, and other foods enjoyed by mice are common librarian staples. *Fast fact:* Librarian Abner Tweed went 43 years without using an oven or microwave (1961–2004).

Cardigans. It may not surprise you to hear that librarians love cardigan sweaters. What you may not know is that there are two varieties of cardigan wearers—ironic and irony-free. The former is typically middle aged or older and enjoys the warmth that a well-made sweater provides in the chilly library setting. The latter resides in the 20–35-year-old age range and is seeking to project the nerdy hipster image. *Fast fact:* The ironic/irony-free librarian schism occurred in late 2003.

Books that haven't been published.
Nothing gets a librarian more excited than reading a book that you haven't, usually so that they can recommend it to you or totally dismiss it before anyone else. "In the know" librarians often use the terms ARC, galley, and advanced copy to describe books that they feel are going to be big. *Fast fact:* Kelly Forte has been called the world's most forward-reading librarian. She is currently reading books that won't be published until 2018, and has even sent a letter to Jon Scieszka's agent, asking that she be allowed to look over Mr. Scieszka's shoulder as he works on his next book.

Tote bags. Librarians have many unnecessary items to carry around on a regular basis and nothing fits the bill like a sharp tote bag. The more obscure the better. Carrying a bag given out at a recent ALA convention? Frowned upon. Carrying around a bag from that Hawaiian grocery store you visited last year? Just right. *Fast fact:* The tote bag was created in 1895 by librarian Lucy Sue Pente to carry her valuable rubber stamps to and from work.

The classics. Librarians would like to make something clear: They love the important works of literature. If it's leather-bound and dusty, librarians support it. Librarians are also constantly bestowing "new classic" status on things ranging from the latest Newbery Medal winner to the digital date-due stamp. *Fast fact:* The most misplaced awarding of "new classic" status occurred in 1992, when Librarian Greg Tackus bestowed the honor on the Whatchamacallit candy bar.

Boldly defying stereotypes. *The scene:* A street corner in Anytown, USA.

Librarian: I'm guessing you assume all librarians are older women with glasses and their hair in buns?

Average Joe: Uh, yeah.

Librarian: Well guess what? (*Dramatic pause*) I'm a man.

Librarians love nothing more than to make you say, "You're not like the librarians I know of." *Fast fact:* Joe Winnan is the world's most unstereotypical librarian. He runs a barber shop and bakery while checking out scent books in his underwater "knowledge cave."

Tiny laptops. There is nothing that gives a librarian more pleasure than pulling out an impressively minuscule computer (sporting an eyestrainingly tiny screen) faster than you can say, "Wikipedia is evil." *Fast fact:* The soon-to-be-released Toshiba DeweyTronic is the world smallest laptop computer. It's so small you can swallow it.

Oddly shaped glasses. Nothing says "I like to read" more than a pair of oddly shaped eyeglasses. The thicker the frames, the better. Oddly shaped lenses are also common. *Fast fact:* Cutting-edge librarian optometrist Charles Hopp has created the world's thickest-framed glasses. To achieve this distinc-

tion, Hopp completely removed the lenses to make room for more frame.

Laughing at obsolete technology. Librarians like to be on the cutting edge when it comes to advances in tech, and derive great joy from mocking technolo-

gies that have become obsolete. Comments such as "I don't even know what this is!" and "Have you ever seen one of these?" are common when outmoded technologies are encountered. Librarians also enjoy labeling technologies obsolete either far too soon or far too late. *Fast fact:* Some librarians have already labeled cellphones obsolete; pointing to a revival in smoke-signal technology that they predict will be the preferred form of communication in the coming years. They are already stockpiling wool blankets.

Hand-selling books. There is nothing that gives a librarian more pleasure than talking someone into reading a book they didn't know they were interested in (or "hand-selling"). Avid hand-sellers have been known to carve notches on their circulation desks for every patron they successfully persuade. *Fast fact:* Overly ambitious librarian Anna Demson holds the record for hand-selling. She once convinced a patron to check out *War and Peace,* the *Two and a Half Men* (Season 4) DVD, and buy a half-eaten bag of Doritos from her lunch.

Small, unseen boom boxes playing soft music. If you hear gentle music emanating from places unknown, chances are you're in a school library, where small boom boxes are often hidden behind desks and shelves, playing music that creates just the right mood. *Fast fact:* In the Uline District Library, a Coby TH-2312 CD player/radio has been playing Lite 96 FM for eight years nonstop. Librarians have been unable to find the device to turn it off.

Not being called librarians. Uncommon titles such as school library media specialist, cybrarian, and media technologist have been created and adopted to inform patrons that important things are going on in the library—things they wouldn't understand. *Fast fact:* Charles Trastel has given himself what is considered to be the most secretive librarian title, changing the sign on his office and business cards to read "Head Wildlife Photographer in charge of Literature Importing/Exporting." Successfully confusing his staff, he has not had to attend a meeting since this change in 2006.

Applying stickers to books. Librarians will do anything to help patrons find the right book, even if it includes completely disguising the book behind an array of labels, barcodes, tags, dots, and reading-level stickers. *Fast fact:* Several library supply companies have begun selling Groucho Marx–inspired glasses with attached false noses to help further the book anonymity.

Foreign-edition covers. Librarians derive great pleasure out of introducing strangers and colleagues to familiar books sporting unfamiliar covers. After

10

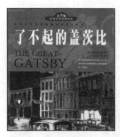

proudly displaying a foreign edition, librarians will typically respond to confused looks with a curt "It's from the UK." *Fast fact:* The most staunch foreign-edition cover supporter, Ellen Blant, refuses to read any book that is written in her native language, resulting in 0.0 books read in the last five years.

Exhaustively precise cataloging. The librarian's mind is a cluttered place, and nothing brings order to the world better than obsessively kept records. If it's a thing, and it's in the library, chances are it has been given a MARC record detailing its weight, color, dimensions, and current mood. *Fast fact:* Librarian Stephen Bredel has been called "The King of Cataloging." In his library he catalogs the individual tissues in boxes of Kleenex, because "they have a way of walking off."

Not weeding. Well before it became reality-show vogue, librarians were the original hoarders. Weeding, or the act of removing unusable materials, has yet to catch on among many in the profession. To librarians, the older and more out-of-date a book is, the more its importance grows. Reality is often altered for support. Dated is turned into "collectible," while damaged quickly becomes "near-mint condition." *Fast fact:* The most extreme case of weeding negligence took place in the Anderton District Library, where a complete set of 100 reference books on Burt Reynolds's moustache was discovered on an out-of-the-way shelf labeled "treasured keepsakes."

SOURCE: Travis Jonker, "Things Librarians Fancy," 100 Scope Notes, October 15, 2009, and June 8, 2010, online at 100scopenotes.com. Reprinted with permission.

The 1992 Librarians and Sex Survey

by Will Manley

YOU ASKED FOR IT; you got it! These are the results of the 1992 Librarians and Sex Survey that *Wilson Library Bulletin* refused to run. They did run the initial survey questionnaire in the June 1992 issue in my "Facing the Public" column and then fired me and destroyed the unsold copies of the magazine. More than 5.000 librarians sent in their questionnaires to me. Here are the results:

Question 1: *Playboy, Playgirl, Playguy.* 40% of the respondents felt that *Playboy* should be included in libraries, 23% felt that *Playgirl* should be included, and 6% felt that *Playguy* should be included.

Question 2: Video ratings. 61% felt that libraries should label their videotapes with G, PG, PG-13, R, NC-17, and X ratings. 39% felt that they should not give labels.

Question 3: R-rated videos and minors. 22% of the respondents felt that libraries should check out R-rated videos to minors not accompanied by adults.

Question 4: X-rated videos. 17% of the respondents felt that libraries should carry X-rated videos.

Question 5: Condom dispensers. 22% of the respondents felt that libraries should have condom dispensers in their bathrooms.

Question 6: Sexual harassment by a supervisor. 14% of the respondents indicated they had been sexually harassed by a library supervisor.

Question 7: Sexual harassment by a patron. 78% of the female respondents and 7% of the male respondents indicated that they had been sexually harassed by a library patron.

Question 8: Sex without love. 20% of the respondents felt that sex without love is by definition bad sex.

Question 9: Nuclear war and Roseanne Barr. 30% of the male respondents indicated that if there were a nuclear war and Roseanne Barr was the only woman on earth to survive, they would have sex with her in order to propagate the species.

Question 10: Nuclear war and Pee-wee Herman. 38% of the female respondents indicated that if there were a nuclear war and Pee-wee Herman was the only man on earth to survive, they would have sex with him in order to propagate the species.

Question 11: AIDS and God. 6% of the respondents felt that AIDS is a punishment from God.

Question 12: Supreme Court Justice Clarence Thomas vs. Anita Hill. 82% of the respondents felt that Anita Hill told the truth in the Senate Judiciary Hearings. [Historical note for Net Genners: Anita Hill accused Clarence Thomas of sexual harassment.]

Question 13: Shakespeare and "the first time." When asked to pick the Shakespearean title that best described their first sexual encounter, 28% chose *The Comedy of Errors;* 23% chose *A Midsummer Night's Dream;* 22% chose *Much Ado About Nothing;* 21% chose *All's Well That Ends Well;* and 6% chose *The Rape of Lucrece.*

Question 14: Genre fiction and sex lives. 38% of the respondents classified their sex life as a "romance," 31% as a fantasy, 22% as a comedy, and 9% as a tragedy.

Question 15: $$$'s for posing nude. 51% of the respondents would pose nude in *Playboy, Playgirl,* or *Playguy* for all the money in Fort Knox; 24% said they would do it for $1 million.

Question 16: Age and virginity loss. 12% lost their virginity from 12 to 15; 22% between 16 and 18; 37% between 19 and 21; 17% between 22 and 25; 5% between 26 and 30; 2% between 31 and 35; 1% between 36 and 100; 4% are virgins.

Question 17: Marriage and celebrities, men. Given a list of 12 celebrities, 27% of the males preferred to marry Kathleen Turner, 25% Jane Fonda, 14% Dolly Parton, 13% Diane Keaton, 8% Diane Sawyer, 6% Madonna, 4% Prince, 2% Elton John, and 1% split between Marla Maples, Yoko Ono, Diana Ross, and Tina Turner.

Question 18: Marriage and celebrities, women. Given a list of 12 celebrities, 60% of the females chose Robert Redford, 18% Patrick Swayze, 7% Woody Allen, 5% Michael Jordan, 4% Martina Navratilova, 3% Cher, 2% Eddie Van Halen, and 1% was split between Prince, Dan Quayle, Arnold Schwarzenegger, Geraldo Rivera, and Michael Jackson.

Question 19: Frequency of sex. 50% of the respondents reported having sex 1–2 times per week; 22%, 3–4 times per week; 21%, 0 times a week; 6%, 5–7 times per week; and 1% have it more than 7 times per week.

Question 20: Public places where librarians have had sex at least once. 63% in a car, 57% in a sleazy motel room, 52% sleeping bag, 43% kitchen floor, 32% hot tub, 20% library, 7% airplane, 8% elevator.

Question 21: Number of sexual partners in their lifetime. 30%, 2–5 partners; 22%, 1 partner; 17%, 6–10; 16%, 11–20; 7%, 21–50; 4%, more than 50; 4%, none.

Question 22: Sex and presidential elections. 72% of the respondents said

10

they would not let a candidate's sex life influence their vote in an election for president.

Question 23: X-rated movies. 61% of the respondents had rented an X-rated movie.

Question 24: Librarians and sex books. 91% had read *The Joy of Sex*, 29% had read *How to Make Love to a Man*, 14% had read *Human Sexual Inadequacy*, and 3% had read *Macho Sluts*.

SOURCE: Will Manley, "The 1992 Librarians and Sex Survey Results," Will Unwound, no. 78, April 11, 2010. Reprinted with permission.

WHIMSY

What is a group of librarians?

NO ONE HAS AN OFFICIAL ANSWER, but many suggestions have been made for a collective noun that describes a group of librarians. I've compiled a list of the best ones from a number of places around the internet.—*GME.*

An access of librarians
An ask of librarians
A backlog of librarians
A cardigan of librarians
A catalog of librarians
A chapter of librarians
A classification of librarians
A collection of librarians
A dewey of librarians
A directory of librarians
An erudition of librarians
A fascicle of librarians
A hush of librarians
An index of librarians
A query of librarians
A renewal of librarians
A ruckus of librarians
A search of librarians
A shelf of librarians
A shush of librarians
A source of librarians
A stack of librarians
A tome of librarians

A group of librarians.

SOURCES: Stephen Abrams, "What Is a Group of Librarians?" Stephen's Lighthouse, May 18, 2009, stephenslighthouse.com; Jeremy Dibbell, "What Do You Call a Group of Librarians?" PhiloBiblos, February 10, 2008, philobiblos.blogspot.com; A. B. Credaro, "Collective Nouns for Librarians," Warrior Librarian Weekly, 2002, warriorlibrarian.com/LOL/ nouns.html; Michael Kelley, "In Search of a Good Collective Noun for Librarians," *Library Journal*, April 21, 2011, www.libraryjournal.com/lj/; "The Collective Noun for Librarians," All Sorts, all-sorts.org/nouns/librarians.

A place called Library

by Larry T. Nix

A COMMUNITY EXISTS in Pennsylvania that is named "Library." Library, Pennsylvania, is an unincorporated community in South Park Township in Allegheny County. It was named in honor of the first library established in the area by John Moore in 1833. The name was a marked improvement over its previous name of "Loafer's Hollow." The community of Library is now served by the  South Park Town Library. A post office was established in Library in 1842. Postmarks on mail that has been mailed from or cancelled in the Library Post Office make nice additions to a collection of postal librariana. It is another case where library history and postal history come together. The January 21, 1931, air mail, special delivery cover shown here has been signed by Library postmaster S. L. Boyer.

SOURCE: Larry T. Nix, "A Place Called Library," Library History Buff Blog, February 4, 2009, online at libraryhistorybuff.blogspot.com/2009/02/place-called-library.html. Reprinted with permission.

Tasks for burned-out librarians

by Will Manley

THERE IS A TON OF STRESS in our libraries with all the budget cutting and understaffing going on. As much as our librarian survivors think they can hang on and do the work of three people, burnout is a reality. The smart director knows that it's important to pull burned-out librarians from their regular posts and give them different duties for a week or two just to mitigate the stress. Here are some suggestions:

- Flicking the lights on and off 15 minutes before closing.
- Watering the real plants.
- Dusting the fake plants.
- Cleaning out the staff refrigerator and taking the refuse to the local hazardous waste facility.
- Putting trash cans under roof leaks.
- Making sure that the toilet paper in all the bathrooms rolls from the top down.
- Watering the library's front lawn with a garden hose.
- Keeping track of all IRS forms.
- Cleaning out the pencil sharpeners.
- Polishing the globe.
- Taking all the hand puppets down to the laundromat for a good cleaning.
- Keeping a fresh supply of pencils and scratch paper by each computer catalog.
- Being the library's Walmart greeter.
- Ringing the bell for the Salvation Army at Christmas time.
- Performing incantations to keep evil spirits out of the library.

10

- Swatting flies.
- Acting as a live sculpture of a librarian in front of the library.
- Serving as the director's car companion so he can drive in the car pool lane on the freeway on his way to meetings.
- Taking the library cat to the vet for its annual checkup.

Question: When do you know the person at the bar is a cataloger?

Answer: When you start talking about your marital problems and she responds, "Don't look at your relationship with Bill as a marriage; look at it as a long-running serial with updates."

SOURCE: Will Manley, "Tasks for Burned-Out Librarians," Will Unwound, no. 623, December 2, 2011. Reprinted with permission.

Oversize
by William Fitch Smyth

It was a tall librarian
　　Who wished to travel far,
So paid for a whole section
　　In a Pullman sleeping car.
But the porter saw him sitting
　　On his berth's soft-cushioned edge,
And yelled: "Get down! You're oversize!
　　You go below the ledge!"

Oh, if!
by William Fitch Smyth

If I were made Librarian
　　I'd bear me like a king.
I'd sit with folded arms and scowl;
　　I'd never do a thing.
But if some visitor should dare
　　To ask me for a book,
I'd thunder: "To the dungeon, knave!"
　　And crush him with a look.

And should some reader seek for aid,
　　I'd shout: "See here, my man!
I'd have you understand that I
　　Am now LIBRARIAN!
Down on your knees, false villain, down!"
　　I'd roar in rabid rage.
But oh, I'm *not* Librarian!
　　I'm just a student page.

SOURCE: William Fitch Smyth, *Little Lyrics for Librarians* (Cleveland: Bazoo Publishing Co., 1910).

INDEX

GEORGE M. EBERHART is a senior editor of *American Libraries* magazine for the American Library Association. Since 2006 he has been the editor of *American Libraries Direct,* ALA's weekly e-newsletter. From 1980 to 1990 he was editor of *College & Research Libraries News,* the news magazine of ALA's Association of College and Research Libraries division. He has also written on the subjects of UFOs, cryptozoology, and postcard collecting. Eberhart holds a bachelor's degree in journalism from Ohio State University and an MLS from the University of Chicago.

You may also be interested in

Digital Libraries and Information Access
Research Perspectives

EDITED BY G. G. CHOWDHURY AND SCHUBERT FOO

Providing an invaluable resource for LIS students, academics, and researchers interested in digital libraries and access—a useful introduction for those developing, managing, or just starting out with digital libraries.

ISBN: 978-1-55570-914-3
256 pages / 6" x 9"

THE LIBRARIAN'S BOOK OF LISTS
GEORGE M. EBERHART
ISBN: 978-0-8389-1063-4

THE WHOLE SCHOOL LIBRARY HANDBOOK 2
EDITED BY BLANCHE WOOLLS AND DAVID V. LOERTSCHER
ISBN: 978-0-8389-1127-3

THE TRANSFORMED LIBRARY: E-BOOKS, EXPERTISE, AND EVOLUTION
JEANNETTE WOODWARD
ISBN: 978-0-8389-1164-8

THE NEW UNIVERSITY LIBRARY: FOUR CASE STUDIES
MATTHEW CONNER
ISBN: 978-0-8389-1193-8

REFLECTING ON THE FUTURE OF ACADEMIC AND PUBLIC LIBRARIES
EDITED BY PETER HERNON AND JOSEPH R. MATTHEWS
ISBN: 978-0-8389-1187-7

GOING BEYOND GOOGLE AGAIN: STRATEGIES FOR USING AND TEACHING THE INVISIBLE WEB
JANE DEVINE AND FRANCINE EGGER-SIDER
ISBN: 978-1-55570-898-6

Order today at alastore.ala.org or 866-746-7252!
ALA Store purchases fund advocacy, awareness, and accreditation programs for library professionals worldwide.